HEROIC POETRY

HEROIC POETRY

BY

C. M. BOWRA

LONDON

MACMILLAN & CO LTD

NEW YORK · ST MARTIN'S PRESS

1961

MACMILLAN AND COMPANY LIMITED

London Bombay Calcutta Madras Melbourne

THE MACMILLAN COMPANY OF CANADA LIMITED

Toronto

ST MARTIN'S PRESS INC

New York

TO

ISAIAH BERLIN

PRINTED IN GREAT BRITAIN

PREFACE

THIS book is a development of some work which I did twenty-five years ago when I was studying the Homeric poems. It seemed to me then that many vexed questions might be clarified by a comparative study of other poems of the same kind. This belief was greatly strengthened when, in 1932, H. M. and N. K. Chadwick published the first volume of their great work *The Growth of Literature*. To it, and its two subsequent volumes, I owe more than I can say, and its influence may be discerned in most parts of my book. Though heroic poetry is only one of several subjects treated by the Chadwicks, their analytical examination of it shows what it is in a number of countries and establishes some of its main characteristics. This present book aims largely at continuing the subject where they stop, first by using material which was not available to them at the time of writing, secondly by trying to make a closer synthesis than they attempted, and thirdly by giving attention to many points on which they did not have time to touch. The result will, I hope, provide a kind of anatomy of heroic poetry and show that there is a general type which persists through many variations. The variations are of course as important as the main type, and I have given considerable space to them. The work is therefore one of comparative literature in the sense that by comparing many examples and aspects of a poetical form it tries to illuminate the nature of that form and the ways in which it works.

Where so much material is available, I have naturally had to limit my choice from it. I have excluded any literature which is not strictly heroic in the sense which I have given to the word. That is why nothing is said about the old Indian epics, in which a truly heroic foundation is overlaid with much literary and theological matter, or about Celtic, either Irish or Welsh, since neither presents many examples of heroic narrative in verse, or about Persian, in which much genuine material has been transformed by later literary poets. I have also excluded from consideration anything written in languages unknown to me, of which I have found no translations available. Thus the reader will find nothing about Albanian or Buryat, though heroic poems have been published in both. For quite different reasons I have confined my study of French heroic poetry to the *Chanson de Roland* and have neglected the whole mass of other *chansons de geste*. My reason for this is partly that the *Chanson de Roland* seems to me the best example of its kind, partly that a close analysis and examination of the other texts would not only take many years but upset the balance of this book.

The texts which I have studied fall into three classes. First, with Greek, whether ancient or modern, French, Spanish, German, and the Slavonic languages I have used the original texts and usually translated them myself, though I am grateful to help from C. K. Scott-Moncrieff's *Roland*, W. A. Morison's versions from the Serb, and Mrs. N. K. Chadwick's from the Russian. Secondly, since I do not know either Anglo-Saxon or Norse, I have used respectively the versions of C. K. Scott-Moncrieff and H. A. Bellows, though I have not entirely confined myself to them. Thirdly, for Asiatic texts, of which no English versions exist, I have used versions in other languages, usually Russian, which I have translated into English. In the exceptional case of *Gilgamish* I have made my own version from the Russian of N. Gumilev and the English of R. Campbell Thompson. In some cases, where no texts have been available, I have used information about them from books of learning, though I have not often done this, and then only when I have had full confidence in the trustworthiness of the author. I fully realise that this is by no means a perfect method. It would certainly have been better to work only with original texts in every case and not to use translations at all. But a work of this kind would require a knowledge of nearly thirty languages, and not only am I myself unlikely ever to acquire such a knowledge, but I do not know of anyone interested in the subject who has it. So I must ask indulgence for a defect which seems to be inevitable if such a work is to be attempted at all.

I am also conscious of other faults in handling this mass of disparate material. The transliteration of unusual names is, I fear, too often inconsistent or incorrect. It has been impossible to avoid a certain amount of repetition, since the same passages illustrate different points in different contexts. The mass of material may discourage some readers by its unfamiliarity, but I have done my best to make it intelligible. Above all, the difficulty of getting books from eastern Europe has prevented me from being as detailed as I should wish on certain points.

I owe thanks to many people for help generously given ; to Mr. A. B. Lord for introducing me to the unique collection of

Jugoslav poems recorded by Milman Parry and now in the Widener Library of Harvard University ; to Mr. F. W. Deakin for the invaluable gift of Karadžić's *Srpske Narodne Pjesme* ; to Professor H. T. Wade-Gery for much helpful criticism ; to Mrs. N. K. Chadwick for the generous gift of a book otherwise unobtainable ; to Professors J. E. Finley, O. Maenchen, and R. M. Dawkins, Dr. G. Katkov, Dr. J. H. Thomas, Mr. A. Andrewes, Mr. J. B. Bamborough, Dr. J. K. Bostock, Mr. W. A. C. H. Dobson, who have given time and trouble to helping me ; and finally to authors and publishers for leave to quote extracts from books — the American Scandinavian Foundation, New York, for H. A. Bellows, *The Poetic Edda* ; Mrs. N. K. Chadwick and the Cambridge University Press for *Russian Heroic Poetry* ; Mr. W. A. Morison and the Cambridge University Press for *The Revolt of the Serbs against the Turks* ; Professor W. J. Entwistle and the Clarendon Press for *European Balladry* ; to the executor of the late C. K. Scott-Moncrieff and Messrs. Chapman & Hall for *The Song of Roland* and *Beowulf* ; to Mr. Arthur Waley and Messrs. Constable & Co., for *170 Chinese Poems* ; Messrs. George Allen & Unwin for *The Book of Songs* ; and the proprietors of *Botteghe Oscure* for *Kutune Shirka*. Finally, I owe a great debt to Miss G. Feith for compiling the Index and to Mr. R. H. Dundas for his careful scrutiny of my proofs. For such errors as remain I alone am responsible,

CONTENTS

I

THE HEROIC POEM

IN their attempts to classify mankind in different types the early
Greek philosophers gave a special place to those men who live
for action and for the honour which comes from it. Such, they
believed, are moved by an important element in the human soul,
the self-assertive principle, which is to be distinguished equally
from the appetites and from the reason and realises itself in brave
doings. They held that the life of action is superior to the pursuit
of profit or the gratification of the senses, that the man who seeks
honour is himself an honourable figure; and when Pythagoras
likened human beings to the different types to be seen at the
Olympic Games, he paid the lovers of honour the compliment
of comparing them with the competing athletes.[1] The Greeks of
the sixth and fifth centuries B.C. regarded the men whom Homer
had called heroes — ἥρωες — as a generation of superior beings
who sought and deserved honour. They believed that Greek
history had contained a heroic age, when the dominant type was
of this kind, and they could point to the testimony of Hesiod,
who, in his analysis of the ages of humanity, places between the
ages of bronze and of iron an age of heroes who fought at Thebes
and at Troy:

> Again on the bountiful earth by heaven was sent
> A worthier race; on righteous deeds they were bent,
> Divine, heroic — as demigods they are known,
> And the boundless earth had their race before our own.
> Some of them met grim war and its battle-fates:
> In the land of Kadmos at Thebes with seven gates
> They fought for Oedipus' flocks disastrously,
> Or were drawn to cross the gulf of mighty sea
> For sake of Helen tossing her beautiful hair,
> And death was the sudden shroud that wrapped them there.[2]

Archaeology and legend suggest that Hesiod was not entirely at
fault and that there was once such a time as he outlines. It left

---

[1] Cicero, *Tusc. Disp.* v, 9.
[2] *Works and Days*, 156-65. Trs. J. Lindsay. In his edition, p. 16, T. A.
Sinclair connects the theory of the Five Ages with the teaching of Zarathustra,
who believed in four ages, each of a thousand years. In that case, as Sinclair
argues, the Heroic Age is Hesiod's addition to an ancient scheme.

memories and traces in Greek epic poetry, and the later Greeks looked back to it with delighted admiration. Homer makes no attempt to conceal its superiority to his own time,[1] and even the critical Heraclitus concedes that such an existence is impressive in its pursuit of honour : for " they choose one thing above all others, immortal glory among mortals ".[2] It is significant that even in the fourth century B.C. Aristotle regarded honour not only as " the prize appointed for the noblest deeds " but as " the greatest of external goods ".[3] In Greece the conception of the heroic life began early and lasted long, and from it, more than from anything else, our own conceptions of heroes and heroism are derived.

The Greeks, however, were not alone in their respect for a superior class of men who lived for honour. The *chevalier* of mediaeval French epic is in every way as heroic as a Greek hero, and acts from similar motives. To the same family belong the Spanish *caballero*, the Anglo-Saxon *cempa*, the Russian *bogatyr*,[4] the Old German *held*, the Norse *jarl*, the Tatar *batyr*, the Serb *yunak*, the Albanian *trim*, and the Uzbek *pavlan*. Sometimes heroic qualities are attributed to a special class of persons who exist otherwise in their own right. For instance, the Jugoslavs regard with peculiar respect the *haiduks*, who led the revolt against the Turks in 1804–13 ; the modern Greeks have since the sixteenth century celebrated the klephts of Epirus, who may have been, as their name suggests, no better than brigands, but were also national champions against the Turks ; the Ossetes of the Caucasus have a large number of stories, often shared with the Chechens and the Cherkesses, about the Narts, who belong to an undated past and have no known origin but are regarded as heroes beyond comparison ;[5] the Ukrainians devote much attention to the Cossacks and their long struggles against the Turks, until the name of cossack, *kozak*, has become a synonym for a great warrior ; in not dissimilar conditions the Bulgars attribute many virtues to enterprising brigands called *yunatsi*. The conception of the hero and of heroic prowess is widely spread, and despite its different settings and manifestations shows the same main char-

---

[1] *Il.* i, 272 ; v, 304 ; xii, 383, 449 ; xx, 287.
[2] Fr. 29, Diels.   [3] *Nic. Eth.* 1123a 20.
[4] The word *bogatyr*, derived from the Persian *bahadur*, occurs in Russian annals from the thirteenth century, but is used there of Tatar warriors ; cf. *Chronicle of Hypatios* on the warriors of Baty Khan in 1240 and 1243. Since the fifteenth century it has replaced old Russian words for " warrior " such as *udalets, khrabr, muzh.*
[5] For theories on the origins of the Narts cf. G. Dumézil, *Légendes sur les Nartes* (Paris, 1930), pp. 1-12.

acteristics, which agree with what the Greeks say of their heroes. An age which believes in the pursuit of honour will naturally wish to express its admiration in a poetry of action and adventure, of bold endeavours and noble examples. Heroic poetry still exists in many parts of the world and has existed in many others, because it answers a real need of the human spirit.

This poetry may be divided into two classes, ancient and modern. To the first belong those poems which have by some whim of chance survived from the past. Such are the Greek *Iliad* and *Odyssey*, the Asiatic *Gilgamish*, preserved fragmentarily in Old Babylonian, Hittite, Assyrian, and New Babylonian, the remains of the Canaanite (Ugaritic) *Aqhat* and *Keret*, the Old German *Hildebrand*, the Anglo-Saxon *Beowulf*, *Maldon*, *Brunanburh* and fragments of *Finnsburh* and *Waldhere*, the Norse poems of the *Elder Edda* and other pieces, some French epics of which the most remarkable is the *Song of Roland*, and the Spanish *Poema del Cid* and fragments of other poems. The last hundred and fifty years have added a large second class of modern heroic poems, taken down from living bards. In Europe, the art is still flourishing, or was till recently, in Russia, especially in remote regions like Lake Onega and the White Sea; in Jugoslavia, both among Christians and Mohammedans; in Bulgaria; in the Ukraine; in Greece; in Esthonia; in Albania. In Asia, it is to be found in the Caucasus among the Armenians and the Ossetes; in the Caspian basin among the Kalmucks; among some Turkic peoples, notably the Uzbeks of what was once Bactria, and the Kara-Kirghiz of the Tien-Shan mountains; among the Yakuts of the river Lena in northern Siberia; the Achins of western Sumatra; the Ainus of the northern Japanese island of Hokkaido, and some tribes of the Arabian peninsula. In Africa it seems to be much less common, but there are traces of it in the Sudan.[1] This list is by no means complete and could easily be increased. There are, no doubt, also regions in which the art exists but has not been recorded by European scholars. There are equally other regions where it once existed but has passed out of currency before the impact of new ideas and ways of life. None the less, the present evidence shows that it is widely spread and that, wherever it occurs, it follows certain easily observed rules. It is therefore a fit subject for study, though any such study must take as much notice of variations as of underlying principles.

[1] Petrović, pp. 190-93, describes an epic poem which celebrates a battle between the fetishists and the Moslems among the Bambara of the French Sudan. Cf. also Mungo Park, *Travels* (edn. 1860), p. 311.

This poetry is inspired by the belief that the honour which men pay to some of their fellows is owed to a real superiority in natural endowments. But of course it is not enough for a man to possess superior qualities; he must realise them in action. In the ordeals of the heroic life his full worth is tested and revealed. It is not even necessary that he should be rewarded by success: the hero who dies in battle after doing his utmost is in some ways more admirable than he who lives. In either case he is honoured because he has made a final effort in courage and endurance, and no more can be asked of him. He gives dignity to the human race by showing of what feats it is capable; he extends the bounds of experience for others and enhances their appreciation of life by the example of his abundant vitality. However much ordinary men feel themselves to fall short of such an ideal, they none the less respect it because it opens up possibilities of adventure and excitement and glory which appeal even to the most modest and most humble. The admiration for great doings lies deep in the human heart, and comforts and cheers even when it does not stir to emulation. Heroes are the champions of man's ambition to pass beyond the oppressive limits of human frailty to a fuller and more vivid life, to win as far as possible a self-sufficient manhood, which refuses to admit that anything is too difficult for it, and is content even in failure, provided that it has made every effort of which it is capable. Since the ideal of action appeals to a vast number of men and opens new chapters of enthralling experience, it becomes matter for poetry of a special kind.

Heroic poetry is essentially narrative and is nearly always remarkable for its objective character. It creates its own world of the imagination in which men act on easily understood principles, and, though it celebrates great doings because of their greatness, it does so not overtly by praise but indirectly by making them speak for themselves and appeal to us in their own right. It wins interest and admiration for its heroes by showing what they are and what they do. This degree of independence and objectivity is due to the pleasure which most men take in a well-told tale and their dislike of having it spoiled by moralising or instruction. Indeed heroic poetry is far from unique in this respect. It has much in common with other kinds of narrative, whether in prose or in verse, whose main purpose is to tell a story in an agreeable and absorbing way. What differentiates heroic poetry is largely its outlook. It works in conditions determined by special conceptions of manhood and honour. It cannot exist unless men believe that human beings are in themselves sufficient

4

objects of interest and that their chief claim is the pursuit of
honour through risk. Since these assumptions are not to be
found in all countries at all times, heroic poetry does not flourish
everywhere. It presupposes a view of existence in which man
plays a central part and exerts his powers in a distinctive way.
Thus, although it bears many resemblances to other primitive
narrative poetry, it is not the same and may well be a development
from it.

There is a narrative poetry which tells for their own sake
stories which are not in any real sense heroic. With this, heroic
poetry has so much in common that it is impossible to make an
absolute distinction between the two kinds. The differences are
of quality and degree, but they are none the less fundamental.
In certain parts of the world there is still a flourishing art of
telling tales in verse, often at considerable length, about the
marvellous doings of men. What counts in them is precisely
this element of the marvellous. It is far more important than any
heroic or even human qualities which may have an incidental
part. This art embodies not a heroic outlook, which admires
man for doing his utmost with his actual, human gifts, but a
more primitive outlook which admires any attempt to pass
beyond man's proper state by magical, non-human means. In
different ways this poetry exists among the Finns, the Altai and
Abakan Tatars, the Khalka Mongols, the Tibetans, and the Sea
Dyaks of Borneo. It presupposes a view of the world in which
man is not the centre of creation but caught between many
unseen powers and influences, and his special interest lies in his
supposed ability to master these and then to do what cannot be
done by the exercise of specifically human gifts. In such societies
the great man is not he who makes the most of his natural qualities
but he who is somehow able to enlist supernatural powers on his
behalf. Of course even the most obviously heroic heroes in
Homer and *Beowulf*, still more in the less sophisticated poetry of
the Kara-Kirghiz or the Uzbeks or the Ossetes or the Kalmucks
or the Yakuts, may at times do something of the kind, but it is
usually exceptional, and their ability to do it is not their first
claim. In more primitive societies this is what really matters,
and it presupposes a different view of manhood and of its possibilities and place in the universe.

In the Finnish *Kalevala*, which is actually not a single poem
but a composition artfully made from a number of original lays by
the scholar Elias Lönnrot, the leading figures are magicians, and
the interest of almost every episode turns on their ability to master

a difficult situation by magic. The actual situation may often resemble something familiar in truly heroic poems, but the management of it is quite different. Take, for instance, the theme of building a boat which is to be found both in *Gilgamish* and the *Odyssey*. In them it is a matter of craft and knowledge; in the *Kalevala* it is a matter of knowing the right spells :

> Then the aged Väinämöinen,
> He the great primaeval sorcerer,
> Fashioned then the boat with wisdom,
> Built with magic songs the vessel,
> From the fragments of an oak-tree,
> Fragments of the shattered oak-tree.
> With a song the keel he fashioned,
> With another, sides he fashioned,
> And he sang again a third time,
> And the rudder he constructed,
> Bound the rib-ends firm together,
> And the joints he fixed together.[1]

What holds good of boat-building, holds equally good of other matters such as fighting or visiting the underworld. In the end it is not strength or courage or even ordinary cunning which wins but a knowledge of the right spells. In *Kogutei*, a traditional poem of the Altai Tatars,[2] it is again supernatural powers which count. The hero is not the man Kogutei but a beaver whose life he spares and whom he takes home. The beaver duly marries a human bride and behaves very like a man, but though he is a great hunter and performs many feats of valour, he is not a human being and does not reflect a heroic outlook. His final triumphs come through magic, and it is clear that he has much of the *shaman* in him when he escapes death at the hands of his brothers-in-law, lays a curse on their whole family, returns to Kogutei, and enriches him by his magical arts.

Although in this poetry great events are usually directed by magic, it does not mean that the men who take part in them lack great qualities. They may often have strength and courage and power to command, but none the less they must practise magic if they wish to succeed. The Sea Dyaks of Borneo, for instance, have long narrative poems about reckless exploits. They have their full share of fighting and of deeds of gallant daring, but sooner or later their warriors resort to magic. In *Klieng's War*

---

[1] *Kalevala*, xvi, 101-12. On the *Kalevala* in general cf. D. Comparetti, *The Traditional Poetry of the Finns* (Eng. Trans.), London, 1898, and C. J. Billson, *Popular Poetry of the Finns*, London, 1900.

[2] *Kogutei: Altaiski Epos*, Moscow, 1935; cf. Chadwick, *Growth*, iii, pp. 99-102.

Raid to the Skies human invaders ascend to the stars by throwing up balls of blue and red thread, an action which may have some connection with the cult of the rainbow and is certainly magical.[1] The main episode of the poem presupposes powers more than human and makes the shamanistic assumption that certain men can scale the sky. So, too, in the fine poems of the Abakan Tatars, or Chakass,[2] an undeniably heroic element expresses itself in stirring scenes of adventure, but even so the issue lies not with human qualities but with forces outside human control, with strange beings who come from nowhere and decide the destinies of men. In such a world the warriors themselves often use magic and think little of flying along the sky on their horses or jumping over a wide sea. Indeed they are so close to the world of beasts and birds and fishes that they seem not to be finally differentiated from them. They are almost natural forces in a universe governed by inexplicable laws to which magic is the only key. If they restrict their efforts to specifically human powers, they are liable to fail, and even the stoutest champion may be foiled by some incalculable intervention from the unknown. In such a society the hero has not reached his true stature because his human capacities are not fully realised, and though he may be concerned with honour, it is not his first or only concern. His life is spent in meeting unforeseen contingencies which make him a plaything of the supernatural.

The difference between shamanistic poetry and heroic poetry proper may be illustrated by a comparison between two examples, in each of which both elements exist but in degrees so different that we can confidently call one shamanistic and the other heroic. The Tibetan poems about King Kesar of Ling are concerned with a great warrior, who may have a historical origin, and is regarded as all that a hero should be.[3] He has indeed many heroic qualities. His portentous birth and boyhood, his destruction of his enemies, his strength and wealth and intelligence, his wars and victories make him look like a hero, but in fact his success comes almost entirely by magic. He is able not only to assume whatever shape he likes, whether human or animal, but to create phantoms which look like living men and frighten his foes into

---

[1] Chadwick, *Growth*, iii, pp. 480-83.
[2] N. Cohn, *Gold Khan*, London, 1946.
[3] G. N. Roerich, "The Epic of King Kesar of Ling" in *Journal of Royal Society of Bengal*, viii, 1942. I owe this reference to Mr. W. A. C. H. Dobson. The poems survive in various dialects of Tibetan, and also in Mongolian and Burushaski. A full paraphrase of the story is given by A. David-Neel, *The Superhuman Life of Gesar of Ling*, London, 1932.

B

surrender. In every crisis he uses magic, and his real place is not with human beings, since he is the incarnation of a god and helped by four divine spirits who succour him in every need. On the other hand the Yakut poems have on the surface many magical elements. Sometimes the heroes themselves are actually shamans ; they are usually able to perform magical acts. But when it comes to war, they rely not on magic but on strength of arm, and that makes all the difference. In the last resort the Yakut poems are heroic and the Tibetan are shamanistic because they presuppose different views of human worth and capacity. In the poems about Kesar what counts is his supernatural power, but in the Yakut poems the main interest is in physical and mental capacity, which may indeed be unusual but is still recognisably human. The difference between shamanistic and heroic poetry is largely one of emphasis, but no poem can be regarded as truly heroic unless the major successes of the hero are achieved by more or less human means.

It is of course possible that sometimes shamanistic elements are later intrusions into a truly heroic art. Indeed it is even possible that this is the case with the poems about King Kesar of Ling. Since the poems seem to be derived from a time before the establishment of Buddhism in Tibet, it is quite likely that the shamanistic elements in them are themselves Buddhistic, and that these have obscured and altered an earlier, more genuinely heroic poetry. But this does not affect the main point that shamanistic poetry is more primitive than heroic and tends to precede it historically. Heroic poetry seems to be a development of narrative from a magical to a more anthropocentric outlook. Such a change may well be gradual, since it must take time to realise the implications of the new outlook and to shape stories to suit it. The process may have been assisted by one or two other kinds of poetry closely related to a heroic point of view, notably the panegyrics and laments which are popular in many countries. The one celebrates a great man's doings to his face, while the other praises him in lamenting his death. The great doings and qualities so commemorated are often of the kind which heroic poets record in objective narrative. Moreover, panegyrics and laments are often in the same style and metres as strictly heroic poems, and indeed in Russian and Tatar literature the two classes have an almost identical manner and vocabulary. Panegyrics and laments resemble heroic poetry in their taste for the nobler human qualities. The great man wins a victory in battle or the games ; he is a famous huntsman, a father of his people, a generous host, a loyal friend, notable alike for courage and wisdom. In such poems honour is assumed to be the right end of life, and a man wins it through great achievements. Both panegyric and lament celebrate an individual's fame at some special crisis, and in so doing endorse a heroic outlook.

Panegyric honours the great man in his presence for something that he has done and is usually composed soon after the event. For instance, one of the oldest relics of Hebrew poetry, the Song of Deborah, composed about 1200 B.C., breathes a heroic spirit in its joy over the rout of a formidable enemy. Though it tells its story with brilliant realism and a fine sense of adventure, it remains a panegyric. If Deborah and Barak really sang it, and it is quite possible that they did, their proclaimed purpose was to praise Jael, the slayer of Sisera :

> Blessed above women shall Jael the wife of Heber the Kenite be,
> Blessed shall she be above all women in the tent.[1]

Panegyrics of this kind are widely spread over the world. They exist not merely among peoples who have a heroic poetry, like the Greeks, the Germanic and Slavonic peoples, the Asiatic Tatars, and some peoples of the Caucasus, but among others who seem never to have had such a poetry, like the Polynesians, the Zulus, the Abyssinians, the Tuareg, and the Galla. Panegyric does not often attain any length and certainly does not compare in scale with long heroic poems. It represents an outlook which is close to the heroic, but it lacks the independence and objectivity of a heroic poem.

Lament is closely allied to panegyric in that it dwells on a great man's achievements, though it does so with sorrow and regret after his death. The heroic temper is often vivid in it, as in another early Hebrew poem, David's lament for Saul and Jonathan (c. 1010 B.C.), with its praise of the dead warriors — " they were swifter than eagles, they were stronger than lions ". But this praise is inspired by contemporary events and delivered by a poet in memory of men whom he has loved and lost :

> Ye daughters of Israel, weep over Saul, who clothed you in scarlet,
>   with other delights, who put ornaments of gold upon your apparel.
> How are the mighty fallen in the midst of the battle ! O Jonathan,
>   thou wast slain in thine high places.
> I am distressed for thee, my brother Jonathan : very pleasant hast
>   thou been unto me : thy love was wonderful, passing the love of
>   women.
> How are the mighty fallen, and the weapons of war perished.[2]

---

[1] Judges v, 24.   [2] II Samuel i, 24-7.

The sense of personal loss, such as David reveals, is essential to
lament, and, though it may easily become a convention, it remains
none the less necessary. Lament is born from grief for the dead,
and though praise is naturally combined with it, grief has the chief
place. The authentic note may be seen in the song which Kiluken
Bahadur sang over the body of Genghiz Khan when it was being
carried on a cart to burial :

> Once thou didst swoop like a falcon ! A rumbling waggon now
>   trundles thee off !
> O my king !
> Hast thou then in truth forsaken thy wife and thy children and
>   the assembly of thy people ?
> O my king !
> Circling in pride like an eagle once thou didst lead us,
> O my king !
> But now thou has stumbled and fallen, like an unbroken colt,
> O my king ! [1]

The lament reflects the spirit of a heroic society not with dramatic
objectivity but with personal intimacy. It shows what men feel
when their lives are touched by loss. The poet is too close to the
actual event to present it with the artistic detachment of heroic
narrative.

None the less the resemblances between panegyric or lament
and heroic poetry are so close that there must be a relation between
them. Historical priority probably belongs to panegyric and
lament, not merely because they are simpler and less objective,
but because they exist in some societies where heroic poetry is
lacking. The reasons for this lack are several. First, it may be
simply an inability to rise beyond a single occasion to the conception of a detached art. This may be the case with some
African peoples, who delight to honour victorious achievements
but address their poems to single real persons and compose
especially for them. How close this spirit is to a heroic outlook
can be seen from a small song of praise composed by court-
minstrels for a king of Uganda :

> Thy feet are hammers,
> Son of the forest.
> Great is the fear of thee ;
> Great is thy wrath :
> Great is thy peace :
> Great is thy power.[2]

[1] Yule-Cordier, *Travels of Marco Polo* (London, 1903), i, p. 351.
[2] Chadwick, *Growth*, iii, p. 579.

The conception of a great man presented in this poem may be matched by that of an Abyssinian lament for a dead chieftain of the Amhara country :

> Alas ! Saba Gadis, the friend of all,
> Has fallen at Daga Shaha by the hand of Oubeshat !
> Alas ! Saba Gadis, the pillar of the poor,
> Has fallen at Daga Shaha, weltering in his blood !
> The people of this country, will they find it a good thing
> To eat ears of corn which have grown in his blood ? [1]

Though these poems, and many others like them, show a real admiration for active and generous manhood, they come from peoples who have no heroic poetry and have never advanced beyond panegyric and lament. The intellectual effort required for such an advance seems to have been beyond their powers.

The limitations of this outlook may be specially illustrated from the poetry of the Zulus. In the first years of the nineteenth century they were organised as an extremely formidable power by their king Chaka, who, by a combination of good tactics and a more than ruthless discipline, made himself a great conqueror and won the fear and respect alike of his subjects and his neighbours. He, we might think, would have been a suitable subject for heroic song, but he seems to have missed this destiny, since all we possess to his memory are panegyrics. In one we see how his soldiers saw him :

> Thou hast finished, finished the nations,
> Where wilt thou go forth to battle now ?
> Hey ! where wilt thou go forth to battle now ?
> Thou hast conquered kings,
> Where wilt thou go forth to battle now ?
> Thou hast finished, finished the nations,
> Where art thou going to battle now ?
> Hurrah ! Hurrah ! Hurrah !
> Where art thou going to battle now ? [2]

This is simple and primitive, the expression of an immediate, violent excitement. A few years later Chaka's successor, Dingan, who was in no sense his peer in ability or intelligence, was celebrated on a larger scale with a greater sense of heroic worth. The second poem praises the king's power and enterprise, and does not shrink from making honourable mention of his murder of his elder brother, Chaka, and his other brother, Umhlangani. Through the 161 lines of his song the poet keeps up a real sense

---

[1] Chadwick, *Growth*, iii, p. 517.
[2] J. Shooter, *The Kafirs of Natal* (London, 1857), p. 268.

of the prodigious prowess and irresistible strength of his master and praises Dingan as the most authentic type of hero. He is of course a great conqueror :

> Thou art a king who crushest the heads of the other kings.
> Thou passest over mountains inaccessible to thy predecessors.
> Thou findest a defile from which there is no way out.
> There thou makest roads, yes, roads.
> Thou takest away the herds from the banks of the Tugela,
> And the herds from the Babanankos, a people skilled in the
>   forging of iron.
> Thou art indeed a vigorous adventurer.

So much is to be expected, but the poet then praises Dingan for other qualities, which are not usually regarded as heroic, though a strict logic might claim that they are — notably for being un-approachable and ruthless :

> Thou makest all the world to keep silence,
> Thou hast silenced even the troops ;
> Thy troops always obey thee :
> Thou sayest, and they go ;
> Thou sayest, and they go again.
> All honour a king whom none can approach.

Though Dingan has murdered Chaka, he is compared and indeed identified with him as a great conqueror :

> Thou art Chaka ; thou causest all people to tremble.
> Thou thunderest like the musket.
> At the fearful noise which thou makest
> The dwellers in the towns flee away.
> Thou are the great shade of the Zulu,
> And thence thou swellest and reachest to all countries.[1]

This undeniably expresses a heroic ideal of an advanced kind, but the poet's art is still confined to panegyric. His outlook is limited to the actual present, and he does not conceive of great events in an objective setting. Indeed this restriction of outlook may be the reason why African tribes have in general no heroic poetry. The present so absorbs and occupies them that they feel no need to traffic with the past and the imaginary. Just as with Dingan the poet speaks only of the immediate past, and that only to show his hero in his present glory, so other African poets seem unwilling or unable to construct songs of heroic action which are enjoyable for their own sake and not some kind of summons to action or an instrument of personal praise.

A second reason for the failure to develop a heroic poetry may

[1] J. Shooter, *The Kafirs of Natal* (London, 1857), p. 310 ff.

be almost the opposite of what seems to operate among the African peoples. The origins of Chinese poetry are lost in a dateless past, and a great mass of early poems has certainly perished. But it seems on the whole improbable that the Chinese ever had a heroic poetry. That they had something like a pre-heroic poetry may be assumed from the traces of rhymed narrative like that in the *Shan-hai-ching* of Yü's fight with a nine-headed dragon.[1] It is also clear that they were capable of producing a poetry of vigorous action, like the piece preserved on stone drums in the Confucian temple at Peking and written about the eighth century B.C. :

> Our chariots are strong,
> Our horses well-matched,
> Our chariots are lovely,
> Our horses are sturdy ;
> Our lord goes a-hunting, goes a-sporting.
> The does and deer so fleet
> Our lord seeks.
> Our horn bows are springy ;
> The bow springs we hold.
> We drive the big beasts.
> They come with thud of hoofs, come in great herds.
> Now we drive, now we stop.
> The does and deer tread warily . . .
> We drive the tall ones ;
> They come charging headlong.
> We have shot the strongest of all, have shot the tallest.[2]

This is a hunting-song, but in its quiet way it recalls heroic narrative. It glories in a successful hunt, in the skill and high spirits of the hunters ; it tells its story with realism and an apt choice of facts ; it reflects the pride of men who set themselves a difficult task and carry it out. But it is not heroic poetry, since it is not an objective narrative but a personal record, and though there is no explicit praise in it, it is really panegyric spoken by the hunters about themselves.

A similar heroic spirit can be seen in other Chinese poems which are unquestionably laments. Ch'ü-Yüan's (332–295 B.C.) *Battle* echoes in a short space the delight of battle and the glory which death in it confers, but though it gives a vivid picture of fighting, it is clearly a lament, as the conclusion shows :

[1] Ch. 8 ; another version in ch. 17. I owe this reference to Professor Otto Maenchen.
[2] Arthur Waley, *The Book of Songs* (London, 1937), p. 290. The poet Han Yü (A.D. 768–824) wrote a poem about the stone-drums ; cf. R. C. Trevelyan, *From the Chinese* (Oxford, 1945), p. 30 ff.

Steadfast to the end, they could not be daunted.
Their bodies were stricken, but their souls have taken Immortality —
Captains among the ghosts, heroes among the dead.[1]

A like spirit informs the anonymous *Fighting South of the Castle*,
written about 124 B.C. It too has a real power of exciting narrative :

> The waters flowed deep,
> And the rushes in the pool were dark.
> The riders fought and were slain :
> Their horses wander neighing.

But it too, at the end, shows that it is a personal tribute to the
dead and not an objective narrative of their doings :

> I think of you, faithful soldiers ;
> Your service shall not be forgotten.
> For in the morning you went out to battle
> And at night you did not return.[2]

Though the Chinese possessed the seeds of a heroic poetry, they
did not allow them to grow. The explanation perhaps is that the
great intellectual forces which set so lasting an impress on Chinese
civilisation were hostile to the heroic spirit with its unfettered
individualism and self-assertion.

Perhaps something of the same kind happened in Israel. The
Hebrews, like the Chinese, had panegyrics, such as the Song of
Deborah [3] and the song which the women sang when Saul and
David returned from battle with the Philistines,[4] and laments,
such as David's for Saul and Jonathan [5] and for Abner.[6] But
there is no evidence that they had a truly heroic poetry. Its place
was largely taken by prose narrative, like that which tells of Saul
and David or of Samson's dealings with the Philistines. These
prose stories have a good deal in common with heroic poetry.
They are tales of adventure told for entertainment ; they abound in
speeches and descriptive details ; they are written from a courtly,
and not from a priestly, point of view and differ considerably
from such stories as those of Elijah and Elisha. On the other
hand they are more historical than heroic. They are episodic,
and their chief characters are more life-like than ideal. Indeed,
apart from Samson, they are hardly heroes in any full sense.
Saul has his kingly qualities and his tragic doom, and David his
vivid and brilliant youth, but fidelity to historical fact lowers the
heroic tone and produces something that is more a chronicle than

---

[1] Arthur Waley, *170 Chinese Poems* (London, 1918), p. 23.
[2] *Ibid.* p. 33.   [3] Judges v.   [4] I Samuel xviii, 7, and xxi, 11.
[5] II Samuel i, 19-27.   [6] *Ibid.* iii, 33 ff.

a saga. In Israel lament and panegyric failed to mature not only into heroic poetry but into heroic saga. The Song of Deborah suggests that the Hebrews might have developed a heroic poetry comparable to that of their Semitic kinsmen in *Gilgamish*, but something held them back. Even though they honoured great figures in their judges and kings, they did not make the most of their opportunities, and after that the growth of priestly rule would certainly have discouraged an art which gave too great an emphasis to the individual hero.[1]

In some countries a heroic poetry may come into existence but fail to be maintained in its full character, and this failure may in some cases be due to artistic considerations. Men may happen to prefer prose to poetry, and then saga becomes the popular art for tales of action. Saga is quite consistent with a purely heroic outlook and is indeed heroic prose. Such seems to have been the case with the Irish. They have an abundant prose which tells of themes like those of heroic poetry, such as violent deaths, cattle-raids, abductions, battles, feasts, and revenges. It has its great heroes like Cuchulainn and Conchobor, abounds in eloquent speeches, describes in detail the warriors' weapons, clothes, and personal appearance. Moreover these prose-tales often contain pieces of verse, usually in the form of speeches but sometimes narrative. In *The Courtship of Ferb*, which tells how Conchobor attacks a wedding-party and causes a great slaughter, the verse is narrative and older than the prose in which it is embedded.[2] Moreover, this verse is sometimes in the form called " rhetorics ", which works with single lines and is probably older than the more usual stanzas. In Ireland there seems once to have been a heroic poetry which for some reason failed to hold the field and survives fragmentarily in prose sagas. Something of the same kind may have happened among the Turcomans, who have a large cycle of prose tales about the hero Kurroglou.[3] They begin with his birth and end with his death, and have an undeniably heroic spirit in their accounts of plundering attacks on caravans, the hero's visits in disguise to the camps of his enemies, the single combats in which he is not always victorious, his unscrupulous revenges. The hero himself often

---

[1] Something of the same kind seems to have happened in Egypt, though there the deterrent force was the power of the Pharaohs, who saw themselves as the companions of the gods ; cf. the victory-song of Thothmes the Great quoted by H. R. Hall, *Ancient History of the Near East*, 4th edn. (London, 1919), p. 250 ff.

[2] A. H. Leahy, *The Courtship of Ferb*, London, 1902, gives both prose and poetry in English translation.

[3] A. Chodzo, *Specimens of the Popular Poetry of Persia*, London, 1842.

breaks into song for which verse is used, but the main narrative is in prose. This art has much in common with the heroic poetry of the Kara-Kirghiz, but though the authors know how to compose poetry, they restrict it and never, it seems, use it for actual narrative. Here, as in Ireland, it looks as if for some technical or artistic reason prose were preferred to verse. The heroic spirit remains, but perhaps because oral improvisation never reached so high a level among the Turcomans as among the Kara-Kirghiz, prose became the usual medium for a story. In restricting verse to songs and speeches made by the heroes the poets show a nicer sense of style than their Irish counterparts. No doubt in this they use many traditional and conventional means, and, since the scale is not usually large, are able to master the problems raised by improvisation. The existence of this anomalous mixed art of prose and verse in two widely separated peoples suggests that, just as in Ireland heroic poetry once existed but was gradually displaced by prose, the same thing may have happened among the Turcomans, who are sufficiently close to the Kara-Kirghiz to have the same poetical forms and may once have had a heroic poetry, but with them, as with the Irish, this seems to have been largely superseded by prose and kept only for dramatic speeches and the like inside a prose-narrative.

Heroic poetry, then, resembles panegyric and lament in its general outlook and primitive pre-heroic poetry in much of its technique. It is dangerous to deduce too much from this, but, if we are right in thinking that panegyric and lament represent a stage earlier than that of objective heroic poetry, it is possible that the latter comes into existence when pre-heroic, shamanistic poetry is touched by the spirit of panegyric or lament, and the result is a new kind of poetry which keeps the form of objective narrative but uses it to tell stories which embody a new ideal of manhood. Once a society has come to see that man will do more by his own efforts than by a belief in magic, and to believe that such efforts do him credit, it alters its whole philosophy. It may well come to its first inklings of such an outlook through its delight in some individual achievement or its grief at some outstanding loss, but it cannot be long before it wishes to see these newly discovered qualities presented on a wider and less impermanent stage, and then it takes to heroic poetry, which tells how great men live and die and fulfil the promise to which they are born. Whether this theory is true or not, it remains likely that heroic poetry learns much on the one side from shamanistic narrative with its ability to tell a story for its own sake, and on the other side from panegyric and lament with their affectionate emphasis on the gifts which win for a man the admiration of his fellows.

Some indication of this process and development may be seen in Russia. In the twelfth century Kiev was the centre of Russian civilisation and had its own school of poetry. There, we may be certain, were produced *byliny* [1] or heroic lays such as still flourish in outlying parts of Russia. From Kiev come many of the persons and events which survive in modern *byliny*, and there too is the landscape which is still described by bards who themselves live and work in quite different surroundings. Of these early *byliny* no example survives. What we have is the *Tale of Igor's Raid*, which was composed in 1187.[2] It tells a heroic story in a grand manner and uses certain devices common in the *byliny*, notably some " fixed " epithets and a kind of " negative comparison " which serves as a simile. It is conceived on a generous scale and is considerably longer than most panegyrics. But it is none the less a panegyric, not a heroic poem. The raid which it records took place in 1185, and the poem tells the dramatic story, draws practical morals from it, and pays a tribute to the reigning house of Kiev. If it resembles a heroic poem in the objectivity of its narrative and in the speeches spoken by its characters, it betrays itself as a panegyric at the close :

> Glory to Igor, son of Svyatoslav,
> To the brave bull, Vsevolod,
> To Vladimir, son of Igor !
> Long live the princes and their men
> Who fight for Christians against infidels !
> Glory to the princes and their men !

The *Tale of Igor's Raid* is on the very edge of heroic poetry, and comes from a society which practised it. In it we can see how closely the two types are related and how easy it must have been to move from panegyric to objective narrative.

At the same time the *Tale of Igor's Raid* knows of an earlier and different kind of poetry, which seems to have been pre-heroic and shamanistic. At the start the poet discusses whether he shall begin his song " in accordance with the facts of the time " and not " like the invention of Boyan ". He then goes on to say :

[1] The word *bylina* (plural *byliny*) is now commonly used for a Russian heroic poem. It was first used by Sakharov in his *Pesni russkago naroda* in 1839, where he took it from the phrase *po bylinam* in the *Tale of Igor's Raid*, which means " according to the facts ".

[2] In *La Geste du Prince Igor* (New York, 1948), p. 146, M. Szeftel dates the composition of the work between September 25th and the end of October 1187. In the same volume, pp. 235-360, R. Jakobson refutes the theory of A. Mazon that the *Tale* is an " Ossianic " composition of the eighteenth century.

> For the seer Boyan, when he wished
> To make a song for any man,
> Would fly in fancy over the trees,
> Race like a grey wolf over the earth,
> Soar like a blue-grey eagle below the clouds.
> Recalling, says he,
> The fights of old times
> He would loose ten falcons
> On a flock of swans ;
> Whichever swan was overtaken
> Was the first to sing a song.
> But indeed Boyan did not loose
> Ten falcons on a flock of swans, my brethren,
> But laid his own magic fingers on the living strings,
> And they themselves would sound forth
> The glory of the princes,
> Of old Yaroslav, of brave Matislav,
> Who slew Rodelya before the Circassian hosts,
> Of Roman, son of Svyatoslav, the handsome.

A little later the poet addresses Boyan and wishes that he were alive to tell of Igor's host :

> O Boyan, nightingale of olden times,
> If only you could sing of these hosts,
> Flitting, nightingale, through the tree of fancy,
> Soaring in your mind beneath the clouds,
> Weaving songs of praise around the present,
> Racing on the Trojan track,
> Across the plains to the mountains.

The poet of the *Tale* distinguishes between the new art of poetry which he himself practises and which, as we see, is realistic and factual, and the older art which Boyan practised. What he says is instructive. When Boyan is called a " seer " and said to race like a wolf or fly like an eagle, we are irresistibly reminded of the words used in popular lays for primitive heroes like Volga Vseslavich :

> He could swim as a pike in the deep seas,
> Fly as a falcon under the clouds,
> Race as a grey wolf over the open plains.[1]

Just as Volga is half a magician or a shaman and able to change his shape, so Boyan surely claimed similar powers for himself and must have been a shamanistic bard who acquired his knowledge by magical means. The poet of the *Tale* rationalises Boyan's powers by adding such words as " in fancy " to his account of them, but the old conception of the bard shines through. More-

[1] Rybnikov, i, p. 10.

over, the comparison between Boyan and the man who catches
swans with falcons makes a special point. Boyan tells of the past,
of which he has no personal knowledge, by a kind of divination.
He sets his powers loose, and the result is a song. This means
that Boyan relied on inspiration to a high degree and no doubt
made special claims to it. Though he told of historical events,
he did so in a pre-heroic way. We can, then, see in Russia a
scheme of development which conforms to our theory of the
origins of heroic poetry. The Russian *byliny*, with their account
of heroes and heroic doings, seem to be derived from a pre-heroic
manner, like that of Boyan, but their spirit owes much to
panegyrics like the *Tale of Igor's Raid*.

A development on similar lines may perhaps have taken place
in ancient Greece, though the evidence is fragmentary and inconclusive. The full fruit of heroic poetry is of course to be
found in the Homeric poems, but there are indications that they
were preceded by poetry of a different kind. The Greeks
attributed their first poetry to Musaeus and Orpheus. They may
never have existed, and certainly nothing of their work survives,
but the legends about them reveal an early view of a poet's nature
and functions. In the first place, he was a magician. Both
Herodotus [1] and Plato [2] attribute magical powers to Musaeus, and
Euripides does to Orpheus.[3] In the second place the early poet
possessed a very special knowledge, not merely of all things on
earth but of the past and the future as well. The words which
Homer uses of the prophet Calchas, that " he knew what is and
what will be and what was before ",[4] are applied in a slightly
different form by Hesiod to himself when he tells how the Muses
appeared to him on Mount Helicon and gave him the gift of
song.[5] If Hesiod claims the powers of a prophet or magician,
he shows his affinity not merely to Musaeus and Orpheus but to
modern shamans who claim a knowledge no less extensive. For
instance, the Swedish ethnographer Castrén met a certain Kögel-
Khan, who said of himself : " I am a shaman who knows the
future, the past, and everything which is taking place in the
present, both above and below the earth ".[6] This knowledge of
history is matched by a knowledge of the physical world. Just as
Tatar sages are said to know the number of stars in the sky, of fish

[1] viii, 96 ; ix, 43. [2] *Rep.* 364e ; *Prot.* 316d. [3] *Alc.* 968, *Cycl.* 646.
[4] *Il.* i, 70. On an Etruscan mirror in the Vatican Calchas is depicted with
wings, a sign, as J. D. Beazley shows, *J.H.S.* lxix (1949), p. 5, that he resembles
a shaman. [5] *Theogony*, 32.
[6] Castrén, *Nordische Reisen und Forschungen*, St. Petersburg (1866), iv,
p. 202.

in the sea, and of flowers on the earth,[1] so Greek legend records that there was once a contest between the seers, Calchas and Mopsos, about the number of figs on a tree, in which Mopsos won.[2] This shamanistic element seems to lurk in the background of Greek poetry, and though there is no trace of it in Homer, it makes an appearance later with Aristeas of Proconnesus, who was said to be able to survey the whole earth by freeing his soul from his body.[3] The Greeks, with their love of fact and reason, disowned the old magical claims, but they lay somewhere in the background and were connected by tradition with their first poetry.

On the other hand the Greeks also had panegyrics and laments and shared the outlook which these represent. Both may be found in Homer. When Achilles kills Hector, he turns to his followers and says :

" Now let us lift up a song of triumph, young men, Achaeans,
Unto our hollow ships let us go and take him with us there.
Great is the fame we have won ; we have killed great Hector,
      the god-like,
Unto whom, as a god, the Trojans prayed in their city." [4]

This is a simple panegyric, which the hero, not entirely out of character, sings with his companions to his own honour. So too when Thetis hears of Patroclus' death, she leads the lamentation and her Nereids join in it.[5] Again, when Patroclus' body is brought to him, Achilles laments in a similar way ; [6] and when Hector's body is brought back to Troy, the Trojan women lament him.[7] Homer knew both panegyrics and laments, and adapted them skilfully to his heroic poem. Of course he is far from any shamanistic claims or practice, but his forerunners who fashioned the mighty measures of Greek heroic poetry may at some early date have found that the respect for human achievement which is reflected in panegyrics and laments opened up new prospects for narrative, and so abandoned the old magical associations.

Heroic poetry lives side by side with panegyric and lament and fulfils its own different function. While they are intended primarily for special persons and special occasions, it is intended for public gatherings and may be performed whenever it is asked for. But there is inevitably some interaction between the two kinds. The same style and metres may be used indiscriminately in both ; the heroic outlook and sometimes heroic themes pass

---

[1] N. K. Chadwick, *Poetry and Prophecy* (London, 1942), p. 2.
[2] Hesiod, fr. 160.   [3] Maximus Tyrius, x, 3.   [4] *Il.* xxii, 391-4.
[5] *Ibid.* xviii, 50-51.   [6] *Ibid.* 315-16.   [7] *Ibid.* xxiv, 720-22.

from one to the other. The result is that each influences the other, and it is not always easy to decide to which kind some poems belong. For instance, the Anglo-Saxon *Brunanburh* tells of the defeat inflicted by Aethelstan on the allied armies of Constantine, king of Scots, and Anlaf, king of Dublin, in 937. It tells its story in a heroic spirit, and looks like a heroic poem in its delight over a victorious action and in its appreciation of the glory which Aethelstan has won. On the other hand it certainly praises Aethelstan and his men and has some airs of a panegyric when it comes to its triumphant close :

> Never in number
> On this island   in years aforetime
> Waxed such dire   destruction of war-men
> Slain by the sword-edge,   since — as the books say,
> Wise old writers, —   from the East wending,
> Angles and Saxons   hither came sailing,
> Over broad billows   broke into Britain,
> Haughty warriors   harried the Welshmen,
> Earls hungry for glory   gat hold of the land.[1]

Brunanburh stands so nicely poised between panegyric and heroic lay that it is pedantic to try to assign it definitely to one or the other class. No doubt it was written to please Aethelstan after the battle, but in doing so the poet copied heroic models and almost succeeded in making the poem stand in its own right.

A similar interaction between heroic poetry and lament can be seen in the Greek *Death of the Emperor Constantine Dragazis*, which must have been composed soon after the capture of Constantinople by the Turks in 1453 and laments both the fall of the city and the death in battle of the last Byzantine Emperor. That it is really a lament is clear from the opening lines :

> O Christian men of East and West, make oh make lamentation,
> Bewail and shed your tears upon the greatness of this ruin.

Having begun like this, it becomes factual and objective. It gives the exact date of the capture, Thursday, May 29th, 1453, and then describes how the conquerors tear down images, break crosses, ride on horseback into churches, kill priests, and rape virgins. This too is perhaps suitable for a lament. But from this the poet passes to what is very like heroic narrative, and tells of the death of the emperor :

> And when Constantine Dragazis, king of Constantinople,
> Heard news of what had come to pass, of hard and heavy matters,
> He made lament, was red with grief, could find no consolation.

[1] *Brunanburh*, 65-73.

His lance he took up in his hand, his sword he girt around him,
And then he mounted on his mare, his mare with the white fetlocks,
And struck with blows the impious dogs, the Turks, the sons of Hagar.
Sixty janissaries he killed, he also killed ten pashas,
But his sword was broken in his hand, and his great lance was
    shattered ;
Alone, alone he waited there, and no one came to help him ;
He lifted up his eyes towards heaven and spoke a prayer :
" O God and Lord omnipotent, who hast the world created,
Take pity on Thy people and take pity on this city ! "
Then a Turk struck him heavily, upon his head he struck him,
And from his charger to the ground fell Constantine the luckless,
And on the ground he lay outstretched, with blood and dust upon him.
From his body they cut the head, and on a pike they fixed it,
And underneath a laurel-tree made burial for his body.[1]

The poem begins like a lament and ends like a heroic lay, but, if it must be classified, it is undeniably a lament.

Another interaction between the two kinds of poem can be seen in many pieces which are not concerned with present events as immediate occasions and are, therefore, strictly speaking, heroic, but are none the less much influenced in their form by lament. Though Welsh poetry contains almost no strictly heroic narrative, it contains a number of laments for figures of the heroic age, like those for Owein, the son of Urien, and Cunedda in the *Book of Taliesin*, and for Urien and Cynddylan in the *Red Book of Hergest*,[2] while Irish has a lament for Cuchulainn by his wife Emer.[3] In other countries lament passes imperceptibly into heroic narrative and leaves a marked impress on many pieces. Some Russian *byliny* look very like laments for historical personages and have even developed a standard shape. For instance, poems on the deaths of Ivan the Terrible, Peter the Great, Catherine II, and Alexander I [4] all follow the same scheme. There is first an overture in which the melancholy scene is set by an appropriate simile ; then the poet describes a young soldier standing on guard ; finally the soldier tells what the sovereign's death means to the army, and what he says is a pure lament. In these poems there is a basis of contemporary history, though of course the authors of the existing versions are far removed in time from the great figures who are mourned. Some pieces in the *Elder Edda*, notably the *First Lay of Guthrun*, make their dramatic effect by speeches in which different characters lament their own woes and

---

[1] Legrand, p. 75 ff. For other versions of the same story cf. Garratt, p. 278 ff. ; Passow, no. cxciv.
[2] Chadwick, *Growth*, i, p. 38.   [3] *Idem*, p. 54.
[4] Chadwick, *R.H.P.* pp. 210, 274, 284, 290.

losses. The Bulgarian *Death of the Warrior Marko* begins with
Marko's mother looking for her son at dawn and asking the sun
where he is, continues with the sun's story of his death, and ends
with the eagles mourning his loss.[1] Some Ukrainian *dumy* are
constructed almost entirely as laments, like *The Prisoner's Complaint*, which begins with five lines telling of a Cossack in prison,
and then continues with forty-seven lines in which he bewails
his woes.[2] In these cases the heroic poem becomes more actual
by borrowing from the lament, but the heroic form still survives.
The story is told for its own sake and has no external reference.
It keeps its distance from its subject and has a dramatic independence as a creation of the imagination rather than as a comment on
a historical event.

The actions related in heroic poetry are primarily those of
human beings. It is anthropocentric in the sense that it celebrates
men by showing of what high deeds they are capable. It therefore
differs from another kind of poetry which resembles it in some
respects and with which it may originally have been united. This
other poetry tells of the doings of gods. Hesiod's *Theogony*,
which is almost purely theological, is composed in the same
metre, and in very much the same language, as the Homeric poems,
while the Norse *Elder Edda*, which is the work of several authors,
contains poems about both men and gods. But the poets themselves seem to have recognised some distinction between the two
kinds. Hesiod opens the *Theogony* by saying that the Muses
have told him to sing of " the race of the Blessed Gods ", while
Homer opens the *Odyssey* by telling the Muse to sing of " a
man ". So too the poems of the *Elder Edda* never confuse the two
subjects and may be divided easily into lays of gods and lays of
men, thus maintaining a distinction which seems to have existed
in old German poetry, of which the two oldest surviving examples
are *Muspili* about the Last Judgment and *Hildebrand* about a
fight between father and son. On the other hand the gods play a
large part in Homer, and the *Odyssey* contains a pure lay of the
gods in Demodocus' song of Ares and Aphrodite. So too in
Gilgamish and in *Aqhat* the gods take a prominent part in the
action. In the early days of heroic poetry this may well have
been common, but the distinction between the two kinds still
holds. Truly heroic poetry deals with men, and though it may
introduce gods into the action, the main interest is in men. In
more modern times lays of the gods have in some countries been
replaced by lays of saints. These are common in Russia and often

[1] Derzhavin, p. 83.   [2] Scherrer, p. 60.

contain heroic elements, like the *Vigil of St. Dmitri*,[1] which is superficially concerned with the victory which Dmitri Donskoi won over the Tatars at Kulikovo in 1378, but is really a poem in honour of God and His Saints who are more responsible than Dmitri for the victory; or in the different poems which tell of the killing of the princes Boris and Gleb, sons of Vladimir I, by their elder brother, Svyatopolk.[2] Wishing to get the whole kingdom for himself, he has them murdered and their bodies cast into the woods, where they remain uncorrupted for thirty years, when divine signs show that they are saints and lead to their burial. So too the Jugoslavs have poems in which the emphasis is not on heroic doings but on suffering and martyrdom, like *Simeun the Foundling*, which is in fact a piece of hagiology in a heroic dress;[3] and, rather differently, the tale of King Stjepan, who is chidden by his ecclesiastics for serving wine to his guests, and when he ceases to do so, is struck on the cheek by an Archangel.[4] In these, as in the Russian poems, the interest turns on a religious scheme of values in which the hero is submerged in the saint or the sinner. In Christian countries saints provide the kind of poetry which pagan countries give to their gods. Just as the Homeric Hymns, which tell stories of the gods, stress the inferiority of men, so Christian poems of saints reject the heroic conception of man as a self-sufficient being, and place him in a subordinate position in a scheme where the chief characters are God and His angels.

It is possible that these poems about gods and saints are the direct progeny of a truly heroic poetry, in which gods and men both take part. That this is an ancient art is clear both from the Homeric poems and from *Gilgamish* and *Aqhat*. The sharp division between the two kinds of lays in the *Elder Edda* looks like a sophisticated development of an art in which gods and men mingled more freely. Both the *Völsungasaga* and Saxo Grammaticus preserve stories in which Othin appears, and it is perhaps significant that the Eddic *Reginsmal* confines to the world of gods an action which the *Saga* divides between gods and men. That such methods existed in old Germanic poetry may be suspected from the story in the *Origo Gentis Langobardorum*[5] in which Ambri and Assi, the Vandal leaders, ask Wodan to give them victory over the Winniles. Wodan replies: " Whomsoever I shall first look upon, when the sun rises, to them will I give

---

[1] Bezsonov, i, p. 673 ff.
[2] *Idem*, p. 625 ff., gives thirteen versions of the poem.
[3] Karadžić, ii, p. 57 ff.   [4] *Idem*, p. 93 ff.
[5] P. 2 ff. ; Paulus Diaconus, i, 8 ; cf. Chadwick, *H.A.* p. 115.

victory ". Then Gambara and her two sons, the Winnile chieftains, Ibor and Aio, ask Fria for her help, and she tells them to come at sunrise with their wives disguised as men by letting down their hair to look like beards. At the moment of sunrise Fria turns the bed on which her husband Wodan lies towards the east and wakes him; he sees the Winniles and asks, " Who are those long-beards? " Fria replies, " As you have given them a name, give them also victory ", and he does. This episode recalls the *Iliad* in that the chief god and his wife take sides in a war between men, and the goddess tricks her husband into giving the victory to her favourites. It looks as if the old Germanic poetry contained stories in which the gods mingled freely in the affairs of men, as they certainly do not in the *Elder Edda*.

These considerations suggest that we can trace a series of stages in the development of primitive narrative poetry. At the start is shamanistic poetry in which the chief character is the magician, and magic is the main means of success. This is touched by the new spirit of a man-centred universe which, appearing separately in panegyric and lament, then invades narrative and produces a heroic poetry in which gods and men both take part. This in turn bifurcates into the poetry of gods and the poetry of men. Heroic poetry proper thus covers the whole of the second stage and half of the third. It is composed in the conviction that its characters belong to a special superior class, which it sets apart in a curious kind of past. Just as the Greeks believed that for a period which lasted for some four generations and had as its main events the sieges of Thebes and of Troy, men were heroes and performed tasks unusually hazardous and glorious, so the Germanic peoples in Germany, Scandinavia, England, Iceland, and Greenland believed in a heroic age of some two centuries which contained the great figures of Ermanaric, Attila, and Theodoric, and had as one of its chief episodes the destruction of the Burgundians by the Huns. Something of the same kind may be seen in mediaeval France with its conception of a heroic society clustered round Charlemagne in his wars against the Saracens; in Armenia with its arrangement of heroic legends round four generations of which the most important is dominated by David of Sasoun and his wars against the Egyptians and the Persians; in Albania with its cycle of tales about wars between the Mohammedan Albanians and the Christian Slavs after the Turkish invasion. Modern scholarship has usually been able to relate these different heroic ages to an established chronology. If there is still some doubt whether the Trojan War took place early in the twelfth century B.C., there is no doubt about the existence of the great Germanic heroes in the fourth, fifth, and sixth centuries A.D., or of Charlemagne about 800, or of David of Sasoun in the tenth century, or of Albanian wars in the fifteenth. But the poets are not interested in dates and hardly mention them; nor, if asked, would they be able to supply them. What matters is a scheme which brings persons and events together and provides a general plan within which the poet can work. The same is true of other cycles for which no historical foundation has been found. The Kara-Kirghiz centre their poems round the great figures of Manas, his son and his grandson; the Kalmucks round Dzhangar; and the Ossetes round the Narts with their leaders, Uryzmag and Batradz. So conceived a heroic age has a unity and completeness. What happens outside it is of little importance and receives scant notice. Round certain places, such as Troy or the Rhine or Aix-la-Chapelle or Sasoun or the Tien-Shan or the borders of Tibet or the Caucasus, memory gathers a number of stories between which there are many interrelations. The different characters who play their parts in such a cycle are sufficiently connected with each other for the whole to present an air of unity. This system has the advantage that by bringing well-known figures into new relations poets can widen the scope of their art and throw new light on old themes.

This simple conception is, however, not universal. Not all countries have heroic ages so clearly defined as those mentioned above. The remains of heroic poetry in Spain suggest that such a cycle never existed there. The *Cid* tells of events in the eleventh century, but fragments of other poems are concerned with earlier periods.[1] The tale of Conde Fernán González belongs to the tenth century, that of the Infante García to the eleventh, as do those of the sons of King Sancho of Navarre and of Sancho II and Zamora. These stories are hardly connected with one another, except that they belong to the history of Castile, and there is no indication either of a heroic age or of a heroic cycle. In modern Greece a long sequence of historical events has inspired poets to many unrelated songs.[2] The earliest events belong to the career of Digenis Akritas, who is thought to have died in 788 on the Anatolian frontier of the Byzantine Empire, but other poems tell of the flight of Alexius Comnenus in 1081, the siege of Adrianople by Amurath in 1361, the fall of Constantinople in 1453, the battle

---

[1] Cf. R. Menéndez Pidal, *Poesía juglaresca y juglares* (Madrid, 1924), p. 317 ff.
[2] Cf. Entwistle, p. 307 ff.

of Lepanto in 1571, the defeat of Ali Pasha by Botzaris in 1792, the defence of Missolonghi in 1824, and events even more modern down to our own time. Though some Jugoslav lays are concerned with the battle of Kosovo, where the Serbian kingdom went down before the Turks in 1389, this is not the only or indeed the most popular centre of interest. Some poems tell of events before it, others of the fifteenth century, or the revolt of 1804, or even of the wars of the twentieth century. The Albanians have poems on Skanderbeg or their fights with the Slavs, but they have many poems on other times and other subjects. Similarly though many of the Russian *byliny* are centred on Vladimir, prince of Kiev, who reigned from 1113 to 1125, many others tell of later events in the times of Ivan the Terrible, the false Dmitri, Peter the Great, Potemkin, Alexander I, Lenin, and Stalin. These later figures are not usually confused with those of an earlier age and tend to fall into independent cycles of their own. The poets treat them as separate parts of their repertory but regard them all as equally heroic. Even when a cycle is firmly established, as it is with the Germanic peoples, the poets sometimes desert it to sing of contemporary events, as in *The Battle of Hafsfjord*, which tells of the victory by which in 872 Harold Fairhaired made himself king of all Norway. So too *Maldon*, which is more austerely and more essentially heroic than any other Anglo-Saxon poem, was composed after a battle between the English and the Norsemen in 991. Evidently the poet thought that such a battle was in the true heroic tradition and should be celebrated accordingly. The strength of such a tradition can be seen in the use of the old alliterative measure for the poem *Scottish Field*, written after the defeat of the Scots by Henry VIII at Flodden in 1513. The heroic spirit may live so long and remain so lively that its poets refuse to confine it to the limits of a cycle, and do not shrink from singing about events of recent times.

Secondly, though we ourselves may like to date a heroic age, if we can, and relate it to some historical scheme, we may well doubt if the poets do anything of the kind. Homer gives no indication of date for the Siege of Troy, and such dates as we have are the production of Greek chronographers who lived centuries after him. *Gilgamish* is equally silent and moves in a self-contained world of the past. The same is true of the Kalmucks, the Kara-Kirghiz, the Uzbeks, and the Ossetes. The author of *Roland* may perhaps assume that his audience knows when his heroes lived, but he does not help with information about it. On the whole, heroic poetry gives no indications of date.

To this general rule there are some exceptions. A very few poems, like a Russian poem on the death of Skopin [1] and a Greek poem on the capture of Constantinople,[2] actually supply dates. The first may be due to literary influence, the second to the importance of an occasion which had become a landmark in history and was remembered as a day of terrible disaster. More commonly, a vague formula connects a story with a remote past. So the Kazak *Sain Batyr* begins with the words :

> When earlier generations lived,
> When forgotten peoples lived . . .[3]

The Norse *Short Lay of Sigurth* and *Atlamál* use a short formula " of old ", while the *First Lay of Helgi Hundingsbane* is rather more elaborate :

> In olden days   when eagles screamed

and the *Lay of Hamther* takes two lines :

> Not now, nor yet   of yesterday was it,
> Long the time   that since hath lapsed.

None the less very little is said, and the poet is plainly indifferent to chronology. The Russian poets do something else. They begin a poem by connecting it with some prince or tsar, as

> Glorious Vladimir of royal Kiev,
> He prepared a glorious honourable feast,

or

> In mother Moscow, in stone-built Moscow,
> Our Tsar was reigning, Ivan Vasilevich.

This is useful chiefly for showing to what cycle an episode belongs. Nor do the poets always use it. Though Ilya of Murom is closely connected with Vladimir, at least one poem neglects the connection and begins :

> Who is there who could tell us about the old days,
> About the old days, and what happened long ago ? [4]

When a modern composer of *byliny*, Marfa Kryukova, begins her *Tale of Lenin*, she follows custom in not worrying too much about dates. She feels that she must say something ; she may even know that Lenin was born in the reign of Alexander II, but she does not trouble to be precise, and places her story simply and firmly in the bad old days :

---

[1] Kireevski, vii, p. 11.
[2] Legrand, p. 75. For another Greek example cf. Baggally, p. 70.
[3] Radlov, iii, p. 205.   [4] Kireevski, i, p. 1.

In those days, in former days,
In those times, in former times,
Under Big-Idol Tsar of foul memory. . . .[1]

The truth is that composers of heroic poetry are not really
interested in chronology and know very little about it. They are
usually unlettered and cannot consult the books in which history
is set out as a sequence of events with dates. For them a heroic
tale has an existence with other tales of the same kind, and its
interest is not consciously historical but broadly and simply
human. So far as they have a conception of a heroic age, it is
artistic. It simplifies a mass of material, relates different stories
to one another, and conjures up a world in which heroes live and
act and die. This is different both from the outlook of panegyrics
and laments which are concerned with some particular occasion
already known to the audience, and from the outlook of romance
which sets its characters in some never-never-land of the fancy.

This art, which is concerned with the great doings of men,
tells stories because men like to hear them. The poet wishes not
to instruct but to delight his audience. Modern travellers who
have studied the performances of heroic poems among the
Russian, the Jugoslavs, and the Asiatic Tatars agree that the
poet's sole aim is to give pleasure. His is an artistic performance,
to which the guests or the crowd enjoy listening. This confirms
what some heroic poets say about their art. Though Hesiod was
not a great composer of heroic songs, he knew about them and
says that, when a man is full of sorrow, he should listen to songs
of glorious deeds and he will be cheered.[2] Homer illustrates how
this happens. His bards claim that their performances give
pleasure and, after holding the company in thrall, are con-
gratulated for their skill.[3] The same thing happens in *Beowulf*
at the feast which follows the rout of Grendel, when there is
recitation and music, and there is no doubt of their success:

The lay was finished,
The gleeman's song. Then glad rose the revel;
Bench-joy brightened.[4]

Heroic poets assume that their task is to give pleasure through
their art, and they depict imaginary bards as doing this. For this
reason heroic poetry is a notably objective art. The poets can
think of no better entertainment than stories of great men and
great doings.

[1] Andreev, p. 523.
[2] *Theogony*, 97-103.
[3] *Od.* i, 337, 347; viii, 44-5.
[4] *Beowulf*, 1066-8.

To this general practice there are some not very significant exceptions. The fervent patriotism of the Jugoslavs overflows into their heroic poetry and often provides its special character. The bards assume, no doubt correctly, that their audiences enjoy hearing of great national efforts. But sometimes this perfectly legitimate interest may become a little didactic, and the poem then becomes a means to inflame patriotism by noble examples. Even so the didactic element is not very aggressive, and we may hardly notice it in such a description of heroic songs as we find in *Haramabaša Ćurta* :

> Then the heroes sang the songs of heroes
> To the music of the maple gusle,
> Songs about the deeds of ancient heroes,
> How this one was famous in the marches
> And how he did honour to his brothers,
> By his courage and fair reputation,
> And still lives to-day in song and story
> As a pride and glory to the nation.[1]

But after all, national pride is a legitimate pleasure, and heroic poetry cannot fail at times to promote it. The same excuse can hardly be made for the many gnomic and moralising passages which give *Beowulf* an almost unique place among heroic poems. Not only does the poet make his characters enounce a number of impeccable maxims, but he himself intersperses improving reflections, as when he points out the different destinies that await the good and the bad after death (184 ff.), or praises the advantages of generosity (20 ff.), or announces that a man must trust in his own strength (1534). He passes laudatory judgment both on Scyld and on Beowulf in the same words — " that was a good king " (11 and 2390) — and, though he praises gentleness and kindness, he is enough of this world to praise the glory which it gives (1387 ff.). The poet might almost be regarded as an early exponent of that moralising for which his countrymen have shown such a predilection in later times, but a more likely explanation is that, since he stands on the threshold between a heroic outlook and a Christian, he is sometimes hard pressed to combine both, and does so only by emphatic maxims which proclaim that, despite his primitive story, he is a good Christian at heart.

Heroic poetry is impersonal, objective, and dramatic. The story is its chief concern. It is not addressed to any single patron, but stands in its own world, complete and independent, and conjures up its figures, their setting and their behaviour. Despite

[1] Morison, p. 10.

30

great differences of skill and quality most poets do what Aristotle says of Homer : " Homer, with little prelude, leaves the stage to his personages, men and women, all of them with characters of their own ".[1] Heroic poetry is indeed close to drama in its lack of criticisms and comments. Whatever direction the poet may give to his story, he keeps it vivid and independent. In primitive societies the audiences who listen to him partake in their imaginations of the events related, as if they themselves were spectators of them. They are held by excitement at what happens, by anticipation of what will come next, by the special appeal of this or that character or episode or description. No doubt they form their own likes and dislikes for characters, their own approvals and disapprovals, but these are natural and simple reactions. The poet's hearers hardly need his help to tell them what to think. They agree with him in a general conception of what men ought to be and follow him easily without fuss as he unfolds his tale.

This dramatic objectivity can be seen in the large part given to speeches delivered by the different characters. Wherever heroic poetry exists, speeches are to be found and are among its peculiar glories. In Homer or *Beowulf* or *Roland* they are conceived on a generous scale. The Kara-Kirghiz and Uzbek poets use them with an even broader scope. One of their functions is to fill in the background of a hero's life with reminiscence and reference, as Homer makes Nestor boast of his lost youth or Phoenix tell of his lurid past. They can also touch on other stories which lie outside the poet's immediate subject, as Homer touches on Heracles or Perseus or Daedalus or Theseus or almost forgotten wars which Priam fought against the Amazons or the Pylians against the Arcadians on the river Celadon, or the poet of *Beowulf* introduces references outside his immediate purview to Sigemund or Heremod or Thryth or the war between the Geats and the Swedes. Speeches also serve to reveal a hero's personality by the way in which he speaks about himself. In Armenian poems about David of Sasoun they give a delightful touch of humanity and humour to the not always very heroic characters. In the poems of the Achins they are said to be composed with a good eye to dramatic effect, and one of the finest passages in the poem *Pochut Muhamat*, which tells of Sumatran wars in the first half of the eighteenth century, is that in which the mother of a young prince urges him not to take part in an expedition to a region where they fight not with cut and thrust but with fortifica-

[1] *Poetics*, 1460a 10.

31

tions and firearms.[1] Speeches are of course useful as a kind of action in themselves, especially when they are parts of a debate or a quarrel, but the emotions which they express and their personal approach to many matters of interest help the poet to display his powers outside the bounds of strict narrative. By identifying himself with his characters he can indulge emotion and sentiment, and adds greatly to the richness and variety of his poetry.

The fascination of dramatic speeches is so great that sometimes they constitute almost complete poems, in which one or more of the characters tell in their own persons what happens. There is a strong tendency towards this in some pieces of the *Elder Edda*, and it is notable that the old Danish poems translated into Latin verse by Saxo Grammaticus all purport to be told by some heroic character who speaks in the first person, though Saxo introduces or explains them with prose passages in the third. It has been thought that this use of the first person is very primitive and anterior to the use of the third. But this seems unlikely for more than one reason. In most primitive peoples the third person is used, and there is no evidence that it has been preceded by the first. Indeed the use of the first is very rare. Outside Saxo's translations, which come from the very end of the Norse heroic tradition, it exists mainly among the Ainus, whose art is highly accomplished, and in some old Turkic inscriptions from the river Orkhon, which are memorials to the dead and follow the convention that the dead man speaks for himself. The third person is the usual instrument for narrative, and when heroic poetry uses the first, it is a sign not of primitive character but of an advanced art which hopes to secure a greater dramatic effect by cutting out the poet as an intermediary and bringing the audience into what looks like direct contact with the heroes and heroines who tell their own tales. We might be tempted to draw other conclusions from such a poem as the Norse *Helgakvitha Hjorvarthssonar*, where all the verse is dramatic, and any elements of narrative are supplied by prose, but the text is certainly composite and corrupt, and too much must not be deduced from it. In general, we may say that the semi-dramatic form of some heroic poetry is due to the poets' desire to present a situation as vividly as possible. Since heroic poetry admits speeches freely, there is after all no reason why a poem, especially a short poem, should not consist of a speech or speeches and very little else. Such an art satisfies the needs of narrative by keeping events vividly before us.

[1] Hurgronje, ii, p. 95.

When a situation is presented through words spoken by one of the characters in it, the audience is made to feel that it listens to some important participant in a great crisis and enjoys a first-hand account of it. When the Ukrainian *dumy*, after a short prelude or introduction, make some hero tell his own story, they give a personal quality to it and show what it means to those who take part in it. A good example of the same art can be seen in a Russian *bylina*, which Richard James, an Oxford graduate, recorded in Moscow in 1619, when he was chaplain to the English merchants there. The poem is close to a lament and no doubt owes much to the traditional form of the Russian *plach*, which is still popular at funerals. It tells of the grief of Ksenya, daughter of Boris Godunov, for her father, who died in 1605, and is thus quite close to the events which it portrays and clothes with a convincing actuality. In its short space it has considerable grace and pathos and a sympathetic understanding of what her situation means to the bereaved princess :

> The little white bird laments,
> The little white quail :
> " Alas, that I so young must mourn !
> They will burn the green oak,
> And destroy my little nest,
> And kill my little fledglings,
> And capture me, the quail."
> The princess laments in Moscow :
> " Alas, that I so young must mourn !
> When the traitor comes to Moscow,
> Grisha Otrepev, the unfrocked priest,
> He will imprison me,
> And, having imprisoned me, will shave off my hair
> And put monastic vows on me.
> But I do not wish to be a nun,
> Or to keep monastic vows.
> The dark cell must be thrown open
> That I may look on fine young men.
> Ah me, our pleasant corridors,
> Who will walk along you,
> After our royal life,
> And after Boris Godunov ?
> Alas, our pleasant halls,
> Who will dwell within you,
> After our royal life,
> And after Boris Godunov ? " [1]

The appeal of this little poem is that it presents a pathetic situation from the view of someone who suffers in it, and this gives

[1] Kireevski, vii, p. 58 ff., Chadwick, *R.H.P.* p. 219 ff.

the directness of a personal revelation. It owes much to the art of the lament, but this has been transposed to a new use in which narrative and drama are united.

Some Norse poems of the *Elder Edda* use a similar dramatic technique with a greater boldness. While the *Second Lay of Guthrun* is spoken throughout by a single character, other poems give an interchange of speeches between two or three or four characters. The dramatic effect is heightened because the poet sometimes plunges straightway into speeches and does not say who the speaker is. The speeches succeed each other in rapid change and counterchange, and though each is short, the whole effect is of a vivid, living scene. There is no need to think that the different parts were originally taken by separate performers. Indeed the *Nornagests Saga* indicates that one performer was enough, since it tells of a stranger's visit to the court of King Olaf Tryggvason and of his recitation of *Brynhild's Hell Ride*, which is entirely a dialogue between Brynhild and a giantess.[1] The dramatic art of the *Elder Edda* is not that of a mimetic rite but an extension of narrative towards drama by making it more concentrated and more vivid. A good performer would no doubt do something towards acting the different parts, but the result is still narrative. The special power of this art can be seen from the *First Lay of Guthrun*. Its subject is Guthrun's grief at Sigurth's death, and it shows this in its tragic strength, first by telling of Guthrun's silence while other women lament their woes :

> Then did Guthrun   think to die
> When she by Sigurth   sorrowing sat ;
> Tears she had not,   nor wrung her hands,
> Nor ever wailed as other women.[2]

Then Guthrun breaks into her lament, and with that, we might almost think the poem should end. But the story is not yet complete. Guthrun's lament awakes qualms in Brynhild and makes her feel bitter regret for encompassing Sigurth's death. The poem is almost a drama, in which speeches take the place of action until the unexpected climax comes.

A special dramatic device used in long heroic poems is that by which an important hero tells part of his own story in the first person. The classic case of this is the tale which Odysseus tells to Alcinous and his court of his wanderings from the sack of Troy to his arrival on Calypso's island. This story has of course

---

[1] Cap. 9 ; cf. N. Kershaw, *Stories and Ballads of the Far Past*, p. 33 ff.
[2] *Guthrúnarkvitha*, i, 1.

been frequently imitated in "literary" epic from Virgil to Voltaire. But Homer is not unique among "primitive" poets in his use of the device. In *Gilgamish* Uta-Napishtim, the Babylonian precursor of Noah, tells the story of the Flood, and in modern times the Kara-Kirghiz bard, Sayakbai Karalaev, does something similar when he makes Alaman Bet tell his own story in some 4500 lines.[1] In long poems this device brings considerable advantages to the composition. It enables Homer to keep his plot in hand and save it from becoming too episodic. The story told by Odysseus has its own coherence because his personality dominates it, whereas, if it were told in the third person, it would certainly disturb the balance of the whole poem. But this method has other advantages. By making the hero tell his own story the poet brings him closer to us and makes his personality more vivid. Just as Homer presents Odysseus' adventurous spirit through the blithe recklessness with which he takes risks and then surmounts them by brilliant improvisations, so in *Gilgamish*, when Uta-Napishtim tells his own story and explains why the gods have given him immortality, we see how different he is from Gilgamish who seeks immortality but is destined not to win it, and Karalaev gives a deeper insight into the character of Alaman Bet, who is by birth a Chinese but has become a Moslem by conversion and is something of an oddity in Kara-Kirghiz society. This device is possible only in narrative of some scale, but is in fact an extension of the dramatic speeches found in short poems like the Russian *byliny* and the Norse *Elder Edda*.

From this it is no great step to composing a whole poem in the first person as if the hero himself were relating it. This is what the Ainus do both for poetical narrative and prose folk-tales. Though it clearly makes the events more immediate and more dramatic, there is no need to assume that it is shamanistic and that the poet identifies himself with the hero. There is no call for him to be anything more than an actor. Of course a simple audience will always tend to identify the actor with the part which he assumes and may well believe that for the moment it hears the hero speaking about himself and his adventures. But this device can be used in quite sophisticated poetry, like the Arabian *The Stealing of the Mare*, in which the story is told by the hero, Abu Zeyd, in the first person. It is true that he sometimes lapses into the third, but that is no more than T. E. Lawrence's friend, King Auda, used to do when he " spoke of himself in the third person and was so sure of his fame that he loved to shout out

[1] *Manas*, pp. 158-232.

stories against himself ".[1]   The highly dramatic character of this poem owes much to its special manner of narration.

Heroic poetry requires a metre, and it is remarkable that, as the Chadwicks have shown,[2] it is nearly always composed not in stanzas but in single lines. The line is the unit of composition, and in any one poem only one kind of line is used. This is obviously true of the dactylic hexameter of the Homeric poems, the line with four " beats " of *Gilgamish*,[3] the accentual alliterative verse of Old German and Anglo-Saxon, the Norse *fornyrthislag* or " old verse " and *málaháttr* or " speech measure ",[4] the verse of the Russian *byliny* with its irregular number of syllables and fixed number of artificially imposed stresses,[5] the ten- and sixteen-syllable trochaic lines of the Jugoslavs,[6] the eight-syllable line of the Bulgarians, the πολιτικὸς στίχος or fifteen-syllable line of the modern Greeks,[7] the sixteen-syllable line, with internal rhymes, of the Achins,[8] and the Ainu line with its two stresses, each marked by a tap of the reciter's stick.   Each line exists in its own right as a metrical unit and is used throughout a poem.

To this general rule there are exceptions both apparent and real.   Apparent exceptions are those cases in which series of lines are bound together by final assonance or rhyme and look like stanzas.   The Kara-Kirghiz, Uzbeks, and Kazaks use a standard line, the *jyr*, of three feet which vary from two to four syllables, and the lines are grouped in sets of varying length which are held together by assonance or the repetition of a word.[9]   In *Roland* the line is of ten syllables, and groups of lines are held by assonance.   In the *Cid* the line varies from ten to over twenty syllables and may have had a fixed number of imposed stresses like the Russian line, while the groups of lines are held by rude rhymes or assonance.   The Albanian lines, with seven or eight syllables and trochaic rhythm, are similarly grouped.   The Armenian line is almost as free as the Russian, but it too tends to form rhyme-

---

[1] *Revolt in the Desert* (London, 1927), p. 94.   [2] *Growth*, iii, p. 751 ff.
[3] The " beat " is not a syllable but a word or word-group.
[4] Philpotts, p. 32 ff.   Perhaps the earliest known example of Germanic verse is the inscription on the golden horn (*c.* A.D. 300), which was stolen from the Copenhagen Museum in 1802: W. P. Ker, *The Dark Ages* (London, 1904), p. 232.
[5] Cf. Entwistle, p. 383.
[6] The sixteen-syllable line, or *bugarštica*, is probably older and may be simply a combination of two eight-syllable lines such as are still used in Bulgarian.
[7] Perhaps the earliest example of this, in a quantitative form, is what Philip of Macedon sang on the field of Chaeronea, Plut. *Dem.* 20: Δημοσθένης Δημοσθένους Παιανιεὺς τάδ' εἶπεν.
[8] Hurgronje, ii, p. 75, the fourth syllable rhymes with the sixteenth, and the eighth with the twelfth.   [9] Radlov, iii, p. xxiv.

groups of very varying length. In all these cases the sets of lines look at first sight like stanzas, but are not really so, since the real essence of a stanza is that it is of a fixed shape and length, and these groups are not. They vary a good deal in length, and the constant element in them is the single line. In principle there is no difference between them and the technique of Homer or *Beowulf*.

A special problem is presented by some poems of the *Elder Edda*, in which, though a single line is used throughout, it tends to fall into regular four-lined stanzas. This is the case with most of the strictly heroic poems which tell a story in a straightforward manner. The line used is based on the old Germanic metre, and we cannot doubt that the Norse technique is derived from a system in which the line, and not the stanza, was the unit. We have, however, to explain why lines tend to fall into stanzas. It is clear that they do not regularly do so, since the Codex Regius, which preserves the poems, presents sometimes groups of six lines and sometimes of two. To attribute this to the editor's or the copyist's errors is almost impossible. The six-lined groups cannot usually be reduced to four lines without spoiling their sense, nor is it always necessary to assume that something is missing from the two-lined groups. On the other hand the tendency to fall into stanzas is undoubtedly present. Perhaps the best explanation is that the collection of these poems was made when they had passed out of current use and were not well remembered, and that those who claimed to know them tended unconsciously to reshape them into something akin to the ballad-stanza which was common in the poetry of the day.

There are, however, more serious exceptions to the general rule than this. Some other poems in the *Elder Edda* are composed in the *ljóthahǎttr* or " chant-metre ", which is undeniably a stanza and not a series of metrically uniform lines. Its form is :

> Who are the heroes   in Hatafjord ?
> The ships are covered with shields ;
> Bravely ye look,   and little ye fear,
> The name of the king would I know.[1]

So far as strictly heroic subjects are concerned, this metre is used only in the third section of the *Lay of Helgi*, and in a single strophe each of *Helgi Hundingsbane II* and the *Lay of Hamther*. In the last two cases it is plainly an intrusion from later versions of the stories, and even in the *Lay of Helgi* it looks as if the

---

[1] *Helgakvitha Hjorvarthssonar*, 12.

collector of the poems, anxious to make the story complete, had used what is really a ballad and not a heroic poem. These cases are not important but they show the beginnings of a process in which the art of heroic poetry is changed into something else. A more violent change has happened to the Ukrainian *dumy*. We may surmise that originally the Ukraine, which is the country of Kiev and the heroic world of Vladimir, had a heroic poetry whose technique resembled the free and easy methods of the *Tale of Igor's Raid*. The modern art may be derived from this since it uses lines of very varying length, but it differs in its use of rhyme, usually in couplets. The system may be seen in *Marusja Boguslavska* :

> This request alone I make you, pass not by Boguslav's town.
> To my father dear and mother make this news known :
> > That my father dear grieve not,
> Alienate not store of treasure, ground or plot,
> > That no store of wealth he save,
> > Neither me, Marusja the slave,
> > Child of Boguslav the priest,
> > Evermore seek to release,
> For become a Turk I am, I'm become a Mussulman,
> > For the Turk's magnificence,
> > And for my concupiscence.[1]

The general effect here is more like that of a song than we expect in a heroic poem. Here too we may see a process of decomposition. The old heroic form has broken down and been replaced by something which is half-way towards song composed in rhymed stanzas.

With these exceptions, which come from regions where a traditional style has begun to decay, heroic poetry uses the single line as its metrical unit of composition and gains certain advantages from it. The superiority of the line over the stanza is that it allows more scope and variety in telling a story. The poet can vary between long and short sentences, and produce unusual effects by breaking or ending a sentence in the middle of a line ; he is free to make full use of conventional formulae and phrases, to introduce descriptions of places and things without having to make them conform to the demands of a stanza. But though the line has these advantages over the stanza, it does not follow that it owes its use to this cause. Heroic poetry seems always to be chanted, usually to some simple stringed instrument, like the Greek lyre, the Serbian *gusle*, the Russian *balalaika*, the Tatar

[1] Entwistle, p. 377 ; Scherrer, p. 67.

koboz, or the Albanian *lahuta*. The music to which poems are sung is usually not a real or a regular tune but a monotonous chant in which the bard often keeps whole lines on a single note. Such indeed is said to be the regular practice in Albania, and the heroic Jugoslav chants recorded by Milman Parry are monotonous and lacking in melody. There certainly seems to be no evidence that a special poem has its own tune. Among famous Russian bards the elder Ryabinin knew only two tunes, and " the Bottle " one.[1] This is quite a different art from the melodies which accompany lyrical poetry, give pleasure for their own sake, and are as likely to obscure as to illustrate the words. Heroic poetry puts the words first and subordinates the music to them. What it uses is really no more than recitative. To use a regular tune like that of a song would have made the task of heroic poets much more difficult and have interfered with the clear presentation of the tales which they have to tell.

This consideration may help to elucidate the troublesome question of the relation of heroic poetry to ballads. At the outset we may notice that many poems called ballads are actually heroic poems. This is true of the Russian *byliny*, the Jugoslav and Bulgarian " national songs ", the lays of Esthonia, Albania, and modern Greece. But other ballads, which really deserve the name, are different. England, France, Germany, Scandinavia, and Rumania have narrative poems which differ from heroic lays in that they are composed in regular stanzas and sung to recurring tunes. Although the spirit of *Edward, my Edward* or *Chevy Chase* or *Sir Patrick Spens* is undeniably heroic, the form is not that of heroic poetry, and the difference of form marks a real difference in function. Such ballads, with their regular tunes and their occasional refrains, belong to song rather than to recitative, and may originally have been accompanied by some sort of dance or mimetic gesture. Their form gives a pleasure different from that of the chanted lay. Music plays a greater part in it, and the narrative not only ceases to be the chief source of interest but tends to be treated in a more impressionistic way which emphasises less the development of a story than certain vivid moments in it. Even the Spanish *romances*, which sometimes look like broken fragments of epic and undoubtedly have some connection with it, are really examples of this art. Their tunes are essential to their performance; they have many lyrical qualities. The distinction between heroic poetry and ballads is not so much of matter and spirit as of form and function and effect.

[1] Rybnikov, i, p. xciii.

Heroic poetry is not only objective but claims to tell the truth, and its claims are in general accepted by its public. In his Preface to the *Heimskringla* or *Saga of the Norse Kings* Snorri Sturluson, who lived from 1178 to 1241, and knew what he was talking about, explains that among his materials are " songs and ballads which our forefathers had for their amusement ", and adds " now, although we cannot say just what truth there may be in these, yet we have the certainty that old and wise men hold them to be true ". The stories may in fact not all be true, but they were thought to be. In considering these words we must remember that one generation's idea of truth differs from another's, and that unlettered societies lack not only scientific history but any conception of scientific truth. For them a story is sufficiently true if it gives the main outlines of events and preserves important names ; it is not impaired by the poet's imaginative treatment of details. Hesiod indeed tells that, when the Muses appeared to him they said :

> We can make false things seem true, so great is our skill,
> For we know how to utter the truth when that is our will.[1]

But few poets and few audiences make so conscious a distinction as this, and on the whole heroic poetry claims to tell its own kind of truth. Its authority is in the first place tradition. Its stories are those which have been handed down by generations and are sanctified by the ages. It is no accident that Russian heroic poems are called either *byliny*, " events of the past ", or *stariny*, " tales of long ago ". Such stories command respect because they are old, and men often assume that their ancestors knew more than they themselves do. The heroic poet speaks with the authority of tradition and passes on what he himself has heard from his elders. A story becomes more respectable by being old and popular. The poet of *Hildebrand* begins by saying simply, " I have heard it said ", just as Yakut and Kalmuck poets often say " as they say " or " as it is said ". In the same way the Norse poet of the *Lament of Oddrun* states his credentials when he begins :

> I have heard it told   in olden tales
> How a maiden came   to Morningland.

In heroic poetry it is commonly assumed that age confers dignity on a story, and that what has been long preserved is likely to be true.

To the authority of tradition some poets add the authority of inspiration by some divine power which it would be improper to

[1] *Theogony*, 27-8. Trs. J. Lindsay.

question. Even Hesiod makes such a claim for himself when he says that the Muses appeared to him on Helicon and gave him a voice to tell of the past and the future.[1] No doubt this is a shamanistic survival, but it fits easily into the heroic scheme, and the audiences accept such a claim. Whatever Homer meant when he told the Muses to tell of the wrath of Achilles or of the man of many wiles, it is clear that he claims some kind of supernatural authority for what he is going to say and assumes that his audience will accept it. His own Phemius, who is the bard at Odysseus' home in Ithaca, says that a god has planted songs in him.[2] In the same way a Kara-Kirghiz bard, whom Radlov knew, said : " I can sing every song ; for God has planted the gift of song in my heart. He gives me the word on my tongue without my having to seek it. I have not learned any of my songs ; everything springs up from my inner being, from myself." [3] Whether by tradition or inspiration, heroic poetry sets out to tell stories which contain some element of truth, and the poet's credulity reflects that of the society in which he lives. There comes, sooner or later, a time when the old stories are no longer believed, and then the old poetry loses its hold on an audience which is now instructed by books and newspapers. When this happens, the poet may still assert his rights and claim that he possesses a special knowledge. When the Kara-Kirghiz bard, Sagymbai Orozbakov, tells in his *Manas* of the destruction of the giantess Kanyshai, he evidently feels that his audience is likely to be sceptical, and makes concessions in advance :

> Everything in this tale you'll find,
> Entanglement of false and true.
> All happened very long ago,
> Eye-witnesses are hard to find !
> To these wonders no one testifies ;
> What was, what not, are here confused.
> This is a tale of long past years,
> An ineffaceable trace of the past.
> The world to-day believes it not.[4]

But until such doubts arise, the bard is regarded as an authority on the past. He provides history as well as poetry. And this, more than anything else, separates heroic poetry from romance which candidly tells stories which everyone knows to be untrue.

The study of heroic poetry depends on material of a very mixed character. In the first place it is still a living art in some countries and may be studied at first hand. It lives by recitation

[1] *Theogony*, 32. [2] *Od.* xxiii, 347. [3] Radlov, v, p. xvii. [4] *Manas*, p. 254.

and is seldom written down except by enquiring scholars from outside. In consequence such texts as we have are almost haphazard records of what has been an enormous mass of recited poetry. This material is none the less of primary importance. The poems show the art as it is really practised by living men, but they suffer from a serious defect. The oral poet usually composes as he recites, and for a successful performance he needs an audience in sympathy with him and eagerly intent on hearing what he has to say. When a stranger, interested in oral poetry for scholarly or scientific reasons, arrives and asks him to recite a poem, the result is not always satisfactory. In the old days when the scholar took down the words in long hand, he was necessarily too slow for the poet and hampered the free flow of his composition. In consequence, as some of the poems recorded by Radlov from the Asiatic Tatars indicate, the poet, deprived of his usual setting and audience and for that reason not at his ease, is even less at his ease when he has to go slowly and pause for his words to be written down. Even with such devices as recording by dictaphone there still remains the difficulty that any stranger may by his mere presence hamper and discourage a poet, especially if he employs some outlandish mechanical apparatus. Though many oral poems have been recorded in the last eighty years, we cannot assume that they are the best of their kind or even the best that an available poet can produce. They are representative in the sense that they are genuine, but their worth is a matter of accident.

Our second source consists of those poems which by some happy chance have survived in written form from the past. These have at least this in common, that they were for some reason written down, often at times when writing was not common and used chiefly for legal documents or sacred books. The Homeric poems, for instance, were probably written down because of their literary excellence, and the handsome manuscript of *Beowulf* suggests that some rich man wished it to be preserved in his library. On the other hand the Oxford manuscript of *Roland* has no such distinction and seems to be a kind of " prompter's copy ", used to refresh the bard's memory when he needed it. Since poems are preserved for quite different reasons, none of which is inevitable, it is clear that many other poems of equal or greater merit have not been preserved, simply because no one thought of having them written down. Even when someone has decided that a poem should be recorded, the dangers are not over. The *Elder Edda*, with its unique collection of old Norse poetry, was written down by someone who could not get complete texts of all the poems and was sometimes forced to combine various poems into one, sometimes unable to say where one poem ended and another began. Even when they have been recorded, poems have to face all the dangers that threaten books. In classical antiquity, perhaps at the library of Alexandria, something was preserved of the heroic epic of Eumelus of Corinth, who lived about 700 B.C. and told of subjects rather outside Homer's range. But of this work there remain only a few lines and a few references.[1] The unique manuscript of *Beowulf* was damaged by fire in 1731, and at the same time *Maldon*, which was discovered in the seventeenth century, was destroyed only five years after Thomas Hearne's *editio princeps* of it. The fragment of *The Fight at Finnsburh*, which survived by an accident in a book-cover at Lambeth, was afterwards lost. Only happy chances have revealed the remains of the Old German *Hildebrand* and the Anglo-Saxon *Waldhere*; for they too were found in book-covers, the one at Cassel and the other at Copenhagen; and since 1945 *Hildebrand* has disappeared. The epic of *Gilgamish* has an even more fortuitous history. Its remains have been unearthed by archaeologists on clay tablets which range from before 2000 B.C. to 600 B.C. and are composed variously in Old Babylonian, Hittite, Assyrian, and New Babylonian. We must be content with what we have and recognise that enormous tracts of heroic poetry have been lost for ever.

Heroic poetry suffers from the special danger that, when it ceases to be fashionable, it disappears. Fortunately the Greeks never abandoned their love for Homer, and that is why his poems are so well preserved. But other countries have been less faithful. Though we know that Charlemagne was interested in " barbarous and ancient songs " and ordered collections of them to be made,[2] nothing survives from his project with the possible exception of *Hildebrand*, which seems at least to have been written down at this time. Indeed *Hildebrand* is the only relic of the great art of heroic song which once flourished in Germany, though its themes survive in Norse and Anglo-Saxon poetry and in later German adaptations. How vigorous and widespread this art was in the fourth, fifth, and sixth centuries A.D. is clear from external evidence not far removed from it in time. Jordanes, himself a Goth, records that his countrymen sang to the lyre songs about their ancestors, notably Eterpamara, Hanala, Fridigernus, and Vidigoia.[3] These were no doubt great figures in their day, but of them only Vidigoia has any place — as Wudga — in existing poetry. In the

---

[1] G. Kinkel, *Epicorum Graecorum Fragenta* (Leipzig, 1877), p. 185 ff.
[2] Egginhard, *Vita Caroli Magni*, 29.   [3] *Getica*, 5.

fifth century Sidonius Apollinaris, bishop of Auvergne, knew of Ostrogothic songs which appealed to King Theodoric II because they " encouraged manliness of spirit ",[1] and suffered from having to listen to Burgundians singing to the lyre.[2] But no Gothic songs survive, and the nearest approach to one is the Norse *Battle of the Goths and the Huns*, which may be based on a Gothic original. Other Germanic peoples practised the same art with a similar fate. In the sixth century Gelimer, king of the Vandals, was himself a minstrel,[3] and about 580 Venantius Fortunatus addresses to Lupus, the Frankish duke of Aquitaine, a poem in which he speaks of barbarians singing to the harp.[4] Paul the Deacon reports that Alboin, king of the Langobards, who died in 572, was sung by Saxons, Bavarians, and other peoples.[5] In the same way we cannot doubt that there was once a Swedish heroic poetry, since there are references to Swedish history in *Beowulf*, a runic monument in Södermanland illustrates the tale of Sigurth,[6] and the Rök stone in Östergötland has enigmatic verses which may refer to Theodoric.[7] There was once a Swedish branch of this Germanic poetry, as there were other branches, but no single text has survived from it.

This lack of old German texts may to some extent be counterbalanced by material derived from original poems which have long been lost. The wealth of old Danish poetry can be seen from the Latin epitomes of Saxo Grammaticus, who wrote about A.D. 1200, when the art was not sufficiently moribund to prevent him collecting interesting stories, like that of Ingeld, who is known to Beowulf, of Hamlet, and many others whose names have survived elsewhere. His worth is proved by his adaptation into Latin verse of the *Bjarkamál*, of which a few lines survive in Norse and show that he was reasonably conscientious. Other stories, which seem to be derived from heroic lays, survive in historians. Procopius' account of the death of Hermegisclus, king of the Warni, looks like a loan from a poem of Frankish origin.[8] Paul the Deacon and the anonymous author of the *Origo Gentis Langobardorum* tell stories which have a truly heroic temper and may well be derived from songs. Alboin's visit to Turisind, whose son he has slain in battle, recalls Homer's account of Priam's visit to Hector ;[9] the battle of the Langobards and the Vandals is Homeric in the role which it gives to the gods in the conduct of human

---

[1] *Ep.* i, 2. [2] *Carm.* 12. [3] Procopius, *Bell. Vand.* ii, 6.
[4] *Carm.* vii, 8, 61 ff. [5] i, 27.
[6] M. P. Nilsson, *Homer and Mycenae* (London, 1933), p. 192.
[7] Stephens, *Handbook of the Old Runic Monuments* (London, 1884), p. 32 ff.
[8] *Bell. Got.* iv, 20. [9] Paulus Diaconus, i, 24.

affairs; [1] the swift retribution for brutal conduct which brings death to Alboin is in the strict tradition of heroic morality.[2] Perhaps, too, even in England legends of the Anglo-Saxon conquest may have survived in poems which were known to the first historians and chroniclers. The story of Hengest, as it is told in the *Historia Britonum*,[3] with its broken promises, its sacrifice of the king's daughter to the invading chief, its four great battles, and its sense of a desperate struggle against an enemy who seems to have limitless reserves of men, must surely come from a poetical source. These passages show how rich the subject-matter of the old Germanic poetry was, and how much has been lost with it.

The same art was practised by other peoples known to the Greeks and Romans. We hear on good authority that in the region of the Guadalquivir in southern Spain the people of the Turditani had songs about their ancient doings,[4] which can hardly have been anything but heroic songs and may possibly have recorded some of the people and events connected with Tartessus, the Tarshish of the Bible and the time-honoured goal of Greek sailors. At the other end of the ancient world, though Attila, king of the Huns, survives for us in Norse poems, he seems not to have lacked his own minstrels. When Priscus visited him on an embassy in 448, two bards recited poems on the king's victories and caused great emotion among those present.[5] Such poems can only have been in the Hunnish language, and, though nothing at all is known about them, we may assume that in them Attila appeared in a more favourable light than in such Norse pieces as *Atlakvitha* and *Atlamál*.

Another serious loss is the heroic poetry of Gaul before the Roman conquest. In the first century B.C. the Gauls not only had an art of panegyric practised by a professional class of minstrels called βάρδοι,[6] from which our word " bard " is derived, but these same men also sang about the dead and events of the past, to the accompaniment of the lyre.[7] In this case we can almost see the transition from panegyric to heroic song. The bard sings the praises of his master and passes by easy stages to those of his ancestors and so from the present occasion to the dateless past. The Gaulish bards were also seers and magicians and had an honoured position in society.[8] So perhaps their heroic poetry was still close to the shamanistic stage. These bards were known to Posidonius in the first century B.C. and their ways were studied

---

[1] *Idem*, i, 8.   [2] *Idem*, ii, 28.   [3] 31-49 and 56.   [4] Strabo, 139.
[5] Müller, *F.H.G.* iv, p. 72.   [6] Posidonius, ap. Athenaeus, vi, 49.
[7] Diodorus, v, 31 ; Lucan, *Phars.* i, 447-9.
[8] Appian, *Celt.* 12.

by him. With the Roman conquest they lost their position and prestige, and though Ammianus Marcellinus knew something about them in the fourth century,[1] he seems to have derived his information from Timagenes, who was more or less a contemporary of Posidonius. No doubt when Gaul was Romanised and the indigenous language was largely replaced by Latin, the old art of heroic song fell into neglect, and that is why we know nothing of its contents.

Something equally catastrophic seems to have happened in Rome itself. In the first century B.C. Cicero laments the loss of old poems which celebrated great events of the past.[2] Such a poetry certainly existed and seems to have been sung on convivial occasions either by boys with or without musical accompaniment, or by the banqueters.[3] There is no need to assume, as Niebuhr did, that this poetry reached epic proportions or had a Homeric quality or even that it resembled the reconstructions of it which Macaulay tried to provide in his *Lays of Ancient Rome*. But at least it provided heroic lays and told tales in verse about such men as Romulus,[4] Coriolanus,[5] and Regulus.[6] Such songs were known to Dionysius of Halicarnassus at a time when Cicero could not lay hands on them. Their contents, at least, survived in oral tradition and may have provided material indirectly for the early books of Livy's history. Such poems would have been composed in the indigenous Saturnian metre, and their existence would explain why in the third century B.C. the Greek slave, Titus Livius Andronicus, translated the *Odyssey* into that measure; it was his way of accommodating Greek heroic poetry to its nearest Latin equivalent. But this early Roman poetry has vanished. It was killed by the imitation of Greek models which became popular with Ennius. Being oral and indigenous it succumbed to the more elegant, literary influences which came from Greece and substituted books for recitation. What happened in these countries may well have happened elsewhere and have left even fewer traces. If we have nothing left of early Roman poetry, we at least know a little about its contents, and that is more than we can claim for the heroic songs of many peoples who must once have had them.[7]

---

[1] xv, 9, 8.
[2] *Brut.* 16, 62; *Tusc. Disp.* i, 2, 3; iv, 2, 3; *Legg.* ii, 21, 62.
[3] Cf. J. Wight Duff, *Literary History of Rome* (London, 1908), p. 72 ff.
[4] Dion. Hal. *Ant. Rom.* i, 79; Plut. *Numa*, 3.
[5] Dion. Hal. *Ant. Rom.* viii, 62; cf. E. M. Steuart in *Classical Quarterly*, xv (1921), pp. 31-7.　　　　　　　　　　[6] Festus, ed. Lindsay, p. 156.
[7] It is also possible that the Etruscans had a heroic poetry like the Roman. At least it is otherwise difficult to explain the occasional appearance on their

When the material is so accidentally and so capriciously preserved, we cannot hope to give a comprehensive study of heroic
poetry or to find a common pattern for all its manifestations.
There may have been, there may still be, forms of it which show
unsuspected peculiarities, but which have been lost or not recorded.
All we can hope is to find what are the main characteristics of this
poetry as we know it and then to examine some of its variations.
The study is both literary and social. This poetry has many
virtues of its own and gives a special kind of pleasure, but it is
also the reflection of the societies which practise it and illustrates
their character and ways of thinking. It has considerable value
for history because it exists in so many countries and ages, but its
claim is not so much for the facts which are embedded in it as
for the light which it throws on the outlook of men and peoples.
For centuries it was a vigorous and popular art. Its known dates
stretch from about 2000 B.C. to the present day, but its beginnings
are lost in an unreckonable past. It reflects a widespread desire
to celebrate man's powers of action and endurance and display.
In most civilised societies it has long ceased to count, and modern
attempts to revive it seldom ring with the authentic note. But in
its own day and its own place it reflects some of the strongest
aspirations of the human spirit, and still remains of permanent
value for all who care for simplicity and strength in human nature
and in the use of words.

works of art of stories which are clearly concerned not with Greek but with
local heroes, like Caile Vipinas and Avle Vipinas on a bronze mirror in London
and on a wall-painting of the Tomba François at Vulci; cf. J. D. Beazley
in *J.H.S.* lxix (1949), pp. 16-17.

II

THE POETRY OF ACTION

THE first concern of heroic poetry is to tell of action, and this affects its character both negatively and positively. Negatively it means that bards avoid much that is common to other kinds of poetry, including narrative — not merely moralising comments and description of things and place for description's sake, but anything that smacks of ulterior or symbolical intentions. Positively it means that heroic poetry makes its first and strongest appeal through its story. Whatever imagination or insight or passion the bards may give to it is subsidiary to the events of which they tell. If it has a central principle it is that the great man must pass through an ordeal to prove his worth and this is almost necessarily some kind of violent action, which not only demands courage, endurance, and enterprise, but, since it involves the risk of life, makes him show to what lengths he is prepared to go in pursuit of honour. For this reason heroic poetry may be concerned with any action in which a man stakes his life on his ideal of what he ought to be. The most obvious field for such action is battle, and with battle much heroic poetry deals. Of course in treating it the poets are interested in much more than ideals of manhood. They like the thrills of battle and know that their audiences also will like them and enjoy their technical details. Sometimes the fighting is on a large scale. The *Iliad* tells of the siege of Troy by the Achaeans; *Roland* of a great battle between Charlemagne's army and the Saracens; the *Cid* of wars in Spain against the Moors; *Maldon* of a deadly struggle between English and Vikings in Essex; *Manas* of a great Kara-Kirghiz expedition against China; the poems on Dzanghar of battles between the Kalmucks and their mysterious enemies, the Mangus; Uzbek *dastans* of wars against the Kalmucks; Achin *hikayats* of wars against the Dutch East India Company; many Jugoslav " national songs " of the defeat by the Turks at Kosovo or the revolt against them at the beginning of the nineteenth century; mediaeval and modern Greek τραγούδια of fights on the frontiers of the Byzantine Empire or of efforts to liberate the homeland; Albanian poems of Skanderbeg's resistance to the Turks, and Armenian poems of wars against the Sultan of Egypt or the Shah of Persia. But of course struggles no less bloody can be fought on almost a domestic scale, like Odysseus' vengeance on the Suitors, or the terrible doom of the sons of Gjuki in Atli's castle, or the deliverance of his home from usurpers by the Uzbek Alpamys. What counts is the thrill of battle, and sometimes this is keener on a small stage than a large.

When human foes are lacking, heroic man fights against powers of nature or monsters. Achilles fights with the river Scamander, Odysseus battles with the sea when his raft is wrecked, and Beowulf takes pride in telling how he swam with Breca for five days and five nights in a wintry sea :

> Weltering waves,   and weather coldest,
> Darkening nights,   and northern wind,
> Rushed on us war-grim ;   rough were the waters.[1]

The struggle with nature passes almost imperceptibly into a struggle with monsters. Just as in his swimming Beowulf defeats fierce creatures of the sea and Odysseus fears that he may be devoured by some fearful fish,[2] so other heroes are often brought into conflict with strange creatures of primaeval imagination. The reality of monsters is taken for granted, and any fight with them demands truly heroic qualities. The dragons slain by Sigurth or Beowulf or Alpamys, the odious Grendel and his Dam who devour the warriors in Hrothgar's hall, the devils who mock and harry Armenian heroes, the one-eyed giants against whom the Narts wage endless war, the fiends who haunt the forests of the Yakuts, the prodigious bull which can kill three hundred men with its breath and is destroyed by Gilgamish and Enkidu, the hideous Tugarin whose head is cut off by Ilya of Murom, are suitable opponents for the heroes whose enterprise and audacity they challenge. In some respects monsters are more formidable than human adversaries because their powers are largely unknown. Any means are justifiable in dealing with them, and it is as heroic to blind Polyphemus as to tear off Grendel's arm.

Battle with men and monsters is not the only field in which a hero can display his worth. There is another large class of actions, which, because it involves risk and calls for courage, is equally suited to him. Much of the appeal of the *Odyssey* comes from the risks which Odysseus takes when he insists on hearing the song of the Sirens or finds his companions drugged by the Lotos-Eaters. In the Arabian poem, *The Stealing of the Mare*,[3] composed by Abu Obeyd in the tenth century, the hero, Abu Zeyd, sets out to steal a priceless mare and faces great dangers in

---

[1] *Beowulf*, 546-8.   [2] *Od.* v, 421.

[3] The poem is admirably translated by W. S. Blunt in *Collected Poems* (London, 1914), ii, pp. 129-217. Perhaps it is not strictly heroic, but it has enough heroic elements to deserve consideration.

doing so. Priam's visit to Achilles to ask for the body of Hector is truly heroic in that he may well be risking his life in approaching his deadly enemy. The Jugoslav poems about Marko Kraljević often turn on the reckless courage with which Marko faces any problem that arises and his complete contempt for anyone who opposes his will. Russian poems are not often concerned with battles but prefer to tell how the heroes behave in a way which ought to ruin them but usually does not, as when Ilya of Murom quarrels with Prince Vladimir and gets the better of it, or the wife of Staver dresses as a man to release her husband and is almost discovered, or Vasili Buslaev breaks the heads of his fellow-townsmen but is saved in time by his mother. Part of our admiration for the hero is that he courts danger for its own sake and in so doing wishes to show of what stuff he is made.

In the absence of enemies or dangerous quests heroes are not content to be idle, and heroic poetry often tells of their attempts to satisfy their lust for honour by athletic pursuits and games which they treat as seriously as battle. Book XXIII of the *Iliad* is a classic case of such games. At the funeral of Patroclus Achilles invites the Achaean heroes to compete, and they do so with full fervour, ability, and even cunning. There were probably similar accounts of games in other Greek poems now lost, like the funeral games of Pelias which were connected with the Argonauts. Nor are they confined to the Greeks. In the Kara-Kirghiz *Bok-Murun* a funeral feast is followed by horse-races and sports.[1] All the most famous heroes attend, and catalogues are given of their names, their peoples, and their horses. In *Manas* the heroes play a game called *ordo* which provokes strong passions:

> They collected the bones,
> They began to play very skilfully,
> They rolled bone upon bone,
> Arousing hatred in their opponents.
> With success, however, they were too excited,
> They exulted too early,
> A cunning visitor closed them round,
> The Devil stupefied them.
> They moved the " Khan " from the spot
> (In *ordo* too there is a " Khan " !)
> That was the last throw.
> None of them noticed
> That the " Khan " stuck on the edge,
> It was not sent over the edge.[2]

[1] Radlov, v, p. 152 ff.
[2] *Manas*, p. 132. The game seems to have some resemblance to bowls or curling, though it is played with bones, *alchiki*.

This leads to a violent quarrel which takes time and tact to settle. Since games involve considerations of honour and glory, they excite violent emotions. That, no doubt, is why heroes are not always scrupulous about their gamesmanship but do anything to win. In the *Iliad* when Ajax wrestles with Odysseus, he whispers to his opponent to make it a sham contest and then proceeds to throw him,[1] and in *Bok-Murun* Er Toshtuk unchivalrously defeats the lady, Ak Saikal, by using supernatural means. Fair play is not indispensable, since what matters is that the hero should show his prowess and be rewarded by success as the manifest token of his superiority.

The success which the cult of honour demands can be gained in many fields of action, but wherever it is found, the conditions tend to show certain fixed characteristics. First, since honour is most easily won by showing superiority to other men, there is often an element of competition. That is why so many poems turn upon boasts and wagers which have to be translated into action. Beowulf and Breca spend five days and nights in the sea because they have boasted that they will.[2] Russian heroes make wagers which concern their honour, as when Dyuk Stepanovich and Churilo Plenkovich boast of their wealth and then compete in houses, food, drink, horses, and clothes. Whoever wins in such a competition is accepted as the better man, and his defeated opponent is treated with contempt. So when Dyuk defeats Churilo, he rubs in the moral :

> " You are not one who should boast,
> Nor are you one who should lay a great wager ;
> Your part should be simply to parade Kiev,
> To parade Kiev at the heels of the women." [3]

In such contests disturbing elements of pride and vanity may be involved. Heroes do not like to think that others surpass them in any respect, and many of them resemble Unferth in *Beowulf*, who pours scorn on Beowulf's swimming-match with Breca :

> For he allowed not ever   that any other man
> More of glory   on this middle-garth
> Should hear, under heaven,   than he himself.[4]

It follows that if a hero boasts, he must make his boast good, and if he fails, he falls below the heroic standard of greatness. The Jugoslav poets like to make Turks fail in this way and be routed

---

[1] *Il.* xxiii, 723 ff.   [2] *Beowulf*, 535 ff.
[3] Rybnikov, i, p. 98 ff. ; Chadwick, *R.H.P.* p. 103 ff.
[4] *Beowulf*, 503-5.

by Christians. So when Musa the Albanian vows to hang all Christians, Marko turns the tables on him and cuts off his head,[1] thus showing their comparative worth. Much heroic poetry acts on these principles, and assumes that competition is indispensable because it shows what a man really is.

Competition need not always be so stern or so intolerant as this. So long as the hero surpasses other men, it is not absolutely necessary that he should humiliate them. This spirit is perhaps not quite so common as we might wish, but it sometimes takes engaging forms. In the Ainu *Kutune Shirka* the hero carries out his task without noticing his rivals and certainly without making them look ridiculous. A rumour has gone round that whoever can catch a golden otter in the sea will win a beautiful maiden and a rich dowry. Heroes gather to the shore and try in turn to catch the otter. First comes the young Man of the East :

> The golden otter
> Glinted like a sword ;
> Then the suck of the tide
> Caught it and pulled it down.
> Once to seaward
> With outstretched hand
> The young man pursued it ;
> Once to landward
> With outstretched hand
> The man made after it ;
> Then fell panting upon the rocks.[2]

After this failure two other warriors, the Man of the Far Island and the Man of the Little Island, make similar efforts and fail in the same way. Then the hero makes an effort and succeeds :

> The golden sea-otter
> Under the foam of the waves
> Was sucked in by the tide,
> And I in my turn
> Plunged into the surf,
> Out to the breakers of the open sea.
> It slipped from my hand,
> But nothing daunted
> I dived again like a sea-bird
> And with one foot trod upon it.
> It looked and saw what I was,
> And so far from fearing me
> It came up and floated between my arms
> Like a water-bird floating.[3]

[1] Karadžić, ii, p. 369 ff.
[2] Trs. Arthur Waley, *Botteghe Oscure*, vii (1951), p. 221.   [3] *Idem*, pp. 222-3.

Here there is an obvious element of competition, but no hostility between the competitors or contempt for those who fail. The hero proves his worth in a quiet and modest way, which is another sign of his superiority.

A second characteristic of heroic narrative is that on the whole it concentrates on the happy few and neglects the others. In the crowded battle-scenes of the *Iliad* very little is said about the rank and file. They are present, and their mass-action in advance or retreat is sketched in a few words or illuminated by an apt simile, but they take no part of importance, and their personal destinies are not thought interesting. When characters of humble lineage, like Dolon or Thersites, are necessary to the story, they are made unpleasant or ridiculous. The same disregard for the crowd appears in *Roland*, where despite lines like

> Common the fight is now and marvellous [1]

or

> Pagans are slain by hundred, by thousands, [2]

the poet's main attention is given to individual heroes, few in number and for that reason greater in renown. The *Cid* shows a similar spirit. The poet is much concerned with the Cid himself and his immediate companions, but hardly with anyone else. In *Manas* the main parts are played by Manas himself and Alaman Bet, and certain important moments are given to other warriors, but the mass of the army receives little attention. Even in the poems on the Serb revolt against the Turks, which was in fact a truly national rising, the poets are interested only in a few leaders. It is true that at times they indicate the wide scale of events in striking lines, like —

> Often did the armies clash in combat,
> In the spreading plainland match their forces,
> In the verdant groves by the Morava,
> Drive each other into the Morava;
> Red the river Morava was tinted
> With the blood of heroes and of horses. [3]

But the main interest is reserved for the great figures, the captains and the chieftains. The same is true of recent Russian and Uzbek poems on the Revolution of 1917 and its subsequent events. In these the heroes may be of humble origin, but they are selected for special treatment, and we do not hear much about the rank and file or the proletariat whose cause they champion. The same

---

[1] *Roland*, 1320. [2] *Ibid.* 1417.
[3] Karadžić, iv, p. 193. Trs. W. A. Morison.

spirit is equally displayed in peace. When the Kara-Kirghiz bard tells of the games held by Bok-Murun, he makes the host say :

> " The lower classes must stand back,
> Only the princes may take their places,
> Take their places to tilt with lances." [1]

Glory is the prerogative of the great, and the heroic world is so constituted that they are offered many chances of winning it.

To this general rule there are some apparent exceptions. There are times in heroic poetry when humble men and women play parts of importance and are treated with sympathy and respect. If Homer's swineherd, Eumaeus, turns out to be a king's son, yet the *Odyssey* has other characters in lowly positions who show a noble spirit, notably Odysseus' old nurse, Euryclea, who is not only devoted to her master but maintains a strict control over the other women of the household, and the goatherd, Melanthius, who plays a minor but not discreditable part in the destruction of the Suitors. Similar characters can be found in the Uzbek *Alpamys*. The shepherd, Kultai, is called " dear friend " by the hero, his master. When Alpamys is away, Kultai does his best to look after his home, and can hardly believe his eyes when his master returns :

> " My beloved, my soul, my child, is it you ? "

To him alone Alpamys confides his identity and uses his help in ejecting strangers from his house. Another shepherd, Kaikubad, helps Alpamys when he is put in prison by a Kalmuck prince, and in return for this Alpamys gives him the prince's daughter in marriage.[2] Yet though these humble characters may have roles of some importance, they are introduced mainly because they help the great and indeed display towards them that self-denying devotion which a hero expects from his servants. They illustrate not a primitive democracy but a truly monarchic or aristocratic world in which service has its own dignity and wins its own honour, but remains essentially subordinate to the heroic circle of the chief characters.

With such assumptions about honour, personal worth, and aristocratic privilege heroic poets proceed to construct their stories, and to make action as vivid and interesting as they can. Though their art is in most respects simple enough, it displays points of interest because it illustrates what a poet must do to create a poetry of action. For instance, he may sometimes produce

---

[1] Radlov, v, p. 171 ; cf. p. 179.   [2] Zhirmunskii-Zarifov, p. 104.

an effect by simply mentioning that something happens and saying no more about it. Some actions are sufficiently significant for the mere thought of them so to excite us that we do not ask for anything else. The momentary impression of a man riding across country or pursuing an enemy or falling in battle may need no more than a bare statement of facts. Yet even this apparently effortless art is less simple than it looks. It implies some selection by the poet from his material, and though this may be largely unconscious, it must be directed by an eye for the essential elements in a situation. Indeed the mere omission of anything which might take our attention from the fundamental significance of an action is itself a highly discriminating task. For instance, in *Roland* the account of fighting takes a new and fiercer turn when Oliver, at the request of Roland, ceases to fight with his spear and draws his sword :

> Then Oliver has drawn his mighty sword
> As his comrade had bidden and implored,
> In knightly wise the blade to him was shewed.[1]

The very simplicity achieves an effect of accomplished art. To have said more might have spoiled the grandeur of the occasion, since what counts is the direct record of events, and for this no comment is needed. The drawing of the sword is momentous because of the results which come from it, and all we need is to hear that it has happened. Much heroic poetry practises this art. Since its first duty is to tell a story, the events of the story must be clear and decisive. Indeed some of the more primitive heroic lays, like those of the Ossetes and the Armenians, have developed a kind of narrative which works mainly in this way and recounts events rapidly on the assumption that what happens is nearly all that matters. Of course for its successful prosecution this art must pick its emphatic events with skill and know what will capture the imagination, but experience teaches how to do this, and such stories are often successful in achieving the desired result.

Since heroic poetry is nearly always recited to a listening audience, the bard has not only to choose subjects which are in themselves attractive but, when he seeks to add something more interesting, he must concentrate on a single mood or effect and avoid complication of any kind. In this respect he differs from the authors of " literary " epic, who, since they write for readers, are able to enrich their work with many echoes and associations and undertones. The oral bard must go straight to the point and keep to it. Otherwise he may confuse his audience and even

[1] *Roland*, 1367-9.

E

spoil the story. So we find that he nearly always concentrates on one aspect of a situation and makes the most of it. Of this Homer provides many examples. Take, for instance, the moment when Achilles has acceded to Priam's request for the body of Hector, and food is spread before them. The crisis is over; the old man has got what he wishes from the slayer of his son. Here indeed is an occasion full of possibilities, but Homer deals with it simply and directly, aiming at one effect only :

Then leapt forth their hands to the good cheer outspread afore them.
But when anon they had ta'en their fill of drinking and eating,
Then Priam in wonder sat mute as he gaz'd on Achilles,
In what prime, yea a man whom no god's beauty could excel ;
And Achilles on comely Priam look'd, marvelling also,
Considering his gracious address and noble bearing :
Till their hearts were appeas'd gazing thus on each other intent.[1]

Homer conveys a single impression, the silence of the meal while the old man and the young man look at each other. It is a triumph of selection. When almost any possibility lay open to him, he decided to do this and nothing more. Heroic poetry proceeds in this way because it must, but takes advantage of it to create situations which look so simple that we respond immediately to them and are caught in a single, overmastering mood.

Fighting is the favourite topic of heroic poetry. Hardly anyone can fail to be interested in a good account of a fight, but there is more than one way of making it attractive. Since battle tests and reveals a hero's worth, interest centres on his performance and his use of his natural gifts. Mere physical strength is hardly ever enough, and the hero who does not back it with skill is of little account. He should combine a powerful arm with a good eye. It is this feeling for strong blows well delivered that enlivens the many single combats of the *Iliad* and *Roland*. To us perhaps they may seem monotonous, but they would be absorbing to audiences who know about hand-to-hand fighting and the warfare of cut and thrust. That is why the poets tell where and how a blow is given, what its effect is, what is remarkable about it. Moreover, since they are concerned with a superior class of fighting men, they like to describe unusual feats of strength and skill, blows of which no ordinary man would be capable but which are to be expected from heroes. The realities of war are thus subjected to a selective process in which the thrills are heightened and the taste for martial details amply satisfied. The poet of *Roland* understands this need. Roland and Oliver deal blows

[1] *Il.* xxiv, 627-33. Trs. Robert Bridges.

which other men could not. They slice men in two from head to seat,[1] or drive spears through a man's shield, hauberk, and body, or cut off heads with a single stroke. Homer's warriors do not acquit themselves quite so splendidly or so simply. Since their main means of offence is the thrown spear, what counts is accuracy of aim and strength of cast. So Homer tells how they throw their spears and what they hit with them, whether the neck or the breast or the belly or the buttocks. The thrill comes from wondering what the cast of a spear will do and from seeing it succeed or fail. For the audience it has all the excitement of a great game, in which the sides are well matched and the issue depends on strength and skill.

The poetry of combat gains in intensity when two great warriors are matched against one other. Then we enjoy the spectacle in its isolation and are not confused as we might be by a general mellay. Part of this enjoyment is almost physical. We identify ourselves with the combatants and feel the tingling of muscles and brawn set purposefully to work. A characteristic example of this is the Kalmuck account of a fight between Khongor and Arsalangin :

> Each strained at the other from the saddle
> Till the eight hoofs of their horses were mingled.
> But neither was victorious.
> They unsheathed their glittering swords from their covers,
> Seven and eight times they dealt each other blows
> Over their bladders,
> But neither was victorious.
> They made haste, they struck each other on their belts,
> They dealt each other blows behind and before,
> They tried tricks of every kind like lions,
> Their strong knees were loosened,
> But neither was victorious.
> They fought like wolves,
> They butted like oxen,
> And then Khongor trod beneath himself
> The lion-like warrior, Arsalangin-batyr.[2]

This is a fight as men feel it in their bodies, and the poet uses the audience's experience to make his sensations real. We feel the strain and the violence of the struggle, the way in which the warriors put their bodies to work until Khongor gets his man down. This kind of art is common in heroic poetry, since it reflects one of the most obvious elements of battle, the sensation

---

[1] Godfrey of Bouillon was credited with cleaving a Turk in two horizontally with one blow at Antioch ; cf. Jenkins, p. 104.
[2] *Dzhangariada*, p. 219.

of physical exertion and effort. It is a simpler form of what
Homer does when he tells how Ajax, assailed by the advancing
Trojans, finds his shoulder wearied by the weight of his great
shield and sweats and is short of breath.[1] Even heroes have
moments when their bodies are unable to endure the strain put
upon them, and then the poet recounts the symptoms of their
exhaustion, and by this means presents the dramatic implications
of the situation.

When a fight is conducted not by two antagonists but by a
number of heroes, who are all in their way equally important, the
drama of battle is more varied and tends to be more confused.
Our attention is turned to a general scene of violence and effort,
of rough-and-tumble, of movements so rapid that the poet cannot
record them all correctly and relies on a general impression of
noise and exertion. For Homer, with his selective taste and his
interest in individual achievement, such scenes are of no interest,
but other poets enjoy them without abating their aristocratic
exclusiveness. When Orozbakov tells how the Kara-Kirghiz engage the Chinese in battle, he confines his story to Manas' forty
great warriors, but for these he creates a scene of general
destruction :

> The forty warriors rushed to the fight,
> Began the fight against the heathen.
> They came in a flood then,
> They were covered in blood.
> They scattered cries here,
> They brandished their pikes here.
> The face of the earth was covered with blood.
> The face of the sky was covered with dust.
> Whoever witnessed the struggle,
> Was robbed of his reason then.
> The earth rose up on its haunches.
> Everything in the world then
> Was inside-out and upside-down.
> Everything that lives on the earth
> Was unrecognisable then.
> Regretting not that they had begun to fight,
> Thousands perished here ;
> Many the khans that fell here,
> Red blood flowed in a river,
> Battle-horses died here,
> Warriors died here,
> Horsemen were thrown down here ;
> If horses were lost here,
> Foot-soldiers were struck down here.[2]

[1] *Il.* xvi, 102 ff.　　　　[2] *Manas*, p. 335.

This is a courageous attempt to describe a general encounter, and in its own way it succeeds. But on the whole such scenes are rare in heroic poetry because in their very nature they are bound to exclude any record of individual achievement. Nor is Orozbakov content to make this his final crisis. From it he moves to a series of personal hand-to-hand fights in which various warriors show their worth. Such a scene is no more than a preliminary to his essential task of showing how the great heroes behave in battle.

A fight may also demand considerable qualities of character, notably the ability to make rapid decisions in a crisis. Then the poetry celebrates the speed of the decision and the passionate force which prompts it and puts it into action. We cannot but admire a hero who turns a threatening situation to victory by taking the boldest possible course in dealing with it. So in *The Stealing of the Mare*, when Abu Zeyd finds himself pursued by a host of enemies, he makes his heroic decision and at once turns and attacks them :

And I turned my mare and sprang, like a lion in the seizing,
And I pressed her flank with my heel and sent her flying forward,
And I charged home on their ranks, nor thought of wound nor danger,
And I smote them with my sword till the air shone with smiting,
And I met them once or twice with stark blows homeward driven.[1]

Because Abu Zeyd has made up his mind to act in this fashion, he defeats his attackers, and we feel that he deserves his triumph, because he has faced the risk so decisively. In *Finnsburh* Hnaef, alone with a few companions in a great hall, makes a similar decision. Someone sees a reflection of light and asks if the horns of the hall are aflame, but Hnaef knows that the light shines from the weapons of approaching enemies, immediately grasps the situation, and makes his choice to fight :

" This nor dawneth from the east,   nor here any dragon flieth,
Nor here on this hall   are the horns burning ;
But the Boar forth bear they,   birds are singing,
Clattereth the grey-sark,   clasheth the war-wood,
Shield to shield answereth.   Now shineth this moon
Waxing under the welkin ;   now arise woeful deeds
Which battle against this people   will bring to pass.
But awaken ye now,   warriors mine,
Take hold of your shields,   as heroes shape you,
Fight in the fore-front,   be firm in courage." [2]

Like Abu Zeyd, Hnaef makes his courageous decision and is rewarded by success, but we do not know this when he makes it,

---

[1] Blunt, ii, pp. 183-4.   [2] *Finnsburh*, 3-12.

and what matters is his temper, which sees immediately what is afoot and takes bold steps to counter it. We are not only thrilled by the apparently desperate situation but roused to admiration for the spirit in which it is faced.

A fighting man is of little account unless he knows his craft and is able not merely to handle his weapons with a strong arm and a sure eye but to act at the right moment in the right way. If he can do this, he wins admiration, as when in *Roland* the heroes appreciate their own and each other's strokes with such comments as, " A baron's stroke in truth " or " Great prowess in that thrust " or " Good baronage indeed " or " He strikes well, our warrant ".[1] To justify such comments the poet tells of prodigious feats of arms against the Saracens. Though the Homeric warriors are less lavish than those of *Roland* in praise for each other's blows, the *Iliad* describes almost every conceivable kind of blow and is precise in its account of them, as when Hector with a blow of his sword slices Ajax's spear in two, or Achilles strikes Hippodamas in the small of the back as he runs away, or Teucer hits Gorgythion with an arrow in his breast with the result that he droops " like a poppy ".[2] These are relatively minor episodes, which show how seriously the poet treats any element in the art of war, but when it comes to great encounters between eminent heroes, there is a natural tendency to make the story even more precise and realistic. Achilles' fight with Hector, despite its foregone conclusion, is treated with great care and detail. So too in other poems like the Kalmuck and Kara-Kirghiz, the poets delight to tell exactly what happens and to show how well matched the heroes are. In *Manas* the fight between the Kara-Kirghiz and the formidable Mahdi-Khan presents an exciting series of events, since he rides on a galloping buffalo and is a deadly archer.[3] The various heroes take him on in turn without success, and he is finally defeated only by a combined attack in which Manas himself and the great Alaman Bet take part. Behind such passages lie a technical knowledge of fighting and a delight in the experienced and dexterous use of arms. They are intended for audiences who know of the subject and like to hear of it.

Heroic poetry develops a special thrill when it makes heroes attempt tasks which are beyond the reach of nearly all other men. On such occasions we admire both the physical endowment which overcomes fearful obstacles and the bold, unflinching spirit which

---

[1] *Roland*, 1280, 1288, 1349, 1609.   [2] *Il.* xvi, 114 ; xx, 402 ; viii, 305.
[3] *Manas*, p. 332 ff.

carries heroes through them. An Ossete poem gives an extreme example of such a situation. The Narts are unable to take a fortress until Batradz comes to their rescue and resorts to a remarkable stratagem:

> Batradz gives orders to the warrior Narts:
> " Bind me with a hawser to an arrow,
> Shoot me with the arrow to the strong fortress ! "
> The Narts were amazed: of what is he thinking?
> But to do what he told them, they all bound him;
> As he commanded, so did they do it.
> " Now lay the arrow on the bow,
> Stretch the string to its full extent,
> And send the arrow flying to the Khyzovsk fortress."
> As he commanded, so did they do it.
> He stretched out his legs and his arms at length —
> Batradz flew to the Khyzovsk fortress,
> He pierced the wall and cut a hole.[1]

This is a strange story and not very easy to visualise, but we can appreciate the spirit in which Batradz sets out to solve a difficult problem, and the self-confidence which carries him through it. In an exaggerated way this poem shows the kind of thing which heroes sometimes do in asserting their heroic worth. They would not attempt such tasks if their physical prowess were not very unusual, and Batradz certainly deserves the epithet of " steel-breasted " which the poets give him. Yet what Batradz does, and the effect which it makes on us, are in principle similar to much that other heroes do in other places. The combination of courage, confidence, and physical powers is essential to the hero's equipment and, when he puts it into action, we admire the way in which it works. The purely physical thrill is hardly ever lacking, but it is strengthened by our appreciation of moral and even of intellectual qualities.

The effects which heroic poets get from battle are similar to what they get from almost any kind of action and are essential to their art. But these effects have a special significance through their connection with the heroic cult of honour. Honour is central to a hero's being, and, if it is questioned or assailed or insulted, he has to assert himself, since he would be untrue to his standards if he failed to do anything to prove his worth. This assumption lies behind most heroic poetry and gives to it its special atmosphere and outlook. The assertion of honour need not always be fierce and bloodthirsty; it may be equally effective if it is quiet. For instance, when Ilya of Murom feels insulted

[1] Dynnik, p. 65.

because Prince Vladimir does not invite him to a feast, he shows
his wrath by damaging the churches of Kiev, and so successful
is he that Vladimir has no choice but to invite him after all. His
arrival shows that he has triumphed :

> There Vladimir, prince of royal Kiev,
> With the Princess Apraxya,
> Went up to the old Cossack, Ilya of Murom ;
> They took him by his white hands,
> They addressed him in the following words :
> " Ah, you old Cossack, Ilya of Murom !
> Your seat was indeed the humblest of all,
> But now your seat is the highest of all at the table !
> Seat yourself at the table of oak." [1]

Honour is satisfied, and all is well, and we cannot but be pleased
that Ilya's outrageous behaviour has ended so happily. So somewhat more grimly in *Manas*, when the khans plot against Manas,
he humiliates them by making them drunk and then imposes his
will upon them. Nor does he try to conceal his contemptuous
satisfaction :

> He looked as the midnight looks,
> He was vexed like an ugly day ;
> He licked his lips like a scabbard,
> His cheeks were strained
> And armoured with moustaches,
> Which were like a sabre from Bokhara.
> Each of those moustaches
> Could almost vie
> With a pike held by a guardsman ;
> Darkness covered his temples.
> The lion shook his locks of hair ;
> So abundantly they grew
> That they would vie with wool.
> Five hairy stockings
> Could be made out of them. [2]

This is Manas in his moment of triumph, and the bold, primitive
imagery catches something of his heroic bearing. This is not a
genial triumph like Ilya's, but it is no less complete and satisfying.

The satisfaction of honour may raise deeper questions than
this, and take more dramatic forms. In the last resort a hero's
honour means more to him than anything else, and, if it comes to
a choice between it and no matter what else, he is almost bound
to follow honour. The issue is raised with great power in *Gilgamish*. Gilgamish and his comrade, Enkidu, have enraged the

---

[1] Gilferding, ii, p. 40 ; Chadwick, *R.H.P.* p. 64.
[2] *Manas*, p. 66 ff.

gods by the enormity of their prowess, and the gods decide on their death. They send a fearful bull to kill them, but the heroes destroy it. As they offer its body in sacrifice, the goddess Ishtar, whose amorous advances Gilgamish has rejected with contumely, takes the stage:

> Ishtar mounted the ramparts of high-walled Erech,
> She went up to the roof-top,
> And gave voice to her wailing:
> " Woe unto Gilgamish, woe unto him
> Who by killing the heavenly bull has made me lament."
> When Enkidu heard the shrieks of Ishtar,
> He wrenched its member from the bull
> And tossed it before her:
> " If I could only have reached thee,
> I would have served thee in the same way,
> I would have dangled its guts on thy flanks ".
> Ishtar assembled the temple-girls, the harlots;
> Over the bull's member she made lamentation.[1]

Honour can scarcely ask for more than this. Gilgamish despises Ishtar who has first made love to him and then conspired to kill him. He treats her with unutterable contempt in a most offensive way, which is all the worse since it has a coarse appropriateness for a goddess of her kind. We cannot but share the hero's almost frenzied delight as he gives her what she deserves.

Often enough, honour must be satisfied by bloodshed, since the hero feels that he has been too deeply insulted for forgiveness or appeasement to be possible, and can hardly continue to exist unless he destroys those who have wounded him in the centre of his being. This is what Odysseus feels about the Suitors who have harried his wife and impoverished his home. So when at last he begins to wreak his vengeance on them, his spirit is triumphant:

Then did he strip off his beggarly rags, the resourceful Odysseus,
And on the broad raised platform he jumped with his bow and his
    quiver
Loaded with arrows fast-flying, and these he emptied before him
Down on the ground at his feet, and thus did he speak to the Suitors:
" Now this impossible task has been done, this labour accomplished.
Now I shall aim at a different mark yet aimed at by no man,
And I shall see if Apollo will grant my prayer to strike it." [2]

Then the slaughter begins with the death of Antinous. If any of the Suitors have had any doubts that this is Odysseus, they now know that it is, and he rubs it in when he mocks them for thinking that he would never return and that they would be able to devour

---

[1] *Gilgamish*, VI, i, 157-69.   [2] *Od.* xxii, 1-7.

his substance, sleep with his serving-women, and pay court to his wife.[1] He proclaims that he will now exact vengeance for all this. Homer makes little attempt to win sympathy or even pity for the Suitors; they have behaved without shame and deserve death. The mood of Odysseus' triumph is that of a man whose honour has been gravely wounded and who at last has a chance to get satisfaction for it. Homer concentrates on this, and the fall of each Suitor is a stage in the process. The slaughter is no doubt brutal, and some might think that the Suitors get more than they deserve, but that is not Homer's view. He is concerned with his hero's wounded honour which only bloodshed can satisfy.

The desire to appease honour may take more passionate forms than this. Odysseus, whose vengeance has been long delayed and carefully plotted, acts almost on a point of principle, but other heroes are so carried away that they act in flaming anger. When Patroclus is killed by Hector, Achilles conceives a bloodthirsty desire for vengeance. He cannot endure the thought that he, the greatest of all warriors, should be robbed of his friend by Hector. This passion sweeps him along until he meets Hector and kills him. Until he has done this, he spares no one, but attacks even the river-god Scamander and shows no mercy to Priam's young son, Lycaon, whom in the past he captured and sold into slavery. Now the sight of him enrages Achilles, who thinks that the dead are rising against him. Lycaon is unarmed and begs for his life, but Achilles is adamant:

" Idiot, offer me not any ransom, nor speak to me of it !
Once on a time or ever his doom-day came to Patroclus,
In those days it was dearer than now to my heart to show mercy
Unto the Trojans, and many I captured or sold into ransom.
But now none shall escape from death, whom god may deliver
Into my hands even here by the walls of Ilion's city,
And of all Trojans the least shall I spare the children of Priam." [2]

Achilles then kills Lycaon and throws his body into the Scamander. Homer shows a true imaginative insight in allowing nothing to stand between heroic honour and its satisfaction in blood. Since Achilles is determined to kill Trojans in return for the death of Patroclus, it is futile for boys like Lycaon to beg mercy from him.

The use which heroic poetry makes of honour means that sooner or later it demands a treatment of human relations. Though the hero may wish to be self-sufficient and in some cases succeed, he has none the less to play his part among other men and women. He is, despite all his pre-eminence, a human being

[1] *Od.* xxii, 35 ff.   [2] *Il.* xxi, 99-105.

and may even possess human affections in an advanced degree. He cannot live entirely for himself, and needs a companion to whom he can unburden his heart and whom he can make the partner of his ambitions. That is why heroic poetry has its great pairs of gifted friends, like Achilles and Patroclus, Roland and Oliver, Gilgamish and Enkidu, the Uzbek Alpamys and Karadzhan, the Armenian brothers Sanasar and Bagdasar. When the hero forms a friendship with a man who is only less heroic than himself, he forms a partnership of a special kind. The participants share both dangers and glory, and the honour of one is the honour of the other. Such friendships are based on mutual respect, and each partner expects and receives the utmost from the other. It is therefore appropriate that the great friendship of Gilgamish and Enkidu should begin with a tremendous fight between them, since this shows each what the other is worth and inspires mutual devotion. A hero's love for his friend is different from his love for his wife or his family, since it is between equals and founded on an identity of ideals and interests. A hero will speak to his friend with a frankness which he will not use to his wife, and consult him on matters which he would never discuss with her.

In such an alliance there is a senior partner, like Achilles or Gilgamish or Roland or Alpamys or Sanasar, and a junior partner like Patroclus or Enkidu or Oliver or Karadzhan or Bagdasar. The senior normally makes proposals and expects them to be carried out, but the junior may offer criticisms and suggestions and is by no means bound to unquestioning subservience. In the end agreement is reached, even if one partner doubts its wisdom. When Gilgamish forms his plan for destroying the ogre Humbaba, Enkidu has serious doubts, but Gilgamish overrules with a heroic appeal :

> " Whom, my friend, does death not conquer ?
> A god, truly, lives for ever in the daylight,
> But the days of mortals are numbered.
> All that they do is but wind.
> But now that thou art afraid of death,
> Thy courage giveth no substance to thee.
> I will be thy vanguard." [1]

To this Enkidu submits, and Humbaba is destroyed by their combined attack. A more serious case of disagreement comes in *Roland* over the blowing of the horn. When he sees the Saracens approaching, Oliver calls on Roland to blow his horn and summon Charlemagne to their aid. He repeats the request three times,

[1] *Gilgamish*, III, iv, 5-11.

and three times Roland refuses.[1] What is for Oliver a wise precaution is impossible for Roland on a point of honour. Since he has promised to guard the army's rear, he cannot ask for help; for that would be to admit that the task is beyond his powers. Oliver is not convinced by his reasoning but gives in unwillingly as to a superior. Later the irony of events reverses the situation. Roland now, seeing that their fight is against hopeless odds, wishes to blow the horn and summon Charlemagne to their aid, but this time Oliver opposes it on the grounds that the Emperor would never forgive them.[2] His opposition is strong and passionate, and the two friends are near to quarrelling; but again Roland has his way, and blows the horn. Of course it is too late, and both heroes are dead before Charlemagne arrives. It might be argued that on both occasions Roland is wrong and Oliver right, but the poetry comes from the tension which arises when the two friends disagree on a fundamental point of honour.

The *Iliad* presents a case of agreement between friends which is no less tragic than any disagreement. When Achilles plans to humiliate the Achaeans by allowing them to be defeated and largely succeeds, his friend, Patroclus, is deeply distressed. He chides Achilles for his hardness of heart and asks for leave to go to battle to help the distressed Achaeans.[3] He acts with perfect justice. He has stood loyally by Achilles until his plan should succeed, and now that the plan has succeeded, he does not wish it to go too far. Achilles allows him to do what he wishes. No doubt he himself has begun to see that he has gone far enough, but his pride does not yet allow him to take part in the battle and reverse the situation. Instead he lends Patroclus his armour and sends him out. The result is that Patroclus is killed and Achilles bitterly regrets his decision. When he hears the news of Patroclus' death, he feels that he is responsible for it and that, if he had been present, he might have saved him.[4] For this sense of failure he must find an outlet, and he finds it in his desire to revenge the death of Patroclus on Hector. In this way he hopes to redeem his own honour and that of his fallen friend. The poetry lies in the powerful human emotions which create such a situation and give significance to it.

A friendship of this kind is founded on deep affection. When Achilles hears of Patroclus' death, he pours ashes on his head and face and garments and lies in the dust tearing his hair. His passionate, uncontrolled nature responds with terrible force to

---

[1] *Roland*, 1051 ff.   [2] *Ibid.* 1702 ff.
[3] *Il.* xvi, 21 ff.   [4] *Ibid.* xviii, 82 and 100.

the feeling of loss, and indeed something essential to his whole being has been taken from him. He has to make a fresh start without an element in his life which he has taken for granted and valued highly. Gilgamish is affected in a similar way by the death of Enkidu. Though he is less directly to blame for this than Achilles is for the death of Patroclus, he is not entirely without responsibility, since the gods kill Enkidu for sharing the activities of Gilgamish. When Enkidu lies dead, Gilgamish laments over him :

> " Hearken to me, Elders, to me shall ye listen.
> I weep for my comrade Enkidu,
> I cry bitterly like a wailing woman.
> My grip is slackened on the axe at my thigh,
> The sword on my belt is removed from my sight.
> My festal attire gives no pleasure to me,
> Sorrow assails me and casts me down in affliction." [1]

He recalls what he and Enkidu did together and walks up and down in front of the dead body, tearing his hair. Then, just as Achilles decides that he must do proper honour to his dead friend, by giving him a magnificent funeral, so Gilgamish promises to do something of the same kind for Enkidu :

> " I Gilgamish, thy friend and thy brother,
> Will give thee a great couch to lie upon,
> Will give thee a splendid couch to lie upon,
> Will set thee on a great throne at my left hand,
> That the lords of Death may kiss thy feet ;
> I will make the people of Erech lament thee,
> I will make them mourn for thee,
> And force maidens and warriors to thy service.
> For thy sake I will make my body bear stains ;
> I will put on a lion's skin and range over the desert." [2]

The splendid rite is the last tribute which the hero can pay to his dead comrade, and he stints nothing in it. Such an end is needed if only to pay due honour to what Gilgamish and Enkidu have done together.

Such friendships usually last till death, but sometimes they are endangered by both partners wishing for something which cannot be shared and each feeling that its acquisition concerns his honour. The Armenian brothers, Sanasar and Bagdasar, present a noble example of heroic affection and identity of aims pursued through many severe ordeals, but unfortunately they both wish to win the same woman, and for this reason they fight. They are not in love with her, since neither has seen her, and indeed the

---

[1] *Gilgamish*, VIII, ii, 1-8.   [2] *Ibid.* 49-iii, 7.

whole quarrel is based on a misunderstanding, since the message which she sends to Sanasar comes by mistake to Bagdasar, who naturally feels insulted when his brother claims priority. Honour demands that they should fight it out, and, being heroes, they do so with full passion and strength. The struggle lasts for one whole day without result, is continued on the next day, and then Sanasar, who is slightly the more powerful of the two, unhorses his brother. At this point his honour is satisfied, but, more than this, his human feelings assert themselves and he at once regrets what he has done :

> " What have I done ! In my strength
> I did not reckon my hand's cunning !
> I have struck, I have killed my brother ! "

Fortunately Bagdasar is not dead. Sanasar carries him to their home and weeps over him until he regains consciousness, and the whole cause of the quarrel is cleared up. Bagdasar not only forgives his brother but acknowledges his own inferiority :

> " Brother, I did not see, alas !
> That you are so much stronger than I !
> But for your sake I am ready to die.
> Let us make peace. You are bolder than I.
> It is finished. I will not raise a hand against you.
> I am your younger brother, you are my elder.
> All that you bid me I will accomplish.
> I will not thwart you, brother.
> Arise, go, take that maiden, win her for yourself." [1]

The result is that both brothers go off in search of the maiden, and, after passing through many dangers together, secure her for Sanasar. In the end their sense of individual honour is transcended by their affection for one another and satisfied by the lure of a new and dangerous quest.

In contrast to a hero's friends we may consider his enemies and the poets' treatment of them. Here on the whole it is perhaps surprising to find that most heroes dislike and despise those whom they oppose in war. For this there is sometimes a religious reason, as when the Christians of *Roland* despise the Saracens, or the Kara-Kirghiz and Uzbeks the Kalmucks, or the Serbs the Turks. In such cases part of the heroes' strength lies in their sense of a superiority which God has granted to them and still favours. In different ways the inferiority of the enemy is stressed to make them less admirable, as *Roland* stresses the treachery and uncontrolled passions of the Saracens, or *Manas* the craft and magic of the

---

[1] *David Sasunskii*, p. 66 ff.

Chinese, or the poems on Marko the brutality of the Turks. There is no question of men meeting each other on equal terms in valiant rivalry; it is a question of right pitted against wrong and striving earnestly to win. Such circumstances hardly permit courtesies on the battlefield or much consideration for the conquered and the captured. Even so honour forbids too great brutality against a defeated foe, and while Charlemagne is content with baptising Saracens, so the Kara-Kirghiz, once the victory is won, are content with loot and do not indulge in indiscriminate slaughter. Even though heroes in these cases are inspired by an exclusive religion, they remain heroic within certain fixed limits. If *Roland* fails to reflect that equality between antagonists, with its mutual respect and its exchanges of courtesies, which existed between Richard Cœur de Lion and Saladin, it still maintains certain rules of behaviour and allows some elementary human rights to the conquered, even if they are heathen, and in this respect the Mohammedan and Buddhist poems of the Tatars and Mongols are not fundamentally different from it.

If religion plays a less dominant part in a heroic outlook, there is a possibility that the two sides in a war may treat each other with considerably more ease and equality. In the *Iliad* the Achaeans and the Trojans fight desperately on the battlefield, but there are no atrocities and very few outbursts of abuse. At times, as when Glaucus and Diomedes meet, friendly relations are established and gifts exchanged, and furious though Achilles' anger is against the whole breed of Priam, he treats the old man himself with great ceremony and consideration when he comes to ransom the body of Hector. Of course in this war, fought for a man's wife, many of the chief warriors take part just to win honour through prowess, and have no reason to hate or despise the other side, which indeed resembles theirs very closely in its religion and way of life. Perhaps something of the same kind existed in the old Germanic poems about war, and for the same reason. In *The Battle of the Goths and the Huns* the fight is indeed fearful, but there is no indication of sharp practice, and Humli, the king of the Huns, insists on observing the inviolability of the messenger sent by the Goths. In *Hildebrand* the fight between father and son is preceded by a dignified interchange of questions and answers about lineage and antecedents. Conversely, when the rules of heroic conduct are broken, as they are at Finnsburh, it is assumed that vengeance must be taken. The Germanic world, like the Homeric, demands a strict code of behaviour between antagonists. Of course the rules are sometimes broken but that is not to be lightly forgiven and may demand a hideous vengeance. In general, however bloodthirsty and fierce war may be, and whatever fury may possess its exponents, they are still bound by a certain code which insists that a hero's opponents are ultimately of the same breed as himself and that he should treat them as he would wish to be treated himself.

Exceptions to this general rule occur when a hero feels that some enemy has struck him in his self-respect or insulted his heroic pride. That is why Achilles has so devouring a hatred for Hector, who in killing Patroclus has dealt Achilles an unforgivable blow. He feels that his life has been ruined and the consciousness that he might have saved Patroclus from death only makes his bitterness greater. His wounded pride can be assuaged only by the death of Hector, and when he has killed him, he still feels unsatisfied and wishes to maltreat his body. His anger ceases when he yields to Priam's entreaties and gives him back the body of Hector. In so doing he regains sanity and his proper, normal self. An even more deadly hatred can be seen in *Atlamál* when Guthrun takes vengeance on her husband, Atli, because he has killed her brothers. She first kills their children and serves them up to him to eat. Nor is this enough for her; she must then tell him of her purpose to kill him:

> " Still more would I seek   to slay thee thyself,
> Enough ill comes seldom   to such as thou art;
> Thou didst folly of old,   such that no one shall find
> In the whole world of men   a match for thy madness.
> Now this that of late   we learned thou hast added,
> Great evil hast grasped,   and thine own death-feast made." [1]

Guthrun differs from Achilles in acting in a way which is perhaps unavoidable in her situation, but like him she breaks the usual rules because her honour has been mortally wounded and drives her to this extremity.

When honour turns to hatred and violence, heroic poetry may develop a special kind of horror. Nor is this alien to its nature. The life of war entails bloodshed and destruction, and the poet necessarily tells of it, but when it passes the mean, it is only another sign that the heroic life is full of perils and that the hero must face this as well as other dangers. In countries which have suffered from Turkish domination the poets often dwell on the hideous actions of the persecuting masters, and tell with brutal frankness of fearful tortures and mutilations. Sometimes these may be simple occasions for vengeful delight, when the Turks

[1] *Atlamál*, 81.

turn on each other, as they do in the Greek poem on the capture
of Gardiki in 1812, when Ali Pasha punishes disobedient officers
and refuses them forgiveness :

" Here, take these men, and drag them out unto the lake's broad
  margin ;
Come take stout timbers with you too, of stout spikes take you plenty.
Off with you ! nail them to the planks, and in the water throw them.
There let them swim the livelong day, the long day let them row there." [1]

When the Turks vent their fiendish ingenuity on their Greek
victims, the situation has to be treated more seriously, but the
poets describe it with the same fascinated horror. There is something specially blood-curdling about the affectation of chivalrous
respect which a vizier maintains when Kitzio Andoni is brought
bound to him :

" Now take him off and bind him fast below unto the plane-tree
And do not torture him at all, seeing that he's a hero ;
Only take hammers up and smite his arms and legs with hammers,
And break his arms and break his legs by beating them with hammers.
For he has slain Albanians and even Veli Ghekas
With thirteen of his followers and other soldiers also.
So torture him for all you can and break him into pieces." [2]

There is a touch of patriotic pride in the way in which the Greek
poet tells how his countryman is tortured by the Turkish vizier.
Such are the risks which klephts take in opposing their infidel
masters, and it is only fair to recognise them. We are rightly
struck with horror, but it is tempered by satisfaction that the
Turks act in character and that the efforts to defeat them are all
the more necessary when things of this kind happen.

In these cases the horrors arise in a struggle between two
peoples, and our sympathies are all on one side. But some horrors
are not so clearly cut as these and invite more mixed feelings.
Indeed there are times when poets indulge in horrors almost for
their own sake as an element in a good story, or at least as a means
to illustrate the straits to which the heroic life may reduce its
participants. On such occasions moral considerations are inevitably raised, and we have no right to assume that the poets themselves are indifferent to them. In this art the Norse *Elder Edda*
shows a considerable accomplishment. In several poems the
crisis comes with some horrifying event, of whose significance the
poet is well aware. This grim temper might be thought to be
due to hard conditions of life in Iceland with the inevitable sequel
that human life is held at a low price, and it is easy to refer it to

---

[1] Passow, ccxix.   [2] Baggally, p. 71.

the world of the Vikings. But it seems to be older than that. Some of the harshest stories go back to the Germanic heroic age, and it might be argued that the Norsemen preserved an original brutality which their kinsmen in England forgot. Whatever the explanation may be, this element is used with skill and power. The stories are usually taut and terse and relate violent events in a short compass. In reducing to a small scale the garrulity of heroic poetry the Norse bards naturally kept the most exciting incidents, and it was inevitable that they should bring a violent tale to a formidable crisis. The result is a use of horror almost without parallel anywhere else. It is true that Greek legends contain horrifying episodes like those of Tantalus and Atreus and Tereus, but it is significant that Homer, who must have known of them, passes them by in silence. But in Norse poetry such stories persisted from its earliest to its latest stages and are almost indispensable to its most individual effects. Though something of the same kind may be found in more primitive branches of heroic poetry, we may doubt whether they are used with so calculated a deliberation and are not due partly to some insensibility in the poets.

Such horrors may do no more than emphasise a hero's heroism and show that in the most appalling and fearful circumstances he does not abate his courage or his style. In such cases the ordeal through which a great man passes takes a peculiarly painful form, but it remains an ordeal whose purpose is to reveal in their true grandeur his bearing and conduct. In the harsh tales of Atli's slaughter of the Sons of Gjuki there are cases of this. The first is when Hogni's heart is cut out of him when he is still alive. In *Atlamál* the poet goes out of his way to praise him :

Then the brave one they seized ; to the warriors bold
No chance was there left to delay his fate longer ;
Loud did Hogni laugh, all the sons of day heard him,
So valiant he was that well he could suffer.[1]

In *Atlakvitha* the poet feels no need for comment, but shows with admiring brevity Hogni's incredible self-command and contempt for pain :

Then Hogni laughed when they cut out the heart
Of the living helm-hammerer ; tears he had not.[2]

The horror of this episode is so great that it leaves us almost breathless, but none the less we are filled with amazed admiration

[1] *Atlamál*, 61.
[2] *Atlakvitha*, 25. The " helm-hammerer " is of course Hogni.

72

for a man who can so gaily submit himself to a hideous doom.
A somewhat similar sensation is aroused when Gunnar is thrown
by Atli into the snake-pit. This occurs both in *Atlakvitha* and
Atlamál, and the treatment of it is very similar. Each tells that
Gunnar, when thrown into the pit, plays his harp, and each omits
to dwell on the fact that this is how he meets his death. Gunnar is
determined never to reveal to Atli the secret of the hidden gold
which Atli wants, and the poet of *Atlakvitha* shows what courage
can do in such a situation :

> By the warriors' host   was the living hero
> Cast in the den   where crawling about
> Within were serpents,   but soon did Gunnar
> With his hand in wrath   on the harp-strings smite ;
> The strings resounded, —   so shall a hero
> A ring-breaker, gold   from his enemies guard.[1]

The poet of *Atlamál* is less interested in the reason for Gunnar's
suffering than in the way in which he surmounts it. He mentions
the significant detail that he plays the harp with his feet — because,
as the audience must know, his hands are bound :

> A harp Gunnar seized,   with his toes he smote it ;
> So well did he strike   that the women all wept,
> And the men, when clear   they heard it, lamented ;
> Full noble was his song,   the rafters burst asunder.[2]

Since Gunnar's heroism survives a hideous situation and a gross
personal indignity, the horror serves to show what a great man he is.

Norse poetry goes much further than this when it deals with
the destruction of children. Such themes were known to Greek
poetry in the tales of Tantalus and Atreus who serve up children
to be eaten at banquets, but the Norse poets use the theme and
others like it with a peculiar horror. When Völund begins to
avenge himself on Nithuth, who has kept him in bondage for many
years, his first step is taken through Nithuth's children, whom he
beguiles into his house and kills. He then proceeds with his
appalling plan :

> Their skulls, once hid   by their hair, he took,
> Set them in silver   and sent them to Nithuth ;
> Gems full fair   from their eyes he fashioned,
> To Nithuth's wife   so wise he gave them.
>
> And from the teeth   of the twain he wrought
> A brooch for the breast,   to Bothvild he sent it.[3]

---

[1] *Atlakvitha*, 34.   [2] *Atlamál*, 62.
[3] *Völundarkvitha*, 25-6.

Nithuth, his wife, and his daughter, Bothvild, are entirely deceived, and the crisis comes when Völund tells them the truth. Now it is clear that Völund's action is dictated by desire for revenge, and, since he has been vilely treated by Nithuth, we have some sympathy for him, but we may still feel qualms about the desperate manner of his vengeance, and it is at least possible that a Norse audience would have felt the same. The poet puts a severe strain on our sympathy, and perhaps the explanation is that Völund is not so much a hero as a magician. As a cunning smith he is outside the code of heroic honour and is expected to practise sinister arts. Völund should be viewed not with respect but with fear and awe, as one who possesses special knowledge and may put it to ugly purposes. When such a man is wronged, his vengeance will be more than usually gruesome, and we must listen to his story with a full apprehension of the fearful means of action which are at his command.

Guthrun also kills children, but they are her own, and she serves them up for her husband to eat. Since he has killed her brothers, she must take vengeance on him, and is determined to make it as complete and ruthless as possible. In *Atlakvitha* we do not hear how Guthrun kills the children, and the first hint that she has done so comes when she says to Atli:

> " Thou mayst eat now, chieftain, within thy dwelling,
> Blithely with Guthrun young beasts fresh slaughtered." [1]

The " young beasts " are her sons by Atli — Erp and Eitil — whose flesh he eats in ignorance. When he has done so, Guthrun tells him the truth, and the first step in her vengeance is complete. The poet stresses that Guthrun weeps neither for her dead brothers nor for her children whom she has herself slain, as if he wished to make her character as grim as he can. In *Atlamál* the episode is told in almost the same outline but with a difference of emphasis. The poet adds pathos to the boys' fate by making them ask Guthrun why she wishes to kill them, and he adds an unexpected touch of horror when she, in telling Atli what has happened, spares him nothing:

> " The skulls of thy boys thou as beer-cups didst have,
> And the draught that I made thee was mixed with their blood.
> I cut out their hearts, on a spit I cooked them.
> I came to thee with them, and calf's flesh I called them;
> Alone didst thou eat them, nor any didst leave,
> Thou didst greedily bite, and thy teeth were busy." [2]

[1] *Atlakvitha*, 36, 3-4. [2] *Atlamál*, 77-8.

74

In both accounts Guthrun's motive is vengeance, and to this extent she resembles Völund. Since her husband has wronged her irredeemably by killing her brothers whose treasure he covets, he is beyond mercy, and up to a point Guthrun acts rightly. But her vengeance takes a dire form, of which the poets are fully conscious. They stress the horror because it shows to what straits Guthrun has been brought and how her heroic temper turns with all its fierceness to exact the utmost humiliation from Atli.

These scenes of horror are connected with something else which receives some prominence in heroic poetry — its sense of the disasters which await the great and its feeling for their imaginative appeal. Such a subject can hardly be avoided. Men who live by violent action will often find that it recoils on them and ruins them. The poet naturally tells of this and in doing so tries to explain it and implicitly comments on it by his treatment of it. On the whole the more primitive kinds of poetry avoid such subjects. The heroes of the Kara-Kirghiz or the Kalmucks or the Yakuts end their days in happiness, honoured and successful. Even Homer avoids closing the *Iliad* on a tragic note. It is true that more than once he points out that Achilles' death is not far distant, but the *Iliad* ends not with it but with the funeral of Hector, while the *Odyssey* may indeed stress that Odysseus is not entirely secure even after he has killed the Suitors, but none the less leaves him in possession of his wife and his home. On the other hand great disasters and catastrophes are faced fearlessly by Jugoslav, French, Norse, and Anglo-Saxon heroes. The question is what poetry is extracted from them.

At the outset it is worth noticing that the calamities of heroic poetry are seldom treated in a truly tragic spirit. What happens in *Roland* or *Maldon* or the Jugoslav poems on Kosovo is indeed a gigantic disaster, but not of the same kind as what happens in *King Oedipus* or *King Lear*. First, when Roland or Byrhtnoth falls after a furious fight, we do not have the same sense of utter desolation and waste that we have in authentic tragedy. It is true that the heroes' efforts may well have been futile, that their armies are destroyed and their enemies triumphant. It is also true that they seem to be caught, often through their own decisions, in a web of disaster from which there is no honourable escape but death. But, even allowing for all this, their deaths are somehow an occasion for pride and satisfaction. We feel not only that their lives are not given in vain, since they have set an example of how a man should behave when he has to pass the final ordeal of manhood, but that by choosing this kind of death he sets a logical and proper goal for himself. The man who has killed others must be ready to be killed himself. There is more than a poetic justice in this; there is an assumption that, since the hero subjects his human gifts to the utmost strain, he will in the end encounter something beyond him, and then it is right for him to be defeated. Secondly, we may well doubt whether the catastrophes of heroic poetry normally evoke pity and fear. Are we really sorry for Roland or for Lazar or the heroes of *Maldon* in their last great fights? Do we not rather feel that it is all somehow splendid and magnificent and what they themselves would have wished for, " a good end to the long cloudy day "? Equally, do we really feel fear for them? Of course we know that they run terrible risks and have no chance of survival. But surely we do not feel fear for them as we do for Lear on the heath or for Oedipus when he begins to discover the whole horrible truth. Indeed the nearer these heroes come to their ends, the greater is our pride and delight in them. This surely is the way in which they should behave when death is near, and if death were not near, they would miss this chance of showing the stuff of which they are made.

Great catastrophes are occasions for heroes to make their greatest efforts and perform their finest feats. This is pre-eminently the case in *Roland*, where not only Roland and Oliver but their companions show strength and skill to a prodigious degree. Although the odds are extravagantly against them, they surpass even their own records, and both Roland and Oliver kill large numbers of enemy before they are themselves wounded. When finally they are mortally struck, their deaths come largely because they are utterly exhausted by their efforts. They have done all and more than all that can be expected of them, and that is why their deaths are hardly matter even for sorrow, let alone for any violent tragic emotions. It is indeed what they would have desired. For, as Charlemagne says,

> " At Aix I was, upon the feast Noel,
> Vaunted them there my valiant chevaliers,
> Of battles great and very hot contests;
> With reason thus I heard Rollant speak then:
> He would not die in any foreign realm
> Ere he'd surpassed his peers and all his men,
> To the foes' land he would have turned his head,
> Conqueringly his gallant life he'ld end." [1]

In such a death there is undeniably something complete and satisfying. The same note may be seen in *Maldon*. When Offa

---

[1] *Roland*, 2860-67.

dies in the fight, his end is both what he would himself have wished and what his companions regard as right and fitting :

> Swiftly was Offa   struck down in battle ;
> Yet what he promised   his prince he accomplished,
> As erstwhile he boasted   to the bestower of rings,
> That they should both of them   ride to the stronghold,
> Unscathed to their home,   or fall with the host,
> Perish of wounds   on the field of war.[1]

The secret of this poetry is that it sees in heroic death the fitting fulfilment of a heroic life. That both Roland and the men of Maldon die in defeat does not matter. It is far more important that their personal honour has been vindicated beyond challenge and that they have justified both their own boasts and the high hopes that others have held of them.

In heroic poetry, death, no matter how disastrous, is usually transcended in glory. But there are some cases where it is authentically tragic and produces a different effect. Such cases come from a conflict between two heroes and relate to some struggle between them which can only be solved by death, and since both protagonists may be noble and attractive, the death of one arouses emotions other than pride and glory. Such is the struggle between Achilles and Hector. It is inevitable that they should meet in deadly conflict, and hardly less inevitable that Hector should lose. He is, heroically speaking, inferior to Achilles, whom he equals neither in speed nor in strength. But humanly he is at least equally attractive, and his fate therefore is bound to concern us. Indeed it has a special claim because on his life so much depends — the fortunes of his old parents, his wife and small son, and the whole existence of Troy. His death is a culmination of his life, and he himself knows that it will come. But when he dies, any sense of satisfaction which it might have brought is overwhelmed in the prospects of disaster which it makes imminent. It is as if with his death the whole of Troy shakes to its foundations.[2] Moreover, Homer emphasises the tragic character of Hector's death by showing its effect on his wife. She is indoors at her loom and gives orders to her servants to heat the bath-water for Hector when he returns from the battlefield. Suddenly she hears a noise of lamentation and goes to find out what it means, only to see her husband's dead body being dragged behind the chariot of Achilles.[3] Such a death is not like Roland's. Hector has too many human ties to win the isolated glory which comes to a great hero when he dies in battle. In his case the only answer to

[1] *Maldon*, 288-93.   [2] *Il.* xxii, 410 ff.   [3] *Ibid.* 437 ff.

death is grief, and this Homer depicts in the lamentations which the women of Troy make for him after his death.

Something similar may be seen in the *Elder Edda* where Sigurth is a great hero, who comes to a terrible end for which there is no consolation in a sense of glorious completeness. Indeed his death is even more painful than Hector's since it is encompassed by a woman who loves him and a man to whom he has given magnificent and devoted service. When Gunnar yields to Brynhild's demand that Sigurth be slain, a situation arises which can strike us only with dismay and horror. Moreover, this death is carried out by methods which destroy any sympathy we might otherwise feel for the killers. They may act on a point of honour, but their action is little short of dishonourable. Gunnar feels that he himself cannot kill Sigurth, since they are bound by oaths of friendship; so he persuades his brother, Gotthorm, who is bound by no such oath, to do the ghastly work for him. Gotthorm attacks Sigurth treacherously when he is asleep in bed, and the one consolation in the whole episode is that Sigurth dies fighting and, before he perishes, kills his slayer:

> In vengeance the hero   rose in the hall,
> And hurled his sword   at the slayer bold;
> At Gotthorm flew   the glittering steel
> Of Gram full hard   from the hand of the king.

> The foeman cleft   asunder fell,
> Forward hands   and head did sink,
> And legs and feet   did backwards fall.[1]

The poet exerts himself to win sympathy for Sigurth and to make his death an occasion for horrified pity. It is a terrible crime, and though the reasons for it may have been unanswerable from a heroic standpoint, the horror of it remains.

The ever-present menace of violent death is a challenge to a hero because it means that in the short and uncertain time at his disposal he must strain his utmost to exert all his capacities and win an imperishable name. But poets are not content always to treat death as a final obliteration. They sometimes tell how heroes face it in an even bolder spirit and seek to master its mysteries by exploring the twilit world of the dead or conversing with spirits. Then for a moment the darkness which wraps human life is broken, and we see something of the dread powers which rule men's destinies. Instead of confining itself to the familiar world, heroic poetry then breaks into the unknown, broadens its range,

[1] *Sigurtharkvitha en Skamma*, 22-3.

and sets its actions in an unfamiliar perspective. Such episodes are an inheritance from shamanistic poetry, which still uses them among the Tibetans, the Abakan Tatars, and the Finns. But what is natural enough for a magician is more surprising in a hero and needs a new interpretation. It is perfectly suitable that the sorcerers of the *Kalevala*, who seek to know all earth's secrets, should visit the god of death, but when the Esthonian Kalevide does so, he acts from an excess of heroism, from a desire to defeat even the final and ineluctable powers who control him. In such an adventure he cannot quite dispense with magic, and in this shows his affinities to the shamans, but his best moments are when he sheds magic for purely human means, as when he is offered a wishing-cap and rod but refuses them as fit only for witches and wizards. In this choice he shows his superiority and proves that, even below the earth, it is the heroic qualities that count. When the crisis comes, the Kalevide fights like a man with the god of death. Sarvik comes with a noise like hundreds of cavalry thundering along a copper roadway; the earth quakes, and the cavern shakes beneath him, but the Kalevide stands undismayed at the entrance, waiting for the onslaught :

> Like the oak-tree in the tempest,
> Or the red glow mid the cloudlets,
> Or the rock amid the hailstorm,
> Or a tower in windy weather.[1]

Though in his struggle with Sarvik the Kalevide uses magic, in the end he wins because of his undaunted courage and obstinate refusal to retreat. The episode shows that, even when they are confronted with supernatural enemies, heroes may triumph by being true to their own rules. By setting the Kalevide in this unwonted situation, the poet throws a fresh light on his prowess and capacity.

When visits to the underworld pass beyond the limits of a shamanistic outlook and are related to a purely heroic attitude, the poets are free to do much with them and ennoble them with great flights of imagination, especially by showing what they mean to the human beings who embark upon them. In the Norse *Brynhild's Hell Ride* Brynhild, after her body has been burned on its pyre, is carried on a waggon to the underworld. On the way she meets a giantess, who blocks her advance and refuses admission to her because she follows Sigurth, who is the husband of another woman. In the dialogue that follows Brynhild triumphs by sheer

[1] Kirby, i, p. 101.

force of character. So far from being ashamed of her actions, she is proud of her valour in battle and of her chaste love for Sigurth :

> " Happy we slept,   one bed we had,
> As he my brother   born had been ;
> Eight were the nights   when neither there
> Loving hand   on the other laid." [1]

Because of this she has lost Sigurth and her own life, but it is none the less a satisfaction to her. Her love will defeat all obstacles in the end, and it is futile for the giantess to try to obstruct her :

> " But yet we shall live   our lives together,
> Sigurth and I.   Sink down, Giantess ! " [2]

By basing his poem on the belief that love is stronger than death, the poet gives a special character to the theme of a journey to the underworld. Of course his version is new and original. His heroine is not alive but dead ; it is her passion for Sigurth which survives and, being no less strong than it was in life, carries all before it. Through the force of her passion Brynhild remains herself, even though her body has been burned. She acts as she ought to act in this strange situation, as if all that is inessential has been purified from her, and what remains is her true, unchanging self. If the giantess stands for those rules which normally guide the conduct and determine the merits of men and women, Brynhild is moved by something stronger and finer, by a spirit unconquerable even after death.

Another powerful variant on the theme of the underworld is presented by *Gilgamish*. Gilgamish's companion, Enkidu, is doomed by the gods to death because the pair of them have insulted Ishtar. Before dying Enkidu dreams what will happen to him and learns of the state of the dead :

> " He seized me and led me
> To the Dwelling of darkness, the home of Ikkalla,
> To the Dwelling from which he who enters never comes forth,
> On the road by which there is no returning,
> To the Dwelling whose tenants are robbed of the daylight,
> Where their food is dust, and mud is their sustenance.
> Like birds they wear a garment of feathers,
> They sit in the darkness and never see the light." [3]

Beyond this the fragments of the text do not permit us to go safely, though it is clear that Enkidu dreams of the gods of the underworld. The poet presents his vision of the dead and gives to it a

---

[1] *Helreith Brynhildar*, 12.   [2] *Ibid.* 14, 3-4.
[3] *Gilgamish*, VII, iv, 33-40.

peculiar appeal because it comes to a hero in the zenith of his glory. What might be no more than a depressing account of the life beyond gains greatly in pathos because it is presented at this time in this tragic and intimate way. Enkidu is humbled by the gods in being made to die, and his punishment is all the harsher because he learns in advance what it is going to be. Nor is the poet content with this. The lesson which Enkidu learns must be brought home also to Gilgamish, and this happens when Gilgamish summons his friend's spirit and questions it about death. Enkidu's spirit speaks unwillingly, knowing that what he has to say can bring nothing but sorrow :

> " I will not tell thee, I will not tell thee ;
> Were I to tell thee what I have seen
> Of the laws of the Underworld, sit down and weep ! " [1]

Gilgamish insists on hearing and forces Enkidu to speak of the dismal fate that awaits the living :

> " The friend thou didst fondle, in whom thou didst rejoice,
> Into his body, as though it were a mantle,
> The worm has made its entry ;
> The bride thou didst fondle, in whom thou didst rejoice,
> Her body is filled with dust." [2]

So the old stories are related to a living fear of death and a knowledge of what it does to the human body. The legend is transformed into a vivid, all too possible experience.

In the *Odyssey* Odysseus goes to the end of the world to consult the ghost of the seer Teiresias about the future. Odysseus does not go beneath the earth, but, guided by Circe's instructions, sails to the stream of Ocean and crosses it to the land of the Cimmerians " wrapped in mist and cloud ". By the Ocean Odysseus digs a trench, into which he pours blood, and hither the ghosts gather, since, if they drink of the blood, they regain for a moment their lost wits and become something like their old selves again. Some of the great heroes of Troy appear and speak in their essential character. First, Agamemnon tells of his murder by his wife. The proud general of the Achaeans has been killed in a brutal and shameful manner in his home and feels angry resentment for it, but he nurses a hope that his son will avenge him, and in the thought of this his pride revives. After him appears Achilles, who asks about his son and is glad to hear of his prowess :

[1] *Ibid.* XII, i, 90-92.   [2] *Ibid.* 93-7.

> And the spirit of fleet-foot Achilles
> Passed with his great long strides going over the asphodel meadow,
> Joyful because I had said that his son gained honour and glory.[1]

The third to appear is Ajax, with whom Odysseus has quarrelled fatally at Troy. Even in death Ajax keeps his old hatred of Odysseus and silently rejects the friendly words addressed to him:

> So did I speak, but he answered to me not a word, and departed
> To Erebus, to mingle where other spirits had gathered.[2]

In this passage Homer shows what awaits heroes after death. Only if they drink blood have they any true consciousness, and even then their thoughts turn to their past lives or to hopes of glory for their sons. This is the background against which the heroic world plays out its drama. Homer uses the theme of a blood-sacrifice to the dead, which is at least as old as the fifteenth century B.C. when it appears on a sarcophagus found at Hagia Triada in Crete,[3] to pass a comment on the terms on which heroic life is held.

If the ghosts of heroes illustrate Homer's attitude towards the love of glory, the scene between Odysseus and his mother is a comment on the affections. Odysseus has been away from home for many years and does not know that his mother is dead. Hers is the first ghost to appear, but he does not speak to her first, because he has to question the ghost of Teiresias before any other. When he has done this, he allows his mother to come near and drink of the blood, and then she knows him and can speak to him. He questions her, especially about her death, and her answer shows the strength of her affection for him:

> " For it was not she, the keen-eyed Archer of Heaven,
> Stole on me unperceived, and painlessly smote with her arrows,
> Nor did a fever attack me, and with its wasting consumption,
> Such as is common with men, drain out the life from the body;
> But it was longing and care for thee, my noble Odysseus,
> And for thy kindness of heart, that robbed me of life and its
>   sweetness." [4]

This stirs Odysseus' love in return, and three times he tries to embrace her, but three times she eludes him " like a shadow or a dream ". He complains of it to her, and her reply reveals the piteous state of the dead:

> " Woe is to me, my son; most wretched art thou above all men.
> Think not the daughter of Zeus, Persephone, wishes to cheat thee;

[1] *Od.* xi, 538-40. [2] *Ibid.* 563-4.
[3] Bossert, p. 48 ff. [4] *Od.* xi, 198-203.

This is the law of mortals, whenever anyone dieth,
Then no longer are flesh and bone held together by sinews,
But by the might of the blazing fire are conquered and wasted.
From that moment when first the breath departs from the white bones,
Flutters the spirit away, and like to a dream it goes drifting." [1]

For Homer love and heroism are equally destroyed by death.
The momentary revival of them in these eerie conditions only
serves to show how utter their obliteration is.

The pathos of Homer's ghosts is that they long to be on earth
and to regain their old lives. The mere presence of Odysseus,
alive and active among them, stirs their faint, wistful longings, and
it is not surprising that, when the ghost of Agamemnon sees him,
it weeps and stretches out hands towards him, although it has
no power or strength to do anything.[2] So in another scene of the
Odyssey the state of the dead is conveyed through a precise and
poignant simile :

> As when bats in the deep hollows of a marvellous cavern
> Screech and flutter about, whenever one of them falleth
> Down from the rock where it clings, and they cleave close one to
> another.[3]

So the dead screech and flutter, showing the meaninglessness and
futility of their existence. But the deepest pathos of their situation is that dimly and vaguely but none the less keenly they are
conscious of the contrast between what they were on earth and
what they are now. At least, when Achilles drinks of the blood
and regains for a moment his old wits, he knows how vastly
inferior his present state is to the lowest that he can imagine
upon earth. He recognises Odysseus and asks him why he has
come to visit the dead, since they are senseless and mere phantoms
of the living. Then, from his momentary knowledge he compares
his present with his past and says :

> " Speak no words unfitting of death, most famous Odysseus.
> Would that I were once more upon earth, the serf of another,
> Even of some poor man, who had not wealth in abundance,
> Than be the king of the realm of those to whom death has befallen." [4]

Against this menacing prospect of a faint, resentful, bloodless
survival in the beyond, this sense that only upon earth is a man
fully in possession of his powers and his intelligence, Homer sets
his living world and marks the contrast between the full-blooded
Odysseus and the fluttering wraiths of his former comrades at

---

[1] *Ibid.* 216-23. [2] *Ibid.* 392-4.
[3] *Ibid.* xxiv, 6-8. [4] *Ibid.* xi, 488-91.

Troy. We can hardly fail to draw the conclusion that for Homer and indeed for other heroic poets, the great deeds of the living are the more worth doing because the chance for them is so brief, and a great darkness awaits everyone afterwards.

If death bounds the heroic span of life, heroes, while they live, have to reckon in the gods with something outside their control and often hostile to their ambitions. The power of the gods limits their activities in many ways and gives a special character to some classes of heroic poetry. They are, or can be, the one thing with which heroes can reach no final settlement or compromise. No doubt many heroes would be content to live without them and feel no need of them, since they put all their trust in their own specifically human powers. In much heroic poetry the gods play no part either on the stage or behind the scenes. It is for instance characteristic of the lays of heroes in the *Elder Edda* that the gods have almost been eliminated from them. Once, it seems, the gods took an active part in Norse stories, but the extant poems have reduced their role almost to nothing. Valkyries may speak in *Hrafnsmal* and *Hakónarmál*, but they do nothing else. It looks as if the Norse poets felt that any interference with human action by the gods somehow lowers its dignity and detracts from the heroes' glory. If gods were to be the subjects of song, they should be confined to special poems about them in which human beings have no part. This is an extreme position and reveals a heroic humanism, which is not very common but is none the less a logical development of a strictly heroic standpoint.

In monotheistic societies divine intervention in heroic actions is rare and usually confined to events outside the sphere of prowess and effort. In *Roland* angels come to carry off Roland's soul to Paradise, but do not help him while he is alive. When Manas dies, God sends an angel to make enquiries about his death and restores him to life, but Manas' great performances are accomplished without divine help. In the poems about Dzhangar the great man is blessed and protected by the saints of Buddhism, but they do not interfere in his battles. We are left to assume that the heroes, strengthened by their faith, whatever it may be, and trusting consciously in it, need no additional support from God. They carry out His will, and all goes well with them. The same is true on a smaller scale of Russian *byliny*, although their Christianity is more implicit than vocal, and of Bulgarian, Armenian, Ukrainian, and Greek poems which tell of fights against infidel Turks. To this general rule of monotheistic poetry there is a small exception in *Roland*, where God twice intervenes to direct the action, first when He sends a supernatural darkness to announce Roland's death,[1] and secondly when He stops the sun to help Charlemagne.[2] Both episodes are built on biblical precedents, but in fact neither really contributes very much to the action, since in the first case Roland will none the less die, and in the second we know that even without this help Charlemagne will chastise the Saracens. The exception is not important and does little to invalidate the general rule that in monotheistic societies heroic poetry gives little active part to God.

There are, however, places in which a monotheistic religion retains relics of older polytheistic beliefs and uses them for narrative. The Ossetes of the Caucasus are in theory Christians, but they keep many memories of an older religion and pre-Christian gods. Just as the hero Batrazd has himself forged by the divine smith Kurdalagon, so other heroes from time to time sojourn in the sky with the gods and have to be summoned to earth to succour their friends in need. The Ossetes seem to be uneasy in their Christianity and to think that when heroism is in question, men need divine support which is unlikely to come from God and His Saints. Indeed to some saints, like St. Nicholas, they are avowedly hostile and attribute various crimes. They prefer to connect their heroes with pagan powers and to explain their performances by these rather than to make any uneasy compromise with Christianity. Their poems come from a time when men were thought to have easy commerce with gods, from whom great men in particular learned much. To these beliefs they adhere because they are necessary to the structure of the heroic world of the Narts. If Christian beliefs have been superimposed on them, they do little to affect either the course or the temper of the stories.

Something of the same kind on a smaller scale can be seen in the part played by the *Vile* in Jugoslav poems. They are supernatural beings of no very obvious origin, akin perhaps to the Valkyries, creatures of storm and mountain who occasionally intervene in human actions. It is usual to translate the word by " fairies ", but that gives too gentle and too fanciful a touch to it. They are fierce female spirits, who take readily to violence. Originally perhaps they were none too friendly to men. So Marko Kraljević fights with a *Vila* who has wounded him because she objects to his singing.[3] But this hostile role seems to have decreased with time until *Vile* have become the friends of heroes. Sometimes they perform neutral actions like prophesying death to

[1] 1431 ff.   [2] 2458 ff.   [3] Karadžić, ii, p. 196 ff.

Marko [1] and to Novak.[2] But more often they are helpful, as when they issue warnings of danger. So after the failure of the revolt against the Turks in 1813, it is a *Vila* who warns Kara-Djorje of dangers to come,[3] and similar warnings are given to the Montenegrin prince Danilo, who reigned from 1851 to 1861, and tell him that the Turkish Sultan is sending a vast host to attack him. Danilo tells the *Vila* to be silent, since he puts his trust in the Russian and Austrian Emperors. The *Vila* then warns him not to indulge false hopes and at last rouses him to battle.[4] Another task of *Vile* is to help soldiers in battle, as when one comes to the wounded Ibro Nukić and restores him to health,[5] or another tends the wounds of Vuk the Dragon-Despot.[6] The *Vile* have a real place in the Jugoslav heroic world. Once perhaps they were more important and took a more active part in the action, but even now they appear as incarnations of strange powers which are interested in the doings of heroes and like to help them on occasions. No doubt the *Vile* belong to some old Slavonic world whose other inmates have disappeared, while they survive because they embody a spirit of wildness and adventure.

When we turn from these cases of survival to polytheistic religions in their full heyday, we find that the gods are much more to the fore and more busy in the action of heroic poetry. The Yakuts, for instance, are one of the few Tatar peoples of Asia who have not embraced Islam, and their religion is still in some sense polytheistic. It is true that they speak of a single, supreme god, but they do not worship him, and he plays little part in their poetry. On the other hand they give a considerable part to good and evil spirits who intermingle with human beings and help to sharpen the conflicts to which they are exposed. Indeed much of Yakut poetry consists of struggles against evil spirits. The heroes are helped by their own shamanistic powers as well as by good spirits, with the result that in the end goodness triumphs. This is a simple outlook, but has its own interest. The doings of the human beings gain something in variety, if not in grandeur, from their middle position between warring spirits; they are at least important enough for evil spirits to wish to harm them and good spirits to protect them. The stories become more vivid because issues of good and evil are at stake, and the sense of heroic values is not diminished, even though the human actors are the victims or beneficiaries of spiritual powers. Of course there

[1] Karadžić, ii, p. 405 ff.   [2] Bogišić, no. 39.
[3] Karadžić, iv, p. 268 ff.   [4] *Idem*, iii, p. 472 ff.
[5] Krauss, p. 394 ff.   [6] Bogišić, no. 16.

is nothing here like the stark human isolation of the Norse poems, but the extension of the struggle into a supernatural sphere gives to the Yakut world a new significance and a more dramatic appeal.

When a polytheistic religion holds the field, the poet may well introduce gods and goddesses into his action, and even construct his plot on the struggles of men against the gods. Such a poetry is possible only when the gods are regarded not as types of goodness but simply as embodiments of power who govern human affairs. There is nothing wrong in opposing them, but it is extremely dangerous. The poet is therefore at liberty, if he chooses, to put the gods in the wrong and the hero in the right, or at least to distribute his praise and blame between them. Something of the kind may be observed in the Canaanite *Aqhat*, which tells how the hero Aqhat comes to his death through the possession of a divine bow which the goddess 'Anat desires. Though his death is accidental in the sense that 'Anat does not wish it and asks for no more than his temporary disablement, its importance is marked by the blight which falls on the earth after it and is not stopped until the assassin, Yatpan, is discovered and punished.[1] Aqhat certainly has a kind of heroic grandeur because he not only refuses the request of 'Anat for the bow but in doing so is none too polite, while 'Anat herself, though innocent of his blood, is indirectly responsible for the blight which falls on the earth and has to be stopped by religious action. There is an undeniable satisfaction in the moment when Aqhat's sister, Yatpan, discovers the murderer and kills him, by making him drink too much and fall asleep, and no doubt we are expected to think this right and proper. Though some of the elements in the story of Aqhat may be derived from a ritual of death and rebirth, it remains a heroic narrative in which the gods are the antagonists of men, and despite their superior powers are neither wholly successful nor completely in the right. In contrast to them Aqhat, with his presumption and insolence, has a heroic stature and independence.

A poet may introduce gods for a more advanced function than this, notably by depicting both men and gods to give a fuller picture of the world in which his heroes live and to provide by contrast a comment on their way of life. Notable cases of this are *Gilgamish* and the Homeric poems. In both there is a contradiction between the ultimate power of the gods and the free and easy way in which the heroes treat them. Just as Gilgamish spends much of his time in trying to defeat the gods' plans for his

[1] Gaster, p. 257 ff.

destruction or to avoid death, which they have decreed for all men, so the Homeric heroes think little of attacking gods and goddesses in battle and treat them as none too serious adversaries. It is possible that both in *Gilgamish* and in Homer a more primitive outlook, which allows men to fight the gods, has been imperfectly combined with a maturer outlook which insists that in the end the gods must always win. But so far as the action of the poems is concerned, the struggles are treated with a fine sense of dramatic possibilities. The gods and goddesses look and behave like human beings and enter easily into the pattern of the narrative. Though they have moments which are beyond any human capacity as when the gods of *Gilgamish* send the Flood, or Homer's Zeus shakes Olympus with his nod, yet on the whole they behave in a human way and are swayed by passions and desires like those of men. Just as Zeus rules none too comfortably over his family of immortals, so Anu treats Ishtar first with a charming candour when he hears of her desire for vengeance on Gilgamish, and then gives in to her importunities. The society of heroes is enlarged by the presence of gods and goddesses, and there is no great difference of manners between them. Through this the poets secure a frame in which to place certain dramatic contrasts.

The gods are essential to the whole scheme of *Gilgamish* since in his struggle with them the hero displays the full scope of his energies and powers. But while this constitutes his heroic life, his actual character is illuminated by contrasts which the poet makes between him and the immortals at two important stages of the story. The first is the splendid scene in which Ishtar offers him her love and he not only refuses it but taunts her with her treatment of her past lovers. Her conduct is fairly criticised by her father, Anu, who tells her :

" Thou didst ask him to give thee the fruit of his body,
Hence he tells thee of thy sins, of thy sins and iniquities." [1]

Ishtar may be a goddess, but she is not at all beyond reproach, whereas Gilgamish has both been heroically truthful in his words to her and shown his superiority to the claims of the flesh. Later, a like contrast is made between him and Siduri, the goddess of wine. She deals not only with wine but with all that is associated with it in the way of ease and indulgence, and her philosophy, which she expounds to Gilgamish, is that of living for the pleasure of the moment. With this he does not even trouble to argue, but states firmly his intention of trying to win immortality and tells of all

---

[1] *Gilgamish*, VI, 88-9.

that he is prepared to risk on this quest. Once again he shows his moral superiority to the gods, and the contrast shows his true worth. If Gilgamish is superior to all other men, he is also in some ways superior to the gods. For this he has to pay, but we feel that what he does or tries to do is itself noble and that he represents, within his human limitations, an exalted ideal of heroism.

In the Homeric poems the gods play a more various part than in *Gilgamish*. They are more active in the *Iliad* than in the *Odyssey*, but in the *Odyssey* at least Athene and to a lesser degree Poseidon are important characters who direct or obstruct the actions of human beings. Homer's gods affect his poetry of action in more than one way. First, they are powers of the spirit, influences and impulses which a modern psychology might ascribe to a man's nature but which the Greeks, not unwisely, saw as external and independent influences coming from another order of being. As such they may complete a man's natural and human gifts, as Athene completes those of Odysseus in the *Odyssey*, where she not only aids and abets him but admires his cunning and does much for his son and family. It is as if he were partly an embodiment of the intellectual qualities which she represents, and for this reason he has a special dignity. Conversely, part of the pathos of Helen is that she is the victim of Aphrodite, who has decreed a destiny for her and refuses to release her from it. When Helen succumbs to Paris, she does not wish to do so, but she cannot help herself because she is the victim of a merciless goddess.[1] Yet there is something in Helen which makes her the victim of Aphrodite — her essential femininity which asserts itself even when she dislikes and condemns it. So too when Athene appears to Achilles and is seen by him alone, so that he does not use his sword to kill Agamemnon, she does no more than strengthen and make explicit what already lies in his own nature.[2] One aspect of Homer's gods is that they make his heroes more truly themselves and therefore more heroic.

A second aspect is that the gods take sides in human struggles for or against individual heroes. Just as Odysseus in the *Odyssey* is supported by Athene and harried by Poseidon, so in the *Iliad* the gods divide into two parties, one of which helps the Trojans and the other the Achaeans. This is perhaps a reflection of beliefs in national deities, but Homer gives to it a purely personal form. The gods act on whims and impulses and seem to embody the many forms which chance may take in human affairs. This

[1] *Il.* iii, 413 ff.   [2] *Ibid.* i, 190 ff.

gives a peculiar character to some of the battles before Troy. What seems at the start to be a not very important war becomes more important because the gods are so concerned with it. And even if their motives are highly subjective and irresponsible, that only adds to the dignity of the men who fight with or against them. Since the important thing is not the cause for which the war began but the desire to win glory through heroism, men have a greater chance of this when the gods take part in the action. It is all the more noble of Diomedes that he does not shrink from fighting even Ares, the god of war,[1] and Hector's death is all the more heroic when Apollo deserts him and leaves him to fight Achilles alone.[2]

In Homer's treatment of the gods the paradox emerges that they are less noble than men, and this is indeed inevitable to his heroic vision of existence. His men are more serious, more constant, more courageous. When they are wounded, they do not howl as Ares does;[3] they do not desert their friends as the gods do; they are faithful to their wives as the gods are not. All this is required of heroes and appropriate to their special calling and position. But the gods are not heroes. Being ageless and immortal, they cannot take such risks as men do, and can do with impunity what men may do at the cost of their lives. In consequence the gods are less impressive than men. They can never know the menace of death which forces a man to fill his life with valorous actions, nor the code of honour which demands that a short life should be rewarded by an undying renown. The gods are free to do what they please, and for that reason behave without responsibility and obligations; and the result is that, despite all their power and magnificence, they are not noble or dignified in a human sense. With men it is different. They are bound by claims and obligations, and in their devotion to these and especially to the ideal of manhood which embodies them they achieve a real nobility. In the Homeric poems, as in *Gilgamish*, man's mortality greatly increases his grandeur, because it means that in his brief career he must do his utmost to realise his ideal of manhood and be prepared in the end to sacrifice everything for it.

---

[1] *Il.* v, 846 ff.   [2] *Ibid.* xxii, 213.   [3] *Ibid.* v, 860.

III

THE HERO

In the poetry of heroic action leading parts are assigned to men of superior gifts, who are presented and accepted as being greater than other men. Though much of their interest lies in what happens to them and in the adventures through which they pass, an equal interest lies in their characters and personalities. Their stories are the more absorbing because they themselves are what they are. The fate of Achilles or Sigurth or Roland is the fate not of an abstract Everyman but of an individual who is both an example of pre-eminent manhood and emphatically himself. Heroes awake not only interest in their doings but admiration and even awe for themselves. Since heroic poetry treats of action and appeals to the love of prowess, its chief figures are men who display prowess to a high degree because their gifts are of a very special order. This does not mean that all heroes are of a single kind. Just as there is more than one kind of human excellence, so there is more than one kind of hero. The different kinds reflect not only different stages of social development but the different metaphysical and theoretical outlooks which the conception of a hero presupposes.

A hero differs from other men in the degree of his powers. In most heroic poetry these are specifically human, even though they are carried beyond the ordinary limitations of humanity. Even when the hero has supernatural powers and is all the more formidable because of them, they do little more than supplement his essentially human gifts. He awakes admiration primarily because he has in rich abundance qualities which other men have to a much less extent. Heroic poetry comes into existence when popular attention concentrates not on a man's magical powers but on his specifically human virtues, and, though the conception of him may keep some relics of an earlier outlook, he is admired because he satisfies new standards which set a high value on any-one who surpasses other men in qualities which all possess to some degree.

In pre-heroic poetry magic plays quite a different part, and the emphasis on human qualities is much less strong. The chief man has pride of place because he is a magician and knows how to control supernatural powers. A typical example can be seen in the Finnish lays incorporated in the *Kalevala*, where the chief characters are not warriors who prevail by strength and courage but magicians who prevail by craft and a special knowledge. For instance, when Väinämöinen, Ilmarinen, and Lemminkainen steal the mysterious Sampo and carry it off in their ship, they are pursued by the Mistress of Pohjola in a war-vessel, and a battle follows, which is fought on very unusual lines. When Väinä-möinen sees the ship coming in pursuit, he creates a reef, on which it is shattered. The Mistress of Pohjola then turns herself into a fearful flying monster and carries her company aloft with her to assault the Finns from the sea. When she settles on the masthead, Lemminkainen attacks her with a sword, but in such a world weapons are useless; and she is defeated only when Väinämöinen assaults her magically with a rudder and an oak-spar. Then she falls down and her company with her.[1] In traditional Finnish poetry the superior man prevails by special knowledge. He is the representative of a society in which the priest-magician is a very important person. But his poetical appeal is limited. He does not stir the common admiration for physical prowess to which heroic poetry appeals.

The emancipation of heroic poetry from the ideal of the magician can be illustrated from two countries near Finland. The indigenous poetry both of Esthonia and of northern Russia shows some resemblances to that of Finland and has certain themes and stories in common. But neither in Finland nor in Russia is the magician the chief character. He may once have been, but he has been superseded by the real hero. The Russian poems come near to the Finnish when they tell of the primitive hero, Volga, who can change his shape into a pike in the sea, a falcon in the sky, and a wolf on the plain, and outwits the Turkish Tsar by becoming a grey wolf which kills his horses and an ermine which ruins his weapons.[2] This is quite in the Finnish manner and suggests that, even if Volga is a distant version of some historical hero like Oleg, he has taken on some char-acteristics of magicians like Väinämöinen. But Volga is not merely or primarily a magician. He uses his gifts to fight for his country and has some marks of a mediaeval prince, when he collects a band, *druzhina*, of faithful companions, in which he is the " elder brother " among " younger brothers ", with whom he hunts and fishes, sees that tribute is properly paid, punishes those who destroy

[1] *Kalevala*, xliii, 99 ff.   [2] Rybnikov, i, p. 10 ff.

bridges, and organises the defence of his country against foreign enemies. In Volga the older type of the magician passes into the true hero but still keeps some of the earlier characteristics.

In the Esthonian lays, which Kreutzwald incorporated into the *Kalevipoeg*, the emancipation is more conscious and more emphatic than in the Russian poems on Volga. The chief hero is the Kalevipoeg, or son of Kalev, known in the *Kalevala* as Kullervo. His father Kalev seems to be an authentic hero, since it is possible that he is the same as Caelic, whom *Widsith* makes king of the Finns.[1] The Kalevipoeg himself is a giant of prodigious strength, but, though what he does is quite beyond ordinary men, he succeeds by the superabundance of his human gifts. His chief enemies are sorcerers and magicians. His mother, Linda, is carried off by a Finnish sorcerer whose suit she has rejected. The Kalevipoeg goes to Finland and slays the sorcerer after a great fight against whole armies of men whom the sorcerer creates by blowing feathers. In this encounter physical prowess meets magical powers and defeats them by force of arm. The difference between Esthonian and Finnish ideals can be seen from the treatment of Kullervo in the *Kalevala*. His character and powers are very much the same as in the *Kalevipoeg*, but he is held up to ridicule as a poor creature who lacks intelligence and comes to a proper end when he kills himself on his own sword. Väinä-möinen passes judgment on him as one who has been badly brought up :

> " Never, people, in the future,
> Rear a child in crooked fashion,
> Rocking them in stupid fashion,
> Soothing them to sleep like strangers.
> Children reared in crooked fashion,
> Boys thus rocked in stupid fashion,
> Grow not up with understanding,
> Nor attain to man's discretion,
> Though they live till they are aged,
> And in body well-developed." [2]

The Esthonian poets treat of Kullervo's death in a different spirit. They too tell that he is killed by his own sword, on which he has set a curse that it may kill his enemy, the sorcerer, but when instead it kills himself, it only helps to show how unheroic and dis-tasteful magic is. The hero ought not to have used it, and since he has, it brings ruin.

The process of change from a shamanistic to a purely heroic

---

[1] *Widsith*, 20, with Chambers' note.
[2] *Kalevala*, xxxvii, 351-60.

outlook may be seen in some Yakut poems in which the chief characters are shamans, but none the less heroic. They need magic because their opponents are usually demons or sorcerers, but when it comes to the final test, it is physical prowess that tells, as when Er Sogotokh fights with Nyurgun:

> They rushed at one another with hands outstretched.
> They began to cut one another with their hands.
> The clatter was like the roll of thunder in a storm.
> They shot out their hands and hammered one another
> With fists on the ribs.
> From that fight a lion wept, they say;
> Hail and snow began to fall, they say;
> The thick wood was bowed, they say.[1]

In another poem the chief characters are two women, who have shamanistic powers, Uolumar and Aigyr. If they are not of the calibre of Guthrun or accustomed to use men's weapons as she does, they are certainly courageous and adventurous, when they are harried and carried off by evil spirits, face the king of the dead, and by a mixture of craft and bravery win their freedom and are restored to their homes, where their valour is rewarded by the birth of sons who do great deeds.[2] The Yakut poets belong to a world where the shaman is still an important person who guides the religious and even the social life of the tribe. They are therefore not likely to pour contempt on him, but they are conscious enough of heroic worth to attribute it even to women who practise magic. They see that, in violent action, strength and courage are in the end more creditable than supernatural gifts.

Once a society conceives of the hero as a human being who possesses to a notable degree gifts of body and mind, the poets tell how he makes his career from the cradle to the grave. He is a marked man from the start, and it is only natural to connect his superiority with unusual birth and breeding. The greatest heroes are thought to be so wonderful that they cannot be wholly human but must have something divine about them. So Gilgamish is " two-thirds divine and one-third human ", and his companion, Enkidu, though not of divine lineage, is made of the desert clay by the goddess Aruru to be the double of Ninurta, the god of war. Achilles, as he is proud to point out to lesser men than himself,[3] is the son of a goddess. So too is the Trojan, Aeneas; [4] and in the previous generation Heracles was the son of Zeus, as was also Perseus. Asiatic heroes are often born in strange

---

[1] Yastremski, p. 28.
[2] *Idem*, pp. 122-54.
[3] *Il.* xxi, 109.
[4] *Ibid.* xx, 208 ff.

circumstances. The Nart Uryzmag is born at the bottom of the sea,[1] while Batrazd is born from a woman who has been kept a virgin in a high tower.[2] The Armenian Bagdasar and Sanasar are born because their mother drinks of a magical spring.[3] Other heroes, like the Kara-Kirghiz Manas and the Uzbek Alpamys, are born when their fathers are far advanced in years, and the births are regarded as the direct work of the gods in answer to prayer. A particularly elaborate case of this is the Canaanite Aqhat, whose father conducts a watch of seven days and nights in the sanctuary of Baal, with the result that Baal intercedes with the supreme god, El, and in due course Aqhat is born.[4]

Whatever a hero's birth may be, and of course it is often natural enough, he is recognised from the start as an extraordinary being whose physical development and characteristics are not those of other men. There is about him something foreordained, and omens of glory accompany his birth. When Helgi Hundingsbane is born, two ravens say :

> " In mailcoat stands   the son of Sigmund,
> A half-day old ;   now day is here ;
> His eyes flash sharp   as the heroes' are,
> He is friend of the wolves ;   full glad we are." [5]

In the same spirit the Kara-Kirghiz, Alaman Bet, who is by birth a Chinese, tells of the signs that accompanied his birth :

> " When I came out of the womb,
> I frightened the lamas with my cries,
> I cried out, it seems, ' Islam ! '
> When I was lifted up from the ground,
> A red flame flashed forth from it." [6]

When Manas is born, his delighted father gives a feast at which the guests prophesy a great future for the child, saying that he will overcome devils and Chinese. While still in the cradle, Manas begins to speak, and his father gives him a horse, proclaiming that he is ready to mount it.[7] When Heracles is still in swaddling bands, he strangles the two snakes which Hera sends to kill him.[8] The hero's career begins early and shows what kind of a man he is going to be.

Once born, the hero grows apace in strength and stature. So the Armenian poets have a formula for his development :

[1] Dumézil, p. 24 ff.
[2] *Idem*, p. 50 ff.
[3] *David Sasunskii*, p. 11 ff.
[4] Gaster, p. 270 ff.
[5] *Helgakvitha Hundingsbana*, i, 6.
[6] *Manas*, p. 175.
[7] Radlov, v, p. 2 ff.
[8] Pindar, *Nem.* i, 37 ff., presumably from an epic source.

> Other children grow by years,
> But David grew by days ; [1]

and show what infant prodigies, like Sanasar and Bagdasar, are in fact like :

> The children grew from day to day.
> They were one year old
> But like boys of five years.
> They went out to play with children,
> But they fought the children, beat them, and made them cry.
> When only five or six years had passed,
> Sanasar and Bagdasar
> Were strong sturdy men. [2]

The Greek, Digenis Akritas, is of the same breed :

> When one year old, he seized a sword ; when two, he took a lance up.
> And when he was but three years old, men took him for a soldier.
> He went abroad, men talked to him, of no man was he frightened. [3]

Digenis mounts his horse, goes off to the mountains, and defies the Saracens, whom he routs in feats of strength and whose horses he takes. If human beings are not available, the young hero may impress his personality on natural things and animals, as the Russian Volga does :

> When Volga Buslavlevich was five years old,
> Lord Volga Buslavlevich went forth over the damp earth ;
> Damp mother earth was rent.
> The wild beasts fled away to the forests,
> The birds flew away to the clouds ;
> And the fish scattered in the blue sea. [4]

A life so begun comes rapidly to its crisis. Manas, after his portentous start, soon moves to a life of action. At ten he shoots an arrow as well as a boy of fourteen, and soon afterwards he is a full-fledged warrior :

> When he grew to be a prince, he overthrew princely dwellings ;
> Sixty stallions, a hundred three-year-old foals
> He drove thither from Kokand ;
> Eighty young mares, a thousand kymkar
> He brought from Bokhara ;
> The Chinese settled in Kashgar
> He drove away to Turfan ;
> The Chinese settled in Turfan
> He drove yet farther to Aksu. [5]

---

[1] *David Sasunskii*, p. 142. [2] *Ibid.* p. 15 ff.
[3] Legrand, p. 187. [4] Gilferding, ii, p. 172.
[5] Radlov, v, p. 6 ; a " kymkar " must be some kind of horse.

At fifteen the Armenian Mher strangles a lion with his own hands ; [1] at sixteen the Kalmuck Dzhangar steals the horses of an enemy ; [2] at fourteen the Uzbek Alpamys invades the country of the Kalmucks.[3] The hero breaks records from the start and is a fully-grown man when others are still boys.

The hero possesses those gifts of body and character which bring success in action and are admired for that reason. He may be strong or swift or enduring or resourceful or eloquent. Not all heroes possess the whole gamut of these qualities but all have some portion of them, and what matters is less their range of gifts, than the degree in which they have one or other of them. A hero differs from other men by his peculiar force and energy. Just as the Greeks define him as one who has a special δύναμις or power, so in all countries he has an abundant, overflowing, assertive force, which expresses itself in action, especially in violent action, and enables him to do what is beyond ordinary mortals. This is commonly displayed in battle, because battle provides the most searching tests not merely of strength and courage but of resource and decision. The greatest heroes are primarily men of war. But even in battle what really counts is the heroic force, the assertive spirit which inspires a man to take prodigious risks and enables him to surmount them successfully or at least to fail with glorious distinction. Their peculiar drive and vigour explains why heroes are often compared to wild animals, as, for instance, the Uzbek warriors are compared to lions, tigers, bears, leopards, wolves, and hyenas,[4] or Homeric warriors are compared to vultures, lions, boars, and the like, while Achilles himself is like some irresistible power of nature, compared in turn to a river in spate, a flaming star, a vulture swooping on its prey, a fire burning a wood or a city, an eagle dropping to seize a lamb or a kid. Hector knows what this power means, when he decides to fight him :

" Him will I face in the fight, though his hands are as fire that
    consumeth,
Hands are as fire that consumeth, his might like glittering iron." [5]

This is the essential hero in his irresistible onslaught and power to destroy.

These qualities are seen at their keenest when a hero's temper is high and his thoughts turn to prowess. The mere prospect of a fight is enough to inflame his passions and make him burn for

---

[1] *David Sasunskii*, p. 107 ff.   [2] Zhirmunskii-Zarifov, p. 321.
[3] *Idem*, p. 323.   [4] *Idem*, p. 306.   [5] *Il.* xx, 371-2.

action, as the Serb hero, Miloš Stoićević, does when he goes out
to fight the Moslems :

> " I am going as my war-horse wishes !
> For my steed is thirsting for the struggle,
> And in my right arm the strength is welling,
> Gladly would it sport awhile with Moslems ;
> At my belt my sword for blood is thirsting,
> It is thirsting for the blood of heroes ;
> I must quench the deep thirst of my sabre,
> Quench it with the blood of Turkish heroes." [1]

The same spirit is present even in the *Kalevala*, though it is
displayed in Kullervo, whom the poets despise. When he sets out
for war, he exults in anticipation of it :

> " If I perish in the battle,
> Sinking on the field of battle,
> Fine mid clash of swords to perish,
> Exquisite the battle-fever." [2]

When a fight begins, heroes deliver blows with astounding force
and an almost delirious delight. The friendship of Gilgamish and
Enkidu begins with a tremendous struggle between them in which
each shows a prodigious energy :

> Enkidu barred the door with his foot,
> He would not allow entry to Gilgamish.
> They grappled and snorted like bulls ;
> The threshold was shattered, the wall quivered,
> As Gilgamish and Enkidu grappled, snorting like bulls,
> The threshold was shattered, the wall quivered.[3]

When Roland sees the Saracens before him, he becomes like a wild
beast :

> When Roland sees that now must be combat,
> More fierce he's found than lion or leopard.[4]

Such a spirit can spread to a whole company when the call is
strong enough and a desperate situation calls for desperate courage.
So the Greeks fought at Missolonghi when it was besieged by the
Turks in 1822 :

The mariners are fighting with cannons and blunderbuses,
The others have unsheathed their swords and fight with naked iron,
The merchants and the artisans are fighting like mad serpents,
They fire their rifles fearfully, they're armed with long sharp daggers.

---

[1] Karadžić, iv, p. 200. Trs. W. A. Morison.
[2] *Kalevala*, xxxvi, 28-32.   [3] *Gilgamish*, ii, vi, 10-15.
[4] *Roland*, 1110-11.

Never a thought they give to death, they hurl themselves like lions,
They cry and call upon the Turks and mock at them with laughter,
They only wait for help to come to fall on them and break them.[1]

The vitality of heroes sharpens their lust for battle and turns into
a superhuman fury and frenzy.

The power which heroes display in action can be felt in their
mere presence. When they appear, other men know them for
superior beings and wonder who they are. So when the Uzbek
hero, Alpamys, first meets the Kalmuck, Karadzhan, who is to
become his devoted friend, Karadzhan says :

" Your beauty is like the moon in the skies,
Your brows I compare to a bent bow,
In shape you are like a grey-blue hawk,
As you sit there, loosening your reins, you are like a lord who
    has countless sheep.
Beautiful lord, whither are you going ?
From what rare diamond were you fashioned ?
Such a warrior as you could not be born from a human mother.
From what nest did you wend your flight ? " [2]

Alpamys belongs to the class of heroes, like Achilles and Sigurth,
who are eminent for their beauty. But beauty is not necessary to
heroes. It is not attributed to Roland or Beowulf or Manas.
Some heroes, like Odysseus, may be undeniably fascinating but
short in stature and stout in build. A hero's appearance reveals
his essential superiority and difference from other men. There is
something about it which reveals unusually strong fires within.
Divine blood may sometimes help, but it too is not essential. It
is their superabundance of life which marks heroes out as it
shines from their eyes or betrays itself in their gestures or their
voices. So the Kalmuck poet describes Dzhangar :

His moustaches are almost like eagles' wings,
The look of his black magical eyes
Is that of a gerfalcon ready to pounce.[3]

The Kara-Kirghiz Manas is of the same breed and strikes equal awe
when his passions are aroused :

The look changed on Manas' face.
In his eyes a furnace blazed.
A living dragon it was. . . .
His look was like the midnight's look,
Angry as a cloudy day.[4]

[1] Legrand, p. 130.   [2] Zhirmunskii-Zarifov, p. 309.
[3] Dzhangariada, p. 97.   [4] Manas, p. 54.

99

Sometimes a fearful appearance is combined with a voice whose tones strike silence and dismay. When Ivan the Terrible is enjoying himself at a banquet, his actions are formidable in their very triviality :

> The terrible Tsar, Ivan Vasilevich, was making merry,
> He walked through his apartments,
> He looked through his glazed window,
> He combed his black curls with a small-toothed comb.

When he opens his mouth and announces that in all his realm there are no more traitors, the effect is appalling :

> Then they trembled before him,
> His subjects were terrified,
> They could not think of an answer.
> The taller of them hid behind the smaller,
> And the smaller for their part were speechless.[1]

Against this modest, untutored effect we may set the magnificent scene in the *Iliad* when Achilles, having decided to go back to battle, stands on the rampart and raises his battle-cry three times :

> Then were the chariot-drivers astounded, who saw the unwearied
> Flame burn over the head of Peleus' son, the great-hearted,
> Terribly, for it was lit by the grey-eyed goddess Athene.
> Three times over the rampart Achilles shouted his war-cry,
> Three times Trojans and allies were sheer amazed and confounded.
> There and then were destroyed twelve men, most noble of Trojans,
> Mid their chariots and spears.[2]

The fear and destruction caused by the mere sight of Achilles and the sound of his voice are a sign of the tremendous force in him.

Though physical strength is an essential part of a hero's endowment, he is no animal or devoid of wits. On the contrary, since wits are another sign that he surpasses other men, there is nothing discreditable in their use to secure some glorious end. Though direct action might be more impressive, there are many occasions when it is impossible. At the lowest level it might be argued that since the hero's chief aim is to exert his own will and get what he wants there is no reason why he should not use guile. When Manas fights Er Kökchö, he wins the first round in a wrestling match ; then Er Kökchö proposes a firing of flint-locks, and Manas misses him, while Er Kökchö hits Manas, who flies away wounded on his horse. When Er Kökchö chivalrously tries to heal Manas' wound, Manas turns and kills his opponent's horse.[3] This is not fair play, but is accepted on the principle that all is permissible

---

[1] Kireevski, vi, p. 55 ; Chadwick, *R.H.P.* p. 194.
[2] *Il.* xviii, 225-31.
[3] Radlov, v, p. 72.

in war. In fact there may be behind it another assumption, that a hero like Manas is so great that he is entitled to exert his powers as he chooses. There are other cases of this kind, notably Mher the Younger in Armenia, but they are not common and certainly not the general rule. Normally, when the hero uses guile, he does so because it is quite as dangerous as force and is, in the given conditions, the only possible means of action.

Craft and stratagem have their own dangers, as Abu Zeyd, the hero of *The Stealing of the Mare*, illustrates in a high degree. He is a formidable man of action, whom no one can withstand in open fight, but for this particular task, the theft of a carefully guarded mare, craft is the only possible means, and justifiable because the undertaking is extremely hazardous and discovery means death. Abu Zeyd enters into his plot with all the bold spirit and love of adventure which he shows on the battlefield, and the high level of his cunning is merely another example of his heroic superiority. The same may be said of Alaman Bet's brilliant adventure at the house of the sorceress Kanyshai. When he disguises himself as a Chinese and walks boldly into her quarters in the middle of a feast, he is alone and a stranger, but he succeeds by the very effrontery of his stratagem. No doubt the same would be true of the lost Greek poem which told how Odysseus disguised himself as a beggar and went into Troy as a spy ; and even the inmates of the Wooden Horse, with all their ingenuity and cunning, did not lack a great element of courage in being willing to risk their lives if they were discovered in the city of their enemies. Perhaps the most authentic heroes are above even stratagems so dangerous as these. We somehow cannot imagine that they would appeal to Achilles or Gilgamish or Sigurth or Roland. But the men who practise them are warriors of high eminence, who resort to guile because they must. Even so their courage is needed throughout.

Of heroes famed for resource Odysseus is the most complete. He too is a great warrior and leader, who uses cunning to get himself out of difficulties into which his headstrong taste for adventure has led him. The classical case of his resourcefulness is his handling of the Cyclops. The one-eyed giant who holds Odysseus in his cave and then decides to eat him is an opponent against whom any stratagem is fair, but Odysseus' predicament is the fruit of his insatiable curiosity and desire for new experiences. There is no need to enter the cave, but Odysseus wishes to know who lives in it on the lonely island, and hopes for a gift from the owner. Once caught, he shows the full range of his talents, and his escape is a masterpiece of imaginative improvisation. It is interesting to compare Homer's version of Odysseus and the Cyclops with Ossete stories of Uryzmag and the one-eyed giant, which have much in common with it. The Ossete hero is trapped for reasons which do him nothing but credit. He has gone out in search of food for the Narts, who are suffering from famine, and finds the giant pasturing his flock. Uryzmag lays hold of the ram, but it makes off with him to the giant, who puts him in a bag and takes him into the cave.[1] In another version the Narts boast against each other about which of them is bravest, and the result is that Uryzmag attacks the giant's flock and follows it into the cave.[2] In both versions Uryzmag behaves in a heroic manner for noble reasons, but his motives are simpler than those of Odysseus and his fate is less intimately connected with his character. Once in the cave, he acts much as Odysseus does and is fully entitled to honour for extracting himself from a desperate situation.

Though most heroes are moved by similar motives and act in similar fashion, there is much variety in the ends to which their actions are devoted. Though the hero's first and most natural need is to display his prowess and win the glory which he feels to be his right, he is ready to do so for some cause which does not immediately concern his personal interest but attracts him because it gives him a chance to show his worth This cause need not be very concrete. Indeed with some of the greatest heroes it is simply an ideal of manhood and prowess to which he feels that he must devote his life. This is what guides Sigurth. Though he is bound by ties of loyalty to Gunnar and serves him honourably, the centre of his being is the conception of manhood which Gripir prophesies to him :

> " With baseness never   thy life is burdened,
> Hero noble,   hold that sure ;
> Lofty as long   as the world shall live,
> Battle-bringer,   thy name shall be." [3]

Sigurth accepts this destiny and acts upon it. He follows his instinctive ambition to be a great warrior. When he kills Fafnir, he tells the dying monster why he has done so — it is a need to show his prowess :

> " My heart did drive me,   my hand fulfilled,
> And my shining sword so sharp." [4]

[1] Dumézil, p. 44.   [2] Dynnik, p. 13 ff.
[3] *Grípisspá*, 23.   [4] *Fafnismal*, 6, 1-2.

This desire for prowess is combined with other noble qualities, which Gripir also foretells:

> " Free of gold-giving,   slow to flee,
> Noble to see,   and sage in speech." [1]

But the root of Sigurth's heroic nature is his unquestioning, unfaltering desire to prove his worth to the utmost limits of his capacity.

Achilles belongs to the same class. Though he plays the chief part in the Trojan War, which is fought to win back for Menelaus the wife whom Paris has abducted, this cause means little to Achilles. When Agamemnon's envoys ask him to return to the fight, he refuses, and one of his reasons is that he does not see why he should risk his life for another man's wife. Then he reveals his true thoughts. His mother has told him that he has a choice of two destinies: he can either stay at Troy and win everlasting renown, or go home to a long and inglorious old age.[2] For the moment he hesitates, but in the end he chooses the first course and follows the promptings of his heroic nature which regards glory as the right aim for such a man as himself. In so doing he obeys the advice which his father once gave him:

> Ever to seek to be best and surpass all others in action.[3]

It is true that, when Achilles goes back to the battle, his uppermost desire is to avenge the death of Patroclus, but even so his heroic nature asserts itself, and his desire for vengeance is transcended in his desire for glory as he exercises his physical gifts and tastes the joys of battle and victory. He slays his opponents with a triumphant pride and mockingly tells them that he is a better man than they. As he makes his bloody progress, and his chariot-wheels are bespattered with blood, there is no doubt what weighs most with him, since the poet says that " the son of Peleus sought to win glory ".[4] Like Sigurth, Achilles is inspired by an ideal of manhood which he thinks that he can realise to a unique degree, and though he has other gifts of counsel, courtesy, and eloquence, they are secondary to his essential and dominating desire to be a great warrior.

The desire for prowess as an end in itself may be illustrated by a remarkable Ossete poem about the hero Batradz, who is so eager to be the ideal and perfect warrior that he applies on a strange errand to the divine smith Kurdalagon, who is a kind of

---

[1] *Grípisspá*, 7, 3-4.   [2] *Il.* ix, 410 ff.
[3] *Ibid.* xi, 784.   [4] *Ibid.* xx, 502.

H

counterpart to Hephaestus. The poem begins by showing what kind of hero Batradz is and what his ambitions are:

> Once Batradz fell strongly a-thinking:
> " I have strength, but I have need of more,
> And not such as with ill luck a strong man will overcome.
> Come, it is better, I will go to the sky,
> I will ascend the sky, go straight to Kurdalagon,
> I will beseech him to temper me ! "
> He went to the sky, straight to Kurdalagon.
> To him Batradz goes, to the heavenly forge.
> " Heavenly smith, smith Kurdalagon !
> Cast me on the furnace, temper me on the forge ! "
> " Think not of it, and dare not to desire it ;
> You will burn up, my Sun, and I have pity for you ;
> Much delight, young man, have you already given me."
> " No. Such is my need, O smith Kurdalagon !
> I beseech you with a great prayer.
> Temper me on the heavenly forge ! "

The smith agrees, and for the first month heats the coals, for the second the sand of the river. Then he beats Batradz on the anvil for a month, and at the end of it thinks that he must be entirely shrivelled up, but Batradz says to him :

> " Your fire has not melted me even a little !
> What game are you playing with me, smith Kurdalagon ?
> It is dull alone in the oven with nothing to do ;
> Give me a lyre, to amuse myself with ! "

Kurdalagon gives him the lyre, heaps up the coal, and sets to work, but still Batradz remains intact. So the tempering begins again, and when Kurdalagon takes another look, Batradz calls out :

> " At last you have tempered me ! How uselessly
>   you continue !
> Take me quickly, cast me into the sea ! "
> And the heavenly smith takes his pincers,
> With the pincers he takes the Nart by his knees,
> Cast him at once into the blue sea.
> The sea foamed and hissed and bubbled,
> And the sea's water all vanished in steam,
> The sea became dry that very day.
> So the body of Batradz was tempered,
> His body turned to blue steel.
> Only his liver remained untempered :
> No water touched it, all vanished in steam.
> When steel Batradz came out of the sea,
> Then was the sea filled again with water.[1]

[1] Dynnik, p. 33 ff.

Achilles, according to Greek legend, was made proof against weapons when his mother dipped him in fire [1] or ambrosia [2] or the river Styx [3]; Batradz makes himself proof by a more exacting and more original method when he hands himself over for treatment by the divine smith.

Heroism for its own sake is perhaps exceptional. More commonly heroes devote their talents to some concrete cause which provides scope for action and an end to which they can direct their efforts. The hero is usually a leader of men and feels an obligation towards those under his command. It is therefore surprising that the kings of heroic story are often hardly heroic in the full sense. They seem so burdened with responsibilities and anxieties that they cannot display a full measure of individual prowess. Homer's Agamemnon, Hrothgar in *Beowulf*, Charlemagne in *Roland*, and Gunnar in the *Elder Edda* are impressive figures but lack the four-square heroism of their subordinates, Achilles, Beowulf, Roland, and Sigurth. The mere fact of being a king sometimes detracts from a man's heroic performance. His duties prevent him from giving all his attention to warlike exploits; he is so occupied with ruling that he must leave the greatest opportunities to others. He may even be prevented by age from acting as he would have done in youth. Of course, when occasion calls, Agamemnon and Charlemagne show their worth in battle, while Gunnar's last hours in Atli's halls are in the highest heroic tradition. On the other hand among Asiatic peoples the king is often the greatest warrior of all, the man who displays in himself all the finest qualities of his people. So Manas, Dzhangar, and Alpamys stand respectively for all that is best in the Kara-Kirghiz, Kalmucks, and Uzbeks. In the great war against the Chinese, it is Manas who in the end takes the lead and attacks the most formidable opponents; when Dzhangar's lands are invaded in his absence by an enemy, he is foremost in reconquering them; Alpamys wins his first fame by leading his people against the Kalmucks. Such kings belong to a more primitive level of society than their European counterparts, and that is perhaps why they are allowed to exert their heroic natures to the full.

There are, however, occasions even in Europe when the king becomes the champion of his people and exerts his heroic powers for it. Though in early life Beowulf kills Grendel from motives of pure heroism, in old age he fights the dragon in a different spirit, to save his people from a deadly pest. He agrees at once to their

[1] Schol. *Il.* xvi, 37. [2] Ap. Rhod. iv, 869.
[3] Quint. Smyrn. iii, 62.

appeal for help and insists on fighting the monster alone. It is his last fight, and he dies from wounds received in it. That is why his subjects lament him as they do :

> So grieved and plained   the Geatish people
> For their Lord's fall,   his hearth-fellows ;
> They said that he was   a World-King,
> Of men the mildest   and to men kindest,
> To his people most pleasant   and for praise most eager.[1]

Another king who gives his life for his people is the Serb, Tsar Lazar, who is killed fighting the Turks at Kosovo. It is he who takes the decision to fight, calls on every Serb to join his army, gives a banquet on the eve of the battle, and dies bravely in the struggle. His national importance is recognised after his death, when his headless body lies uncorrupted on the field of Kosovo for forty years :

> Pecked not by the eagles and the ravens,
> Trampled not by horses or by heroes,[2]

until the head is miraculously joined to it and the remains put in a shrine. In Tsar Lazar the Serbs have a type of their own sufferings and sacrifices, and for this reason he has a special place in their national poetry.

If kings do not often hold pride of place, their followers and liegemen do, and there are many notable examples of men who perform heroic actions out of loyalty to a suzerain or sovereign. Though Charlemagne cuts no great figure in *Roland*, he commands astonishing loyalty and receives wonderful service. Though Roland does not shrink from disputing the Emperor's decisions in council, in the end he obeys them, notably when he is told to command the rear-guard of the army, though he knows that this is due to Ganelon's plot to encompass his death. When he first receives the orders, he bursts out in anger, but he accepts them none the less. Once he has undertaken the task, honour forbids him to ask for help, and that is why he refuses to blow his horn. He feels that such an action would be to betray his overlord's trust in him :

> " A thousand score stout men he set apart,
> And well he knows, not one will prove coward.
> Man for his lord should suffer with good heart,
> Of bitter cold and great heat bear the smart,
> His blood let drain, and all his flesh be scarred." [3]

[1] *Beowulf*, 3178-82.   [2] Karadžić, ii, p. 296.
[3] *Roland*, 1115-19.

This of course is the spirit of chivalry as the twelfth century conceived it. Roland must act in a truly feudal spirit to his overlord, but that does not prevent him from being a complete hero.

The relative positions of suzerain and hero can produce their own drama of personal relations. In the Kara-Kirghiz poems a special interest attaches to the friendship between the great prince, Manas, and his subordinate, Alaman Bet. Alaman Bet is by origin a Kalmuck or a Chinese. He attaches himself to Manas because a previous attempt to serve the Ulgur prince, Er Kökchö, has failed through the envy of his colleagues.[1] He chooses Manas for no better reason than to find a career of adventure, but, once his choice is made, he does his duty with such loyalty that he has a very special place in Manas' regard and affection. The degree of Manas' trust in him is shown by what Manas says to his captains before the start of the great expedition :

> " To Alaman Bet alone is known
> The distant road to China.
> Let him be our guide,
> Let him enable us to look
> On China, though it be with only one eye.
> If he falls into a lake,
> We shall float across the lake after him !
> If he moves in circles,
> In circles we shall go after him ;
> If he hurls himself on the wind,
> On the wind we shall fly after him.
> If he bristles with wild beasts,
> We shall join our spears after him ;
> If suddenly he feels sorrow,
> Then we shall lament with him." [2]

Alaman Bet is a notable example of the heroic subordinate who shapes his life in the service of a master and is rewarded by the trust in which he is held.

Another cause which a hero may serve is religion. The heroic temper might not at first sight seem to be perfectly attuned to the self-sacrificing ideals of Christianity and Buddhism, but in practice no difficulty arises. *Roland* is set in a war between the Christian paladins of Charlemagne and the infidel Saracens. The Christian spirit is often present and does much for the action. The Christians fight to convert the infidels, and Charlemagne insists on the baptism of the captured and the conquered. He celebrates Mass and Matins in his camp, and, when he takes the

[1] Radlov, v, p. 32 ff. ; cf. p. 515.   [2] *Manas*, p. 83.

field to avenge Roland's death, God shows His favour by stopping
the sun in its course. This faith is woven into the heroic scheme
without any great strain. The Christians despise and hate the
infidels for their worship of false gods and their lack of chivalry
and honour. The struggle is presented as between right and
wrong, truth and falsehood, and this gives an emphatic character
to the issues at stake. It is therefore appropriate that, when the
Saracens are defeated, they should turn on their own gods and
curse them as useless and unrewarding, and on the other hand
that the Christians should be confident that to die for their cause
is to win Paradise. The Archbishop, Turpin, has no doubts
about the worthiness of the issue and, before the battle begins,
tells the host :

> " My lords barons, Charles left us here for this ;
> He is our King, well may we die for him :
> To Christendom good service offering.
> Battle you'll have, you all are bound to it,
> For with your eyes you see the Sarrazins.
> Pray for God's grace, confessing Him your sins !
> For your souls' health I'll absolution give ;
> So, though you die, blest martyrs shall you live,
> Thrones you shall win in the great Paradis." [1]

He then gives absolution and benediction, and the fight begins.
Later, when Roland is stricken to death, he confesses his sins and
is carried by angels to Paradise, thus reaping the reward which he
has himself asked for the dead on the mountain-side :

> " Lords and Barons, may God to you be kind !
> And all your souls redeem for Paradise !
> And let you there mid holy flowers lie ! " [2]

The scheme is clear and simple and fits well into the cult of
honour. Roland seeks always to display his valour because he is
confident that he acts in the holiest of causes and that the glory
which he desires will be found not merely in the memories of
men but in heaven.

No other religion informs its poetry with so complete a
scheme as this, but there are times when Islam does something
like it. The Kara-Kirghiz heroes are Mohammedans and proud
of it. It is true that they seem to have been recently converted,
since an echo of this survives in reference to the Uigur prince,
Er Kökchö :

> Who opened the doors of Paradise,
> Who opened the closed doors of the bazaars. [3]

[1] *Roland*, 1127-35.   [2] *Ibid.* 1854-6.   [3] Radlov, v, p. 18.

But, like other converts, the Kara-Kirghiz feel some contempt for those who do not share their spiritual advantages. It is true that they disobey the Prophet to the extent of drinking brandy on many suitable occasions, but their own laxity does not affect their habitual reference to Buddhists and others as " unclean " or their shocked disapproval of the Kalmucks as men " who cut up pork and tie it on saddles ". That there is a basis of religious experience behind this faith is clear enough from Orozbakov's account of the vision of Paradise which Alaman Bet learns from his mother.[1] It is of course a place of material and sensual joys, but none the less, the poet implies, worth winning, and indeed Alaman Bet is converted to Islam by the prospect of it. But on the whole the Mohammedan faith of the Kara-Kirghiz has little of the crusading zeal which we find in the Christian paladins of *Roland*. It is largely a national and racial affair. Though Alaman Bet tactfully murmurs the word " Islam " as soon as he is born and early embraces the faith, he does not feel perfectly at home among the Kara-Kirghiz, since he is by birth a Chinese, and complains to Manas :

> " Those who are born of Kirghiz blood
> Cast reproaches at me because
> I am born of a Chinese stock.
> They say : ' You are a Kalmuck, you,
> You are not truly one of us ;
> No true believer gives to you
> The lofty rights that we possess.
> You have the same rights as a slave,
> You're not our brother, despised slave,
> You are a heathen, hypocrite ! '
> Such the abuse they cast on me." [2]

In effect the Kara-Kirghiz believe that, because they are Mohammedans, they are more civilised and more heroic than Buddhists or idolaters and belong to a superior order of manhood.

On the other hand, though the Kara-Kirghiz identify their religion with their national pride, they are more tolerant of other faiths than are the Christians of *Roland*. In time of peace they invite Kalmucks and heathen Kara-Nogai to their festivals, and at the feast of Bok-Murun both parties mix in a friendly spirit, though it is assumed to be right and proper that in the games the Kara-Kirghiz should win all the events. So too in war, though the struggle may be indeed bloody, the Kara-Kirghiz respect their enemies, and the poets present them in an almost heroic light. It is true that they use magic to protect themselves, which the

[1] *Manas*, p. 94. [2] *Ibid.* p. 197.

Kara-Kirghiz themselves do not, and that some of their leading figures are of monstrous size and shape. None the less it takes all the efforts of the Kara-Kirghiz to defeat Mahdi-Khan and Kongyr Bai. Moreover the poets give to these alien chieftains sentiments which would sound well on the lips of any Kara-Kirghiz. Though Kongyr Bai may begin by claiming that he is safe from attack because of his magical protections:

> " No sword frightens us,
> And nothing terrifies us.
> My country is my shield,
> My mountain is my defence.
> Live; be not afraid of destruction:
> Meet your death-hour in your beds ",[1]

yet when real danger faces him, he rises to the occasion and tells his followers:

> " If death is our fate, we shall die.
> We are not at all afraid of death!
> Did you come here only to have a look?
> Only to scare the foe with your numbers? "[2]

The Kara-Kirghiz must have adversaries worthy of them such as the Chinese in fact are. It is therefore intelligible that the most distinguished warrior in the Kara-Kirghiz army, Alaman Bet, is by origin a Chinese.

The Kalmucks, whom the Kara-Kirghiz fight and despise as unbelievers, are Buddhists, and the spirits and saints of Buddhism receive more attention in the Kalmuck poems than do the Christian saints in *Roland*. They take no part in the action, but their presence in the background is emphasised at some length, and the poems usually begin with a tribute to the visible tokens of their power in Dzhangar's mountainous realm. The poet insists that the faith and religious standing of the Kalmucks is beyond reproach:

> The four seas of Shartak are theirs,
> Four yellow shrines are theirs,
> A lama is theirs,
> A manifest Buddha incarnate.
> The Buddha's blessings are theirs.[3]

Of this faith Dzhangar is the representative and the champion:

> He affirmed the universal rule like a rock,
> He rejoiced radiant with the Buddhist faith like a sun.[4]

[1] *Manas*, p. 248.　　　　　　　　　[2] *Ibid.* p. 334.
[3] *Dzhangariada*, p. 95.　　　　　　　[4] *Ibid.* p. 142.

One incarnation of the Buddha has breathed on his cheek; another watches over him as he sleeps.[1] A special lama looks after him :

> The lama Alisha watches and protects his arms and legs,
> His pure beautiful breast,
> His heart like a young moon,
> The red thread of his life.[2]

Inspired by an exclusive confidence, Dzhangar and his companions are in every way convinced that they have divine support and that their war against the vampire people of the Mangus is a war between those whom the gods love and those whom the gods hate. But, though the Kalmuck heroes regard themselves as chosen instruments of heaven, they are recognisably human and act as heroes usually do, following their desire for glory in a familiar way. Like the Kara-Kirghiz they have so strong a faith that they do not need magic but are able to get what they want by force of arms. Their religion gives them an inspiring purpose in battle, but they are primarily moved by the desire for glory.

What religion does in these cases is done more often and more easily by love of country. In many cases this is almost unconscious, and rises to the surface only when it is challenged. So the Uzbek hero, Yusuf, tells an enemy what his country means to him :

> " Our country is a good country.
> The winters in it are like spring.
> Gardeners watch over its gardens,
> And its trees are rich with fruit.
> Its old women rest in white carts,
> But the young busy themselves as they will.
> Maidens and youths are constant in love,
> Their time is filled with joy and delights." [3]

Another hero says :

> " My country is my life,
> My country is my soul." [4]

Such feelings are common enough, and it is only natural that at times heroes should share them and fight for them. He who fights and dies for his country is known to Homer and portrayed in the *Iliad*, not indeed among the Achaeans, who fight to get back Menelaus' wife from Paris, but among the Trojans, who fight to defend their city and their homes. Hector is the earliest hero who exerts all his powers on behalf of his country. When

---

[1] *Ibid*. p. 96.
[2] *Ibid*. p. 146.
[3] Zhirmunskii-Zarifov, p. 317.
[4] *Idem*, p. 317.

the seer Polydamas tells him that the omens are hostile, Hector defies them and says :

" Only one omen is best, to fight in defence of your country." [1]

Later, when his men are discouraged and seem likely to abandon the struggle, Hector appeals to them in the language of pure patriotism :

> " All of you, keep to the fight by the ships, and if any among you,
> Struck by a javelin or spear, get his end of doom and destruction,
> So let him die. No dishonour is it to fall for his country,
> Leaving behind him his wife and his children alive and uninjured,
> Leaving his home and possessions unharmed, so be the Achaeans
> Sail away hence on ships to the much loved land which begat
> them." [2]

Hector thinks not so much of glory as of home and family and city. In his heart he knows that Troy will fall, but none the less he is ready to do all that he can to avert or postpone the evil day. He acts like a hero and has a glorious triumph when he comes near to burning the Achaean ships. But he hardly thinks of displaying his personal prowess. In many ways the most human and most attractive figure in the *Iliad*, he is not its chief hero. Homer draws a contrast between him and Achilles, between the human champion of hearth and home and the half-divine hero who has very few ties or loyalties. Perhaps in Hector we may see the emergence of a new ideal of manhood, of the conception that a man fulfils himself better in the service of his city than in the satisfaction of his own honour, and in that case Hector stands on the boundary between the heroic world and the city-state which replaced it. Yet Hector has much of the attractiveness and nobility which belong to the true hero. Inferior as he is to Achilles in strength and speed, he is a formidable warrior who is carried on by his impetuous might. In him love of country is the driving motive, but through it he realises a destiny which is certainly heroic.

A hero, conceived as Hector is, is the representative of his people, their spokesman and their exemplar. From this it is no long step to finding a hero not in a great prince or leader but in some less eminent person who has his great hour in a crisis, or in a group of persons who show their worth when their country is in peril. Such is the case with the Anglo-Saxon *Maldon*, in which perhaps the chief character and in some sense the hero is Byrhtnoth. It is he who gives the first defiant answer to the Viking invaders and in so doing speaks for his king and country :

[1] *Il.* xii, 243.   [2] *Ibid.* xv, 494-9.

" Seamen's messenger, take word to thy masters,
Tell to thy people more hateful tidings,
That here stands a noble earl with his soldiers,
Who will dare to stand in defence of this land,
Land of Aethelred, lord and master,
Its people and soil." [1]

When Byrhtnoth is killed, his comrades maintain his defiant spirit
and show themselves worthy of him. Aelfwine appeals to the
men to fight on for the sake of their dead lord and to justify
boasts made in the past :

" Remember what time at the mead we talked
When on the benches our boasts we made,
Heroes in hall of the hard encounter ;
Now may be kenned whose courage avails." [2]

In turn different warriors, Offa, Leofsunu, and Dunnere, give
support to this call, until the Old Companion, seeing that the fight
is now going against the English, speaks in the ultimate eloquence
of heroic resistance, as he calls for a last effort :

" Will shall be harder, heart the bolder,
Mood the more, as our might lessens." [3]

In fighting for their country the men of *Maldon* are moved by a
truly heroic spirit and act in accordance with its immemorial rules.
In them the group shows the old pride of the individual and
reveals that it knows what is expected of it in an hour of desperate
effort.

When a country is under foreign domination, there is a
tendency for every man to become a hero who resists or fights
the conquerors. This may be seen in more than one country
under the Turkish rule. Many Greek poems of the last two
centuries tell of otherwise obscure persons who have struck a blow
for their people against the foreign tyrants. There is the captain,
Malamos, who refuses at the last moment to make submission
to the Turks, because they are treacherous, and goes back to the
mountains.[4] There is Xepateras, who fights alone and is threatened
by a whole army, but none the less refuses to submit and cuts off
the head of the Turk who asks him to.[5] There is the captain,
Tsolkas, who for three days and three nights, without water or
food or help, fights his way through the Turkish lines.[6] There
is Master John, of Crete, who raises a rebellion, but is captured

---

[1] *Maldon*, 49-54.   [2] *Ibid.* 211-15 ; cf. *Beowulf*, 2630 ff.
[3] *Maldon*, 312-13.   [4] Legrand, p. 80.
[5] *Idem*. p. 84.   [6] *Idem*, p. 88.

by the Turks and thrown to the fishes.[1] There is the mother of
the sons of Lazos who denounces her sons for leaving their strong-
hold in Olympus and says she will curse them if they join the
Turks.[2] There is the patriarch Gregory who is hanged by
Turkish janissaries in front of his church.[3] The episodes are small,
and the characters not too prominent, but a heroic air is given to
them by their participation in a great cause and their reckless
defiance of the Turks.

The Jugoslav poems on the resistance to the Turks present a
more varied scheme than the Greek both in temper and in episode.
There are times when this resistance takes on a truly heroic
character and every Serb becomes a hero. Such is the spirit of
the poems on Kosovo, and it is concentrated in the words which
King Lazar sends round when he summons his people to battle :

> " He who is a Serb, with Serbian forebears,
> And of Serbian blood and Serbian nurture,
> And comes not to battle at Kosovo,
> He shall ne'er be blessed with descendants,
> With descendants, either male or female,
> And beneath his hand shall nothing flourish,
> Neither yellow wine nor waving cornfield :
> Let him rot together with his children ! " [4]

The call is answered on a wide scale and the Serbian people goes
to Kosovo, to be defeated and lose its independence. The heroes
go in the knowledge of what awaits them, but are not afraid of it.
Jugovíću Vojine represents a general view when he says :

> " I must go to battle at Kosovo,
> Shed my life-blood for the cross of glory,
> Perish for my faith with all my brothers." [5]

This is the authentic spirit of Jugoslav heroism, but it is not its
only form. The poems on the revolt against the Turks in 1804-13
are on the surface less noble in that they speak less of sacrifice
and are less conscious of defeat and death. But they are none
the less heroic. The patriots fight gaily and gallantly for their
country, and the poems reflect their confidence and pride. In this
struggle, as at Kosovo, no single figure has a dominating position,
but heroism is shared by different characters who harass Turkish
governors or tax-collectors or janissaries ; the great events like the
battle of Deligrad or the taking of Belgrade are the work of many
men working together for a common end. This revolt too fails,

---

[1] Legrand, p. 98 ff.   [2] *Idem*, p. 116.   [3] *Idem*, p. 124.
[4] Karadžić, ii, p. 271. Trs. W. A. Morison.   [5] *Idem*, p. 264.

but this adds to the nobility of the great effort which has been made for liberty. The poet records the end :

> Then the Turks the land once more did conquer,
> Evil deeds they did throughout the country ;
> They enslaved the slim Šumadian women
> And they slew the young men of Šumádija.
> Had but one been there to stand and witness,
> And to listen to the fearsome clamour,
> How the wolves were howling in the mountains,
> In the villages the Turks were singing ! [1]

The Jugoslav sense of heroism both glorifies any man who fights for his country and gives him a tragic dignity because in the end he fails.

Since the Jugoslavs have created this poetry of national heroism, it is paradoxical that their chief hero should be Marko Kraljević, who is not of this breed, and whose patriotism has an ambiguous quality. At least, he is in the Sultan's service. For this there may be a historical justification, since in fact many Jugoslav leaders found a living by giving their somewhat dubious loyalty to the Commander of the Faithful. The poets accept the fact and get over it as best they can by showing in what a jaunty, independent spirit Marko treats his master. He disobeys his orders about not drinking wine in Ramadan, cuts up janissaries, persuades the Serbs not to pay taxes, and bullies the Sultan himself. When Marko kills the Turk who has his father's sword, he stalks fiercely into the presence of the Sultan, who has summoned him, and says without fear :

> " Yes, if God himself had giv'n the sabre
> To the Sultan, I had slain the Sultan." [2]

Marko appealed to a people under the Turkish yoke. The Serbs had to find a way of life which did not detract too much from their own honour, and created in him a man who accepted the real situation and was yet able to maintain his style and freedom. His life is not that of the single-minded, uncompromising hero, but in the mixed world of Turkish Serbia he shows that love of country still means something to the servant of an alien despot.

The hero who champions a people's rights has taken a new form in modern times when the world " people " is used less of a race or a nation than of the nameless masses who are helpless to assert their rights without a leader. When such a leader appears, he may in favourable circumstances take on the attributes of a

[1] Karadžić, iv, p. 269. Trs. W. A. Morison.   [2] *Idem*, ii, p. 316.

hero. In northern Russia the Revolution of 1917 has inspired poems in which Lenin is a hero in this sense. In Marfa Kryukova's *Tale of Lenin* the hard sardonic realist who created the Soviet system has taken on many attributes of the traditional *bogatyr*. The tale begins with the arrest and execution of Lenin's brother for an attempt on the life of the Tsar Alexander III, and Lenin's mother calls on her children to fight for their brother and " for the truth, the people's truth ". Lenin promises to do so and explains that he feels in himself the confidence to succeed :

> " For I feel in me a great power :
> Were that ring in an oaken pillar,
> I'd wrench it out, myself with my comrades,
> With that faithful bodyguard of mine —
> I'd then turn about the whole damp mother earth !
> Well am I trained in wise learning,
> For I have read one magic little book,
> Now I know where to find the ring,
> Now I know how to turn about the whole earth,
> The whole earth, our whole dear Russia." [1]

Kryukova writes in the traditional style and transforms her modern themes into the accepted language of Russian poetry. So here she uses an ancient theme from folk-lore, the magic ring which gives wonderful powers, rather as the primitive giant Svyatogor boasts :

> " If I should take to walking on the earth,
> I would fasten a ring to heaven,
> I would bind an iron chain to the ring,
> I would drag the sky down to mother earth,
> I would turn the earth on its end,
> And I would confound earth with heaven ! " [2]

Lenin's ring is more up-to-date. For he has learned about it from a book, which is no other than Marx's *Das Kapital*. The modern hero uses his own kind of magic. The ring is the symbol of the strength which Lenin offers. So later in the poem, when he returns to Russia for the Revolution, the ring again is mentioned, and this time the people share his use of it :

> The whole people gathered and thronged,
> They all thronged and gathered,
> Up to that marvellous pillar.
> They gathered in a mighty force,
> They laid hold of the little ring, the magic one,
> Hard it was to wrench the little ring,
> With stout force they wrenched it,

[1] Kaun, p. 186.   [2] Chadwick, *R.H.P.* p. 51.

Turned about the land of our glorious mother Russia,
To another side, the just side,
And took away the keys of little Russia
From those landlords, from factory owners.[1]

So far Lenin, the hero, relies largely on magic and is entitled to do so because he has the knowledge and craftiness worthy of a hero.

Lenin is also a fighter. He has his own idea of the struggle which awaits him :

" It will not be the honour of a man of prowess,
Nor a knight's glorious fame ;
To kill a Tsar is a small gain,
You kill one Tsar, and another Tsar rises.
We must fight, we must fight in another way —
Against all princes, against all nobles,
Against the whole order up to now ! " [2]

So Lenin becomes the champion of the common people in a great fight. Like other heroes he gathers his company or *druzhina*, which consists of " factory workers " and " learned men " and is a " great people's force ". Even when the people entrusts him with the " golden keys of the whole land ", his efforts are not over. After the Revolution comes the Civil War, and the attempt on Lenin's life by " a fierce snake ". While Lenin is ill, his loyal comrade, Stalin, " rises in the stirrups " and addresses the soldiers :

" Hey you fellow-soldiers of the Red Army,
Hey you famous factory workers,
Hey you peasants, tillers of black soil,
A time has come, a most hard time,
A time has come, a most warlike time,
We must gather our last strength,
With our valorous valour we must crush our enemies,
Crush our enemies, scatter all doers of evil." [3]

Stalin's speech has the desired result. The Red soldiers hurl the invading generals into various seas, swamps, and rivers. The victory is won, and now Lenin dies. Physical nature weeps for him, and the earth is soaked in the tears of his mourners. The whole framework and style of the tale are traditional, but it suits the stirring events of modern history. Lenin appears as the champion of a people and acts as a champion should. His reward is the glory which he wins after death.

The career of a hero needs, at least for artistic completeness, some kind of realisation. The efforts and the preparations must

---

[1] Kaun, p. 188.   [2] *Idem*, p. 186.   [3] *Idem*, p. 189.

lead to an impressive end. Such an end is often a triumphant success which shows the hero's worth and wins him his due of glory. So the Kara-Kirghiz *Manas* ends with the capture of Peking, and the Kalmuck poems with feasts to celebrate victories; so the *Odyssey* ends with Odysseus being reunited to his wife, the *Cid* with the reinstatement of the hero in royal favour and the marriage of his daughters to kings. Other poets seem to feel that they must provide something more complete and final and that the only right close is the end of the hero's life. So the Armenian David is killed almost casually when drinking at a stream; so Beowulf exerts his strength for the last time in killing a dragon and is himself killed. In such cases the death comes appropriately without exciting any powerful emotions. In such a hero's life there are no paradoxes; he encounters difficulties and overcomes them until his span is finished. Such a view concentrates on the hero's powers and successes and raises no difficult questions about his calling or his position in the scheme of human action.

Not all heroes, however, are conceived in this way. Often enough their careers seem to lead inevitably to disaster and to find their culmination in it. When this happens, the story gains greatly in depth and strength, since the hero who comes to such an end seems in his last hours to be most truly himself and to make his greatest efforts. His life, instead of ending quietly, ends in a blaze of glory which illumines his whole achievement and character. If he dies after a heroic struggle, he shows that, when it comes to the final test, he is ready to sacrifice himself for his ideal of manhood. Such deaths are naturally more moving and more exalting than any quiet end, and it is not surprising that the poets make much of them. Moreover they raise questions about motives and standards of behaviour which increase the dramatic reality of the story, and give the poet considerable opportunities to present the kind of spiritual conflict which illustrates important issues in the heroic outlook. On such occasions it is difficult to escape from a sense of doom which will be fulfilled, whatever human beings do to prevent it; the hero, no less than other men, must meet his destined end. So the story passes from the record of bold achievements to something graver and grander and suggests dark considerations about the place of man in the world and the hopeless fight which he puts up against his doom. Such an outlook seems on the whole to exist mainly in aristocratic societies, perhaps because they are not quite easy about the heroic ideal and feel that, great though its rewards are, it demands a price which is no less great, and that in the last resort the hero fulfils his destiny by meeting his doom when circumstances arise which he challenges but is unable to defeat.

This sense of doom is effectively displayed in the theme of the disastrous choice, in which the hero is confronted by having to choose between two courses, each of which is in some way evil. He makes his decision, and whatever it is, it means disaster. The *Elder Edda* gives good examples of this. When Gunnar believes that his wife, Brynhild, has slept with Sigurth, he is torn between two fearful alternatives : either he can do nothing, and in that case he dishonours himself as a man and a husband, or he can kill Sigurth, and in that case he breaks his faith to a devoted friend. In the *Short Lay of Sigurth* the issue is perfectly clear. Brynhild demands the death of Sigurth and says that otherwise she will leave Gunnar. Gunnar consults Hogni and tells him how much he loves Brynhild :

> " More than all to me is Brynhild,
> Buthli's child, the best of women ;
> My very life would I sooner lose
> Than yield the love of yonder maid." [1]

Though Hogni advises him to do nothing, Gunnar decides that Sigurth must be killed and avoids the point of honour by getting his brother, Gotthorm, to do it. The means are certainly questionable, but Gunnar is in an impossible position. He believes, quite wrongly since Sigurth is innocent, that he must avenge his wife's honour if he is to keep her love, and in that case Sigurth must die. In this moment Gunnar is the victim of doom, and Brynhild, who is near to being a murderess, wins sympathy by her conception of her own honour and by her decision to kill herself once she has had her vengeance.

Guthrun is faced with a similar choice in *Atlamál* and *Atlakvitha*. Despite many differences the two poems tell what is in outline the same story. Guthrun is torn between two loyalties, one to her husband, Atli, and the other to her brothers, whom Atli kills. Since the Norse heroic world would recognise both loyalties, the poets know that Guthrun has to make a terrible choice. They tell that she decides to be loyal to her brothers and kill her husband, but they explain her decision differently. In *Atlakvitha* she kills Atli because he has violated his oath to his guests and so set himself beyond any obligation which she may feel to him. The point is not made very clearly, but Gunnar foretells it before his death,[2] and it can hardly be doubted. In *Atlamál* Guthrun is moved by the consideration that in the last

---

[1] *Sigurtharkvitha en Skamma*, 15.   [2] *Atlakvitha*, 32.

resort blood is thicker than any adopted tie and that she must avenge her dead brothers. The poet dwells on Guthrun's feelings and especially on her love for her brother Hogni. When she hears of his death, she tells Atli that she cannot forgive him :

> " Our childhood we had   in a single house,
> We played many a game,   in the grove we grew ;
> Then Grimhild gave us   gold and necklaces ;
> Thou shalt ne'er make amends   for my brother's murder,
> Nor ever shalt win me   to think it was well." [1]

Guthrun makes her choice, which may well be right according to her own code but is none the less ghastly.

Gunnar and Guthrun are moved largely by instinctive, unreasonable passion, he by love for Brynhild, she by feelings of kinship. But there is another kind of choice which is made with full knowledge and is none the less disastrous. The hero is faced with alternatives which he weighs carefully, and chooses the one which brings disaster. Many lands have a story of the father who fights with his son. This is in any case a painful theme, but it assumes a special grandeur in *Hildebrand*. Unfortunately the poem is incomplete, and we do not know what the end was, but what survives abounds in tragic possibilities. The old warrior, Hildebrand, has been an exile for thirty years when he meets in battle a young man who prepares to fight him in single combat. This, though Hildebrand does not know it, is his son Hadubrand. Before beginning to fight, Hildebrand asks Hadubrand who he is and finds out at once that it is his son. He begins to tell him the truth :

> " But High God knows   in heaven above,
> That thou never yet   with such near kin man,
> Hero brave,   hast held thy parley ! "

He then unwinds a gold ring from his arm and offers it to Hadubrand with the words " In love now I give it thee ". But Hadubrand refuses it, because he thinks that his adversary is lying and trying to trap him. Hildebrand is thus faced with a fearful choice. He must either refuse battle and incur the charge of cowardice or fight his own son. He decides on the second course, and his words show what his motives are :

> " Now my own sweet son   with sword must hew me,
> Fell me with falchion,   or fall at my hands !
> — Yet 'tis easily done,   if thou doughty be,
> From so old a man   his arms to take,
> To seize the spoil,   if such strength be thine.

[1] *Atlamál*, 68.

> Most infamous were he   of East Goth folk
> Who should keep thee from combat   so keenly desired,
> From fight with foe !   Let the fated one try
> Whether now his trappings   be taken from him
> Or both of these breast-plates   he boasts as his own." [1]

Hildebrand decides to fight because he is a warrior who believes that he cannot in honour refuse a challenge. We do not know how the poem told the end of the story. In later versions, like the fifteenth-century *Der vater mit dem sun* of Kasper von der Rön,[2] and a broadsheet of 1515,[3] the end comes happily with the mutual recognition of father and son. But it looks as if the Old German poem ended with Hadubrand's death, since it is couched in a grim and tragic tone, and such was the version known to Saxo Grammaticus.[4] But in either case, whatever the sequel is, the choice which Hildebrand has to face is indeed grave. Human affections pull him in one direction, but honour forces him in another.

A special form of the disastrous choice can be seen in the Jugoslav poem, *The Fall of the Serbian Kingdom*. The prophet Elias comes to Tsar Lazar with a message from the Mother of God which offers him a choice :

> " Tsar Lazar, thou prince of noble lineage,
> What wilt thou now choose to be thy kingdom ?
> Say, dost thou desire a heavenly kingdom,
> Or dost thou prefer an earthly kingdom ? " [5]

If Lazar takes the first alternative, he will be destroyed with his army; if the second, he will destroy the enemy. The choice is difficult, especially for a hero, since the introduction of a celestial reward puts his calculations out. The ordinary hero would undoubtedly accept the second alternative, but, since Lazar is the champion of the Christian Serbs against the infidel Turks, he must in the end choose the first. In his situation this is the heroic thing to do. It means his own death and the destruction of his kingdom, but as a man of honour he must do the utmost for his faith, and so he decides :

> " If I now should choose an earthly kingdom,
> Lo, an earthly kingdom is but fleeting,
> But God's kingdom shall endure for ever." [6]

Indeed in Lazar's choice we may with some reason detect a high heroic pride, even though it is placed in a Christian setting. If a

---

[1] *Hildebrand*, 53-62.   [2] Henrici, *Das deutsche Heldenbuch*, p. 301 ff.
[3] Von Liliencron, *Deutsches Leben im Volkslied um 1530*, p. 84 ff.
[4] Holder, p. 244.   [5] Karadžić, ii, p. 268.   [6] *Idem*, p. 269.

hero is offered a choice between victory and a magnificent disaster, it is almost necessary for him to choose the disaster, since it shows the degree of sacrifice which he is prepared to make. Lazar's desire for a heavenly kingdom is essentially not very different from the hope of Paradise which sustains Roland in his last fight at Roncesvalles. The heroic spirit is easily attached to great ideals of this kind but remains none the less heroic. The poet, of course, approves Lazar's decision and gives a benediction to it :

> All was done with honour, all was holy,
> God's will was fulfilled upon Kosovo.[1]

The identification of honour with God's will does not mean that Lazar's sense of honour is not of the noblest and highest kind. Though his position is unusual and outside the usual heroic way of life, it enables him to behave in a way worthy of his position and to fulfil his destiny with glory.

Different from the disastrous choice is the disastrous mistake. There are many forms of this, and in all a decision is made wrongly through some miscalculation or defect of character. The result is always some catastrophe which might otherwise have been averted. The usual cause of such decisions is the hero's pride which forbids him to take any course which he thinks dishonourable or below his dignity. His high spirit drives him on, and so, when disaster follows, it seems inevitable and almost appropriate. Such is the case in *Maldon*. The Vikings have landed their force on an island in the river. Here they can do little harm, since their only way out is across a causeway held by the English troops. When they try to force a passage across it, they are easily stopped. The right tactics would have been to keep the Vikings on the island until they were forced to take to their ships or were all killed in efforts to reach the mainland. But the heroic world does not act in this way. The Vikings ask to be allowed to cross over and fight on the mainland, and Byrhtnoth allows them to do so :

> " Now is space yielded.   Come with speed hither,
> Warriors to battle.   God alone wots
> Who will hold fast   in the field of battle." [2]

The result is that the English lose the advantage of their position, and are defeated and destroyed in the fight that follows on the open land. Byrhtnoth's motives are not unlike Hildebrand's. He feels that as a soldier he cannot refuse his opponent a chance to fight, and the existing position seems likely to end in a stalemate.

Karadžić, ii, p. 270.   [2] *Maldon*, 93-5.

But, unlike Hildebrand, he takes a wrong decision because he allows his sense of honour to override his real duty. But he would not be judged in this way. His end is glorious because he obeys the dictates of heroic honour and prefers death to an inglorious success.

A somewhat similar mistake is made by Roland in the beginning of the fight at Roncesvalles. As a loyal liegeman of Charlemagne he undertakes to command the rear-guard of the army, though he knows that treachery is afoot and that his task is exceedingly hazardous. So far he does what he must do, and no criticism is permissible. But in so far as his task is to guard the rear, he should take every thought to do it properly. When he takes up his position, Roland sees the advancing hosts of Saracens and knows that all his fears are confirmed. His comrade Oliver grasps the realities of the situation and three times calls on Roland to sound his horn ; for then Charlemagne will hear and come to their help. But Roland refuses, and his words show his character and motives :

> " Never, by God," then answers him Rollanz,
> " Shall it be said by any living man,
> That for pagans I took my horn in hand !
> Never by me shall he reproach my clan.
> When I am come into the battle grand,
> And blows lay on, by hundred, by thousand,
> Of Durendal bloodied you'll see the brand.
> Franks are good men ; like vassals brave they'll stand ;
> Nay, Spanish men from death have no warrant." [1]

Roland refuses because of his heroic pride. He is confident that his strength of arm will do all that is needed, and this confidence is an essential part of his character. Later, when he is wounded to the point of death, he admits his mistake and sounds his horn, but it is then too late to save himself or his companions. But though Roland dies because of this mistake, no one would wish it otherwise. The mistake is characteristic of him, and in making it he is essentially himself, while his death is all the more glorious because he has fought against tremendous odds.

Achilles is not a tragic hero in the same sense as Roland, but over him too hangs a like sense of doom. He is fated to die young and glorious and is fully conscious of his fate. He himself speaks of it more than once and it is foretold to him by his own horse and by the dying Hector.[2] What makes it more poignant is that in the short time before him he makes a great error in abstaining

---

[1] *Roland*, 1073-81.   [2] *Il.* xix, 409 ff. ; xxii, 358 ff.

from battle and in consequence loses his friend Patroclus. He makes this decision because he feels, rightly enough, that Agamemnon has insulted him by demanding from him a girl who is his legitimate booty. As a hero who lives for honour he cannot endure the affront, and his answer is to humble Agamemnon by refusing to help him in battle. But, though this abstention undeniably harms Agamemnon and humiliates the Achaeans to the point of begging Achilles to return to the fight, in the end it harms Achilles himself more. When, instead of fighting himself, he allows Patroclus to take the field, he sends him to his death, and his remorse and anger at this so dominate him that he rages with fury and treats his enemies with less than customary chivalry. The tragedy of Achilles is less in his misfortunes than in his soul. For this Homer creates an incomparable end when Achilles is touched by the entreaties of old Priam and gives back Hector's body. With this act of courtesy Achilles' wrath is healed, and he is himself again. None the less, though the *Iliad* ends in a harmony of reconciliation, the harm has been done. The great hero has passed through a dark chapter and behaved in a way unworthy of himself. With him, as with Roland, this is inevitable because his heroic nature makes him extremely sensitive about his honour, and the force which is so formidable on the battlefield turns all too easily into fierce wrath against his friends. But, even when he is most furious, he is still the great hero, who accomplishes wonderful feats of prowess and has no equal in the acts of war.

The wrathful temper which harms Achilles finds a striking parallel in the Norse *Lay of Hamther*. Guthrun sends her two sons, Hamther and Sorli, to avenge their sister, Svanhild, on Jormunrek, who has done her brutally to death. They set out on their task, and are joined by their bastard half-brother, Erp. He offers his help to them, no doubt because he too feels that he has obligations to Svanhild and that these men are his brothers. But they reject his offer with scorn, and Erp cannot but reply with anger and insult :

> Then Erp spake forth,   his words were few,
> As haughty he sat   on his horse's back :
> " To the timid 'tis ill   the way to tell ".
> A bastard they   the bold one called.[1]

A fight follows, and Erp is killed. The short, brutal episode shows on both sides how the heroic spirit works. Erp, wishing to show his worth, makes a generous offer, and when it is rejected, has to

[1] *Hamthismál*, 16.

fight for his honour; the brothers, in their proud notion of themselves, do not want his help and reject it in excess of self-confidence.
For this they pay. After they have wounded Jormunrek to death
and are ready to depart, the dying king calls his men to his rescue.
If Erp had been there to help them, the brothers would have
killed their attackers, but as it is they are defeated, and before
they die, see that their doom is the result of their fatal mistake
in killing him. Hamther accepts his fate, and though he admits
his mistake, he is not ashamed of it:

> " His head were off now   if Erp were living,
> The brother so keen   whom we killed on the road,
> The warrior noble, —   'twas the Norns that drove me
> The hero to slay   who in fight should be holy.
>
> " We have greatly fought,   o'er the Goths do we stand
> By our blades laid low,   like eagles on branches;
> Great our fame though we die   to-day or to-morrow;
> None outlives the night   when the Norns have spoken."
>
> Then Sorli beside   the gable sank,
> And Hamther fell   at the back of the house.[1]

The tragic mistake seems to be inevitable to the heroic temper and
provides some of its most poignant and most splendid moments.

The hero who finds troubles in himself, may find other troubles
in his circumstances, and resist them with the same energy which
he bestows on his human adversaries. In his desire to be himself
he may seek to war against the whole condition of life or against
the gods who impose it. Though few heroic poems make men
engage in unremitting warfare with the gods, such struggles take
place and have a peculiar quality. The heroes of the *Iliad* engage
gods and goddesses in fight in the plain of Troy, and though for
a short time they seem to get the better of the encounter, it is
clear before long that they are committed to an impossible task.
So though Diomedes does not shrink from defying Apollo when
the god protects Aeneas, he gives way when the divine voice tells
him to yield because there is no equality between the immortal
gods and men who walk the earth.[2] Even Achilles, who defies
the river-god Scamander and is ready to fight with him, is forced
to run away from him, " for the gods are stronger than men ".[3]
Odysseus owes many of his troubles to having angered Poseidon,
nearly meets his death when Poseidon wrecks his raft, and is safe
only when he reaches land. Homer's moderation forbade him
to allow his heroes to venture too much against the gods or to

---

[1] *Ibid.* 28 and 30-31.   [2] *Il.* v, 440 ff.   [3] *Ibid.* xxi, 264.

come too violently into conflict with them. Those in Greek legend who went further than this, like Tantalus, who sought to avoid death by deceit, or Ixion, who violated Hera, the wife of Zeus, provided examples of hideous sin and condign punishment. It was dangerous to set men too clearly against the gods, and Homer avoids it.

The issue is raised on a larger scale and in a bolder spirit in *Gilgamish*, which is nothing less than the story of a hero who tries to surmount his human limitations and fails. At the beginning of the poem Gilgamish is so sure of himself that he allows nothing to obstruct his will. No man and no woman is safe from his violence, and his ways are so outrageous that in response to prayers from the men of Erech, where Gilgamish rules, the gods decide to create another hero no less mighty who shall overcome him. So Enkidu, a strange creature of the wilds, is made from the desert clay. But Gilgamish frustrates the gods' plan by vanquishing Enkidu in fight and then forming a devoted friendship with him. The two heroes show their valour by destroying the ogre Humbaba, and this leads to a second struggle with the gods. The goddess Ishtar falls in love with Gilgamish and makes him an offer of marriage which he rejects with scorn. He reminds her of those lovers whom she has betrayed or maltreated and heaps abuse on her. She is so enraged that she asks her father, Anu, to make a heavenly bull to kill both Gilgamish and Enkidu. But this too fails. The bull is a terrible monster, but the heroes destroy it. After this the gods decide that Enkidu, though not Gilgamish, must die. So in his second round with the gods Gilgamish is still undefeated, but he has lost his friend, and his troubles now take a new turn.

After this deliverance Gilgamish continues his struggles with the conditions of human life, and the poem takes a noble grandeur as it shows how he fails. The death of Enkidu is a bitter blow to him, first because he has lost a devoted comrade whom he loved, then because it reveals the horror and the reality of death. He sees that he himself, with his enormous powers, must also die. The thought of death haunts him, and he struggles against it, hoping that he can somehow avoid it :

" Shall I, after roaming as a wanderer up and down the desert,
Lay my head in earth's bowels and sleep through the years for ever ?
Let my eyes see the sun and be sated with brightness ;
For darkness is far away if brightness be widespread.
When will the dead man look on the light of the sun ? "[1]

[1] *Gilgamish*, IX, ii, 10-14.

In this spirit Gilgamish devotes all his energy to seeking release from death and goes on a long and hazardous journey to the end of the world to find Uta-Napishtim, the Babylonian Noah, who alone among men is exempt from death and should be able to help him. This quest is the culmination of Gilgamish's life, his final heroic effort to break the bonds of mortality. He pursues it with unremitting courage, thinks nothing of the hardships which he has to undergo, and pays no attention to Siduri, the goddess of wine, when she propounds her gospel of pleasure and ease. He rejects her advice that he should be content with the ordinary happiness of men, and pushes on in his quest. He knows that it is impossible for a hero like himself to live a life of unadventurous pleasure.

In due course Gilgamish finds Uta-Napishtim and hears the story of the flood and why the gods have exempted Uta-Napishtim from death. The lesson is that Uta-Napishtim has been so rewarded because of his perfect obedience to the gods. As Gilgamish is unlikely to win immortality for such a reason, he tries, at Uta-Napishtim's suggestion, other ways of escaping death. First he must consult the gods how to do it, and Uta-Napishtim tells him that he must stay awake for six nights and six days. But this is too much for Gilgamish: he falls asleep and has to be woken and told that he has failed. It seems that his mighty physical frame is too insistent in its demands, and prevents him from finding the self-control and detachment which are necessary for converse with the gods. So on his homeward journey Gilgamish tries an alternative course and fetches from the bottom of the sea a plant which gives eternal youth, but, when he has got it, a serpent seizes it, and he loses this chance also. He comes home heavy with failure and calls up the ghost of Enkidu, only to hear of the dismal state of the dead. The poem ends with a conversation between him and the ghost:

" He who dies in war, hast thou seen him ? " " I have seen him !
His mother and father lift his head, his wife is bowed over him."
" He whose body lies in the desert, hast thou seen him ? " " I have
     seen him !
His spirit does not rest in the earth in peace."
" He whose ghost has none to tend him, hast thou seen him ? " " I
     have seen him.
He drinks the lees from cups and eats crumbs thrown in the street." [1]

So *Gilgamish* ends on a note of failure and emptiness. More consciously than any other heroic poem it stresses the limitations

[1] *Ibid.* XII, i, 149-54.

of the heroic state and its inability to win all that it desires, but at the same time it gives a peculiar grandeur to the hero who makes such efforts to realise his nature in all its potentialities. More even than Homer, the poet of *Gilgamish* sets his heroic achievements against a background of darkness and death which make them all the more splendid because they are done for their own sake without any hope or prospect of posthumous reward. Indeed Gilgamish would be much less impressive if he succeeded in finding immortality. His failure is a tribute to his unrelenting conflict against the rules which govern human existence.

The splendour which irradiates a hero in the hour of defeat or death is a special feature of heroic poetry. Though the heroes know the struggle to be hopeless, they continue to maintain it and give to it the fullest measure of their capacities. This is the glory of their setting, the light which shines with more than usual brightness on their last hours. And what is true of individuals may also be true of nations when they seem to lose their life in some overwhelming catastrophe. The Russian heroic age came to a terrible end when Kiev was destroyed by Mongol invaders in 1240. Such a catastrophe could not fail to leave traces of itself in song, and the mediaeval *Tale of the Ruin of the Russian Land*, composed not long after the event, is a lament which reveals the extent of the disaster. The story survived in popular memory and passed into the different versions of a heroic story on the fall of the Russian heroes. The versions vary much in detail, but in the main agree that at a certain time Vladimir is attacked by enemies and summons all his knights to fight them. At first the Russians are successful and destroy the invading army. Finding that their shoulders are not weary and their weapons not blunted, they boast, and the boast takes a fatal form. Some knight, Alyosha Popovich or another, utters the deadly words :

> " Though they set against us a supernatural army,
> An army which is not of this world,
> We shall utterly conquer such an army." [1]

God hears the boast, and two unknown warriors appear and challenge the chief Russian knights :

> " Grant a combat with us !
> We are two, you seven. No matter ! "

The Russians accept the challenge, but, as they cut the strangers in two, each half becomes a new, living warrior. The fight lasts all

[1] Sokolov, p. 99 ff. ; cf. Trautmann, i, p. 176 ff.

day and the enemies grow in number and courage. At last they
are overcome by panic :

> They fled to the stony hills,
> To the dark caves.
> When a prince flies to the mountain,
> There he is turned to stone ;
> When a second flies,
> There he is turned to stone ;
> When a third flies,
> There he is turned to stone.
> Since that time there are no more heroes
> in the Russian land.

In this tale the Russian heroic world perishes because it defies
God. In the end its heroic pride is too much for it. It pays the
last price and is no more.

Just as the power of Kiev fell before the Mongols, so the old
Serbian kingdom perished at Kosovo in 1389, when Tsar Lazar
and his allies were overwhelmed by the Turkish army of Sultan
Murad, who was himself killed. Round this catastrophic event
memories gathered and inspired a cycle of poems which told of
events before and after the battle, though with no great taste for
the subject of the battle itself. Unlike the Russians, the Serbs
have not turned this disaster into a myth or a fable, and, though
there is a supernatural element in the choice offered to Tsar
Lazar, the rest of the poems are realistic and factual. The events
which they describe might well have happened, even if they did
not actually happen in this way. The enemies who defeat the
Serbs are not supernatural beings but Turks who wish to conquer
Serbia. Nor is there any suggestion that the Serbs are punished
for pride. On the contrary their destruction is due to Tsar
Lazar's decision to prefer a supernatural to an earthly kingdom, and
by religious and moral standards that is beyond reproach. The
extent of the destruction is enormous, as the Maiden of Kosovo
hears :

> " Dost thou see, dear soul, those battle-lances,
> Where they lie most thickly piled together ?
> There has flowed the life-blood of the heroes ;
> To the stirrups of the faithful horses,
> To the stirrups and the girths it mounted,
> Mounted to the heroes' silken girdles." [1]

Nor is Kosovo a battle in which only eminent heroes take part ; it
is fought by the whole Serbian people and is their last heroic
ordeal.

[1] Karadžić, ii, p. 290. Trs. Helen Rootham.

The paradox of the disaster at Kosovo is that it is caused by treachery. The poems agree that the Turks defeated the Serbs because at a crucial moment of the battle Vuk Brancović led away his troops and turned the scale against his own side. This seems in fact not to have happened, but legend has canonised it. The issue is stated simply in *The Fall of the Serbian Empire* :

> Tsar Lazar and all his mighty warriors
> There had overwhelm'd the unbelievers,
> But — the curse of God be on the traitor,
> On Vuk Brancović — he left his kinsman,
> He deserted him upon Kosovo ;
> And the Turks o'erwhelmed Lazar the glorious,
> And the Tsar fell on the field of battle ;
> And with him did perish all his army,
> Seven and seventy thousand chosen warriors.[1]

Just as Ganelon betrays Roland to the disaster of Roncesvalles, so Vuk betrays Lazar to the disaster at Kosovo. But whereas Roncesvalles is soon avenged by Charlemagne, there is no one left to avenge Kosovo ; for the whole nation has perished at it. The two cases show the doom which the heroic world carries in its very being. The man who lives for his own honour feels all too easily any slights laid upon it and is jealous to the point of treachery of those who surpass him. Ganelon and Vuk are driven by injured pride to betray their comrades. In their own judgment there is nothing wrong in this, since pride provides their whole scale and scheme of values. They act much as Achilles does when he abstains from battle, but they carry out their purposes more relentlessly and do not repent in time. The heroic system breaks down through its own nature. Yet even so the disaster of Kosovo remains glorious in Serb memory because of the heroism which the nation as a whole showed at it.

A catastrophe of this kind, whether it happens to an individual or to a nation, provides a satisfying end to a heroic legend. It is somehow right that great warriors should die, as they have lived, in battle, and refuse to surrender to powers stronger than themselves. It means that they are ready to sacrifice their lives for an ideal of a heroic manhood which will never yield but will always do its utmost in prowess and endurance. There must always come a point when heroes encounter an enemy whom they cannot subdue and then, if they shirk the issue, they are unworthy of themselves. At last comes the obstacle which cannot be surmounted, the fight which is too much even for the greatest and

[1] Karadžić, ii, p. 271. Trs. Helen Rootham.

strongest hero. He may fall to foul play like Sigurth or to treachery and overwhelming force like Roland or to something almost accidental and trivial like Achilles to the arrow of Paris. When he so falls, his life is completed and rounded off, as it can hardly be if he lives to safe old age. The Greeks thought Achilles a greater hero than Odysseus, because he dies young in battle, while Odysseus, after all his adventures, will die among a contented people from a death " ever so gentle " which comes from the sea.[1] To his heroic career the final fitting touch is lacking. Of this fatality the greatest heroes are often conscious. They know that their lives may be short, but this is only a greater incentive to fill them with action and glory. When Gripir tells Sigurth his future, Sigurth is not downcast but says simply :

" Now fare thee well ! Our fates we shun not ",[2]

and accepts almost gladly what lies before him. Achilles too knows that his life is short and that he will be killed in battle, and, though for a passing moment this makes him hate the thought of battle and wish to go home, it soon makes him an even greater hero than before and stirs him to speak the terrible words with which he refuses mercy to Lycaon :

" See what a man I am also, both strong and comely to look on,
Great was the father who bred me, a goddess the mother who bore me ;
Yet over me stand death and overmastering fortune.
To me a dawn shall come, or a noontide hour, or an evening,
When some man shall deprive me of life in the heat of the battle,
Casting at me with a spear or an arrow shot from a bow-string." [3]

In his consciousness that his life is short Achilles becomes more active and more heroic. In this he is typical of all doomed heroes whose short careers reflect in their crowded eventfulness the bursting ardours of the heroic soul.

[1] *Od.* xi, 134 ff. [2] *Grípisspá*, 52, 1. [3] *Il.* xxi, 108-13.

IV

THE REALISTIC BACKGROUND

In assuming that what they tell is in the main true, heroic poets treat it with realism and objectivity. However strange some of their episodes may be, the narrative is made, so far as possible, to conform to life as they see it. They employ many themes which give a greater solidity and verisimilitude to their tales. Since heroes move in what is assumed to be a real world, their background and their circumstances must be depicted, and, when their quests carry them into unusual places, these must be made real to audiences who know nothing of them and wish to hear what they are like. At the same time heroic poetry does not indulge in description for its own sake. Since its main concern is with heroes and their doings, it would fail in its duty if it were to spend too much time on mere decoration. It does not provide such scenes of imaginary beauty as we find in romance or " literary " epic. The heroic poet keeps his eye on his characters and their doings and does not waste energy on irrelevant detail, but detail which is to the point he likes and provides in abundance. It is indeed necessary to his purpose. It may at one time reflect his hero's character, at another show in what circumstances he carries out his designs. In general it brings the story closer to life and makes it more substantial. Of course the descriptions may add to the charm of the poetry, and the poet is often conscious of this and takes advantage of it. But it is not his primary purpose. Since a hero lives and moves, it is necessary to tell how he lives and in what places he moves, and by this means heroic poetry secures much of its fullness and independence.

Description of natural scenery is rare in heroic poetry, nor is it difficult to see why. This is an art which flourishes in societies which do not live in towns and know the country so well that they take it for granted and feel no call to make much of it. They lack not only the modern city-dweller's desire for it as a place of escape but the whole romantic conception of it as a home of secrets and mysteries. For them indeed towns hardly exist, and, when they exist, are certainly more wonderful than any wonders of nature, since they are the exception and the country is the rule. This does not mean that nature is nothing to heroic poets or that they are not interested in the background against which their characters play their parts. They are interested in nature at least as a background, and if hardly any show such a loving observation of it as Homer does in his similes, most of them, sooner or later, pay some attention to it, and, when they do, not only open new prospects to the eye but add to the solidity of their imagined worlds.

In general it may be said that heroic poets describe natural scenes when they are to fulfil some special function in the story. The nature of such functions varies and may be anything from a need to create a convincing setting for an event to a desire to stress some contrast or unusual situation. At one extreme are those poets who describe the scene in which an action takes place because it is unfamiliar to their audiences and must be presented clearly to them if the story is to make its proper effect. Such effects are to be found in the poetry of the Kalmucks, who lived till very recently on the western shore of the Caspian after their great migration in the seventeenth century, but whose heroic legends are derived from their original home in central Asia on the northern borders of Tibet. The poets take some care to describe the homeland of the great Dzhangar, if only because it is very unlike their present country and has for them an almost sacred character as the cradle of their race and religion and the setting of their heroic past. That is no doubt why the *Song of the Wars of Dzhangar with the Black Prince* begins with an elaborate account of the region in the Altai where Dzhangar rules, and especially of the inland sea of Shartak:

> Up and down move the waters of the broad sea of Shartak.
> Its waters weave ice into silver.
> It has corals and pearls on its surface.
> It flowers with every kind of water-lily.
> Whosoever drinks from the waters of that sea,
> He is free from death for ever,
> Or is born again for ever
> In the land of the three and thirty Holy Ones
> In the very hour when it is fated for him to die.
> From that sea come eight thousand rivers.
> They flow and ripple at every door
> Of forty million subjects, with sandy streams,
> From endless time never freezing
> In all four seasons of the year.[1]

This is a land of wonder as it is remembered after two centuries of exile, but it is none the less suitable to the heroic figures who

[1] *Dzhangariada*, p. 95.

live near it. They are so far above ordinary men that their dwellings must be close to the gods.

Something of the same kind may be seen in the Yakuts. They once lived in the region of Lake Baikal but were pushed northwards by the Buryats and now inhabit the tundra and forests of northern Siberia round the river Lena. Like the Kalmucks, they brought with them tales which preserve memories of a landscape unlike that which is now theirs. That is why they take pains to describe the setting in which events take place. So the poem *Er Sogotokh* begins with an account of where the hero lives :

> On our blessed earth,
> With a border of mountains about it,
> — They will not be removed —
> With strong upright mountains about it,
> — They will not be shaken —
> With mountains of stone about it,
> — They will not quiver —
> Where is the top of the earth,
> With water in the midst,
> Covered with turf,
> Lived a certain rich man.[1]

This is unlike anything in the poet's own country and must be made real to his audience. It has the mysterious appeal of the remote and unfamiliar, and even if it reflects the landscape of the Baikal region, it has been glorified by years of separation. In *The Deathless Knight* the scene is set with like detail but in a different landscape. This time the poet is concerned with a vast open space, and he describes it carefully, because it too is unlike his familiar tundra :

> In the glistening middle of the earth,
> On a dazzling white open plain,
> — Though it race for the whole day long
> The stork does not fly over it —
> Amidst the white spaces of a white open plain
> — The crane cannot fly around it —
> There settled and lives, they say,
> In rich state, with many possessions,
> Bai Kharakhkhan-Toion.[2]

This setting too must be made vivid if the hero, who lives in it, is to be understood by the audience. Part of his situation is that he lives in this remote world; it explains why such strange things happen to him. The Yakut poets draw on tradition to create

[1] Yastremski, p. 13. [2] *Idem*, p. 100.

unusual landscapes, but their art is none the less disciplined by a factual realism which makes their descriptions significant.

Once or twice Homer has to tell of remote regions which no man in his audience could have seen. Odysseus' wanderings take him to many strange places, and the legends about them may well have travelled far both in space and in time. For instance, he sails to Circe's home, which tradition connected with the remote east. Her island, Aeaea, may indeed be a reflection of some place in the Black Sea, visited by early explorers, who left traces of their discoveries in stories of the Argonauts. Homer knows that Aeaea is far away, since he says that there the Dawn has her halls and dancing-places and the Sun his risings.[1] But when he comes to describe it, he makes it like any attractive Greek island. At first sight it looks uninhabited, and wild stags rove on it, but soon Odysseus sees smoke rising and descries the palace of Circe,[2] made of polished stones in an open ground.[3] What might have been a pure fairy-tale becomes circumstantial and convincing. Again, it is possible that in his account of the Laestrygonians with their rocky coast, their monstrous giantess, and their long northern day, Homer repeats far-travelled legends of Scandinavia, which may have come to the Aegean by the same route as the amber-traders from the Baltic. He sees that this is a wild, forbidding place and deftly sketches it in four lines, telling how the harbour has a narrow entrance enclosed by steep rocks, with jutting headlands facing each other at the entrance.[4] The description would apply to many Norwegian fjords and is poetically appropriate for the hard people of the Laestrygonians.

With Circe and the Laestrygonians Homer merely gives a short sketch of the physical surroundings, but once at least circumstances compel him to attempt more and to show what he can do with natural beauty. When Odysseus is wrecked on Calypso's island far away to the west, it is important to the story that he is a castaway in a place where no human beings and hardly even any gods ever go. It is also important that Calypso, who loves him and wishes to keep him with her for ever, should have a home worthy of her divine nature and rich in attractions to seduce the hero into staying with her instead of returning home. The beauty of her dwelling can hardly be that of the familiar world; it must be remote and wild and outside human society. So Homer makes her live in a cave which has its own charms and graces. When Hermes is sent by the gods to tell her to release

---

[1] *Od.* xii, 3-4.   [2] *Ibid.* x, 149-50.
[3] *Ibid.* 210-11.   [4] *Ibid.* v, 63-73.

Odysseus, he is greeted by a sight to gladden the eyes.[1] Calypso sits in her dwelling plying her golden shuttle, while outside is a scene of great beauty and brilliance. Round about is a wood of alder, poplar, and cypress, in which many land-birds and sea-birds nest, while on the cave clusters a vine. Four streams are there, and meadows of violet and parsley. No wonder that even an immortal, on seeing it, would be delighted in his heart. Homer means us to enjoy the scene, since it plays an important part in his story. It is from this beauty and from the loving company of Calypso that Odysseus must tear himself away, if he is to go home, and even then he will find that many troubles await him. In his heroic life he must reject this ease and beauty and face stern tasks and hard conditions.

Description of this kind can hardly be expected in the many passages of heroic poetry which treat of war. Yet the setting of a battle may well be important to it, and there are times when the poets feel that they must complete the picture by some hint of a natural background. Nature lays down rules for the seasons of warfare, which the heroes must observe. It is true that in much heroic poetry scant attention is paid to the time of year, perhaps because in many countries warfare is confined to the summer and the audiences do not need to be told so. Sometimes, however, the poet sees that physical conditions are relevant to his tale and makes something of them. For instance, Jugoslav poets have a good eye for the time of year. When Harambaša Ćurta goes out to harass the Turks, it is still winter, when even haiduks are expected to be resting in peace. So the poet stresses the loneliness of the countryside :

> Ćurta hastened to the Travnik highway
> Through the virgin snow, on painful pathways
> And untrodden tracks, where no man wanders
> Save the haiduk, when in search of booty
> He by stealth descends upon the highways,
> And except the dusky-coated wolf-pack
> That in secret creeps about the cow-byres,
> Passes from one sheepfold to another,
> Watching sharply for the meat it feeds on.[2]

This is a winter scene, described in some detail, because it is unusual. Conversely, when the spring comes, it is time for action, and the first leaves and flowers are a challenge to brave exploits. Like their Serb opponents, the Turks too turn to action :

> When at last dawned bright St. George's feast-day,
> And the mountain-sides with leaves were covered,

[1] *Od.* x, 87 ff.   [2] Morison, p. 22.

And the black earth gay with grass and blossoms,
And the lambkins sported in the meadows,
And the horses in the plain were hobbled,
And the wooded hills were decked with mallows,
Then the vizier indited letters.[1]

The poet suggests how the revival of life in spring makes men also active. If the Turks are getting busy, the Serbs too must be up and doing.

Homer hardly connects the Trojan War with nature in this way, but he is not indifferent to its natural background. He marks the mountains which are visible from the plain of Troy, and once or twice mentions local features which have their own interest, like the two streams, one cold and one hot, which are the source of the river Scamander.[2] Past these streams Achilles pursues Hector in the last fight, and Homer pauses to tell of them, turning for a moment our attention from the fierce struggle to the natural scene. Perhaps this place was connected by legend with the fight of Achilles and Hector, but in the poem it has its own function of reminding us that even a struggle like this takes place among natural surroundings. Homer, however, displays a more remarkable art earlier in Achilles' career of vengeful fury. When he fights the river-god Scamander, Hephaestus, the fire-god, comes to the river's help and burns the countryside and makes the water boil :

Burned were the poplar-trees and the myrtle-bushes and rushes,
Burned also were the grass and the meadowsweet and the parsley,
Which grew abundantly by the beautiful streams of the river ;
Troubled too were the eels and the fishes that swam in the eddies
Leaping this way and that in the beautiful streams of the river,
Troubled sore by the breath of the cunning fire-god Hephaestus.[3]

Such trees and plants as the fire consumes may still be seen on the plain of Troy by the banks of the Simois and the Scamander. Homer is convincingly realistic in this scene of which he cannot have seen the like, showing what things happen when a hero fights with a god.

A hint of natural scenery may stress the atmosphere of some grave occasion. So in the Norse *Atlakvitha*, when Gunnar and his companions ride on their doomed expedition to Atli, there is something appropriate about the places through which they pass on their horses :

Then let the bold heroes   their bit-champing horses
On the mountains gallop,   and through Myrkwood the secret.[4]

---

[1] Karadžić, iv, p. 185. Trs. Morison.   [2] *Il.* xxii, 147-52.
[3] *Ibid.* xxi, 350-55.   [4] *Atlakvitha*, 13, 1-2.

The background of mountain and dark forest is merely hinted at, but is enough to call up the wild scenes through which Gunnar and his companions make their long journey. Another small and striking touch can be seen in the *Short Lay of Sigurth*, where Brynhild, who is married to Gunnar but secretly in love with Sigurth, cannot display her feelings and goes out alone with them at night :

> Oft did she go   with grieving heart
> On the glacier's ice   at even-tide,
> When Guthrun then   to her bed was gone,
> And the bedclothes Sigurth   about her laid.[1]

The introduction of the glacier shows Brynhild's need to be alone with forbidding powers of nature when her rival and the man whom they both love are in bed. There is a parallel between her outward state and the chill hopelessness of her situation. So an even smaller touch adds magic to the moment when the smith, Völund, is discovered in his hiding-place by Nithuth's men :

> By night went his men,   their mail-coats were studded,
> Their shields in the waning   moonlight shone.[2]

The moonlight not only explains why Völund is out — he hunts at night — but gives an eerie atmosphere to the sinister plot against him.

These touches are strictly subordinated to the story and important mainly for it, but there are times when poets make use of a situation to indulge a taste for a little description for its own sake. This is not very common, but when it comes, it adds an unexpected touch of colour to the story. For instance, in the Kara-Kirghiz *Manas*, when Alaman Bet quarrels with Chubak, the weather suddenly turns foul, and, though the poet makes use of this to show how Manas separates the heroes in the middle of a hideous storm, the storm itself receives a full amount of attention as something impressive and interesting in itself :

> Suddenly the storm grew wild ;
> Everything around was darkened,
> Black clouds came over the sky,
> Thunder roared in the mountains,
> Suddenly rain poured from the sky —
> Such rain no man had ever seen !
> Piercing snowflakes fell in swarms
> And blinded the eyes.
> To their knees it swept the horses.
> People could not open their eyes —
> It burned their eyes with piercing snow.

---

[1] *Sigurtharkvitha en Skamma*, 8.   [2] *Völundarkvitha*, 9, 3-4.

138

> People could not open their lips —
> It froze their tongues with frost.
> From the north it blew with a storm,
> From the south it soaked them with rain,
> From the east a hurricane blew on them,
> From the west a water-spout fell on them.[1]

This is something of a show-piece, neatly introduced at an important stage in the action, but more than the actual story really needs. In contrast to its fierce temper we may set another piece, which the poet obviously enjoys, from the Ainu *Kutune Shirka*. When the hero, in search of a mysterious golden otter, comes to the sea, which he has never seen before, he pauses to say something about it :

> And coming from the sea
> A pleasant breeze blew on me and the face of the sea
> Was wrinkled like a reed-mat.
> And on it the sea-birds
> Tucking their heads under their tails,
> Bobbing up their heads from under their tails
> Called to one another
> With sweet voices across the sea.[2]

That, after, all is what a young man might see in the sea on looking at it for the first time, but it is none the less a charming piece of poetry for its own sake. In both these passages the poets go rather beyond the usual limits which heroic poetry allows to descriptions of nature, but they are careful to fit their observations into the story.

The art of adapting the background to the tone and temper of events can be seen in *Roland*, when the poet prepares the setting for the grim fight in the pass at Roncesvalles. He sketches, very briefly, the scene :

> High are the peaks, the valleys shadowful,
> Swarthy the rocks, the narrows wonderful.[3]

It is only a hint, but it does something important. The whole scene rises before our eyes and remains with us through the long account of the fight. It is appropriate that such a struggle should take place in these wild surroundings. It is moreover a preparation for a bolder and grander effect which comes later when the poet makes nature take part in the catastrophe of Roland and his peers. When the Franks meet the Saracens in the pass, an unearthly tempest and darkness possess the earth :

---

[1] *Manas*, p. 150.
[2] Trs. Arthur Waley, *Botteghe Oscure*, vii (1951), p. 219.
[3] *Roland*, 814-15.

Torment arose, right marvellous, in France,
Tempest there was, of wind and thunder black,
With rain and hail, so much could not be spanned ;
Fell thunderbolts often on every hand,
And verily the earth quaked in answer back
From Saint Michael of Peril unto Sanz,
From Besunçun to the harbour of Guitsand ;
No house stood there but straight its walls must crack ;
In full midday the darkness was so grand,
Save the sky split, no light was in the land.[1]

Almost certainly the poet has in mind the darkness which covered
the earth at the Crucifixion. His battle is itself a tremendous
Christian sacrifice, in which Roland and his companions lay down
their lives for their faith. So perhaps the audience would see it
and would for that reason accept the miracle. It marks the true
meaning of the battle, and, though its events are beyond experience, they are described with a factual realism which makes them
convincing. The extent and the horror of the great darkness are
seen with a clear, firm vision.

The poet of *Roland* combines this idea with another. The
vast storm has a meaning which men do not see :

Beheld these things with terror every man,
And many said : " We in the Judgement stand ;
The end of time is presently at hand ".
They spake no truth ; they did not understand ;
'Twas the great day of mourning for Rollant.[2]

When nature mourns for Roland in this awful, tragic way, the
poet allows himself something beyond the usual scope of heroic
poetry. Yet what he says is understandable enough. When a
hero dies, the world is so much the poorer that even inanimate
nature may be imagined as feeling his loss. A similar idea,
conceived in a gentler and quieter spirit, may be seen in some
Bulgarian poems. They use the theme less for death than for
parting, but their touch is sure and successful. When Liben
leaves the forest, he says good-bye to it, and the forest, which
speaks to nobody else, speaks to him. It reminds him of what he
has done in it and continues :

" Hitherto, my warrior Liben,
The old mountain was your mother,
And your lover the green forest
In its dress of tufted leafage,
Freshened by the gentle breezes ;

[1] *Roland*, 1423-32.   [2] *Ibid.* 1433-7.

140

> Grasses made your bed for sleeping,
> Leaves of trees provided cover,
> Limpid streamlets gave you water,
> In the woods birds carolled for you,
> For you, Liben, was their message :
> ' Make glad with the heroes, Liben,
> For the forest makes glad with you,
> And for you makes glad the mountain,
> And for you make glad fresh waters.' " [1]

This has no such heights and depths as the mourning of nature in
Roland but it is more lyrical.   A simpler, if similar note is struck
in another poem where the hero plots a dangerous enterprise :

> The green forest was lamenting,
> Both the forest and the mountain,
> And the leaves within the forest,
> And the birds among the woodlands,
> And the grasses in the meadows,
> For the gallant hero Pantcho. [2]

Such pieces portray the intimacy with nature which the hero has
enjoyed, and comes quite easily in its context.   The literary fancy,
which has been unfairly denigrated as the " pathetic fallacy ",
has here a real truth to experience.   When the poet makes the
forest speak or weep, he portrays in a vivid way what are really
the hero's own thoughts, his feelings about leaving a place where
he has long found a happy life.

This sense of animate nature is characteristic of Slavonic
poetry.   In some Russian poems it takes a special form when
nature weeps for some great man's death.   This may be quite
simple as in a poem on the death of Ivan the Terrible :

> Now, our father, bright moon !
> Why do you not shine as of old,
> Not as of old, not as in the past ?
> Why do you not rise from behind the cloud,
> But hide yourself in a black mist ? [3]

The greater the dead man, the greater the distress, and it is
right that in her *Tale of Lenin* Marfa Kryukova should put on a
full-dress performance.   After comparing Lenin's death to the
setting sun, the moon, and a star, she advances from symbol
to description and makes creatures of nature share the distress of
men :

> Birds flew up then like falcons high to the skies,
> Fishes then sank to the depth of the seas,

[1] Dozon, p. 38.   [2] *Ibid.* p. 46.
[3] Kireevski, vi, p. 206 ; Chadwick, *R.H.P.* p. 206.

141

Martens scampered over the islands,
Friendly bears scattered through the dark woods,
And people put on black clothes,
Black clothes they put on, sorrowful clothes.[1]

Lenin's death is seen as a cosmic event which disturbs the course of nature. In this case nature is not so much lamenting for him as distressed and frightened. The hero is set on a vast stage in which men and animals have come equally under his spell and responded to his efforts to master and change the world. Behind Kryukova's bold vision is the traditional idea that a hero is so closely bound to his surroundings that they are inevitably affected by any change in their relations with him.

This general assumption takes a special form in a number of Greek poems, in which nature is so closely connected with the lives of the klephts and their struggles with the Turks that she cannot but show human emotions when anything happens to her friends. It is above all the mountains who play such a part. A hero climbs them by moonlight and hears them speaking to the winds and saying that it is not the snows and hailstones which trouble them but the Turk, Deli Achmet, who treads upon them.[2] Another two mountains talk about the klephts going down to the plains, and one asks the plain to look after them; otherwise it will melt its snows onto the plain and turn it into a sea.[3] When the klephts are attacked by the Turks, Mount Maina is wet with weeping.[4] When the snows begin to cover the mountains, the klepht must go to the plains and risk capture and death, but when spring comes the mountains are the home of freedom and hope, and Olympus and Kissabos are justified in debating which does more for him:

Olympus — see! — and Kissabos, two mountains in a quarrel:
Which shall pour down the heavy rain, which shall pour down the
    snowstorm.
'Twas Kissabos that sent the rain, Olympus sent the snowstorm.
Olympus turned his mighty head, to Kissabos thus spake he:
" Nay, scold me not, Sir Kissabos, by feet of Turks betrampled,
For I am Olympus full of years, in all the world renownèd,
And forty-two my summits are, and sixty-two my fountains;
And on each peak a banner free, 'neath every branch an outlaw ".[5]

In this way the Greek poets make nature the background for the seasonal warfare of the klephts.

In marked contrast to their treatment of nature is the way

---

[1] Kaun, p. 191. [2] Garnett, p. 310. [3] *Idem*, p. 311.
[4] *Idem*, p. 321. [5] Politis, 23. Trs. W. J. Entwistle.

in which heroic poets treat the work of men's hands, especially their dwellings. Dwellings are important because they reflect a man's style and character. They are visible emblems of his worth and pride and ambition, and, more subtly, they reflect the undercurrents of his being. It is right and proper that, when the poet of *Beowulf* presents his picture of a wise and good king in Hrothgar, he should make him build a great hall to be a sign of his royal dignity and a proper place for his hospitable entertainment of guests. The hall is an achievement of stylish craftsmanship :

> Broad of gable,   and bright with gold :
> That was the fairest,   mid folk of earth,
> Of houses 'neath heaven,   where Hrothgar lived,
> And the gleam of it lightened   o'er lands afar.[1]

It is this hall which is to be defiled by the man-eating raids of Grendel, and there is a tragic and ironical contrast between its builder's intentions and its actual fate. As a sinister counterpart to it we may set the halls of Atli, king of the Huns, as the Norse poet sketches them. They are the true home of a man of blood, a warrior who plots a hideous end for his guests :

> Then they saw Atli's halls,   and his watch-towers high,
> On the walls so lofty   stood the warriors of Buthli ;
> The hall of the southrons   with seats was surrounded,
> With targets bound   and shields full bright.[2]

The Norse poets can seldom spare time to describe a hero's dwelling, and in this case the poet probably does so because it adds to the impression of embattled power which he wishes Atli to make.

The Asiatic poets also describe dwellings, though they are usually different from the European kind. The great Manas has an appropriate home in a fortress, guarded, like Atli's, by armed warriors :

> His fortress, full of people,
> Seethes like a large kettle ;
> In that fortress Manas has
> Abundance of every possession ;
> That fortress is more solid than a hill.
> In its windows of pewter
> Are twelve unsleeping guards,
> Each one in rank a warrior.
> Each of the guards holds
> A knife of chased steel.[3]

[1] *Beowulf*, 308-11.   [2] *Atlakvitha*, 14.   [3] *Manas*, p. 34.

Here the emphasis is on the impregnability of Manas' dwelling. The Kalmuck poets aim at a different effect. The great hero, Dzhangar, lives not in a fortress but in a tent, as befits his nomadic nation:

> Beautiful arise the motley yellow domes.
> They are adorned with diamonds of four colours.
> On each summit are stablished
> His invincible sceptres.
> He raises it up in the centre of all earth's kingdoms.
> They have built each fold of it outwards,
> They have built it over the abyss.
> At a height of two hundred yards
> Above the clouds of the sky
> Stands the motley yellow chamber.[1]

The Kalmuck poet sees the home of Dzhangar through a pardonable mist of home-sickness. This is what a people who have moved to the Caspian believe their old home in the Altai to be. It is a glorification of the nomad's tent, and remains, despite all its size and decorations, simple enough. Tents can present other charms than these. In Arabia they are the normal type of lodging, and the poet of *The Stealing of the Mare* is ready with a surprise for the hero, Abu Zeyd, when he comes in disguise to the dwelling of his enemy. The Arabian poet has a more observant eye than the Kalmuck, and his description has its own delightful realism:

> And I cast my eyes around, and lo, like the stars for number,
> Stood the tents in their ranks, as it were the Pleiades in heaven,
> Each a cluster of stars ; and among them a pavilion
> Set for a leader of men ; and mares were tethered round it,
> And dromedaries trained as it were for a distant riding ;
> And hard beside a tent of silk, a fair refreshment
> To the eyes as rain on the hills, the blest abode of women.
> And next in a lofty place, set on a windy platform,
> As it were a fortress in size, the booth of the great council,
> Wonderful in its spread, its length full sixty paces.
> And tears came to my eyes, for none in the world was like it.[2]

In this the imagination is tempered by a solid sense of fact. This is the kind of encampment which every Arabian would wish to be his own.

The Russian poets lack this refinement of observation, but their descriptions of dwellings have a native charm and truth. Sometimes they are unexpectedly modest. When Sadko finds the Tsar of the Sea, the royal dwelling is only an *izba* or hut ; [3] it is

[1] *Dzhangariada*, p. 96. [2] Blunt, ii, p. 144.
[3] Kireevski, v, p. 43.

true that it is a very special hut, " built all of w
none the less the kind of hut in which a Russian pe
Rather more bourgeois in its solidity and comfort is
which Dyuk Stepanovich boasts to Prince Vladimir, co
more than favourably with the standard of homes at Kiev

> The floors are of white hazel-wood,
> The balustrades are made of silver,
> Crimson carpets are spread.[1]

This is wealth as a Russian peasant sees it from outside.   More
adventurous is the house of the rake, Churilo Plenkovich, which
fills Prince Vladimir with awe and envy and suits the extravagant
character of its owner :

> The floor was of pure silver,
> The stoves were all of glazed tiles,
> The pillars were covered with silver,
> Churilo's ceiling was covered with black sable,
> On his walls were printed curtains,
> In the curtains were sash windows,
> The hall was a copy of the sky.
> The full moon of heaven rode aloft.[2]

The poet makes skilful use of an unexpected piece of information,
and models Churilo's home on the apartment of the daughters of
Tsar Alexis in the Kremlin, where the wall was painted with
frescoes and the part round the windows represented a blue sky
with white clouds.[3]   This is the height of splendour and well
suited to Churilo's smart and extravagant tastes.

The Yakuts resemble the Russians in the limited range of their
experience and in their sense of the close relation between a man's
house and his character, but they spend more time in describing
dwellings, partly because their stories are set in remote regions
on which any information is interesting.   In *The Deathless Knight*
the home of Bai-Kharakhkhan, his wife, and eighteen children, is
presented at some length for audiences who are presumably
interested in the building of houses in a densely forested country
and know something about it.   First the setting is described ;
then the solidity of the structure :

> Like an ox lying down after drinking water,
> The main door has a hanging
> Of the skins of eight fine bears ;
> Seven men could not open it.

[1] Rybnikov, i, p. 101.   [2] *Idem*, ii, p. 528.
[3] Cf. Chadwick, *R.H.P.* p. 96, with reference to Rambaud, " Les Tsarines
de Moscou ", *Revue des Deux Mondes* (1873), p. 516.

> The walls are such that a strong horse
> Charging against them would lose its breath ;
> They are made from strong larch-trees.
> There are small windows
> In nine places on every wall,
> A door with such fastenings
> That eight men cannot open it ;
> With such bolts of larch-wood,
> That ten men cannot move it.[1]

This building may be made of simple materials in a simple way, but it is in its own way a fortress, impressive to an uneducated audience and worthy of the strange character who lives in it.

Though dwellings are usually described because they are essential to the story, there is no reason why poets should not appreciate their charm and give to them an attractive poetry. The Ainu poet of *Kutune Shirka* does this with some success for the home of his hero. The hero has lived indoors all his life until he receives supernatural promptings to go abroad and catch a mysterious golden otter. The first sight that greets him is that of his own home, which moves him to great delight :

> Then I went out at the door,
> And saw what in all my life
> Never once yet I had seen —
> What it was like outside my home,
> Outside the house where I was reared.
> So this was our Castle !
> Never could I have guessed
> How beautiful it was.
> The fencing done long ago
> Standing so crooked ;
> The new fencing
> So high and straight.
> The old fencing like a black cloud,
> The new fencing like a white cloud.
> They stretched around the castle
> Like a great mass of cloud —
> So pleasant, so lovely !
> The crossbars laid on top
> Zigzagged as the fence ran.
> The stakes below
> Were swallowed deep in the earth.
> In the tie-holes below
> Rats had made their nest.
> In the tie-holes above
> Little birds had made their nest.
> Here and there, with spaces between,

[1] Yastremski, p. 100.

The holes were patches of black.
And when the wind blew into them
There was a lovely music
Like the voices of small birds.
Across the hillside, across the shore
Many zigzag paths
Elbowed their way.
The marks of digging-sticks far off
Showed faintly black ;
The marks of sickles far off
Showed faintly white.
The ways went pleasantly ;
They were beautiful, they were lovely.[1]

The poet is evidently determined to describe the best kind of Ainu dwelling and does so by the ingenious ruse that his hero has never seen his own home from the outside before. He relies entirely on truth and observation for his success, and such is his feeling for dwellings of this kind that he can easily dispense with fancy or exaggeration. He feels the poetical appeal of such a scene, and has a painter's eye for its lines and perspectives. If the Yakut poet likes strength and solidity, the Ainu likes grace and elegance.

Such descriptions are usually based on a firm foundation of familiar fact. The audience must first feel familiar with the imagined scene, and only when that is assured is the poet free to add his touches of fancy. Homer makes his heroes live in real palaces. Of course their style has a Mediterranean grandeur such as is not to be found in Asia, and his taste and experience are much closer to our own. He does not often indulge in description, but when he does, he has an eye for visible splendour. When Telemachus arrives at Sparta and sees the palace of Menelaus, he is amazed at its brilliance, for on the high-roofed house there is a glitter as of the sun or the moon.[2] It is only a slight touch, but it is appropriate to the palace of a great prince who has amassed great wealth on his long wanderings. The theme, merely suggested here, is developed at length for the palace of Alcinous in Phaeacia. This too has a glitter as of the sun or moon, and understandably, since the walls are of bronze, the doors of gold, the door-posts and lintels of silver, while dogs of gold and silver guard the entries.[3] Into this imaginary palace Homer has perhaps put remote legends and memories of Minoan or Mycenean times when gold was plentiful and kings lived in great palaces like those of Cnossus and

---

[1] Trs. Arthur Waley, *Botteghe Oscure*, vii (1951), pp. 218-19.
[2] *Od.* iv, 45-6. [3] *Ibid.* vii, 84-94.

Mycenae. Though none of his audience would have seen such a palace, except in ruins, it would be accepted as right and proper for Alcinous, who reigns in a fabulous island far from other men and enjoys peculiar wealth and glory.

Unlike palaces, gardens play little part in heroic poetry, partly perhaps because the heroic world hardly knows what they are, partly because the taste for them is rather too luxurious for the heroic temper. Their real home is in a world of courtship and courtesy and ease. It is true that *Roland* allows something of the kind to the Saracens, but it denies them to Charlemagne in his palace at Aix, while the stark world of *Beowulf* and the *Elder Edda* is remarkable more for rude rocks and rough seas than for bowers and fountains. None the less gardens sometimes appear and help to complete the picture of the splendour in which a great man lives. They are not, as in romance, settings for love and sentiment, but an adjunct of power and wealth. Homer once gives his powers to such a domain, when he describes at considerable length the garden and orchard of Alcinous. Outside the palace is the great orchard, surrounded by a wall, where fruit-trees, pear, pomegranate, apple, fig, and olive, flourish all the year round, so that there is never any lack of either fruit or blossom. Here some grapes are dried and trodden, while others are still ripening on the trees. Here too are flower-beds, and two springs, one of which flows through the garden, and the other under the threshold of the court to the house, where men draw water from it.[1] This miraculous garden is both beautiful and functional, and it is characteristic of Alcinous that his *douceur de vivre* should be founded on so unusual and so admirable a system of supply. Homer describes it so factually and with so obvious a belief in its reality that we take his word for it and enjoy it as something entirely possible in the magical world of Phaeacia.

A similar theme is used with quite a different intention in a modern Greek poem on Digenis Akritas. In *The Dying Digenis* the poet begins by showing the hero in all his power and splendour, the great man who builds a castle and a garden worthy of his noble name and superior nature :

Akritas built a citadel, Akritas built a garden,
Upon a plain, a grassy place, a site for them well suited.
All the plants growing in the world he brought to it and planted ;
All the vines growing in the world he brought to it and planted ;
All waters flowing in the world he brought and made them channels,
All the birds singing in the world he brought and made nests for them.
Unceasingly they sang, and sang : " May Akritas live for ever ! "[2]

[1] *Od.* vii, 112-32.   [2] Legrand, p. 195.

148

This is how a hero likes to display his greatness. He assumes that he has the power and the right to express himself on this royal scale and to sack the world for delights to please his eye and ear. So far he resembles Alcinous, but the more modern Greek poet is not like Homer. He will not leave it at that. Digenis' pride, it seems, is not justified after all, and the great display is only a preliminary to his death. One Sunday morning the birds change their tune and sing " Akritas will die ". In defiance of this he goes out to shoot them and to kill what animals he can. He finds none and meets instead Charon, with whom he struggles and is defeated. He accepts his defeat and prepares for death :

> " Come here, my lady beautiful, and make my death-bed ready ;
> Put flowers on for coverlet, with musc perfume the pillows ;
> Then go, my lady beautiful, to hear what say the neighbours."

The great hero must die like any other man, and in the end his proud magnificence is no more than the signal for his final defeat.

Closer even than his dwelling to a hero are his weapons. Since through them he wins the renown which he seeks, they must be worthy of him. So heroic poetry loves to dwell on some weapon or piece of armour with meticulous, professional care. That is why the forging of weapons is a grave affair. Sometimes the means used are natural enough, as when Gilgamish and Enkidu prepare for their expedition against the ogre Humbaba, and give orders which are carried out :

> The workmen prepared the mould, and cast monstrous axes ;
> They cast celts, each of three talents' weight ;
> They cast monstrous knives, with hilts each of two talents' weight,
> And blades, of thirty manas each, to fit them ;
> The gold inlay of each sword was thirty manas.
> Gilgamish and Enkidu were laden each with ten talents.[1]

That is professional and factual. The heroes carry weapons of prodigious weight, which only shows how splendid they are. But not all weapons are so innocent as these. Often enough magic or poison is used to make them more deadly. So the sword, Hrunting, with which Beowulf hopes to kill Grendel's Dam, has had a special treatment as well as considerable use :

> Iron was its edge, all etched with poison,
> With battle-blood hardened, nor blenched it at fight
> In hero's hand who held it ever.[2]

So too the sword which the Valkyrie gives to Helgi Hundingsbane is engraved with snakes to indicate its power to destroy, and has

---

[1] *Gilgamish*, III, iii, 30-35.   [2] *Beowulf*, 1459-61.

miraculous powers which may be expected to bring victory to its
possessor :

> In the hilt is fame,   in the haft is courage,
> In the point is fear,   for its owner's foes ;
> On the blade there lies   a blood-flecked snake,
> And a serpent's tail   round the flat is twisted.[1]

Heroic weapons are not forged without much time and trouble.
The resources of earth are ransacked to give them a final strength,
and magical powers are called in to help. So the forging of
Manas' sword is a lengthy and exacting business :

> They cut down a multitude of woods
> To smelt the sword in the furnace !
> They slaughtered a multitude of oxen
> And brought their skins for the sword,
> To smelt a terrible sword !
> Often the smith prayed,
> Karataz pleaded with passion,
> Saying " Help me, God ! "
> For the tempering of that sword.
> So hot was the steel,
> They emptied cold streams.
> Many a stream was dried up !
> They were unable to finish it,
> They dared not, they were exhausted,
> The forty skilled masters
> From the distant land of Egypt.
> The most renowned smith
> In winter and summer hammered
> Manas' sword for fights to come. . . .
> In hideous days of strain and slaughter
> They beat out for him that sword ;
> In mirages of the blue sky
> A fortune-teller tempered the sword,
> Spirits put charms upon the sword,
> In snake's poison was dipped the sword.[2]

The hero, who is unlike other men, must have a sword unlike
other swords, and his strength and skill, which seem to be almost
supernatural, must be exercised on a weapon fashioned by more
than human art. Such swords help to complete their masters'
personalities and have an interest of their own for audiences who
know the good points of a weapon and what it means to its
possessor.

In such a world the smith who makes weapons has a peculiar
renown and is often thought to be a god or a demi-god. In Germanic legend the great smith is Völund, or, as the English called

---

[1] *Helgakvitha Hjorvarthssonar*, 9.   [2] *Manas*, p. 326 ; cf. Radlov, v, p. 43.

him, Weyland Smith. Though his life is regarded by the poet of
Deor as a classic case of suffering, he surpasses all other smiths in
skill. No doubt that is why he is put in chains and made to work
by Nithuth, from whom in due time he exacts a hideous revenge.
It is he who makes Beowulf's corslet [1] and Waldhere's sword,[2]
and is known to the author of *Waltharius* for his *Wielandia
fabrica*.[3] In the Norse *Lay of Völund* he speaks with pride of his
own handicraft :

> " At Nithuth's girdle   gleams the sword
> That I sharpened keen   with cunningest craft,
> And hardened the steel   with highest skill ;
> The bright blade far   forever is borne,
> Nor back shall I see it   borne to the smithy." [4]

Völund is so fine a smith that he is thought to be a magician, and
his final revenge on Nithuth shows his talents. In him perhaps
the Norse imagination has glorified the Finnish magicians known
to legend, since he is connected with Finland and his place in
the Norse world is somewhat ambiguous. He stands outside the
common rut as a great smith should. From a magician to a god
is but a small step, and it is natural that poets should make some
of the greatest smiths divine. The Ossete Kurdalagon lives in the
sky but helps men with superhuman feats on his forge. The most
famous divine smith is Hephaestus, and it is right that, when
Achilles' armour has been stripped from Patroclus' body by
Hector, new armour should be made for Achilles by Hephaestus.
Thetis comes to him and asks him to make the armour, and he
agrees in a few courteous words. Then, like a real smith, he sets
to work, and Homer describes the scene with a firm, realistic eye.
Of course this forge is more powerful than any forge used by men,
but it works on the same principles and shows that its smith is a
supreme master of his craft. He sets twenty bellows in action,
and throws bronze, tin, silver, and gold into the fire. Then he
sets his anvil on its block, and takes in one hand his hammer and
in the other his bellows.[5] Hephaestus works in ideal conditions
beyond human reach. Even his bellows obey his orders as if they
were his servants. But his manner of work is that of all smiths,
and the weapons which he makes are to be used in human warfare.

In contrast to the way in which Achilles has his armour made
for him by a divine smith, we may set another hero who has to seek
out a smith for himself and then prove his worth in choosing from
the weapons which are offered to him. When the Esthonian

---

[1] *Beowulf*, 455.   [2] *Waldhere*, 2.   [3] *Waltharius*, 964.
[4] *Völundarkvitha*, 19.   [5] *Il.* xviii, 468-77.

Kalevide visits a Finnish smith, whom he finds with some trouble, he is first presented with an armful of swords, from which he picks the longest. He bends it into a hoop, but it straightens itself out. He then strikes it on a massive rock, and the blade is shivered to pieces. He asks scornfully :

> " Who has mixed up children's playthings
> With arms meant for grown-up warriors ? "

More swords are brought in, and the Kalevide chooses one which he brings down on the anvil. The sword cuts deep into it, but the sharp edge is blunted. The smith then says that he has one sword worthy of the hero's strength if he is rich enough to buy it, and states a fabulous price, including horses, milch kine, oxen, calves, wheat, barley, rye, dollars, bracelets, gold coins, silver brooches, the third of a kingdom, and the dowries of three maidens. Then a sword is fetched from a cupboard. The smith and his sons have worked at it for seven years and made it from seven kinds of iron with seven charms and tempered it in seven different waters from those of the sea and Lake Peipus to rain-water. The Kalevide receives it with reverence, whirls it like a fiery wheel, till it whistles through the air like a tempest that breaks oaks and unroofs houses. Then he brings down the edge like a flash of lightning on the anvil and cleaves it to the ground without in any way hurting the sword. The Kalevide thanks the smith and promises to pay his price.[1] Such a sword has more than a touch of magic in it, and it is significant that this smith also is a Finn. But the Kalevide gets the sword because of his heroic strength and superb swordsmanship. A lesser man would never had been able to test weapons as he does.

The weapons made in these unusual conditions develop their own personalities and often have their own names. If the Greeks do not give names to their weapons, the Germanic peoples, the French, and the Tatars do. Sigurth's sword is called Gram. It was made for him by Regin and was said to be so sharp that when he thrust it into the Rhine and let a strand of wool drift against it with the stream, it cleft the strand as if it were water. With this sword Sigurth cleaves Regin's anvil and kills the dragon Fafnir. Waldhere's sword, Mimming, is one of Weyland's masterpieces, and that is why in the fight with Gutthere Hildegyth encourages Waldhere with a reminder that he has an incomparable weapon :

> " Indeed Weyland's   work not faileth
> Any among men   who the Mimming can,
> The hoary one handle.   Oft in the host hath fallen
> Blood-sweating and sword-wounded   swain after other." [2]

[1] Kirby, i, p. 42 ff.   [2] *Waldhere*, 2-5.

Another famous sword is Hrunting, which Unferth lends to Beowulf for his attack on Grendel's Dam :

> never in battle had it failed
> Any man   whose arm had clasped it,
> Who the way of terror   dared to tread,
> The field of foemen ;   'twas not the first time
> That an excellent work   it was to accomplish.[1]

Actually Hrunting fails Beowulf in his encounter with the Dam, but perhaps that is not its fault, since the conditions of fight are highly unusual and the foe is no human opponent.   In *Roland* is a sword no less renowned than these.   Roland's Durendal is also reputed to be the work of Weland and is the gift of Charlemagne.   It has accompanied Roland on his great exploits and, before he dies, he addresses it with affectionate remembrance of what it has done and of all the places in which they have tasted victory together.[2]

Something of the same kind may be seen among some Asiatic peoples.   The Kalmuck poet gives the measurements and materials of Dzhangar's great spear :

> The guardian of his life, his spear,
> With its shaft of sandalwood,
> Is made of six thousand stocks of that wood.
> Its striking point is made
> From three hundred and fifty clamped roes' horns,
> But on it is woven a cover
> Wound of six thousand sheep tendons.
> The point of the spear is of diamond.
> It has sixteen blades,
> Crushing with terror every living thing.[3]

Everything in the heroic world of the Kalmucks is on a large scale, and this spear conforms to accepted standards, but despite its size it is built on a real model and shows that the poet knows about weapons.   With this spear we may compare the gun of the Kara-Kirghiz Manas.   It may sound more modern, and perhaps it is, but to the poet it is hardly less wonderful.   It deals death in a way worthy of its master, and his affection for it is shown by its having a name " Ak-kelte " :

> His right eye shoots flames —
> Bullets pour out from Ak-kelte,
> A hot coal flies from his left eye —
> Bullets pour out from Ak-kelte !

[1] *Beowulf*, 1460-64.   [2] *Roland*, 2316-37.
[3] *Dzhangariada*, p. 98.

153

Indifferent is Ak-kelte,
Be the enemy far or near,
It throws the enemy in the dust !
A heart of steel has Ak-kelte !
Its muzzle brings death.
Thicker than fog smoke comes from it.
Its aim is a marvel, its bullets death ! [1]

The hero's weapon is both an instrument and an emblem of his terrible power. It rounds off his nature and helps him to fulfil his potentialities.

If a hero pursues his projects on the sea, he needs a ship, and though ships are not very common in heroic poetry, they are to be found in it and provide interesting cases of realistic description. Of course a hero knows both how to make a ship and how to sail it : that is part of his general competence and mastery of affairs. He is both craftsman and mariner and does by his own knowledge and wits what sorcerers like Väinämöinen do by spells. If need arises, he can build a boat to compete with the best. He may even have to build something out of the ordinary, and then he has a chance to display his accomplishment. This is true of Odysseus. On the remote island of Ogygia, whose only other inhabitant is a goddess, he hears that he may at last go home, and for this he has to build himself some kind of craft. There is no one to help him, and all that he has is an abundance of well-seasoned wood which will float easily. Calypso vaguely tells him to build a raft, and we might expect that he would make something very simple and primitive, but in fact Odysseus is too good a sailor and too cunning a workman to be content with that. What he builds is in fact a seaworthy boat which can be controlled by one man. He first cuts twenty planks and shapes and smoothes them. Then he sets to work as boat-builders still do in Greece. With gimlet and hammer he fastens together a hull, to which he adds decks fore and aft in the usual Homeric manner. Then he fits it with ribs and planks, sets in it a mast with a yard-arm, and adds a rudder. [2] So far the craft is the usual Homeric ship, though doubtless built on a small scale, since it has only to take a crew of one. On the whole this is the kind of ship depicted on Geometric vases of the eighth century B.C., though there is no evidence that it has anything like the ram with which, for purposes of war, they were fitted. Nor is it clear that Odysseus' mast resembles other Homeric masts in being fitted with a box which enables it to be taken down when sails are useless and oars must be taken up

---

[1] *Manas*, p. 327.　　　　[2] *Od.* v, 246-57.

instead. Odysseus intends to sail and has no oars. In another point Odysseus goes his own way. He puts a fence round the boat to prevent it being swamped, and this device is still used in Greece. Leake saw a gunwale enveloped with withies " to protect it from the waves or from the danger of a sudden heel ".[1] Odysseus knows his job and does it skilfully. It is not his fault if he is wrecked; that is the doing of Poseidon, god of the sea.

A second early craft is the remarkable ark described in *Gilgamish*, which Uta-Napishtim builds at the command of the gods. Though this Babylonian Noah is not a hero in the same sense as Gilgamish, he is an important person who takes part in great events. The gods warn him that a deluge is coming and give him orders :

> " Pull down a dwelling and fashion a vessel ;
> Abandon possessions and seek life ;
> Disregard thy hoard and save life.
> Embark every creature on thy vessel.
> The vessel which thou art to fashion,
> Let its measure be apt, and its length to match,
> Launch it on the deep." [2]

Uta-Napishtim did what he was told, and later, with a craftsman's pride, tells Gilgamish how he built the vessel :

> " On the fifth day I laid out the shape ;
> Her sides were a hundred and twenty cubits high,
> And her deck a hundred and twenty cubits long.
> I laid down the shape of her fore-part and fashioned it.
> Six times I cross-pinned her,
> Sevenfold I divided her deck,
> Ninefold I divided her inwards.
> I hammered the caulking within her,
> I found a measuring pole.
> All that was needful I added,
> I smeared the hull with six *shar* of bitumen
> And I smeared the inside with three *shar* of pitch." [3]

The result is that the ark survives the deluge, and Uta-Napishtim and his family are the only human beings who do not perish. It is clear that the poet of *Gilgamish* takes as professional an interest as Homer in ship-building. Both poets see that on occasions like these the great man must be able to beat craftsmen at their own craft.

The hero both makes his boat and sails it. The poet of *Beowulf* appreciates the point and makes his hero first build his

---

[1] *Travels in the Morea*, i, p. 499, quoted by H. Michell in *Classical Review*, lxii (1938), p. 44.
[2] *Gilgamish*, xi, i, 24-30.   [3] *Ibid*. 56-66.

ship and then put it to sea. Beowulf sets about it methodically.
He chooses his companions and his expert pilot, and between them
the ship is built and launched :

> He had, good man,   from the Geatish people
> Champions chosen,   of those that keenest
> Might be found :   with fourteen else
> The sound-wood he sought ;   a sailor shewed them,
> A lake-crafty man,   the land-marks.
> On time went ;   on the waves was their ship,
> A boat under bergs.   The boys all ready
> Stepped on the stem ;   the stream was washing
> The sound on the sand ;   those seamen bare
> Into the breast of the bark   bright adornments,
> Wondrous war-armour ;   well out they shoved her,
> (Wights willing to journey)   with wooden beams bounden.
> Went then over the waves,   as the wind drave her,
> The foamy necked floater,   to a fowl best likened.[1]

At first sight perhaps the mannerisms of Anglo-Saxon poetry may
conceal the essential realism and truthfulness of this description,
but it is soon clear that Beowulf knows his job and attacks it with
confidence and competence. The same of course is true of Odysseus. When he leaves Calypso's island on his new craft, he sets
out on unknown seas and has to find his own course without charts
or information of any kind. He proceeds in a quiet, purposeful
way. He spreads his sails and catches the wind, which carries him
along, while he sits and steers. He guides himself mainly by the
stars, watching the Pleiades and Boötes and being careful to observe
Calypso's instruction to keep the Bear on his left. So for seven
days and nights he sails.[2] Homer presents the action simply, but
it is clear that Odysseus' seamanship has no flaws. A third member
in the trio of heroes who both build boats and manage them is
Gilgamish. When he comes to the Waters of Death, he meets
Ur-Shanabi, the boatman of Uta-Napishtim, who tells him to
build a boat, and Gilgamish sets about at once to do so :

> He took the axe in his hand,
> And drew the glaive from his belt,
> Went to the forest and fashioned poles of five *gar*,
> He made knops of bitumen and added sockets. . . .
> Gilgamish and Ur-Shanabi fared forth in the vessel,
> They launched the boat on the waves,
> And themselves embarked on her.[3]

As they draw near to the other side, the navigation becomes
difficult, and the poet realistically describes how Ur-Shanabi makes
Gilgamish take soundings with his pole until they make a safe

[1] *Beowulf*, 205-18.   [2] *Od.* v, 269-78.   [3] *Gilgamish*, x, iii, 44-8.

landing. Heroes are good sailors because it is part of their job to know how to build and manage boats, and when the poets tell of this, they make the details convincing, so that those in the audience who know the sea will be suitably interested.

More important than a hero's boat, and perhaps more important even than his armour, is his horse. No animal invites so technical or so discriminating a knowledge or excites stronger affection and admiration. Heroic poets know about horses and study them with professional appreciation. In heroic societies the horse has more than one function. It is in the first place an article of wealth. A man is known by the quantity and quality of his horses and is naturally proud of them. If raiding is still an honourable pursuit, horses are among the first objects of loot. In the second place, the horse is invaluable in war — the hero's most trusted friend, which may often save him in dangerous situations and provide inestimable service in overcoming his enemies. When war gives place to games or other tests of prowess, horse-racing is one of the most favoured ways for heroes to compete against each other. In the third place, a knowledge of horses is one of the most prized branches of knowledge. The man who really knows about them is respected as few other men are, and, conversely, ignorance of them invites contempt. These elements are constant in heroic poetry, since they represent a natural attitude, and, though there are interesting variations on them, they exist in most countries and follow similar lines.

By universal consent one of the most important things about a horse is its pedigree, and, just as heroes are superior to other men through their lineage, so their horses are superior to other horses by their birth and resemble their masters in a divine origin or at least in having been trained by gods, like the horses of Eumelus at Troy, which are second only to those of Achilles, swift as birds and alike in their coats, age, and height, and worthy of the nurture which Apollo gave them in Perea.[1] Sigurth's horse, Grani, was given to him when he was a boy by Othin and was sprung from Othin's own horse, Sleipnir.[2] Other horses have origins even more remarkable, like the horse of Manas, which is called Ak-kula and reveals its unusual birth in its behaviour :

> If night without moon is on the earth,
> If earth is lost in mist and gloom,
> The horse's ears shine upon it,
> As if lights were kindled in them !
> A whirlwind made its mother pregnant.[3]

[1] *Il.* ii, 763-7.   [2] *Völsungasaga*, 13.   [3] *Manas*, p. 326.

Ak-kula is of the same breed as Achilles' horses, Xanthus and Balios, " Brown " and " Dapple ", who fly with the winds and are the children of the Harpy Podarge — " the Swift-footed " — born by her to the West Wind when she fed in a meadow by the streams of Ocean.[1] Since horses travel as fast as the wind, it is right to assume that they are sometimes its children. The delightful Armenian horse, Dzhalali, has an even more mysterious origin. When Sanasar dives into the sea and finds a splendid dwelling :

> He sees ; a horse is tethered,
> A horse with a saddle of mother-of-pearl.[2]

The Mother of God appears to him and tells him that the horse is his. In such mysteries are the origins of great horses hidden.

The poetry of horses must be both convincing and charming, if it is to do justice to them and their owners and show what great men these are. But within these limits it can vary from expert observation to rapturous fancy. Sometimes it is enough to describe a real horse as it appears to those who know about horses. So a Jugoslav poet describes the horse of the Turk, Birčanin Ílija, with an eye to its speed and beauty :

> 'Twas an Arab steed of fiery temper,
> White as is the snow upon the mountains ;
> Had it no caparison or harness
> From the snow it ne'er could be distinguished ;
> If it did not stamp its feet, or whinny
> In its equine converse with the dapple,
> Didst thou not perceive the glaring eyeball
> That was from its noble head protruding —
> With a single blow it might be severed
> And the sabre would not touch the forehead ! —
> Easily 'twould pass thee by unnoticed.[3]

If we wish to see a real battle-horse in the grand manner, it is the charger which Archbishop Turpin took from an enemy slain in Denmark and rides into battle against the Saracens. The poet tells of it with care for its bone and breeding :

> That charger is swift, and of noble race ;
> Fine are his hoofs, his legs are smooth and straight,
> Short are his thighs, broad crupper he displays,
> Long are his ribs, aloft his spine is raised,
> White is his tail, and yellow is his mane,
> Little his ears, and tawny all his face ;
> No beast is there can match him in the race.[4]

---

[1] *Il.* xvi, 149-51.
[3] Morison, p. 25.
[2] *David Sasunskii*, p. 43.
[4] *Roland*, 1651-8.

This is the right horse for a warrior in full armour. It lives up to its form and is the Archbishop's valiant ally in his last desperate battle.

Horses are not always portrayed realistically like this. Oriental poets sometimes glorify the points of a horse with metaphor and hyperbole. So *The Stealing of the Mare*, which is concerned with a creature of surpassing beauty and rarity, gives proper emphasis to it :

> Spare is her head and lean, her ears set close together ;
> Her forelock is a net, her forehead a lamp lighted,
> Illumining the tribe, her neck curved like a palm branch,
> Her wither clean and sharp. Upon her chest and throttle
> An amulet hangs of gold. Her forelegs are twin lances,
> Her hoofs fly forward faster ever than flies the whirlwind.
> Her tail bone held aloft, yet the hairs sweep the gravel ;
> Her height twice eight, sixteen, taller than all the horses.[1]

There is poetic licence in this, but it hardly extends beyond some apt images, and in the main the poet knows his subject and bases himself on fact. From this kind of eulogy it is but a small step to something that sounds more unusual. The Kalmuck poet, who glorifies Dzhangar, glorifies his horse with him and takes us into what looks like a world of wonder. This is a Mongolian horse, detailed with an abundance of Asiatic rhetoric :

> Its neck, like a swan's, is nine spans long,
> Its blowing mane is not to be caught . . .
> Its ears are like the lips of a water-lily,
> Its eyes are bright as a hawk's,
> Its teeth are white as clenched claws,
> Its tusks are like piercing gimlets ;
> Its croup is like that of a black bear,
> Its curly brown-silver tail is eighty-one spans long,
> Its step is light, its four black hoofs are like swords,
> It will go without rest, it will not pause,
> It will go through the world and not be overtaken.[2]

There is exaggeration in this, but not so much as there might seem at first sight. The points made are real enough, but they are made in the language of imaginative eulogy and suit the superhuman order to which Dzhangar and everything that concerns him belong.

Since his horse means so much to him, a hero forms a special intimacy with it. The Homeric heroes take their horses into their confidence and appeal to them for generous help and utmost effort. So Hector reminds his horses, Chestnut, Brightfoot, and Gleamer, what good treatment they have received from himself and Andro-

[1] Blunt, ii, p. 147.   [2] *Dzhangariada*, p. 98.

mache, how they have had abundance of barley and even of wine given to them, and asks them now to repay this kindness.[1] In his household, horses receive special attention and are treated almost as members of the family. He is on intimate terms with them and speaks to them as old retainers. In the same way, but with no appeal to benefits received, Achilles calls to his horses to go out with him and rescue the body of Patroclus,[2] and in the horse-race at the funeral-games Antilochus urges his horses to defeat those of Menelaus and threatens them that, if they lose, they will not only get no food from Nestor but may even be killed.[3] In this there is an element of playful humour, suitable to the spirit in which the games are conducted, but it is none the less intimate. The Homeric heroes treat their horses as tried companions and expect the most from them.

Something of the same kind may be seen at a more primitive level in the Uzbek poems. When the hero, Alpamys, being only fourteen years old, chooses a horse, he knows what he is doing and picks one called Baichibar, who serves him all through his career. When he is selected and mounted by the young hero, the horse is assailed by powerful emotions :

> Baichibar, like a dromedary, felt his knees sink,
> From his eyes poured tears mixed with blood,
> He pricked up his ears and three times made a mighty bound,
> But Alpamys did not let him go.
> He at once made him feel his immeasurable strength.
> Baichibar now spoke a word to himself,
> That on him there sits a man
> Whom he cannot throw over his tail to his feet.
> " It means that he is my master ",
> Thought Baichibar and became quiet.[4]

Once the horse accepts its master as worthy of it, it becomes his best and most faithful friend. The show of resistance at the start shows that it too has a heroic nature and is not prepared to give its devotion to any but the best commander. The Uzbek heroes also treat their horses with a Homeric intimacy and remind them of what they have done for them. Even if Khushkelli speaks with oriental flamboyance and rotundity, his sentiments are not ultimately very different from Hector's :

> " I have given you human milk that you may be sharp-sighted
>   as a man,
> I have given you mare's milk that you may outstrip all in my
>   people,

---

[1] *Il.* viii, 184-90.
[2] *Ibid.* xix, 400.
[3] *Ibid.* xxiii, 403-5.
[4] Zhirmunskii-Zarifov, p. 356.

I have given you cow's milk that your mouth may be like a calf's,
I have given you mule's milk that your spirit may be strong,
I have given you jennet's milk that you may know the way like
    a jennet,
I have given you sheep's milk that you may be gentle as a sheep,
I have given you goat's milk that you may always·leap like a goat,
I have given you camel's milk that you may carry loads patiently
    like a camel,
I have given you dog's milk that you may go forward like a dog,
I have given you snake's milk, that you may crawl forward like
    a snake,
I have given you chamois' milk that you may climb slopes like
    a chamois,
I have given you deer's milk that you may be keen of sight as
    a deer,
I have given you bear's milk that you may be brave as a bear." [1]

This by no means exhausts the catalogue. The poet has of course
an ulterior purpose in using this elaborate device. It may serve a
use in the narrative, but it also helps to enumerate all the qualities
which a warrior would like to have in his horse. None the less it
shows, in however exaggerated a manner, what the warrior is
prepared to do for his horse to make it surpass all other horses in
his heroic world.

One of the most remarkable relations between a hero and his
horse is that between Marko Kraljević and Šarac. Šarac plays a
large part in the varied adventures of his master and is inseparable
from him. There is nothing that Marko will not do for his horse.
He gives it wine to drink, embraces and kisses it, promises it
horseshoes of gold and silver, and conversely threatens it with
hideous punishments. The result is that there is little that Šarac
cannot do. In pursuit of a *Vila* or mountain-spirit it leaps the
length of three spears into the air. It treads down its master's
enemies in battle, and, while Marko engages a Moor in fight, goes
for the Moor's horse, puts its teeth into it, and tears off its right
ear. When Marko and Šarac both grow old, they go out together
and, when Šarac stumbles and sheds tears, Marko knows that no
good awaits them. So he addresses Šarac in affectionate words :

" What ails, Šarac ? My good horse, what ails thee ?
We have shared a hundred years and sixty,
Never yet till now has thy foot failed thee,
But to-day thou stumblest as thou goest,
And, God knows, no good thing this forebodeth.
Of us twain, the one will lose his head, sure,
Be it my head or be it thine haply." [2]

[1] *Idem*, p. 359.   [2] Karadžić, ii, p. 405.

Knowing that his own end is near, Marko kills and buries Šarac, that he may not fall into the hands of the Turks and " carry their copper water-pots ". A hero like Marko is more intimately affectionate with his horse than with any human companion.

Naturally enough, in such conditions horses develop their characters, which, so far as loyalty and courage are concerned, are often the equal of their masters'. So Sigurth's horse, Grani, resembles him in its unflinching loyalty and taste for great adventures. It will do for him what it will not do for another. So when Gunnar mounts it and tries to pass through the flames to Brynhild, Grani refuses to move, but, when Sigurth mounts it, it goes at once. When he is killed, Grani is the first to lament him, as Hogni notices :

> " The gray horse mourns   by his master dead." [1]

Grani is a heroic horse of the truest breed. The Armenian horse, Dzhalali, is a family horse which serves and survives several generations. It is ready to do quite menial duties and does them with great success, as when unguided it carries the infant David from Armenia to Egypt. It is full of cunning as well as strength, and when the Sultan of Egypt tries to imprison it behind a high wall, Dzhalali is more than equal to the occasion :

> Then Melik's eyes began to flame.
> He said :
> " Ho ! shut the doors fast !
> If the horse Dzhalali falls into our hands,
> We shall keep it ! "
> They shut the doors, and in that same moment
> A hundred horsemen surrounded the horse,
> And wished to catch it.
> Then the stallion Dzhalali said to itself :
> " O Lord ! how shall I escape ? "
> He leaped to the left, he leaped to the right,
> He flew to the wall.
> He prayed : " Lord, give me strength to leap over the wall.
> I shall not escape — I shall be lost here."
> Then the leaping horse Dzhalali gathered his strength,
> And the people could not stop him.
> There was a wall eight feet high,
> But the leaper leaped, leaped over it
> And vanished in the distance.[2]

This is the way in which a hero, placed in similar circumstances, would like to behave. The horse Dzhalali is so well trained to heroic actions that it knows what to do in an unforeseen crisis.

[1] *Brot af Sigurtharkvithu*, 7, 3.　　　　　　[2] *David Sasunskii*, p. 140.

In such matters as houses, gardens, weapons, ships, and horses heroic poets practise on the whole a realistic art, using these elements of common life to add to the persuasiveness and solidity of their narratives. But this task is matched by another of an opposite kind. Heroic tales often deal with the unknown or the impossible, which have to be made credible to the audience. This too demands a kind of realism. Untutored fancy must be guided by a keen sense of how such things would happen. Situations of which the poet and his audience know nothing must be woven into the text of the poem without too great a jump from ordinary life to impossible fancy. The treatment of horses may illustrate this just as it illustrates the needs of ordinary life. We pass almost imperceptibly from the possible to the impossible. It is an easy assumption that a horse is capable of thinking and feeling, and it is but a small step to making it interpret its master's fears and desires. So a Kalmuck horse sees what its master wants and acts accordingly :

> His swift grey horse heard these words in his mind.
> It lifted its fore-legs under its chin,
> It jumped over three high hills one after the other,
> It raised its beautiful hind-legs up to its tail and bolted,
> It bolted and from behind it, like a rifle bullet,
> With a whistle fly clods of earth from its hoofs.
> To the sky whirls in twelve streams
> Cloudy red dust from its four beautiful hoofs.
> Beautiful as a sea-shell
> The foam rises on its head.[1]

Despite the exaggeration, the main effect is realistic and convincing, since this is a very superior horse from whom much is to be expected. So too when Marko Kraljević hears that the Turks are exacting a marriage-tax from the people of Kosovo, he gets into a fury which he communicates to his horse :

> Urging Šarac he went to Kosovo,
> And he spurred good Šarac into fury,
> From his hoofs a living flame came flashing,
> And a blue flame rose up from his nostrils.[2]

Beneath the lively fancy is the sensible notion that a horse knows what its master wants and does its best to please him.

Exaggeration of a horse's performances may be carried quite far, especially when it comes to their covering wide stretches of country at a great speed. Just as Russian horses think little of leaping from mountain to mountain or crossing rivers and lakes at

---

[1] *Dzhangariada*, p. 119.   [2] Karadžić, ii, p. 387.

one stride, so Uzbek horses are similarly gifted :

> If he meets a ravine, he jumps over it ;
> If he meets a hill-side, he passes it ;
> If he meets a level place, he makes play with it
> If he meets a river, he springs over it ;
> If he meets a gully, he leaps over it.

or

> Holes and low places he does not notice,
> On the road he pays no attention to them.[1]

Natural obstacles present little trouble to heroic horses and tend to inspire rather than to discourage them. So Dzhalali, the horse of David of Sasoun, deals lightly with distances and atmospheric disturbances :

> When David set out on his journey,
> So thick a fog fell on the earth
> That he could not see the way anywhere.
> But like a dove Dzhalali flew through the fog.
> " This is the work of God's hand ",
> Said David,
> " It is better now to give rein
> To my horse Dzhalali
> To race wheresoever he will."
> Such is Dzhalali ! He flew and flew
> And accomplished a seven days' journey in an hour.
> He lighted on the peak of a mountain,
> He leaped on the crest of a mountain, and stood still.
> Suddenly the fog flew away.[2]

The horse may be subject to its master's will but it does much that is beyond his powers, and in describing how this happens the poets provide some charming variations on the old theme of the rider and his mount.

If a horse can do such feats in the course of an ordinary journey, it is capable of even more when its master's honour is to be tested by battle or something else equally stringent. Such a test may be a wager between two heroes on the relative worth of their horses, and in the ensuing contest the better horse wins, and with it the better master. The Russian poet, for instance, tells of the wager between Dyuk Stepanovich and Churilo Plenkovich and of the part which their horses play in it :

> Then Dyuk bestrode his good steed,
> And rode with young Churilo Plenkovich
> Over the glorious, free, open plain ;
> And they rode away beyond the free, open plain,

---

[1] Zhirmunskii-Zarifov, p. 371.   [2] *David Sasunskii*, p. 236.

With their whole equine strength,
And leapt across the river, mother Dnêpr,
On their good heroic steeds ;
Young Dyuk Stepanovich, the prince's son,
He leapt across the river, mother Dnêpr,
On his good heroic steed,
And with a single equine bound
He leapt quite a whole verst beyond ;
And he looked over his right shoulder,
When his comrade did not follow him,
Young Churilushka Oplenkovich,
Churilo Plenkovich had gone splash into the middle
    of the Dnêpr.[1]

Much of the phraseology here comes from the ordinary mechanics
of equitation, but the episode has a new point because the horse is
treated as a superequine creature with very unusual gifts.

If a horse can think, it is but a small step to make it speak.
It is only another sign of the close intimacy which exists between
the mount and its rider. In shamanistic poetry this is common
enough. The Tibetan Kesar is saved from disaster by his horse's
prescience,[2] and in the poems of the Abakan Tatars horses often
speak.[3] The belief passes easily into heroic poetry where the horse
has many of the qualities of its master and is often superior to
him in constancy and courage. At times it keeps him to the mark
by resolving his fears and doubts. So in the Kazak *Sain Batyr*,
when the hero prepares himself for a dangerous enterprise, he has
some misgivings, but his horse resolves them for him :

He took out his saddle and saddle-cover,
Calling on God he went to his horse ;
When he put on the saddle and saddle-cover,
When he tightened the girth,
The horse opened its mouth,
It spoke like a man :
" Sain, hero, be not afraid !
Flee not, because they are many.
The strength that God has given thee,
Display it on this quest !
The outspread hosts,
If thou severest them not, it is thy fault !
If I let myself fall before the arrows, it is my fault.
I will advance blithely,
I will go gracefully like a maiden." [4]

Hero and horse make, as it were, a bargain on how to behave in
battle and agree that, if each does his part properly, all will be well.

---

[1] Rybnikov, i, p. 108 ; Chadwick, *R.H.P.* p. 113.   [2] David-Neel, p. 107.
[3] Cohn, p. 40 ff., p. 80 ff.   [4] Radlov, iii, p. 253 ; cf. Orlov, p. 61.

The admirable Armenian horse, Dzhalali, addresses David with the privileged frankness of an old family retainer. David is a brave fighter, but has reasonable fears about the outcome of the battle which awaits him. Dzhalali will have none of them and chides him, promising that he need have no doubts so far as his horse is concerned :

> " Ah, man of little faith, why this fear ?
> As many as your sword shall smite,
> So many shall I scorch with my fiery breath !
> As many as your sword shall smite,
> So many shall I throw down with my breast !
> As many as your sword shall smite,
> So many shall I crush with my hoofs !
> Lose not heart !   Spur me on !
> You shall not be parted from me." [1]

With such a partner the hero has little to fear.   David's confidence is restored, and he goes gaily to battle.

When danger is afoot, horses are often quicker to detect it than their masters.   The Tatar poets often dwell on this point and like to show a horse's intelligence at work.   It is credited with insight and knowledge beyond its master's, and is often able to warn him of danger ahead or to inform him of something of which he is ignorant.   When a Kazak hero wishes to go on an expedition, his horse warns him against it :

> The Busurman Tsar went on a journey,
> Vasyanka went in pursuit of him.
> Then his good horse spoke to him
> In a clever human voice :
> " Go not, Vasinka, unarmed,
> Go not to the people of the Busurmans,
> The people of the Busurmans are crafty and cunning :
> We can neither of us live among them." [2]

So, when the Russian Dobrynya is long absent from home, and his wife, in the belief that he is dead, is about to marry Alyosha Popovich, his horse somehow knows it and breaks the news to its master :

> Now Dobrynya chanced to be at Tsargrad,
> And Dobrynya's horse stumbled :
> " Oh, you food for wolves, you bear's skin !
> Why are you stumbling to-day ? "
> The good steed addressed him,
> Addressed him in human voice :
> " Ah, my beloved master !

[1] *David Sasunskii*, p. 240.   [2] Orlov, p. 37.

You see not the misfortune which has befallen you ;
Your young wife Nastasya Nikulichna
Has married bold Alyosha Popovich ;
They are holding a feast for three days ;
To-day they go to holy Church,
To receive the crowns of gold." [1]

Sometimes the hero gets annoyed when his horse warns him of danger, as Ilya of Murom does when his horse stumbles on the way to Nightingale the Robber.[2] But the horse, being a good servant, does not complain and continues bravely to do what is expected of it.

Even when it is parted from its master a horse will keep its loyalty and intelligence and power of speech. Marko's horse, Šarac, shows itself at its best in the episode of his master's encounter with Philip the Magyar. Marko is drinking in a tavern and Šarac stands on guard outside, when Philip comes up and tries to force his way inside, horse and all. Šarac rises to the occasion :

By the tavern door was Šarac tethered.
Philip urged his gray Arab mare onward,
He would have her enter the new tavern,
But the war-horse Šarac would not let him.
With his hoofs upon her ribs he struck her ;
Then Philip the Magyar waxed in anger,
He took up his studded mace, and with it
Made to smite Šarac before the tavern.
But Šarac cried out before the tavern :
" God of mercy, woe is me, who must now
Meet my death this morning by the tavern
At the hands of great Philip the Magyar,
When my famous lord is not far distant ! " [3]

Marko tells Šarac to let Philip pass, with the result that Marko cuts off Philip's head. Šarac shares his master's recklessness and gaiety. He is not afraid to cry out when he sees danger, but even at the most critical moments he keeps his wits and remains in command of himself and his circumstances.

It is not always easy for a man to win the confidence of a horse. He must first prove his worth and his claims and show that he is likely to be a worthy master. When David of Sasoun first finds the horse Dzhalali, which belonged to his father, Mher, and has been hidden away for years, he has to impress his personality on a creature which has its full share of heroic pride and independence. Dzhalali does not know who David is and is not impressed by him

---

[1] Rybnikov, i, p. 165 ; Chadwick, *R.H.P.* p. 84.
[2] Rybnikov, i, p. 17.   [3] Karadžić, ii, p. 325.

at his first appearance. He is naturally suspicious and takes some convincing before he is ready to co-operate:

> Dzhalali saw that it was not Mher before him.
> The horse thundered with its hoofs on the earth,
> And fire spurted from the earth.
> In human speech the horse spoke:
> " You are dust, and to dust I shall turn you!
> What are you going to do with me?"
> David said: " I shall sit on your back!"
> Dzhalali speaks: " I shall lift you up to the height,
> I shall strike you on the sun and burn you up!"
> David said: " I shall turn round
> And hide under your belly!"
> The horse said: " Then I shall fall on a mountain,
> I shall let you fall, I shall cut you to pieces on a crag!"
> David said: " I shall return,
> And I shall sit on your back!"
> The horse said: " If that is so,
> You are my master, and I am your horse!"
> David answered the horse:
> " You have not had a master, but I will be he!
> They have not fed you or watered you, but I will feed and water
>   you!
> They have not combed you, but I will comb you and soap you!"[1]

By this kind of persuasion Dzhalali is broken in and becomes David's faithful servant.

When its master dies, a horse feels that its life is ended and has no meaning. When Manas is killed, his horse is inconsolable:

> Manas' horse, the cream-coloured,
> By the ground of the day-dwelling,
> By the ground of the night-dwelling,
> Gurgled and drank not water,
> Foamed and ate not grass.
> On its ribs black flies gather.
> It howls and stands by the house,
> Lies down by the grave of Manas,
> Is parched like a stone image.
> On the ground of the day-dwelling,
> On the ground of the night-dwelling,
> It neighs and looks at the sky.[2]

Indeed so great is the grief of Manas' horse and of the hawk and the hound with it, that God sends angels down to ask its cause, and this leads to Manas' resurrection. Here indeed the horse does not actually speak, though we might presume that its grief is too great for words. What a horse may feel about a lost master can be seen

[1] *David Sasunskii*, p. 231 ff.   [2] Radlov, v, p. 123.

from the Bulgarian *Warrior and Horse*, which tells how a warrior lies dead, with a bullet in his breast, while hawks fly above, and his white horse beats the earth with its hoofs and calls him :

> " Rise up quickly, my brave master,
> Set your foot in the steel stirrup,
> Stretch your hand forth to the bridle.
> Mother at your home laments you,
> Day and night she weeps in sorrow ;
> No more will you leap, my hero,
> At late eve or early morning,
> Out of tavern into tavern.
> You will feast no more, my hero,
> With your valorous companions —
> In the cold grave you lie buried." [1]

The poet's simple and sincere imagination pictures the horse lamenting for its master with the loyalty of a devoted servant.

Sometimes the theme of a horse's devotion inspires heroic poetry to what is more than pleasant fancy. Sigurth's horse, Grani, shares his dangers and triumphs and accompanies him in his great undertakings. It is also with him at his death. In the *Second Lay of Guthrun*, when Guthrun tells the story of this death, she relates how she first discovered what had happened :

> From the Thing ran Grani   with thundering feet,
> But thence did Sigurth   himself come never ;
> Covered with sweat   was the saddle-bearer,
> Wont the warrior's   weight to bear.
>
> Weeping I sought   with Grani to speak,
> With tear-wet cheeks   for the tale I asked ;
> The head of Grani   was bowed to the grass,
> The steed knew well   his master was slain. [2]

The horse's silence is more effective and more moving than any speech, and the poet shows how well he understands the human experience behind the traditional theme of the faithful horse, as he shapes it to a new success which is both close to common life and yet profoundly tragic. Another striking variation on this theme occurs in the *Iliad*. When at last Achilles goes again to the battlefield, Homer prepares with care the preliminaries to the great episode. After getting into his chariot, Achilles addresses his horses and tells them that their task is to bring the body of Patroclus back from the battlefield. Then the horse, Xanthus, bows its head until its mane reaches the ground, and the goddess Hera gives it a voice :

---

[1] Derzhavin, p. 91.   [2] *Guthrúnarkvitha*, ii, 4-5.

" In very truth shall we save you this time, O mighty Achilles ;
Yet is the day of your doom very near ; and truly in no wise
Are we to blame, but a powerful god and masterful fortune.
Nay, it was not because we were sluggish or slow that the Trojans
Stripped the armour away from the shoulders and breast of
      Patroclus ;
Nay, but the noblest of gods, who has fair-haired Leto for mother,
Slew him among the foremost and gave great glory to Hector.
As for us, we could race as fast as the breath of the West Wind,
Whom they say is the lightest of winds ; but you shall in battle
Meet your death from a god and a man ; for so is it fated." [1]

Homer moves with consummate skill from the ordinary theme of
a hero driving to battle to a forecast of his death from his horse.
With his Greek moderation and wisdom he first makes the horse
understand what Achilles says, and then he explains the miraculous
sequel by attributing it to a goddess. All is kept in hand ; for even
the prophetic words of the horse are explicable on the ancient
belief that horses have gifts of prophecy.[2] The essential realism
of the scene is maintained when Achilles is angry with the horse
and tells it that he knows well of his impending doom but will
continue to fight until the Trojans have had enough of war.

Another testing subject with which a heroic poet has to deal
is monsters. Though he almost certainly believes in their existence, he cannot know what they are like, but has none the less to
make them credible and fearful. Of course tradition helps him up
to a point, but tradition may be ill informed and not give him much
to work with. The situation is naturally quite different with
" literary " poets who present monsters in the full knowledge that
they are imaginary and that the play of imagination round them is
fully permissible. Camoens and Racine and Ariosto can produce
their monsters of the deep and describe them in lively detail
because no one will contradict. The same is also true of such
semi-allegorical figures as Virgil's Rumour and Milton's Sin. In
such cases what matters is the oddity of the presentation, the very
monstrosity of the monster, who, being outside actual experience,
is exempt from the laws of biology. With heroic poets it is
different. They believe that monsters exist and are fearful and
hideous, but beyond that they have little to guide them, and their
presentation of them is determined by these conditions. They
must somehow convince their audiences and create the right
degree of fear and horror.

The simplest way to present a monster is to assume that

---

[1] *Il.* xix, 408-18.
[2] E. Samter, *Volkskunde in Homer* (Berlin, 1923), p. 89 ff.

everyone knows what it is and that it therefore needs no description. Such a method is legitimate when the poet and his audience share some fundamental convictions about the supernatural creatures which exist in the world. This is the case with the Armenians whose poems are full of malignant devils. These play a considerable part in the action and cause much trouble to the heroes, but their appearance is not described, presumably because the poet and his audience are sufficiently in agreement about it for description to be unnecessary. What matters is not the devils' appearance but their actions, and these the poets present realistically as human enough to be intelligible. This art may be illustrated from an episode in which the hero Mher deals with a devil. He is prevented from drinking at a fountain by two of the devil's servants and, after killing them, finds the devil's cave and his wife, who falls in love with him and offers him help. He retires and waits for his chance. Then the story proceeds and shows how the White Devil, as he is called, behaves:

> The White Devil drank and ate,
> He got drunk. He wanted water.
> Long, long he looked from the mountain;
> His water-carriers do not bring him water.
> He says: " Has some ill chance befallen them?
> I scent that a human warrior has encountered them."
> The White Devil got up and sat
> On a whirlwind-horse, hurried to the spring,
> He looks suddenly: on the path to his cave
> Sits someone terrible like a mountain,
> His fire-breathing horse pastures by him,
> And beneath the rock groans a water-carrier.
> The White Devil called out to Mher:
> " Hey, human! Neither birds on the wing nor snakes
>   on the belly
> Fly hither or crawl hither.
> How have you dared to come hither to me?" [1]

Mher reveals his identity and says that he has come to fight. Then the story comes rapidly to its end: the White Devil makes a dishonest proposal:

> " Aye, aye, it is good to visit here!
> Arise, come into my dwelling,
> We will feast till the morning.
> We will fight it out afterwards!"
> " No!" answered Mher. " My forefathers left me a testament.
> Whenever you meet an enemy, delay not to fight with him."

[1] *David Sasunskii*, p. 115.

> Then the Devil drove his horse at Mher,
> And Mher drove his horse at the Devil.
> Three days and three nights they fought,
> Neither achieved anything.
> As soon as Mher seized the Devil,
> He sank his hand into his body,
> As if the Devil were made of dough.
> Only on the third day did Mher kill him.[1]

Except for the neat touch that the Devil is made of a substance like dough, his presentation is on recognisably human lines. He is a sly and treacherous creature whose actions are sufficiently like those of men not to require detailed description.

This is the simplest way to deal with monsters, but it is possible only if the audience knows about them and does not ask for fuller information. More often something lurid is expected, but the poets are usually economical in what they say and do not take too many risks. They conform to their own kind of realism in dealing with these creatures of the unknown. The result is that even when they seem to be presenting a clear picture, they leave much vague and undescribed. Take, for instance, the Russian poet's account of the monster, Tugarin, whom Alyosha Popovich encounters :

> " I have seen Tugarin the Dragon's son ;
> Tugarin is twenty feet high,
> The span between his sloping shoulders is seven feet,
> Between his eyes is the width of a tempered arrow,
> The horse beneath him is like a ferocious wild beast,
> From his jaws pour burning flames,
> From his ears comes a column of smoke." [2]

All that Alyosha says is that Tugarin is of monstrous size and belches flame and smoke. That is enough to make him formidable and hideous, but leaves enough unsaid for him not to become unconvincing. In other descriptions of Tugarin wings are added, but an air of vagueness is maintained and probability is not unduly outraged.

The poet of *Gilgamish* employs a similar art in a more accomplished manner when he tells of the expedition of Gilgamish and Enkidu against Humbaba. He guards a forest of cedars, which Gilgamish wishes to possess, and has been given special powers by the Sun-god and the Storm-god, but his appearance and habits are left vague. The poet tells of him :

---

[1] *David Sasunskii*, p. 116.
[2] Kireevski, ii, p. 72. For other accounts cf. Sokolov, pp. 38, 42-4, 124.

> To guard the Forest of Cedars,
> To terrify mortals, Enlil has appointed him,
> Has appointed Humbaba, whose roar is a whirlwind,
> Flame is in his jaws, and his breath is death !
> If in the forest he hears a tread on the road,
> He asks " Who is this who comes to the Forest ? "
> To guard the Forest of Cedars,
> To terrify mortals, Enlil has appointed him,
> And evil will seize whosoever comes to the Forest.[1]

Even when it comes to the fight between the heroes and Humbaba, the poet is no more explicit. What wins the day is Gilgamish's prayer to the Sun-god who sends eight winds, against which Humbaba is helpless. In his desperate straits, he behaves like a man and asks for mercy :

> " Gilgamish, stay thy hand.
> Be thou now my master, and I will be thy henchman :
> Regard not the words which I boastfully spoke against thee."

The offer is refused, and Humbaba's head is cut off. Though he is a fearful brute, the poet makes him real partly by leaving him vague, partly by making him behave like a human being. So the main difficulties in his presentation are surmounted.

The method of *Gilgamish* is on the whole that of most heroic poets. Of the many dragons who play a part in these stories very few receive detailed attention. Indeed the poets seldom do more than mention their fiery breath. So the Norse poet who tells of Fafnir, the dragon slain by Sigurth, says no more than

> The fiery dragon　　alone thou shalt fight
> That greedy lies　　at Gnitaheith.[2]

Everyone will admit that a dragon is greedy and fiery, and the poet feels no call to say more. Nor is the dragon of *Beowulf* character-ised any more precisely, though he plays a considerable part and causes the hero's death. He guards a hoard of gold, like Fafnir, and attacks anyone who comes near, but though his attacks are deadly, his method of delivering them is left vague. Indeed almost his only characteristic is the belching of flames. On this the poet dwells both when the dragon's peace is first disturbed :

> Then the enemy began　　to spit forth embers,
> To burn the bright houses ;　　a blazing light shone
> Awful to all men ;[3]

and when he comes out of his cave to fight Beowulf :

[1] *Gilgamish*, III, iv, 1-8.　　　　[2] *Grípisspá*, 11, 1-2.
[3] *Beowulf*, 2312-14.

> Came then the burning one,   bowed and creeping,
> Speeding to his doom.[1]

In the last encounter the poet risks a little more. After all, he has to tell how the dragon kills Beowulf and is itself killed. So he plucks up his courage and says :

> Then the tribe's scather   a third time,
> The fearsome fire-dragon,   his feud remembered,
> Rushed on that gallant one,   when room he gave him,
> Hot battle-grim   all his neck he grasped
> In bitter tooth-bones ;   he bloodied was
> With his soul's gore ;   that sweat in streams gushed.[2]

The dragon, it seems, can bite, as well as breathe flame, but its main outlines are still dim. It is a creature of horror and dread, and there is no call to present it too concretely.

Dragons of course are familiar enough to the untutored imagination and do not really require exact delineation. But sometimes heroic poets have to deal with more unusual monsters. Yet even in these cases they tend to follow the same technique and to rely on vague horror and undefined dread. This is certainly what the poet of *Beowulf* does for Grendel and his Dam, and in so doing secures some of his greatest successes. What counts with Grendel is not what he looks like but what he does, and on his first appearance the poet is careful to stress this and nothing else :

> The monster of unhealing,
> Grim and greedy,   was speedily yare,
> Fierce and furious,   and took from their beds
> Thirty thegns.[3]

When Grendel returns to Hrothgar's hall and is engaged by Beowulf in single combat, the air of mystery is maintained, as befits an episode in the darkness of night. The monster seizes a sleeping man, drinks his blood, and eats his flesh. Beowulf comes to grips with Grendel and wrestles with him, eventually tearing off his arm. But, beyond the fact that Grendel has an arm, little is said about him. But the arm is used skilfully for poetic purposes. It is nailed up for all men to see :

> 'Twas a token clear,
> When that battle-hero   the hand laid down,
> The arm and the oxter   (it was all there together,
> Grendel's grip !)   under the groined roof.[4]

A similar art is applied to Grendel's Dam, when Beowulf sees her in her lair :

[1] *Beowulf*, 2569-70.   [2] *Ibid.* 2688-93.
[3] *Ibid.* 120-23.   [4] *Ibid.* 834-7.

> The good one grew ware then   of the ground-lying wolf,
> A mighty mer-wife.[1]

Beowulf wrestles with her, as he did with Grendel, and finally cuts off her head, but that is about all we hear about her. Such monsters are the more monstrous for being kept mysterious.

In general, heroic poets treat monsters with a vagueness tempered by realism, but there are some exceptions, for which we can usually find a reason. The Kazak poet who tells of Alpamys is on the whole factual and realistic, but he lets himself go on a revolting creature whom the hero destroys :

> His breast is big as a shield,
> His beak is high as a hill,
> His single tusk is like a hoe,
> His throat is like a huge grave.
> Where he sits, he fills the space of a six-windowed dwelling.
> His ears are like a warrior's shield,
> His nose is like a crushed husk of millet,
> His eyes are like deep darkness,
> His footstep is like a flaming hearth,
> His mouth is like a spit,
> His single tusk is like a knife,
> His nostrils are like a cave,
> His chin is big as a basket.[2]

The poet, who knows what the real world is like, seems to have tried to imagine a monster and to present him as he would actually appear. Though some of his comparisons indicate no more than size, others give visual impressions, and though these are not very precise, they create a sufficient effect of hugeness and horror. So too in his *Manas* Orozbakov describes the giant, Malgun, who guards the entry to China. No doubt he comes from ancient legend, and the poet, who is sufficiently modern and aware of the difficulties, does his best with him :

> Only Malgun remained far off,
> Suspicions crept into his soul.
> Like a hillock is his head,
> Like a house is his club,
> Like thunder he coughs !
> Malgun was brought hither
> From the city of the giants.
> Like walls are his shoulders ;
> In the words of human speech
> He has been taught by many khans.
> They have placed him on guard,
> Bullets do not pierce him ;

[1] *Ibid.* 1518-19.   [2] Orlov, p. 31.

An iron cuirass is on his body,
They have clothed him in a coat of steel !
The first on guard is Malgun,
A renowned sentry is Malgun.[1]

Compared with the Kazak monster, Malgun is a little prosaic and ordinary, since Orozbakov is so eager to fit him into a human scheme of things that he has been economical in mentioning his monstrous characteristics. None the less he remains a formidable and unusual creature, and we are naturally interested to hear how the Kara-Kirghiz heroes, who rely on force of arms and skill of hand to deal with their enemies, will treat him. The attack lasts for six days, and even the great Alaman Bet is unable to pierce with his spear into the giant's defences, since every stroke is countered by his enormous club. Malgun's only weak point is his neck, since this is not protected, and for this Alaman Bet and young Syrgak eventually go, with the result that they cut it through with a sword. Orozbakov gives reality to Malgun by the fight with him, in which good blows are given on both sides and in the end skill triumphs over magical defences. Malgun has his place in the story because he represents the supernatural guards which the Chinese use to defend their lands, but he is rightly defeated by purely human strength, since anything else would be below the level of the Kara-Kirghiz. To stress this little lesson the poet takes care to make Malgun a formidable monster.

When a Yakut poet sets out to describe a demon, he works in rather different circumstances, since the audience believe in demons and accord them an important position in their religious beliefs. No doubt he draws upon current views and trusts that his picture will be accepted as convincing. The result is certainly precise :

He had a single black leg,
Which grew like a pillar of bone ;
His huge crafty arm
Grew from his breast-bone.
He had only one eye
In the middle of his forehead,
Like a frozen pond.
The bridge of his nose was huge
As the back-bone of a lean ox.
His full beard resembled
An old breast-covering of bear-skin.
In the middle of his mouth
Gaped something like a gully,

[1] *Manas*, p. 248 ff.

> And there stood out six huge green teeth,
> Each enormous as an axe,
> And a dark tongue
> Like a green spleen.[1]

Since the Yakuts believe in demons, the poet makes his monster conform to their fears.

In this respect Homer too is an exception to the general rule. He has not many monsters, but such as he has he deals with in his own way. He has the clear Greek vision of visible things and does not traffic in the vague or the indefinite. He essays the difficult task of presenting monsters vividly to the eye and tries to make them look real. Sometimes he calls up a terrible appearance in the fewest possible words and leaves it at that, as when the Chimaera, killed by Bellerophon, with its hybrid nature and fiery breath, is dismissed in two lines :

> Lion in front, with the back part a snake, and a goat in the middle,
> Breathing the terrible breath of fire irresistibly flaming.[2]

The matter is dispatched so quickly that we have no time to suspect absurdity or to ask more precisely what such a creature looks like. So too when Odysseus' companions encounter a giantess among the Laestrygonians, she is left impressively vague :

> There was a woman as big as a mountain, and greatly they loathed her.[3]

No more needs to be said, since the whole effect of appalling size is conveyed by the loathing felt by the men for the giantess. Scylla is less tractable. She is related to sea-monsters, and any account of her must appeal to a love of sea-yarns and their terrors. So Homer takes a big risk when he makes Circe describe Scylla, who barks with a voice as loud as a new-born puppy's, and has twelve feet, and twelve necks, on each of which is a head with three rows of thick teeth set closely together.[4] Scylla is a very advanced version of a polyp, and the careful enumeration of her limbs suggests a kinship with the giant squids and krakens of sea-yarns. The Aegean world had its tales of sea-monsters and saw them with a vivid imagination, as Minoan and Mycenean gems and seals show.[5] Homer may have learned something from this tradition, and here he does his best to use it. He takes a great risk, but succeeds in surmounting it just because he is precise and exact.

In contrast with this bold experiment we may set Homer's

---

[1] Yastremski, p. 27.   [2] *Il.* vi, 181-2.
[3] *Od.* x, 113.   [4] *Ibid.* xii, 85-94.
[5] H. Dussaud, *Les Civilisations préhelléniques* (Paris, 1914), p. 417 ff.

treatment of the Cyclops, Polyphemus. He is a one-eyed, man-eating giant, and the subject, though popular enough in legend and folk-lore, needs tactful handling. Homer attacks the difficulties with confident mastery, and depicts the monstrosity of Polyphemus with an unwavering grip on reality. When he is first seen, he is sleeping among his flocks outside his cave :

> There asleep was a man, gigantic, who used to look after
> Flocks far away from the others, alone ; nor used he to mingle
> With any others, but lived by himself, ferocious and lawless.
> He was a monster, enormous in bulk, nor did he resemble
> Men who live upon bread, but was like a forested headland
> Jutting out among mountains, and seen apart from the others.[1]

Polyphemus is undeniably an awful creature, who acts up to form when he eats Odysseus' comrades, after dashing them on the floor " like puppies ". He has no friends even among his fellow Cyclops, and is peculiarly loathsome when he falls into a drunken sleep. Yet these horrible qualities have something human in them, if only as a perversion or exaggeration of human failings. Homer even makes Polyphemus almost win our sympathy when, after his one eye has been put out, he addresses his ram affectionately and asks it why it no longer goes first from the cave but lags behind the flock. Polyphemus is convincing because he is, for better and for worse, somehow human. What might have been an impersonal ogre, a man-eating monster with no real identity, becomes a primitive pastoral giant, disgusting and bestial, but at times almost pathetic and always convincing.

Heroic poetry, then, gives verisimilitude and solidity to even its most improbable themes, partly by making them fit into a visible world, partly by relating them to common experience. It enables its audiences to see miraculous events and monsters and provokes certain feelings about them. Such episodes create an immediate, vivid impression, and there is no doubt about what impression the poet means to make. He is able to do this because his art is always concerned with the vivid presentation of things and events. Just because he is accustomed to describing armour and houses and ships, he is able to describe other matters outside his experience but not beyond his imagination. In this the very simplicity of his outlook is a great asset. He sees things from a single angle, without hesitations or qualifications, and is able to give to them that unity of impression which makes them real.

[1] *Od.* ix, 187-92.

V

THE MECHANICS OF NARRATIVE

No reader of heroic poetry can fail to notice that it abounds in detailed descriptions of actions which are in themselves trivial, and would be omitted by a novelist or narrative-poet working in modern conditions. These are the mechanics of narrative and are needed to keep the story coherent and objective. Without them the audience might fail to follow what happens and might complain that the poet does not do his job properly. But these passages can be made attractive and illuminating and add their own kind of poetry to the general effect. They do not draw too much attention to themselves; they are not show-pieces, but within their limitations they can have an unobtrusive charm and increase our pleasure by the light which they throw on the characters and the circumstances of their lives. Indeed the poets often go beyond the immediate purpose of such passages and give some new turn or unexpected decoration which we pause to enjoy. The different branches of heroic poetry all employ them to some degree and for very similar purposes, and in many cases what might be the mere mechanics of narrative are turned to a genuinely poetical end.

First, heroic poetry often deals with arrivals and departures. The entrances and exits of its characters are usually treated with care and precision. A hero comes as a stranger to some great house and is welcomed and entertained, but the manner of his arrival may illustrate the elaboration of heroic manners and the way in which great men treat one another. Hospitality and courtesy are heroic virtues and must be displayed even when they do not mean very much for the story. So in *Beowulf* the hero arrives in his ship with his company at a foreign shore. They are seen by a guard who rides off to examine them. He explains who he himself is and what his duties are, asks the visitors who they are, admits that they are plainly no common folk, and urges them to comply with the usual formalities. Beowulf gives a courteous answer and explains that he comes on an errand of friendship. The guard, without committing himself to accepting all that Beowulf says, then guides the party to Hrothgar's hall, where Wulfgar meets them, and again they are questioned. This, it seems, is the correct procedure before introducing visitors to the king's presence :

> He hied then in haste   where Hrothgar sate,
> Old and hoary   amid his band of earls.
> He stepped forth, strong-hearted,   till he stood by the shoulders
> Of the Lord of the Danes.   He knew the law of the doughty.[1]

Once in the presence of the king, Beowulf establishes his identity and position. Hrothgar recognises him as a friend of his family and makes a formal speech of welcome. He sees that Beowulf has come to help him and offers him all that he has. In this arrival and welcome there is a kind of ritual. The visitor must be identified and questioned, and then, if his answers prove satisfactory, he is received as an old friend. In a world where enemies are many, some degree of caution is necessary, but it does not prevent the host from behaving in a generous and princely manner.

In Homer there are many cases of strangers arriving at the courts of princes, but there is a lack of such precautions as are taken in *Beowulf*, as if the Homeric world in its islands and isolated valleys had less fear of sudden incursions by enemies. In each case much the same routine is followed. When a visitor arrives, he is welcomed by his host, who is careful at first not to ask his name. He is first washed and fed ; then the formalities take place, and ties are found between the guest and the host. This is the way in which Telemachus welcomes Athene when she comes in disguise to Ithaca,[2] and Menelaus welcomes Telemachus at Sparta.[3] This is also the procedure in more unusual circumstances. When Odysseus ventures into the palace of Circe, she does not ask him who he is but gives him a drink which should turn him into a beast. Then the ritual goes a little wrong. Odysseus attacks her with his sword, as if intending to kill her, and then she asks him who he is.[4] The familiar frame is kept, even if the proceedings are unusual. Another slight variation is made with Odysseus' arrival in Phaeacia. He is thrown up from the sea and borrows garments from the king's daughter, Nausicaa, who guides him to the palace but modestly leaves him to make his own entry. He walks straight in and kneels before the queen in supplication.[5] Despite the unusual circumstances, she behaves with perfect correctness. Odysseus is washed and fed, and then the questions come. This is of course a special case and receives rather more than the usual treatment. But it shows how Homer

---

[1] *Beowulf*, 356-9.   [2] *Od.* i, 103 ff.   [3] *Ibid.* iv, 20 ff.
[4] *Ibid.* x, 312 ff.   [5] *Ibid.* vii, 139 ff.

sees the human side of such an occasion and uses it to illustrate
the personalities of his characters.

Kara-Kirghiz poets resemble *Beowulf* and Homer in their
careful account of heroic arrivals. In one poem Alaman Bet
comes to the dwelling of the great Manas. A guard questions him
courteously but firmly, and Alaman Bet replies in the same tone
without revealing who he is :

> " I seek nothing, I am a traveller,
> I ask now about my way,
> I come here from a land of princes,
> Let word go to thy master,
> I come here from a land of princes,
> Let word go to thy master." [1]

The guard admits Alaman Bet to Manas' presence, and Manas
asks him who he is. Alaman Bet replies at length with a family
history, and at the end of it reveals his name. The effect on Manas
is immediate. He answers shortly :

> " If you are the son of Kara Khan,
> If you are the hero Alaman Bet,
> Now give me your hand." [2]

The guest is welcomed as a friend, and Manas spares nothing to
make him at home and to load him with gifts. Just as the Homeric
heroes are feasted after arrival, so is Alaman Bet, for whom
Manas himself orders refreshment in the usual Kara-Kirghiz
style :

> " Put the kettle quickly on the fire,
> Then put fresh cream into it,
> And sugar in it also,
> And get good tea ready for us.
> Put it before Alaman Bet !
> Let him put hot food in his mouth
> And have something to feast his eyes." [3]

This is indeed a special occasion, since it is the beginning of the
great and lasting friendship between Manas and Alaman Bet, but
the poet uses for it the machinery which the Kara-Kirghiz use for
all arrivals of strangers. None the less what might be quite
insignificant gathers dignity and interest from the context in
which it is set.

Not all arrivals are as simple as this. A hero, however great,
may arrive in such a condition that his prospective host or hostess is
troubled and hardly knows what to do about him. The poet has
then to recast the traditional technique to meet such a disturbance

---

[1] Radlov, v, p. 55. [2] *Idem*, p. 57. [3] *Idem*, p. 57.

in the usual routine. So, when Gilgamish, on his journey to the end of the world, comes to the home of Siduri, the wine-maker, she sees him coming and is thoroughly alarmed by his weather-beaten, haggard appearance :

> The wine-maker looked in the distance ;
> She took thought with herself and said :
> " This is one who would ravish a woman.
> Whither does he advance ? . . ."
> As soon as the wine-maker saw him, she barred the postern,
> She barred her inner door, she barred her chamber.

Gilgamish hears the noise and speaks to her, asking why she has shut the door, and she answers :

> " Why is thy vigour wasted, thy countenance fallen ?
> Thy spirit sunken, thy cheerfulness gone ?
> There is sorrow in thy belly,
> Thy face is of one who has gone a far journey,
> With cold and heat is thy face weathered." [1]

Gilgamish does his best to ease her misgivings by telling her something of his story. He explains that his woebegone air comes not from his journey but from the death of Enkidu, of whom he speaks in moving words at some length, thus telling her of his quest for immortality. She takes up the subject with zest and puts to him her own philosophy of living for pleasure and the passing moment. The episode has an almost metaphysical importance in the story of Gilgamish, but is introduced by an ingenious variation on the familiar theme of a hero's arrival.

There are of course times when heroes meet with anything but a courteous reception, but even then the poets tend to observe something of the familiar pattern, though they vary it to suit the changed circumstances, as Homer does in his account of Odysseus and the Cyclops. Odysseus comes uninvited into the Cyclops' cave, when its owner is out with the flocks. When he returns, he asks the usual questions — who are his visitors, where do they come from, where is their ship. He asks them rudely and suggests that the visitors are pirates. This justifies Odysseus in answering as he does. He says, truly, that he comes from Troy, but, suspecting the Cyclops' intentions, says untruly that his ship has been wrecked. He does not yet say who he is, since convention demands that that should wait until he has eaten. Instead of offering his visitors food the Cyclops eats two of them, and then, according to pattern, asks Odysseus who he is. Odysseus follows the rules and

[1] *Gilgamish*, x, i, 15 ff.

answers, but again untruthfully, that his name is " No-man ", a piece of deception which stands him in good stead later. Finally, it is customary for hosts to give gifts to their guests, and Odysseus hopes for one from the Cyclops. The theme is nicely developed and reaches its climax when the Cyclops, beginning to get drunk on the excellent wine which Odysseus has brought, says :

> " I shall eat No-man the last, when the rest of the company's
> finished,
> After I've eaten the others, and this is the gift I shall give you." [1]

In this episode the traditional elements are present, but put to a new purpose to suit the brutal character of the Cyclops.

In another passage Homer adapts the traditional theme quite differently but with no less success. When Priam goes to ransom the body of Hector from Achilles, he faces great danger. Achilles is the deadly enemy of Priam's house, and the old man goes alone to him. He walks straight into the tent, where Achilles, who has just eaten after his long fast, is with two companions. He does not see Priam come in :

> And Priam entering unperceiv'd till he well was among them,
> Clasp'd his knees and seized his hands all humbly to kiss them,
> Those dread murderous hands which his sons so many had slain.
> As when a man whom spite of fate hath curs'd in his own land
> For homicide, that he fleeth abroad and seeketh asylum
> With some lord, and they that see him are fill'd with amazement.
> Ev'n so now Achilles was amaz'd as he saw Priam enter,
> And the men all were amaz'd and lookt upon each other in turn.[2]

Both Priam and Achilles know who the other is, and there is no need for questions about names. Moreover, Priam comes on a very special and dangerous errand. So he does the wisest and safest thing in taking up the position of a suppliant, which entitles him to certain rights of sanctuary. He at once declares the nature of his errand, and Achilles is moved by the old man's pathos and in due course agrees to yield Hector's body. All this is unusual and outside the conventional course. But once the agreement about the body has been reached, convention asserts itself. Achilles insists that his guest shall have supper and spend the night in his quarters. Even in these conditions the heroic code of manners is maintained.

Departures are no less decorous than arrivals and are treated with the same degree of detail. *Beowulf* presents a pattern which may be paralleled elsewhere. When Beowulf leaves Hrothgar, the

---

[1] *Od.* ix, 369-70. [2] *Il.* xxiv, 477-84. Trs. Robert Bridges.

episode is treated at some length. First speeches are interchanged, Beowulf speaking first and saying how ready he is to return at any time when he is needed, and Hrothgar declaring his affection for Beowulf. Next, handsome gifts are presented, and the friends part :

> Kissed then   the King well-born,
> Baron of Shieldings,   that best of thegns,
> And clasped his neck ;   coursed his tears,
> That hoary beard.   Both things he looked for,
> Ancient and old,   but one thing rather,
> That, some time, each   might see the other,
> Proud minds in a meeting.[1]

Beowulf and his party then proceed to their ship and are greeted by the same guard who challenged them on their arrival. Beowulf gives a gold-mounted sword to the man who watches over the ship, goes aboard, and sails off. It is an elaborate ceremony in which each stage is traditional and correct but has also its human interest, whether in Hrothgar's genuine affection for Beowulf, or Beowulf's no less genuine desire to help him, or the delight which Beowulf's company take in their gifts, or the courtesy of the guard. In a sense the whole episode is unnecessary for the story. Beowulf has killed the monsters, and there is nothing left for him but to go home. The poet might have dismissed him in a few lines, but he has good reasons for preferring an expansive manner. It gives a dignified close to the adventures which have taken place and enables him to stress certain points about the way in which heroes behave.

Homer uses a not dissimilar pattern for the departures of his heroes. It consists of the presentation of gifts, the delivery of speeches, the pouring of libations, and the provision of transport. When Telemachus leaves Sparta, Menelaus offers to give him a silver bowl with gold edges and a chariot with three horses.[2] When Odysseus leaves Phaeacia, he is loaded with rich gifts and put on a miraculous ship which goes its own way without sails or oars.[3] Just as Menelaus makes a farewell speech and pours a libation to the gods, so Alcinous makes a speech in which he asks his companions to make a last contribution of gifts and performs a sacrifice and a libation to Zeus. When the formalities are concluded, the actual departure is made quickly. Telemachus whips up his horses ; Odysseus wraps himself up on board and goes to sleep. The general pattern is the same, but Homer introduces small differences which illustrate the idiosyncrasies of his characters. While Telemachus is modest about both gifts and trans-

[1] *Beowulf*, 1870-76.   [2] *Od.* iv, 589 ff., 615 ff.
[3] *Ibid.* xiii, 8 ff., 81 ff.

port, Odysseus shows no such restraint, and while Menelaus is the old family friend, Alcinous is a little ostentatious and pleased with himself for treating his guest so well. So too with their wives. While Arete provides Odysseus with homely necessities like food and wine, Helen interprets omens to mean that all will soon be well in Ithaca and the Suitors destroyed. In both cases unimportant occasions are enriched with significant details, and the heroes are sent on their way in proper style.

In these cases the hero is simply going home. When he sets out from home on some perilous quest, a somewhat different technique is used. On such occasions prayers and good wishes are needed, and the poets do not omit them. So when Priam prepares to ransom the body of Hector from Achilles, he is told by his wife, Hecuba, to pour a libation to Zeus before he starts. He does this in due form and utters a prayer with it.[1] When Gilgamish and Enkidu depart to destroy the ogre Humbaba, they are seen off by the elders of Erech, who give them advice and a blessing, and then Gilgamish offers up a prayer to Shamash :

> " Here I present myself, Shamash,
> And lift up my hands ;
> Grant that my life may be spared hereafter,
> Bring me back again to the ramparts of Erech,
> Spread thy shield above me." [2]

Before the Yakut heroes proceed on their adventures, they go down on their knees before the fire on the hearth and pray to the spirit of fire, asking for help in the struggles which lie ahead. If the heroes do not offer up these prayers for themselves, their kinsfolk do so for them.[3] Even in the short scope of the Edda poems there is still room for such a rite. When Gunnar and his companions set out to visit Atli, they go with evil omens and dark forebodings, but Hogni's wife, Kostbera, maintains the heroic form, when she bids them farewell :

> " May ye sail now happy,   and victory have ;
> To fare well I bid ye,   may nought your way bar ! " [4]

The Yakuts provide a more elaborate formula for the parents of any hero to say before he sets out :

> " Bear yourself in front with protection like a rock
> From a powerful blessing on your soul,
> Burning with flame, and go your way.
> Bear yourself behind with the support
> Of a powerful blessing from home on your soul." [5]

[1] *Ibid.* xxiv, 287 ff., 302 ff.   [2] *Gilgamish*, III, vi, 36-40.
[3] Yastremski, p. 3.   [4] *Atlamál*, 31.   [5] Yastremski, p. 4.

However dark the prospects may be, the heroic system demands that they be faced with courage and confidence, and departing heroes must start on their quests with the air of going to victory.

A second piece of mechanism is concerned with a hero's rising in the morning. When he gets up, details are given which show how he pursues the ordinary routine of life. It is part of his human condition, of his likeness to other men. Russian poets like to describe how a hero rises from sleep and tend to do so in a stock way, as for Alyosha Popovich:

> Alyosha woke from sleep,
> Got up early, very, very early
> Washed himself at break of day,
> Dried himself with a white towel,
> And turned to the east to pray to God.[1]

So in her *Tale of Lenin* Marfa Kryukova tells that, when the hero comes out of hiding to control the Revolution, he starts his day like any ancient *bogatyr*:

> On a morning it was, on an early morning,
> At the rising of the fair red sun,
> That Ilich stepped out of his little tent,
> He washed his face
> With cold spring water,
> He wiped his face with a little towel.[2]

Lenin, as we might expect, does not say morning prayers, but otherwise his rising is very like Alyosha's, and in both cases the poet uses this device to start an adventurous story in as natural a way as possible. In essence this is akin to Homer's art. When Telemachus has to face the elders of Ithaca with a grave decision about the Suitors, he begins his day in a quiet, customary manner:

> But when the Daughter of Dawn stretched forth her roseate fingers,
> Then from his slumber arose the belovèd son of Odysseus,
> Speedily put on his clothes and fastened a sword from his shoulder,
> And on his gleaming feet he bound his beautiful sandals.[3]

It is all very ordinary and commonplace, but has its own charm in the narrative.

Parallel to the scenes of getting up are those of going to bed, which provide a note of rest and quiet after an eventful day. Homer often describes how his heroes rest after battle or travel, as when Telemachus and Peisistratus stay with Menelaus and are guided to their beds on the verandah by slaves with torches.[3] Even more domestic is the account of Telemachus on Ithaca when, after an exciting day, the old slave Euryclea lights him to his bedroom:

[1] Kireevski, ii, p. 71.   [2] Kaun, p. 188.   [3] *Od.* iv, 296 ff.

Then did he open the door himself of his well-fashioned chamber,
Sat on the side of the bed and took off his soft woollen garment,
And then into the hands of the wise old woman he gave it.
She then, when she had brushed and neatly folded the garment,
Put it to hang on a peg at the side of the well-fretted bedstead,
Quietly went from the room and pulled the door by the handle
Shaped as a ring, and then with the thong she drew the bolt
    forward.
Wrapped there all night long in his fleecy sheepskin he slumbered.[1]

There is little essential difference between this and the sleep
which Beowulf enjoys after vanquishing Grendel. He too is
conducted to his room by a retainer and takes his rest with delight :

>   Before all things the Geat,
> Rough shield-warrior,   for rest was longing ;
> Weary of his swimming,   swiftly the hall-thegn
> Guided him forth,   who was come from far ;
> He that worshipfully   watched over all
> The needs of a thegn,   such things as in those days
> Sea-wanderers   might be wanting.
> Rested him then, roomy-hearted ;   the roof towered,
> Gaping and gold-decked ;   the guest within slept,
> Until the black raven   of heaven's blessings
> Boded, blithe-hearted.[2]

The elaborate style hides to some degree the simplicity of the
action which the poet describes, but his art is of the same kind as
Homer's in its attention to tranquil, domestic details.

Sometimes, if the theme of going to bed is a preliminary to
some fearful event, a contrast is made between the usual routine of
night and what comes after it. A nice variation comes in *Beowulf*
before the fight with Grendel. Beowulf knows what awaits him
in the night and is ready to face the monster, but, contrary to
expectation, he does not keep his armour on but undresses almost
as if he were going to bed :

> However the Geats' prince   gladly trusted
> In his moody might,   in his Maker's Mercy.
> Then he did off   his iron byrny,
> His helm from his head,   gave his hilted sword,
> Choicest of irons,   to his armour-bearer,
> And bade him hold   the battle-harness.[3]

He explains that he does this for reasons of heroic pride, that,
since he considers himself every whit as good as Grendel, he will
fight him without weapons in his own way. Then he proceeds to
go to sleep :

---

[1] *Ibid.* i, 436-43.   [2] *Beowulf*, 1792-1802.   [3] *Ibid.* 669-74.

Laid him down then the Champion,   a cheek-bolster took
The face of the earl.[1]

The structure of this small episode is based on the familiar way in
which a hero goes to sleep, but it receives a new character through
the unusual considerations which prompt his action and the
conditions which force him to it.   Conversely, the imminence of
disaster may interfere with the ordinary routine of rest.   When
Charlemagne has left Roland to fight in the Pass, he bivouacs his
army and prepares himself for sleep.   But he feels that something
is amiss, and does not undress :

> That Emperour is lying in a mead ;
> By's head, so brave, he's placed his mighty spear ;
> On such a night unarmed he will not be.
> He's donned his white hauberk, with broidery,
> Has laced his helm, jewelled with golden beads,
> Girt on Joiuse, there never was its peer,
> Whereon each day thirty fresh hues appear.[2]

Charlemagne is full of fears about Roland, and, even when he falls
asleep, he has troubling dreams.   In this case the ordinary theme is
reversed.   The hero sleeps in his clothes and even keeps his armour
on, a touch which is the more effective because it provides a
contrast to the standard passages in which he goes to sleep in the
ordinary way.

Closely related to accounts of rising and going to bed are those
of a hero or heroine dressing.   This is often enough quite unimportant, but it may be used for a significant purpose, especially to
show how clothes betray the character of their owner.   How well
the apparel can proclaim the man can be seen from the way in
which Marko Kraljević, after deciding that he must get married,
puts on all his finery :

> Marko then put on his cloth of velvet,
> On his head a silver-crested kalpak,
> On his legs his breeches, clasps upon them,
> And each clasp was worth a golden ducat :
> And he girded on his inlaid sabre,
> To the ground hung down its golden tassels,
> And a sheath of gold contained that sabre,
> Sharp of blade it was and sweet to handle ;
> And his servants brought to him his charger,
> And they set on it a gilded saddle ;
> To its hoofs fell down the horse's trappings ;
> Over it they put a dappled lynx-skin,
> With a bridle made of steel they curbed it.[3]

---

[1] *Beowulf*, 688-9.   [2] *Roland*, 2496-511.   [3] Karadžić, ii, p. 205.

This is not only picturesque and delightful but illuminates Marko's character and the gay spirit in which he goes to seek a bride. As a counterpart we may quote the Kara-Kirghiz account of how Ak Erkach, the wife of an Uigur prince, sees the hero Alaman Bet riding towards her house and prepares to greet him:

> Her beautifully decked head-dress
> She set upon her head.
> To the right her hair she parted,
> On the right side she arranged it.
> To the left her hair she parted,
> On the left side she arranged it.
> Her thick snood of gold
> She fixed to the end of the moon ;
> Her thick snood of silver
> She fixed to the end of the sun.
> Like a puppy she whimpered ;
> She showed her teeth in laughter,
> With her breath she shed fragrance.
> She frisked like a little lamb ;
> Her ringlets fell to her shoulders.[1]

Ak Erkach is hardly a heroine, but she moves in a heroic world and behaves as such a woman should. Her action is a tribute to the kind of men with whom she consorts. The poet enjoys not only the refinements of her toilet with its elaborate coiffure and its ornaments shaped like the sun and the moon but makes it reveal her character and provide an amusing contrast to the formidable hero whom she hopes to impress.

Of course feminine toilet is more adapted than masculine to varied treatment, and in developing the familiar theme a poet may allow himself considerable liberty. What is applicable to a mere woman is still more applicable to a goddess, since she may be expected to display her graces on a more formidable scale. This is what Homer does with Hera. She wishes to entice her husband, Zeus, from Mount Ida where he is watching the battle and inter-fering with her plans for its progress. So in a purposeful and crafty spirit she plots to use all her charms on him. Homer takes up the traditional theme of dressing, uses its full resources, and makes a great show with them. Though Hera's toilet might occur almost anywhere in the *Iliad* as part of its machinery, it receives careful attention here because it is important for the plot. She first washes her skin with ambrosia and anoints it with a sweet oil which, if it is so much as shaken, sends its scent to heaven and earth. She then does her hair, tying it in plaits, and afterwards puts

[1] Radlov, v, p. 37.

on a garment, made by Athene and embroidered with many patterns, and fastens it with golden pins and a girdle with golden tassels. She puts on ear-rings, each of which has three drops. When she has finally put on her head-dress and her sandals, she is ready for work.[1] This is indeed a full-dress occasion, and Homer makes Hera's toilet as magnificent as possible.

The theme of dress may also be adapted to the needs of other special occasions. When something is afoot, the poets may take care to show how their characters clothe themselves, since this is a necessary part of the whole effect. For instance, in *Roland* when Ganelon sets out to the Saracens with intent to betray Roland, he puts on all his finery in order to make as good an impression as possible :

> Guenès the count goes to his hostelry,
> Finds for his road his garments and his gear,
> All of the best he takes that may appear :
> Spurs of fine gold he fastens on his feet,
> And to his side Murglès, his sword of steel.
> On Tachebrun, his charger next he leaps,
> His uncle holds the stirrup, Guinemere.[2]

Ganelon is on a fell errand, but he is none the less a great noble with his own style and splendour. Here his care for his appearance serves a double task. In the first place it is a kind of defiance to Roland and others who have derided him and made him wish to assert his pride, and in the second place he goes as an ambassador of Charlemagne and must be worthy, at least in appearance, of his master. Other heroes in *Roland* dress themselves in the same way, but special attention is given to Ganelon because his departure is the sign for an important development in the story. So too the poet of *Gilgamish* more than once insists that his hero is cleansed and clothed. The first occasion looks simple enough. When Gilgamish comes back from the slaying of Humbaba, he is stained with blood and removes the traces of the fight :

> He washes his stains,
> He cleanses his tattered garments,
> He braids his hair over his shoulders,
> He lays aside his dirty garments,
> He clothes himself in clean ones,
> He puts on armlets,
> He girds his body with a baldric,
> Gilgamish binds his fillet,
> He girds himself with a baldric.[3]

---

[1] *Il.* xiv, 170-86.   [2] *Roland*, 342-8.
[3] *Gilgamish*, VI, i, 1-5.

This may seem a merely mechanical interlude to mark the end of a bloody episode. But it is more than that. It is because Gilgamish does this, that the goddess Ishtar realises his beauty and wishes him to be her husband, and from that much follows. Again, later in the poem, before leaving Uta-Napishtim at the end of the world, Gilgamish is bathed and given fresh clothing :

> Ur-Shanabi took him,
> And led him where he might bathe him.
> He washed his stains in the water like snow,
> He put off his pelts,
> And the sea bore them away ;
> Fair did his body appear ;
> He renewed the fillet on his head,
> He garbed himself in a mantle
> To clothe his nakedness,
> Such that when he reached his city
> Or finished his journey,
> The mantle would not betray its age
> But keep its freshness.[1]

This too has a definite purpose. Gilgamish still hopes to win immortality and still has a chance of doing so. For this reason it is unfitting that he should be unkempt and filthy as he is after his long journey to Uta-Napishtim. So the poet describes in detail the cleansing and the clothing which have almost a ritual significance and are relevant to his main theme.

Heroic poetry naturally abounds in accounts of warriors arming themselves. Such are necessary to keep up the reality of a world at war and to show with what weapons a hero fights. The audience knows about weapons and will listen attentively to any mention of them. Homer usually describes such scenes of arming in a succinct and economical way, omitting nothing that matters but not worrying about details. When he lets himself go, as he does with the shield of Achilles or on a lesser scale with the armour of Agamemnon, he has a special purpose in wishing to display his hero's might through his accoutrements. Sometimes he gives the elementary details but no more, as a necessary preliminary to the record of some action. It may seem unexciting but is none the less needed, especially when the armour belongs to some important hero like Hector or Paris. Other poets do much the same thing, and are not afraid of introducing passages which are useful pieces of mechanism but little more. In a heroic world most warriors use the same arms, and the variations between them are confined to such matters as size and weight and decoration. If a warrior likes

[1] *Ibid.* XI, i, 246-54.

something out of the way, we are told about it, and a special point is made of it. But ordinarily much is taken for granted. When descriptions of armour are needed, they are provided, but not too much time is given to them.

However, when the hero sets out on an unusual errand, the nature of his arms may be of some importance, especially when he sets out to fight some monster, whose habits are unfamiliar to the audience and arouse curiosity about the way to tackle it. So, when Gilgamish goes to fight Humbaba, his townsmen see that he is properly armed :

> They brought monstrous axes,
> Into his hand they gave the bow and the quiver ;
> He took a celt and slung on his quiver ;
> He took another celt and fastened a knife to his girdle.[1]

The weapons show how Gilgamish starts on a strange quest. Although in fact he kills Humbaba less by his own weapons than by the help of winds sent by the Sun-god, yet he cuts off Humbaba's head ; so his arms, though not so effective as his townsmen may have hoped, are not entirely useless. A similar technique may be seen in *Beowulf*. When the hero prepares to fight Grendel's Dam, he does not rely, as with Grendel himself, on his bare hands but arms himself carefully. The point of honour which prevented him from taking on an unarmed Grendel with weapons no longer operates, since, it seems, he is afraid of the Dam's hideous grip and arms himself against it. So the poet describes the arming at length and throws in a comment or two to show what it means :

> He would in his war-byrny   braided by hand,
> Broad and broidered with skill,   brave the deep sound ;
> Well could it shelter   the sheath of his bones
> That the battle-grip   might not his breast,
> Nor the angry clutch   his spirit injure ;
> But the white helmet   his head warded,
> Which on the mere's floor   was to mingle,
> To seek the sound's tumult —   with treasure made worthy,
> With fine chains compassed,   as in former days
> The weapon-smith wrought it,   with wonders adorned it,
> Beset it with swine-figures,   so that since then no
> Brand nor battle-blade   managed to bite it.[2]

Beowulf puts on the best armour that he can find, and the poet takes pride in it. But even this armour is not going to be enough. His helmet, as is carefully pointed out, will fall off in the monster's

---

[1] *Gilgamish*, III, vi, 10-13.
[2] *Beowulf*, 1443-54. For the " swine-figures " cf. Klaeber, Plate 3, for a helmet from Vendel, Uppland, made at the close of the seventh century.

den, and the sword which he takes with him will prove to be useless. The old theme is used to show how even the best weapons may not be sufficient for so fierce an encounter as that which Beowulf faces.

Sometimes the clothes or the armour which a hero puts on are connected with a special occasion in his life and derive additional interest from it. In the Ainu *Kutune Shirka* the hero has led a very cloistered life until he hears of the golden otter. One night he cannot sleep because the gods keep him awake, and he tosses on his bed. It is still dark, and his brother and sister are snoring. Then he makes his decision :

> Suddenly, there on my bed,
> I stretched myself, and at one bound
> I was up on my feet.
> I went to the treasure-pile,
> I fumbled about in it
> And pulled out a basket,
> A basket finely-lacquered.
> The cords that bound it
> One after another I untied ;
> I tilted off the cover.
> I plunged my hand into the basket :
> An embroidered coat,
> A graven belt-sword,
> A belt clasped with gold,
> A little golden helmet —
> All of them together
> I tumbled out.
> The embroidered coat
> I thrust myself into,
> The golden clasped belt
> I wound about me.
> The cords of the little helmet
> I tied for myself,
> So that it sat firm on my head.
> The graven sword
> I thrust through my belt.
> And though I tell it of myself,
> I looked splendid as a god,
> Splendid as a great god
> Returning in glory.
> And there upon the mat,
> Though I had never seen them,
> I copied deeds of battle, deeds of war,
> Spreading my shoulders, whirling round
> and round.[1]

[1] Trs. Arthur Waley, *Botteghe Oscure*, vii (1951), pp. 217-18.

At divine prompting the young hero has suddenly found himself and his calling. Though it is a new thing for him to put on armour or make use of it, he does so naturally and easily and knows exactly what he is doing. Of course he enjoys the process and takes pride in his unaccustomed accoutrements. The armour itself has nothing unusual about it; what matters is its relevance to the occasion.

Closely allied to descriptions of dressing and arming are those of heroes who disguise themselves or have their appearance in some way altered. Here too the poet operates on an accepted idea of what a hero's dress and appearance ought to be and secures his effects by the kind of change which something may produce in it. His first duty is to explain what the change is and what results it produces. When he has done that, he can secure other effects which are less essential but add to the variety of the poetry. This may be done shortly and swiftly, if the poet has an eye for the main point. When Alaman Bet wishes to insinuate himself into the household of the sorceress Kanyshai, it is well for him to be disguised, since, if he appears as a Kara-Kirghiz, he will be killed at once. He reconnoitres the ground, finds a watering-place frequented by guards, and sees at it one of them filling twelve ox-skins with water:

> Alaman Bet rose in front of him,
> Cut off his head in a moment,
> Threw it into the clear stream,
> And over his own clothes put
> The clothes of that guard;
> His pig-tail, like a stick,
> He fastened to his own head.
> He took up the twelve ox-skins
> Filled to the brim with water,
> Did Alaman Bet, the great hero,
> And went straight to the household
> Of the sorceress giantess.[1]

This is short and simple but decisive. Alaman Bet is sufficiently disguised for his purpose and ready for the adventures which await him, while for the Kara-Kirghiz audience his action shows not only his swift power of decision but his superiority to vulgar considerations in not shrinking from disguising himself as a despised Chinese.

Of course if a hero is renowned for his cunning, his disguise will reflect it and show what a good actor he is. So in *The Stealing of the Mare* Abu Zeyd tells how he makes himself look like a

[1] *Manas*, p. 256.

wandering beggar before he goes to the encampment of his worst
enemy to steal his mare :

And I reached my hand to my wallet and found in it things needful,
And I took from it an onion and an egg-shell of the ostrich,
And made a fire on the ground with twigs of the wild willow,
And in a golden bowl I mixed and turned the ingredients,
Then whitened I my beard and limned my face with wrinkles,
Lowering my brows a little and darkening one of my eyelids,
And I crooked my back like a bow, a bow bent for the shooting,
And donned my clothes of disguise, that seeing none might know me.[1]

This is almost professional in its accomplishment and befits the
wily spirit of Abu Zeyd. Later in the poem he has to disguise
himself anew. He has stolen the mare, but the girl who helped
him to do so is in trouble because of it, and he has to go back to
help her. This time his disguise is even more skilful, and he is
every whit as proud of it :

And I took from my back my wallet, and shook the dust from its
    leather,
And I loosed the buttons all, and searched its inner recesses,
And took from it a dress should serve me for disguisement,
Unguents and oil of salghan, and red beans and essalkam,
And I roasted them on the fire till they were ripe and ruddy.
And I whitened my beard with chalk, and pulled down my
    mustachios,
And dyed my face with saffron till my cheeks glowed like apples ;
And I wrinkled the skin of my brows and crooked my back like a
    bent bow,
And leaned upon my staff. For am I not, O people,
A man of infinite wiles, a cunning man, a deceiver ?
And over the rest of my clothes I set the garb of a dervish,
And held a pot in my hand, even of the pots of the beggars.[2]

Here, as in Homer's account of Hera's beautifying process, the
poet uses stock themes with much brilliance and dash to secure a
special effect. Each item in the catalogue of the " make up " may
be stock, but the result is exciting and dramatic. It shows that
Abu Zeyd, the great hero, enjoys himself on such an errand as
much as Odysseus does. Indeed we may imagine that, when he
prepared himself to go as a spy into Troy, Odysseus took similar
care to disguise himself. For, as Helen tells the story :

Bruising himself with unseemly blows, and over his shoulders
Throwing a hideous rag, like some poor drudge of the household,
Into the fine broad streets of the enemies' city he entered,
In his disguise appearing a different person, a beggar,
He who was far from such when among the ships of Achaeans.[3]

[1] Blunt, ii, p. 144. [2] *Idem*, pp. 190-91. [3] *Od.* iv, 244-8.

In such adventures the paradox of the hero who assumes a lowly guise calls for detailed treatment.

A special interest attaches to those women who for some reason put on men's clothing. They may not necessarily wish to be thought to be men, or have any other reason than that such clothing is useful for some specific purpose. So when the Bulgarian girl, Penka, wishes to pay a last visit to the haiduks, with whom she has consorted in the past, she does not wish to pass for a man but simply to dress as men do, because that is demanded by the adventurous conditions of their life. She tells her mother:

> " I have a request to make you,
> Then address it to my father:
> That he give to me a dowry,
> Give me also a man's costume,
> Give me too a pair of pistols,
> Give me too a Frankish sabre,
> Give me too a great long rifle;
> Like a man I wish to live now,
> For two days or three days, mother,
> Or maybe for three hours only,
> On the mountain with the haiduks." [1]

Penka duly dresses herself in this style, visits the haiduks, and takes a stately farewell of them. Nothing remarkable is attempted, but the male clothing gives a touch of colour and character. When the Russian heroine, the wife of Staver, hears that her husband has been thrown into prison by Vladimir, she sees that she alone can rescue him and must use her wits to do so. She must go to the court and see what can be done there: so she disguises herself as a man. The poet pays little attention to the action and treats it in a very matter-of-fact way, as a mere piece of mechanics:

> Very, very quickly she ran to the barber,
> Cut off her hair like a young man,
> Transformed herself into Vasili Mikulich,
> Collected a bold company
> Of forty bold archers,
> Forty bold wrestlers,
> And rode to the city of Kiev. [2]

This too is perfectly factual and straightforward. Staver's wife is engaged on a bold errand, for which disguise is necessary, but she treats this transformation of herself from Vasilissa Mikulichna into Vasili Mikulich in a nonchalant spirit, as if it were part of the ordinary conduct of life.

[1] Dozon, p. 28. [2] Rybnikov, i, p. 204.

This device can be given a greater complexity when the issues involved are less simple. In the Canaanite *Aqhat*, Aqhat's father, Daniel, decides that he must exact vengeance for the murder of his son, but he does not know who the murderer is. He himself is too old to do anything; so he turns to his daughter, Paghat, who is renowned chiefly for her excellent conduct of domestic affairs, and charges her with the task. She proceeds with some care:

> She fetches up a fish from the sea,
> Washes and rouges herself
> With the red dye of that cosmetic of the sea
> Which comes from the " wild ox " whose emission
>   is on the sea.
> Then she takes and puts on the garb of a warrior,
> Places the knife in its sheath,
> Places the sword in its scabbard ;
> And above she dons the garb of a woman,
> But beneath that of a soldier.[1]

Paghat does a double task. She both emphasises her femininity by painting her face with some mysterious substance which may be connected with the cuttle-fish, and arms herself like a man underneath her woman's clothing. She knows what she is doing. She hopes, when she has found the murderer, to allure him with her charms and then to kill him. And this in fact she does. When by a happy chance she comes upon Yatpan, he welcomes her and offers her wine. Attracted, no doubt, by her beauty, he boasts of the men whom he has killed, and so reveals himself as the murderer. He then gets drunk, and Paghat has no difficulty in killing him. Her disguise is peculiar but needed for a special purpose. That is why it is described with some care.

A third item in the mechanics of narrative consists of feasts, entertainments and the like. Poets are not ashamed to speak, even at some length, about eating and drinking. Heroes have healthy appetites as befit their ebullient vitality and their life of action. It is fitting that when he goes spying, Odysseus should have three meals in the course of a night.[2] It is the other side of his ability to spend two days and two nights without food in the sea. The notice which poets take of food and drink is a tribute to the physical virtues of their heroes. But it is also more than this. The giving of feasts is a sign of princely generosity and splendour. By his conduct of convivial occasions the hero shows a new side of his mastery of men and things. Since food and drink are a

---

[1] Gaster, p. 309 ff. ; cf. Gordon, p. 100. The " wild ox " is variously explained as the whale, the ray-fish, and the cuttle-fish.
[2] *Il*. ix, 91 ff., 218 ff. ; x, 578.

necessary part of life, the heroic world insists that they should be
treated with style and dignity.

Descriptions of feasts are often enough perfunctory, as if they
were introduced mainly to keep the story going. This is what
Homer on the whole does. The great man entertains guests, but
not too much bother is made about it, nor usually do we hear
more than—

He set before them a feast to give their hearts' satisfaction ;
They stretched hands to the dainties which lay all ready before them.[1]

The Russian poets do the same kind of thing, though not quite
with the Homeric brevity. At Prince Vladimir's court the
Princess Apraxya carves swans for the guests to eat, while they sit
in order of eminence at oaken tables and eat " sweet food " and
drink " honeyed drink ". This is the stock form, of which the
main elements are hardly varied. The Norse poets are even more
succinct, as when Knefröth comes to Atli with his fatal invitation
to Gunnar :

To Gjuki's home came he   and to Gunnar's dwelling,
With benches round the hearth,   and to the beer so sweet.
Then the followers, hiding   their falseness, all drank
Their wine in the war-hall,   of the Huns' wrath wary.[2]

In another version the messengers are received with princely
hospitality :

Then the famed ones brought mead,   and fair was the feast,
Full many were the horns,   till the men had drunk deep.[3]

The feast must be mentioned if the setting and the situation are
to be understood, but there is no need to elaborate it.

This economy is often abandoned when the needs of the
narrative demand something more detailed. Homer, for instance,
is well aware that when Odysseus sets out on his perilous voyage
from Calypso, he needs meat and drink :

The goddess set in the boat one skin of red wine, and another
Large one filled with water, and store of food in a wallet,
And many dainties she set therein to his heart's satisfaction.[4]

We do not hear that Odysseus eats and drinks of this supply, but
it is enough that it is mentioned. It shows the practical spirit in
which he sets out on his voyage. A Jugoslav poet is less shy about
speaking of a meal *al fresco*. When Birčanin Ilija is out in the

[1] *Il.* ix, 90-91, 220-21 ; xxiv, 626-7 ; *Od.* i, 148-9, etc.
[2] *Atlakvitha*, 1-2.   [3] *Atlamál*, 8, 1-2.   [4] *Od.* v, 265-7.

country on a dubious quest, he thinks of food and eats a comfort-
able luncheon, despite the presence of danger :

> Then the servant brought the bag with victuals,
> Things to eat and drink he took from out it
> In accordance with his master's orders.
> Ílija quickly seized the wooden bottle
> That was wound around with plaited rushes
> And was filled with potent šljívovica
> That was rather older than Ílija.
> And he drew out cakes of bread unleavened,
> With the cakes dried meat and cheese producing,
> That they might eat something with the brandy.[1]

This is a picnic held in a hurry, but the poet enjoys telling how
even in such a moment the hero lives up to his standards by doing
himself well.

The pleasures of eating and drinking may not always be very
dignified, and some poets like to tell how heroes get drunk. This
is not to the taste of Homer, who uses the adjective " heavy with
wine " as a term of abuse and contempt,[2] and whose chief drunkard
is the Cyclops. But other poets are more tolerant. Indeed, a
Kalmuck regards it as a desirable element in a convivial occasion :

> In the beautiful wood in the spring-time,
> In the motley yellow chamber like a picture,
> With his six thousand and twelve warriors
> As beautiful as the sun,
> At the tables set for vodka,
> He drinks and makes merry.
> His warriors grow hot and drunken
> With the wine with which Dzhangar regales them.[3]

There are of course no hints of unseemly behaviour. The heroes
still conduct themselves with heroic propriety. Indeed delight in
drink and intoxication are often regarded as proper to a hero,
worthy of his physical strength and ebullient nature. The
Armenian hero, David of Sasoun, is not above being drunk for
several days even in a time of danger and crisis, and the poet seems
to approve of his behaviour as showing his superiority to ordinary
rules. When David has succeeded in winning Khandut to be his
bride, he celebrates his success with wine :

> David said : " Where have we a cask of wine ?
> I shall have bread and begin to eat.
> From my soul I wish to wash off the dust.
> Here I cannot wash my tongue.

---

[1] Morison, p. 28. [2] *Il.* i, 225.
[3] *Dzhangariada*, p. 110.

Am I a sparrow to pour water on myself,
Am I a camel to drink from a spoon ? "
They hurried to the house in search of a great cup,
And the cup was as big as a basin.
They gave David to drink from that cup.
David was drunk and became gay.
Drunkenness took David and carried him off.
David was drunk, he hung his head on his breast.[1]

In this condition David looks an easy prey to his enemies, who prepare to kill him, but each time that he raises his head, they are frightened and do nothing, with the result that, when David recovers, he kills them. Even in drink a hero keeps his essential nature.

In the Kara-Kirghiz *Manas* the theme of a feast is used for a special purpose. The khans have plotted against Manas, and he skilfully contrives to humiliate them. He invites them to his dwelling, and his wife, Kanykai, helps him to entertain them so handsomely that they repent of their plans and acknowledge Manas' power and superiority. Here too the theme of drunkenness has a part. In making her guests drunk Kanykai behaves as a hostess should, but the khans show their inferior nature by succumbing too quickly to the drinks which she provides. She sets about her task in a conscientious spirit :

> To boil the flesh of a white horse,
> That she might entertain the warriors,
> Generous Kanykai gave orders.
> On empty stomachs the guests began to drink.
> Strong arak made them drunk ;
> They were drugged then
> By drinking kumys,
> They were bewitched then
> By the tables painted with pictures,
> They made jests then
> To the generous maidens.
> There was a buzzing in their heads,
> Their bowels began to burn,
> Drops of sweat glistened on their lips,
> Their tongues were loosened.
> Fresh drinks Kanykai
> Now had brought to them,
> Joy she poured out to them ;
> Modesty humbled them.[2]

The intoxication which is suitable enough for David in a moment of triumph is not equally suitable for the khans. They show their

[1] *David Sasunskii*, p. 273.　　　　　[2] *Manas*, p. 96.

inferiority to the great man against whom they have plotted and who now humbles them.

In contrast with these drunken revels we may set the scene in *Beowulf* when Hrothgar gives a feast to celebrate the rout of Grendel. The poet insists that this is highly decorous :

> Nor have I heard that a muster   of men so many
> About their booty-giver   bare themselves better.[1]

He is less interested in the pleasures of eating and drinking than in the gifts which are presented and the spirit in which they are received. The king gives Beowulf an ensign of gold and a suit of armour, and Beowulf accepts them with dignified gratitude. The company celebrates a notable occasion in good fellowship, and the poet applauds their temper :

> Nor have I heard that more friendliwise   four treasures
> Any gold-girdled   groups of men
> At the ale-benches each   upon other bestowed.[2]

The presentation of gifts is followed by a lay from the court-minstrel in the Homeric manner, and after it more gifts are bestowed. Then the queen, Wealhtheow, makes a speech to Beowulf, wishing him fame and happiness and wealth and hoping that he will help her sons as he has helped her husband. She ends with praise of her own court for its unity and obedience :

> " Here is every earl   by the others trusted,
> Mild of mood,   to the Master loyal,
> The thegns are kindly,   the commons all in readiness.
> Drinking, the nobles   do as I bid them." [3]

This is certainly not like the spirit of Tatar or Armenian revels. The poet's Christian outlook and love of decorum have invaded his ideas of what heroes should do when they relax.

On some occasions songs are sung at feasts for the amusement and pleasure of the guests and for no other reason. In Phaeacia Odysseus hears not only heroic songs but the scandalous lay of Ares and Aphrodite, which is not intended to do anything more than amuse. At such times the host or hostess takes pains to see that the bard or the singers do their task with a high degree of accomplishment and win the admiration of the chief guest. So in *The Stealing of the Mare* Abu Zeyd is entertained on a royal scale by the maiden, Alia, whose life he has saved. Both the feast and the music are on an unusually high level and reveal a refined taste for good living :

[1] *Beowulf*, 1011-12.   [2] *Ibid.* 1027-9.   [3] *Ibid.* 1128-31.

And when the meal was done then poured they fair potations,
Drinking in jewelled cups with skilled musicians and singers,
(Where should the like be found ?) for they sang in such sweet
measure
That, if a bird had heard, it had stooped from its way in heaven.
In figure and trope they sang, of four-and-twenty stanzas.
And Alia chose eight players, the cunningest among them,
Four for the lute and viol, and four for hymns and chauntings.
Each sate him down and played, and they sang with pleasant voices.[1]

In a world where song and music are appreciated by everyone, and
judged by exacting standards, only the best is good enough for the
hero, especially when, like Abu Zeyd, he has saved the life of his
hostess.

It is but a small way from singing to dancing, and on festal
occasions the dance often occurs as a fitting accompaniment to
general rejoicing. The poet may describe it in a simple and
matter-of-fact way as a small part in a general subject. So the
Ossete poet does not trouble to say too much about a dance, which
forms a minor part of his story :

> Sometimes the Narts went to the public square,
> Gathered for the dance on the open playground,
> They danced the *simd* — no simple dance is it —
> Such a dance is it that the earth shivered,
> The earth quaked beneath the young men's feet.[2]

The Bulgarian poet treats a dance in a similar manner in the *Tale of
Kolio*, where Kolio collects men together by the power of his music :

> Kolio obeyed his orders,
> And he took with him his bag-pipe
> And he went to Stambul city,
> To Stambul of seven towers,
> To the inn of seven towers,
> Where the Sultan's beasts are slaughtered.
> Kolio played upon his bag-pipe,
> And the young men gathered round him,
> They were thirty and three hundred,
> Some three hundred new companions.
> Kolio led them off with him,
> Led them to the captain Pancho.[3]

In these cases the dance and song are merely a part of a more
important action, but the poet pauses for a moment on them just
to make them vivid, before going on to his main theme.

It is not quite the same thing when a dance or other display is
held at some important festival. Then the poet may wish to make

---

[1] Blunt, ii, p. 178. [2] Dynnik, p. 47. [3] Dozon, p. 47.

something special of it. Weddings and the like may demand
dances as a necessary part of the ritual. So an Esthonian poem tells
how, when two great heroes are married, one of them gives a great
display with his bride :

> After this they danced the cross-dance,
> Waltzed the waltzes of Esthonia,
> And they danced the Arju dances,
> And the dances of the West Land ;
> And they danced upon the gravel,
> And they trampled on the greensward,
> Starry youth and maiden Salme
> Thus their nuptials held in rapture.[1]

Homer seems to have known something of the same kind. He
speaks of " the dancing-place which Daedalus made in broad
Cnossus for the fair-haired Ariadne ",[2] and perhaps he records
memories of dances held in the great courtyard of the Minoan
palace. So too at the court of Alcinous, after Demodocus has sung
of Ares and Aphrodite, two dancers of special excellence do a turn
in which they bend backwards, throw a ball up, leap, and catch it
while still themselves in the air. After this they dance with many
changes, and the other men, who stand round, beat time on the
ground.[3] Wilder and more varied but hardly different in kind is
the scene of gaiety described by a Yakut poet :

> Nine days and nights on end the feast lasted,
> And they played every play without growing weary.
> Then the women danced !
> Then the strong men struggled !
> Then the runners competed in speed !
> Then friend with friend in rivalry
> Tried to leap on one leg !
> Nine days and nights on end, they say,
> They danced and played.
> Then the hungry man ate his fill.
> Then the lean man made merry.[4]

In hardly any of these cases are the dances indispensable to the
story, but they give substance and solidity to it.

There is at least one case where a dance really affects the action,
and then the poet has to do something special about it. When
Alaman Bet insinuates himself, disguised as a Chinese, into the
house of the sorceress, Kanyshai, he finds a feast in progress and
joins in the dancing. But here the poet has a special concern. His
account of the actual dancing is short and conventional. What

[1] Kirby, i, p. 14.   [2] *Il.* xviii, 590 ff.
[3] *Od.* viii, 370 ff.   [4] Yastremski, p. 45.

interests him particularly are its results. Alaman Bet is surrounded
by enemies, but boldly dances away, and his dancing has a notable
result on Kanyshai :

> Kanyshai on her throne,
> On her golden throne,
> Watches how Alaman dances :
> His dancing steals away her wits !
> Her body grows weary,
> She sighs for Alaman,
> Her passions are inflamed,
> She dreams of bliss,
> That Alaman embraces her,
> That Alaman kisses her.
> She is sick with desire,
> She is weak before Alaman,
> She sees his hot lips,
> She sees his white teeth,
> She sees his round hands,
> She sees his strong limbs !
> Her memory fails, she swoons,
> She comes back to consciousness,
> Fires consume her within.[1]

In this condition Kanyshai is in no condition to resist Alaman Bet
when he pretends to make love to her ; she delivers herself into
his power and is killed.

A fourth common theme is that of sailing. Unknown to
inland peoples, it naturally appeals to those who live by the sea,
and has developed standard forms and interesting variations. Its
basic elements are short descriptions of putting a ship to sea,
travelling, and coming to shore. Such at least is necessary to move
a hero from one place to another, and in its simplest form the
theme often occurs. But it often does more than describe a mere
change of place by the hero. The poets know the sea too well not
to introduce some additional poetry which has its own charm.
Homer sets the tone when he tells how Telemachus prepares a
ship and puts to sea. Homer's audience, we may be sure, knows
all about ships and will be interested and critical about any factual
details. The ship of imagination must be every whit as real as a
ship of common life. Homer is aware of this and shows that he
understands about sailing. First, the ship is made ready :

> Smart at the word they obeyed, and raised up the mast made of
>   pine-wood,
> Firm in the deep mast-box they fixed it and tied it with forestays,
> Hoisting the white sails up with twisted halyards of ox-hide.[2]

[1] *Manas*, p. 257.　　　　　　　　　　[2] *Od*. ii, 424-6.

The professional preliminary establishes the ship's reality, but from this Homer advances to tell how the ship starts and gets under way, and to this he gives his own quiet poetry, though it is only an incidental feature in the narrative :

Under the breeze the sail bellied out ; the blue wave was divided
Roaring about her bows, as the ship gathered way through the water.
Over the waves she darted in haste to accomplish her journey.
Then in the swift black ship they set to tighten the tackle
And bowls brim-full of wine they put for themselves on the benches,
Pouring out some to the gods who are ageless and everlasting,
Chiefly to that great daughter of Zeus, the grey-eyed Athene.
All night long till the morning the good ship passed on her journey.[1]

The ship of Telemachus sails as other ships sail, and Homer's account of her keeps to familiar facts, but from them he extracts a charming poetry, not merely in the sense of the ship making her own way with the wind behind her but in the account of what is done aboard in the performance of the rites customary to men at sea. When the ship comes to land, the ritual is fixed and the same proceedings usually take place. The ship is driven on to the beach, and then the crew take off the sails and furl them, and come to land. This done, they turn the ship round, so that she can start again when occasion demands.[2] It is all very simple and straightforward, but correct and true to fact. Homer might have omitted these details and indeed said no more than that Telemachus sails from one place to another. But by making the voyage circumstantial he gives an additional strength and charm to his story.

Something of the same kind may be seen in *Beowulf*, where the poet feels to some degree the appeal of ships and the sea, though scarcely with Homer's discerning eye for its many beauties. His epithets and descriptive phrases are picturesque enough and show that at least his teachers were sea-faring men who knew the lure of great waters. He exercises his own kind of art when he tells how Beowulf sails home after his adventures in Jutland. Beneath the mannered style we can detect not only a sound sense of fact but a delight in recalling how a ship gets going before a wind and takes the waves lightly :

Then was to the mast   one of the mer-sheets,
A sail, rope-fastened ;   the sea-wood roared ;
Nor that wave-floater   did the wind over the waters
Hinder from sailing ;   the sea-goer started,
Floated, foamy-necked,   forth over the waves,
The banded stem   over brimming streams.[3]

[1] *Ibid.* 427-34.   [2] *Ibid.* iii, 10-11.   [3] *Beowulf*, 1905-10.

If this is an Anglo-Saxon counterpart to Telemachus' voyage, we may also compare his landing at Pylos with Beowulf's in Jutland. Nor in this is the Anglo-Saxon poet entirely inferior. He catches at least the charm of the moment when land is sighted, and speaks of it with a decorous thrill:

> on the second day
> Her winding stem   had waded so far
> That the sailors   land could see,
> Shore-cliffs shining,   mountains sheer,
> Spreading sea-nesses.[1]

The landing itself is dismissed quickly, almost without any detail except that the ship is made fast. The Anglo-Saxon poet has a less steady eye than Homer, and at this point hurries unwontedly to get on with his story.

It may be doubted whether the poet of *Roland* knew the sea so well as Homer or the poet of *Beowulf*, and indeed ships only once play an important part in his poem. Baligant comes from Babylon to help the Saracen king, Marsilies, and he has to come by sea. The poet's interest is less in sailing than in the preparations and appearance of a great fleet:

> His great dromonds, he made them all ready,
> Barges and skiffs and ships and galleries;
> Neath Alexandre, a haven next the sea,
> In readiness he gat his whole navy.
> That was in May, first summer of the year,
> All of his hosts he launched upon the sea.[2]

Once prepared, the fleet puts to sea, but what interests the poet is not the technical details of its voyage but its brilliance, and he dwells with a special insistence on the lights which gleam on it at night:

> Great are the hosts of that opposèd race;
> With speed they sail, they steer and navigate,
> High on their yards at their mast-heads they place
> Lanterns enough, and carbuncles so great
> Thence, from above, such light they dissipate
> The sea's more clear at midnight than by day.
> And when they come into the land of Spain
> All that country lightens and shines again.[3]

This case presents points of interest. The poet clearly feels that he must tell how Baligant gets from Egypt to Spain and therefore goes through the usual mechanism of building a fleet and putting it to sea. But the actual sailing is either too dull or too unfamiliar for

---

[1] *Beowulf*, 219-23.   [2] *Roland*, 2624-9.   [3] *Ibid.* 2630-37.

him to say anything about it. He concentrates instead on the fleet's brightness at night, and no doubt this is intended to stress the wealth and brilliance of the men who come from the East to help Marsilies. He says nothing which is impossible, and he is quite within the navigation of his time in making the fleet sail up the Ebro, since it was said to be navigable even beyond Saragossa. But the factual element is subordinated, not without art, to the impression of brilliance.

The Norse poets seldom have time to speak of the mere mechanism of sailing, and if they do so, it is because it is relevant to their story. For instance, in *Atlamál* when Gjuki and his companions go to Atli, they go by sea, as suits a poem said to have been composed in Greenland. The poet gives only a quatrain to the voyage, but in it shows the heroic strength of his characters and their eagerness to get to their goal :

> Full stoutly they rowed,　and the keel clove asunder,
> Their backs strained at the oars,　and their strength was fierce.
> The oar-loops were burst,　the thole-pins were broken,
> Nor the ship made they fast　ere from her they fared.[1]

When, however, ships play an essential part in the action, the poet gives them their due recognition and shows how well he understands their ways. This is the case with one of the poems on Helgi Hundingsbane. When he takes his fleet into Stafnsnes the poet dwells on its gallant air :

> Soon off Stafnsnes　stood the ships,
> Fair they glided　and gay with gold.[2]

Once in harbour, Helgi prepares for battle, and the poet gives a clear account of clearing the decks and waking the sailors :

> The ship's tents soon　the chieftain struck,
> And waked the throng　of warriors all ;
> The heroes the red of　dawn beheld ;
> And on the masts　the gallant men
> Made fast the sails　in Varinsfjord.[3]

At each move of Helgi's fleet the poet finds something to say which both illustrates the action and is an implicit comment on Helgi's behaviour, as when he defies the elements and sails into the rough sea :

> Helgi bade higher　hoist the sails,
> Nor did the ships'-folk　shun the waves.[4]

[1] *Atlamál*, 34.　　　[2] *Helgakvitha Hundingsbana*, i, 24, 1-2.
[3] *Ibid.* 27.　　　[4] *Ibid.* 30, 1-2.

This was composed by a man who felt the call of ships and knew that their management betrays a man's nature. His Helgi is a proud, reckless seaman who flaunts his character at sea.

A ship may reflect its owner's character in the splendour of its equipage and tackle. On such an occasion the poet, although following formulaic lines, may add a detail or so which gives an additional touch of style and brilliance, as the Russian poet does in his account of the visit of Nightingale Budimirovich to Prince Vladimir. His notion of ships is traditional, but by no means incorrect, and he uses the formulae for old-fashioned sailing-ships to produce a special effect of wealth and grandeur :

> Bravely were the ships adorned,
> Bravely were the ships bedecked.
> Stem and stern were shaped like an aurochs,
> The broad sides were in the fashion of an elk.
> The sails were of rich damask,
> The ships' anchors were of steel,
> The anchors had silver rings,
> The ropes were of the seven silks ;
> Where the rudder was, it was hung
> With precious sables from foreign lands ;
> Where the eyebrows should be, it was decked
> With precious foreign fox-skins ;
> In the place of the eyes it was inset
> With sapphire stones from foreign lands.[1]

Nightingale Budimirovich is a considerable person, who comes on an important errand, to seek the hand of Vladimir's niece in marriage. He must make a good impression and be worthy of the princess. A similar delight in a ship's appearance and a similar sense of the light which it throws on the owner may be seen in the Ukrainian *Samijlo Kishka* :

> From the city of Trebizond a galley advanced,
> Decked and adorned with three colours.
> The first of these colours,
> These are the banners of blue-gold ;
> The second of these colours,
> These are the cannons on the deck ;
> The third of these colours,
> These are the Turkish tents of white linen.
> On this galley walks Alkan Pasha,
> Young prince of Trebizond,
> Surrounded by his chosen men.[2]

The young Turkish prince has his own style and makes it felt even when he is at sea. Again, when a fleet sails to battle it may somehow

[1] Gilferding, i, p. 527 ; Chadwick, *R.H.P.* p. 116 ff.   [2] Scherrer, p. 72.

reflect the determined, warlike temper of its captain and his companions. This is the case in the Norse *Battle of Hafsfjord* when Harold Fairhaired sails into Hafsfjord to fight Kjötvi the Wealthy : [1]

> A fleet came from the east,   with figure-heads gaping,
> And with carved beaks,   in desire for battle,
> With warriors laden   and with white shields,
> With spears from the west,   and with swords from France.
>
> The berserks were howling,   the wolf-coats bawling ;
> Swords were clashing ;   war was in full swing.[2]

So too in *Hrafnsmal* the king's ships are briefly described with an eye to their master's wealth and power :

> Deep ships he commands
> With reddened stripes   and crimson shields,
> With tarred oars   and foam-splashed awnings.

The ship reveals the man, and a finely decked ship is testimony to its captain's greatness.

Ships may sometimes sail in unfamiliar seas and encounter unaccustomed dangers. Then the old mechanism has to be refurbished, and the formulae adapted to new uses. A modern Russian bard attempts such a task in telling of the adventures of the Russian ship *Chelyuskin* in the Arctic. Though the theme is contemporary, the treatment is, as far as possible, traditional. When the ship sails into the ice-floe, the captain faces danger in a truly heroic spirit :

> There, when evil enemies encountered them,
> Evil enemies, swimming blocks of ice,
> Long did they fight with those unfriendly ones ;
> They could not in any way escape their blows.
> Then a blow struck the *Chelyuskin* on the nose,
> The timber broke, the water poured in . . .
> Beard-to-the-knees, Captain Voronin,
> Did not wince at that blow,
> At the blow of that unfriendly rock.
> Beard-to-the-knees began to give orders,
> Captain Voronin began to give commands,
> That quickly, very quickly, all should be mended ;
> He summoned the master-locksmiths,
> By the speed of the masters all was repaired ;
> And the ship flew forward on her way
> In the ocean-sea of ice.[3]

Here an unprecedented situation is presented in words derived from quite a different world, but the treatment of the blocks of ice

---

[1] Kershaw, p. 90.   [2] *Idem*, p. 83.
[3] Nechaev, p. 287. No name is given for the author of the poem.

as attacking enemies and of the captain and his men as heroes fighting against fierce antagonists gives a new interest to the theme of sailing in dangerous seas.

A fifth conventional theme is that of horses and riding. The earliest exponent of this is Homer, whose heroes do not ride horses but drive them in chariots. So they go to battle, where the chariot plays a large part, or in peace-time visit their friends. Homer likes sometimes to give attention to the preparation of a chariot before it goes out. If he usually does this in a brief and even perfunctory way, he once at least devotes some care to it. When Priam sets out to ask Achilles for the body of Hector, sixteen lines are given to the preparation of his chariot. Priam's sons take down the chariot from where it is propped against a wall, take down the yoke, and fasten the yoke-band to it, being careful to see that the knot is secure.[1] The careful description is not necessary to the story, but it provides a dignified start and assumes that, since Priam is embarking on an important errand, anything concerned with it is interesting. Equally, when travellers reach their destinations, Homer tells how they dismount from their chariots and look after their horses. The chariot is propped up on end against a wall, and the horses are given corn and barley.[2] Homer prefers to dwell on the beginning and end of such journeys and says little about the journeys themselves, which he usually dismisses briefly in some such line as —

Then did he whip up the horses, and they sped eagerly onward.[3]

The important thing in this case is to mark the start and the end of a journey, and this is done simply and circumstantially.

Homer's method is paralleled in various other countries. When a hero sets out on his horse, we often hear something about his start, as when the Serb hero, Marko Kraljević, sets out :

> Then did he go down into his stable,
> And made ready his stout charger Šarac.
> First he covered him with a grey bear-skin,
> Then he bridled him with a steel bridle ;
> And he hung his heavy mace upon him,
> With a sword on either side about him,
> Flung himself upon the back of Šarac.[4]

Russian poets give fewer details but seldom fail to say something about saddling a horse before the hero goes out, as Dyuk does before his contest with Churilo :

[1] *Il.* xxiv, 265 ff. [2] *Od.* iv, 39 ff.
[3] *Ibid.* iii, 494. [4] Karadžić, ii, p. 231.

> Young Dyuk Stepanovich, the prince's son,
> Went into the spacious courtyard,
> And with his own hands saddled his good horse ;
> He saddled it and made it ready.[1]

So too his rival, the stylish Churilo, also saddles his horse :

> He saddles it with twelve saddles,
> He girds it with twelve girths,
> The girths were of silk,
> And the girth-straps of gold.[2]

When the Kalmuck, Khongor, gets ready for a dangerous expedition, the saddling of his horse is an important event :

> At the door of the hall
> He began to saddle his restive hot horse.
> He straightened and put on it a black saddle-cloth.
> On the four spans of tall withers
> He laid a saddle of forged gold,
> With a front arch of dull silver,
> With a saddle-tree of black sandalwood.
> He put on a breast-plate of yellow silk,
> Fitting it to the black breast-muscles.
> He clothed its tail in a cover
> Twenty-five times as long as a swan's neck.[3]

In each case, whether shortly or at length, the poet goes through the routine of telling how a horse is saddled, and in so doing adds something to our conception of the rider's character and purpose.

As the rider goes on his way, nothing much may happen to him, but few poets will be entirely silent about it. They may say no more than a very few words to indicate that so far all goes according to plan, as the Ossete poets do in their tales of Amran and his brothers. For them the merest reference suffices, like

> Day began to shine. They rode on,

or

> The brothers went on further,

or

> They rode on. They came to a valley.[4]

This is the minimum that such poetry demands, and it suffices to keep the audience aware of what is happening. So even the Norse poets of the *Elder Edda*, whose concentrated art usually leaves little place for the mechanics of narrative, sometimes pause to tell of someone riding and to add some small vivid touch, as when

[1] Rybnikov, i, p. 108. [2] Nechaev, p. 133.
[3] *Dzhangariada*, p. 114 ff. [4] *Amran*, pp. 45, 86, 49.

Guthrun relates how she and the Sons of Gjuki come to Atli's hall:

> Soon on horseback   each hero was,
> And the foreign women   in wagons faring;
> A week through lands   so cold we went; [1]

or when the heroes arrive at the hall and ride into it in all their clatter and splendour:

> Great was the clatter   of gilded hoofs
> When Gjuki's sons   through the gateway rode; [2]

or the sons of Guthrun set out on their fell mission to take vengeance from Jormunrek for the death of Svanhild:

> From the courtyard they fared,   and fury they breathed;
> The youths swiftly went   o'er the mountain wet,
> On their Hunnish steeds,   death's vengeance to have. [3]

In each of these cases something is added, whether to show the length and character of the journey or the pride of the horsemen or the spirit in which they ride. The brief sketches give a momentary glimpse of what happens and fit into the general pattern of the story. The poets keep their plots continuous by using this almost mechanical device, but at the same time succeed in making even the mechanics significant.

As the rider goes on his road, he may pass over country which the poet thinks worthy of mention, and the way in which the rider and horse take it throws light on them. So when Dobrynya is in a great hurry to reach Kiev before his wife marries Alyosha, he makes great demands of his horse:

> He took his silken whip,
> He beat his horse about the legs,
> About his legs, his hind legs,
> So that his horse set off at a gallop,
> From mountain to mountain, from hill to hill,
> Leaping rivers and lakes,
> Stretching his legs in full stride.
> It is not a bright falcon in full flight,
> It is a noble young man racing in his course. [4]

Though this is a special occasion and Dobrynya is in a great hurry, the poet tells of his passage much as any Russian poet tells of heroes riding even though they have nothing much to hurry about. The point is that, when heroes mount their horses, this is the way in which they should proceed. The Russian tradition

[1] *Guthrúnarkvitha*, ii, 36, 1-3.   [2] *Oddrúnargrátr*, 26, 1-2.
[3] *Hamthismál*, 12.   [4] Rybnikov, i, p. 165 ff.

is indeed remarkably stereotyped in this as in other matters, and it is perhaps profitable to contrast with it what a Kara-Kirghiz poet does when his heroes ride across country. When Alaman Bet and the young Syrgak ride in front of the army, the poet has an eye for the country through which they pass and its forbidding nature :

> On inaccessible mountain peaks,
> From summit to summit,
> Where waters flow not on the road,
> And no signs of grass can be found,
> Where the eyes see no feathered things,
> On the dented spurs of the mountains,
> Where the heat fails not all year round,
> Along the banks of dried-up rivers,
> On the sands of desolate valleys,
> Alaman Bet, son of Aziz Khan,
> Together with young Syrgak,
> By ways long known to them
> Hastened forward, spared not their horses,
> Without halting, for many days.[1]

Here the Kara-Kirghiz poet follows the tradition of his national art in using details to make a picture more real and more interesting. He describes a convincing landscape, such as we might expect to lie on the long road from the Tien-Shan to China and worthy of the heroes who pass through it and think little of its dangers. They have indeed a task to do, and their journey is part of it. So it deserves some attention, and the poet is right to make much of it.

The theme of riding is not confined to single riders or to pairs. There are times when whole companies and even armies go out on horseback and demand that something should be said about them. The mere effect of numbers is impressive enough, and much is added when the riders are proud and splendid in their best accoutrements. So the *Song of Roland* can, when grand events are afoot, rise to the occasion in high style. The Saracens make an impressive show when Roland and Oliver first see them at Roncesvalles :

> Fair shines the sun, the day is bright and clear,
> Light burns again from all their polished gear.
> A thousand horns they sound, more proud to seem ;
> Great is the noise, the Franks its echo hear.[2]

Later, when Charlemagne comes back to the battlefield and prepares to fight Baligant's army, the different Frankish columns,

[1] *Manas*, p. 236.   [2] *Roland*, 1002-5.

all of them on horseback, are treated with some attention and each receives some little distinguishing touch, like the Normans, whose horses " charge and prance ",[1] or the Bretons who " canter in the manner of barons ".[2] The poet knows something about cavalry and sees that the muster of a great army before its advance into Spain is an occasion for display. When all are gathered, the forward movement begins with some majesty :

> That Emperor canters in noble array,
> Over his sark all of his beard displays ;
> For love of him all others do the same,
> Five score thousand Franks are thereby made plain,
> They pass those peaks, those rocks and those mountains,
> Those terrible narrows and those deep vales,
> Then issue from the passes and the wastes
> Till they come into the March of Spain.[3]

This is a military movement on a big scale and requires careful handling. The poet gives force and speed to it and creates his own simple poetry for a large army of horsemen on the move.

With matters such as arrivals and departures, getting up and going to bed, feasts and celebrations, sailing, and riding, heroic poets fill in the interstices between their more impressive and exciting occasions. They may use these themes simply to keep the narrative going, to make clear what happens, and to maintain an air of reality. They may also use them for their own sake, because even simple matters of this kind may have a quiet charm and be interesting in their own right. So far they pursue the mechanics of narrative and are perfectly justified in doing so in an art which seeks to create a complete world of its own, sufficiently like the familiar world to cause no embarrassment. But sometimes they advance beyond these obvious needs and turn a familiar theme into something else, which sheds light on the hero's character or surroundings or has its own excitement from what happens. In this respect, as in others, heroic poetry uses its traditional devices freely and fruitfully, but feels no obligation to confine itself within them. If the poet chooses, he can leave tradition behind and try something new which has none the less a traditional background.

[1] *Roland*, 3047.   [2] *Ibid*. 3054.   [3] *Ibid*. 3121-8.

VI

THE TECHNIQUE OF COMPOSITION:
LANGUAGE

Almost without exception, heroic poetry is in the first place intended not for a reading but for a listening public. Famous poems may be written down to preserve them from oblivion, and in due course there comes a time, as came in France in the thirteenth century, when reading begins to have a vogue. But this comes when heroic poetry has passed its prime and begun to turn into something else. Both ancient and modern evidence points to the conclusion that the heroic poet composes what is to be heard and that his whole technique presupposes an audience listening to recitation. Ancient poems, like the *Odyssey* and *Beowulf*, show how bards at the courts of Odysseus and Hrothgar recite lays of heroic action to appreciative companies. Mediaeval French and Spanish epics abound in lines in which the poet addresses his public with such phrases as " I shall tell you " or " you will see " or " you have heard ".[1] Modern observers among the Jugoslavs, Russians, Greeks, Albanians, Ainus, and Asiatic Tatars report that it is the regular practice to chant or recite a heroic poem, and collections of such poems are made, directly or indirectly, from those who so perform them. An art which works in these conditions is necessarily different from one which caters for books and reading. It has its own peculiarities of technique which arise from the way in which the bard has to work. He has before him an audience, often large, which listens to him, and he has to keep its attention, to make everything clear and interesting, and, above all, not to lose the thread of his narrative. Though in matters of detail a listening public is less exacting than individual readers, it is more exacting about main episodes. It cannot skip the dull parts, and it insists on understanding what is told.

Recitation is the normal practice of heroic poetry because the societies in which it was born and bred were originally illiterate. But it is no longer confined to totally illiterate peoples. Indeed, in the modern world totally illiterate peoples seem not to have

---

[1] *Cid*, 2764, 3671, 1423; *Aliscans*, 249; *Gui de Bourgogne*, 4302; cf. R. Menéndez Pidal, *Poesía juglaresca y juglares*, p. 330 ff.

passed beyond the pre-heroic stage, if they have even reached so far, while heroic poetry is common among peoples who know something of writing. The different texts of *Gilgamish*, whether Babylonian or Hittite or Assyrian, come from societies in which the cuneiform script was used not merely for religious and legal texts but for hymns and annals. Homer mentions writing only once, and then in a mysterious way, when he tells of the " deadly signs " which Proetus, king of Corinth, writes in a " folded tablet " and sends to the king of Lycia with intent to compass the death of Bellerophon; [1] but this is probably a traditional feature in an ancient story and does not discredit the probability that writing existed in Homer's time and that he must have known its use. In the Norse *Atlamál* Guthrun tries to communicate with her brothers in a runic message and warn them of the doom which Atli is preparing for them, but Vingi tampers with the text and prevents it from being understood. [2] Nor in modern times are heroes necessarily illiterate. The Kara-Kirghiz Alaman Bet has no difficulty in reading the Koran when he becomes a Moslem. [3] Russian, Jugoslav, and Armenian heroes commonly write and read letters. Heroic poetry often exists in societies where writing is practised in some form. It can even exist by the side of a written literature which is contained in books. *Roland* mentions both Homer and Virgil, [4] and it is possible that Virgil was known, if only indirectly, to the author of *Beowulf*. [5] Of course the bards themselves tend to stand outside the world of letters and to rely on the spoken word, but even this rule has its exceptions. There are in Russia to-day singers of traditional songs, like Marfa Kryukova and Peter Ryabinin-Andreev, who are fond of reading but none the less compose poems for recitation in the old manner, partly because many among their audiences are illiterate, but chiefly because this kind of recitation is expected of them. Heroic poetry aims at recitation, and this explains many of its peculiarities.

Much heroic poetry is not only recited, but actually improvised. There are degrees and kinds of improvisation, and there are places where poets have passed beyond it to a more considered kind of composition, but improvisation is common and may well be the fundamental method of performance. The bard who recites a poem composes it in the act of recitation. This state of affairs would seem almost incredible if it were not guaranteed by impeccable witnesses. It is the normal practice among Russian bards. Gilferding observed that among the peasants of Lake Onega a

---

[1] *Il.* vi, 168-70 ; cf. Lorimer, p. 474. [2] *Atlamál*, 1.
[3] Radlov, v, p. 11.   [4] *Roland*, 2616.   [5] Klaeber, p. cxxi.

singer never sang a *bylina* twice in the same way,[1] and his evidence is confirmed by Rybnikov, who took down songs from the same singers on the same subjects as those heard by Gilferding, and we can examine the two sets of records.[2] For instance, the famous bard, Trofim Grigorevich Ryabinin, sang twenty-four lays to Rybnikov and eighteen to Gilferding, and the subjects of eight of these are common to both lists, but not one poem is identical with another. The main outlines are the same, but the details and the length differ, and the explanation is that Ryabinin created a new version of a poem each time that he recited it. He did not recall a text verbally but improvised a fresh text round certain fixed features in the story. Often enough the difference between two versions lies mainly in the varying space given to conventional themes and makes practically no difference to the total effect, but this is not always the case. When Ryabinin sang of Ilya of Murom and Tsar Kalin to Rybnikov [3] he gave quite a different story from that which he sang later to Gilferding.[4] The first version has 289 verses, and the second 616, and the difference of scale is to be explained by more than a mere expansion of common themes. The second poem has different episodes and almost a different temper. What is true of Ryabinin is true of other bards from the same district whose poems were recorded by Rybnikov and Gilferding, and the evidence is conclusive that here at least the bard does not repeat himself exactly but improvises afresh on each occasion.

Evidence for the practice of Jugoslav bards is not so complete as it is for Russian, but it indicates a similar state of affairs. Matthias Murko examined the methods of performance in Jugoslavia and discovered that the bards rely mainly on improvisation.[5] A bard may hear a poem only two or three times and be able to reproduce it, but he will not do so in the same words. To some extent each performance is a new creation. No bard repeats the same poem exactly word for word. Indeed in the course of years he may introduce such changes into a subject that it becomes unrecognisable. As he gets used to a theme, he may expand and enrich it until his final version is two or three times as long as his first. These observations were confirmed by Milman Parry in the thirties of this century. He too found that each performance by a poet produced what was virtually a new poem. Indeed, when he asked a poet to recite the same poem in the same words as on a previous occasion, the poet agreed to do so but produced in fact

[1] Gilferding, i, p. 32. [2] Chettéoui, p. 26 ff.
[3] Rybnikov, i, p. 35 ff. [4] Gilferding, ii, No. 75.
[5] *Zeitschr. d. Vereins f. Volkskunde* (Berlin, 1909), p. 13 ff.; *Sitzungsberichte d. k. k. Akademie in Wien*, Bd. 176 (1914–15).

something different. It is of course possible that some poems
have reached a kind of finality, and no one would dare to give them
a new form. But that is because they have been written down and
circulated and become widely known. Their texts have been
fixed, and they have passed into a national heritage. This is the
case with some of the poems about Kosovo which Vuk Karadžić
published in 1814. They have become classics, but that does not
mean that Karadžić himself repeated them from memory. The
poems which he published were collected by him from the bards
who sang them. Nor indeed has his collection prevented new
poems from being composed on the same subjects. Such are still
composed, as Murko and Parry found. The Jugoslav art of heroic
poetry is still one of improvisation.

A third example of improvisation can be found among the
Kara-Kirghiz. Their poetry was taken down by the great scholar,
V. Radlov, in the last forty years of the nineteenth century. His
account of what happens is explicit:

> Every minstrel who has any skill at all always improvises his songs
> according to the inspiration of the moment, so that he is not in a
> position to recite a song twice in exactly the same form. . . . The
> improvising minstrel sings without reflection, simply from his inner
> being, that which is known to him as soon as the incentive to sing
> comes from without, just as the words flow from the tongue of a
> speaker without his producing intentionally and consciously the articu-
> lations necessary to produce them, as soon as the course of his thoughts
> requires this or that word.[1]

Radlov describes authentic improvisation and notes some important results which follow from it. The minstrel needs an audience
to get him going. In its presence he finds that his imagination
works freely. The more the audience enjoys his skill in choosing
the right expressions, the better he does his work. The way
in which a Kara-Kirghiz bard works is described by the Russian
traveller Venyukov, who was attached to an expeditionary column
in 1860 and watched with admiration the extemporary performance of a minstrel:

> Every evening he attracted round him a crowd of gaping admirers,
> who greedily listened to his stories and songs. His imagination was
> remarkably fertile in creating feats for his hero — the son of some Khan
> — and took most daring flights into the regions of marvel. The greater
> part of the rapturous recitation was improvised by him as he proceeded,
> the subject alone being borrowed from some tradition.[2]

[1] Radlov, v, p. xvi; cf. Chadwick, *Growth*, iii, p. 182.
[2] J. and R. Michell, *The Russians in Central Asia* (London, 1865), p. 186;
cf. Chadwick, *Growth*, iii, p. 179.

This art is still practised among the Kara-Kirghiz, and recent versions of the epic of *Manas* were taken down from two bards who improvised as they recited. Improvisation is the first and earliest form of heroic poetry, and has left its marks on the whole technique of the art.

The Russians, Jugoslavs, and Kara-Kirghiz show how improvisation works, and we are well informed about their methods. But they are not the only people to practise it. Though full evidence is lacking, there is little doubt that this kind of improvisation is practised also by the Ossetes, the Kalmucks, the Yakuts, the Ainus, and the modern Greeks. When examples of their poems exist in many variants, there seems so little probability of there being any standard or fixed form that we must assume that the minstrel re-creates the traditional material in his own way. Indeed, improvisation must have been the normal practice in any society where the bard might be called at a moment's notice to recite a poem on a new subject. When Beowulf routs Grendel, his action immediately becomes a subject for a song by Hrothgar's bard:

> Who had made many vaunts,   and was mindful of verses,
> Stored with sagas,   and songs of old,
> Bound word to word   in well-knit rime,
> Welded his lay;   this warrior soon
> Of Beowulf's quest   right cleverly sung.[1]

If this is not absolute improvisation, it is very close to it. The bard may have had some warning of what he has got to do, but he certainly has not had time to polish a complete poem in his head. When Odysseus at the court of Alcinous calls on the bard, Demodocus, for a song, he tells him what to sing, and Demodocus, without more ado, proceeds to tell how the Achaeans set fire to their camp and embarked on their ships.[2] He is sufficiently master of his technique and his material to provide without preparation or pause a poem on the recent subject for which he is asked. Moreover, he seems to work in a special way, since Alcinous says of him:

> The god has given him singing,
> And to give joy with his song as his spirit commands him to utter.[3]

If Demodocus' spirit urges him to sing, the suggestion is that he does not repeat the songs of others or even songs which he has himself prepared previously but follows his inspiration wherever it takes him. So too in Ithaca the bard Phemius says of himself:

---

[1] *Beowulf*, 868-72.   [2] *Od*. viii, 44-5.   [3] *Ibid*. xiii, 44-5.

My own teacher am I, and in my soul God has planted
All the approaches of song.[1]

Phemius disclaims any debt to earlier singers and says that he is
divinely inspired. The word, οἶμαι, which he uses of his songs
means literally " ways " or " approaches " and suggests that he
can approach any theme. Perhaps even more striking is the
passage in the Homeric Hymn to Hermes, in which the young god
begins to sing, ἐξ αὐτοσχεδίης,[2] which can only mean " im-
promptu ". We can hardly doubt that improvisation was known
both to Homer and to the author of *Beowulf*. We need not assume
that they themselves practised it, but their art may well have been
affected by it.

This evidence suggests that improvisation is a normal practice
among composers of heroic poetry. The minstrel, whether in
Jutland or Ithaca, in Russia or Jugoslavia, learns his craft, including his stories, and creates a new poem each time that he performs.
Naturally this demands special powers, and it is not surprising that
minstrels claim to have supernatural support. The ancient Greek
poets said that their words came from the Muse. This must mean
that in composition they exercised a power akin in some ways to
what modern poets call inspiration, but which they were almost
able to summon at will when they found themselves confronted by
an audience calling for a song. Nor were they wrong in calling the
Muses the Daughters of Memory ; for such inspiration works only
because the poet has memorised many devices and phrases which
help him to compose. So Homer begins both the *Iliad* and the
Odyssey with invocations to the Muse, whether to sing of the
wrath of Achilles or of the man of many wiles. So too Hesiod
makes a similar claim when he says that he was taught poetry by
the Muses,[3] when he was keeping sheep on the slopes of Helicon.
Nor are such claims confined to antiquity, since, as we have seen,
a Kara-Kirghiz bard told Radlov that God had implanted the gift
of song in his heart and that he could sing of any theme, although
he had learned none of his songs.[4] This remarkable activity of the
creative spirit lies behind much heroic poetry and dictates to it
some of its special characteristics.

When we say that a poet improvises, it is important to know
exactly what we mean. It is not a wild flood of words which flows
from his lips but an orderly stream which his hearers find familiar
in vocabulary and in metre. Though each version which he gives
of a story may differ in details and turns of phrase, these details

[1] *Od.* xxii, 347-8. [2] *Hom. Hymn*, iv, 55.
[3] *Theogony*, 22 ff. [4] Radlov, v, p. xviii ; cf. *sup.* p. 41.

come from his repertory and are themselves formalised and traditional. Improvisation is based on what Radlov calls " elements of production ". The poet learns in the first place a number of stories and becomes acquainted with their chief persons and their main characteristics; these provide him with the material for his work. Normally he restricts himself to these accepted and familiar stories, and, though he may often change them or add to them, they are the basis of his craft. In the second place he learns a large number of formulae, both short and long, suited to the metre in which he composes, and these enable him to rise immediately to most needs that his subject forces on him. These formulae are in the main traditional; for, once a good formula has been found, poets use it freely without considerations of copyright. If formulae prove useful, they may last for centuries, and there is no call to abandon them just because they are familiar. Indeed their familiarity gives them a special dignity and commands respect. For instance the modern Russian minstrel, Marfa Kryukova, speaks of " stone-built Moscow " in a poem on a contemporary subject because it is the usual formula for any reference to Moscow and occurs in countless poems, of which the oldest known to us is that on the failure of the Crimean Tsar, as Richard James recorded it in 1619.

Improvised heroic poetry could hardly exist without formulae. The task of composition would be too difficult and too uncertain for almost any bard. He could not trust himself to complete a poem without hesitating for a phrase or even breaking down when he began to be tired or found his concentration disturbed. Of course, even as it is, poets break down, and the scholars who have recorded the Russian *byliny* show how sometimes the bards forsake verse for prose, no doubt because the strain of poetical composition is too much for them. But this is a failure in professional honour, and may even do them harm, since the case of the Altai Tatars, who are said never to listen again to a bard who breaks down,[1] may not be unique. But if the bard has his formulae at his command, they will help him to surmount almost any difficulty. His poem will not always be of the finest quality, but it will at least be a poem so long as his technique is at work. For instance, Radlov records that the Kara-Kirghiz bard who sang *The Birth of Manas* seemed not to be at his best or entirely at his ease because the subject was not in his usual repertory,[2] but his command of formulae enabled him to produce something tolerably interesting and coherent. The use of formulae is fundamental to improvised

[1] *Kogutei*, p. 7 ff.   [2] Radlov, v, p. xiii.

oral poetry, which could not really exist without them. Of course the more skilful minstrels not only know more formulae than their less gifted fellows but use them more adroitly and even add to their number with others of their own creation. But the formula remains the foundation of improvised poetry.

A formula is a set of words which is used, with little or no change, whenever the situation with which it deals occurs. It may thus be very short like the familiar combinations of nouns and adjectives which occur in most heroic poetry; it may be a single line, or it may be a set of lines up to a dozen or so in number. In principle all these formulae are of the same kind and perform the same function of helping the poet to surmount such and such a need when it occurs. But in practice formulae fall into at least two classes. On the one side are the noun-adjective combinations, like " blue sea " or " dark death ", in which a noun, whether it applies to a common object or an individual person, is usually accompanied by what is called a " fixed epithet ". The phrase is not entirely happy, since in the first place the noun may sometimes occur without its usual epithet, and in the second place it may sometimes have another epithet. But the noun-adjective combination has a special character because in it the epithet, being formulaic, performs no very obvious function so far as the narrative is concerned. It is easy to call it " decorative ", but that is to put too great an emphasis on it, since we may become so used to it that we hardly notice it when it occurs, and in that case there is not much point in speaking of its decorative value. Its task is to help the poet in composition, and though it hardly ever troubles us and may have its own charm, it is not really useful so far as the story is concerned. On the other hand there are repeated phrases, which may be parts of lines, or single whole lines, or sets of whole lines. These differ from the noun-adjective combinations in being strictly functional and necessary to the narrative. They have of course their own charm and may at times have considerable poetical appeal, but their first duty is to deal with the machinery of action, to tell how certain recurring events happen. Since these events may not be very interesting in themselves, little is lost by recording them in formulaic words.

Not all heroic poetry shows these two kinds of formulaic elements on the same scale. Indeed it may on the whole be divided into two classes. In one the formulae are used abundantly and follow certain rules; in the other there are many traces of them but they are not ubiquitous. To the first class belong the lays of the Russians, the Jugoslavs, the Kara-Kirghiz, the Kalmucks, and the Yakuts, and no doubt an examination of other languages would show similar results. If we can establish the principles by which they are used in these five languages, we should be able to see what the formula does for a large class of poetry, and from that we can advance to consider the second class in which it is used somewhat differently.

Noun-adjective combinations seem to be an ancient possession of the Slavonic peoples. They are already present in the *Tale of Igor's Raid*, composed in 1187, which speaks of " grey wolves ", " open plain ", " scarlet shields ", " black ravens ", " tempered sabres ", " green grass ", " Frankish steel ", and " valiant retinue ". They are not quite fixed or constant, but it is clear that even at this date the poet felt the need for them. Indeed some of these combinations may be older than this, since a certain number of them occur both in Russian and Jugoslav poems and may derive from a common ancestry before the Slavonic peoples had been divided into their present branches. Such are " white town ", " white hand ", " white face ", " bitter tears ", " good hero ", and " good steed ". From this common basis the Russians and the Jugoslavs have developed separately their own combinations. The Russians habitually speak of " damp mother earth ", " free open plain ", " silken bowstring ", " stone-built Moscow ", " honeyed drinks ", " sweet food ", " oaken table ", " blue sea ", " splendid honourable feast ", " dark forest ", " white breast ", " rebellious head ", " green garden " and the like. The Jugoslavs similarly speak of " black earth ", " broad highway ", " wide plain ", " green mountains ", " cool wine ", " sugared cakes ", " heavy maces ", " helpless children ", and " skilful barbers ". The same technique is used for proper names whether of places or of persons. The Russians speak of " glorious city of Kiev ", " Novgorod the great ", " glorious rich city of Volhynia ", " Vladimir, prince of royal Kiev ", " Sadko the merchant, the rich stranger ", " Ilya of Murom, the old Cossack ", " the terrible Tsar, Ivan Vasilevich ", " bold Alyosha Popovich ", " young Volga Svyatoslavovich ", and " Tugarin, the Dragon's son ". So too the Jugoslavs speak of " fair Miroč mountain ", " Rudnik the white town ", " level Krágujevac ", " Vučitrn the white-walled village ", " Vuk the Firedrake ", " the spiritual head, the Archimandrite ", " Novak Krstović, the swift champion of Montenegro ", " mighty Philip the Magyar ". The Slavonic noun-combinations are not in themselves very exciting, but they have an ancient lineage and show how the technique is used without literary pretences or ambitions.

As a counterpart to these European examples we may set the

practice of three Asiatic peoples. In Kara-Kirghiz poems noun-adjective combinations are extremely common. In addition to the formulae for simple things like " red sun ", " tall horse ", " golden bed ", " white milk ", " sweet sugar ", " princely dwelling ", " strong brandy ", " high, black cap ", " black sweat ", " white breast ", " white foam ", there are other more elaborate and more striking like " golden tent of white camel's hair ", " leopard-skin saddle-cloth ", " waterless steppe ", " blue falconer's drum ". The chief heroes are distinguished by vivid titles like " Alaman Bet the tiger-like ", " Adshu Bai the sharp-tongued ", " Er Joloi with a mouth like a drinking-horn ", " bald-pated Kongyr Bai ", " Kanykai, daughter of princes ", " Bakai Khan, son of the rich ", " Semätäi, the young hero ", while places and peoples receive a fullness of attention outside anything in Slavonic poetry, like " Bokhara of the seven gates ", " the jabbering Chinese whose language no one understands " or " the stinking Kalmucks, with round tasselled caps, who cut up pork and tie it to saddles ". The noun-adjective combinations are extremely common and more elaborate than in Slavonic poetry. They have indeed developed their own brilliance. They are not usually necessary to the plot, but they throw a sidelight on its events and characters.

Something similar can be seen among the Kalmucks, whose poetry abounds in formulae of a great richness and variety. The noun-adjective combinations include such fine specimens as " motley yellow domes " for tents, " silver-bottomed streams ", " high white mountains ", " saddles strong as an anvil ", " golden yellow road ", " red dust ", " humped earth ", " glancing eyes, proud with drinking ", " stance like a grown sandalwood tree ", " setting fiery sun ", " old yellow-headed swan ", " silken garment worth a million silver kopecs ". Numbers play a mysterious part and perform their own functions, as in " land of thirty-three saints " or " six thousand and twelve chosen warriors " of Dzhangar's company. The heroes have elaborate Mongolian titles, but are also called by simpler names. Dzhangar is " khan " or " ruler " or " renowned " or " terrible "; Ulan-Khongor is " of the red bay " or " the tower " or " the drunken "; other warriors are " white champion of lions ", " blinding sun ", " red medley of storms ". Places are similarly distinguished, whether mountains like " the lion Altai " and " Samban, source of winds ", or waters like " the holy sea of Bumba " or " the flowing stream, Artai ". Indeed the Kalmuck poems are so loaded with formulaic phrases that at times the action is rather obstructed by them, though it is fair to say that, when a crisis comes, it is usually managed with economy and speed.

Like the Kara-Kirghiz poems, those of the Kalmucks suggest a people deeply interested in poetry, and this may partly account for this richness. But age too may have something to do with it. The Kalmuck formulae seem to be of considerable antiquity and look as if they had been polished and elaborated with the passage of years.

A third Asiatic people whose poetry abounds in noun-adjective combination are the Yakuts, who use them almost as abundantly as the Kara-Kirghiz and the Kalmucks. Their favourite forms are usually quite simple, like " black mother night ", " red day ", " blessed world ", " iron pillar ", " silver-breasted lark ", " good horse ", " white tufted clouds ", " echoing, wide sky ", " silver sables ", " mighty thunder ", " sturdy tree ", " fiery star ", " iron cradle ", " yellow butter ". The human characters are also decorated with epithets, though these are sometimes woven into their names and are almost indistinguishable from them. Still there are such cases as " Suodal, the one-legged warrior ", " Karakhkhan, the rich lord ", " Yukeiden, the beautiful white butterfly ", and " Dzhessin, the old warrior ". The Yakut world lies in remote regions of Siberia and lacks the scope which the Kara-Kirghiz have gained from their contacts with China, or the Kalmucks from memories of the time when they lived on the edges of Tibet. Yet their poetry has the same general character and shows the same main characteristics, one of which is its frequent use of noun-adjective combinations.

Though such combinations are to be found not merely in the poetry of the peoples just examined but in others as well, their purpose is not immediately obvious. They are not always elegant or delightful; indeed sometimes they are flat and feeble. Aesthetic considerations cannot be the original reason for their existence. Nor at first sight are they of great use to the bard in improvisation. We might think that he could dispense with them, since on the whole they are short and do not carry him far. Of course they serve to keep clear the personality of a man or a woman or the main characteristics of a place, but that does not explain why they are so commonly and so consistently used not merely of people but of things and even of very commonplace things which need no such means to distinguish them. It is also true that many of them must be traditional, and this may be the reason why poets use them now, but it does not explain why they came into existence in many different countries. They must serve a use in the composition of a poem, and the answer is that they make the poet's task easier. In so far as a noun qualified by an adjective takes longer to say than an unaccompanied noun, it helps the poet and enables him to think ahead for just that particle of time which is necessary in improvising. They are not his only means for doing this, but they are a not unimportant means. By loosening the texture of his poetry through these largely otiose words, the poet can proceed more calmly and more confidently. Moreover, the formula, which exists for this reason, serves a secondary purpose. When we listen to the recitation of an improvised poem, the fixed phrases become so familiar that we hardly notice them. When they occur, our attention is momentarily slackened and our minds rested. The formulae are important to oral improvised poetry because they make it easier for the audience to listen as well as for the poet to compose.

When poetry abounds in noun-adjective combinations, it has also repeated lines and sets of lines, which are the indispensable links in a story and do an unassuming task for it. Their frequent occurrence in the Russian *byliny* shows how the poets rely on them. Indeed the Russian minstrels seem to use formulaic phrases for almost any ordinary occasion. A man sets out to do something:

> He flung his boots on his bare feet,
> His fur-cloak over his shoulder,
> His sable cap over one ear.

He goes out for sport:

> Shooting geese, white swans,
> And little feathered grey ducks.

He destroys his enemies:

He trampled them down with his horse and slew them with his spear,
He trampled down and slew the host in a short time.

He abuses his horse:

> " Ho, you food for wolves, you grass-bag;
> Will you not go on, or can you not carry me? "

He rides into a palace:

> He entered the spacious court-yard,
> He stood his horse in the middle of the court-yard,
> He went into the palace of white stone.

Time passes:

> Day after day, as the rain falls,
> Week after week, as the grass grows,
> Year after year, as the river flows.

A company of guests is frightened:

> They could not think of a reply,
> The taller of them hid behind the lesser,
> And the lesser for their part were speechless.

Such passages, and many others of the same kind, are extremely common. They may vary in small respects from poet to poet, but they play a large part in the composition of *byliny*. No poem is without them, and in most they take up considerable space.

Much the same can be said of the Jugoslav poems. Their opening lines are highly conventional and standardised. In addition to the stock themes of birds flying, warriors drinking or riding out, we find such lines as

> God of mercy, what a mighty marvel!

or

> In a vision dreamed a pretty maiden

or

> Rose a maiden early in the morning.

But the great mass of such formulaic lines and sets of lines are to be found in the main episodes of the poems. They are contrived to meet recurrent needs, and are in fact used when such needs arise. A well set-up man appears in a standard guise:

> Never was a man of greater stature,
> Never was a man more broad of shoulder;
> What a knightly aspect was the hero's!

A battle begins:

> God in Heaven, thanks for Thy great goodness!
> Often did the armies clash in combat,
> In the spreading plainland match their forces.

It continues:

> Many of the army then were slaughtered,
> Filled with deep dismay were those remaining

A hero prepares to go out:

> Then he girded on his rich-wrought sabre,
> And he cast his wolf-skin cloak about him.

A new day begins:

> When the day was dawning on the morrow.

An old man is described:

> With a white beard all his breast is covered,
> And it reaches to his silken girdle.

227

A maiden praises a man :

> When he speaks, it's like a ringdove cooing,
> When he laughs, it's like the sun's warmth spreading.

The Turks assert their domination :

> Evil deeds they did throughout the country.

Nor are these formulaic passages always short. They sometimes extend to a dozen or more lines, and often to half a dozen. Jugoslav formulaic repetitions differ from the Russians in that they vary less from poem to poem in minor details and tend to follow a strict model. But they perform a similar function and are indispensable to the mechanics of a story.

When we turn from the European to the Asiatic poems, we find very much the same technique. The Kara-Kirghiz poets delight in standard groups of lines and show their usual individuality in them. They use them for such matters as the coming of night :

> In the west night fell,
> Ominous shadows fell,

or for a horse galloping :

> It flies from crest to crest
> On the white hot hills,
> On the endless slopes,

or for the coming of morning :

> When the dawn of day broke,
> And the constellation of the Wain set,
> When the sun rose up bright.

The ordinary machinery of the tales is usually dealt with in such ways. But there are other formulaic passages which are more ingenious and adapted to less expected situations, as when servants welcome a stranger :

> One took his white horse,
> One opened the door,
> One secured it after the fashion of the Sarts ;
> Out of the great golden chest
> They brought strong brandy ;

or when a hero is born :

> His upper half was of gold,
> His lower half was of silver,
> After two days he said " Mother ",
> After seven days he said " Father ".

or goes out to track his runaway slaves :

> Your steps I will trace
> To the waterless steppe.
> Kudai will cause you to come in my way.
> I will ride to bring this about,
> All alone against a thousand foes.

The Kara-Kirghiz compose on a large scale and have plenty of room for highly developed formulaic passages. In them, as in their noun-adjective combinations, a vigorous and creative tradition is at work.

The Kalmuck art is very similar. Formulae are, if anything, more abundant than in the Kara-Kirghiz poems and are often quite long. The great hero, Dzhangar, is often described in the same words, as he is introduced :

> Under his motley yellow dome
> He has passed all his time,
> As they say, at the point of his spear ;

or when he sits in state :

> Higher than everyone,
> On his golden lion throne.

His dwelling is praised in conventional form :

> The dwelling of the high ruler,
> A wonder of wonders in all lands under the sun,
> In all the lands of the eight thousand khans.

A notable warrior is introduced :

> See what a warrior commands
> The seven circles around him.

When he saddles his horse

> He sat on his stallion,
> He set his heavy bear-skin on his shoulder,
> And went forth to meet his famous enemy.

Time of day is indicated :

> When the yellow sun rises over the earth

or

> In the dawn before the sunrise.

With such phrases and many others like them the Kalmucks build up elaborate patterns, and at times whole long passages are made of such formulaic elements. Many of the phrases occur several times within a short space, and there is no doubt that they are the poet's instruments of composition.

The poetry of the Yakuts is equally rich in formulaic elements of this kind. Their methods of narration is less impeded than that of the Kalmucks, and their formulae tend to be less detailed, but are none the less useful. The Yakut stories are set in a vast land where woods are haunted by demons and the weather is fierce and faithless. So the formulae help the presentation of this natural setting. A thunderstorm comes :

> Thunder roared above,
> And heavy rain poured down.

Night descends in high style :

> Shadows of black night thickened,
> Black mother-night began,
> Gray mother-night covered all.

The forest has its beauty and its mystery :

> The bark on it was of silver,
> The needles of gold,
> The bosses of silver, enormous.

The movements of characters are often described in formulae :

> Thither he departed,
> He went straight to the west.

Even demons introduce themselves with an agreeable convention :

> My songs are a thick cloud,
> My cry snow and rain,
> My chant a black mist,
> My tidings a hurricane !

A story ends simply, in some such form as

> Then they lived in wealth and happiness.

The circumstances of Yakut poetry may be unusual, but its formulae are operated in very much the same way as elsewhere.

These five languages, Russian, Jugoslav, Kara-Kirghiz, Kalmuck, and Yakut, show the formulae at work, whether in noun-adjective combinations or in repeated lines and passages. A similar art is practised by other Tatar peoples of Asia, like the Uzbeks, by the Ossetes, the Ainus, the modern Greeks, the Albanians, and the Bulgars. Indeed this seems to be the normal technique for poetry which is composed and recited orally, with no thought of being written down or read. But though this poetry abounds in formulae, it is hardly ever entirely formulaic. It seems usually to leave something for the bard to do. Formulae are commonest when he is not very gifted or not quite himself or forced to sing on a subject which he has had little time to prepare.

If formulae are indispensable to the improvising bard, they are also helpful to any listening audience. First, just as the bard rests himself for a fragment of a second while he uses a noun-adjective combination, so too the audience on hearing it can also ease its attention, since the phrase is familiar and demands no effort of comprehension. Since listening to a poem is by no means easy even for people trained to it, any such small help is worth having. Secondly, most formulae are traditional and familiar, and their very familiarity makes the audience feel at home and know in what world of the imagination it is moving. When we consider how conservative most primitive peoples are in their tastes and how much they dislike innovation on any substantial scale, we can see that they will like to be comforted in this way. If they know where they are, they will enjoy all the more the slight novelties which the bard may introduce into his telling of an old tale. For this reason the formulae come to be liked for their own sake as old friends, and the omission of them would leave the audience uneasy and unsatisfied, as if they had not had their proper poetical fare. Thirdly, if a poet has mastered the old formulae, he can then, no doubt with caution, proceed to invent new ones which suit the traditional tone but add something unfamiliar to the subject. His success in this will be judged by the ease with which he fits his new formulae into the old structure, and it is notable that, when modern Russian bards introduce new formulae for modern characters, they are careful to acclimatise them to the ancient technique. So, though the existence of formulae is due in the first place to the needs of bards in improvisation, their persistence and survival are no less due to the demands of audiences who expect them, like them, and even need them if they are to respond fully to what the bard says.

It is clear that in oral poetry there is also an element of what may be called free invention. The bard is so well in control of himself and his tale that he is able to invent without pause for thought. No doubt he has planned beforehand what he is going to say, and with the tenacious memory of the unlettered is able to carry it without trouble in his head. But for this he must have considerable ability and time to sort his material out. He may also be assisted by the fact that some subjects are so popular and so often treated that he will know all their main points and be able to add improvements at his ease. Indeed some such explanation as this may account for the Jugoslav poems on Kosovo, which have indeed certain formulaic elements but leave them behind for their high moments. The texts, as we have them, were collected by

Vuk Karadžić at the beginning of the nineteenth century and represent versions current at that time. By then their themes, which may be as old as the fourteenth century, were so well known that a poet could easily leave formulae behind and pass to free invention, especially as none of these poems is at all long, and it is easier for a poet to invent freely when he knows that only a short performance is expected of him. If we compare these pieces with some of the long poems recorded by Milman Parry in 1934, we see a great difference in the use of formulae. Parry's bards were urged to sing a long tale and did so by employing formulae freely. With Karadžić's bards it was different. A poem of a hundred or so lines is more easily composed and retained in the head than a poem of several thousand. In this kind of poetry it is not a question of abandoning formulae altogether, but of reducing the part played by them in a short poem.

There is no fundamental or necessary reason why an oral poet should not supplement his traditional language with new elements of his own making. In Sagymbai Orozbakov's version of *Manas* there are recurring phrases which are undeniably formulaic but look as if they were his own invention or at least learned by him from someone who has changed the old manner of dealing with familiar subjects. They are not what the poets known to Radlov used in similar situations, and Orozbakov shows that one poet does not necessarily use the same formulae as another. Perhaps in composing a poem on a very large scale he felt that he must be more original and varied than his predecessors who did not reach a quarter of his length. The coming of night is, for instance, a stock theme in Kara-Kirghiz, as in other heroic poetry, but in Orozbakov's *Manas* it has a new form:

> Rolling shadows fell,
> Ominous night fell,
> All grew deaf around,
> The earth vanished around.[1]

So too when a great company assembles, it is dealt with formulaically:

> They came from forty ends of the earth,
> They numbered forty regiments.[2]

These cases look conventional enough, and, though we cannot be certain that they are not the poet's invention, or at least the product of the school to which he belongs, they show that even for quite simple purposes it is permissible and possible to produce

[1] *Manas*, p. 51.   [2] *Ibid.* p. 52.

variant formulae which are not those in common use. Of course their function is the same as that of the conventional formulae, and we soon become accustomed to them and treat them in the same way. If in this case we can compare new poems with old and establish the presence of innovations, it may well be possible that, if we could do the same in other cases, we might find a considerable element of invention even in well-worn and familiar topics. It seems clear that in oral poetry, even when formulae are common owing to the requirements of improvisation, there remains a large element of non-formulaic language which the skilful poet so harmonises with the traditional mannerisms that we hardly notice it. If formulae imply improvisation, it does not rely wholly upon them but often creates its own means of expression.

Compared with these poems the Homeric poems present a special problem. No one can dispute the formulaic character of Homer's language. Indeed it suggests a derivation from a long tradition of oral composition. He abounds in both classes of formulae. In the first twenty-five lines of the *Iliad* there are at least twenty-five formulae of one kind or another, and in the first twenty-five lines of the *Odyssey* there are about thirty-three.[1] Nor are these passages exceptional; they give a fair sample of how the poems are composed. There is hardly a passage in either poem in which there are not many small formulae, while about a third of each poem consists of lines or blocks of lines repeated elsewhere. Nor is this a characteristic of Homer alone; it is no less true of other poems like those of Hesiod, the Homeric Hymns, and the fragments of lost epics. At the start it is clear that the formula plays a more important part in ancient Greek heroic poetry than in any oral poetry which we have examined. There seems to be hardly any department into which it does not penetrate. It is present equally in the machinery of narrative and in the highest flights of poetry, though here it is managed with uncommon tact and seldom makes itself noticeable. Homer clearly derives his art from a powerful tradition which has worked out formulae for almost every occasion, and his task was to make a good use of them.

Homer's noun-adjective combinations have a range and a variety unequalled by any other heroic poet. There is hardly a person or a thing which has not got its distinguishing adjective, and many of these have an entrancing appeal. No doubt some of the epithets for his heroes are intended to do no more than tell

[1] Parry, *Studies*, i, p. 118 ff.

who they are and establish their credentials in our memories. That is why Achilles is " son of Peleus ", Agamemnon " son of Atreus ", Odysseus " son of Laertes ". That too is why Agamemnon is also " king of men ", Nestor " the Gerenian knight ", and Eumaeus " the noble swineherd ". Such epithets fix a character and give him his place in the story. But Homer goes far beyond this. Many of his adjectives are purely and delightfully decorative. Nothing but pleasure is given by such epithets as " of the glancing helmet " for Hector, " long-robed " for Helen or Thetis, " white-armed " for Hera, " cloud-gathering " for Zeus, " plague of men " for Ares. Nor are gods and heroes the only recipients of this attention. All animals and things are treated equally and in each case a touch of poetry makes the phrase live, whether in the " loudly-resounding " or " wine-dark " or " echoing " sea, or " shadowy mountains ", or " rosy-fingered dawn ", or death " who lays at length ", or " windless " sky, or " long-shadowing " spear, or " echoing " rivers, or " mountain-bred " lion, or " shameless " fly, or " windy " Troy, or Mycenae " rich in gold ", or " hollow " Lacedaemon. Such epithets, and many others like them, must have been evolved by a long process in which poets eliminated much that seemed dull or pointless and kept those epithets which have both charm and truth. If we compare Homer's noun-adjective combinations with those of the Russian or Jugoslav poets, we find a vast difference of quality between them. While the Russian and Jugoslav phrases are strictly useful, Homer's are not only useful but imaginative and illuminating.

This wealth of noun-adjective combinations is matched by an equal wealth of repeated lines and passages. There is hardly a situation for which Homer has not a formulaic line or passage. He has them for all the machinery of narrative, for speech and answer, morning and evening, sleeping and waking, weapons, ships putting to sea and coming to land, feasts and sacrifices, greeting and farewell, marriage and death. He has formulae for what might seem to be not very common occurrences like the two dogs who accompany a prince when he goes out, the slave woman with whom a man will not sleep for fear of his wife's anger, fruit-trees that make a pleasant place, sea-birds on the shore, the ragged garb of a beggar, the horse-hair plume that nods on a helmet, the stones of which a house or a wall is built, the treasure that lies at the bottom of a chest, the noise that a key makes when it is turned in a lock. Moreover, Homer uses his formulae with an unexpected rigour. The mechanism of the narrative is conveyed through formulae which are never altered so long as the metrical requirements are the same. When dawn comes, it is always :

> Now when the early-born rose-fingered Dawn had arisen.

Night comes :

> When the sun had gone down, and darkness had followed upon it.

A man falls in battle :

> Down he fell with a crash, and loud rang his armour upon him.

A feast ends :

> When they had put from them all desire for eating and drinking.

A man dies :

> Then did dark-coloured death and powerful destiny take him.

When a formula meets his need, Homer uses it without change, even though it extends to several lines, as when heroes get ready their chariots, or their ships, or when food is served, or a sacrifice conducted. The convention is powerful, and Homer observes it rigorously.

In dealing with noun-adjective combinations, which usually occupy only part of a line, Homer is equally strict, though he follows different rules. Roughly, as Milman Parry has shown,[1] it may be said that the formula in a given case is determined by the needs of the metrical structure and by the place which the formula has to take in it. In a given place or part of the line the same thing or person is always represented by the same formula, and variations are determined entirely by what case the appropriate substantive is in. There are, for instance, 36 different noun-adjective combinations for Achilles. The number is large because his name is used in all five cases, but the use of each combination is decided by the place which it has to occupy in the line. In several hundred cases there are only two exceptions : one, when Achilles is called not πόδας ὠκύς but μεγάθυμος,[2] the other when he is addressed not as θεοῖς ἐπιείκελ' Ἀχιλλεῦ but as διίφιλε φαίδιμ' Ἀχιλλεῦ.[3] The same rule applies to other persons and things, and exceptions are very few.[4] The combination used is settled by its place in the line and its case, and at that place hardly any other combination is used. Technique so described may sound very complicated and artificial. We feel that the poet must

---

[1] *L'Épithète traditionnelle dans Homère* and *Les Formules et la métrique d'Homère*, both Paris, 1928.

[2] *Il.* xxiii, 168.   [3] *Ibid.* xxii, 216.

[4] Examples are discussed by Parry in *L'Épithète traditionnelle*, p. 221 ff.

master considerable gymnastics before he can control so curious an art. But in fact the Homeric language is not in the least complicated to read. Homer is one of the most straightforward and direct of poets; he is seldom ambiguous or obscure, nor does his attachment to formulae mean that he is sometimes slightly off the point; his words flow with a remarkably natural movement which presents a marked contrast to the hesitations and circumvolutions of *Beowulf*. The fact that, with all his strict observance of these rules, he is still perfectly easy and natural reflects the greatest credit both on him and on them. They have clearly succeeded in their task of making poetry easier for the poet, and though no doubt it took time and labour to master them, Homer's years of apprenticeship were well rewarded by the style which it gave him.

If we compare Homer's use of language with that of any of the peoples whose improvised poetry we have examined, we see that, though it resembles them in having its origin in improvisation and serves similar ends, it differs in more than one respect. We cannot say that his language is older than any of theirs, since we know nothing of its beginnings except that they must lie in a distant past. But it has certainly been organised for poetry to a degree which is not to be found elsewhere. This may partly be due to its metre. The heroic hexameter, based on the quantity of syllables and formed on a " falling " rhythm of six dactyls, of which the last is truncated, is a much stricter and more exacting metre than those of the Russians, Jugoslavs, or Asiatic Tatars. It has indeed its licences, notably in its artificial lengthening of short syllables and its occasional tolerance of hiatus between vowels, but this only emphasises how rigorous it is in other ways, and how difficult it is to fit the Greek language into this demanding and exacting form. Now a poet who improvises in a difficult metre is faced with a much sterner task than, say, a Russian poet whose line is determined neither by the quantity of syllables nor by their number but by accents which he himself puts on in chanting. It follows that, in order to make improvisation in the Greek hexameter possible, a technique had to be invented which provided minstrels with a great array of phrases and indeed prepared them for almost any emergency. That is why Homer has far more formulae than even the most formulaic poets from other countries. For them relatively easy metres allowed a degree of free composition; for the Greeks free composition was almost out of the question, and the formula must always be ready to help.

This difference of metre accounts for another difference, which is most marked between Homer and the Russian minstrels, though it is important also between him and the Jugoslavs. Whenever he deals with a standard situation, he uses, as we have seen, the same form of words, for the good reason that these fit the metre and it would be a waste of labour to invent an alternative form. Now the Russians are in some ways more conventional than Homer; at least they begin episodes with much less invention and variety than he does. But in such beginnings, which are a good example of formulaic practice, they do not confine themselves to a single form of words for a single theme. They keep the substance but make various changes in the form. An extremely common example of such an opening is the theme of a feast given by Prince Vladimir. But this occurs with several minor variations. Trofim Ryabinin begins his *Ilya's Quarrel with Vladimir*:

> Glorious Vladimir of royal Kiev,
> He prepared a glorious, honourable feast
> For his host of princes and boyars,
> And glorious, mighty powerful heroes.[1]

The bard known as " the Bottle " begins his *Staver*:

> In the glorious city of Kiev,
> It happened that gracious Prince Vladimir
> Made a banquet, an honourable feast,
> For his company of princes and boyars.[2]

Another bard, L. Tupitsyn, begins his *Dobrynya and Vasili, Casimir's Son*:

> By generous prince Vladimir,
> The little sun, the son of Svyatoslav,
> Was given an honourable feast,
> For many knights and boyars,
> For every bold woman-warrior,
> For all his gallant company.[3]

Almost every poet has his own way of treating this theme, though the details which he adds or omits are of very little importance either to the poetry or to the story. Nor indeed do single poets confine themselves to a single form of words. For instance, Ryabinin begins his *Dobrynya and Vasili, Casimir's Son* with an opening somewhat different from what he uses in *Ilya's Quarrel with Vladimir*:

> By the glorious prince Vladimir
> Was given a feast, a banquet
> For mighty princes, for boyars,
> For powerful Russian warriors.[4]

[1] Gilferding, ii, p. 38. [2] Rybnikov, i, p. 202.
[3] Andreev, p. 123. [4] Rybnikov, i, p. 43.

Since the Russian minstrel is not restricted to a very exact metre, he is able to vary his language in a way that Homer does not and indeed cannot.

The metre of Jugoslav heroic poetry is much stricter than that of Russian. It is based on accent and is normally a trochaic pentameter like

God of mercy ! what a mighty marvel !

It allows licences with accent but no more than are allowed in quite regular English verse equally based on accent. For this reason many of its formulae remain fixed and are not liable to variation, especially the single lines which occur so frequently at the beginning of a poem. None the less this metre is better adapted to Jugoslav than the hexameter is to Greek, and easier to compose. Indeed the Jugoslav metre has shown its adaptability by the way in which it can accommodate almost any proper name or account of technical events. But the ease with which the Jugoslav metre adapts itself to new themes means that it lacks the suppleness and variety of the Greek hexameter, and in consequence its formulae are less carefully woven into the text. They stand out prominently, often at the beginning of a line, like the theme of a person rising early, which nearly always appears in the same place :

In the morning rose a Turkish maiden . . .

In the morning Marko rose up early . . .

In the morning Oblak made all ready . . .

or the theme of drinking wine, which varies only between singular and plural in the verb :

Drinking wine sat thirty chiefs together . . .

Drinking wine sat Musa the Albanian . . .

Drinking wine sat the King's son Marko . . .

The Jugoslav method differs from Homer's in an important respect. Whereas Homer has a different formula for every place in the line and is so able to vary a given theme in many ways, the Jugoslavs have a standard formula and allot the same place in the line to it, with the result that they are far more monotonous. Similarly, when they use complete lines or blocks of lines, their introduction of them is more marked than in Homer because they normally start with the beginning of one line and end with the end of another. The Jugoslav art is less advanced than Homer's, and for this reason its formulae draw more attention to themselves.

Another difference between Greek poetry and the poetry not only of the Slavonic peoples but of others can be seen in the management of a difficulty caused by the use of noun-adjective combinations. If a noun has an adjective attached to it, there must be times sooner or later when this adjective is not so much otiose as absurd. This happens often enough in Russian poems. The hero, Dyuk Stepanovich, comes from Galicia, which has the epithet " accursed " because, like Poland and Lithuania, it belongs to the Roman Church and is viewed with disapproval by the Orthodox Russians. Ordinarily this does not matter, but there is some absurdity when Dyuk, in answer to Vladimir's question who he is, says :

> " I come from accursed Galicia." [1]

So too Russia, because of its attachment to the Orthodox Church, is always " Holy Russia ", but it is absurd when the Turkish Sultan plans an attack on it and says :

> " I shall go into Holy Russia." [2]

There are similar misfits in Jugoslav poems, as when the standard epithet for hands, " white ", is applied to Moors, who are themselves called " black ".[3] Something of the same kind can be seen in Bulgarian when Marko deals with a Moor :

> And he cut his fair-haired head off.[4]

Since by convention all heads are " fair-haired ", the adjective is used even for a Moor. So too a dead formula may account for a difficulty at the end of the Norse *Atlamál* :

> Then did Atli die,   and his heirs' grief doubled.[5]

Since all Atli's heirs are dead, the last phrase is meaningless and has been introduced because it is often used for deaths. We might think that Homer, with his greater number of noun-adjective combinations, would often fall into this trap. Nor is he entirely safe from it. It is, for instance, a little disturbing to find that Eriphyle's husband is called " dear " when she plots his death,[6] or that the dirty linen which Nausicaa washes is " shining ",[7] as if it were clean. But such cases are not in fact very common. Homer usually seems to see when a contradiction is involved and surmounts it to secure an ironical contrast. When Achilles sulks in his tent, he is still " fleet-footed ", and the adjective compares

---

[1] Rybnikov, i, p. 100.
[2] Gilferding, ii, p. 174.
[3] Drerup, p. 461.
[4] Dozon, p. 64.
[5] *Atlamál*, 98, 2.   [6] *Od.* xi, 327.   [7] *Ibid.* vi, 26.

him as he normally is with what he is now.[1] When the waters of
the Scamander are fouled with blood, the River-god calls them
beautiful,[2] which is of course their usual and proper condition.
When Homer says that the " life-giving " earth covers Helen's
brothers in death,[3] he marks the ironical contrast in the nature of
the earth which both feeds and buries us.[4] This is a delicate art
which Homer usually manages with skill. Of course it might be
argued that such epithets are so otiose that nobody takes much
notice of them. This is no doubt true in many cases, but none the
less it is a finer art to make a conscious use of such formulae than
to treat them as if they had no function.

When we look at Homer's use of language, a paradox emerges.
On the one hand his use of formulae is more extensive, more
homogeneous and more governed by rules than any other poetry.
On the other hand the range of his effects is greater, and his
purely poetical achievement is far richer and more subtle than any
other heroic poet's. The explanation of this is probably that he
stands in the middle of an important change produced by the introduction of writing. That it came in the eighth century we can
hardly doubt, and it is quite possible that its special character was
determined by a desire to use it to record poetry.[5] In this case
we can understand Homer's ambiguous position. Behind him
lie centuries of oral performance, largely improvised, with all its
wealth of formulae adapted to an exacting metre ; these he knows
and uses fully. But if he also knows writing and is able to commit
his poems to it, he is enabled to give a far greater precision and
care to what he says than any improvising poet ever can. Since it
is almost impossible to believe that the *Iliad* and *Odyssey* were
ever improvised, and the richness of their poetry suggests some
reliance on writing, we may see in them examples of what happens
when writing comes to help the oral bard. He continues to compose in the same manner as before, but with a far greater care and
effectiveness. He can omit and correct and rearrange and take his
time as the improvising poet cannot, and the result is a great
enrichment of his texture. Indeed the dazzling use which Homer
makes of his traditional formulae is perhaps an indication that he
has passed beyond their purely functional use in composition to

---

[1] *Il.* i, 489.   [2] *Ibid.* xxi, 218.   [3] *Ibid.* iii, 243.
[4] There are other places in which a traditional epithet contradicts the
sense of a passage, without perhaps our noticing it, as when the sky is called
" starry ", though it is day, at *Il.* xv, 371, *Od.* ix, 527, xii, 380, or Ajax calls
Hector " great-hearted " at *Il.* xiv, 440, or Zeus refers to the villainous Aegisthus
as " blameless " at *Od.* i, 29. For Aristarchus' treatment of this point cf.
Parry, *L'Epithète traditionnelle*, p. 148 ff.
[5] I owe this suggestion to H. T. Wade-Gery.

something that is almost purely poetical. Perhaps he learned his craft in the old tradition, but in his lifetime the alphabet appeared, and he had the insight to see what great advantages it brought in turning the old technique to a nobler and richer purpose.

If Homer represents the transition from improvised, oral poetry to a poetry which relies to some extent on writing, other heroic poems show what happens when writing is well established and commonly used. *Gilgamish* survives in written texts of four different languages, and we might expect it to be a purely literary composition with no signs of oral usage and formulae. Yet it has its fair share of them. For noun-adjective combinations it offers " handsome couch ", " generous mantle ", " Erech the high-walled ", or " the broad-marketed ", " crest like an aurochs ", " the lady Ishtar ", " the Sun-god in heaven ", " Humbaba whose roar is a whirlwind ", " the cedar-forest, terror to mortals ", "Uta-Napishtim the distant", and "Ninsun, the glorious queen". Its repeated lines are not very common but include :

> Gilgamish opened his mouth and spake,

> Roaming the desert like a hunter,

> He takes his axe in his hand,
> He draws his dagger from his belt,

> Comrade and henchman who chased
> The ass of the mountains, the pard of the desert.

Though the Assyrian poet of *Gilgamish* certainly owes much to books, and may well have composed his poem to be read by the learned few, his style remains largely that of oral composition. He has, it is true, a greater degree of free composition and fewer formulaic passages than we find in Homer, but that no doubt is because he is more accustomed to writing and relies more upon it. None the less he maintains the manners of oral composition in some important respects. This may be due in the first place to his sense that he belongs to a tradition and must write in a tradi-tional way. But it must also be partly due to the needs of recita-tion. His poem would normally be recited and would thus need the devices which are proper to recitation and indeed almost indispensable to it.

The example of *Gilgamish* suggests that the existence of writing need not necessarily interfere very much with the formulaic character of heroic poetry, though it naturally gives more oppor-tunity for free composition. Such conditions may perhaps explain the character of the language of *Beowulf* and other

Anglo-Saxon poems and the *Elder Edda*. We may be fairly sure that the author of *Beowulf* was able to read, and since the fragments of *Finnsburh* and *Waldhere* cannot be far from him in date, it is at least possible that their authors were in the same case. With the *Elder Edda* the possibility is hardly less. That some of the poems are ultimately derived from an illiterate society is beyond doubt, but in their present form, broken and corrupt though they are, they must have been written down, or for that matter remembered, if not actually composed, at a time when reading and writing were not uncommon. But both the Anglo-Saxon and the Norse poems retain formulae in the same way as *Gilgamish*, and no doubt for the same reason. They preserve a technique which goes back to the Germanic mainland and is at least as old as the fourth century A.D. and probably much older, and such a tradition is not lightly abandoned, even when its original usefulness for improvisation is no longer urgent. Equally the Norse and Anglo-Saxon audiences, knowing that these poems preserved memories of a distant past, might well expect them to be composed in a traditional manner in which formulae play their ancient, almost hieratic part. Indeed the respect for formulae can be seen in the way in which *Beowulf* uses them for Christian matters which lie outside the old heathen, Germanic tradition but are assimilated to the ancient style. They belong to the art and are expected from any practitioner of it.

Whatever the relations of Anglo-Saxon heroic poetry may have been to an earlier Germanic tradition, it is clear that to some extent it employs formulae. These are obvious in *Beowulf* and *Finnsburh* and survive somewhat diluted in *Maldon*. They fall, as usual, into two classes, noun-adjective combinations and repeated phrases, though the unit in the latter is less usually the whole line than the half-line. The noun-adjective combinations are numerous. They include such familiar phrases as " grey sea ", " hollow ship ", " windy cliffs ", " lofty halls ". The great man is " lord of men " or " lord of knights " ; the king is " keeper of troops " ; the hero is " rampart of a nation ". More peculiar and more characteristic of the Anglo-Saxon temper are the "kennings", artificial synonyms, which present things by referring only to some special aspect of them. By this means the sea is " the whale's road " or " the gannets' bath ", a soldier is a " helmet-bearer ", the sun " the world's great candle ", to make a speech " to unlock a word-hoard ", fire " the branches' foe ", and to die " to leave earth's joys ". These are quite as integral a part of the Anglo-Saxon style as the more ordinary noun-adjective combinations.

The minstrel would learn them and find them useful in helping him to keep up the special tone at which this kind of poetry aimed. Such phrases have no parallel in Homer or Slavonic poetry, but they are not alien to Asiatic taste, and they certainly belong to a tradition of oral improvised poetry. Like the noun-adjective combinations, they help the poet in his task by providing him with ready-made aids.

Longer phrases which help the mechanism of the action are equally present in *Beowulf*, and several hundred examples of them have been noted. Some of these are complete lines like

> The gift firm-set   which God had sent him (1271, 2182)
> And the fighters were fallen,   the fierce Shieldings (252, 3005)
> Ere he might go   to the ground beneath (1496, 2770).

But these are exceptional. The more truly formulaic element in *Beowulf* is the half-line like

> Hoard-warden of heroes (1047, 1852)
> Jewel of athelings (130, 2342)
> Picked band of thegns (400, 1627)
> Young spear-warrior (2674, 2811)
> Good and gallant (602, 2349)
> Massacre fierce (2250, 2537)
> Hard, hand-linked (322, 551).
>   (of mail-coats)

Since many of these half-lines are concerned with the details of fighting, they are likely to come from an old tradition. In *Beowulf* they play a part half-way between noun-adjective combinations and repeated lines. Since they are not in themselves complete, they provide only part of a sentence; the rest must be provided by the poet to suit his needs. But they perform a useful function in dealing with many ordinary actions. The poet may, if he likes, eschew them, but he can equally use them and relate them to his poem by the words with which he completes them into whole lines.

These half-lines are part of a wider method used by Anglo-Saxon poets for composition. The original method of composition seems to have been through a verse matrix, which is a half-line with double alliteration.[1] What counts is precisely the existence of certain phrases which can be altered to suit different needs and then, without much trouble, completed with a second half-line. The different ways in which this can be done can be seen from

---

[1] E. D. Laborde, *Byrhtnoth and Maldon*, p. 54; *M.L.R.* xix, p. 410 ff.

Maldon, where the poet knows the old artifices and uses them quietly and efficiently. These matrices usually consist of three words. This provides a unit which the bard can alter to suit his needs, while keeping the essential element of alliteration. Such a matrix may be seen in *Maldon* in

gār tō gūþe (13)
(spear to fight).

This can be transformed either at the end into

gār and gōd swurd (237)
(spear and good sword)

or at the beginning into

guman tō gūþe (94)
(warriors to fight).

This device enables proper names to be introduced without too much difficulty, as in

Godrīc fram gūþe (187)
(Godric from fight)

or

Godrīc tō gūþe (321)
(Godric to fight).

On this basis the poet works. It seems to be an inheritance from the old Germanic poetry, and may be detected not only in *Beowulf* but in the *Elder Edda*. Of course it is different from the static formulae of many poetries, but it rises from like causes. The bard who has this instrument at his command is able to improvise, at least on familiar subjects, without much difficulty. The peculiar nature of the device is due to the alliterative character of Germanic poetry, which naturally has to be treated differently from a poetry based on quantity, like Greek, or on the number of syllables and accents, like Jugoslav.

A comparison of *Beowulf* or *Maldon* with modern improvised poems or with Homer shows some points of difference in technique. In the first place, *Beowulf* is unusual in using a great many synonyms. There are, for instance, some thirty for " hall " or " house ", twenty-six for " king ", nine for " ship ", seventeen for " sword ", twenty-three for " retainers ". Of course Homer also uses synonyms, but not on this scale. Nor is *Beowulf* compelled by necessities of metre to use such a variety. Many of these synonyms begin with the same letter and, so far as the metre is concerned, one beginning with each different letter would be enough. Like the " kennings ", they are a feature of the elevated style, invented not so much to help the poet in the task of improvisation as to enable him to maintain the required tone. Of course some of them would help in improvisation, and no doubt all would be more or less useful. But that is not their first purpose. The Anglo-Saxon art of heroic poetry aims more consciously at a special kind of effect than the Russian or the Jugoslav, no doubt because it is a court-poetry, whereas they, at least in their modern form, belong to peasants and humble people who do not ask for too much complication.

In the second place, *Beowulf* treats certain standard themes neither with the free, if monotonous, treatment of the Russian *byliny* nor with Homer's strict adherence to formulae. This may be examined for such common themes as the feast and going to bed. There are three feasts in *Beowulf*, the first after Beowulf's arrival at Hrothgar's court,[1] the second after the rout of Grendel,[2] and the third after the slaying of the Dam.[3] Each is treated quite differently with no trace of stock phrases. So too with going to bed. After each of these feasts the poet tells how Hrothgar goes to bed,[4] and in each case treats it differently. This is not in the least like Homer's standard and formulaic handling of such occasions. Since the actions described are purely mechanical, we might expect them to be treated mechanically, but they are not. The poet will expend eight lines on a topic which hardly affects the narrative, and give to it his personal attention, selecting on each occasion some different element in the very familiar action. This method differs both from Homer and from most modern oral poetry, in both of which such matters are dismissed summarily as necessary to the reality of the story but no more. The Anglo-Saxon style has its formulae, but it does not use them as Homer does. And this is probably due to the different metre. The unit is the half-line, and most formulae are formed as half-lines; since there is no great difficulty in completing one half-line with another in alliteration, the Anglo-Saxon poets seem to have felt that they could dispense with longer formulaic phrases and use even single formulaic lines sparingly.

In general, despite these differences of technique, which are due to differences of metre and ultimately of language, the Anglo-Saxon poets resemble the Russians and the Jugoslavs and even the Asiatic peoples in combining formulae with free composition. The differences are not of kind but of degree, and this is probably due to the appearance of writing in England before *Beowulf* was

---

[1] *Beowulf*, 491-8. [2] *Ibid.* 1010-17.
[3] *Ibid.* 1785-9. [4] *Ibid.* 662-6, 1235-8, 1789-92.

composed. Like the Homeric poems and *Gilgamish*, its texture suggests that the poet did not improvise but was able to work slowly and carefully, and this implies some help from writing. In this there is no difficulty. Writing was common enough in England about 700 when the poem seems to have been written. The poet, with his theological interests, may well have been in contact with clerical circles to whom books were familiar. The poem must have been written down long before it was copied in its present manuscript about 1000, and there is no reason to think that it was not written down at the time of composition. No doubt the old Germanic poetry about Arminius or even the first poems on Attila were improvised, and to them and their kind the poet of *Beowulf* owes the main elements of his style. But he has brought it up to date and used many opportunities to escape from a purely formulaic language. We can hardly doubt that he composed for recitation, and for this reason he keeps many elements of the old oral style. That such was expected of him is clear from his Christian and theological passages, which cannot owe anything to the old Germanic poetry, but have none the less been assimilated to its manner.

The *Elder Edda* shows similar, if fewer, traces of an improvising past. For noun-adjective combinations we can quote, " lofty " buildings, " high-legged " stags, horses " trained to coursing ", and kings " lords of land ". In the *Lay of Völund* there are repeated lines like

> Maids of the south,   spinners of flax,
> Völund home   from his hunting came,[1]

In the *Lays of Guthrun* I and II a formulaic phrase is used for Sigurth :

> As the spear-leek grows   above the grass.

In *Guthrúnarhvöt* there is an even more primitive kind of formula :

> Then Hamther spake,   the high of heart.

We cannot doubt that the Norse poems of the *Elder Edda* are derived from a tradition which once used formulae. Their diminution may have been dictated by a desire to make the poems as concentrated and concise as possible, to remove any extraneous or unnecessary detail. Just as the poets omit much of the machinery of narrative, so too they are sparing in their use of formulae. Since every word is expected to do its full work, the standing epithets and fixed phrases have often been omitted or replaced by others which

---

[1] This is perhaps a special case ; cf. *inf.* p. 261.

go more directly to the point. So the usual apparatus of introducing speeches is largely abandoned, and the characters often
begin without the poet saying who speaks. Such changes were
easy, partly because the poems are usually short and would not be
difficult for a poet to compose in his head and remember for recitation, partly because the subjects are so familiar that any poet would
know that he need not make himself perfectly clear on every point.

The linguistic technique of the Anglo-Saxon and Norse poems
is a natural result of oral composition. They have sufficient traces
of formulae to betray both their origins and their own practice.
The same can hardly be said of the *Cid* and *Roland*, which stand
outside the main scheme and raise special problems. Both were,
so far as we can see, composed in writing. It is certain that their
authors could read, and, though the poems would no doubt be
recited, there is here no question of purely oral composition. The
origins of the two poems are probably different. If *Roland* is
something of a sport, the *Cid* certainly shares many characteristics
with other heroic poetry. Even if these are partly due to a literary
origin, some may be traced back to a past when oral composition
was the rule.

The *Cid* reveals traces both of noun-adjective combinations
and of repeated lines, though neither conforms very closely to
other models. Some of the characters, it is true, have their
epithets, like " Martín Antolínez, the loyal citizen ", " God,
spiritual father of us all ", " Galindo García, the valiant lance ",
" Minaya, the illustrious knight ", but these epithets are by no
means constant, and they usually perform some slight function in
their context instead of being merely decorative or otiose as are
most epithets in improvised heroic poetry. Thus Martín Antolínez
is called " loyal citizen " because his prowess is needed at that
moment. Though the persons of the *Cid* are clear enough in their
simple outlines, that is not because they are distinguished by
characterising epithets but because they show themselves in speech
and action. To this general paucity of noun-adjective combinations there is one great exception — the Cid himself. He is
called variously " the Cid Ruy Diaz ", " the Campeador ", " the
good Cid Campeador ", " the fortunate Cid ", " Cid of the
beautiful beard ", " the Cid of Vivar ", " illustrious Campeador ".
This variety is all the more remarkable because of the comparative
absence of titles for other characters. It is surely possible that in
treating his hero like this the poet follows a tradition which he
otherwise neglects. The Cid is honoured in this way because he
is a fit companion for the heroes of old and worthy to be men-

tioned in an archaic manner. Such titles are of course perfectly to the point, but they suggest that the poet has either invented them or adapted them from an older tradition in order to give a heroic status to his chief character.

More striking than these titles is the way in which the poet of the *Cid* devotes certain recurring lines to his hero. He commonly says of him that he " girt on his sword in a good hour ". The formula is not quite constant but shows minor variations, like

Ya Canpeador, en buena çinxiestes espada,
(O Campeador, in a good hour thou didst gird on thy sword)

Mio Çid Roy Díaz, el que en buena çinxo espada,
(My Cid, Ruy Diaz, who in a good hour girt on his sword)

Fabló mio Çid, el que en buen ora çinxo espada,
(So spoke the Cid, who in a good hour girt on his sword)

Merced, Canpeador, en buen ora çinxiestes espada,
(Thank you, Campeador, in a good hour thou didst gird on thy sword.)

This is plainly formulaic. The notion that the Cid " girt on his sword in a good hour " has little direct connection with the contexts in which it occurs. It is decorative, but not especially so, and it has all the marks of being derived from a formulaic style. It almost takes the place of a noun-adjective combination and does very much the same kind of task. Instead of qualifying the Cid with an adjective, the poet makes a laudatory statement about him. Nor is this the only case of such a formula. The poet is hardly less fond of another, which also takes slightly different forms :

Ya Canpeador, en buen ora fostes naçido,
(O Campeador, thou wast born in a good hour)

Dixo el Çid, el que en buen ora nasco,
(Then spoke the Cid who was born in a good hour)

Fabló mio Çid, Roy Díaz, el que en buen ora fue nado.
(Then spake the Cid, Ruy Diaz, who was born in a good hour.)

These formulaic expressions suggest two considerations. First, the variation which exists inside each recalls the Russian habit of varying a formula, as opposed to the strict Homeric adherence to it ; and this is largely due to considerations of metre. The Spanish line, which greatly varies the number of its syllables and has no very marked rhythm, resembles the Russian and not the Greek line in this respect. The Spanish formula is not forced into an absolutely fixed shape, and in fact has not got one. Yet it is plainly a formula, and no doubt its origins are to be found in the needs of improvisation — there is no need to think that it was first

used of the Cid — but it has not the finality of formulae fashioned
for strict metres like those of the Greeks or even the Jugoslavs.
Secondly, we can see why the poet sometimes uses one of these
kinds of formulae and sometimes the other. His lines are bound
together by assonance in the final syllable. They are not formed
in regular strophes, and the number of lines in a section varies
greatly. But in each section the final assonance must be preserved. Now the formula of girding on the sword belongs to lines
whose assonance is *a*, while that of being born in a good hour
belongs to lines whose assonance is *o*. By such aids to metre
composition is made easier for the poet.

The *Cid* stands apart in its use of formulae. On the one hand
it uses them, even if sparingly and in a special way ; on the other
hand its movement is generally so akin to that of prose narrative
that the main impression made is not at all formulaic. This would
seem to indicate that originally there was an oral poetry in Spain
which used formulae to some extent, but that the poet of the *Cid*
wrote his poem when this old style had been largely superseded.
So far his manner might suggest that he uses formulae out of
respect for the past. But it may be possible, though it cannot be
proved, that oral poetry in Spain never developed formulae on
any great scale. To judge by the extant remains of Spanish heroic
poetry, not merely in the *Cid* but in fragments of other poems
restored from the chronicles, this style was always factual and even
prosaic. The elastic nature of the heroic line, with its lack of
fixed accent and its ability to vary greatly its number of syllables,
suggests that oral composition can never have presented such
difficulties as it does for the Greek hexameter or even the old
Germanic metres. In that case the bard may not have needed
formulae so much as in these other cases, and that would explain
why there are so few of them. Of course the *Cid* was composed in
an age when writing was quite common and the poet was probably
an educated man. So it is conceivable that the comparative
absence of formulae in his work is due to his reliance on writing.
None the less his poem was intended for recitation, as he himself
says more than once, and we would expect him to show more traces
of formulae than he does, simply because they are useful in recitation. Though there can be no certainty in the matter, on the whole
it looks as if in Spain heroic poetry never used formulae so freely
as elsewhere, and that the *Cid* has almost passed beyond them.

Roland also presents a peculiar case. As we shall see later, it
looks as if French heroic poetry came into existence about the
year 1000, and was influenced not by indigenous French lays but

by Latin poems of the type of *Waltharius*. Since these poems are sometimes based on German vernacular originals, of the type of *Waldhere*, they contain echoes of formulae even in their pseudo-Virgilian dress. *Roland*, which might be expected to have no formulae at all, has in fact a fair share of them. It is true that so far as proper names are concerned, noun-adjective combinations hardly exist. The nearest is " sweet France ", but otherwise both places and people go for the most part unadorned. With ordinary things the case is different. *Roland* has its simple combinations like " green olive-branches ", " green grass ", " spurs of gold ", " Alexandrian silk ", " golden hilt ", " good sword ", " good spear ", " good hauberk ". In their unpretentious air these combinations look traditional and conventional, and though it is hard to believe that they are derived from Latin learning, it is possible that they come from an old vernacular usage through Latin adaptations. At the same time it should be noticed that the poet often advances beyond them to a greater elaboration, as when he dwells with admiring care on the points of a piece of armour instead of dismissing it briefly with a single adjective. So he speaks of

> Gird on their swords of tried steel Viennese,
> Fine shields they have, and spears Valentinese. (997-8)

> Their helmets gleam, with gold are jewellèd,
> Also their shields, their hauberks orfreyèd. (1031-2)

> His horse he pricks with his fine spurs of gold. (1738)

Of course in such matters the poet speaks of what he knows and his audience expects to hear. He therefore adds a touch of professional knowledge and gives an individual quality to his details.

Though most of *Roland* is occupied with fighting and treats of it with knowledge and precision, the poet on the whole avoids repeating himself verbally on such matters as wounds and deaths. Here he differs from Homer. Homer tends to have a set formula for each kind of wound, but *Roland* describes fewer kinds without any set form. For instance, in the first great fight seven successive sections speak of different single combats, and in each the substance is much the same. A blow breaks the opponent's shield and pierces his hauberk, so that he is killed. But this is expressed in a number of ways :

> So his good shield is nothing worth at all,
> Shatters the boss, was fashioned of crystal,
> One half of it downward to earth flies off ;
> Right to the flesh has through his hauberk torn. (1262-5)

> The shield he breaks, the hauberk unmetals,
> And his good spear drives into his vitals. (1270-71)

> The shield he breaks, with golden flowers tooled,
> That good hauberk for him is nothing proof. (1276-7)

> The shield he breaks, its golden boss above,
> The hauberk too, its doubled mail undoes. (1283-4)

> The shield he breaks and shatters on his neck,
> The hauberk too, he has its chinguard rent. (1292-3)

> Upon the shield, before its leathern band,
> Slices it through, the white with the scarlat,
> The hauberk too, has torn its folds apart. (1298-1300)

> The shield he breaks, the hauberk tears and splits. (1305)

To modern taste these variations on a single theme may not be very interesting, but to their original audience they had no doubt the appeal which details of battle have for soldiers. The poet's sense of battle may not be very varied, but it is at least vigorous and intense.

This series of passages illustrates an important element in the technique of *Roland*. In five out of the seven the poet describes the breaking of the shield in the same words, " l'escut li fraint ". This is for all practical purposes a formula, which is used as a basis for variation. In some ways it resembles the formulaic half-lines which are common in *Beowulf*. In *Roland* the short phrases usually come at the beginning of a line and are then completed with varying sequences to suit the required assonance. For instance, the setting of the fight at Roncesvalles is conveyed by the formula " halt sunt li pui " — " high are the peaks " — but each time that it occurs it is completed differently. It comes first when Charlemagne's main army goes through the pass :

> Halt sunt li pui e li val tenebrus. (814)
> (High are the peaks, the valleys shadowful.)

When Roland at last decides to blow his horn, the formula conveys through what country the blast rings :

> Halt sunt li pui e la voiz est mult lunge. (1755)
> (High are the peaks, afar it rings and loud.)

It makes a third appearance when Charlemagne's forces begin to come back to Roncesvalles :

> Halt sunt li pui e tenebrus e grant. (1830)
> (High are the peaks and shadowful and grand.)

And its last appearance is when Roland swoons before death :

> Halt sunt li pui e mult halt sunt li arbres. (2271)
> (High are the peaks, the trees are very high.)

On each occasion the formula serves a somewhat different purpose by having a different conclusion. But the reappearances serve to emphasise the setting of the battle and to remind us of the conditions in which it is fought. The poet uses it consciously with a fine sense of its worth, but it is none the less a formula.[1]

Roland poses a special question about the use of formulae. It is no longer possible to believe that its technique is derived from a long tradition of indigenous lays, and even if it owes something to earlier poems written from 1000 onwards, its background and antecedents are quite different from those of traditional oral poems. We might indeed expect *Roland* to have few or no formulae, and yet it has a certain number of them, which resemble to some extent the half-lines of Anglo-Saxon poetry. This cannot be an accident, and, if we exclude the possibility of any real debt to a traditional art, the most natural explanation is that French heroic poetry, which was undoubtedly recited and may even have been to some degree improvised, was forced by the conditions of its performance to create a style in which formulae came to play a part because of the minstrels' and the audience's needs. They were just as necessary to him as to any bard who has to perform in public and to keep the attention of his hearers without too great a strain on them. When Taillefer performed at Hastings, we need not necessarily assume that he knew his poem by heart; it is at least equally likely that he knew the outlines of the story and the means to make a poem of it, but the actual presentation may have been his own, and for it he would need some of the aids which oral recitation seems to find indispensable.

In general, we may say that the language of heroic poetry falls into two classes. In one it is derived directly from the needs of improvisation and helps the poet in this arduous task. This is the earlier form and accounts for the existence of formulae on a large scale in most heroic poems. If a bard is not very original, he may, like some Russian bards, confine himself almost entirely to formulae, and the result may give satisfaction but not be very interesting. But if he has some genuine talent, there is no need for him so to confine himself. He may well invent new formulae of his own and compose passages which are not formulaic. Such a

---

[1] Like *Beowulf*, *Roland* rarely repeats complete lines. The only examples are 576 and 3755 ; 2943 and 4001 ; 2646 and 3345 ; 1412 and 3381 ; 828 and 3613.

technique helps not only the poet but the audience, which finds
the formulae restful and familiar and proper to this kind of art.
At its best this kind of art can produce poetry as rich and varied
as that of the Kara-Kirghiz; at its worst it tends to be conventional and jejune, like some Russian poems. A great change comes
with the introduction of writing which allows a poet to compose
with far greater care and with much more time at his disposal.
Though this allows him to indulge in free composition, if he wishes,
he none the less tends to use formulae to some degree, just because
they are still useful and traditional. After all, every poet has to
use the means at his disposal, and, when no other kind of narrative
poetry is known to him, he will naturally compose as his predecessors have done before him. The result is that the difference
between oral, improvised poetry and semi-literate poetry is not
one of kind but of degree. Both use language in much the same
way, even if for different reasons, and though we may rightly
differentiate the art of the Tatars from that of *Roland* or the
Elder Edda, the two are not fundamentally dissimilar. In the end
it remains true that heroic poetry remains faithful to its peculiar
use of language because it has to be recited.

VII

THE TECHNIQUE OF COMPOSITION: DEVICES OF NARRATIVE

Just as the oral poet learns formulaic phrases which help him in the art of composition, so he also learns certain devices which enable him to surmount the many difficulties inherent in telling a story. Through them he knows how to start and how to finish, how to cause suspense and to maintain interest, how to avoid monotony and to vary the tone and texture of his work. Of course some of these devices are expressed in formulae, but even then the placing of them requires a sound judgment and a good sense of the audience's needs, and the poet shows his skill as much in his omission of them when they are not really needed as in his adroit use of them when they are. Moreover, just as the formulae exist because they are useful, but develop their own poetical charm, so the devices of narrative, which are in the first place indispensable to telling a story, also develop their own individuality and appeal. The audience knows that they exist, expects them to be used, greets them as old acquaintances, and applauds the poet who uses them expertly. It likes to see a familiar device turned to a new purpose or developed in a new direction. In considering such devices we have of course to ask what their fundamental use is and also what poetical success the poet gains through them, how he advances beyond their mere utility to make them attractive.

We may first look at repetitions. In many heroic poems a passage is repeated, almost word for word, very soon after its first appearance. Obviously this is no accident. A simple example may help to illustrate the problem. In the Bulgarian poem *The Visit* a husband says at the start to his wife:

> " Knead a white unleavened pudding,
> Pour some wine out, yellow-coloured,
> In this yellow wooden bottle ;
> Then, my wife, come, let us travel
> On a visit to your mother,
> To your mother and your father ;
> For nine years have come upon us
> Since I brought you from them hither ;
> We have visited them never." [1]

[1] Dozon, p. 55 ff.

254

The wife at first refuses; then the husband repeats his orders in exactly the same words, with the result that we see how insistent he is and what importance he attaches to his project. The wife does what she is told, and the poet tells how she

> Kneads a white, unleavened pudding,
> Pours some wine out, yellow-coloured,
> In a yellow wooden bottle.

A little later in the poem, when they enter a forest, the husband says:

> " Sing, my dear, a ringing ditty,
> With your own voice sing a ditty,
> Sounding like two voices singing,
> So your mother well may hear it,
> Father and your mother hear it,
> Know that we come on a visit,
> And let them come out to meet us."

Again the wife hesitates, and again the husband repeats his orders in exactly the same words, and again the wife carries them out:

> So she sang a ringing ditty,
> With her own voice sang a ditty,
> Sounding like two voices singing.

This may be unsophisticated, but it is clearly conscious and deliberate. The whole poem has 182 lines, and of these a large proportion consists of repetitions. There must be some explanation of it.

If we put modern poetry out of our heads and assume, as best we can, the simple mentality of an audience listening to this poem, we begin to understand why the poet uses this device. In the first place the repeated orders which the husband gives and the poet's repetition of them after him show that the details are important and intended to be noticed. They may seem trivial to us, but in the story they have their relevance and impress what happens on the memory. Secondly, the details do not lose in interest by being repeated. In fact, they gain. They somehow assume a special significance, suited to the simple mind, which likes precise facts and feels at home with them. It is clear that the husband has a purpose and means to carry it out. It may be trivial but has none the less its own interest, which the repetitions make, more vivid and suggestive. Thirdly, the device gives a firmer personality both to the husband and to the wife, to him because he is so insistent and to her because at first she hesitates and then obeys. This is a way in which husbands and wives are expected to behave, and the emphasis does justice to it. Fourthly, the device is a preliminary to what happens later. The husband and his wife are set upon by brigands who hear her song, and, though the husband kills the rest of them, he fails to kill the chieftain, who demands his wife from him, and thence exciting results follow. Both the song and the idea of the visit which precedes it are woven into the story and important to it. The poet stresses the way in which the action starts, that the conclusion may be seen in its proper perspective.

The art of this little piece has many parallels in heroic poetry, and in each case the motives for using it are similar to those mentioned above. A common form is for the poet first to retail something that happens and then to make a character repeat it in the same or almost the same words. In the Russian poem which tells of Ilya's quarrel with Vladimir, the device is used with admirable simplicity. Because Ilya is not asked to Vladimir's feast, he creates havoc in Kiev :

> He began to wander through the city of Kiev,
> And to stroll about the holy mother churches ;
> And he broke all the crosses on the churches,
> He shot off all the gilded balls.

This is duly reported by a messenger to Vladimir with only such changes of language as are required by a change from the past to the present tense :

> " He wanders through the city of Kiev,
> And strolls about the holy mother churches ;
> And he has broken all the crosses on the churches,
> He has shot off all the gilded balls." [1]

This repetition leaves no doubt about what Ilya does in his offended pride. Its details, being curious and amusing, gain by repetition ; it illustrates the heroic character of Ilya who is not likely to submit to insults from Vladimir, and it is important to the story, since Vladimir is so frightened by Ilya's behaviour that he decides to appease him by asking him to the feast after all.

Very similar is the kind of repetition in which first an order is given and later the same words are used as closely as possible to show that it is carried out. So in the Jugoslav *Marriage of Djuro of Smerderevo* Marko, on arriving at Dubrovnik, gives orders to his companions :

> " Give your horses up, but not your weapons,
> And sit down in armour at the tables,
> Drink of the dark wine above your weapons."

[1] Gilferding, ii, p. 38 ff. ; Chadwick, *R.H.P.* p. 62.

His orders are carried out:

> They gave up their horses, not their weapons,
> And sat down in armour at the tables,
> Drank of the dark wine above their weapons.[1]

Marko wishes to impress his host with the power and strength of his warriors, and his action has its bearing on the story later when he rescues his host's lady from a dungeon. The theme is worked in neatly, since the host asks why the men behave like this, and Marko answers with confident assurance that it is a Serbian custom; but the poet's real purpose in the repetition is to stress a point which might otherwise escape notice. Not all poets are so economical of the device as this. Many delight in it for its own sake as an almost ritualistic procedure which imparts an additional dignity to a point by repeating it. So when the Canaanite poet of *Aqhat* tells how Daniel decides to make a tour of neighbouring lands, he first makes him call to his daughter:

> " Hearken, O Paghat,
> Thou that carriest water on thy shoulders,
> That brushest the dew from the barley,
> That knowest the courses of the stars;
> Saddle an ass, hitch a foal;
> Set upon it my silver reins,
> My golden bridles." [2]

The poet goes on immediately to tell how Paghat carries out the orders, and uses almost the same words:

> Paghat obeys,
> Even she who carries the water on her shoulders,
> Who brushes the dew from the barley,
> Who knows the courses of the stars;
> Straightway she saddles an ass,
> Straightway she hitches a foal,
> Straightway she lifts up her father,
> Seats him on the back of the ass,
> On the gaily-trapped back of the foal.

The repetition serves to make perfectly clear what the orders imply, that Paghat is to saddle an ass for her father to ride upon. The whole little action gains in ceremony by this decorous carrying out of orders, but we may suspect that the poet has another motive than this. Daniel speaks to his daughter as to one whose whole life is engaged in household tasks from dawn till dark — that is why she knows the courses of the stars — and this has some importance for the story, since later Paghat is to prove that she is much more

---

[1] Karadžić, ii, p. 437 ff.　　　　[2] Gaster, p. 297; Gordon, p. 95.

than this, when she goes out to find Yatpan, who has killed her brother, and kills him in return for it.

Most repetitions are of only a few lines, but sometimes they are much longer. For instance, in the Canaanite *Keret* the god El appears to Keret in a dream and gives him precise instructions about organising an expedition against Edom (Udm) and marrying the king's daughter. This takes about a hundred lines, and is followed immediately by an account of the same length, in as far as possible the same words, in which Keret carries out the instructions.[1] At one or two points, as in the behaviour of the king of Edom, the passage is slightly expanded, but apart from this it is a remarkable case of repetition, which, even if the whole poem were of a considerable length, would be very noticeable. Of course it serves to show how Keret carries out a god's commands and is so far what a king ought to be. It also illustrates his character in his high-handed treatment of the king of Edom and his insistence on marrying his daughter. But it is difficult not to suspect that the poet has some other motive. Perhaps, like the poet of *Aqhat*, he has a ritualistic feeling for what happens and likes to make it more impressive and stately by repetition. This is the more justified since his theme concerns the relations of gods with men, and may appropriately be treated in the style which the Semitic poets use for religious subjects. Indeed repetition in more than one form seems to be a marked characteristic of the Canaanite epics, and in it we may see the influence of theological poetry in which, like other Semites, the Canaanites delighted. Just as in a hymn points are stressed by frequent repetition, so in a story concerning the gods it is again used to impart a religious dignity.

Sometimes the same passage is repeated several times, but for this there is usually a special reason. The poet has something out of the way to say and feels that it must be repeated if it is to make its full impression. A simple example comes from the Ossete *The Last Expedition of Uryzmag*. The hero, Uryzmag, is taken prisoner and shut up in a tower by a giant. He offers ransom in mysterious terms, which the giant foolishly accepts without knowing what they mean :

> " We offer ten thousand cattle, each with one horn,
> And ten thousand cattle, each with two horns,
> And ten thousand cattle, each with three horns,
> And ten thousand cattle, each with four horns,
> And ten thousand cattle, each with five horns." [2]

[1] Gordon, p. 68 ff.
[2] Dynnik, p. 21 ff. ; cf. Dumézil, pp. 45-6.

This formula occurs three times more, first when Uryzmag tells it to the messenger who is to carry the news of the offer to the Narts, then by the messenger to the Narts, then by the Narts themselves, when, puzzled by the words, they take them to their wise woman, Satana, for elucidation. The message is cryptic and oracular and central to the plot, since through it Uryzmag conveys instructions which are unintelligible to his captor and which only Satana will understand. As she expounds it, it means :

> " An ox with one horn, that is a warrior with an axe,
> An ox with two horns, that is a warrior on horse-back,
> An ox with three horns, that is a horseman with a spear,
> An ox with four horns, that is a spearman in a breast-plate,
> An ox with five horns, that is a warrior in full armour."

The passage occurs four times because it is alluring in itself, shows Uryzmag's craft and Satana's wisdom, and is essential to the story, since through this message Uryzmag outwits his captor and is in due course delivered by an army of Narts.

A special type of repetition is that in which an action is itself repeated. The poet may do this to stress the emotional character of a situation, or to provide a contrast with something that is to come later. A striking example of the first may be seen in the *First Lay of Guthrun*. The scene is set after Sigurth's death, when Guthrun is so broken with grief that she sits by his body without speaking or even weeping. Wives of other warriors come and try to comfort her by telling of their own sorrows. First, Gjaflaug tells how she has lost five husbands and eight brothers. But Guthrun says nothing :

> Grieving could not   Guthrun weep,
> Such grief she had   for her husband dead,
> And so grim her heart   by the hero's body.[1]

Then Herborg, at greater length than Gjaflaug, tells another tragic tale, but again Guthrun remains silent, and again the poet uses the same three lines. The repetition is extraordinarily effective. It shows that Guthrun has not noticed what is happening but remains frozen in her grief. This type of repetition may be slightly varied to produce a somewhat different effect. So in an Armenian poem, when Sasoun is in danger, Mher the Younger goes to call on the spirits of his parents. He first summons his mother, and from under the earth a voice answers :

> " My son, how can I help you ?
> My son, how can I help you ?

[1] *Guthrúnarkvitha*, i, 5.

259

There is no blood in my face,
The light of my eyes has long gone out.
Scorpions and snakes
Have plaited their nests above me.
You have had enough of wandering, my son,
Enough of wandering . . .
Your place is at the Bird Rock,
Go up to the Bird Rock." [1]

Mher then calls on his father's spirit and receives almost an identical answer but with the important addition that he is to dwell alive in a cave until the end of the world. Mher's strange destiny is not revealed until he has repeated his question, and the repeated answer gives a special force to the final message when it comes.

A special form of this kind of repetition is when the poet deals with a ritual which demands that an action should be performed several times in succession. The Canaanite *Aqhat*, which is considerably interested in Semitic rites, does this at least twice. When Daniel decides to ask the gods for a son, he performs the rite of incubation and stays as a suppliant in a sanctuary in order to obtain an oracle by a dream or some other means. After telling how Daniel goes to the sanctuary, the poet describes his actions for seven days, on each of which he does the same thing:

Behold one day and a second,
Clothed in the loincloth,
Clothed in the loincloth, Daniel gives food to the gods,
Clothed in the loincloth, he gives drink to the holy ones. [2]

This is repeated once for the third and fourth days, and once again for the fifth, sixth, and seventh days. On the seventh day Daniel's prayers are answered. Here the repetition of the action, and the even more emphatic repetition of its elements, stress its ritual nature. So later in the poem, when the son is born, Daniel celebrates it with a feast and invites " daughters of melody " to his house. Just as modern Arabs celebrate the birth of a child with seven days of entertainment by female singers and musicians, so Daniel does the same, and the poet emphasises the formality of the occasion by a series of repetitions, of which the first sets the pattern:

Behold, for one day and a second
He gave the singing women to eat,
And the daughters of melody, the Swallows, to drink.

This happens again, in very much the same words, for the third and fourth days, and again for the fifth and sixth:

[1] *David Sasunskii*, p. 324 ff.   [2] Gaster, p. 270.

> Then on the seventh day,
> The singing women depart from his house,
> The daughters of melody, the Swallows.[1]

The unpretentious device conveys the solemn, formal character of the feast.

A poet may also use repetition to show the difference between a first and a second occasion or to provide a kind of rehearsal for an action performed fully later. Two events are thus brought together, and the second becomes more significant through its association with the first, especially if the full implications of what happens are not revealed till the second occasion. This is done with skilful effect in the Norse *Lay of Völund*. When Völund plots vengeance on Nithuth, he decides to kill Nithuth's sons. One day the two boys come to his house, and he shows them a chest filled with gold :

> They came to the chest,   and they craved the keys,
> The evil was open   when in they looked ;
> To the boys it seemed   that gems they saw,
> Gold in plenty   and precious stones.[2]

This looks harmless enough, but the words " the evil was open " are a dark and ambiguous hint of something to come. The chest is called " the evil " not on the principle that all gold is evil but because it is to be the cause of the boys' deaths. As we read the words, we do not see any great significance in them, but their full purport is revealed later. The boys go away after being invited to come back the next day. They come back, go to the chest, and are killed. The poet picks up the theme by repeating two lines and then shows what he has had in mind all the time :

> They came to the chest,   and they craved the keys,
> The evil was open   when in they looked ;
> He smote off their heads,   and their feet he hid
> Under the sooty   straps of the bellows.[3]

The repetition here is used with subtle art. The first time is a kind of rehearsal for the second, when the words " the evil " reveal their full significance in the light of Völund's merciless trick.

Emphasis is the special task of repetitions, but it is not always needed, and the poet is not compelled to repeat passages even when we expect him to do so. He may wish to create some other effect, notably surprise, by keeping something in reserve so that, after telling how a command is given, he then, somewhat differently, tells how it is carried out. So when the Russian poet relates how

---

[1] *Idem*, p. 277.   [2] *Völundarkvitha*, 21.   [3] *Ibid.* 24.

Nightingale Budimirovich visits Prince Vladimir, he stresses the visitor's wealth and state, especially in the orders which he gives before disembarking from his ship :

> " Lower a silver gangway,
> Lower a second one covered with gold,
> Lower a third of whale-bone.
> Take pleasant gifts,
> Marten-skins and fox-furs from foreign lands."

The main impression is made, and there is no need to repeat all the details in the same words. But, since our curiosity has been aroused by the unusual orders about the gangways, the poet must explain what they mean and does so by varying the form of words :

> They took the gifts in their white hands ;
> His mother took figured damask,
> And he himself his lyre of maple-wood,
> And he crossed the gilded gangway,
> His mother crossed the silver one,
> And all his company the gangway of whale-bone.[1]

Here it is a question not of emphasising something important to the plot but of drawing attention to the special character of Nightingale's visit. Our curiosity is first aroused and then satisfied.

Since repetitions are an accepted part of a poet's art, it is natural that he should play with them and vary their use. One variation is to turn them to an unexpected result. An order is given but not carried out, or an intention stated but not fulfilled. Then the poet repeats his formula fully but with negatives throughout to show the failure of some plan or idea. A simple example of this comes from the Jugoslav *Marko's Ploughing*, a short poem whose appeal turns almost wholly on such a point. Marko's mother is tired of her son's endless fights with the Turks and tells him to take to a different kind of life :

> " Take thou up the plough and take thou oxen,
> Plough with them the hill and plough the valley,
> Then, my son, sow thou thereon the wheat-seed."

Marko half obeys his mother, but not entirely :

> He took up the plough, and he took oxen,
> But he ploughed not either hill or valley,
> But he ploughed with them the Sultan's highway.[2]

---

[1] Gilferding, i, p. 157 ; Chadwick, *R.H.P.* p. 118.
[2] Karadžić, ii, p. 403.

The result is that he is soon engaged in fight again with the Turks, kills them, and comes back with their gold to his mother :

" See ", said he, " what I have done with ploughing."

The formula is more or less preserved, but the effect is unexpected, and the repetition is skilfully used to stress the strange result. Somewhat similar is the art of the Bulgarian *The Beginnings of the Turkish Empire*. The villagers tell their leader that they have forgotten God and must build churches. He takes up their words and makes an ingenious use of them by what is in effect a double repetition. He says that it is useless to build churches, but that none the less they must build them :

> " 'Tis not fitting to build churches,
> All of gold and all of silver ;
> For our empire will be finished,
> And the Turkish empire starting.
> They will break to bits the churches,
> Of the silver fashion saddles,
> Melt the gold down into bridles ;
> Let us none the less build churches,
> Made of white stone and of marble,
> With white chalk and yellow plaster."
> To his words the townsfolk listened,
> And began to build the churches
> Made of white stone and of marble,
> With white chalk and yellow plaster.[1]

The movement is more complicated than in *Marko's Ploughing*, but the variation on the repeated phrases, first negative, and then positive, applies a familiar technique with neatness and ingenuity.

An impressive example of negative repetition comes from *Gilgamish*. Gilgamish wishes to summon the ghost of his dead comrade, Enkidu, and sets about the task with some cunning. He asks what he must do to avoid being haunted by the dead and receives elaborate, explicit instructions :

> " If thou comest to the temple, put on clean clothing ;
> Like a townsman shalt thou come to it.
> Be not anointed with sweet oil from a cruse,
> Nor let its fragrance gather around thee ;
> Set not bow to the earth,
> Lest those shot down by thy bow gather around thee ;
> Carry not a stick in thy hand,
> Lest ghosts gibber against thee ;
> Put no shoe on the sole of thy foot,
> Nor make a sound on the ground ;

[1] Dozon, p. 67.

S

The wife whom thou lovest, kiss her not,
The wife whom thou hatest, chastise her not;
The child whom thou lovest, kiss him not,
The child whom thou hatest, chastise him not." [1]

Gilgamish then does just the opposite of what he is told, and the poet tells of this in the same order and with only such changes as are required by Gilgamish's violation of the rules. The art of repetition receives a new and subtle turn, and it is clear that the poet is a master of it.

In such repetitions there may be a number of different items, each of which has its own importance, and it is essential that each should be equally emphatic. For this reason an ingenious method is sometimes used by which the items are first stated in one order and then repeated in the reverse order. The reason for this is that in absorbing such lists the audience, in its interest in what is coming later, may forget what comes earlier, and this technique serves to keep all the items fresh in the memory. A charming example comes from the Jugoslav *Marko drinks Wine in Ramadan*, which begins with an order given by the Sultan and with Marko's immediate disregard of it :

Sultan Suleiman gave cry an order,
That no man should drink of wine in Ramadan,
That no man should put on green apparel,
That no man should gird a sword about him,
That no man should dance a dance with women.
Only Marko danced a dance with women,
Marko girded on a well-forged sabre,
Marko garbed himself in green apparel,
Marko drank of wine, red wine, in Ramadan. [2]

By this neat device all the items in Marko's behaviour are kept clear and emphatic, and there is a certain charm in the way in which they are repeated in reverse order, so that the drinking of wine stands out as his chief offence.

The same technique is used by Homer, especially in dealing with complicated questions and answers. For instance, when Odysseus arrives as an unknown stranger at the court of Alcinous, the queen, Arete, asks him three questions, who is he, who gave him his garments (which she recognises as belonging to her own household), and whether he came over the sea. Odysseus answers these questions in the opposite order. First, he tells at some length of his wanderings at sea ; next, he says that he landed naked and that Arete's daughter, Nausicaa, gave him the garments which

[1] *Gilgamish*, XII, i, 15-27.   [2] Karadžić, ii, p. 395.

he is wearing; his name he does not tell but keeps in reserve to surprise his hosts later.[1] Again, when Odysseus meets the ghost of his mother, he asks her a series of questions, seven in all, about her own death, did she die of disease or by the gentle arrows of Artemis, about Laertes and about Telemachus, whether his estates and power are safe or have been taken by another, and about Penelope. His mother answers these questions in exactly the opposite order, beginning with news of Penelope, then tells him that no one has taken his power and estates which are safe, continues with Telemachus and Laertes, and ends by saying that she herself died not from the gentle arrows of Artemis, nor from disease, but for longing for Odysseus.[2] Not only is the audience kept fully aware of the situation in its many aspects, but Homer secures a wonderful effect through the last words which come as a triumphant climax.

The repetitions so far considered belong to a special department of the poet's technique which is concerned with stressing something within a short space. Each time the passage is repeated we recall that it has already been used and relate its later appearances to its earlier. When a poet composes, as Homer does, on a large scale, the use of repetition may be different. He has his recurring formulaic passages for many kinds of action, and he uses them frequently. Nor, when he repeats a passage after a considerable interval, do we necessarily remember where it last appeared and what purpose it then served. But Homer uses these repetitions with discrimination. He does not introduce them on every suitable occasion but varies their introduction to mark stages or emphasis in his story. He has, for instance, a set of eight lines which tell how a guest is washed and fed, and in the *Odyssey* he uses this six times, but always as a prelude to some new development in the action — for the first appearance of Athene in Ithaca which sets the plot going,[3] for the first colloquy between Telemachus and Menelaus which precedes the stories of what happened to the heroes of Troy,[4] for the reception of Odysseus in Phaeacia with its promise that he will be sent safely home,[5] for the moment when Circe has promised to turn back his comrades into their proper human shape,[6] for the departure of Telemachus from Sparta with its propitious omens and Helen's prophecy of success,[7] and for Telemachus' story of his adventures to Penelope with the solemn words of the seer, Theoclymenus, that Odysseus has already

[1] *Od.* vii, 237 ff. [2] *Ibid.* xi, 171-203 ; cf. Bassett, pp. 120-22.
[3] *Od.* i, 136 ff. [4] *Ibid.* iv, 52 ff. [5] *Ibid.* vii, 172 ff.
[6] *Ibid.* x, 368 ff. [7] *Ibid.* xv, 135 ff.

arrived in Ithaca.[1] On other occasions guests arrive and the formulaic passage might be used, but it is not, and the natural conclusion is that it creates an effect which prepares us for new developments. It gives a pause in the action and leads us from one episode to another. Not all poets are so skilful at this as Homer, but the use of the set passage in the long poem is not simply a convenience for the poet; it can also do a special work in its context.

Homer also illustrates the art of omitting set passages unless they have something special to do. He has, for instance, a form of several lines which tells how a warrior arms. But he does not use it invariably. When all is ready for the duel between Hector and Ajax, he says no more than Ajax " armed himself in bright bronze ".[2] He uses similar shortened forms for the arming of Paris, Idomeneus, and Athene.[3] But on four occasions he uses a full form, and each has its significance. The first is before the duel between Paris and Menelaus, which is the first fighting in the *Iliad* and the prelude to the general battle;[4] the second is when Agamemnon, in the absence of Achilles, prepares for a great onslaught;[5] the third is before the counter-attack led by Patroclus which saves the Achaean forces from destruction and drives the Trojans back to Troy;[6] and the fourth is when Achilles finally decides to go back to the fight.[7] Each is a special occasion since it marks a new and important stage in the development of the action. It is true that the four cases are not quite alike, and that in each Homer, after using a set form for the start, then adds to it differently in each case. But this only shows how he sees each occasion in its own light and adapts his formula to it with some piece of relevant information about Agamemnon's shield and breast-plate or the chariot and horses of Patroclus and Achilles. Homer is such a master of his craft that he makes his formulaic passages vary with their contexts and the needs of his narrative.

Repetitions are commonest in formulaic poetry but there is one important feature of this style which survives in almost all branches of heroic verse. Similes have their roots very deep in poetical art. They are already impressive in *Gilgamish*, where Enkidu's hair sprouts " like barley "; he himself sways " like mountain corn "; Gilgamish laments for him " like a wailing woman " or " like a lioness robbed of her cubs "; in the Flood bodies glut the sea " like fish-spawn "; the tempest and the deluge fight " like an embattled army "; the gods come to a

---

[1] *Od.* xvii, 91 ff.   [2] *Il.* vii, 206.
[3] *Ibid.* vi, 504 ; xiii, 241 ; viii, 388.   [4] *Ibid.* iii, 328 ff.
[5] *Ibid.* xi, 16 ff.   [6] *Ibid.* xvi, 130 ff.   [7] *Ibid.* xix, 369 ff.

sacrifice " like flies "; sleep comes " like a breeze ". Similes, as Gilgamish uses them, belong to a very ancient habit of speech. They do something which direct description cannot do, in stressing aspects of a situation which appeal to the eye or the feelings but are too indeterminate for direct statement. No doubt a highly developed language might say the same kind of thing, without resorting to similes, by some precise account of what happens. But, even so, much would be lost, since the simile catches those emotional and imaginative associations which lie beyond the reach of literal statement. The simile is as essential to heroic poetry as to any other because it conveys fleeting shades and tones which would otherwise be lost.

Comparisons may be extremely simple and short, and in most heroic poetry similes consist of a very few words. Such are to be found constantly in Homer, as when he says that a shield is " like a tower ", that Apollo comes down " like the night ", that Thetis rises from the sea " like a mist ", that a cloud is " blacker than pitch ", that Agamemnon surveys his forces " like a ram ", that Athene comes " like a sea-bird ", that warriors are " like lions or boars ". Such comparisons are immediately to the point; they illuminate the situation for a moment, and then the poet goes on with the story. This kind of illustration serves a truly poetical purpose in bringing together things which are commonly kept apart. The poet almost identifies one object with another and creates in the minds of his hearers a similar identification. When Homer's gods descend like the night or rise like the mist, they are for the moment almost equated with night or mist and have such a look and movement. In such comparisons a real element of identity is presupposed, and to this the poet draws attention.

At the same time a simile not only illustrates but creates a special effect because it is drawn from some sphere of reality not closely related to that in which the action itself takes place. It turns our minds to this and makes us for the moment forget the action in the thought of something else. It thus gives relief and respite, especially in accounts of battle and fighting which may not be monotonous to their right hearers but at least tend to awake a narrow range of emotional response. The excitements and the thrills of fighting, even the pity and fear which it arouses, may come in so strong a flood as to overwhelm us and dull our sensibilities. Even the smallest simile may help in this and enable us to regain our interest. So when a Jugoslav hero leaps to the attack,

As a mountain falcon spreads its pinions,

we not only see him more vividly but feel differently about him. The mention of the bird conjures up a different world of experience and adds a new note of colour to the picture. The small simile nearly always has this effect, even when it is not concerned with battle. It takes our minds momentarily away from the scenes of violence, and so refreshes them and enables them to listen again with a new attention.

The size and character of similes vary considerably from one class of heroic poetry to another. There are even some poems which lack them altogether, like *Hildebrand* and *Maldon*. These poems are short, and it may be that in their restricted compass poets do not feel any need to embellish the story, but give all their time to making the most of its essential facts. Or it may be that their temper is so austerely heroic that even a simile is felt to be out of place, an unnecessary decoration or unworthy concession to human frailty. Certainly these two cases seem to be exceptional. Similes occur in *Beowulf* and in the *Elder Edda*, and there is no reason to think that they did not exist in the old Germanic poetry which lies behind both *Hildebrand* and *Maldon*. There is also a comparative paucity of similes in the Armenian poems, and here there is no question of space, since the poets compose on quite a generous scale. But this art, as it is now practised, must have lost much which it once had, and the comparative absence of similes is probably due to the passage of time which has taken away much else. With these exceptions, for which there may be special reasons, similes are to be found in most heroic poetry wherever it exists.

Similes are usually short and consist of no more than a few words. That this is in origin formulaic is clear not merely from Homer but from other poets who improvise or are close to improvisation. It is, for instance, normal in Jugoslav poems, where warriors are " like burning coals " or " mountain wolf-packs ", with moustaches " black as midnight ", or roar for booty " like bullocks ", where a woman hisses " like a furious serpent ", villages rise in revolt " like the grass-blades ", bullets fly " like hailstones from the sky ", women lament " like cuckoos " or " like swallows ", men ride together " like a pair of pigeons " or " like two tall mountains ", a warrior casts his cudgel " like a maiden playing with an apple ", a man's throat is slit " like a white lamb's ", eyes pierce through the darkness " like a prowling wolf's at midnight ", or a horse races " like a star across the cloudless heavens ". Similes of this kind are much less common in Russian poems, but they have their part in the Russian tradition and may be seen in the *Tale of Igor's Raid*, where warriors run like wolves, fly like falcons, creep like weasels, swim like ducks. As we shall see, the characteristic Russian simile is different, but the ordinary simile is known to the poets who tell how ships fly " like falcons " or " like white hawks ", or how the heathen are " like black crows ", or roar " like beasts ".

The Asiatic peoples are quite as fond of similes as the European. The poetry of the Kara-Kirghiz abounds in them. Warriors are commonly compared to leopards or camels or tigers or bears ; their eyes are like flames ; a woman's eyes sparkle like mirrors ; tears are like drops of rain or hail in spring ; words are like hawks. The Kalmucks have an equal abundance. A flag is like the yellow sun ; a hero beautiful as the meeting of friends ; dust rises like the white clouds of the sky ; deer are as numerous as the stars ; tears are like hail ; warriors are like lions ; a woman's face is like the full moon. Despite the small scale of their composition, the Ossetes manage to introduce similes into their poems and tell how a warrior disguises himself in a skin " like a leathern bottle ", or strikes at his enemy " like an arrow ", or roars " like thunder in the sky ", or looks at his opponent " as an eagle looks at a sparrow ", how a man disappears " like water poured from a cup on the sand ". Such similes are certainly formulaic, since they are repeated when there is need for them. They add to the variety of the poetry, and their repetition contributes to the general effect.

The same art can be seen in a modified form in poems which have moved further from improvisation, and prove that this device still has its charm and usefulness. In *Beowulf* the work of such similes is largely done by the " kennings ", but there are a few genuine similes like

> The foamy-flecked floater   to a fowl best likened (218).

> In his eyes there shone
> The leaping flame likest   a light unlovely (727-8).

> Was the stem of each nail   to steel best likened (985).

In *Roland* there are no " kennings " but there are some simple similes. The Franks are " fiercer than lions ", the Saracens " blacker than ink on the pen ", a man's head " white as a flower in summer ", bears " white as driven snows ", a horseman " swifter than a falcon ". As the poet gets further away from formulae, he uses similes less freely, but when he uses them, they are clearly traditional. He owes them to an ancient art and at times resorts to them to make a point clear.

A special kind of simile, found chiefly in Slavonic countries and often called " epic antithesis ", is really a negative comparison. In it a statement is first made or a question asked ; then it is contradicted or denied. This device enables the poet to hint at a state of mind and then to make it clear, and in so doing to give a fuller significance to what he describes by creating expectation and surprise. The first traces of this can be seen in the *Tale of Igor's Raid*, when Igor escapes from the Polovtsy :

> It was not the magpies chattering ;
> In pursuit of Igor
> Gzak rides with Konchak.

This reflects a natural experience. First a sound is suggested, which might be the chatter of magpies ; then it is clear that it is something else, the chatter of Igor's pursuers. But the impression of a simile remains because the sound of the pursuit is really like the confused babble of magpies. This device is found in all branches of Slavonic poetry, and may well be an inheritance from a distant past. A good example comes from the Bulgarian *Death of the Warrior Marko* :

> With a red light was the sunrise flaming
> On the beautiful Wallachian country.
> No, it was not sunrise in the heaven ;
> 'Twas his mother seeking her son, Marko.[1]

Precisely the same device is used by Ukrainian poets, as when captives lament in prison :

On Holy Sunday it is not the grey-blue eagles who have begun to cry,
It is the poor captives in their harsh captivity who have begun to cry.[2]

Or when a Cossack leaves his home :

> On Sunday in the morning,
> It is not the clocks that sound,
> It is voices which sound in the house at the end of the village.
> The father and the mother send their son to a foreign land.[3]

The same device is commonly used by Jugoslav poets, especially to introduce a poem by a striking appeal to the imagination. So *Marko Kralević and General Vuka* begins with a scene of revel in the castle of a Turk who has captured three Serb warriors :

> Is it thunder, or is it an earthquake ?
> No it is not thunder nor an earthquake ;
> They are firing cannons in the castle,
> In the mighty castle of Varadin.[4]

[1] Derzhavin, p. 83. [2] Scherrer, p. 58.
[3] *Idem*, p. 114. [4] Karadžić, ii, p. 224.

The noise of the cannons is presented first through the image of thunder or earthquake, then in its true character. Again, in *Miloš Stoićević and Meho Orugdžijć* a mother's lament is presented by the same indirect approach :

> Loud a grey-blue cuckoo-bird lamented
> On the hillock over Bíjeljina ;
> 'Twas no grey-blue cuckoo that lamented,
> But the mother of Orugdžijć Meho.[1]

Such passages perform the same function as ordinary similes, but in a more striking way. Our curiosity is first aroused, then satisfied, and we receive a complex impression of what is happening through the poet's double presentation of it.

This device is exploited with much skill by Russian poets who greatly prefer it to the ordinary simile. A good example can be seen in Ryabinin's account of the murder of the Tsarevich Dmitri by Boris Godunov :

> It is no whirlwind rolling along the valley,
> It is not feather-grass bowing to the earth,
> It is an eagle flying under the clouds ;
> Keenly he looks at the Moscow River
> And the palace of white stone,
> And its green garden,
> And the golden palace of the royal city.
> It is not a cruel serpent rearing itself up,
> It is a cowardly dog raising a steel knife.
> It has fallen not into the water nor on the earth,
> It has fallen on to the white breast of the Tsar's son,
> None other than the Tsar's son Dmitri.[2]

Here there are in effect three comparisons. First, the flight of an eagle is like a wind or grass moving : then, the murderous stroke of Boris is like the bite of a snake ; lastly, the fall of the knife on the young man's breast is like something falling on earth or water. The negative comparisons create an impression which is both visual and emotional ; they show both what the crime looks like and what it means. Sometimes this art is used for a purely emotional or psychological purpose, as when a poet describes the fury of Ivan the Terrible against the towns of Pskov and Novgorod :

> It is not the blue sea which is stirring,
> It is not the wet pine-wood which is on fire,
> It is the terrible Tsar Ivan Vasilevich who is aflame,
> Saying that he must punish Novgorod and Pskov ;[3]

[1] *Ibid.* iv, p. 196. Trs. W. A. Morison.
[2] Kireevski, vii, p. 1.　　　　　　　[3] Rybnikov, i, p. 115.

or the impression of awe and fear which a Russian general makes
at the time of Peter the Great's war against Charles XII of Sweden :

> It is not a threatening cloud which has come up,
> Nor a heavy fall of sleet descending ;
> From the glorious town of Pskov
> The great royal boyar has arisen,
> Count Boris, the lord Petrovich Sheremetev,
> With all his cavalry and dragoons,
> With all his Muscovite infantry.[1]

In such cases the parallel is not visible but emotional. The images
reflect the temper of the Tsar and the threatening appearance of the
general, and set the tone for the poem which follows.

In these cases an additional emphasis is often secured through
an accumulation of comparisons. The poet feels that one is not
enough for his purpose and adds one or two more to make his
meaning quite clear. This is a technique pursued by many users
of similes. It draws attention to more than one aspect of a complex
situation and shows how much the poet sees in it. When the Kara-
Kirghiz poet describes a sorceress, he says :

> Like a bride, with covered face,
> Dzhestumshyk, the copper-lipped,
> Hunts there for human beings,
> As an evil spider hunts for flies.[2]

In appearance the sorceress is like a bride ; in character like a
spider. The elements so accumulated are unpretentious enough
in themselves but gain by being placed in new combinations.
Thus, though the poets of the *Elder Edda* seldom use similes, yet,
when they do, they like to accumulate them. The elements are
plainly traditional — a man is like a stag or a tree or a jewel —
but variations are secured through new conjunctions, as for
instance :

> Helgi rose   above heroes all
> Like the lofty ash   above lowly thorns,
> Or the noble stag,   with dew besprinkled,
> Bearing his head   above all beasts.[3]

Sigurth is praised in much the same way by Guthrun :

> " So was my Sigurth   o'er Gjuki's sons,
> As the spear-leek grown   above the grass,
> Or the jewel bright   borne on the band,
> The precious stone   that princes wear " ;[4]

---

[1] Kireevski, viii, p. 129; Chadwick *R.H.P.* p. 271.   [2] *Manas*, p. 76.
[3] *Helgakvitha Hundingsbana*, ii, 37.   [4] *Guthrunárkvitha*, i, 17.

or

> So Sigurth rose   o'er Gjuki's sons
> As the leek grows green   above the grass,
> Or the stag o'er all   the beasts doth stand,
> Or as glow-red gold   above silver grey.[1]

Though the separate elements in these similes are simple and even conventional, something is gained by their juxtaposition. Helgi or Sigurth is suggested in his whole being, in his height and strength, his superiority and brilliance and beauty. Each simile makes its contribution, but the total result is more than the mere sum of them.

When a poet wishes to produce a particularly striking effect, he may pile up similes in this way, taking care that each adds something new. So the Kara-Kirghiz poet conveys the speed and ferocity of Alaman Bet in action :

> He flashed like a whirlwind,
> He made the light of noon like night,
> He made summer into winter,
> And with a thick veil
> He covered the empty steppe.[2]

In a similar manner the Kalmuck poet lets himself go on the great hero, Dzhangar :

> Look at him from behind,
> He is slender as a tall cypress ;
> Look at him from in front,
> It is as if he had a hungry lion's grip
> Who leaps from the crest of a hill.
> Look at him from the side,
> He is like a full moon on the fifteenth night.
> In the muscles between his shoulders
> He is almost like a loaded camel.
> His lustreless silver hair
> Stays like a fallen full-grown cypress.[3]

This portrait from every angle leaves little unsaid. Nor is this technique confined to men. It is equally suited to feminine charms, and a Kara-Kirghiz poet uses it very prettily when he expands on the charms of Ak Saikal :

> The snow falls to the black earth,
> Look at the snow, it is like her flesh ;
> A drop of blood falls on the snow,
> Look at the blood, it is like her face.

[1] *Ibid.* ii, 2.   [2] *Manas*, p. 240.
[3] *Dzhangariada*, p. 97.

> Her mouth is like a foxglove,
> Her teeth are rows of pearls,
> Like feathers her eyebrows,
> Black berries her eyes,
> Like sugar is the maiden.[1]

A similar technique and not dissimilar comparisons are used by a Jugoslav poet for the same purpose :

> Fine of waist is she, and tall of figure,
> And her hair is like a wreath of silk-threads ;
> Her two eyes are like two precious jewels,
> And like leeches from the sea her eyebrows ;
> In her cheeks a crimson rose is blooming,
> And her teeth two strings of pearls resemble,
> And her mouth a little box of sugar ;
> When she speaks, 'tis like a pigeon cooing,
> Like the sound of sprinkled pearls her laughter,
> And her walk is like a peahen's gliding.[2]

Most of these comparisons are formulaic and traditional, but their combination is new and charming. The poet sets out an inventory of the young woman's attractions, and she emerges from it in all her grace and gaiety.

These accumulated similes belong to what is on the whole an unsophisticated poetry, but they are also used by poets who are more conscious of their literary calling and know well what they are doing. In *The Stealing of the Mare*, when Ganimeh comes to ask Abu Zeyd for help, she praises him for his chivalry in a series of comparisons :

> " Thus have I come to thee on my soul's faith, Salameh,
> Thee the champion proved of all whose hearts are doubting,
> Thee the doer of right, the scourge of the oppressor,
> Thee the breeze in autumn, thee the winter's coolness,
> Thee the morning's warmth after a night of watching,
> Thee the wanderer's joy, well of the living water,
> Thee to thy foeman's lips as colocynth of the desert,
> Thee the river Nile in the full day of his flooding,
> When he hath mounted high and covereth the islands." [3]

With this we may compare the way in which a list may be used not for praise but for abuse and be equally effective in its own task. In *Gilgamish*, when the goddess Ishtar falls in love with the hero and makes him an offer of marriage, which he rejects with scorn, he is inspired to a series of comparisons :

> " Thou art a ruin which gives no shelter to man from the weather,
> Thou art a back door which resists not wind or storm,

---

[1] Radlov, v, p. 392.   [2] Morison, p. xxx.   [3] Blunt, ii, p. 136.

Thou art a palace which breaks in pieces the heroes within it,
Thou art a pitfall whose covering gives way,
Thou art pitch which defiles the man who carries it,
Thou art a bottle which leaks on him who carries it,
Thou art limestone which lets stone ramparts fall and crumble,
Thou art chalcedony which fails to guard in an enemy's land,
Thou art a sandal which causes its owner to stumble." [1]

The devastating list shows up the goddess Ishtar for the untrustworthy being that she is.

The small simile inevitably becomes bigger as the poets see its uses for varying the texture of their poetry. It may be expanded into several lines by the addition of details inside a single frame. So though *The Stealing of the Mare* is fond of similes in sequence, it also knows the use of a fuller, single simile, as when Abu Zeyd is surrounded by enemies in a fight :

And they pressed me left and right as the high banks of a river,
Even the river Nile in the full day of its flooding,
When the whirlpools sweep with might and overwhelm the bridges. [2]

Even poets who are sparing of similes sometimes do this or come near to it. So *Roland*, in which the similes are sparse and short, expands them at least into a single whole line when Roland pursues the Saracens :

Even as a stag before the hounds goes flying,
Before Rollanz the pagans scatter, frightened. [3]

So too the poet of *Beowulf* evidently feels that the mysterious melting of Beowulf's sword in the lair of Grendel's Dam demands something more than a short comparison, and spreads himself on it :

Then that sword began
From the sweat of death   in icicle drops,
The war-bill, to wane ;   that was something wondrous
That it all melted,   to ice most likened. [4]

So the Norse poet makes Guthrun describe her widowhood :

Lonely am I   as the forest aspen,
Of kindred bare   as the fir of its boughs,
My joys are all lost   as the leaves of the tree
When the scather of twigs   from the warm day turns. [5]

The art of comparison has passed beyond the equivalence of a single point and advanced to something more complex. So the Kara-Kirghiz poet describes the warriors of Manas :

---

[1] *Gilgamish*, VI, i, 33-41.   [2] Blunt, ii, p. 184.
[3] *Roland*, 1874-5.   [4] *Beowulf*, 1605-8.   [5] *Hamthismál*, 5.

> As the grass of the wormwood on the steppe
> Passes beyond the sandy wastes,
> As on the other side the grass
> Passes into the waving blue. . . .[1]

The wide landscape is evoked to show the size of the host. By this extension of the simple simile the poets not only make their comparisons more vivid and more precise but give a longer respite in the record of action.

In Homer the long simile plays a large part. He is the source of all the long similes which are so attractive in Virgil, Camoens, Ariosto, Tasso, and Milton. Though he frequently uses short similes, his long similes are hardly less frequent and represent a more advanced art. By them he illustrates the central character of an event by comparing it to some other event of quite a different kind. He stresses what seems to him important and does not attempt the impossible task of trying to find a comparison on every point. What he stresses is some essential quality which two events have in common. When the Achaeans in battle are white with dust, it is like a threshing-floor covered with chaff.[2] All that concerns Homer for the moment is the visual impression of whiteness. Again, when Priam and the old men of Troy talk on the city-wall, and are compared to cicadas chirruping on a tree,[3] the comparison is of sound and of the effect which it makes. By such means Homer makes his actions vivid to the eye and the ear. He first speaks of them plainly and then enlarges the concept of them by some comparison which emphasises a special quality in them. He helps us to select from a complex experience what is really essential and central.

Of course this art inevitably passes beyond the appeal of sight or sound and helps to stress the appeal of some situation to the imagination by drawing attention to its actual character. Take, for instance, the occasion when the Achaeans stand firm against the onslaught of Hector and his Trojans :

> Like to a tower they held, firm fastened, just as a grey rock
> Rising high in the air, at the side of the silvery-grey sea,
> Waits and endures the attacks of the winds that whistle against it
> And of the full-bellied waves that break into foam all about it.[4]

Both sight and sound play some part in the comparison, but there is something else more important. The defence of the Achaean warriors has the strength and majesty of a wall of rock, and that

---

[1] *Manas*, p. 75.
[2] *Il.* v, 499 ff.
[3] *Ibid.* iii, 151 ff.
[4] *Ibid.* xv, 618-21.

is what principally matters. The visual impression passes into something else and adds a new dimension to the issue at stake. Again, when Priam comes to Achilles to ransom the body of his dead son, Hector, Achilles is dumbfounded at the old man's courage, and Homer emphasises this in a simile :

> As when a man whom spite of fate hath curs'd in his own land
> For homicide, that he fleeth abroad and seeketh asylum
> With some lord, and they that see him are fill'd with amazement.[1]

At first sight we might think that the simile is not very exact, that Priam is less suitably compared to a murderer than Achilles would be. But Homer has his eye on a special point, and his simile stresses it. The amazement which Achilles feels is not merely surprise at Priam's courage but is coloured by dark emotions related to the world of carnage in which he lives and of which his killing of Hector is a signal example. In this world passions of hatred and revenge cloud the judgment, and the unexpected appearance of Priam is in its own way as strange as the arrival of a homicide in quest of asylum with a rich lord. What matters is the identity of emotional and imaginative effect, the light which the simile throws on the event which it illustrates. The mixed emotions and the sinister implications of bloodshed are implicit in the simile as in the dramatic situation.

In his desire to create this identity of character and atmosphere Homer sometimes tends to pass beyond the limits of exact comparison so far as sight is concerned. He begins a simile with something plainly visual, and then adds something else which is not visual and seems to have no direct relation to the original situation. Take, for instance, the scene where the Trojans camp in the plain and light their camp-fires :

> As when in heaven the stars around the moon in its splendour
> Shine very bright, when the air is silent without any wind's breath,
> And all the mountains are clear, and the peaks of the lofty hill-
> ranges,
> And every valley ; from high the limitless heaven is open,
> And every star can be seen ; and at heart the shepherd is joyful.[2]

The camp-fires are visually like the stars on a windless night but the introduction of the shepherd and his gladness is a new idea. It sums up the calm and peacefulness of such an occasion. Even in war there are these moments, and Homer touches dexterously and lightly on them. Again, when Odysseus enters the hall before beginning to kill the Suitors, he debates with himself what to do,

---

[1] *Ibid.* xxiv, 480-82. Trs. Robert Bridges.   [2] *Il.* viii, 551-5.

and the movements of his thought are compared to something
visible :

> Even as over a fire that rises up crackling and flaming
> A man turns this way and that a paunch full of blood and of suet,
> And very greatly desires that it shall be speedily roasted.[1]

The visible image adds exactness and clarity to the movements
of Odysseus' mind, but what really matters is his eagerness to get
to work, and that is what Homer conveys. Odysseus is as im-
patient as a man cooking a haggis, and that is the chief point.

Homer's similes are vivid pictures of different corners of life.
Each lives on its own and reveals some unsuspected or hidden
quality in a situation. But because they are complete, they tend
sometimes to pass beyond mere comparison, even of character and
atmosphere, and to introduce something which is, strictly speaking,
irrelevant. The picture takes command, and the poet so enjoys it
that he completes it with some charming touch which makes us
almost forget why the simile has been introduced. A striking
example of this is when Menelaus is wounded and his hip stained
with blood :

> As when a Carian woman, or maybe Maeonian, staineth
> Ivory with red dye as a cheek-decoration for horses ;
> Safe in a chamber it lies ; many horsemen are eager to wear it,
> But in a king's treasure-chamber it lies to be a decoration
> Worn by his horse and to bring great glory to whoso may drive it.[2]

The first point of the comparison is of course between the colour
of blood on the skin and of scarlet stain on ivory. The implied
comparison may go further and hint at the fascination which even
such a wound may have. But then the comparison really ceases.
The last two lines leave the original situation behind and complete
the picture for its own sake. Again, when Asius is killed by
Idomeneus :

> Down he fell with a crash as an oak may fall or a poplar,
> Or as a lofty pine, which men who work on the mountains
> Fell with new-sharpened axes to make a plank for a great ship.[3]

The fall of the warrior is well likened to the felling of a tall tree,
but the reference to the ship's timber is not strictly to the point.
It helps to fill in the picture and make it more interesting. Homer
does not often expand his similes in this way, but his reasons for
doing so may be surmised. He wishes not only to illustrate an
occasion in his story but to provide some relief from what might
otherwise be too monotonous. These little glimpses into worlds

[1] *Od.* xx, 25-7.   [2] *Il.* iv, 141-5.   [3] *Ibid.* xiii, 389-91.

which have nothing to do with war give a momentary respite and send us back refreshed to the fighting.

In his similes Homer uses formulaic phrases as he does elsewhere, and the remarkable thing is how finely he uses them, how little sense of strain is felt at their reappearance in different circumstances. But he does more than this; he repeats actual similes, either in whole or in part, to illustrate quite different situations. On this many theories have been built, but we cannot doubt that Homer did it because the similes existed and were ready for use. It was up to him to see that they were used effectively and relevantly. For instance, he twice makes a comparison between a man going to battle and a horse going to pasture:

> As when a stallion, fed with barley-meal in the stable,
> Breaks his tether and runs off stamping over the country,
> Being accustomed to bathe in the streams of the broad-flowing
> river,
> Glorying; high he raises his head, and the mane on his shoulders
> Floats all about him; he puts his trust in his prowess, and swiftly
> His legs carry him off to the haunts where the mares are at pasture.[1]

This is admirably to the point for Paris, who goes to war rather as he goes to love. But it is used again for Hector,[2] and we might feel that for him it is less appropriate. Yet in the context it is right enough. Hector too goes to battle like an eager stallion. We must forget that the simile has been used for Paris and dismiss its associations with him. It takes its colour from its new setting and works very well. Again, Ajax is pressed back by the advancing Trojans:

> As when a glittering lion retreats from a steading of oxen,
> Driven away in much haste by the dogs and the men of the pasture,
> Who will never allow him to pick the best of the oxen,
> All night waiting for him; and he, for flesh very eager,
> Goes to his task but achieves not a thing; for many the javelins
> Flung by their fearless hands come to meet him upon his arrival,
> And many torches aflame, which he fears, though he be very eager.[3]

Ajax's unwilling retirement is well caught in this simile, but Homer uses it again to tell how Menelaus leaves the battle to look for Antilochus.[4] The occasion is less exciting and there is hardly any fight in it. But the simile is appropriate enough. Menelaus does not wish to leave the battle and is therefore like the lion which retreats unwillingly. The context colours the simile and gives it rather a different meaning. As commonly with formulae, the

[1] *Ibid.* vi, 506-11.
[3] *Ibid.* xi, 548-54.
[2] *Ibid.* xv, 263 ff.
[4] *Ibid.* xvii, 657 ff.

colour is partly provided by the situation, and we must look to that, and not to other places where the same form of words has been used.

Another traditional element in heroic poetry is concerned with getting a story started. This too is often formulaic and part of the technique which a bard inherits from tradition and learns from his masters. This is not to say that all heroic poems begin on conventional lines with a stock theme. There are many of them which show the poet's ability to start with something striking of his own invention. But the majority start in a familiar way, and the reason for it is that, just as the audiences like formulae and repetitions, so too they like stock openings. They feel immediately at home; their uncertain attention is caught without difficulty by the familiarity of the theme, and they listen to see how it is developed and what new point is given to it. The result is that there are certain openings which occur in more than one country or language and show the way in which heroic poets work, wherever they may live. These openings are, naturally enough, commonest in short lays, but they are to be found also in long poems, and even in very long poems, as means to start new episodes. Their use is an interesting commentary on the development of heroic poetry from short lay to full-scale epic. The poet of the epic knows the art of the lay and has probably been brought up on it; so when he advances to composition on a large scale, he still uses the devices which belong to the lay and weaves them into a larger whole. The themes which open poems or episodes may often be quite simple and conventional, but it is instructive to see how they are made to fit into a narrative of action.

First, there is the theme of the feast. In Russian poetry no theme is commoner. The great man gives a feast, and at it a boast or a wager is made which has to be justified by action. It does not matter whether the great man is Vladimir or Ivan the Terrible or another. The procedure is usually the same and expressed in very similar words. It looks as if such an opening were devised to cover the moments when the bard begins his performance and has not yet caught the full attention of his audience. It is completely conventional and unadventurous, but good enough to engage attention and set the story going. The feast is described, and then the story proper begins. Staver boasts that his wife can deceive Vladimir, and in due course she does; the talk turns to the wealth of Churilo Plenkovich, and Vladimir rides out to see for himself; Vladimir gives a feast and forgets to ask Ilya to it, with humiliating consequences for himself; Ivan the

Terrible boasts that there are no traitors in his realm, and his son, Ivan, says that the other son, Fedor, is one. The feast is useful for more than one reason. It allows a number of heroes to be gathered together and to compete with each other in boasts and challenges; it shows familiar characters at their ease, ready to face any new call to action; above all it gives no indication of what is coming next. In so starting his tale the bard keeps the audience in the dark as to what is going to happen, and so prepares for the surprise which he intends to create.

The Jugoslavs resemble the Russians in using the theme of the feast, though their practice is a little different. It is usually very short, not more than a line or two, and it depicts not so much a feast at the house of a king or prince, though it does this in the famous account of the feast before Kosovo, as of warriors drinking together and depicted rapidly in such opening lines as

> Three young Serbian chieftains sat a-drinking,

or

> Thirty captains sat at wine together,

or

> Marko sat at supper with his mother,

or

> Musa the Albanian was drinking
> Wine in Istambul, in the white tavern.

The words differ slightly according to the character or characters to be introduced, but the plan is the same. The warriors sit and drink; then someone boasts or makes a wager or news arrives, and stirring events are set in action. Philip the Magyar boasts that he will put Marko's head on a tower of Karlovatz; Marko carries out his plan of feigning sick in order to trap a Turkish adversary; letters come to him, and he goes to the Sultan; Musa boasts that he will become a brigand and does so. The Jugoslav openings resemble the Russian in the great freedom which they leave to the poet to develop what sequel he will. They set a simple scene, which makes almost anything possible.

A feast may also provide an opening for a longer poem, and in that case it may be set out at some length as a useful way of introducing a hero and his companions and showing how they live. That is what Kalmuck poets do more than once for Dzhangar. In *Dzhangar's War with the Black Prince* the poet begins with a long account of the hero, his dwelling, his horse, weapons, wife, and companions, and all this leads up to a feast at which the hero's praises are sung by a minstrel. This is followed immediately by a similar feast at the court of his enemy, the Black Prince, and only

after this does the main action begin.[1] A somewhat similar technique is used in another poem which tells of Dzhangar's victory
over the seven warriors of Khan Zambal, though there the poet
dispenses with the enemy's feast.[2] The Kalmuck poets use the
theme of the feast because it enables them to present a whole
company of heroes in their splendour, and then to achieve a fine
contrast between their dignified calm when they are at rest and
their irrepressible energy when they are in action. Into this
setting is woven the theme of the boast which has to be justified
by action, as when the Black Knight says :

> " Is there in all the world under the sun,
> Under the sun or under the moon,
> Such a man as could be matched with my strength ? "

The boast, once made, has to be justified, and the Black Knight is
defeated by Dzhangar.

A second popular theme is that of knights who ride abroad and
encounter adventures. This is extremely common in Slavonic
poetry whether in Russia or Jugoslavia or the Ukraine. The
Russians start with their usual simplicity, describing how a rider
crosses the open plain and then meets someone, and adventures
follow. Ilya of Murom encounters the giant Svyatogor or Nightingale the Robber; Alyosha and a companion find an inscription on
a stone which takes them to Kiev; Svyatogor rides out and comes
to his death. The Jugoslavs have a similar technique, though they
maintain their habitual brevity, in such phrases as

> Two sworn brothers rode abroad together,

or

> Marko, king's son, rode out in the morning.

Then follow the adventures. Marko goes to Tsarigrad and be-
friends a powerful Turk, or finds that the Turks have instituted
a marriage-tax in Kosovo and abolishes it. So the Ukrainian
Cossack Holota begins in a similar way :

> Across the fields of Kilia,
> On the great highway of the Hordes,
> Rides the cossack Holota,
> Who fears not fire nor steel nor the three marches.[3]

He soon picks up a Tatar and engages him in battle. This is a
good Slavonic technique and is similar in essential respects to the
theme of a feast. A warrior riding over the plain has the world
before him, and anything may be expected to happen.

[1] *Dzhangariada*, p. 108 ff.   [2] *Ibid.* p. 153 ff.
[3] Scherrer, p. 122.

The theme of the rider can also introduce an episode in a longer poem, and still keep its typical character. So, when in a Kalmuck poem the hero Khongor rides out to find an enemy, he sees something in the distance :

> On his fiery horse he leaped
> On the southern peak of a hill
> And saw that from the setting sun
> Arose a thin red dust.
> Speak of a whirlwind — this is no whirlwind.
> Speak of a snow hurricane — this is no hurricane.
> It must be dust from a brave war-horse,
> It draws near to the warrior Ulan-Khongor,
> On the slope of a high white hill
> A warrior draws near, armed with a long spear. . . .[1]

Khongor addresses the stranger, and each declares who he is, with the result that they know that they are enemies and serve masters who are at war. Then Khongor comes to the final words :

> " Before you get acquainted with me,
> Do you not wish to taste my sword,
> Such as there is not in all the world ? "

The fight begins and is conducted in a truly heroic manner :

> They mingled their cold, black sabres,
> Each smote the other on the shoulder-blade,
> Stoutly on their protective battle-armour.
> Their living black blood lashed their noses and mouths.[2]

In the result Khongor wins. The episode is part of the whole poem but complete and satisfying in itself, as if the bard were using the old device of starting a short lay with the theme of a warrior riding out into the country.

A third popular theme for starting a poem is the flight of birds. Birds, of course, are creatures of augury, and their flight may foretell the future. So a tale may well begin with them because they suggest that something important is going to happen. When Helgi Hundingsbane is born, ravens watch from a tree and prophesy his future. In the *Hrafnsmal* they tell a Valkyrie of the doings of Harold Fairhaired. But more interesting perhaps is the account, most likely based on a poem, which Procopius gives of events in the year shortly before war broke out between the Warni and the Angli.[3] When Hermegisclus, king of the Warni, was out riding with his chieftains, he saw a bird sitting on a tree who croaked loudly. The king, either because he understood what the

---

[1] *Dzhangariada*, p. 218.   [2] *Ibid.* p. 219.
[3] *Bell. Goth.* iv, 20.

bird said or had other intimations, claimed that it had prophesied his death forty days later. He then made his last dispensations and died on the fortieth day. This is the authentic pattern of prophecies uttered by birds. The hero suddenly has the gift for understanding what they say, and, for good or ill, what they foretell comes to pass. So too, after Sigurth has killed Fafnir and drunk of his blood, he hears the nuthatches singing and understands their song, which warns him against Regin, whom he then kills, and tells him about Brynhild, how she is asleep on a mountain with a wall of flame around her.[1] The nuthatches start Sigurth on a new adventure, which is to be the cause of his greatest glory and his death. The *Elder Edda* is on the whole not fond of supernatural elements of this kind, but we can hardly doubt that the theme of birds was once common in Germanic poetry and has survived in these cases.

The theme of birds is extremely common in Jugoslav poems, in which they either forecast or give warning about coming events. The simplest way of treating them is to make them messengers, whose appearance and behaviour tell that something has happened, as in *The Battle of Mišar* :

> Through the air came flying two black ravens,
> From the far extending plain of Mišar
> And from Šabac, from the white walled city ;
> Bloody were their beaks unto the eyeballs
> And their legs unto the knees were bloody.[2]

The wife of a Turkish general sees them and asks if they have news of her husband who has gathered a great army to subdue the Serbs, and the birds reply that his army has been defeated. She continues to ask them questions until she has heard the whole story, with a technique that recalls *The Maiden of Kosovo*, where a battle and its details are reported by a series of answers to questions, though by human agents. In *The Battle of Mišar* the birds give a more eerie and menacing atmosphere to the story. Their role suggests that the defeat of the Turkish army is a great natural catastrophe in which even physical nature is concerned. *The Taking of Belgrade* opens in a similar way but develops differently. At the start the birds arrive :

> Through the air came flying two bald ravens,
> Flew across the whole of level Srijem,
> Tired and hungry fell, and curses uttered :
> " Land of Srijem, may thy green be withered
> And thy townships all be drowned in sorrow !

---

[1] *Fafnismal*, 32 ff.   [2] Karadžić, iv, p. 177 ; Morison, p. 74.

Is there in all Srijem not one hero
Blood to spill, engaged in mortal combat ?
From the last three days have we two ravens
Over all the mountain-chains been flying,
Over all the forests, fields, and meadows ;
Nowhere on the soil could we discover
Meat of horses, or the flesh of heroes ;
What is this ?   Misfortune fall upon thee ! " [1]

This is a more sinister and more imaginative idea than making the
birds mere messengers.   They look for dead bodies and fail to
find them.   A shepherd-boy curses them for wanting war, and they
fly off to the wife of a Turkish chieftain, who drives them away
with stones, and then to her horror sees a large army pitched
before her town.   Then the story develops its full strength and tells
of the taking of Belgrade.   The technique is more advanced than
in *The Battle of Mišar*, and a comparison between the two poems
shows how differently the stock opening can be used.

This theme of birds is used abundantly by modern Greek
poets with some ingenious variations.   The bird, as we might
expect, is sometimes no more than a bringer of news.   So a poem
on events of 1770, *Nikostaras*, begins rather as a Jugoslav poem
might :

From Verrhia a little bird has started on its journey,
From rock to rock it makes its way, from refuge unto refuge,
The klephts interrogate the birds, to it the klephts put questions :
" Whence comest thou, O little bird ?   O little bird, whence com'st
    thou ? " [2]

The bird replies that it goes from Verrhia to Agrapha to bring a
message to his friends from a leader who has been fighting for
three days and three nights in the snow.   Nikostaras hears the
message and calls his men to arm and go with him to cut the
crossing over the river and join the forces of Lambrakis.   More
curious is the opening of the poem which tells of the capture of
Trebizond in 1461 :

A bird from Trebizond, a bird comes flying from the city ;
It settles not upon the vines, nor settles in the gardens.
But into Hili fortress goes and there it ends its journey.
One of its wings it flutters then, and it is soaked in blood-stains,
The other wing it flutters too, which bears a written message. [3]

The message tells grave news of conquest by the Turks, and the
poem comes quickly to its close with a note of mourning.   Greek
poetry provides another variant on the stock opening when the

[1] Morison, p. 104 ff.   [2] Politis, p. 93.   [3] *Idem*, p. 77.

birds are not augurs or messengers but representatives of public opinion or some sort of spiritual agency which urges a man to action :

> Three little birds were wandering in the klephts' hiding places,
> They sought to find Dimotsios, that he might be a captain.[1]

Dimotsios refuses because he is too old and has sons who can act for him.   But the birds insist :

> " 'Tis you alone we wish to have, 'tis you we love and cherish."

Dimotsios promises to do something.   Then a pasha passes with some prisoners, and Dimotsios cries out to him to free them.   The traditional bird has developed a new character and become almost an indication of powers at work in the old captain.

A fourth way of opening a poem is to bring two characters together and from this to evolve a scene of action.   A special form of this occurs in battle-scenes.   Two warriors are somehow separated from the general throng and confront one another. They hold a parley, asking each other about their names and families, and after this they fight.   This theme resembles that of a rider going out to seek an enemy, but differs in its setting.   The background of the battlefield is essential to it, and gives it a peculiar distinction.   A noble example of this theme can be seen in a short poem, the Old German *Hildebrand*.   It starts without explanation with two warriors meeting on the battlefield :

> I have heard it told
> That Hildebrand and Hadubrand   between the hosts
> Challenged each other   to single combat.
> Father and son   set their panoply right,
> Made their armour ready,   girt their swords on corslets,
> Did the heroes then   when they rode to the fray.

Yet even with this simple start the strange situation is soon apparent.   The two men, though neither yet knows it, are father and son, and the development is made with a menacing sense of doom.   They engage in a parley, and it is clear to Hildebrand that this is his son, though the son does not believe it and insists on fighting.   What might be only a useful start is woven into the essential structure of the story.

In longer poems which are extensively concerned with war this scheme is used to isolate individual combats and give them a certain completeness.   Homer certainly knew of it and uses it for some hand-to-hand combats in the *Iliad*.   When Achilles and

----

[1] Politis, p. 89.

Aeneas meet before Troy, the scheme is used with a nice sense of its quality. Homer, like the poet of *Hildebrand*, goes straight to the point and dispenses with preliminaries :

> Two men of valour surpassing
> Went to the space between the two hosts, both eager for battle,
> Aeneas, son of Anchises, and godlike Achilles.[1]

Since they know each other, there is no need for explanations, and they begin to fight. But the old scheme has its claims, and Homer soon presents an interesting variation on it. Achilles interrupts the fighting to tell Aeneas to retreat, and then Aeneas replies with a full history of his descent, though he begins by saying that it is familiar to both of them.[2] Aeneas does this because he has to assert his claim to be as good a man as Achilles, since after all both are sons of a mortal father and an immortal mother. Then the gods intervene and break off the fight, but not before we have seen that the two men are well matched and that Aeneas can stand up to Achilles as hardly anyone else can.

A second ingenious variation which Homer makes of this theme comes in the middle of another general battle. While Achaeans and Trojans engage in battle, two warriors meet, and their meeting is described in the traditional way :

> Glaucus, Hippolochus' son, and Tydeus' son, Diomedes,
> Came together between the two hosts, both eager for battle.[3]

Diomedes, who has not seen Glaucus before, asks him who he is, wonders if he is a god, and says that, if he is, he will not fight him, since it will bring him a terrible doom. He speaks gravely and courteously, and Glaucus answers him in the same spirit. After saying that there is really no reason to ask a man who he is, since the generations of men are like those of leaves, he tells his ancestry and with it the story of his grandfather, Bellerophon. This shows Diomedes that their families have old ties, and for this reason he refuses to fight, and insists instead that they shall exchange armour. On this the episode ends. It is a model of its kind. The art of the short lay is used with much skill inside a large frame, and much of the success depends on the way in which Homer uses an old device to take him straight to the point at the start.

A fifth type of opening consists of persons arriving with news or the like, with the result that some important action has to be taken. This device enables the poet to start an action at its proper beginning, to move from a scene of peace to scenes of violence, and

---

[1] *Il.* xx, 158-60.   [2] *Ibid.* 203 ff.   [3] *Ibid.* vi, 119-20.

to depict various persons in characteristic roles. The simplest form is when a messenger arrives who is no more than a bringer of news and has no importance beyond that. So in the Russian *The Youth of Churilo Plenkovich* the bard combines this theme with that of a feast. As Prince Vladimir holds a feast, he sees a crowd of people coming, beating the ground with their heads. They make complaint to him :

> " Dear Sun of ours, Prince Vladimir !
> Give us, Master, a just judgment,
> Against Churilo Plenkovich.
> To-day, when we were at the river Soroga,
> Strangers appeared ;
> They cast fishing-nets —
> The strands were of seven silks,
> The nets had floats of silver,
> And gilded sinkers.
> They caught dace,
> But for us, dear master, there is no catch,
> And for thee, Sire, there is not a fresh morsel.
> And we have no guerdon from thee ;
> They all call themselves, announce themselves to be
> Churilo's company." [1]

This deputation is immediately followed by another, which complains that Churilo shoots all the birds in the countryside ; then comes a third with a like complaint about the wild animals. The result is that Vladimir sets out to see Churilo for himself, and from that much follows. Though the people who bring news are anonymous, and interesting mainly as victims of Churilo's rapacity, the device is effective since it moves at once to the dramatic issue and shows how Vladimir behaves when faced by an urgent problem.

The device is more dramatic and more intimate when the news is brought by a single person who is closely involved in what happens, since this provides an opportunity for hearing at first hand a story of suffering or injustice and makes us curious about the result. This is the case in the Jugoslav *Marko Kraljević and the Twelve Moors*, which begins with Marko taking his ease in comfort :

> Marko, King's son, set up his pavilion,
> In the harsh land of the Moorish people,
> Sate him down to drink in his pavilion,
> But before his glass of wine was finished,
> Came a slave-girl running to him quickly,
> Went into the tent of King's son Marko.

[1] Rybnikov, ii, p. 524 ; Chadwick, *R.H.P.* p. 92.

The girl tells that she is maltreated by twelve Moors, who scourge her and make her kiss them. Marko welcomes her kindly, covers her with his mantle, and gives her a glass of wine :

> " There ", quoth he, " now drink thy fill, O damsel,
> From this day the sun hath risen on thee,
> Seeing thou art come to my pavilion." [1]

Marko then takes on the Moors and kills them. The girl he hands over to his mother for care, and later sees that she finds a good husband. Though the poem is too short for the girl to have any definite personality, she has at least a situation and the interest which comes from it, and the device of making her bring news of her own plight helps to knit the poem together.

This device is put to a highly dramatic use in the Norse legend of the sons of Heithrekr. The legitimate son, Angantyr, is king of the Goths, while the illegitimate son, Hlöthr, has been brought up among the Huns and has nothing. After a short statement of the general situation, the poet of *The Battle of the Goths and the Huns* [2] plunges into the story by making Hlöthr himself come to Angantyr :

> Hlöthr rode from the east,   Heithrekr's heir,
> Till he came to the garth,   where the Goths dwell,
> To Arheimar,   to ask for his heritage.
> Here Angantyr held   Heithrekr's funeral feast.

Hlöthr enters the hall and is welcomed by Angantyr, who asks him to join in the feast. Hlöthr refuses and demands half of Angantyr's possessions. Angantyr offers a handsome compromise, but says that he will rather fight than concede all that Hlöthr demands. Hlöthr goes back to the Huns, gets them to declare war, and in due course is killed in battle. This is a tragic tale in the true heroic vein, and its main action turns on the conflict between the two brothers. It is therefore suitable that at the start they should be brought together and their different characters revealed. While Hlöthr is aggressive and vain, as suits the bastard, Angantyr is generous and proud. He is ready to treat Hlöthr well, but honour forbids that he should yield all that is demanded of him. The opening lines prepare the way for the grim story that follows.

This technique may be used in a longer poem to start a chain of dramatic events. Such is the case with the Norse *Atlakvitha*. Atli, king of the Huns, plots the death of Gunnar and his companions in order to gain their wealth. To secure his end, he

[1] Karadžić, ii, p. 314.   [2] Kershaw, p. 142 ff.

decides to invite them to his court, and sends a messenger asking
them to come. The poem begins with the arrival of the messenger :

> Atli sent   of old to Gunnar
> A keen-witted rider,   Knefröth did men call him ;
> To Gjuki's home came he   and to Gunnar's dwelling,
> With benches round the hearth   and to the beer, so sweet.[1]

Knefröth brings not news but an invitation, and he sets it out with
cunning eloquence :

> " Now Atli has sent me   his errand to ride,
> On my bit-champing steed   through Myrkwood the secret,
> To bid you, Gunnar,   to his benches to come,
> With helms round the hearth,   and Atli's home seek.
>
> Shields shall ye choose there,   and shafts made of ash-wood,
> Gold-adorned helmets,   and slaves out of Hunland,
> Silver-gilt saddle-cloths,   shirts of bright scarlet,
> With lances and spears too,   and bit-champing steeds.
>
> The field shall be given you   of wide Gnitaheith,
> With loud-ringing lances,   and stems gold-o'erlaid,
> Treasures full huge,   and the home of Danp,
> And the mighty forest   that Myrkwood is called." [2]

Since the poet composes on a relatively full scale, he is able to make
Knefröth tell his tale in this detailed manner and thereby to show
how treacherous Atli and his agent are. He then develops his
story with a dramatic sense of its possibilities. At first Gunnar
sees no reason to accept the invitation ; he has abundant riches
and does not need what Atli offers him. But he feels that his
honour is somehow at stake and that he must go. Then the long
cruel series of events follows. Since the main interest now lies
with Gunnar and Atli, no more is said of Knefröth who has played
his part and disappears. But the theme of the invitation is used
with great ability. It shows the mixed feelings with which Gunnar
receives it and the heroic spirit in which he decides to take the
risk.

The arrival of a visitor with important news opens at least one
long heroic poem. The *Odyssey* starts with the visit of Athene to
Ithaca, where, in the long absence of his father, Telemachus is
sorely troubled by the Suitors who devour his substance. She
comes in the form of Mentes, prince of the Taphians, and is first
seen by Telemachus, who says courteously :

> " Welcome, guest, to our hall, and when you have finished your supper,
> Then do, I pray you to tell anything we may do in your service." [3]

[1] *Atlakvitha*, 1.   [2] *Ibid.* 3-5.   [3] *Od.* i, 123-4.

This is the correct way to greet a stranger, and what follows is equally correct. After the necessary preliminaries, Athene asks about the Suitors, and Telemachus tells her of his plight. Then she breaks her news :

> " Know this for sure that he is not dead, the godlike Odysseus.
> Nay, but he still is alive, tho' the broad sea-water withholds him
> Far on a sea-girt isle, and cruel people restrain him,
> Savages hold him back, tho' he longs very greatly to leave them." [1]

This is important news, but Telemachus is slow to believe it. Athene persists in her story and tells him that he must go to Pylos and Sparta to get news of his father. Any hesitation which he still feels is dispersed when Athene changes into a sea-bird and flies away. He then knows that she is a goddess and accepts her message and her orders. So the action of the *Odyssey* is set in motion. Athene's visit to Ithaca breaks a situation which has lasted for years. The Suitors have cowed Penelope and her son into inaction, and divine intervention is needed to break it, but Homer uses for this the old theme of a visitor arriving with important news.

Lastly, dreams play a large part in starting heroic poems. They have several advantages. They are interesting in themselves and present incidents unlike those of ordinary life ; they create a sense of destiny or of issues which have to be faced ; they often come at important moments and decide the course which the action takes. There is of course something fatalistic in the idea that dreams foretell the future and that it cannot be avoided, but such fatalism is common enough among most peoples and is easily combined with a belief that a man normally shapes his own destiny. So far as the story is concerned, the dream helps to set the central theme in a prominent place and to prepare the way to the crisis and make it more impressive when it comes. Dreams need not necessarily be of disaster, though they often are, since their unearthly character is well suited to the blows of fate or circumstance. The forecast of coming events invokes both doom and mystery. The ways of the gods are strange, and it is not for man to understand them fully, but, if he is wise, he will take the hints given to him, especially when they come in sleep, when his ordinary powers are relaxed and he is free to receive messages from another world.

The simplest kind of dream is that which gives a more or less literal forecast of coming events. So in the Jugoslav *Taking of Úžice* a Turkish woman, the wife of a great soldier, dreams as she lies on her soft cushions :

[1] *Ibid.* 196-9.

> Strange her dream, and on a strange day dreamed she,
> On the Friday, on the Turkish Sunday ;
> Dreamed a dream, and in her dream she witnessed
> How the radiant sky was clothed in darkness
> Suddenly o'er Úžice in Serbia,
> Then from end to end was rent asunder ;
> All the stars careered to the horizon
> And on Úžice the moon fell blood-stained ;
> From the east the lightning sent its flashes,
> And they slew the Turks within the city.[1]

When the husband explains that this means a slaughter of Turks by Serbs, he does not do anything very clever, since the dream itself has shown Turks being slain at Úžice, and that gives a clear enough clue. Immediately after the interpretation, the dream begins to be fulfilled by the arrival of a Serb army outside Úžice. The dream has by then done its work, and is no more mentioned. Its purpose is to create an atmosphere of impending doom, to set the tone for the story which follows. The capture of Úžice is presented as a foreordained, inevitable event against which any action is useless.

With this relatively intelligible dream we may compare another which is more mysterious. In the Russian *Prince Roman* the main theme is a dream and its accomplishment. The situation is set out at the start :

> Once upon a time lived Prince Roman Mitrievich,
> He slept with his wife, and she dreamed in the night
> That her ring fell from her right hand,
> From the ring-finger of her right hand, the middle finger,
> And was shattered into tiny fragments.

The prince is troubled by the dream and unable to interpret it ; so he suggests that it be published abroad that others may find what it means. But the princess rejects the suggestion, because she is ready with her own interpretation :

> " I myself will judge my dream,
> I myself will interpret my dream :
> There will speed towards me from over the sea
> Three ships, three black ships,
> They will carry me, Marya, over the blue sea,
> Over the blue salt sea,
> To Yagailo, the son of Manuelo." [2]

This is what happens, and the princess is right. Why she interprets the dream in this sense remains a mystery. The poet does

---

[1] Morison, p. 115.
[2] Kireevski, v, p. 92 ; Chadwick, *R.H.P.* p. 168.

not claim to understand it himself and gives no explanation. Here the sense of doom works with a special force. The victim is not only warned that something will happen to her but able by some unexplained process to interpret the enigmatic images in which the presage comes. The technique used suggests the presence of incalculable forces which make themselves known by means not intelligible to ordinary men.

Dreams, then, are useful because they give a sense of destiny. So, when a poet has enough space at his disposal and wishes to tell a story which, in his view, illustrates the power of fate, he may well make use of dreams and even accumulate them to add to his effect. This is what the Norse poet does in *Atlamál*. A message comes from Atli to Gunnar asking him to go to him, and before a decision is taken, the poet prepares a brooding atmosphere of dread by his use of dreams. First, Kostbera, wife of Hogni, who knows from reading a runic message from Guthrun that something is amiss, dreams three dreams and reports them to her husband. In the first she sees her bed-covering catch fire and flames bursting through the walls of her home; in the second, a bear breaking pillars, brandishing his claws, and seizing many victims with his mouth; in the third, an eagle flying through the house and sprinkling its dwellers with blood. To the reader who knows the story the three dreams are perhaps intelligible enough, in that they suggest the catastrophe which awaits the sons of Gjuki when they go to Atli. But Kostbera, who sees that something is wrong, hardly attempts to interpret them, except in the third case when she sees that the eagle is Atli's spirit. But her husband will have nothing of it. He has his own interpretations : in the first dream he sees no more than a warning that her bed-cover, which is of little value, will soon be burned; in the second, he sees a presage of rough weather :

" Now a storm is brewing, and wild it grows swiftly,
A dream of an ice-bear means a gale from the east " ; [1]

in the third, he sees only a forecast that oxen will be slaughtered. He remains obdurately confident and tells his wife :

" True is Atli's heart, whatever thou dreamest." [2]

In the circumstances she can do nothing but be silent. In this set of dreams the poet not only creates a sense of doom but sketches the helplessness of its victims. Kostbera does not know what her dreams portend, and Hogni rejects the notion that it is anything bad.

[1] *Atlamál*, 17. [2] *Ibid.* 19, 3.

These three dreams are followed by four others, dreamed this time by Glaumvor, the wife of Gunnar. Unlike Kostbera's dreams, Glaumvor's are almost literal and certainly easy to interpret. In the first she sees a gallows and her husband, still alive, being bitten by serpents; in the second, a sword driven through his body and wolves howling at his head and feet; in the third, a river flowing through the hall and breaking over the feet of Gunnar's brothers; in the fourth, dead women come to her in sad garments and summon Gunnar to them. Here again the audience will know the answers. Glaumvor dreams of the future when Gunnar will be put in the serpents' den, his body pierced, his brothers killed, and his soul fetched by the Norns. On hearing of these dreams Gunnar is less sceptical than Hogni, or rather becomes less sceptical as he hears of one dream after another. His answer to the first is lost; the second he treats as no more than a forecast of hunting; his answer to the third is also lost; but with the fourth he seems to be a little shaken. At least he does not reject it, but simply reaffirms his purpose to go to Atli; and indeed foresees that all may not be well:

> " Too late is thy speaking, for so is it settled;
> From the faring I turn not, the going is fixed,
> Though likely it is that our lives shall be short." [1]

In the two sets of dreams the poet uses a slightly different method. In the first they are obscure, and Hogni remains unpersuaded; in the second they are relatively clear, and in the end Gunnar sees that something is wrong. By adopting this double technique the poet shows his familiarity with the ways in which dreams can be used in heroic poetry. His purpose is evidently to show both how inexorable destiny works on the sons of Gjuki and how heroic they are in facing it when they know it.

Dreams can also be used to start the separate episodes of a longer poem. Of this an outstanding example is *Gilgamish*. In our existing text, which is sadly fragmentary in parts, there are no less than seven dreams, and in the full text there may well have been more. All these seven occur before important changes in the action and make some contribution to them. They are on the whole easy to interpret, and the heroes have no great doubts about them. The first comes before Gilgamish's struggle with Enkidu. He sees a great figure falling onto him. It is too strong for him, and he ends by holding it to his breast like a woman. This, as Gilgamish's mother explains, is the great friend whom he

---

[1] *Atlamál*, 26.

is soon to make after struggling with him. So the friendship with
Enkidu is foreshadowed. He then recounts a second dream in
which an axe falls into Erech, and he presents it to his mother;
and this too she explains to mean that he will make a great friend.
The second set of dreams come just before the fight with Humbaba,
which is the next great episode after Gilgamish and Enkidu have
made their alliance. The account of the first dream is lost. In the
second Gilgamish sees himself and Enkidu standing on a mountain
peak which begins to topple, and Enkidu knows that this means
that they will conquer Humbaba. In a third dream Gilgamish sees
something more frightening:

> The firmament roared, the earth resounded,
> The day was black with rising darkness and lightning flashes,
> Flames were kindled, and there too was Pestilence
> Filled to overflowing, Death was gorged.
> The glare faded, the fires faded,
> The brands turned to ashes.[1]

The interpretation is missing, but it must surely have referred to
Humbaba, " whose roar is a whirlwind ", and have portended his
defeat. Lastly, when Enkidu is about to die, he dreams of death
as a man with a dark face and the claws of a lion, who sets on him
and overcomes him; then he dreams of the underworld in all its
emptiness and drabness. So in each of these three episodes, the
formation of a friendship between Gilgamish and Enkidu, the
attack on Humbaba, and the death of Enkidu, the poet puts dreams
in the forefront of his narrative. By this means he may to some
extent spoil the effect of surprise in what follows, but he achieves
something else no less important. The dreams show the grandeur
of what the heroes do and are an imaginative and illuminating
comment on it.

Roland uses dreams less freely than *Gilgamish*, but with a good
sense of their dramatic possibilities. They are used on two great
occasions, first after Charlemagne has commanded Roland to
command the rear-guard, the second before his counter-attack on
the Saracens. On each occasion the Emperor dreams two dreams,
and on neither is he disturbed by them to the point of waking.
These dreams are symbolic, but not difficult to interpret. On the
first occasion the first dream presents the traitor Ganelon in his
own person, though his activities are a little unusual:

> That Emperour, rich Charlès, lies asleep;
> Dreams that he stands in the great pass of Size,
> In his two hands his ashen spear he sees;

[1] *Gilgamish*, v, iii, 15-19.

> Guenès the count that spear from him doth seize,
> Brandishes it and twists it with such ease,
> That flown into the sky the flinders seem.[1]

We need not press the meaning of the spear too far. It is Charlemagne's chief weapon of defence, and may mean his rear-guard or Roland or both. It strikes a note of warning against treachery and danger, and leaves no doubt who the traitor is. The second dream is more complicated:

> And after this another vision saw,
> In France, at Aix, in his Chapelle once more,
> That his right arm an evil bear did gnaw;
> Out of Ardennes he saw a leopard stalk,
> His body dear did savagely assault;
> But then there dashed a harrier from the hall,
> Leaping in the air he sped to Charlès' call,
> By the right ear that felon bear he caught,
> And furiously the leopard next he fought.
> Of battle great the Franks then seemed to talk,
> Yet which might win they knew not, in his thought.[2]

This belongs to the familiar class of animal-dreams and needs some elucidation. The Emperor's right arm is Roland, for so he is called elsewhere.[3] The bear and the leopard are the Saracens. They may even be the king Marsilies and his uncle, the Algalife, but there is no need to be too precise about this. The harrier is again Roland, who comes to Charlemagne's defence. This dream is not so much a warning as a prophecy, and it is characteristic of Charlemagne that he pays little attention to it. He is used to danger and does not trouble too much about it in advance.

The second occasion when Charlemagne dreams follows rather a similar pattern. First comes Saint Gabriel who warns him that another battle awaits him and leaves him in doubt of its outcome. After natural portents of thunder and wind have fallen on the army, wild beasts and monsters feed on the soldiers, whom the Emperor is unable to help; then

> Out of a wood came a great lion then,
> 'Twas very proud and fierce and terrible;
> His body dear sought out, and on him leapt,
> Each in his arms, wrestling, the other held;
> But he knew not which conquered, nor which fell.[4]

This dream forecasts accurately what is to come. The great Pagan army under Baligant is like a tempest and inflicts great losses on the Christian army. Its leader, Baligant, is like a lion

[1] *Roland*, 718-23.   [2] *Ibid.* 725-35.
[3] *Ibid.* 597.   [4] *Ibid.* 2549-53.

whom Charlemagne must subdue. The dream is meant to instil fear and watchfulness but the Emperor, as is his wont, sleeps on. It is followed by another which is a little more mysterious :

> Him seemed in France, at Aix, on a terrace,
> And that he held a bruin by two chains ;
> Out of Ardenne saw thirty bears that came,
> And each of them words, as a man might, spake :
> Said to him : " Sire, give him to us again !
> It is not right that he with you remain,
> He's of our kin, and we must lend him aid."
> A harrier fair ran out of his palace,
> Among them all the greatest bear assailed
> On the green grass, beyond his friends some way.
> There saw the King marvellous give and take ;
> But he knew not which fell, nor which o'ercame.[1]

This dream refers to the traitor Ganelon, who is the chained bear and is supported by his thirty kinsmen. The most powerful of these, Pinabel, is challenged by Thierry of Anjou, who is the harrier. This dream forecasts what is to happen later in the poem, but leaves both the action and its outcome obscure. It is a warning to the Emperor about the efforts which will be made later to save Ganelon from his doom. To the audience, who may not know exactly what is going to happen, it suggests even more troubles in store for Charlemagne. The dreams in *Roland* foretell what is coming without saying too much about it.

A noteworthy and unusual variant of the dream-motive comes early in the *Iliad*. The dream comes from the gods, but Zeus, who sends it, intends to deceive Agamemnon by it ; for by this means the Achaeans will lose many men, and Achilles will be asked to go back to battle with full honours. The dream tells Agamemnon to order the Achaeans to arm, since now is the time fated for the capture of Troy. Agamemnon believes the dream, and can hardly do otherwise, since dreams come from Zeus, but behaves very peculiarly. He makes a speech in the assembly of chieftains, in which, in order to test the spirit of his army, he announces that he has decided to abandon the siege and go home. The result is panic and confusion, and the situation is saved only by the purposeful wisdom of Odysseus. In this unusual situation Homer puts the old theme of the dream to an uncommon purpose. Perhaps he wishes to suggest that since the dream is deceitful and represents no real will of the gods, it creates unwise ideas in Agamemnon's mind and leads to a general panic. We may possibly discern Homer's basic reasons for this remarkable device. He seems to

[1] *Ibid.* 2556-67.

wish in the first place to get his armies into movement after the quarrel of Achilles and Agamemnon, and for this he needs a scene of general activity; and in the second place he is able to show Agamemnon as the troubled, care-ridden, none too confident leader that he is. To secure these ends Homer takes the traditional theme of the dream and gives to it an unexpected turn. Here, as often elsewhere, he seems to feel that it is not enough to use an old device in a familiar way : he must see what new surprise he can create through it. So he starts with the unusual conception of a deceitful dream and proceeds to a scene of confusion and dismay. In any case he succeeds in creating a situation in which the Achaean army is marshalled and the main first movement of the *Iliad* is set going. If the *Odyssey* begins with the familiar theme of someone arriving with news, the start of the *Iliad* owes something to the theme of a dream, even though it is unlike most other dreams and has a special complication.

VIII

SOME PECULIARITIES OF COMPOSITION

HEROIC poetry has in the past been misunderstood and misjudged because it works by rules different from those which apply to poets who write books. Much of the " Higher Criticism " of the Homeric poems, *Beowulf*, and *Roland* suffers from the serious defect that its standards belong to a reading, not to a listening, public and that it takes no account of the special circumstances of oral composition. For instance, when the Abbé d'Aubignac wrote his *Conjectures académiques* in 1664 and argued that the *Iliad* and *Odyssey* were a number of independent songs collected by Lycurgus at Sparta in the eighth century B.C.,[1] he was guided primarily by the literary ideals of France in his time and failed to see that Homer did not share them. Again, when F. A. Wolf attacked the unity of Homer in his *Prolegomena* in 1795, he based part of his argument on the assumption that writing did not exist in Homer's time and that without it no poet could have composed poems so long as the *Iliad* and the *Odyssey*. This, as we now know, is a fallacy, and Wolf's main arguments are outmoded. But his spirit survives, even to-day, when the nature of oral composition has been carefully studied, and some scholars continue to criticise heroic poetry as if it were composed in the same way as a modern novel. This is to approach a complex subject with unwarranted presuppositions and leads almost always to error. Since oral poets compose in special conditions, their work shows special character-istics, and examination of these will help not only to remove current misconceptions but to show the difficulties in which these poems are composed.

The conditions of oral performance may mean that sooner or later a poet contradicts himself or muddles something in his narrative. There are few heroic poems in which some such contradiction cannot be found. The poet so concentrates on his immediate task that he may not remember all that has gone before or foresee all that will come later. The chances are that any such slip will be of little importance, since, if the poet does not notice

---

[1] Cf. J. B. Bury, *C.A.H.* ii, p. 502.

it, it is not likely that his audience will notice it either. But when his poem is written down and subjected to the sharp eyes of critical scholars, what was originally a trivial slip may be regarded as a grave error and made a foundation for bold theories of multiple authorship. We must remember that most heroic poems are composed for one performance only and that the audience has no written text before it. It cannot turn pages back to see if what comes later agrees with what has come before, and it is not likely to subject a poem to minute criticism. Since it follows a tale with its ears and has to keep its attention on the sequence of events told by the bard, it has no time to ask inconvenient questions. It is interested in the main elements of a tale and the way in which they are treated. The poet therefore is not much concerned to make everything consistent and may well fall into what we may regard as serious faults.

One source of such contradictions seems to be the existence of formulae which the poet uses whenever they suit his purpose. In his attachment to them he may not see that sometimes they betray him into saying what he might otherwise have avoided. For instance, the *Iliad* is guilty of one famous contradiction. At one place Pylaemenes, king of the Paphlagonians, is killed by Menelaus, and at another he is alive at the funeral of his son. It is true that Pylaemenes is a quite unimportant person and that slips equally grave or equally trivial may be found in poets so careful as Virgil and Dante. But in this case we may surmise what the cause of the slip was. When Pylaemenes is killed, Homer knows what he is doing and gives four lines to it :

> Then did they find in the field Pylaemenes, tireless in battle,
> The Paphlagonian people he ruled, a spear-man high-hearted.
> Unto him Atreus' son, Menelaus, famed with the spear-shaft,
> Went as he stood in his place and struck with a spear on the collar.[1]

Much later in the poem Pylaemenes' son, Harpalion, is killed by Meriones. His companions carry him off on a shield to Troy :

> And with them went also his father, lamenting,
> Yet did he not receive any recompense for his dead son.[2]

This is beyond dispute a mistake, but we can account for it. The lines in which the father laments and follows the corpse are probably traditional and formulaic. Pylaemenes is not mentioned by name in them, and Homer, in employing a familiar form of words, has for the moment forgotten its full implications.

[1] *Il.* v, 576-9.   [2] *Ibid.* xiii, 658-9.

A similar mistake may be found in *Beowulf*, where the poet seems to be in some doubt about the sex of Grendel's Dam. She is normally feminine, but in three places she seems to be masculine :

> He who in dread waters   his dwelling must keep (1260)
> I swear to you this,   that he shall not escape me (1392)
> Nor on ocean ground,   go where he will (1394).

This inconsistency has not escaped the critics, who have suggested that they either reflect an earlier version of the story, in which Beowulf kills Grendel in the cave, or are transferred from the fight with him to the fight with the Dam. There is an easier solution than either of these. It is that the poet operates with formulaic phrases which do not quite fit his subject. If the first case concerns monsters, the others need not necessarily do so, and it looks as if the poet, employing a traditional means, failed to see that it was not entirely appropriate here. There are other examples of such misfits in *Beowulf*.[1] They would hardly trouble an audience used to formulaic poetry and not very interested in the precise sex of a monster.

Formulae may account for some contradictions, but they do not account for all. Some are quite clearly due to slips of memory. With no written text to help him the poet may well falter and not notice it, particularly if it does not really affect the main course of his narrative. Homer is sometimes guilty of this. Though most of the accusations against him have been disproved, there are one or two cases where he errs on the side of vagueness, if not of contradiction. For instance, in the *Odyssey*, when Odysseus is transformed into a beggar by Athene, she destroys the " brown hair " on his head :[2] later, when she restores him, he has a blue-black beard.[3] Of course a hero like Odysseus may well combine brown hair with a blue-black beard, but one cannot help wondering whether Homer really gave thought to the matter and did not slightly change his conception of Odysseus' appearance. Less excusable is the treatment of the gods in Book I of the *Iliad*. Athene comes down to see Achilles [4] and soon afterwards goes back to Olympus to the other gods,[5] though a little later we hear that they have all gone to the land of the Ethiopians for twelve days.[6] This does not matter, but it is an undeniable slip. Something of the same kind may be seen in *Roland*. Before Roland dies he takes his famous oliphant and

---

[1] *E.g.* 1344, 1379, 1887, 2421, 2685.   [2] *Od.* xiii, 431.
[3] *Ibid.* xvi, 176.   [4] *Il.* i, 194.   [5] *Ibid.* 221.   [6] *Ibid.* 424 ff.

breaks it on the head of a pagan who is trying to kill him. He is glad to kill the enemy, but sorry to smash his oliphant :

> " But my great one, my olifant I broke ;
> Fallen from it the crystal and the gold." [1]

Later, after Roland's death, the oliphant is found by Charles near his body and entrusted to Guineman. So far there is no contradiction, but, when the battle against Baligant's army takes place, the horn seems to be whole and sound and able to do its old work ; for it is blown, and sounds louder than all the other horns :

> Above them all boomed the olifant again,[2]

> And the olifant sounds over all its knell.[3]

If the oliphant is really broken, as we have been led to think, this after-life is impossible. The point is of no importance, but there it is.

The real reason why oral poets make slips like these is that their conditions of performance force them to concentrate on one thing at a time. They must at all costs make themselves clear to their audiences and cannot encumber their poems with too many details. If they do, they lose attention through putting too great a strain on it. The result is that in concentrating on a given scene they may neglect or forget something which precedes it. This may not be important and indeed seldom is, but it is not what we would expect from a modern novelist or a writer of " literary " epic. Each separate scene tends to develop its own character and to have its own fullness. It is therefore not surprising that it may sometimes cause contradictions in the main narrative. When Harpalion is killed, the poet feels that he must make someone mourn for him ; for without that his death is incomplete and lacks pathos. Tradition supplies the mourner in the dead youth's father, and a contradiction arises. When Charlemagne orders horns to be blown, it is obviously right that among them should be the famous oliphant of Roland, and it is mentioned, even at the cost of contradicting what has been said before. On an ordinary reading such contradictions are hardly noticeable, but, when they are noticed, they may cause uneasiness. But that is because we are accustomed to reading poems instead of listening to them.

This condition explains some peculiarities of heroic poetry, and especially its tendency to omit much that we might expect to be mentioned. The oral poet does not tidy up his loose ends but leaves them as soon as they have served their purpose, with

---

[1] *Roland*, 2295-6.   [2] *Ibid.* 3119.   [3] *Ibid.* 3302.

the result that we may feel that he neglects minor details in his story. This kind of omission takes different forms. First, a character may be introduced and play a part of some importance, only to disappear without anything being said about it. For instance, in the Norse *Atlakvitha* the action is set in motion by the arrival at Gunnar's court of Atli's messenger and agent, Knefröth. His part is important, since he has to persuade Gunnar to come on a visit to Atli, and there are good reasons why Gunnar should not go. Knefröth presents his case skilfully, and succeeds in his task:

> And Knefröth spake loudly,   his words were crafty,
> The hero from the south,   on the high bench sitting.[1]

But once Knefröth has had his say, no more is heard about him. He has played his part, and the poet turns to the next item on his programme, the speeches which Gunnar and Hogni and their wives make about the expedition. In this he has no need of Knefröth, and any mention of him might interfere with the direct and forceful presentation of a leading theme. Again, in *Roland* the Saracen, Blancandrin, plays a very important part. He urges King Marsilies to feign submission to Charles (24 ff.), is the chief of the embassy which comes with a false offer of surrender (68), addresses Charles (122 ff.), rides off with Ganelon and plots Roland's death with him (414), and conducts the tricky negotiations between Ganelon and Marsile, when it looks as if Ganelon has overplayed his part and is likely to be killed by the Saracens (506-11). But after this he disappears, and nothing at all is said of him. Though he is an important figure in the Saracen army, " very wise " and " a gallant knight ", he takes no part in any of the battles or of the events which follow them. Once the poet has used him for a special purpose, he dismisses him without a word and moves on to another topic in which Blancandrin's services are no longer needed. Homer does something of the same kind in the *Iliad* with Thersites. When Agamemnon unwisely calls an assembly and says that he intends to give up the siege of Troy, he excites dismay and panic, and the first to speak is Thersites, a man of no lineage and no account, on whose ugly appearance Homer dwells with some relish. He reviles Agamemnon and is punished for it by Odysseus who, after saying what he thinks of him, strikes him on the back and shoulders with a sceptre and leaves a great weal on them. He sits down humiliated, and the crowd applauds the action.[2] That is the end of him. We are not even told that he

---

[1] *Atlakvitha*, 2, 3-4.   [2] *Il.* ii, 211 ff.

leaves the assembly. It is enough that he has played his part and is needed no longer. Immediately afterwards Homer turns to a different theme.

If important characters can be dismissed in this perfunctory way, we need not be surprised if actions which have some importance at one stage of a story are later forgotten or neglected. Homer understands how to do this. He seldom stresses a small point beyond its immediate usefulness. For instance, Achilles lays down his spear, but fifty lines later has it in his hand,[1] though we are not told that he has picked it up. Poseidon arrives at the battlefield in a chariot drawn by horses with golden manes, and shackles them with golden shackles.[2] When he leaves the field, nothing is said of either horses or chariot.[3] Zeus watches the battle from Mount Ida,[4] but soon after is back on Olympus without our being told that he has gone there.[5] These are not errors of memory but a necessary economy in an art which treats of one thing at a time. To elaborate all the implications of such themes would be to overburden the narrative. So Homer lets well alone and leaves us to fill in the gaps if we wish to. The same thing can be seen in *Roland* in the case of the hostages which Charles demands from the Saracens and duly receives. The poet pays some attention to them. Blancandrin suggests that they should be sent :

> " Send hostages, should he demand surety,
> Ten or a score, our loyal oath to bind." [6]

In due course they arrive, accompanied by Ganelon, who presents them to the Emperor :

> " Tribute I bring you, very great and rare,
> And twenty men ; look after them with care." [7]

But once the hostages are delivered, nothing more is heard of them. Although they are a surety for the good behaviour of the Saracens, and should be killed when the Saracens break their word, the poet does not mention them. He has more interesting and more important matters in hand, and the hostages can be forgotten. So too in *Beowulf*, Hrothgar's queen, Wealhtheow, comes to the feast in honour of Beowulf, pledges his health, and makes a speech in his honour.[8] But once she has done her duty, no more is said about her, and we are not told that she leaves the hall, but have to infer it later when Hrothgar goes to join her :

[1] *Il.* xxi, 17 and 67.   [2] *Ibid.* xiii, 23.   [3] *Ibid.* xiv, 293.
[4] *Ibid.* 157.   [5] *Ibid.* xvi, 431.   [6] *Roland*, 40-41.
[7] *Ibid.* 678-9.   [8] *Beowulf*, 614 ff.

He would the War-Chief,   Wealhtheow, seek,
A Queen for his couch.[1]

Similarly, the sword Hrunting, which belongs to Unferth, has some importance in the fight with Grendel's Dam. Unferth lends it to Beowulf, and the poet describes it at length.[2] Later, when Beowulf sets out for home, Unferth offers him the sword as a gift,[3] though no word has been said about it having returned meanwhile to Unferth's possession. These details do not matter. The important thing is to focus attention on the main events, and this is done by an adroit art of omission.

Omission is practised with some skill by Homer when the personal relations of his characters seem likely to interfere with the development of the story. He is too good a poet to neglect the poetical possibilities of such relations, but he so places their great moments that they attract attention before the plot really demands them. For instance, the wonderful scene between Hector and Andromache on the walls of Troy has in it much of a last scene between husband and wife.[4] After it we feel that they may never meet again and that they have said their final words to one another. But in fact the plot of the *Iliad* suggests that they do meet again. For soon afterwards all the Trojan heroes go back to Troy, and we must assume that Hector is among them.[5] But Homer has placed his scene between Hector and Andromache in conditions which allow nothing to interfere with it, and he is not going to spoil it later by any anti-climax or make it subordinate to some other theme. So, too, when Odysseus leaves Calypso on her remote island, Homer presents a charming scene of farewell between them, when Calypso, with a forbearance not always to be found in goddesses, wishes him good speed in his departure, though she feels that she is in no way inferior to the wife whom he longs to see. He accepts what she says but insists that he must go.[6] This is the last scene between them in the *Odyssey*, but we may infer that it is not the last occasion when they see one another. For after it Odysseus spends four days building his boat and Calypso helps him by providing sails and food. Homer wishes to deal with one theme at a time, and the farewell must be done with before the boat-building is begun. The farewell comes first, because the boat-building prepares the way to Odysseus' voyage and is a necessary, immediate preliminary to it. A similar technique is used with Nausicaa. In the first hours of Odysseus' arrival on Phaeacia she plays a leading part. She saves his life,

---

[1] *Ibid.* 664-5. [2] *Ibid.* 1455 ff. [3] *Ibid.* 1807 ff.
[4] *Il.* vi, 390 ff. [5] *Ibid.* vii, 477. [6] *Od.* v, 202 ff.

gives him food and drink and clothing, and brings him to her parents' palace. Then she disappears, except for one short and charming moment when Odysseus meets her on the threshold when he is coming from the bath.[1] She reminds him of what she has done for him, and he thanks her for it. That is all. He has still much before him in Phaeacia, but she is not mentioned again. Attention is now turned to Odysseus' relations with the king and queen, his recital of his adventures, and his preparations to return home. In each of these cases Homer uses the same technique and justifies it abundantly.

Oral composition creates special problems for the presentation of character and motives. The poet addresses an audience of simple people who may well appreciate the salient points of a personality but must not be expected to understand any complicated psychology. Even if the poet himself has considerable insight into character and understands mixed motives, he will hardly carry his audience with him. Nor would the conditions of performance allow any great elaboration, even if he wished to practise it. Just as oral composition insists that one event at a time is sufficient and that irrelevant or unnecessary additions must be avoided, so in the presentation of character it seems to insist that one mood or motive is enough at a time and that to attempt more is to blur the clarity which is indispensable to success. This may be a limitation on the presentation of character, but it has at least the advantage that many heroic persons have a simplicity which is delightfully real and convincing, even if it is not very subtle. Odysseus and Gilgamish, Roland and Alaman Bet, are not complicated like the characters of a modern novel, but they have their own rich kind of being and act in accordance with their own inner necessities. On the whole the characters of heroic poetry are of this kind, but there are places where the convolutions of the story demand a greater complexity of character, and then the poet has to evolve his own technique of adapting his needs to the conditions of composition.

The poet solves this problem by presenting not a complex situation in a hero's soul at a given moment but a series of psychological states which may look inconsistent, as they appear in succession, but are actually consistent enough if we see that this is a way of treating what is really a single problem. A good example of this may be found in *Roland*. The treachery of Ganelon is fundamental to the whole poem, and the poet knows how important it is. He also knows that it is not at all simple or

[1] *Od*. viii, 456 ff.

obvious. A distinguished warrior like Ganelon does not become a traitor without some powerful motive, and such a motive may itself be complex. The poet has clearly given thought to this question and found his solution for it, but he proceeds according to the demands of oral composition and sets out his scheme in a series of statements which may look contradictory to those who are not used to this art. The treacherous plan begins in Ganelon's mind when Roland suggests that he, Ganelon, should be sent on a dangerous mission to the Saracens. Ganelon is enraged by the suggestion and bursts into a furious outburst :

> " Fool, wherefore art so wrathful ?
> All men know well that I am thy good-father ;
> Thou hast decreed, to Marsiliun I travel.
> Then if God grant that I return hereafter,
> I'll follow thee with such a force of passion
> That will endure so long as life may last thee." [1]

Here Ganelon's anger turns on a point of honour. He is perfectly willing to be sent by the Emperor on this mission, as his subsequent words make clear, but he cannot endure that Roland should suggest that he should go, since this implies that he would not volunteer of his own accord. This behaviour is quite in accord with heroic rules of honour, and the poet presents it with some care. In his anger Ganelon almost betrays his purpose when he says

> " There I will work a little trickery,
> This mighty wrath of mine I'll thus let free." [2]

This is the first stage in Ganelon's career of treachery. His pride has been wounded, and he decides to avenge it on Roland who has humiliated him before the Emperor and his peers.

Behind this, however, lies something else. As the poem advances, it is revealed that Ganelon has long hated Roland because of his pride and presumption. This becomes clear when Ganelon rides off with Blancandrin and begins to plot Roland's destruction. He argues that peace is impossible so long as Roland lives, and says that his pride will in the end destroy him :

> " His cruel pride must shortly him confound,
> Each day t'wards death he goes a little down,
> When he be slain, shall peace once more abound." [3]

Even before he proposes his plot to Marsilies and is still acting as Charles' ambassador and repeating what he has been told to say, Ganelon cannot but let slip a word of abuse of Roland for his

[1] *Roland*, 286-91. [2] *Ibid*. 300-301. [3] *Ibid*. 389-91.

pride, when he tells of the proposed division of Spain which the Emperor offers :

> " One half of Spain he'll render as your fief,
> The rest Rollanz, his nephew, shall receive,
> Proud parcener in him you'll have indeed." [1]

Much later, when Ganelon faces condemnation for treason, he repeats this view of Roland and advances it as a reason for his treachery :

> " Hatred of me had Rollant, his nephew ;
> So he decreed death for me and dolour." [2]

Ganelon holds to the last his view that Roland wished to destroy him by sending him on the mission to Marsilies.

A third element in the portrayal of Ganelon is the poet's suggestion that he is avaricious and takes bribes from the enemy. The gifts which he receives are enumerated at some length, and, as he receives each, Ganelon suggests that he is party to a bargain, which he seals by some such words as " So be it, as you command " or " It shall be done ". Much later the same theme is taken up when Ganelon gives as a reason for disliking Roland his tendency to take too great a share of spoil :

> " He did from me much gold and wealth forfeit,
> Whence to destroy and slay him did I seek." [3]

This completes the poet's conception of Ganelon's psychology, and in the final picture the different elements cohere without difficulty. He has always hated Roland, partly because in his avarice he thinks that Roland deprives him of his just profits, partly because Roland has always been overbearing with him. This old hatred reaches a climax when Roland suggests that Ganelon should go on the embassy. Ganelon then feels that Roland wishes to have him killed and is furious that he should be made to look like a coward. The poet sees Ganelon's character and motives quite clearly, but presents them piecemeal as his narrative demands.

The poet of *Beowulf* attempts a more complex piece of psychology when he portrays Unferth, whose name means " mar peace ", and whose history does not dispose us to like him, since he has killed his brother [4] and is, according to Beowulf, destined to receive his punishment in Hell.[5] On his first appearance he makes an unfavourable impression, when he questions Beowulf about his swimming-match with Breca and suggests that, since

---

[1] *Roland*, 472-4.   [2] *Ibid.* 3771-2.   [3] *Ibid.* 3758-9.
[4] *Beowulf*, 587 ff., 1167 ff.   [5] *Ibid.* 588 ff.

Beowulf lost in it, he is not likely to do better in his encounter with Grendel. His words justify the poet's description of him as the most envious of men.[1] Beowulf answers him, but the poet omits to tell us how this answer affects Unferth, thus leaving us in the dark about his future development. The picture so presented is of an aristocratic Thersites, or even of the wicked counsellor who sows discord and envy in an honourable and courteous court. But later the poet corrects this. When Beowulf prepares to assault Grendel's Dam, Unferth hands him the sword Hrunting, and the poet explains how this change of mind has come:

> Indeed he recalled not,   Ecglaf's kinsman
> Strong in might,   what he had spoken before,
> With wine drunken,   when that weapon he lent
> To a better swordsman ;   himself, he durst not
> Under the rush of the waves   risk his life,
> Act with lordship ;   lost he thereby glory,
> An excellent fame.[2]

Unferth, who at first sight seemed the incarnation of envy, is now seen to be a not very brave man, who becomes braver in his cups, but is still capable of a generous action. In him the poet attempts something difficult and has to advance by bold steps which may create uneasiness. But he could hardly do otherwise. His technique demands that a man should be presented in emphatic, hard lines, and if he is at all complicated, his qualities must be revealed in turn until a complete picture of him emerges.

In the extended scale of a large epic the presentation of character presents greater difficulties and may lead to greater misunderstanding, as with Achilles in the *Iliad*. The plot of the *Iliad* turns, as the poet says at the outset, on the wrath of Achilles, and Book I tells how this began. Agamemnon insists upon taking from Achilles the captive girl Briseis, and Achilles resents this as an affront to his pride. At first he wishes to kill Agamemnon, but is prevented from doing so by the intervention of Athene. He retires to his tent and asks his mother, the goddess Thetis, to help him. He has now formed his plan. He has yielded Briseis to Agamemnon, but cherishes a bitter resentment, and his consolation now is the hope that he will see Agamemnon and the other Achaean chieftains humiliated by defeat when he is absent from battle. He believes, correctly enough, that in his absence the Trojans will prevail and the Achaeans do little against them. In this his injured pride hopes to find satisfaction and revenge. His plan is quite explicit. Thetis is to ask Zeus

[1] *Ibid.* 501 ff.   [2] *Ibid.* 1465-71.

If he be willing to grant his succour unto the Trojans,
And to defeat the Achaeans among their ships at the sea-shore,
Slaying them so that they learn what boons their king has bestowed
    them ;
And Agamemnon, who rules far and wide, son of Atreus, may also
Know of his doom, that he failed to honour the best of Achaeans.[1]

This is a perfectly clear scheme, and the *Iliad* begins with it. Just as Ganelon, in his sense of injury against Roland, plots his destruction and his army's, so Achilles plots the defeat of Agamemnon and his army that he himself may be missed and so honoured. To this his injured pride drives him.

Achilles' plan works. Before long he is so sorely needed that Agamemnon and the other leaders decide to make amends to him in the hope that he will return to the battlefield. Agamemnon is prepared to humble himself, and his offers of amends are on a royal scale. But Achilles rejects them categorically. In presenting this the poet may seem to make Achilles' behaviour inconsistent with his original motives of wrath and injured pride. He now asserts that a man's life is worth more than any riches and urges the Achaeans to go away and think of some other plan. Now this point of view is not inconsistent with Achilles' first outburst of wrath against Agamemnon. He has had time to think about his grievances and formed a general theory about them. This is true to his character and to life, but Homer does not show how Achilles has passed from his first wild wrath to a meditative and determined melancholy. The lack of intervening links is due to the conditions of oral recitation. All the poetry must be given to the present situation, in which Achilles rejects the offers of Agamemnon. To make the rejection effective Homer puts Achilles in this grave mood and gives him an abundance of high poetry. When it comes to this scene, the audience will have forgotten, more or less, about the original wrath and be interested mainly in what Achilles now feels and says. This Homer presents with great imagination and power. It is not inconsistent with what has preceded it, and is indeed a subtle development of it, but we must supply for ourselves the steps in the process which has led from the one stage to the other.

The third stage in Achilles' story is after his rejection of the embassy. He watches the battle and knows that the Achaeans are suffering humiliation and defeat according to his plan. Then he says to Patroclus some words which have caused much trouble to the commentators :

[1] *Il.* i, 408-12.

" Now, as I think, the Achaeans will stand by my knees in petition.
On them cometh a need they cannot endure any longer." [1]

This is Achilles' hour of triumph, and in it he speaks as if he had
not recently received an embassy asking for his help. The
contradiction is perhaps more apparent than real. When the
embassy came, there was still hope of an Achaean recovery, as
Diomedes said at the time ; now the situation is desperate. Then
the proposals made were handsome but not abject, but this is what
Achilles now expects. The later words can in fact be squared
with the earlier occasion, though we may still feel that they are
awkward. So indeed they are, if we forget the conditions of oral
composition. But since the poet concentrates on the present
moment and makes everything of it, he does not refer, even by
implication, to the earlier occasion, but thinks only of the present
crisis. In consequence, he uses a theme which is perfectly to the
point and causes trouble only when we connect it too closely
with what has happened before. Since his audience is not likely
to do that, there is no real trouble. In these three scenes Homer
develops Achilles' character from his first outbreak of wrath
through his deeper thoughts on life and death to the moment
when his plan seems successful and his triumph complete.

Another result of the poet's concentration on his immediate
task is that he may neglect chronology at the expense of coherence.
For instance, Homer places the events of his *Iliad* in the tenth
and last year of the siege of Troy. This he says more than once,[2]
and it is important to his main plan. The crisis of the *Iliad* is the
death of Hector, and, when he is dead, Troy is ready for capture.
But though this is the main plan, there are certain episodes which
do not fit easily into it and have made scholars suggest that Homer
at times follows a tradition which made the Trojan War last for
only a few months. Certainly in the first books of the *Iliad* there
are episodes which would be more suited to the beginning of a war
than to its tenth year. When Homer gives a catalogue of the
Achaean forces as they gathered at Aulis before setting out for
Troy, he goes back to the beginning of the war. When Helen
points out to Priam from the walls of Troy the chief Achaean
leaders, she does what would be probable in the first year of the
war, but is hardly probable in the tenth. When Menelaus fights
Paris in single combat, they do what the two men most concerned
with the origin of the war might well have done at its start but can
hardly have left until near its end, especially as both sides agree to

---

[1] *Il.* xi, 609-10.
[2] *Ibid.* ii, 134, 295, 328 ff. ; xii, 15 ; xxiv, 765.

end the war according to the result of this duel. On these occasions we undoubtedly feel that the tenth year of the war is an odd time for such events to happen and wonder why Homer has arranged things in this way.

In answer to these doubts we may in the first place note that, though Homer says at least five times that the war has lasted for ten years, he does this only when its long duration is relevant to some immediate point in the story. In Book II, for instance, it is relevant, since it is part of Agamemnon's plan to test the morale of the army to say that the war has lasted too long. In Book XII it is relevant to the great dyke which the Achaeans build to protect their ships and which lasts till the end of the war. In Book XXIV it is relevant to Helen's complaint that she has been away a long time from her home and her family. The ten years' duration of the war is known to Homer and used by him when he can make a special point with it. It is, as it were, at the back of his mind and comes to the front when occasions arise which are connected with it. Then he mentions it in order that he may drive some point home. But this does not mean that he is always thinking of it or always feels a need to stress it. On the contrary, with that lack of interest in chronology which seems to be natural to the oral poet's outlook, he sometimes disregards it completely, and we can see what he gains by doing so.

Homer's poem is an *Iliad*, a poem on the siege of Troy, but his sense of craftsmanship forbids him to treat it episodically as a mere chronicle. He takes instead a crisis and builds episodes round it. None the less he wishes to keep to his theme of the siege, if only to provide a wide stage for his main characters. He has thus to deal with two large armies, each containing a number of famous heroes. He cannot take it for granted that his audience will know what heroes are fighting on each side, or what their titles and histories and kingdoms are. So to make his position clear he includes in his poem a Catalogue of the Achaean forces as they gathered at Aulis before sailing to Troy and another, shorter Catalogue of their Trojan opponents. The first of these Catalogues is chronologically out of place, since it portrays a state of affairs ten years earlier than the main events of the *Iliad* and is not even placed at Troy. Nor is it entirely in harmony with the rest of the poem. In its enumeration of the Achaean kingdoms it mentions several heroes who have little or no part in the main text, while others are already dead before the plot opens. Nor does its account of their relative importance, judged by the size of their domains and the number of their ships, correspond with that of the rest of the poem. Odysseus, for instance, is of little account in the Catalogue, but of great account in the main poem. Homer treats this historical document as it deserves. It gives his credentials, but, after presenting it, he can go his own way, not indeed in defiance of it, but certainly not worrying too much about it. It helps to justify him in making his poem an *Iliad* and shows the world in which his events are set. It does not matter that it belongs to an earlier date than the last year of the siege of Troy or that much of its information is irrelevant to the story. It is useful where it comes, since it sets the stage and gives the necessary information on the army-lists of the opposing forces in the Trojan War.

A little later Homer makes Helen and Priam watch the Achaean forces from the wall of Troy, and in answer to Priam's questions Helen identifies Agamemnon, Odysseus, and Ajax. It does not matter that Priam has had nearly ten years to learn who they are. For the moment we forget that it is the tenth year of war, and are interested to make the acquaintance of the chief Achaean leaders and to know what they look like. The heroes whom Helen describes in their physical appearance and in some of their habits are going to play a large part, and there is undeniably an advantage in having them presented in this vivid way. No doubt any poem on the Trojan War would have some such means of identification, and Homer was right in not allowing his theme of the tenth year to prevent him from using this useful device. So too with the duel between Paris and Menelaus. The appropriate time for this was certainly before the general slaughter began at the start, when it would have saved much trouble to have the issue settled by the two men for whom the war was fought. This duel may well have been a traditional element in the story of Troy and is anyhow a good theme, since it brings the two heroes face to face. The fact that it fails to produce any decisive result makes it easier to introduce it into a late stage of the war, and there is nothing wrong in Homer's use of it. But of course when the original audiences heard of it, they would hardly trouble about the time of its occurrence but accept it as an episode which is exciting for its own sake.

Time presents another difficulty to the oral poet. He has no easy way to depict contemporaneous actions. In a book this presents no difficulty, but the oral poet, with his concentration on one thing at a time, has no ready means to suggest that something else happens somewhere else at a given time. His method is to neglect the difficulty and present as happening in sequence events which really happen simultaneously. This is what the poet of *Roland* does in the battle of Roncesvalles. We are presented with a series of small encounters which might suggest to a prosaic mind that when Roland is fighting a Saracen, Oliver, Turpin, and the rest do nothing. Of course the poet does not mean this, but he has no available means to depict actions occurring at the same time. Homer is clearly troubled by the same difficulty in the fighting-scenes of the *Iliad*. At one point he says that the fighting went on

While the morning endured and the holy day was still waxing,[1]

and suggests that it is getting towards noon. Then much later he says that the fighting went on

While the sun in its march bestrode the centre of heaven.[2]

Between the two there can at the best be only a few hours, but an enormous lot of fighting has taken place. Various warriors have gone out, done their best, and retired. The audience, hearing perhaps the poem piecemeal, will not be much troubled by the lack of precise indications of time, and Homer's only way to convey many contemporaneous actions is to set them out in a series. At the beginning of the *Odyssey* he is faced by a graver problem. He has two main themes which he develops separately at some length; first, Telemachus' situation in Ithaca and his voyage in search of news, then Odysseus' departure from Ogygia. He begins the first with a council in heaven which sends Athene to Ithaca, where she gets things moving. This carries on the story for four books, but then Odysseus too has to be started. The subject has been broached at the first council, but some of the audience may not have heard this, and others may have forgotten its details. So Homer tells of it again. This second council is really the same as the first, but this time it leads not to the arrival of Athene in Ithaca but the arrival of Hermes in Ogygia with orders to Calypso to send Odysseus away. The technique is primitive, and other poets do not use it, but we can see that for Homer, who had to keep each section of his story clear and coherent, it was a useful device.

In addition to the special difficulties caused by oral composition the heroic poet has to face others arising from the nature of his material. This material is for the most part traditional. He learns the outlines of stories when he learns his formulae and devices, and to them on the whole he adheres. He may of course some-

---

[1] *Il.* xi, 84.　　　　　　　　　[2] *Ibid.* xvi, 777.

times invent a new story, but his audience will normally expect him to tell familiar tales, even if he gives them his own individual stamp. He is free to invent details within a given frame and even to alter quite important elements in the plot. In composition he draws upon the traditional stories and tells them in his own way. This too has its perils. Since the stories are both traditional and changeable, he may fail to make all his points clear or to make the most of a dramatic opportunity. Since he probably knows several variant versions of any single story, he may confuse them and produce something which is neither very clear nor very dramatic. Of course good poets know this danger and usually surmount it, but others, who are less confident or less gifted, may fall into it and produce something indecisive or muddled. This is hardly true of those poets whose poems were written down long ago, but it is applicable to existing bards whose oral performances have been recorded in recent years, and through their occasional failures we can see what difficulties faced Homer and the poets of *Roland* and *Beowulf*.

An experienced bard, who knows his stories well and has told them many times, may suffer from over-confidence and careless-ness about details. He may do his work so easily and so mechanic-ally that he preserves certain points without fully understanding their significance or making it plain. For instance, a famous Russian bard called " the Bottle " tells the story of Staver's wife, who seeks to rescue her husband by disguising herself as a man and coming to Vladimir's court. Vladimir and his womenfolk are a little suspicious of her and all too ready to examine any evidence she may provide of her sex. One of the tests turns on her going to bed, and the imprint she leaves on the bedding. " The Bottle " tells of this in a muddled way. The alleged man, for no obvious reason, acts as follows :

> When he entered the warm bed
> And lay down on the wooden bedstead,
> He laid his head where his feet should be
> And laid his feet on the pillow.
> When Vladimir of royal Kiev arrived
> And looked into the warm bed,
> There are the broad heroic shoulders.[1]

To understand the full import of this manœuvre and its effect on Vladimir we must look at another version, in which Vladimir promises his daughter to make the test in words which leave no obscurity :

---

[1] Rybnikov, i, p. 207 ; Chadwick, *R.H.P.* p. 128.

" We will ensconce him in the royal feather bed.
If he is a man, there will be a little hollow where his shoulders have
    pressed,
But if a woman, it will be under the hips." [1]

Staver's wife foresees this difficulty and surmounts it by lying
with her feet on the pillow. "The Bottle", whether from
forgetfulness or carelessness, has left the point obscure.

Another Russian bard, Fedotov, makes similar slips in his
delightful account of Vasili Buslaev. Vasili is a bumptious
playboy, whose exuberant spirits take the form of attacking his
fellow townsmen and causing much trouble and annoyance. His
mother does her best to bring him to reason, but her first efforts
meet with humiliating failure, and in dealing with these Fedotov
shows an uncertain touch. After trying in vain to persuade the
citizens of Novgorod to accept gifts in amends from Vasili, she
behaves in what looks like an inexplicable way :

> Then the honourable widow Amelfa Timoferovna
> Turned away from the honourable feast,
> And kicked with her right foot
> That cudgel of maple-wood —
> And the cudgel flew away behind the fence,
> Behind the fence, scattering everything in its course.
> Vasili slept till dawn and took his ease,
> Unconscious of the misfortunes which had befallen him.[2]

To understand this we must look at other versions of the story,
in which we find that Vasili's mother has hidden his club, given
him a sleeping potion and locked him up. Later in the poem a
similar obscurity arises. Vasili has gone out with his club,

> And an old monk from the Andronova monastery met Vasili,
> On the bridge over the Volkhov,
> Wearing on his head the great bell of St. Sophia.

Fedotov has here omitted to tell that after Vasili has fought for
some time and killed a number of citizens, the others go to his
mother who advises them to persuade his godfather, an old monk,
to appease him. The monk does his best, but is killed by Vasili.
Perhaps the audience would know the story well enough not to be
troubled by this important omission, but none the less it illustrates
a difficulty in oral composition.

The nature of the traditional material may create curious
situations. If a story has a wide popularity and is told by many
poets, it may grow into different versions which seem to have little

---

[1] Gilferding, ii, p. 410.
[2] Rybnikov, i, p. 373 ; Chadwick, *R.H.P.* p. 148.

connection with one another and are eventually treated as separate episodes in a hero's career. We can in such cases discern a basic story and see how it has been developed in different directions. But of course a poet, who is interested in all that happens to a hero, may not see or care that two or more stories are essentially variations of a single one and may even combine them in one poem. This sometimes leads to curious results. A favourite Russian story is of the fight between Alyosha Popovich and Tugarin, the Dragon's son. There are of course many kinds of fight, and Alyosha kills Tugarin in more than one way. But this variety has led to an odd result in the version recorded by Kirsha Danilov.[1] This falls into two parts. In the first part Alyosha encounters Tugarin, refuses his offer of friendship, cuts off his head, takes off his robe, and rides off to Vladimir. It is a complete story and needs no more than it says. But the bard then continues to tell how Tugarin follows Alyosha to Kiev and the two engage in single combat which ends with Tugarin's death. What has happened is quite clear. The poet knew of two stories. In one Alyosha kills Tugarin in the country, in the other in Kiev. For some reason the poet feels that he must tell both and does so by the clumsy expedient of bringing Tugarin to life after he has been killed.

Such cases show how a poet can fail when he uses two variant versions of a single theme, but other poets can do this and make a success of it. If the basic theme is sufficiently simple and the variations sufficiently ingenious, we will hardly notice that a single theme has been used twice, nor will we resent it if we do. It is, for instance, possible that in *Beowulf* the twofold scheme by which Beowulf first fights Grendel in Hrothgar's hall and then fights his Dam in her cave is really a double use of a single theme by which the hero fights a monster and its mother. In the parallel stories, like that of Ormr the Strong, the hero encounters both the monster and its dam in their cave and defeats them there. It is possible that the poet of *Beowulf* knew of a version in which the hero's exploits were not in the hall but in the cave, since he makes Beowulf see Grendel's body lying in the cave and cut off the head:

> For that loss repaid him
> The raging champion,   inas resting he saw
> Grendel lie,   of war grown weary,
> All unliving,   as erstwhile had left him
> The battle in Heorot.   His body sprang aside
> When he after death   endured that stroke.[2]

[1] Kireevski, ii, p. 74 ff.
[2] *Beowulf*, 1584-9.

The poet combines his two themes neatly, and there is no contra-diction or awkwardness. And we can see why he does it. By having two fights, one in the hall and one in the cave, he creates a richer situation and is able to exploit suspense more fully. Each fight is differentiated and has its own character, and we do not feel that the poet repeats himself.

It is possible that something of the same kind may be seen in *Gilgamish*. When Gilgamish asks Uta-Napishtim for the secret of immortality, he is told that he must keep awake for six days and six nights that he may pray and find out who will assemble the gods to help him in his need. Gilgamish tries to do this, but through human weakness fails. After this he is told a second way of becoming immortal; he must fetch a plant from the bottom of the sea. This he succeeds in doing, but a serpent steals the plant, and he is again frustrated. The two scenes are quite separate, and their appearance in succession stresses the almost impossible difficulty which faces Gilgamish in trying to do what he wishes. But we may suspect that originally these were alternative versions of the way in which Gilgamish tries to escape from death. For his story one such episode is sufficient, since it illustrates the inability of men to break the laws of the gods, but we can see why the poet combines two. In the first Gilgamish fails because he is a man, and sleep overcomes him; in the second he fails through the malignity of chance, which sends a serpent to snatch his prize when he has secured it. The repetition enhances the sense of failure and is no doubt used for that reason.

The combination of variants on a basic theme may be detected more than once in the *Odyssey*. The most basic theme of all is the return of the hero after many years to his home, where he is faced by enemies and not recognised by his wife. Such stories were told of other men than Odysseus, and there are many possible variations. At one point we can see how Homer combines two of them. The returned hero is a great archer, renowned for his prowess and able to do with the bow what hardly anyone else can do. In the process of revealing who he is he has to show his strength and skill at the expense of his enemies. Here Homer uses two themes which may once have been alternatives. The first is that in which Odysseus is able to string the bow when all the Suitors fail; the second when he does his exhibition shot down the line of axes arranged in the hall. The first shows his strength, since he alone is able to bend the bow and string it; the second shows his skill, since the shot causes wonder and amazement. In the *Odyssey* the two are combined and both are a preparation to the killing of the Suitors. But originally we may suspect each was used separately and need not have been turned to any other purpose than to show the hero's superiority. Homer works both episodes skilfully into his plot. The stringing of the bow humiliates and frightens the Suitors and makes them aware that they are confronted with a dangerous enemy; the preparations for the shot, with the suggestion that there is to be a competition, mean that Odysseus is well supplied with arrows with which he can soon proceed to kill the Suitors. There is no contradiction or awkwardness, and the two variants are used for two distinct and differentiated actions.

Another example of this art from the *Odyssey* may be seen in the episodes of Circe and of Calypso. In Odysseus' sojourn with both there are certain obvious similarities. Each is a goddess who lives on a remote island; each loves Odysseus and gets some satisfaction from him, though not enough; each in the end releases him to go home. Behind the two episodes is the common theme of the goddess who loves a man and has in due course to send him back to his human wife whom he loves more than her. But from this common basis Homer has worked out variations so great that the two episodes are quite different. Circe lives in a palace, Calypso in a cave. Circe is a witch who turns men into beasts; Calypso is a gentle and hospitable hostess. Odysseus arrives at Circe's island with his companions on a ship, at Calypso's island alone as a castaway from shipwreck. Circe releases Odysseus because he asks her to, Calypso because the gods tell her to do so. Circe tells Odysseus where to sail and what to do; Calypso merely helps him with food and sails for his voyage. It has even been surmised that Homer invented Calypso because he had to make Odysseus stay somewhere for a long time before he returns home.[1] Be that as it may, it is clear that the names, Circe and Calypso, indicate some original difference of character. Circe, " the hawk ", was once a witch; Calypso, " the concealer ", is the kind of divine being with whom a man lives outside the common world. The differentiation between the two may well have begun before Homer. What he does is to make the most of it, so that we do not notice that he is using two variants of a fundamental theme.

The combination of variants in a single poem like the *Odyssey* receives some illustration from the different forms which a single story may take in separate short poems. This shows how free poets are to develop and elaborate a familiar theme and how elastic

[1] W. J. Woodhouse, *The Composition of Homer's Odyssey* (Oxford, 1930), p. 215 ff.

such themes are. Tradition may provide a poet with material but it leaves him considerable liberty in handling it. Provided that he keeps the outline and certain main features, he may fill in the rest as he likes. Thus, some Russian themes are very popular, and numerous versions of them have been recorded, but though no one poem is exactly like another, the main structure of the narrative seems to be reasonably constant, though the details vary a great deal. For instance, the story of Sadko, the rich merchant of Novgorod, may go back to a time when Novgorod succeeded Kiev as the centre of Russian civilisation. Poems on Sadko come from widely separated parts of Russia, and yet on the whole there is a common basis to them. In all Sadko, who is a poor musician, becomes a friend of the Tsar of the Sea or some similar character, and gains great wealth from it. How this happens varies. In Sorokin's version [1] Sadko is a poor musician, who, finding that his songs are no longer liked in Novgorod, retires to Lake Ilmen, where the Tsar of the Sea appears to him, tells him that he will reward him for his music, and advises him to wager his head against all the wealth of Novgorod that there are gold fishes in Lake Ilmen. Sadko takes his advice, makes the wager and wins it, and with his profits furnishes a fleet of thirty ships. A different version is that recorded by Kirsha Danilov.[2] Sadko is a stranger from the Volga, who comes to seek his fortune in Novgorod. The Volga has asked him to convey greetings to Lake Ilmen, and when Sadko does so, a youth appears who gives advice similar to that in Sorokin's version and leads to a similar conclusion. In Danilov's version Sadko is not a native of Novgorod and does not deal directly with the Tsar of the Sea. What the two versions have in common are the advice that comes from Lake Ilmen and the wealth which it brings. No doubt the differences are partly to be explained by the fact that Danilov's version comes from the Volga region, and that is why the Volga is introduced into it. But even so the main outlines are kept, though the story must already have had some centuries of existence when Danilov recorded his version.

A similar kind of variation can be seen in two Jugoslav lays which tell how Marko Kraljević recognises and recovers his dead father's sword. In both the father is wounded in battle and asks help from a Turk who kills him and takes his sword; in due course Marko comes accidentally upon the sword, sees from the inscription that it belonged to his father, kills the Turkish owner and secures it. Within this frame the variations are considerable. In

[1] Rybnikov, ii, p. 243 ff.   [2] Kireevski, v, p. 41 ff.

one case the possessor of the sword is a soldier in the Turkish army,[1] in the other a merchant crying his wares, among which is the sword.[2] In the one case the sword is passed from hand to hand because no one can draw it from its scabbard until Marko takes it and does so; in the other case there is no such test, and the names on the blade identify the sword as having belonged to Marko's father. These differences make some difference to the poems. The first is more ingeniously constructed than the other, and there is a certain fitness in the way in which Marko gets the sword from the man who actually killed his father rather than from a stranger, and this allows Marko a proper revenge when he kills the Moor and throws his body into the river where his father's body was thrown. There are many cases of such variants, and they rise from the practice of oral composition. The bard re-creates an old story in his own way and gives it a new interest. The existence of such variants shows how fluid oral tradition is and helps to explain how, when a poet composes on a larger scale, he has many possibilities to choose from and must show his skill in adapting them to his general scheme.

The shape of a story need not necessarily mean that the same character is always connected with certain events. The events may be detached from him and connected with someone else. In this way heroic poetry enriches its contents and brings old characters into new settings or new characters into old settings. When a poet takes a new theme and adapts it to his repertory, it is quite likely that he will build it on a traditional structure and use themes which have been used before for quite different circumstances. For instance, the Jugoslav lay of *Lazar Mutap and the Ethiopian*[3] is concerned with a historical figure of the revolt of 1803, but the story told by the poet has little connection with history or with the period in which it is placed. In it Lazar solves the question of paying taxes by fighting a Moorish chieftain and cutting off his head. This is a traditional theme connected with Marko Kraljević,[4] who is historically senior to Lazar Mutap by several centuries. In the two poems the details of the taxes are different, but the main situation and its solution are similar, and even details, like the part played by the hero's horse, are also similar. When Marko rides out in fury to exact justice from the Moors, his horse, Šarac, strikes fire from his hoofs and breathes it from his nostrils; Lazar's horse does not quite do this, but at least it reflects the angry haste of its master:

[1] Karadžić, ii, p. 312 ff.
[3] *Idem*, iv, p. 355 ff.; Morison, p. 164 ff.
[2] *Idem*, p. 317 ff.
[4] Karadžić, ii, p. 384 ff.

Then he mounted on his furious war-horse,
Straight across the level plain proceeded
Like a star across the cloudless heavens.

Of course this poem may have owed something consciously to the other, but, even if it did, it still shows that a new subject can be set going by incorporating elements canonised by tradition for other and older subjects.

If a story has sufficient appeal and possibilities, it may have a long history and be adapted to many different characters. The *Odyssey* provides a hint of such a history in the treatment of Nausicaa. Behind it we may discern a story in which a hero is shipwrecked and washed up on an unknown shore where he is tended by the king's daughter. An early version of this can be seen in an Egyptian story of about 2000 B.C.[1] In this a man is shipwrecked and thrown up on an island, where he hides in a laurel-bush. To him comes a beautiful snake, inlaid with gold and lapis lazuli, who asks him who he is, takes him off to a wonderful lair which shows how rich the country is, loads him with gifts, and sends him home on a ship. This is in the main the story of Odysseus on Phaeacia, with two significant exceptions. The snake is only a snake and not a human being; not a charming girl but the ruler of the land. On this ancient theme, which may have reached him by long and indirect ways through many changes and variations, Homer has grafted another ancient story. The stranger who saves the shipwrecked man is not only a king's daughter but falls in love with him and in the end marries him. This cannot happen to Odysseus, who has to go home to Penelope, but Homer is aware of the story's associations and touches delicately on them. When Odysseus makes his appeal for help to Nausicaa, he speaks almost as a lover, comparing her to a young palm-shoot and calling her parents and brothers thrice blessed in her.[2] He even refers to the prospect of her marriage, as Athene has referred to it earlier when she sends her out to the place where Odysseus has landed.[3] Homer is conscious that in this theme marriage has its part, and makes Odysseus touch on it gently and deftly. The meeting of Odysseus and Nausicaa is the ripe fruit of two ancient stocks. What were originally general themes that might be used for any hero and any maiden are here brought together and given a marvellous distinction.

Since an oral poet operates with stories which are often familiar, he may sometimes produce a surprising effect by seeming to lead

---

[1] A. Wiedemann, *Altägyptische Sagen und Märchen* (Leipzig, 1906), p. 25 ff.
[2] *Od.* vi, 149 ff.　　　　　[3] *Ibid.* 27 ff.

up to one result while actually leading to another. This is made easier for him by the elastic nature of his material. Since a story has many variants, the audience is never quite sure which he will use, and he may astonish them by doing something unexpected by producing something that is after all new and original. Perhaps something of this kind can be seen in *Roland* when the poet pauses in the middle of the battle to condemn Ganelon for his treachery and to forecast the fate which awaits him later.

> Evil service, that day, Guenes rendered them,
> To Sarraguce going, his own to sell.
> After he lost his members and his head,
> In court, at Aix, to gallows-tree condemned;
> And thirty more with him, of his kindred,
> Were hanged, a thing they never did expect.[1]

We are led to expect that Ganelon will be hanged, and the same idea is assumed later when Pinabel assures him that all will be well with him:

> " Straightway you'll be delivered.
> Is there one Frank that you to hang committeth? " [2]

In the end Ganelon is not hanged but tied to four stallions and torn to pieces. No doubt in some versions hanging was his end, and the audience would expect it here too, but the poet has in store something more gruesome, of which he gives no hint, but skilfully sets a false trail until the actual death comes as an effective surprise.

Perhaps something of the same kind may be seen in *Beowulf*. When Beowulf arms himself for the encounter with Grendel's Dam, his armour is described at some length: first his corslet, then his helmet, and lastly the sword, Hrunting, which has been lent to him by Unferth. Of this sword the poet says that it has never failed in battle and suggests that once again it will do good work:

> 'twas not the first time
> That an excellent work   it was to accomplish.[3]

But when it comes to the actual struggle with the Dam, this promise is not fulfilled. When Beowulf attacks her with it, it fails him:

> Then her guest found
> That his battle-gleamer   would not bite,
> Nor fetch to her heart,   but the edge of it failed
> The lord in his need.   It had lasted many
> Hard-fought meetings,   helms oft had shorn,

---

[1] *Roland*, 1406-11.   [2] *Ibid.* 3788-9.   [3] *Beowulf*, 1463-4.

Fated men's war-coats ;   this was the first time
For the goodly weapon   that its glory waned.[1]

This can hardly be a slip, since it comes very soon after the earlier statement about the sword, and it is easier to suppose that the poet first leads us to expect one thing and then provides something different. We can perhaps see why he does this. Hrunting is indeed a marvellous sword, but not so strange or so marvellous as the sword which Beowulf finds on the floor of the monster's cave, and drives into her neck. This is an unexpected development, but not so unexpected as when, after cutting off Grendel's head, the sword dissolves like ice. The poet has planned his little surprise and brings it off very nicely.

The art of surprise is practised by Homer in an important crisis of the *Iliad*. When Patroclus is killed by Hector, Achilles is not content until he has exacted a full and final vengeance from the slayer of his friend. It is quite possible that in some older versions of the episode Achilles first dragged Hector alive behind his chariot and then cut off his head and threw his body to the dogs.[2] Homer's treatment takes note and even advantage of such stories. He leads us to think that this is what Achilles will do in the *Iliad*. Before Achilles goes out in pursuit of Hector, he says to the dead Patroclus :

" I shall not pay you the last due rites until I have brought here
Hector's armour and head, the great-hearted hero who killed
      you." [3]

Later he threatens to throw Hector's body to the dogs :

                              " Hector, son of Priam,
I shall not give to the fire but throw to the dogs to be eaten." [4]

We are led to expect some appalling end of this kind, but what happens is quite different. Aphrodite keeps the dogs away and anoints the corpse with ambrosia to save it from decay, while Apollo sheds a dark cloud over it lest the sunbeams breed worms in it. Homer has no intention of allowing Achilles to treat a dead man in this unfitting way. But he has more in reserve than this. The end of the *Iliad* is preceded by the marvellous scene in which Achilles' wrath is healed by the compassion which he feels for old Priam when he comes to ransom Hector's body. That, we may believe, is Homer's own invention, and to secure it he could not allow the body of Hector to be maltreated or mutilated.

[1] *Beowulf*, 1522-8. [2] Cf. Virgil, *Aen*. ii, 273.
[3] *Il*. xviii, 334-5. [4] *Ibid*. xxiii, 183-5.

Another kind of misunderstanding is due to the difficulties which the oral poet encounters when he composes on a long scale. As we have seen, he naturally arranges his poem in episodes, which may be recited separately almost as independent poems, but none the less he builds these into a whole and has to keep his eye on the general result. Sooner or later he may find that an episode loses much of its meaning unless the audience knows what has come before. He may of course take this knowledge for granted and go boldly ahead. But sometimes this is difficult, especially when he comes to the end of a long story and feels a natural desire to make a neat ending which sums up what has happened before. Homer seems to have felt something of this kind in the *Odyssey*. In Book XXIII, when Odysseus after twenty years' absence has at last been united to his wife, they naturally tell one another what has happened in the interval, but whereas Penelope's tale receives three lines, that of Odysseus receives thirty-three and is nothing less than a summary of all that has befallen him between the departure from Troy and his arrival at Ithaca.[1] In other words, it is a synopsis of what the *Odyssey* has told, and must have been introduced for this reason. It looks as if Homer felt a need to recapitulate his tale before advancing to his last stage. This passage has caused some trouble and even in antiquity some scholars thought that it and what follows were additions to an *Odyssey* which closed with the reunion of Odysseus and Penelope. Yet we can perhaps surmise Homer's motives in providing this synopsis. His long tale is coming to an end, but he has still something to tell. Before he gets on to that, he must tidy up the manifold adventures of Odysseus and put them in their final setting. The recapitulation of them provides a contrast with the peaceful reunion with Penelope. After all these dangers and mishaps Odysseus has at last come home. Since the main theme of the poem is his return, it is reasonable to show at the end what it has been and what it has cost.

A more remarkable example of this device can be seen in *Beowulf*. On returning home Beowulf tells Hygelac what has happened to him and relates the story of his fights with Grendel and the Dam together with a digression on the Heathobards, which takes 150 lines.[2] It is true that it adds something to what the poet has already told, notably that the thegn killed by Grendel is called Hondscio, that Grendel intended to carry off Beowulf in a kind of game-bag, and that Beowulf succeeded in cutting off the Dam's head with his sword. But clearly it was not to add these small

[1] *Od.* xxiii, 310-43.　　　　[2] *Beowulf*, 2000-2151.

touches that the poet composed this long summary. It seems more likely that he felt some need of it to end the first part of his story, which tells of the hero's adventures in Jutland. He comes home and reports on his adventures to Hygelac, who is suitably impressed and rewards him handsomely. Of course it was necessary for Beowulf to tell what has happened, but was it necessary for the poet to report it at such length? Could he not rather have dismissed it in a few lines? Nothing is explained by claiming that the passage is an interpolation, since any argument for inserting such a passage is equally applicable to its having been put in by the poet himself. Obviously he saw some advantage to be gained by it. Perhaps he felt that his tale needed a dignified and quiet ending, neither too abrupt nor too exciting, and this he secures in his own way by a summary of events. But it may also be possible that Beowulf's return might be liable for use as a separate episode, and in that case it would lack its full significance and meaning unless the poet told shortly what had preceded it. In either case we can hardly doubt that the poet himself composed it, since it would not be in the interest of any interpolator merely to repeat what has already been said at greater length before.

Sometimes the close of a longer poem presents another difficulty. After reaching his climax and finishing it off, the poet seems unable to abandon his poem but moves on to what looks almost like a new episode or even a hint of a new poem to come. Instead of tidying up all the loose threads, he introduces some fresh prospect which suggests that further action is in the offing. Something of the kind happens in the *Odyssey*. After Odysseus has slain the Suitors and been recognised by his wife and old father, we might expect the story to end, but, before it does, Homer tells how some men of Ithaca, who have been friends of the Suitors, begin to attack Odysseus but are stopped by the intervention of Athene. The effect of this is peculiar. After so many excitements it comes rather as an anti-climax, and after the sense of triumph it strikes a note of uneasiness and uncertainty. So perhaps the poet intended, but his reasons are not easy to determine. He may of course have felt that a man like Odysseus, whose life has been passed in danger, is not likely to find any lasting peace, even after he has killed the enemies in his home. There may well be truth in this. The heroic world so lives on excitement that to some of its poets the mere thought of ease is almost untenable. Yet it is remarkable that Homer, with his well-designed poem, should have ended it in this uneasy way. The opposition of the men of Ithaca seems almost alien to his main subject and outside the actual adventures of Odysseus. Another explanation is perhaps better. Heroic tales belong, as we have seen, to cycles in the sense that certain heroes have certain episodes connected with them. That Odysseus had a career after his return to Ithaca is clear from the remains of the *Telegony*, which told of further travels of the hero and finally of his death.[1] Now the *Telegony*, which is said to have been written by Eugammon of Cyrene, is certainly later than the *Odyssey*, but the story which it told may well have been of ancient date and familiar to Homer. In ending the *Odyssey* as he did, he may have wished to leave the door open for Odysseus' further adventures, of which he knew that other poets, if not he himself, would tell sooner or later, and that it would be unwise to be too final and definite in ending his poem on a note of complete success.

An unusually surprising and indeed sensational close is that of the Ainu *Kutune Shirka*. The hero has fallen in love with a maiden called Nishap-tashum, which means " Miss Malinger ". After first saving her life and then rescuing her from enemies who have carried her off, he leaves her at home while he goes out to finish off his enemies. Exhausted by his battles, he lies on the ground and a beautiful girl appears and bends over him and sings :

> " If such a hero
> Fell to my hand,
> What a boon to my village ! "

Fortunately Nishap-tashum knows that he is in danger, appears at his side and puts a spell on the girl. The hero goes up to the girl from behind and undoes the strings of her bodice. Then comes the climax :

> Her young breasts
> That were like snowballs
> I fondled with my hand.
> She looked back over her shoulder
> And cried out, " Is that you ?
> I thought you were dead."
> But while she was saying these words,
> I hewed her limb from limb
> And heard the swish of her soul,
> Her evil soul as it rose.
> Then Malinger came to me and said :
> " Women should do battle with women,
> And this my evil sister
> Should have fallen to my hand.

[1] Allen, v, p. 109.

Y

> But now that, before I could slay her,
> A godlike hero
> Has meted punishment,
> We have no more to fear ;
> Let us go back to our home."
> But I thought to myself :
> " Where is this village of Peshutun
> That the girl said she came from ?
> If without destroying it
> I were now to go back home,
> Would it not be said that I was afraid ? "
> That was what I thought to myself.[1]

That is the end of the poem, and no known version carries the story further. Here surely the poet is trying to do two things at once, to finish his story and leave an opening for a new start. The first need is met by Malinger's suggestion that she and the hero should go home, the second by his intention to destroy the village of Peshutun ; and with this calculated ambiguity the poet stops.

No less remarkable in a different way is the end of *Roland*. Charlemagne has avenged the death of Roland, had Ganelon executed, and the Saracen queen baptised. There is, we might think, nothing more to say : all loose ends have been tidied up, and the story is finished. But then the poet adds fourteen lines :

> When the Emperour his justice hath achieved,
> His mighty wrath's abated from its heat,
> And Bramimunde has christening received.
> Passes the day, the darkness is grown deep,
> And now the King in's vaulted chamber sleeps.
> Saint Gabriel is come from God, and speaks :
> " Summon the hosts, Charlès, of thine Empire,
> Go thou by force into the land of Bire,
> King Vivien thou'lt succour there, at Imphe,
> In the city which pagans have besieged.
> The Christians there implore thee and beseech."
> Right loth to go, that Emperour was he :
> " God ! " said the King : " My life is hard indeed ! "
> Tears filled his eyes, he tore his snowy beard.[2]

It is certainly tempting to think that the poet intended this remarkable close to show how the Christian king, Charlemagne, is never allowed to rest from fighting the heathen. Just as the poem begins with his false assumption that he has finally conquered the Saracens, so it ends with the truth that he must go on fighting them. This is the lesson which the fight at Roncesvalles has to

---

[1] Trs. Arthur Waley, *Botteghe Oscure*, vii (1951), pp. 233-4.
[2] *Roland*, 3988-4001.

teach. Yet though we cannot deny that the end of *Roland* may produce this effect on us and that we may be right to feel it, we must also recognise the possibility that the poet, like Homer in the *Odyssey*, keeps a door open for other poems about further adventures of Charlemagne. Whether he ever wrote such a poem is doubtful, and indeed King Vivien and the land of Bire have no known place in the many poems on Charlemagne, though a Count Vivianus led the troops of Charles the Bald against an invasion of Bretons and Norsemen.[1] It is at least possible that the poet knew of some story in which Charlemagne went to Vivien's rescue, and thought it wise to connect the end of *Roland* with it.

[1] Suchier, *Chanson de Guillaume*, p. liv.

IX

SCALE AND DEVELOPMENT

Heroic poetry varies in scale from the short lay to the long epic. At one end are pieces like the Russian *bylina* of 23 lines on Napoleon's invasion; at the other end are the *Odyssey* with 12,000 lines, the *Iliad* with 15,000, and Sagymbai Orozbakov's version of *Manas* with 40,000. Between these limits almost any length is possible. Ossete poems seem seldom to pass beyond 500. The poems of the *Elder Edda* vary from about 40 in the *Third Lay of Guthrun* to 384 in *Atlamál*. *Beowulf* has 3182 lines, the *Cid* 3730, *Roland* 4002, and the Assyrian text of *Gilgamish* may have had about 3500, which is the average length of the Kalmuck poems on Dzhangar. Yakut poems are sometimes onger than this, as are some Kara-Kirghiz and Kazak poems recorded by Radlov. A heroic poet is not confined to any strict limits of length and can operate on a large or a small scale. Though it is wrong to assume that there is a natural and inevitable growth from the short to the long poem, there seems to be a tendency for later poets to be more expansive than earlier poets in the same tradition. Three Jugoslav poets, whose work was recorded by Milman Parry, passed beyond 10,000 lines, which is much longer than anything recorded a century earlier by Karadžić. Radlov gives no hint that Kara-Kirghiz bards of his acquaintance composed on so enormous a scale as the more modern Orozbakov. At the same time the emergence of the long poem does not mean the disappearance of the short. Greek literature offers not only the *Iliad* and the *Odyssey* but the *Shield of Heracles*, a poem of 480 lines, typical of a class which is now represented only by small fragments. Though the Anglo-Saxon *Fight at Finnsburh* is a mere fragment, it seems to come from a short poem composed quite differently from the leisurely and expansive *Beowulf*. In our own time Russian *byliny* range from 40 lines in Peter Pavlovich's *Dobrynya and Marinka*[1] to about 2000 in Marfa Kryukova's *Tale of Lenin*. Modern Greek and Albanian poems vary greatly in length from under a hundred lines to several thousands. Long and short poems may come from the same society and the same poet, and

---

[1] Nechaev, p. 268.

their length depends less on his circumstances than on his immediate needs and personal whims and ability.

It might be thought that a poet must adapt his length to the time at his disposal for recitation; that, if he has only an hour or two, his poem will have to be short. This no doubt accounts for many short poems, but it seems to be a relatively unimportant consideration. Heroic poems are often recited at festivals or on holidays or during longer winter evenings when time is no obstacle, and yet in Russia or Jugoslavia the result is usually not a single long poem but a number of short poems. For instance, at Zagreb, between January 2nd and February 15th, 1887, Salko Vojniković sang ninety lays with a total of 80,000 ten-syllabled lines.[1] So far as time was concerned, he could have produced a single poem twice as long as the *Iliad* and *Odyssey* combined, but he preferred to sing a number of short poems, no doubt because this was the kind of art which he liked and in which he felt that he excelled. Conversely, when long poems are the fashion and poets possess the art of composing them, there is no need to compress a large subject into a short compass just because time is short. It is just as good to take a single episode and treat it with full attention. It is possible that Homer developed his art in conditions like this. At least, many parts of the *Iliad* may be isolated and treated as complete poems. They lose something by being detached from the main structure, but they are still sufficiently complete and independent. If the *Roland* which Taillefer sang at Hastings bore any resemblance to our existing text in the Oxford manuscript, it can hardly have been sung complete, and it is possible that Taillefer sang no more than a part of it. The length of a poem depends on several factors, of which the chief are the poet's time and taste. But since the length varies, the art of the poem varies also, and both short and long poems have appropriate techniques. It is wrong to assume that the short lay is an imperfect preliminary to the full epic.

The short lay has its own characteristics and standards. It can be roughly divided into two classes. The first, which is much commoner, treats a single subject, the second a series of episodes, and this difference dictates a considerable difference of manner. For while the first kind can to some degree expand on its single topic and present it with some detail, the second can do little more than touch on a number of topics without treating any fully. The distinction may well be inherent in the nature of heroic poetry, since an audience may wish to hear, or a poet to tell, equally about

[1] M. Murko in *N. Jahrbücher f. d. kl. Alt.* (1919), p. 294.

a single event or a wide sweep of legend. The difference can be seen in Norse poetry, where the *Second Lay of Guthrun* deals with a single tragic crisis, while *The Prophecy of Gripir* is little more than a catalogue of the different events which make up the career of Sigurth. While Homer's Demodocus sings of single adventures like the quarrel of the Achaean princes or the Wooden Horse, Odysseus himself gives Penelope a complete sketch of his wanderings in thirty lines. In *Beowulf* the hero tells of the single theme of his swimming with Breca, while the account of the Scyldings prefixed to the poem is a sketch of family history for several generations. The single theme is naturally more popular than the episodic, since it is inevitably more dramatic and more interesting, but the episodic poem has its own uses, if only to keep the structure of a hero's career intact and provide useful material for any poet who wishes to expatiate on some episode in it.

As we have seen, the short poem may be introduced in a formulaic manner with some conventional opening. Even so the poet must soon get on to his subject, since he has little time to waste. This on the whole happens. In *The Fall of the Serbian Empire* the opening is made with the common theme of birds flying :

> From Jerusalem, the holy city,
> Came a swift, grey bird, a falcon, flying,
> And he carried in his beak a swallow.[1]

This tells us little, but we hear at once that the falcon is the prophet Elias, and the swallow a message from God to Tsar Lazar, and at once the tragic story begins to unfold. In the same way a favourite Bulgarian opening is to say that someone " has become a brigand " and to move from this to an exciting story. For instance, in *Dragana and Ivancho* the theme is used in its common form :

> Since Ivan became a brigand,
> And his sister, too, Draganka,
> On the roads there passed no convoys
> For the Sultan or his vizirs.[2]

Then at once the amusing and exciting story begins by which Draganka plants a garden to beguile travellers and ends by slaughtering a Turkish convoy. Of course not all poems which open with conventional formulae are equally successful at getting a story going. There is often enough a tendency to waste time on the formulae, which are so familiar that the poet produces them almost without thinking. This is sometimes the case with Russian

[1] Karadžić, ii, p. 268. [2] Dozon, p. 29.

poems, and it is obviously a danger that threatens this kind of
start. None the less there is no reason why a formulaic opening
should necessarily prevent a poet from moving at once to his main
events and developing them in their full implications.

Short poems may equally well begin with an opening which is
not formulaic but goes straight to the heart of the matter in
question. Since time and space are short, the poet may dispense
with preliminaries and explanations and start in the middle of an
action which indeed explains itself. So the *First Lay of Guthrun*,
which tells of Guthrun's grief as she sits by the dead body of
Sigurth, begins with her sorrow-stricken silence :

> Then did Guthrun   think to die,
> When she by Sigurth   sorrowing sat ;
> Tears she had not,   nor wrung her hands,
> Nor ever wailed,   as other women.[1]

So too an Armenian poem of the fifth century A.D. tells how the
Persian king, Shapukh, plots the defeat of the Armenian king,
Arshak :

> Then the Persian king, Shapukh, summoned
> His star-gazers, mages, and wonder-workers.[2]

The Ossete *Last Expedition of Uryzmag* begins appropriately with
the old age of the hero :

> Uryzmag, most renowned of the Narts, grew old,
> His beard turned to white,
> His old legs cannot carry him,
> He cannot stretch the bow-string in his hands.[3]

Yet in this condition he still shows his heroic worth, and that is
the subject of the poem. Sometimes the Russian poets abandon
their beloved formulae for something more unusual and closer to
their special themes, like the piece on Prince Roman's murder of
his wife :

> Prince Roman murdered his wife,
> He murdered his wife, he tore her corpse,
> He tore her corpse and threw it in the river ; [4]

or the short and charming piece on Prince Vasili :

> In the blue sea,
> In the quiet bay,
> Was Prince Vasili drowned
> Through the weight of his gold crown.[5]

---

[1] *Guthrúnarkvitha*, i, 1.   [2] Arutyunyan, p. 41.
[3] Dynnik, p. 18.
[4] Kireevski, v, p. 108 ; Chadwick, *R.H.P.* p. 164.
[5] Kireevski, v, p. 66 ; Chadwick, *R.H.P.* p. 182.

From this the poet moves at once to the grief of the widowed princess and her decision to become a nun. This is the art of the single episode. The poet sees that he must make the most of it and goes straight to the point at the start.

Since in such poems the story is told in a short compass, we must not look for many incidental decorations. What counts is the central, significant event, the surprise which it awakes and the force with which it strikes us. The poet's task is to choose the telling detail, the single touch which brings home the meaning of his story. So the first hint of the disaster of Kosovo comes to the wife of Tsar Lazar when his servant comes on his horse to her:

> In his left hand, see, he bears his right hand,
> He has countless wounds upon his body,
> And his horse is bathed in blood beneath him.[1]

In the Norse *Third Lay of Guthrun*, when Atli doubts the virtue of his wife, Guthrun, and insists on putting her to the ordeal of dipping her hand in a kettle of boiling water, the crisis comes with no comment or ornament:

> To the bottom she reached   with hand so bright,
> And forth she brought   the flashing stones:
> " Behold, ye warriors,   well am I cleared
> Of sin by the kettle's   sacred boiling." [2]

In the short Russian piece on Napoleon's invasion of 1812 the drama consists entirely of a contrast between the hesitant Tsar Alexander and the brave general Kutuzov, and the climax comes when Kutuzov dismisses the Tsar's doubts:

> " Fear not, fear not, Tsar Alexander, do not be dismayed!
> We will welcome him half-way, that dog of an enemy.
> We will prepare him delicacies of bombs and bullets,
> As an entrée we will offer him cannon-balls,
> As a side-dish we will give him deadly grape-shot,
> So that his warriors will march home again under their banners." [3]

In the Esthonian *The Herald of War* the story is of a man who carries secret orders to gather a host for war. He meets on his way various figures who indicate the horror of war, and the climax comes when he decides not to deliver his message:

> Thereupon I took the mandate
> Which I carried in my wallet,
> And amid the depths I sunk it,
> Underneath the waves of ocean,

---

[1] Karadžić, ii, p. 280.   [2] *Guthrúnarkvitha*, iii, 8.
[3] Kireevski, x, p. 2 ; Chadwick, *R.H.P.* p. 288.

Till the waves to foam had torn it,
And to mud had quite reduced it,
While the fishes fled before it.
Thus was hushed the sound of warfare,
Thus was lost the news of battle.[1]

The art of the short lay consists largely of creating this sense of crisis and leading rapidly to the single dramatic moment. For this reason much is omitted that might be attractive but would interfere with the direct march of events.

The other kind of short lay, which deals episodically with a man's career or a series of related events, has naturally a different manner. No great problems are presented by the life of a single hero, since this has its own continuity and unity. Such a poem is satisfactory enough as a work of art. It begins early in the hero's career and guides him through its main events to an effective close. A typical example of this is the modern Russian poem on the revolutionary hero Chapai, as the bard Dityatev tells it.[2] It begins with Chapai's humble origin and simple home and his departure from it to make a living as a wandering minstrel. Then it tells how he joins the army to fight the Germans and meets revolutionaries. With them he joins the forces against Kolchak. Then he meets a woman, Katharine, who helps him in his work and becomes an efficient machine-gunner. So the story proceeds through a series of episodes, in which Chapai carries out tasks for Lenin and is a relentless foe of the White armies. In the end he is killed in battle and honoured after death. It is the story of a revolutionary hero depicted in a series of separate scenes. The traditional method is used, but through it the poet secures his own little surprises in the individual situations. There is an ingenious combination between old and new themes when Chapai first gets ready for civil war :

He took with him his sharp sabre,
He took with him his heavy club,
He took with him his steel knife
And his Maxim machine-gun.[3]

There is a simple charm about the appearance of the courageous Katharine :

She was beautiful in her beauty,
In complexion she was white,
Her eyes were like a bright hawk's,
Her eyebrows were black sable,
Her speech was very gentle.[4]

---

[1] Kirby, ii, p. 292. [2] Andreev, p. 508 ff.
[3] *Idem*, p. 511. [4] *Idem*, p. 512.

There is a sense of straightforward decision in the way in which Chapai rides into the Kremlin to see Lenin:

> He went to stone-built Moscow,
> To stone-built Moscow, to the Kremlin itself.
> He did not enquire of the guards at the entrance
> But swung through the wall of the Kremlin,
> He led his horse by the bridle-rein,
> And came to the tall door of the Kremlin.[1]

This is more than a purely formulaic art. The episodes have their own interest, and within the limited space at his disposal the poet does much to keep them lively. This is a suitable technique for the episodic lay and shows what can be done with a series of not too closely related actions.

If a poet is not too hampered by limitations of space, he may sometimes combine the techniques of the two kinds of poem and use an episodic introduction to lead up to some crisis which provides his main theme. This happens in two poems of the *Elder Edda*, and in both it is fully justified. The *First Lay of Helgi Hundingsbane* begins with the hero's birth and the omens and dooms that accompany it. It then touches on his childhood and tells how at the age of fifteen he slays Hunding. This occupies about a quarter of the surviving poem, and after it the poet is ready for his main subject, which is Helgi's love for the Valkyrie, Sigrun. His efforts to win her from her pledged husband occupy the rest of the poem, which ends with Helgi's triumph and the prospect of greater glories. Here the preliminaries show how the hero's early life is a preparation for later victories and how he is marked from the start to be a great figure and fit mate for a Valkyrie:

> Mighty he grew in the midst of his friends,
> The fair-born elm, in fortune's glow.[2]

The poet does not skimp details in his preliminaries, but makes each contribute something to the account of Helgi's upbringing. So too in the *Short Lay of Sigurth* the poet begins with an episodic biography, telling how Sigurth forms ties with the sons of Gjuki, helps Gunnar to win Brynhild, and himself marries Guthrun; then having set the scene and introduced the characters, he moves to the complex plot of Sigurth's death at the hands of the sons of Gjuki. Here is a masterly combination of different themes, the unflinching nobility of Sigurth, the heart-rending devotion of Guthrun, the merciless pride of Brynhild, and the hesitation of Gunnar about encompassing the death of his sworn friend. The

---

[1] Andreev, p. 513. [2] *Helgakvitha Hundingsbana*, i, 9, 1-2.

crisis comes with a great crash, and its fearful character is shown in Guthrun's grief at it :

> In a swoon she sank   when Sigurth died ;
> So hard she smote   her hands together
> That all the cups   in the cupboard rang,
> And loud in the courtyard   cried the geese.[1]

At this point the story has a terrible force which does not abate as the poet advances to show the storm in Brynhild's soul, her scornful treatment of Guthrun's grief, her preparations for her own death, and her dying prophecy which foretells in a brief compass the events still to come. This is a complex story with several notable characters. Its central point is Sigurth, and that no doubt is why the poem recounts his early history and leaves no doubts of his relations with the other men and women.

When a lay has three thousand lines or more and may be classed as a short epic, its art is not very different in essentials from that of the short lay. Elements which exist in the short lay are developed and expanded but nothing ultimately new is introduced. Poets who compose on the scale of *Roland* or *Beowulf* may well know the shorter art and learn from it before they advance to a larger scope. But of course the new scope raises new problems, of which the first is construction. On this scale it is no longer possible to confine the issue to a single crisis. There must be a series of actions, and the technique will be to some degree episodic. The problem is to make the episodes hang together and produce a single result. Not all poets succeed in this, though most make some attempt at it. The poet's task is to provide some kind of necessary connection between the different episodes, and the closer the connection, the better the construction. When improvisation rules, construction at a high level is not at all easy, and we can hardly be surprised if few poets are really successful at it.

The easiest way to construct a long lay or short epic is to tell a series of events in the life of a single character. This is to apply a technique of the short lay on a wider scale, and to enrich a series of episodes by various kinds of expansion and decoration. So the Kara-Kirghiz *Joloi*, which has 5322 lines and tells a well-ordered story,[2] begins with the hero lying on the ground, indifferent to the theft of his father's horses and the appeals of his family to get them back. At length he is set to action by his sister and sister-in-law and rides out in search of the horses. He kills the thief, Ak Khan, and seizes his wife, while his wonderful horse carries off for him

---

[1] *Sigurtharkvitha en Skamma*, 29.   [2] Radlov, v, pp. 372-528.

Ak Saikal, the daughter of a great chief, who becomes his wife. Numerous episodes follow. Joloi's sister, Kardygach, marries a Kalmuck prince, Karacha, and they usurp Joloi's principality while he is imprisoned by another Kalmuck. Later Joloi's son, Bolot, is born, and Kardygach and Karacha try to kill him. He is rescued and brought up in a nomadic settlement by Joloi's two wives, and in due course is restored to his father and married. This is a complex story, well arranged and well told, but its structure is essentially episodic. The different parts are complete in themselves but are bound together by the personality and career of Joloi. It is a good example of straightforward narrative in which there is a guiding plan, but the connections between the parts are not at all elaborate or subtle. Many poems are constructed in this way, and their interest lies in the appeal which the poet gives to the separate episodes.

When a poet constructs long lays he not only is influenced by the technique of short lays but may even have to construct his poem in such a way that it may be recited in sections or in part. This means that he will so arrange his episodes that some may, if necessary, be omitted or kept in reserve until he is asked to sing them. This may account for the way in which the Yakuts construct their poems. These are not only episodic but tend to fall into two or three main sections which are almost separate poems. For instance, *Er Sogotokh* tells how a hero sets out to win a wife : he finds a wife for another man, kills successively and separately three opponents, and eventually reaches the home of a woman whom he wishes to marry and is betrothed to her. Here, we might think, the story should end, but it is followed by a long sequel, in which the hero's son, Basymdzhi, has his own adventures, which include two fights and a marriage.[1] The son's career is mingled up to a point with the father's, but the second part of the poem is really separable and may perhaps have been composed for recitation as a sequel when the audience asked for more. So too in *Kulun-Kullustur* the first and main part tells of four victorious encounters between the hero and various monsters and other enemies and ends with his winning a bride. The sequel tells how the bride disappears and is brought back after considerable risks and efforts.[2] Of course these poems may often have been recited complete, and they have their own unity which depends not only on the hero's personality but on links between the main part and the sequel. But the manner of their construction suggests that the bard was not sure of being able always to recite them in their

[1] Yastremski, pp. 13-55.　　　　[2] *Idem*, pp. 56-76.

entirety, and so used a technique which allows omissions and additions.

When we turn from these modern oral poems to poems written down in the past, we see much the same technique and the same conditions of construction. *Gilgamish* is, on the face of it, an episodic poem in which a series of events is held together by the hero's personality. It tells in sequence of Gilgamish's rule over Erech, of the creation of Enkidu by the gods to overcome him, of his victory over Enkidu and the formation of a fast friendship with him, of their expedition against the ogre Humbaba and destruction of him, of Ishtar's love for Gilgamish and his contemptuous rejection of it, of the creation by the gods of a bull intended to kill both Gilgamish and Enkidu, and their killing of it, of the death of Enkidu and Gilgamish's grief and attempts to escape death himself, which take him to Uta-Napishtim but end in failure, when he summons up the ghost of Enkidu from the dead. Any or all of these episodes may once have been matter for separate poems, and in *Gilgamish*, where they are combined, they still have a certain independence from each other. So far as the mutilated text allows us to see, each episode comes to an emphatic end, as when, after being defeated by Gilgamish, Enkidu says to him:

> " One, and one only, did thy mother bear thee;
> Ninsun, cow of the steer-folds, exalted thy head above heroes,
> Enlil dowered thee with kingship over men," [1]

or Humbaba is killed:

> They cut off the head of Humbaba.[2]

But though the episodes are thus separable, they are subordinated to a majestic plan which makes them parts of a great poem. The central theme of *Gilgamish* is that even the greatest of heroes cannot escape mortality. The poet develops this first by showing how mighty a hero Gilgamish is and then by telling of his failure to win immortality. To this central idea the parts contribute, and the episodic construction is transcended in a great, unifying plan. This is a much more subtle art than that of *Joloi* or other episodic poems, in which the only unifying factor is the hero's career and personality.

The same kind of technique may be observed in a modern Russian poem, Marfa Kryukova's *Tale of Lenin*. Though it has no more than 2000 lines, it tells of the main episodes in Lenin's life from the execution of his brother for an attempt on the life

---

[1] *Gilgamish*, II, vi, 31-3.   [2] *Ibid.* V, vi, 37.

of Alexander III to his own death. It describes Lenin's formation
of a revolutionary party, his action in the Revolution of 1905, the
outbreak of war in 1914, the arrival in St. Petersburg, the rise to
power, the Civil War, the attempt on Lenin's life, the rise of
Stalin, the treason of Trotsky, and Lenin's death and funeral.
The episodes are separable both in history and in the poem, but
they are held together not merely by Lenin's identity but by his
revolutionary aims. The main theme is set at the start when Lenin
tells his mother not to grieve for her elder son's death, since the
fight will be carried on without him :

> " Do not grieve, dear mother, do not sorrow.
> We will indeed take a great vow among us,
> A great vow to battle for the people's truth !
> Wet not, beloved mother, thy fair face,
> Spoil not thy bright eyes." [1]

The promise made at the beginning is carried out by stages
through the poem, and the death at the end is the fitting con-
summation of the hero's life, duly honoured by the way in which
his tomb on the Red Square at Moscow is made, according to
Kryukova's ingenious fancy, of precious stones :

> All peoples carried these stones,
> Each people brought one stone apiece.
> The peoples built a little house of death,
> Therein lies Ilich and sleeps in peace. [2]

The *Tale of Lenin* has little in common with *Gilgamish* either in
style or in subject, but its technique of construction is similar in
its adaptation of single episodes to a main design.

The way in which a detachable sequel is added to a heroic
poem, as it is among the Yakuts, finds some sort of parallel both
in *Beowulf* and in *Roland*. In *Beowulf* the first main story is
finished when Beowulf, having killed both Grendel and his Dam,
leaves Hrothgar and sails home. The episode of the dragon
which follows is not only quite separate but set much later in the
hero's life. It is, moreover, less imaginative and less exciting than
the fights with Grendel and his Dam ; the characters introduced
are less interesting than such men as Hrothgar and Unferth ; the
setting is less attractive than the great hall in Jutland. If, as we
may surmise, the poet composed it to satisfy demands for more
poetry about Beowulf, he was perhaps not very happy in his
choice of a subject. But we can see why he did so. The poet of

[1] Kaun, p. 186.   [2] *Idem*, p. 191.

Beowulf is a moralist, eager to show what a good man is. In the first part he has shown Beowulf as the brave hero, but though he has given him all the worthiest qualities of a hero, he has not shown his gift for kingship and command. The sequel does this, and almost illustrates a thesis that he who is brave when young will become a good king in his mature years. The emphasis is on kingly virtue, and the excellence of Beowulf is displayed in his readiness to give his life for his people. To the poet's ethical taste this is perhaps a more serious subject than the fight with Grendel. Artistically, perhaps, the sequel is not a great success, but morally it must have meant much to the poet.

The structure of *Roland* is more complicated and more skilfully contrived. The whole has a shape which is mutilated by the removal of any section. Ganelon's treachery leads to the fight in the pass and Roland's death, and Roland's last blast on his horn brings Charlemagne into battle, which is necessary both for moral and for poetic justice. Even the arrival of the great army under Baligant is necessary; for otherwise Charlemagne would not have opponents worthy of his metal. No doubt it would have been easy to end the poem with Roland's death, and so other poems on the subject may have ended. But that is just what our poet does not do. The blowing of the horn, all the more effective because Roland has previously refused to blow it, makes Charlemagne's intervention inevitable. So too the final episode of Ganelon's trial and execution is part of a well-conceived plan. Just as the poem begins with his crime, so it ends with his punishment. Critics sometimes complain that the vengeance exacted by Charlemagne from the Saracens is too long and that the interest of the poem lags towards the end. But that is only because the poet treats seriously not only the whole question of treachery but the conflict between the Christian Franks and the infidel Saracens. His story is the story of Roland but it is also an important episode in the long wars between the Christians and their enemies, and a resounding defeat of the Saracens is the only way in which the disaster of Roncesvalles can be properly requited. Indeed, if the poem had ended with Roland's death, or if the last part had been much shorter than it is, we should miss this highly important aspect of the poet's vision. The story of Roland is an example of the crusading spirit, of its extraordinary prowess and the sacrifices which it is ready to make, and that is why the story had so strong and lasting an appeal for the mediaeval mind. The poet expands his work to a large scale because that is the way to show Christendom at work in its strength and glory. He has taken the old device of the sequel and merged it so skilfully into his design that we cannot dispense with it.

The art of constructing a poem on such a scale may be illustrated by a comparison between *Roland* and the Spanish *Cid*. The *Cid* has solid virtues, but as a piece of poetical architecture it leaves something to be desired. It falls roughly into two parts. In the first, the Cid, driven out in disgrace by the king from Castile, conducts a campaign against the Moors in which he is uniformly successful; in the second, he is taken back into favour and his daughters are married to two rich nobles, the Counts of Cárrión, who treat them abominably and are in due course punished. The poem may be criticised on two counts. First, the campaign against the Moors is undoubtedly monotonous. The Cid takes a number of towns, and wins rich booty, much of which he sends back to the king. This is told in a precise, factual way which looks historically accurate but lacks dramatic development or much dramatic interest. Secondly, the latter part, with its account of the Counts of Carrión, is much more vivid and interesting, but its connection with the first part is uncomfortably loose. There is a real difference of tone and temper between the record of battles and the gross behaviour of the Counts. It almost looks as if the poet used two different sources and combined them into a single poem. This is not a case of a poem with a sequel. The theme of the Counts is introduced while the Cid is still at war, and gains greater prominence when he is restored to favour. Even if the poet did not combine two stories known to him, he has two different ways of telling a story, and the result is incongruous. The *Cid*, unlike *Roland*, is an attempt to combine a factual military tale with something quite different in spirit.

The extension of scale from the short lay to the long is secured by different means, and a glance at some of them may help to show how the poets work when they move towards this more advanced kind of art. First, as we might expect, the individual episodes are more extensive and more detailed. What the short lay dismisses in a few lines may receive a large space. This makes greater demands on the poet's invention, and he is not always more successful than his predecessor or competitor in a smaller field. For instance, the familiar theme of the hero's fight with a dragon is often treated by Russian poets in stories of how Ilya of Murom or Alyosha Popovich fights Tugarin, the Dragon's son. Since their space is short, they have no difficulty in keeping the story interesting, and there is often a touch of ironical humour in the monster's efforts to trick the knight into friendship. The advantage of the short treatment is that it allows the poet to introduce a few small touches without making any of them so emphatic as to strain our credulity. With this simple art we may compare the episode of Beowulf and the Dragon, which takes nearly a thousand lines and is a highly elaborated affair. The poet expands by different means. He gives the history of the treasure which the dragon guards, adds details about Beowulf's career, introduces various characters who know about the dragon and have something to say about it, describes its various forays and fights, makes much ado with the final fight between it and Beowulf, and brings Beowulf to his death and funeral with some style. All this is beyond the scope of the short lay, and certainly gives opportunities for different kinds of poetry. The Anglo-Saxon poet is even able to moralise on the dangers of wealth and to associate his dragon with its wickedness. This is perhaps a doubtful gain, but it illustrates the way in which a theme can be developed. The poet's task is to find unexploited implications in his subject and make as much of them as he can. He is exposed to greater risk of failure than the composers of short lays, but of course, when he succeeds, his kind of success is beyond their reach.

This art of expansion can be seen in the treatment of battle. In *Maldon* a fierce fight between English and Vikings is told in some 300 lines ; in *Roland* two battles between Franks and Saracens take 3000. The comparison here is not so much of quality, since each is in its own way a remarkable performance, as of method. The Anglo-Saxon poet economises space, while the Norman-French poet is spendthrift of it. Each for instance has to describe hand-to-hand combats, but, while *Roland* does this many times, *Maldon* does it rarely and, as it were, only in chosen, exemplary cases, so that even Byrhtnoth's exploits are confined to a very small number of adversaries, while the other chieftains have to be satisfied with one combat each. This is not the way in which *Roland* describes one encounter after another, gives to each its own individuality and makes the chief characters take on a series of enemies in turn. *Maldon*, with its limited space, has to choose significant episodes, and even with these it must be brief and factual ; *Roland* with its many heroic combats, invents new and ingenious ways of dealing death. Secondly, the greater scale of *Roland* demands a larger number of actors than is possible in *Maldon*. *Maldon* has indeed its chosen few who play their parts and say their words in a noble and memorable manner, but *Roland* has not only its great Franks like Roland, Oliver, and Turpin ; it has also a large number of Saracens, each of whom is introduced with some words on his history and character. But the Vikings of *Maldon* remain anonymous and uncharacterised. There is no time to tell of anything but the actual fight and what is said and done during it. If the long poem has abundance and variety, the short lay has its own austere and economical power.

Secondly, the extension of scale allows a fuller handling of the incidental elements which play so large a part in heroic poetry. These, as we have seen, add to its realism and are always in some degree present. But while the short lay can only touch on them, the long poem can develop their possibilities and give them a new character. This is true of all the usual machining elements, like armour and ships and horses, but the long poem is also able to develop some themes which are not of this kind, since though they add much to the story, they are not indispensable to it. They give it a greater variety or depth through the new light which they throw on the hero or the nature of his experience. For instance, in the Yakut *Er Sogotokh* the hero fights various monsters and devils, but at one point he meets a different kind of opponent, which is introduced after a certain Kulut has refused to fight him. The episode does not call for much heroic effort by Er Sogotokh, and is introduced more for its variety than for necessity. The hero stands by the edge of a fiery sea:

> Over that sea no bird flies,
> On its floor no mouse crawls.
> They came there; he began to look.
> From the shore of the sea
> A fire blazes with blue uproar.
> Beyond the fire there flew a black, fiery bird
> With wings of iron,
> Like two long stripes of an elm-tree,
> With feathers like sabres,
> With a flaming, iron back, seven sagenes long,
> With a neck three sagenes long,
> With an iron tail like an elm twisted into a tube,
> With a huge head like a vat,
> With eyes like a cup,
> With cunning iron claws.[1]

The bird, so fully described, is soon dealt with. The hero kills it at once without difficulty, and it has not done much to make him assert his courage. But we can see why it has been introduced. This is the fire-bird of Indian legend, whose fame has somehow wandered into the far North, and the poet wishes to bring it into

[1] Yastremski, p. 26.

344

his story. In it he adds something which is not only decorative but contributes to the strangeness of Er Sogotokh's adventures.

Another advantage of this freedom to introduce additional themes is that it may enable the poet to give an unexpected touch of humanity to a story which is almost too austerely heroic. In *Maldon* there is no time or place for such concessions to human tenderness, but once at least in *Roland* the poet passes beyond his male society and its concentration on battle to something else. When at last Roland wishes to blow his horn, Oliver opposes him on the grounds that it is dishonourable to summon their liege lord so late in the battle when Roland might have summoned him before. Oliver backs his case with an unexpected argument:

> " Now by my beard, hereafter
> If I may see my gentle sister Alde,
> She in her arms, I swear, will never clasp you." [1]

Oliver's sister, Alde, is betrothed to Roland, and in his chivalrous pride Oliver tells Roland that he will now never marry her. This is the first mention of Alde in the poem, and it comes with a sudden stroke of reference to what seems a very different and distant world. Roland does not take up the point but asks Oliver why he is angry, and that is all we hear of Alde for the moment. Much later, when Charles has defeated the Saracens and returned to Aix, Alde comes to him and says:

> " Where's Rollanz the Captain,
> Who sware to me, he'ld have me for his mate ? " [2]

Charles weeps and tells her that Roland is dead. All he can do is to offer his son Lewis as a husband in Roland's place. The effect of his words is catastrophic:

> Alde answered him : " That word to me is strange.
> Never, please God, His Angels and his Saints,
> When Rollant's dead shall I alive remain ! "
> Her colour fails, at th' feet of Charlemain
> She falls ; she's dead. Her soul God's Mercy awaits !
> Barons of France weep therefore and complain.[3]

This is Alde's only appearance in the poem, and yet it has its own pathos, as it breaks across the grim story and introduces an unexpected note of tenderness.

Of a different temper but of equal dramatic advantage is a scene which varies the austere movement of the *Cid*. When he sets out on his campaign, the hero needs money. This is not a

[1] *Roland*, 1719-21.   [2] *Ibid.* 3709-10.   [3] *Ibid.* 3717-22.

consideration which usually troubles heroes, but the practical Spanish poet feels that it is relevant and secures one of his best moments through it. The Cid, despite his high standard of honour, is not above financial trickery. He fills two chests with sand and fastens them securely. He then sends Martín Antolínez to make a deal with two Jews, Raquel and Vidas. Martín explains the situation to them : his master is off in a hurry and cannot take his treasure with him ; so he wishes to leave it in secret custody with the Jews. The Jews are delighted and suggest a deal : if they may keep the chests, they are willing to let the Cid have six hundred marks for them. Antolínez agrees, but asks that, since he has done them a good turn, he himself should receive something for his services, and gets thirty marks. He returns to the Cid and reports the excellent bargain. The Cid, with unconscious humour on the part of the poet, then asks God for His blessing and makes ready for his departure.[1] The trick played on the Jews is a piece of comic relief. It is not necessary, since the Cid could easily have set out without money, but the poet, with an unwonted whimsicality, varies his story with this engaging episode.

Still another advantage of the longer poem is that it can develop the characters and motives of its leading persons, partly through their actions, partly through their words. In the short lay the nearest approach to this kind of success is in the Norse poems where the behaviour of figures like Guthrun and Brynhild and Hogni is so forthright that we feel that they are clear-cut characters. But actually what concerns us is less their characters than their destinies. We assume that they are simple, violent beings, and interpret their motives through their actions. In most short lays there is even less characterisation than this. The Russian heroes, for instance, are usually rather colourless and it is not surprising that the same story may be told about different people. Some, like Churilo Plenkovich, have character-parts as reckless play-boys, but that is exceptional, and even Churilo's character consists of little more than uncontrolled appetites and a boastful recklessness. The great warrior Ilya of Murom has little personality, and others like Dyuk and Staver and Dobrynya have less. The same is true of the Jugoslav heroes. With the notable exception of Marko Kraljević, whose character is built up in a number of different poems, the other heroes have little personal identity except their love of their country and their hatred of the Turks. Even the traitor Vuk Brancović is without outline or motives. The short lay, whether practised by Russians or Jugoslavs or

[1] *Cid*, 78 ff.

Ossetes or Bulgars, has no time to depict personalities. The most it can do is to create situations in which a man behaves in a way which makes us think that he is this or that sort of human being. The longer poem has space at its disposal and allows the poet to indulge his interest in human beings and to uncover the springs of their behaviour.

This skill is displayed most obviously with the leading heroes, who gain through it unexpected traits and become more solid and more interesting. It is, for instance, essential that Gilgamish should be a great warrior, but the poet fills in the outline of his character with other qualities, like his affection for his mother, his contempt for the fickle goddess Ishtar, his all too human inability to keep awake for six days and six nights, his obsessing horror and fear of death. These make him more impressive and his destiny more tragic. We understand why the death of Enkidu sends him to the end of the world to ask Uta-Napishtim about the secret of everlasting life. In *Roland*, where the characters are on the whole rough-hewn from solid blocks, there are moments when the poet surprises us with a sudden touch of insight, as when Oliver insists that it is dishonourable to blow the horn just because they are in dire straits,[1] or Turpin composes the quarrel between him and Roland,[2] or Charlemagne clumsily tries to comfort Alde for Roland's death.[3] These are small and simple touches, but they add humanity to the otherwise austere and majestic figures. In *Beowulf* the poet plainly delights in Hrothgar, who shows a real grief for his thanes when they are destroyed hideously by monsters,[4] is genuinely fond of Beowulf,[5] and has a touch of melancholy which suits his age and experience and comes out in his long moral discourse on the vanity of power.[6] Even in the *Cid* the characters have a certain unity of being, like the hero himself with his devoted loyalty to the king who has exiled him; the unscrupulous, cowardly, and cynical Counts of Carrión, who leave their wives almost to die of hunger and neglect; the worthy Martín Antolínez, who is glad to do anything for his master. The chief persons of long poems are usually real enough. Of course there is little subtlety or elaboration in their portraiture, but the main outlines are clear enough for us to know what kind of men they are.

A third means of expansion consists of showing both sides of a conflict from their respective points of view. This is almost impossible in the short lay which has to concentrate on a single

---

[1] *Roland*, 1715 ff.   [2] *Ibid.* 1737 ff.
[3] *Ibid.* 3713 ff.   [4] *Beowulf*, 129 ff., 473 ff., 1322 ff.
[5] *Ibid.* 1870 ff.   [6] *Ibid.* 1724 ff.

situation. Even in *Atlakvitha* and *Atlamál* little attempt is made
to elaborate Atli's intentions in asking Gunnar to his court or to
show the process by which he comes to do so. The poets have
enough to do without extending the field of their narrative. But
in longer poems this is easily done and adds much to the variety of
the story. For instance, the Kalmuck poem on Dzhangar's war
with the Black Prince begins with an elaborate account of Dzhangar
and his companions and then moves to the other side and gives a
picture of his great enemy, who is in his own way hardly less
formidable. With this the action begins, since it is at the Black
Prince's dwelling that a plot is hatched to attack Dzhangar. After
the description of the Kalmuck heroes at rest we turn to a similar
scene :

> With their countless chosen warriors
> In their motley yellow tent
> They sit and drink wine,
> Draining a hundred flagons.[1]

The camp of the enemy is not a contrast but a parallel. Despite
their differences and their enmity the Kalmucks and their foes
behave in much the same way, and the interest of their conflict
comes largely from this. We want to know how these well-matched
antagonists will fare when they meet in battle.

In *Roland* the poet gives some attention to the enemy and even
sets certain scenes among the Saracens. In this he shows a good
judgment, notably after the fight in the pass where Roland and
Oliver, at the cost of their own lives, have routed the enemy.
The Saracens flee back to Spain, and the poet gives some time
to showing what they do there and how they recover their forces
for another battle. Into this situation he works ideas which add
considerably to the wealth of his poem. First, the Saracens are
Pagans who have been defeated. Their false gods have done
nothing for them. So they turn on them and maltreat them :

> Then Apollin in's grotto they surround,
> And threaten him, and ugly words pronounce :
> " Such shame on us, vile god ! why bringest thou ?
> This is our king ; wherefore dost him confound ?
> Who served thee oft, ill recompense hath found."
> Then they take off his sceptre and his crown,
> With their hands hang him from a column down,
> Among their feet trample him on the ground,
> With great cudgels they batter him and trounce.
> From Tervagant his carbuncle they impound,
> And Mahumet into a ditch fling out,
> Where swine and dogs defile him and devour.[2]

---

[1] *Dzhangariada*, p. 111.   [2] *Roland*, 2580-91.

By this admirable scene the poet presents a contrast between the Christian and the pagan ways of life. The Christians fight in the confidence that their God will sustain them; the pagans find that their gods fail them. Secondly, this change of scene to the Saracen country enables the poet to expand on a theme which meant much to his time, the richness and splendour of the East. He does this by introducing a new character in Baligant, who comes with a great army from Babylon. His arrival is an occasion of some brilliance :

> Clear is that day, and the sun radiant.
> Out of his barge issues their admiral,
> Espaneliz goes forth at his right hand,
> Seventeen kings follow him in a band,
> Counts, too, and dukes ; I cannot tell of that.
> Where in a field, midway, a laurel stands,
> On the green grass they spread a white silk mat,
> Set a fald-stool there, made of olifant ;
> Sits him thereon the pagan Baligant.[1]

This too presents a contrast to the simplicity of life practised by Charlemagne and his knights. The poet of *Roland* not only widens the sphere of his narrative by changing the scene but stresses some points which mean much to him and his audience.

The *Cid* uses this same device to show the contrast between the hero on his campaign and the king in his court. When the Cid collects booty, he sends part of it to the king, and the poet shows what then happens at the court of Castile. The king is displeased with the Cid, and can hardly be expected to welcome his messenger. But the Cid plans wisely. He sends Minaya Albar Fáñez to the king with a rich share of the booty taken from the Moors. Minaya does his task well, offers the booty in a spirit of respectful homage, and says nothing about the Cid's being returned to honour. The king is pleased, accepts the booty on the specious plea that it comes from the Moors, gives back his fiefs and lands to Minaya, and allows those who wish to help the Cid. But about the Cid himself he does not at the moment wish to hear anything, and says that it is too soon to forgive a man who has been in disgrace for only three weeks.[2] An impression has been made, and forgiveness, if not in sight, is no longer out of the question. Later, after the capture of Valencia, the Cid again sends Minaya to the king, and again Minaya plays his part well, but this time he speaks freely of the Cid's victories, and this time the king is pleased and says so. He then approves the proposal that the Counts of Carrión should marry the Cid's daughters, and the breach is healed.[3] These two

[1] *Ibid.* 2646-54. [2] *Cid*, 873 ff. [3] *Ibid.* 1308 ff.

scenes are simple and not very dramatic, but they are important in the structure of the poem because they present the other side of the picture, the court circles in which the Cid has been traduced and badly treated, and the character of the king, who is easily swayed and too ready to believe what he hears. It is not surprising that the Cid is not at home in such circles and that he makes enemies in them.

A fourth method of expansion is not so common as these, but is well illustrated both in *Beowulf* and in *Gilgamish*. The poet, either in his own person or through some character, tells stories which are not immediately connected with the plot. In *Beowulf* the telling of such stories is one of the chief means of expansion and largely responsible for the poem being so long as it is. Some of the stories so told are obviously relevant to the hero's character like his inglorious youth, his swimming match with Breca, his early adventures. In these we see how the hero grew to manhood and prepared himself for his future exploits. So too the story of the Scylding line which begins the poem is useful as a historical preparation and background for characters who are to take leading parts later. But the other stories are less obviously to the point. They are introduced skilfully enough, often by comparison or contrast, but their relevance is not always obvious. For instance, the story of the arrogant queen, Thryth, is introduced by a slender thread, in that the poet has just mentioned the good queen, Hygd, and thinks that this justifies a digression. Again, the story of Freawaru and the war of the Danes and the Heathobards is introduced by Beowulf's father because Freawaru is Hrothgar's daughter and Beowulf has visited Hrothgar. The connection is natural enough but not very cogent. Perhaps in these episodes the poet seeks to point some moral, but on the whole he seems to bring them in because they belong to a body of legend to which he wishes to relate Beowulf. He may have felt that his own story had too unreal and too legendary an air and needed to be connected with more genuinely historical events.

The art of *Gilgamish* is not like this. The only story told by a character is Uta-Napishtim's tale of the flood, and the connection of this with the main plot is quite clear. Gilgamish wishes to know how Uta-Napishtim became immortal and hears that it was a gift from the gods in reward for his behaviour. After the Flood the god Enlil comes to him and blesses him and says :

" Hitherto Uta-Napishtim has been mortal,
Now Uta-Napishtim and his wife shall be like the gods." [1]

[1] *Gilgamish*, x, i, 193-4.

So far the story is entirely relevant to the rest of the poem. When Gilgamish meets the only two human beings who have escaped from death, he hears that their immortality is a reward from the gods. For him this is impossible; if he is to gain immortality, he must win it for himself, and in this he fails. Thus Uta-Napishtim's story is implicitly an ironical comment on Gilgamish's quest for immortality. Moreover, it implies a moral which the poet surely intended to be drawn. Uta-Napishtim is the favoured of the gods whose will he has carried out, but the same cannot be said of Gilgamish, whose life is spent largely in combating their will. The story of the flood is in fact a comment on Gilgamish's way of life and passes judgment on it. A hero who defies the gods can hardly expect to be rewarded by them.

In these several ways the art of the short lay is adapted to the more extended scale of the longer poem. The process is quite natural and may still be observed in some parts of the world. It depends on a poet's ability and taste and circumstances. Not all poets are able or willing to attempt it, and many seem content with short lays. But the longer poem is not only an efficient and successful form of narrative but, by showing how the outline of a tale can be enriched and expanded, points out the possibilities of composition on a still greater scale. Beyond it lies the heroic epic, the poem composed on a truly grand scale, with a certain elaboration in its main plan and its episodes. Such epics are not nearly so common as short lays or longer poems, but they are sufficiently distinguished to deserve special attention. We are fortunate in knowing how one or two of them were composed, and from this we can advance to a consideration of others of whose origin we know next to nothing. We can hardly doubt that all these epics belong to a single class and were composed in much the same way. If we can see what this is, we should be able to understand more about their character and methods.

The Moslem bards of Jugoslavia often compose poems of 3000 or 4000 lines, but in some few cases they are known to have reached as many as 12,000 lines. In 1934 Milman Parry found a bard in Southern Serbia, a Moslem called Avdo Mededović aged about sixty, who would sing for about two hours in the morning and for another two hours in the afternoon, resting for five or ten minutes every half-hour. To sing a long song took him two weeks with a week's rest in between to recover his voice. The result was an epic poem on Osman Delibegović and Pavičević Luka, which has about 12,000 lines. Since the text of the poem has not yet been published, it may be convenient to reproduce the summary of it made by Parry's assistant, A. B. Lord :

The song of Osman Delibegović and Pavičević Luka opens in the city of Osek, where its lord, Osman Delibegović, rose very early one morning and, after having his coffee and saying his morning prayers, went with his servant, Husejin, to the battlements of the city to look out over the rich plain. As he was admiring the green fields, he saw a cloud and from it emerged a young man of heroic mien riding upon a chestnut steed. Osman did not recognise him, but, when the rider approached, Osman did him homage and asked who he was and whence he came. The boy said that his name was Silić Jusuf and that he came from Kajnidže. His mother was Osman's sister. Jusuf had never heard of his uncle until one day long after his father's death he had asked his mother whether he had any kin, and she had told him of her brother, the mighty lord of Osek. So he had sought out his uncle. Osman was pleased beyond words, and declared a festival in honour of his newly found nephew. He gathered all the nobles together and introduced the boy to them. Not long after Jusuf's arrival, Osman again saw a cloud of dust on the far side of the river Drava, and from it came forth a mighty warrior of gigantic stature arrayed in the panoply of battle. Osman could not make out whether he was friend or foe ; so he despatched some of his own men to greet the stranger and bring him into his presence, first having laid aside his sword and spear and rifle. The stranger of course refused to do this because his mother had warned him in his youth never to appear before any ruler without his weapons. She would rather see him dead and buried. In spite of this Osman agreed to see him and, when the unknown hero had been ushered into the hall, Osman asked him his name and whence he came. He replied that he was from a far-off kingdom, from the city of Kajsar, and that his name was Pavičević Luka, of one of the best families of Kajsar. He had fallen in love with Jela, the daughter of General Vuk, but she had spurned him, and he had sworn revenge : he would become a Turk and go to Osek to ask its ruler to raise a mighty army to reduce the city of Kajsar to ashes. As he left Kajsar, he had come upon three captives, two young girls and a boy. He had discovered that they were the children of Osman Delibegović, and they had given him a letter to their father asking him to come to Kajsar and rescue them from captivity. Luka gave the letter to Osman, and the old man wept for joy at receiving news of his lost children. He accepted Luka as a foster-son and again declared a festival, at which he presented Pavičević Luka to all the nobles of his court. Finally the time came to learn from Luka the strategy which was to be followed in the impending campaign, to determine the forces needed, and to gather them together. The singer does this at very great length and with consummate skill, avoiding in so far as possible the monotony of verbal repetition. Luka enumerated the cities and towns they must pass through, the garrisons which they must leave in them, and the destruction which he personally, with the youth Jusuf at his side, would bring to his enemies. Osman dictated messages to the Turkish chieftains and despatched them. The various contingents arrived at Osek and are described in considerable detail. All of this activity is covered in approximately 5000 lines. At last the army was ready and set out for Kajsar. Every battle along the way is described in detail, and in each Pavičević Luka distinguished himself by his prowess in single-handed combats. When they arrived before the gates of Kajsar and encamped, Luka suddenly discovered that Hrnjičić Halil had disappeared. Osman had hesitated in asking the young Halil to join the expedition because he was famous for his way with women, and Luka had sworn vengeance upon anyone who might disturb Jela. Luka therefore sent Halil's renowned brother, Mujo, the commander-in-chief of the armies, together with the comic hero, Tale of Orašac, to get Halil and bring him back. They discovered him with Jela in the city, returned with him, and brought about a reconciliation between Halil and Luka. All the male inhabitants of the city were at a religious festival in the cathedral. They were surprised there by the Moslems and slaughtered; the church itself was desecrated and left in ruins. Then the Turkish army entered Kajsar. Luka took Jela, and there is a touching scene of reunion between Osman and his captive children. The city was pillaged and burned to the ground. Finally the armies were ready to return to Osek. The journey back was a series of battles because in each place where garrisons had been left behind by the advancing army they had been destroyed, and it was necessary to retake each city. On their return to Osek the heroes made a count of the army and discovered that of 220,000 men only 60,000 had returned, and of that 60,000 half were wounded. The spoils were then divided and rich gifts were sent to every family which had lost a warrior. Osman then gathered his nobles together and they sent messengers to Sultan Sulejman in Stanbol to tell the Sultan of their victory and to find out whether he was angry at them for having made the expedition without asking his permission. Sulejman was overjoyed and amazed at the reports and requested the leaders to come to Stanbol. When they arrived they were welcomed with great honour and were richly rewarded by the Sultan. Luka became a Moslem and was made Dizdar of Banjaluka, where the Sultan promised to build him a palace. After a period of festivity the heroes returned to Bosnia and preparations were made as ordered by the Sultan for the wedding between Luka, now named Mahmut, and Jela, whom Osman had adopted and given the Turkish name of Mejruša. The poem ends with an elaborate account of the gathering of wedding guests in Banjaluka, their journey to Osek, and the festivities associated with the wedding.

Such is the abstract of this poem, and we can see that it is an epic constructed on a well-conceived plan, and not a series of separate lays joined together by superficial transitions.

It is, then, clear beyond dispute that, whatever may have been said to the contrary, it is quite possible to construct an oral epic of 12,000 lines. The bard in this case could not read or write, and seems to have composed the poem as he went on. No doubt he formed certain plans in his head and was helped in his execution of them by the formulaic elements which belong to his art and appear abundantly in his poem. The result is a poem which has its complex plot, its variety of incidents and characters, its full-scale descriptions and speeches. Other Jugoslav poems, also recorded by Parry, show the same kind of composition and character, though one of them at least is much more episodic in construction than this poem. In these cases the impulse to compose a long poem came from outside, in Parry's request for it. But once he had been asked for it, the poet had no great difficulty in providing it. The psychological process of composition must remain a mystery, but at least we know that the poets were able, by following a routine of recitation and pauses, to produce poems as long as the *Odyssey*. This is a fundamental fact of first importance.

A similar art of composition on a large scale can be found among the Uzbeks. The bard Pulkan (1874–1941), who was a simple shepherd by origin and never learned to read or write, was not only the author of some seventy different poems, most of some length, but composed one called *Kiron-Khan*, which has more than 20,000 lines.[1] Unfortunately the text is not available, and we are unable to see what its methods of construction are. Since the normal length of an Uzbek poem is about 3000-4000 lines, this shows how a bard can extend himself when he feels a call to do so. More is known about another long Uzbek poem, the *Alpamys* of Fazil,[2] which has about 14,000 lines as opposed to a Kazak version of the same story which has 2500 and a Karakalpak which has 3000. Of Fazil's poem something is known. It tells the story of the hero from his birth to his final triumph over his enemies and has a well-conceived plan into which the different episodes fall. Alpamys fights the Kalmucks and has varying fortunes with them, being put into prison at one time for seven years by their prince. When he escapes, he finds his house occupied by enemies, rather as Odysseus finds his in Ithaca, and triumphs over them in the same way, although at first he has almost no friends but an old servant and no advantage but his skill with the bow. The hero is assisted by his unwavering friend, Karadzhan, his sister, Kaldir-gach, and his beloved, Barchin, to say nothing of his wonderful horse, Baichibar. The actions of this group are developed with a full sense of their personalities and many combinations and variations in their relationships. The poem is one of many on Alpamys, and nine other versions are known in Uzbek. None of these is on anything like the same scale, and Fazil shows how a bard who has enough inventive power can extend a story to a large

---

[1] Zhirmunskii-Zarifov, p. 47.
[2] *Idem*, pp. 61-9. Part of the poem is translated into Russian in *Antologiya uzbeksoi poezii* (Moscow, 1950), pp. 20-40.

scale without making it look at all inflated. Part of his gift lies in the speeches which he gives to his characters and which abound in eloquence and dramatic strength. In this poem expansion comes easily because the poet has mastered the fundamentals of his story and seen what new possibilities it contains.

From these long Jugoslav and Uzbek poems we may turn to the work of two relatively modern Kara-Kirghiz bards, about whom we are less well informed than about the Jugoslavs, but whose achievement is clearly even more remarkable. In 1946 a committee of Russian scholars published a Russian translation of a long epic called *Manas*. This is a combination of two poems by different authors, but that need not trouble us, since the two parts are quite distinct. The larger part tells the story of Manas' great expedition against China; the shorter tells the life-story of Manas' comrade, Alaman Bet. The two are quite separate, and the editors are careful to show their limits. The first is the work of Sagymbai Orozbakov, who was born in 1867 and died in 1930, the second of Sayakbai Karalaev, who was born in 1894 and was still alive in 1946. Both poems derive from an old and popular tradition. In the middle of the eighteenth century a bard called Keldybek composed poems on the subject; a hundred years or so later Radlov included several poems on Manas and his cycle in his collection from the Kara-Kirghiz; and to-day the popularity of the subject is indicated by the common use of the word *manaschi* for any man who is able to sing songs of this kind. But between these older works, so far as we know them, and the *Manas* of Orozbakov there is an enormous difference of scale. The poems published by Radlov do not pass beyond 6000 lines, but Orozbakov's *Manas*, without Karalaev's addition, has about 40,000 lines. So much we can examine and control for ourselves, and it is certainly an astonishing achievement. But the Russian editors give other information which is even more remarkable.[1] According to them, between 1922 and 1926 Orozbakov composed some 250,000 verses. Of these a considerable proportion seem to have been variants on the main theme, but the final result, as taken down from Orozbakov by Abdrakhmanov Ibrahim, was not only *Manas*, as we have it, but two sequels to it on an equal scale, *Semätäi*, which tells of Manas' son, and *Seitek*, which tells of his grandson. Unfortunately these two sequels have not been published, and no information is available about them. Even so the published *Manas*, with its 40,000 lines, is a remarkable enough performance. Since Orozbakov could not read nor write, he com-

[1] E. Mozolkov in *Manas*, p. 10.

posed the poem orally, and it was taken down from him, like the rest of his work, between 1922 and 1926. Sayakbai Karalaev seems to have worked in the same way. Though his published poem on Alaman Bet has only some 4000 lines, he is credited with a poem or cycle of poems on Manas which reaches the astonishing figure of 400,000 lines.[1] Since this represents a total output and includes figures for variant versions of the same story, it does not mean that any single poem is of this length. None the less it shows that Orozbakov is not a unique phenomenon and that in this century Kara-Kirghiz poets have discovered a gift for oral composition on a gigantic scale.

Before we consider the nature and significance of poems on this large scale, it may be useful to clear away certain other poems which seem to resemble them but are in fact quite different, although they pass as traditional epics. The Finnish *Kalevala*, for instance, is sometimes called the national epic of Finland. So in practice it may have become, but it was not such in its origins. It is in fact a composition made by the scholar Elias Lönnrot and published first in 1833 and then, in an enlarged form, in 1849. Lönnrot collected oral poems and pieced them together into a whole, but in so doing did not shrink from mutilating many of them and from transferring passages from their right contexts to other contexts where they suited his plan better. He did not conceal what he had done, and the work is in no sense an imposture. Indeed Lönnrot may well have believed that he was restoring a lost epic from broken pieces. Actually he did nothing of the kind. There is no likelihood that such an epic ever existed or that, if it did, Lönnrot's reconstruction is right. The stories which he included are usually known in many other versions, all of which are equally authentic. Indeed the whole conception of such a lost epic seems to be a romantic illusion. Epics are more likely to grow out of short lays by a natural process of expansion than to be broken up into them. The *Kalevala* contains genuine materials, but as a long poem it provides no basis of comparison, since such unity as it has is the work of a scholar working with scissors and paste.

The composition of the *Kalevala* was followed in 1857 and the following years by the Esthonian *Kalevipoeg*. It was perhaps the fruit of a society of Esthonian scholars founded in 1838, which collected oral poems, but the actual work for it was done by F. R. Kreutzwald, who followed very much the same lines as Lönnrot and fitted separate lays together in the same ruthless way. Unfortunately, while Lönnrot left his papers behind him so that

[1] E. Mozolkov in *Manas*, p. 18,

his methods may be examined, Kreutzwald destroyed his, so that it is now impossible to control his work. None the less there is no doubt that the *Kalevipoeg* is a literary construction in the same sense as the *Kalevala* and provides no evidence whatsoever on the normal process of growth in heroic poetry. In recent years something similar has been done for Armenian poems about David of Sasoun, his parents, and his son. In 1939 there appeared a Russian book, *David of Sasoun*, which gives a translation of what looks like a complicated epic of four heroic generations. This was compiled from genuine Armenian materials, with far less adaptation or adjustment than Lönnrot and Kreutzwald made, but the single form in which they are presented is the work of modern scholars. The editors made selections from a large number of oral versions and fitted them together. Though this contains material of the highest value, it throws no light on our present problem. The so-called epic is no more than a learned arrangement of single, independent lays. The same criticism may be made of some other attempts to create large-scale epics out of short lays, like the attempts to construct a single Jugoslav epic of Kosovo,[1] or a single Russian epic on the circle of Vladimir.[2] These constructions betray themselves by many inconsistencies of tone and manner and story, and in any case are quite irrelevant to our enquiry. If we wish to know how a full heroic epic comes into existence, we can find our best material among the Jugoslavs and the Kara-Kirghiz.

The example of these poems is obviously relevant to any discussion of the composition of the *Iliad* and the *Odyssey*. When in 1837 Karl Lachmann advanced his theory that the *Iliad* was a compilation made of various short lays, one of his arguments was that so long a poem could not be composed without the aid of writing. We know now that this argument is worthless. When bards can neither read nor write, their powers of memory may seem prodigious to us who rely on books and paper. What has been done in this century by Avdo Mededović and Sagymbai Orozbakov can equally have been done in the past. There is no *a priori* reason why the *Iliad* and the *Odyssey* should not have been composed in much the same way as *Osman Delibegović* and *Manas*. As we have seen, their very extensive use of formulae indicates that they were composed in a tradition of improvisation and their many devices of narrative belong to an oral art. If we cannot deny that

[1] Notably by S. J. Stojković, *Lazarica* (Belgrade, 1903), and L. Dimitrijević, *Kosovo* (Sarajevo, 1924).

[2] The latest attempt is by N. V. Vodovozov, *Russkii narodnyi epos* (Moscow, 1947).

they are oral poems, we can surely admit that they reached their present form through some such process as may be observed among the Kara-Kirghiz and the Jugoslavs. Just as in both these societies the existence of short and medium lays has ended in long epic, so something of the same kind may have happened in Greece. Since Homer tells of short lays sung by Phemius and Demodocus, he knew of their existence, though his own art was different. It seems legitimate to conclude that the *Iliad* and *Odyssey* presuppose an art of oral composition which dealt with poems of varying length, but that the long epic was an unusual phenomenon which both owed much to the technique of the shorter lay and had to create its own means to tell a complex story on a large scale.

Oral composition on a large scale implies certain conditions which are not prevalent everywhere. First, it is clear that poets like Mededović, Fazil, Orozbakov, and Karalaev are able to compose easily because they have at their command a large number both of stories and of devices, including formulae. This would not be the case if poetical composition were an uncommon art restricted to a few famous bards, but when a country has a large number of bards, all of whom tell more or less the same stories in more or less the same kind of poetical language, it is obviously easier to make use of these resources and combine them in a long poem. In Jugoslavia Parry found that most villages had at least one bard, who knew other bards elsewhere; the Uzbek respect for bards is shown by the conferring of titles on them, such as *bakshi*, *shair*, *dzhirov*, each of which has its own implications and distinctiveness; among the Kara-Kirghiz heroic song is a national art, which almost everyone admires and most try to practise. When heroic song is an occupation of every day and practised by all sorts of persons, it is clearly easier to master its technique and therefore, if occasion arises, to produce a poem of a length beyond the powers of bards who lack such support and resources. Secondly, the tradition of Jugoslav, Uzbek, and Kara-Kirghiz poems is rich and ancient. It has lasted for centuries and evolved all kinds of useful devices, which the poet is at full liberty to use. He may invent stories if he wishes, but his audience is usually content if he chooses from the mass of old material the subjects which suit his taste and talents. Such conditions may well account for the scale on which these poets compose, and also for the scale of the Homeric poems. The large number of stories which survive from the Greek heroic age imply a widespread and popular art, and the Homeric poems profit much from being the fruit of a long tradition. Homer, in fact, seems to have been well placed for the composition of poems as long as the *Iliad* and the *Odyssey*, and the modern parallels may illustrate the conditions in which he was able to do so.

When the poet moves from the technique of the short epic of 4000 lines to the long epic of 12,000 lines or more, he faces serious problems of composition. He must arrange his material in such a way that his audience accepts his poem as a unity and not a collection. It must have some kind of shape. The simplest way to do this is to tell the story of a hero's life in a series of episodes, each of which is more or less complete in itself but related to what precedes and connected by the identity of the hero. This is done in medium lays, like Kryukova's *Tale of Lenin*, and it is also done in long epics like those of some Jugoslav bards. But though this is the simplest way, it is also the least satisfactory. What is perhaps tolerable in a short epic becomes an obstacle to enjoyment when it is applied on a large scale. We miss the central structure and wonder why the poet has chosen to compose a single poem instead of a series of poems. Aristotle saw this difficulty when he explained that unity of plot does not consist in having one man as its subject :

An infinity of things befall that one man, some of which it is impossible to reduce to unity ; and in like manner there are many actions of one man which cannot be made to form one action. One sees, therefore, the mistake of all the poets who have written a *Heracleid*, a *Theseid*, or similar poems ; they suppose that, because Heracles was one man, the story also of Heracles must be one story.[1]

The method which Aristotle deplores is common enough, and it has produced no better results in our time than in his. The episodic poems of modern peoples are still open to his criticism, even when they are told with considerable skill like Karalaev's account of Alaman Bet. It is when the poets attempt some more complex kind of composition that they achieve more interesting results.

A good example of such composition may be seen in Mededović's *Osman Delibegović*. This is not a tale in which one character holds the stage and plays the others off it. It has two main characters in Osman and Luka, and others only less important in Jusuf and Halil. The plot follows a logical and consistent development. First, comes the setting of the stage with the arrival of different characters and the preparations for war ; then the main action in the war with its diverse incidents and its successful conclusion ; finally the sequel with its tale of rewards and

[1] *Poetics*, 1451a, 20 ff. Trs. I. Bywater.

2 A

successes. This is a good plot, well balanced and well arranged. The sequence of action has a logical development and moves towards its extended crisis with a variety of interest. Themes suggested early are developed later, like Luka's loss of his children and subsequent discovery of them or Halil's amorous tendencies and dalliance with Jela. The personal and private fortunes of the main characters are woven into the fortunes of armies and cities, if not of nations, and the extension of scale in the narrative allows a far greater stage on which the events can be played. Heroic achievements on the battlefield are varied by domestic scenes and stately festivals. The composition of *Osman Delibegović* is the work of a skilful craftsman, who knows that an epic must have a shapely and balanced design and be held together by certain main themes and characters and lines of development.

The task which Orozbakov set himself in his *Manas* was more difficult. 40,000 lines is a great length, through which it is difficult to keep a main design clear. But Orozbakov had the sense not to attempt anything too elaborate. His main scheme is simple and dominating. He tells of a great expedition of the Kara-Kirghiz led by Manas against the Chinese. This is the thread which holds the poem together, and nearly all the incidents lead up to this or contribute to it. On this basis the poem falls into six sections. First, the various subordinate khans plot against Manas. He sends for them, humbles them, and reduces them to discipline. He announces his plan for an expedition, and the section closes with a great speech about what lies ahead and what is expected of one army. In the second part, the preparations for the expedition are told in some detail. The different hosts assemble and get ready to set out; Manas consults his wife Kanykai, who prophesies the successful outcome of the expedition. The character of the hero Alaman Bet assumes a special prominence, and is revealed in his long conversation with Manas and his quarrel with Chubak. In the third part the expedition has set out, and we hear of the part played by Alaman Bet in going before the main army and removing various sinister obstacles, including a one-eyed giant and the sorceress Kanyshai. These episodes prepare the way for the army to enter China, while Alaman Bet goes forward on his own adventures and has a curious episode with a woman called Burlucha. The fourth part is quite short and tells first of Alaman Bet's meeting with the Chinese hero Karagul, who flies off in fear to his master, Kongyr Bai, and then of a splendid fight between Alaman Bet and Karagul, who have met again. Kongyr Bai now gets ready for battle and sets out to face Manas. In the fifth part the fighting is fast and furious, and Manas begins to play a dominant role, fighting three famous warriors. He is caught in a dangerous position but saved by the skill and cunning of Bakai. The army has now almost reached its goal. In the sixth and last part, the expedition succeeds in its aims. Kongyr Bai is defeated and killed, and another formidable enemy, Mahdi, Khan, is routed by Manas. The poem ends with the triumphal entry of the Kirghiz into the Chinese capital.

Manas is not episodic. Its design moves towards a final climax, and skill is displayed in making the different parts fall into the whole. The conspiracy of the khans sets the action going and, in doing so, shows what a hero Manas is and why he goes to war. The various adventures of Alaman Bet may stand a little outside the main theme but they contribute to it since they help the advance of the army. The last two parts, with their rich variety of combats and mass movements, are a fitting crisis to what has gone before and end the poem on a resounding note of victory. The large scale allows for a high degree of characterisation, and the poet develops his action through a variety of well-delineated personalities. If for a time Alaman Bet steals the applause, Manas displaces him when he takes the stage again and proves his pre-eminence. The minor figures, like Manas' wife Kanykai, or the various Chinese leaders, have their own personalities, and much is gained by ingenious contrasts between them and the Kirghiz heroes. The landscape changes with the advance of the army, and the length of its march enables the poet to give many hints of natural surroundings and strange places. *Manas* is well constructed and follows a single plan. Of course it has its digressions and its supplementary episodes, but these are fitted into the main frame. The whole has a bold design carried to a successful conclusion.

From such well-constructed epics as *Osman Delibegović* and *Manas* we may turn to the *Iliad* and the *Odyssey*. Aristotle had no doubts about their excellence:

> The structure of the two Homeric poems is as perfect as can be, and the action in them is as nearly as possible one action.[1]

To see what he means with reference to the *Iliad* we may quote some other words of his:

> He [Homer] did not attempt to deal even with the Trojan war in its entirety, though it was a whole with a definite beginning and end — through a feeling apparently that it was too long a story to be taken in in

[1] *Poetics*, 1462b, 10. Trs. I. Bywater.

one view, or if not that, too complicated from the variety of incident in it. As it is, he has singled out one section of the whole ; many of the other incidents, however, he brings in as episodes, using the Catalogue of the Ships, for instance, and other episodes to relieve the uniformity of his narrative.[1]

This is true so far as it goes, and must be respected as coming from a great authority. But though Aristotle saw the superiority of the *Iliad* to other heroic poems constructed episodically, he did not see that the *Iliad* does rather more than he says and is in fact an adventurous piece of composition. It has both a special theme and a general theme. The special theme, as the poet announces in the first line, is the wrath of Achilles ; the general theme is the Siege of Troy, and that is why the poem is not an *Achilleid* but an *Iliad*. The two themes are closely interwoven and often overlap. But they must be considered separately if we wish to understand what Homer does.

Homer's special theme is the wrath of Achilles, and in his opening lines he speaks of it and its results. From the mass of possible subjects in the career of a great hero he chooses one poignant episode. We do not know why he did so, but we can see what advantages he gains from it. The wrath is both heroic and tragic. It is a fault in a great character, but also a fault inherent in the whole heroic scheme of life. Achilles' anger, when his pride is wounded by Agamemnon, is the final realisation of the life which makes honour its chief end. Homer could not have chosen a theme better suited to a heroic poem. This wrath provides the machinery of the action. Because Achilles is angry and keeps away from battle, his comrades in war are defeated and Hector comes near to burning the Achaean ships. With such a subject there was no need to close the poem with the death of Achilles. His end falls outside the *Iliad* and has less interest than his tragic wrath, which leads to the death of Patroclus and his own moral degradation when he purposes to mutilate the body of Hector. None the less Homer is aware of Achilles' death and uses it to emphasise the position in which Achilles' action puts him. His death is not far away, and is referred to more than once, by Thetis when she comes to comfort her son,[2] by Achilles himself to Lycaon,[3] by his horses when he drives out to battle,[4] and by Hector in his last words.[5] The death of Achilles lies in the background and makes his present conduct more tragic. In the short time at his disposal he falls below heroic standards and wastes the precious days. This is the special theme

---

[1] *Poetics*, 1459a, 31 ff. Trs. I. Bywater.   [2] *Il.* i, 417 ff.
[3] *Ibid.* xxi, 108 ff.   [4] *Ibid.* xix, 409 ff.   [5] *Ibid.* xxii, 358 ff.

of the *Iliad*, with which it begins and ends, and from which most of its action arises.

The *Iliad* is also a poem about Troy and the Trojan War in its tenth and last year. To complete his picture Homer presents in contrast to the camp-life of the Achaeans the civic life of Troy with its old men like Priam, its women like Helen and Andromache, its children like Astyanax. Like the death of Achilles, the fall of Troy lies outside the *Iliad*, but is none the less suggested with a subtle art. Hector foretells it to Andromache on the walls of Troy,[1] and when he is killed, it is as if all Troy were shaken to its foundations ;[2] so closely is its destiny bound up with his life, and so certain is it that his death means its fall. Just as the wrath of Achilles is more tragic than his death and is chosen as a main theme for that reason, so the death of Hector, who embodies the resistance of Troy, is more significant than the actual fall which will come inevitably after his death. Since the destiny of Troy comes from war, the *Iliad* has to be a tale of war. So Homer describes a long series of battles which are ended by Achilles' deadly return to the field and his victorious struggle with Hector. These battles may take us away from the theme of the wrath, but they are connected with it, first when the different Achaeans are unable to withstand the Trojan onslaught because Achilles refuses to fight, afterwards when in his own battles Achilles gluts his wrath in deadly and unrelenting action. The theme of Troy is combined with the theme of the wrath, and, though the poem expands and luxuriates as it advances, nothing would have happened in this way if Achilles had not at the start been angry with Agamemnon.

This complex subject is placed in a noble and well-balanced scheme. The *Iliad* begins with the wrath of Achilles and ends when that wrath is healed by the surrender of Hector's dead body to Priam. The first and the last books are constructed on similar plans. In each book Thetis intervenes with Zeus on behalf of her son, first to ask that he may gain honour by the defeat of the Achaeans, then that he may be allowed to end his wrath and give up Hector's body. Inside this frame events follow a well-designed plan. The first part tells what happens when Achilles abstains from battle, and this closes with the episode of the first embassy to him. The second part brings the disaster closer and ends with the death of Patroclus. The third is concerned with Achilles' return to battle, his slaying of Hector, and the funeral-games of Patroclus. Inside this frame there is a rich variety of episodes, and in many Achilles has no part. But no episode is without its import-

---

[1] *Ibid.* vi, 448.　　　　[2] *Ibid.* xxii, 410-11.

ance for the whole design. The most detailed account of this or that hero's actions in battle is always relevant because it shows how even the best warriors like Diomedes or Ajax are unable to stem the tide of Trojan advance or to take the place of the absent Achilles.

The design of the *Odyssey* is unlike that of the *Iliad*. When at the start the poet tells the Muse to sing of a man, he seems to suggest that he is going to tell of a hero's career in an episodic manner, but what he does is different. His story is of the return of Odysseus. It begins, so far as Odysseus is concerned, with the gods' decision to let him leave Ogygia, where he has been living with Calypso, and it ends with his final triumph over enemies at home and his union with his wife. It is thus in the main a straight-forward account of a hero's return after many years to his home and family. Aristotle sums up the plot correctly when he says:

A certain man has been abroad many years; Poseidon is ever on the watch for him, and he is all alone. Matters at home too have come to this, that his substance is being wasted and his son's death plotted by suitors to his wife. Then he arrives there himself after his grievous sufferings; reveals himself, and falls on his enemies; and the end is his salvation and their death.[1]

In the *Odyssey* there is no connection between the theme of the return and some wider issue, nor does the poet ever pass far from his hero, except for a clear purpose. Odysseus is always kept before our minds even when he is not on the stage. The characters are fewer and less various than in the *Iliad*, and there is no hint of great events menacing in the background. All is self-contained and complete; the theme of the hero's return dominates the poem from beginning to end.

Homer, however, elaborates this fundamental theme in more than one way. First, he evidently feels a need to show what Odysseus' absence from Ithaca means to his family and his friends. That is why he devotes the first four books to the fortunes of Odysseus' son, Telemachus. This enables us to see to what a plight Ithaca has come in its master's absence. The Suitors distress his wife, bully his son, and devour his substance. In due course they plot the death of Telemachus, and after that no one can feel it wrong that they should be killed by Odysseus. This picture of Ithaca is needed to show how much Odysseus is needed and what difficulties he will encounter when he arrives. But Homer does more than this. He sends Telemachus on a voyage to Nestor at Pylos and to Menelaus at Sparta to find out news of

[1] *Poetics*, 1455b, 17 ff. Trs. I. Bywater.

his father. The actual news that he finds is scanty, but the voyage does something else for the story. It shows how Telemachus, though little more than a boy, almost grows up as he gets away from home and his mother and is thereby the more ready to help his father when he returns. It also introduces us to important figures of the tale of Troy, like Nestor, Helen, and Menelaus, and incidentally fills in the gap between the point where the *Iliad* ends and the *Odyssey* begins. In various stories told by the characters we hear of the main events in the capture of Troy and the return of the Achaean heroes. This is an incidental gain. The first purpose of these early books is to set the stage and introduce the characters, so that, when Odysseus arrives, all is ready for him.

The *Odyssey* also employs a second device to which there is no real parallel in the *Iliad*. After leaving Ogygia Odysseus does not go straight home. He is shipwrecked on Phaeacia, and in addition to having a royal welcome there, which ends in his receiving gifts appropriate to the returned wanderer, he tells the story of his wanderings between the departure from Troy and his arrival at Ogygia. In this scheme Homer gains two advantages. First, the whole episode of Odysseus' time in Phaeacia is not only of great brilliance and beauty but provides a remarkable contrast to what he is going to find in Ithaca. The Phaeacians seem to enjoy an endless holiday and to have no troubles or difficulties, and it is characteristic of Odysseus that, while he is there, his mind is always on his return home. The Phaeacian splendours leave him cold. Secondly, the story which Odysseus tells covers a number of adventures, which if told in the leisurely manner of the main narrative would take up a great deal of time and upset the balance of the main design. As it is, their method of narration is always crisper than the main story. Moreover, Homer varies the scale of the individual adventures with some skill. The Lotus-eaters and the Laestrygonians are each dismissed in a few lines, while the visit to the Cyclops and the summoning of the ghosts at the end of the world are displayed with considerably more detail. In this there is a great advantage. If each episode had been related at full length, the accumulative effect might have been rather stupefying, while the variation of scale makes some of the adventures look like rather minor affairs which Odysseus, with characteristic disregard of danger, does not think worthy of more than a brief mention.

The *Iliad* and the *Odyssey*, then, are in their different ways skilfully contrived compositions, whose structure is more advanced than that of the Jugoslav and Kara-Kirghiz epics. But all four cases show that an oral poem may be well and nobly shaped and that it is not only literary poets who know how to compose on a large scale. Of course in all four cases the traditional devices of oral poetry are very much in evidence. The themes which give body to *Osman Delibegović* come largely from the stock material of improvising bards. Its arrivals, journeys, feasts, battles, and the like are all traditional and expressed to a large degree in formulaic language. Much the same is true of *Manas*, with its single combats, sports, journeys, and festivals. Nor are the *Iliad* and the *Odyssey* lacking in similar elements, though perhaps they treat them more economically or with a more adventurous spirit. All four poems do more than this in their elaboration of subjects which may not be mechanical but are common enough in heroic poetry, like the gathering of armies, the enumeration of men and horses, the meeting of persons long separated, the rich rewards given for heroic exploits, the relations between husbands and wives or fathers and sons, the faithfulness of old retainers, and the stored wisdom of elderly warriors. These poems are all products of long traditions of oral poetry. The poets are able to compose on this scale because they have at their disposal a language fitted to almost any need, a large number of helpful devices to speed the story, and an equally large number of topics which may be introduced when occasion demands.

These poems have risen from a tradition designed for poems less extensive, and they show the marks of this origin. The bards in each case know the art of the short lay and make use of it in their full epics. This can be seen most clearly in the apparently independent character of many episodes. The poet starts an episode and deals with it so completely that there is no reason why it should not be taken and recited as a separate poem. This is, for instance, the case with the meeting between Osman and Jusuf. It is the theme of the lost relative who comes back and is warmly welcomed and handsomely entertained. The attack on Osek is an equally self-contained story which can be enjoyed without any knowledge of what precedes or follows it. The same is true of many parts of *Manas*. The plot of the khans against Manas and his humiliation of them is an admirable tale about a hero and his unruly subordinates. Alaman Bet's adventures are all equally enjoyable for their own sake, and so indeed are the great single fights in which Manas shows his prowess. The same applies to the *Iliad*. The careers on the battlefield, while Achilles is away, of the various Achaean warriors, the scenes between Glaucus and Diomedes or Hector and Andromache, the funeral-games of Patroclus, the ransoming of Hector's body, may be enjoyed as separate poems and keep much of their art. Homer introduces them abruptly and then carries them through with so keen a concentration that they are entirely satisfying in themselves. This does not mean that such episodes were originally composed separately and then incorporated into the great poem. No doubt many of them were told often either by the poet himself or by other poets, and that may account for some elements in his technique. But he has retold them to suit his commanding plan and fitted them into it. In doing so he still keeps many traces of the old art which belonged to the short lay. In the *Odyssey* this is less obvious. Odysseus' wanderings may have once been material for separate lays and can still be enjoyed as such. So to some extent can parts of Telemachus' voyage, but on the whole the *Odyssey* shows fewer traces of this technique than the *Iliad*, and it is tempting to think that Homer, who knew of the art of the short lay, used it to some degree in the *Iliad* but passed largely beyond it in the *Odyssey*.

X

TRADITION AND TRANSMISSION

HEROIC poetry is maintained by a tradition, in the sense that its exponents learn their craft from their elders and practise it in much the same way. This craft includes a knowledge not merely of metre and formulae but of stories, themes, and literary devices. A poem once composed and recited is usually lost, unless by some rare chance someone writes it down. None the less the same story will be told again and again, in slightly different forms, by the same bard and by other bards, and may in these conditions have a life of many centuries. We may therefore speak of the transmission of poems, though it is not actual poems which are transmitted but their substance and their technique. Such a transmission is quite different from that of written texts in manuscripts, as has happened with the literature of Greece and Rome. Then one scribe copies a text, and in due course his copy is copied by another, until what was first written down before the Christian era survives in manuscripts from the Dark and Middle Ages. Heroic poems, like the *Iliad* and the *Odyssey*, may be written down in this way and raise their own problems about transmission, but that is not our immediate concern. The transmission of heroic poems normally happens not in writing but in recited words and presents its own special problems. At the start we may ask how this happens.

It is sometimes claimed that heroic poems are transmitted orally by being memorised and that, when a poet composes a poem, someone else learns it by heart, and this process goes on for centuries, without any help from writing and without seriously changing the texts. This is obviously quite a different thing from the way in which the Sons of Homer learned the Homeric poems in order to recite them, or the *jongleurs* of mediaeval France learned *chansons de geste*. In these cases a written text is presupposed, and the Sons of Homer or the *jongleurs* consult it. In most cases written texts do not exist, and the bard is supposed to learn complete poems by heart through hearing them recited. This may be a possible thing to do, but there is little evidence that it is actually done. In their thorough analysis of the subject the Chadwicks are unable to find any authentic cases where such a process is applied to heroic poetry. It is true that genealogies are memorised and preserved for long periods in Africa and Polynesia, but a genealogy is not a heroic poem, and the accurate preservation of it is demanded for political and family reasons.[1] On the face of it memorisation of heroic poetry seems unlikely. The tendency in all countries where we can check it is to pass on the substance of a poem but not its exact words, and this seems entirely natural. There is, however, one case which is certainly exceptional if it is correctly reported. Rastko Petrović describes an epic poem which he heard in the Sudan :

If it had not been for Vuillé, I would never have known of the importance and meaning of Koulikoro. I would have avoided this place as all other travellers have, which has the same meaning for the negroes as it has for us. It was here that Vuillé discovered the great epic of Sumanguru and wrote it down. The legend had it that in this village, whose name means " under the mountain ", a decisive battle took place between Sundujat, the Moslem leader and chief of the Malinka, and Sumanguru, the leader of the Fetichists and chief of the Bambara. This battle must have taken place in the 12th or 13th century. Sumanguru was killed at Koulikoro, after being defeated, according to Malinka tradition, but unconquerable, according to the Bambara. A special group of singers, old men called Djale, sing the glory of Sumanguru, the hero of the Fetichists, to the accompaniment of a native violin, which they strike as if it were a *tambura*. The epic is about ten thousand lines long and in an archaic tongue, and it is handed from father to son in specific families. The neighbouring tribes also know the whole epic by heart, word for word, though they do not understand a word of it.[2]

This looks impressive, but a closer examination suggests doubts. First, though the Bambara assert that the poem has been passed down unchanged for a thousand years, they have no possible means of knowing that it has. Indeed primitive peoples are likely to make such assertions just because the poem is traditional. Moreover, in such a period it must have suffered considerable changes and can hardly have kept its primitive form. The Bambara's idea of passing down a poem word for word may mean no more than that the main outlines of a story are passed on. Secondly, it is surely unlikely that neighbouring tribes, who do not know the Bambara language, should know the whole poem by heart. They may know some of its phrases or some of its contents, but Vuillé's statement on this point is highly questionable. It seems much more probable that the tale of Koulikoro has been transmitted in the same way as other subjects of heroic song and, though it may have a history of

[1] Chadwick, *Growth*, iii, p. 867 ff.
[2] R. Petrović, *Afrika* (Belgrade, 1930), p. 190 ff. I owe this reference to Mr. A. B. Lord.

eight hundred years, the chances are that in this period it has suffered many changes. With this dubious exception it seems clear that heroic poems are not transmitted from generation to generation by being memorised.

Another exceptional but better authenticated kind of transmission is when a poet is able to read and has at his disposal poems in written texts, which he uses as the basis for his own work. This is different from the mere copying of texts, such as must have happened to the Homeric poems after their first recording, or to *Beowulf* in the interval between its first recording about 700 and the existing manuscript of about 1000. It means that a poem still has its chief life through recitation and remains oral but that the poet uses material which he has gathered from books. This is certainly the case with *Gilgamish*. The study here is not simple owing to the mutilated condition of the tablets, but we can at least compare the Assyrian text, which was written in the seventh century B.C. and is the longest and best preserved, with the remains of the Old Babylonian text, which was written about 2000 B.C. It is clear that, though there are minor points of difference, there is on the whole a great similarity both in main outlines and in details. For instance, when Enkidu mourns the loss of his love after the fight with Gilgamish, Gilgamish comforts him with almost the same words in both versions. Such a similarity can be explained only by the Assyrian poet knowing something of the old version. This need not have been the precise Babylonian text which we have, but he must have derived much from some text very like it. This did not prevent him from making his own changes, and adapting the old story to suit his own taste, but the fact that in the seventh century *Gilgamish* has so much in common with the Old Babylonian version shows what books can do to maintain a tradition of heroic poetry.

The relevance of written texts also concerns *Roland*. The Oxford manuscript may be dated to about 1160 and the poem which it contains seems to have been composed very shortly before, about 1158.[1] We have here, then, a text written very soon after the composition of a poem, but the poem itself is not the first on the subject and owes something to earlier works which the author must have known from written texts. There is no difficulty about this in the eleventh century, when writing was common in clerical circles, and *Roland* may have a clerical origin. The poet seems to have drawn on two sources. The first was an earlier poem, which may have been composed about 1000 and have passed into a wide

[1] Mireaux, p. 82 ff.

currency, no doubt in different forms, like the *cantilena Rollandi* which was sung at Hastings in 1066. From this the poet of our *Roland* seems to have derived the main outlines of his story except for the episode of Baligant. But in addition to this he seems to have used a more mysterious source, to which he refers more than once :

> In Chronicles of Franks is written down (1443)
> In charters and in briefs is written clear (1683)
> *Gesta Francor'* these thirty columns prove (3262)
> Written it is, and in an ancient geste (3742).

If the poet is to be believed, and there is no reason why he should not, he used a *Gesta Francorum* as a source for certain elements in his story. Moreover, he tells us something about it :

> So tell the tale, he that was there says thus,
> The brave Saint Giles, whom God made marvellous,
> Who charters wrote for th' Minster at Loüm ;
> Nothing he's heard that does not know this much. (2095-8)

The poet asserts that he uses a work written by St. Giles, who was present at Roncesvalles. We do not know whether this book was in prose or in verse, but its title suggests prose, and in that case the poet will have versified some of its contents. But what was it? Since St. Giles is often connected with the story of Roland, this may have been an imaginary account of the battle, purporting to be written by the saint either as a witness present at it or from a vision. In that case it would bear some resemblance to the *Chronicle of Turpin*, which Bédier connects with the pilgrimage-routes to Santiago da Compostella and assigns to the middle of the twelfth century.[1] For men of that age a book ascribed to St. Giles would carry considerable authority, and we can hardly doubt that the poet of *Roland* used the *Gesta Francorum* to supplement what he learned from an earlier poem or poems on Roncesvalles.

In modern times there is naturally a greater chance than in the past that bards will learn from books. In Russia, where until recently the mass of the population was illiterate, there were exceptions even at the beginning of the nineteenth century, when Trofim Ryabinin's teacher, Ivan Kokozhin, transcribed *byliny* in St. Petersburg and used to read them in his own village,[2] and it is at least possible that Ryabinin learned some of his subjects from him. In modern times Marfa Kryukova and other Russian bards are able to read, and this certainly helps them in the composition of poems on contemporary themes like Kryukova's *Tale of Lenin*.

[1] Bédier, *Légendes*, iii, p. 42 ff. ; *Commentaire*, p. 26 ff.
[2] Chettéoui, p. 16.

The famous Uzbek bard, Ergash Dzhumanbulbul (1870–1938), learned to read after he had grown up and picked up new themes from books.[1] None the less it is noteworthy that these modern bards continue, despite their reading, to maintain the traditional manner and technique, since after all, though they may themselves be able to read, their art remains oral and is directed to listening and largely illiterate audiences. That is why it must maintain old methods and ways. On the whole, books play little part in the transmission of heroic poetry. They may sometimes intervene and create an unusual situation for it, but normally it lives by word of mouth.

The beginnings of nearly all heroic poetry are lost for us in a remote and unrecorded past. In most cases the earliest examples come from societies where it is already well established and has found its own character. Its first known appearance among the Germanic peoples is in the region east of the Rhine at the beginning of the Christian era. Writing his *Germania* in A.D. 98 Tacitus says that the Germans celebrate their gods " in ancient songs, which are the only kinds of records and annals which they possess ".[2] This proves at least that the Germans had songs which took the place of records and may have resembled the lays of the gods in the *Elder Edda*. But that they were not confined to the gods is clear from Tacitus' next statement that such songs told of the origin of the Germanic tribes. Nor were these their only subjects. For elsewhere, speaking of Arminius, prince of the Cherusci, Tacitus says " he is still sung among barbarian peoples ",[3] that is, Germans. There can be no doubt that in the first century A.D. the Germans had songs both about the mythical past and about recent heroes like Arminius, who was born about 18 B.C. and died in A.D. 16. Before this we know nothing, but it is clear that in Germany heroic poetry was a well-established art at the beginning of the first century, though it may even then have had a long past behind it.

The Slavonic peoples present a more complex problem. The first Russian poems seem to go back to Vladimir II, prince of Kiev, in the twelfth century, but possibly not much before him, since the wise Boyan, to whom the *Tale of Igor's Raid* refers, seems to have been a shamanistic bard,[4] and no stories can be traced back to events before this time. In Jugoslavia heroic poetry certainly existed before Kosovo in 1389, since it tells of Tsar Dušan, who reigned from 1331 to 1356; and Nicephorus Gregoras, who in

[1] Zhirmunskii-Zarifov, p. 45.
[2] *Germania*, 3.
[3] *Annals*, ii, 88.
[4] Cf. *sup*. p. 18.

1326 travelled in the land of the Serbs with a Greek mission to their ruler, Stjepan Uroš, describes how on a night in the valley of the Strumica some of his followers sang " about famous men of whose glorious deeds he heard, but saw nothing ".[1] With Kosovo Serbian poetry reached its heroic maturity, but there is no need to think that it was then more than a century old. On the other hand, it is possible that both it and Russian poetry are ultimately derived from a common Slavonic original, since both use very similar noun-adjective combinations, which are so undistinguished that they suggest a single source, and both use a peculiar kind of negative comparison which does the work of a simile and is not to be found elsewhere except in some regions which have been under Slavonic influence.[2] On the other hand it is clear that the division between the two kinds of poetry must have come very early, not merely because the Slavs were split into northern and southern divisions in the eighth century, but because the vast difference between the free Russian metre and the trochaic Jugoslav ten-syllable and sixteen-syllable lines indicates an early breach of the ancient technique. Indeed, if there was once an original Slavonic poetry, it is more likely to have been shamanistic than heroic, since no heroic stories seem to be common to the Russians and the Jugoslavs. So far as our very inadequate evidence allows us to judge, heroic poetry appeared in Russia in the eleventh or twelfth century with the political emergence of Kiev, and in Serbia in the thirteenth or fourteenth with the consolidation of the Serbian kingdom.

Far more ancient that any of these is the poetry of the Semitic peoples of Asia, of which the chief remains are *Gilgamish* and the Canaanite (Ugaritic) poems from Ras Shamra. Since the earliest tablets of *Gilgamish* are in Old Babylonian and date from before 2000 B.C., it is our oldest surviving specimen. Its high accomplishment suggests that it comes from a well-established tradition, but of this we know nothing. All that we can say is that since the story of the flood, which is told by Uta-Napishtim in *Gilgamish*, goes back to a Sumerian story of the fourth millennium, some of the material used is extremely ancient. But this material need not be heroic. Uta-Napishtim is not a hero as Gilgamish is, and his story seems rather to come from some religious poem of a kind which may well have existed in Babylonia hundreds of years before a heroic outlook developed and demanded its own kind of poetry. The Canaanite poems from Ras Shamra, notably *Aqhat* and *Keret*, come from the thirteenth century B.C., but since they

---

[1] *Byzantine History*, viii, 14.　　　　　[2] Cf. *sup.* p. 270.

are closely related to religious poems and are indeed contemporary with purely religious pieces like *Baal and 'Anat*, it is tenable that among the Canaanites heroic poetry was still of recent growth and that we need not assume any very long tradition behind it.

When we turn to the Tatar peoples of Asia, we find that it is possible to date an early appearance of their heroic poetry. The heroic spirit is already clear in poems from the river Orkhon, a tributary of the Yenisei, inscribed on graves of the eighth century A.D. They celebrate the doings of Bilga-kagan and his brother, Kul-tegin, and make the dead ruler speak in the first person with such words as

> " I did not sleep at night,
> I did not know rest by day,
> I united our tribes,
> I did not allow them to fight with each other
> As water fights with flames." [1]

There is almost a hint of a future language for heroic poetry in such a passage as this about Kul-tegin :

> " Before everyone on Tadik-churi's gray horse
> He hurled himself to battle ;
> Then and there that horse fell.
> A second time he hurled himself to battle
> On the gray horse of Ishbar-yamtar ;
> That horse also fell.
> A third time he mounted the saddled bay horse
>   of Iegin-silig-bey ;
> That horse also fell.[1]

This is the technique not of epitaphs or even of panegyrics but of heroic narrative. To this time, when the various Tatar tribes were united under a powerful ruler, may belong the formation of their heroic poetry.

A little later it is undeniably in existence. The admirable philologist, Mahmud of Kashgar, who flourished in the second half of the eleventh century, knew certain pieces of old Tatar heroic poetry which he quotes in translation. Their matter goes back to the time of Bilga-kagan, and they themselves cannot be much later. One piece tells of the conquest of the Tanguts, who lived between the Uigurs and China, between 762 and 850 ; another of a war between the Mohammedan Turks and the Buddhistic Uigurs and comes from soon after 840. In these poems there is a fierce, wild spirit which delights in battle and glory. The poets go straight to the point and convey the delirious delight of battle :

[1] Zhirmunskii-Zarifov, p. 9.

> At night we fell upon them,
> From every side we surrounded them;

or

> In anger like a lion I fell on my foe,
> I roared, I cut off warriors' heads;
> Who dares now to stand against me?

or

> His wound was grievous,
> Blood flowed and hardened;
> Though wounded, he climbed to the top of a hill;
> Who now can overtake him? [1]

The metre of these poems is usually the seven- or eight-syllabled line still used by most Tatar peoples, and we can see in them the remote ancestors of Tatar poems collected in the last hundred years.

In Armenia the beginnings of heroic poetry are hard to discern. It centres round David of Sasoun, who reigned in the tenth century, and to this at least the tradition must go back. But it is certainly older. If the fragments on Vaagn and Artashes [2] are too magical to be admissible as evidence, the same cannot be said about a piece of some 280 lines contained in the *Armenian History* of Pavstos Byuzandatsi about Shapukh, king of Persia, and Arshak, king of Armenia, who lived in the fourth century. When this was composed, the shamanistic outlook had given place to something more human and more heroic, which values the high doings of men for their own sake. It is realistic and factual and yet noble and impressive, especially in the scene where the two kings meet on soil brought from both their countries:

> Such was the law,
> That the Persian and Armenian kings
> Should sit together on a single throne.
> On that day some guests had seated themselves;
> All the kings who were there sat on high,
> But afterwards, lower than all, lower than all,
> On earth which had been brought from Armenia,
> The people of Arshak sat.
> According to rank they all sat at first,
> Last of all they sate Arshak.
> There Arshak sat, insulted, but not for long.
> He arose and cried to king Shapukh:
> " Where are you sitting? That is my place!
> Away from it! I will sit there myself!
> That is the immemorial place of the Armenian king!
> When I return home,
> I shall take cruel vengeance for everything! "

[1] *Idem*, p. 11.   [2] Arutyunyan, p. 39.

375   2 B

The Persian king Shapukh
Bade a chain be put on Arshak's neck
And his hands and legs be bound in irons.
He commanded him to be imprisoned in the fortress of Andmish,
Which is now called Anush.
There the Armenian king was kept for all his days.[1]

This poem comes from the heyday of Armenian heroic song. It has an aristocratic independence, which is not afraid of telling a story against its own side and lacks the self-conscious patriotism of later Armenian poems. When this was written, Armenia had discovered what heroic poetry is and could produce poets able to write it.

In these cases there are at least some indications that heroic poetry existed at a certain time and is therefore at least as old as that. Unfortunately, in other cases we have not even so much information as this. The poetry of the Kalmucks presents a peculiar problem. It is possible that it is ultimately derived from the same source as that of the Tatar peoples, but has gone its own way because the Kalmucks were Buddhists while the Tatar peoples were Mohammedans. But it seems unlikely that this is the case, since the manners and technique of Kalmuck poetry have very little in common with those of the Tatars. The poems give very few indications of time, and we do not know when, if ever, Dzhangar and his forty warriors lived. If Khongor lived, as is possible, about 1500,[2] the poems would be at least as old as that. But they may well be older. The kingdom of Dzhangar, as described in the poems, seems to reflect historical conditions of the thirteenth and fourteenth centuries.[3] The kingdom of Bumba coincides, so far as can be seen, with the historical realm of Mongol princes who ruled over Tibet and Tangut. With this the social system of the poems agrees. Dzhangar is the head of a feudal system, described as " four ruling councils " and " four independent peoples ", a state of affairs which hardly survived the Mongol conquest of China, and suggests that the Kalmuck poems are derived from a time in the thirteenth century or earlier before the Yüan dynasty ruled in Peking. It may well have older antecedents than this, but nothing is known of them.

The origins of Greek heroic poetry are equally matter for conjecture. If Homer refers to bards older than himself, like Thamyris, they may well be fictitious, and the same may be said of other bards, like Orpheus, whom Greek legend regarded as

---

[1] Arutyunyan, p. 44 ff.   [2] Cf. *inf*. p. 518.
[3] S. A. Kozin in *Dzhangariada*, p. 78 ff.

pioneers in the art of song. On the other hand the siege of Troy may well be a historical fact. The site known as VIIA at Hissarlik contains the remains of a city destroyed by fire about 1200 B.C.[1] Hittite records of the fourteenth century indicate that at this period the Achaeans (Ahhijawa) were powerful and busy in Asia Minor,[2] and since Troy guards the best and easiest route from Europe to Asia, it is not surprising if they attacked it.[3] Such an event may well have captured the imagination and become a subject for heroic song at an early date, and in that case the tradition which Homer inherited will go back at least to the twelfth century. It may indeed be older than this. There are indications that Homer knew of certain things whose memory can only have survived through poetry, notably the wealth of Egyptian Thebes,[4] which belongs to the middle of the fourteenth century, the strange kingship of Minos in Crete [5] which must go back at least to the late Mycenean age, the use for gods of adjectives derived from birds and animals, certain pieces of armour such as Odysseus' helmet covered with swine-teeth,[6] the cup of Nestor with doves carved on it,[7] dim memories of embalming the dead.[8] It has even been argued with some persuasiveness that the dactylic hexameter with its many artificialities of scansion and its unusual system of equating dactyls with spondees in a " falling " rhythm, comes from a language which was not even Indo-European, and has been adapted to Greek with some difficulty.[9] Without postulating any great dependence on pre-Greek poetry, which may well have been shamanistic and not heroic, we may at least assume that Greek heroic poetry, which found its full flower in Homer, is at least as old as the heroic age which the Greeks themselves placed in the thirteenth and twelfth centuries. A tradition which told of the siege of Troy and of other great events not far removed from it in date could survive best in poetry, and to this poetry, with all its resources and material, Homer must owe much of his own art.

There remain one or two cases in which the origin of a tradition is not so much obscure as disputed, in that a certain amount of evidence exists but has been very variously interpreted. The first case is Spain. Our main document, the *Cid*, was composed about 1140 and shows what heroic epic was. Nor is it the only specimen of its kind. Fragments of other poems have been reconstituted

---

[1] Lorimer, p. 36. [2] *Idem*, p. 88.
[3] Bowra, *T.D.* p. 156 ff. [4] *Od.* iv, 125 ff. ; cf. Lorimer, pp. 95-9.
[5] *Od.* xix, 179. [6] *Il.* x, 261-5.
[7] *Ibid.* xi, 632-7. [8] *Ibid.* vii, 85 ; xvi, 456, 674.
[9] A. Meillet, *Les Origines indo-européennes des mètres grecs* (Paris, 1923), pp. 37-71.

from chronicles which have incorporated them so completely that reconstruction is easy and relatively certain. Thus to the *First General Chronicle of Spain* we owe the relics of four poems, on the seven Infantes of Lara, the siege of Zamora, Bernardo del Carpio, and Count Fernán González. All these are concerned with Castile and suggest that Spanish heroic poetry was mainly a Castilian art. But how old this art is has not been settled. It is unlikely that it goes back to the Germanic poems of the Visigothic conquerors and their descendants, since it has very little in common with what we know of Germanic song. Nor on the other hand does it seem to be a late invention, derived from the French *chansons de geste*, since it differs greatly from them in its metre which is rough and ready and has no regular number of syllables. Perhaps the simplest solution is that it came into existence in the tenth century, since some of the poems record events of this time, like the seven Infantes of Lara, who are connected with events of 980, and Fernán González, who died in 970. It is true that the Spanish tradition would be much older if it went back to certain events of the eighth century with which it deals. In the *Chronica Gothorum*, falsely attributed to St. Isidore, there is a story of the daughter of Count Julian which is based on a poem and claims to tell of events connected with the fall of the Gothic monarchy in 711. But this is pure romance, the invention of a later age, which has reached its present stage after a devious course through various chronicles. We cannot safely put the beginnings of Spanish poetry much before the beginning of the tenth century. And that, after all, is a likely time for it, since by then the language had begun to settle into its new shape and to escape from its late Latin roots. Since too this was a time when the northern kingdoms began to take shape, and men's thoughts turned to campaigns against the Moors, it would be a suitable period for the emergence of a heroic spirit like that which Charlemagne had encouraged a century earlier in France. The metre remains a mystery, but it is at least possible that it was derived from metrical lives of saints and the like, which were in currency soon after 800, and would naturally be used by poets who had quite different stories to tell but no other form ready to hand.

The origins of French heroic poetry have occasioned much debate. The fundamental difference between the French tradition and others is that the story of Roncesvalles, as told in *Roland*, does not derive from an oral tradition but from some literary source such as Egginhard's Life of Charlemagne, and the same is true to some extent of most other French heroic subjects. *Roland* was certainly composed some centuries after the battle of 778, and it is clear that the gap was not bridged by any tradition of heroic poetry and that all efforts to prove the existence of *cantilenae* or the like are futile. On this point the destructive criticism of Joseph Bédier has been merciless. Each alleged poem from the vital period has been discredited, and it is now all but certain that French heroic poetry did not emerge before the eleventh century, but in this century the figure of Roland comes into great prominence, and it is natural to conclude that this is due to some poem about him. This poem is not that of the Oxford manuscript, which is not likely to be earlier than 1158, but seems to have been known to our poet. We have first to establish the emergence of Roland and then try to find an explanation for it.

By the end of the eleventh century Roland has become the type of what a soldier ought to be. When Raoul of Caen praises two crusaders, he compares them to Roland and Oliver.[1] When between 1090 and 1110 Raoul le Tourtier tells the story of Ami and Amile, he speaks of the sword which Charlemagne gave to Roland.[2] When Robert Guiscard lay on his death-bed in 1085, he compared Bohemond with Roland.[3] Between 1086 and 1106 Gérard de Montalais had two sons called Roland and Oliver.[4] At the consecration of the church of Saint-Pé-de-Génerés in 1096 two men called by these names were present,[5] and would have received the names some time before. A " cantilena Rollandi " is said to have been sung at Hastings.[6] A charter of Saint-Victor-de-Marseille, dated to 1055, names as witnesses two men called Roland and Oliver,[7] who would hardly have been so christened if the heroes had not already been famous towards the beginning of the eleventh century. These scattered scraps of evidence indicate beyond doubt that Roland came into fame soon after 1000. Before that date he is not known except in Egginhard's reference, but after it he has a renown which spreads to most parts of Europe. In this interval French heroic poetry seems to have come into existence.

In France, then, we are confronted with a special situation. Heroic poetry is not descended from an ancient traditional art but comes suddenly to life on a large scale. Its creation must have been, if not actually deliberate, at least forced by very special

[1] *Historiens des croisades occidentales*, iii, p. 627.
[2] *Epist.* ii, 229 ff.
[3] Ordericus Vitalis, ed. Prévost et Delisle, iii, p. 185.
[4] Mireaux, p. 109.
[5] M. F. Lot, *Romania*, liv (1928), p. 379.
[6] William of Malmesbury, ed. Stubbs, iii, p. 302.
[7] Mireaux, p. 113.

circumstances. At some time in the eleventh century French heroic poetry was born in a way that seems to have no parallel elsewhere. In a society which did not cultivate lament or panegyric and had nothing resembling pre-heroic narrative stories of Charlemagne or other great kings and paladins, Roland appeared and made an enormous impression. This poetry evidently responded to a current belief that France was enjoying something like a heroic age and needed this resuscitation of the past to sustain it. We may well believe that this was partly due to the Crusades, which combined Christian fervour with tremendous prowess, and, though poems about Roland were almost certainly current some time before Peter the Hermit preached the First Crusade, they may be attributed to the growing interest in the wars against the Saracens in Spain. It is true that such wars were on no great scale, but they may still have captured the popular imagination. In 1015 Cluniac monasteries propounded the suggestion that to die in Saracen land in battle against the heathen was to win a martyr's crown; in 1018 Roger I of Tosny led his Normans on such an enterprise; in 1033 Burgundians enrolled by Odilon, abbot of Cluny, followed their example.[1] In such an atmosphere the story of Charlemagne, who had been a great Christian king and was reputed to have conquered Spain, provided an inspiring precedent, and it may well be that this was responsible for the poems about Roland which came into existence at the time. As the century grew older, the crusading spirit grew more vigorous, and continued to thrive all through the next century. Our *Roland* comes from this time, and, though it derives its subject from the early enthusiasm for the invasion of Spain, it has been greatly strengthened by events which actually took place in Palestine. If it comes from the court of Henry II, that would be natural enough, since Henry's son, Richard Cœur de Lion, was to be one of the most eminent crusaders of his age, and Henry himself liked to claim kinship with men who fought for Charlemagne. In *Roland* the Crusades produced a poem which reflected their spirit and ideals.

Once heroic poetry has come into existence, it may take one or other of two courses. It may expand with an expanding people, until it covers a wide area of space and adapts itself to new linguistic conditions, when a language is broken into different branches, each of which becomes increasingly distinct and separate; or it can stay within a limited area and proceed on limited lines with no great change of either language or manner.

[1] Bédier, *Commentaire*, p. 15 ff.

The first alternative is well illustrated by the poetry of the Germanic peoples. If its first appearance is with Arminius, it is clear that in the next three or four centuries it had a vigorous life among most branches of the Germans. For the first part of this period our information is limited to the Goths, of whom their country-man, Jordanes, says that they used to celebrate the deeds of their famous men in songs which had an almost historical manner.[1] One such song told of the migration under Filimer to the Black Sea and may be as early as the second century;[2] another told of the king Ostrogotha, a contemporary of the Roman emperor, Philip the Arabian, who ruled from 244 to 249.[3] In the fourth century we may perhaps place the songs about Vidigoia, who was killed in battle against the Sarmatians.[4] At this period the Goths were on the move, and their successes inspired them to song.

In the fourth century and later our evidence is more varied. That the old art still existed on the Rhine, as it did in the time of Arminius, may perhaps be deduced from the words of the Emperor Julian, who, when soldiering on the frontier, noticed with distaste the barbarians' addiction to songs :

I notice the barbarians beyond the Rhine singing wild songs composed in language like the croaking of harsh-voiced birds, and rejoicing in their tunes.[5]

To this time must belong what looks like a Langobardic song preserved in a prose history about a battle between the Langobards and the Vandals.[6] Since in it the armies pray respectively to Wodan and Fria, it must be earlier than the conversion of the Langobards to Christianity about 400. In the next two centuries we hear of songs sung by Vandals, Franks, and Bavarians, and we can hardly resist the conclusion that at this period heroic poetry was the favourite art of the Germanic peoples. From the continent it spread to the islands and there it found a new lease of life. If the Angles and Saxons practised it in their old homes, they brought it with them to England, while others took it first to Norway and then to Iceland and Greenland. In Germany itself it certainly continued to exist, although the only surviving testimony is the fragment of *Hildebrand*, which was written down about 800. None the less, stories survived and found their way into later poetry when it was being transformed into romance. In all these places the bards kept the old Germanic metre, even if they adapted it to the

---

[1] *Getica*, 5. [2] *Ibid.* 40. [3] *Ibid.* 4. [4] *Ibid.* 34.
[5] *Misopogon*, ed. Hertlein, p. 434.
[6] *Origo Gentis Langobardorun*, ed. Pertz, p. 2 ; cf. Paulus Diaconus, *Hist. Lang.* i, 8 ; cf. *sup.* p. 24.

needs of new languages, and at the same time remained faithful to the great stories of the fifth and sixth centuries. Though the Germanic art spread far and wide, it kept its identity and essential characteristics.

To this development Tatar poetry provides a kind of parallel. If it came into existence in Siberia on the river Orkhon, it spread far from there and had a varied history. Its chief exponents to-day are the Kara-Kirghiz, the Uzbeks, and the Yakuts, but it has also been practised to some degree by the Turcomans, the Kazaks, and the Crimean Tatars. It is true that the Turcomans now prefer prose saga to verse and that the Kazaks tend to mix the two, but some stories survive in different forms among all the different peoples, and the original form of verse is still used. In this development the Yakuts have tended to go their own way, no doubt because they are isolated in the frozen fastnesses of Northern Siberia. But apart from this the Turkic art has kept its main lines and seems to have done so for some time. One or two instances serve to show how it has worked and flourished. The Persian historian, Rashid-ad-Din, writing in the thirteenth century, knows of a poem about Oguz-khan and his six sons, each of whom has a mythological name, his own totem, and his own seal.[1] Writing about 1660, Abulglazi also knows of Oguz-khan and quotes some lines which show how the poets treated him :

> He was a ruler, he built a golden house,
> In rivalry with it the sky was ashamed ;
> He drove 900 horses and 9000 sheep.[2]

The same Abulglazi knew of poems about Alpamys, who is still a favourite with Uzbek bards. Like the Germanic, the Turkic peoples have carried their heroic poetry over vast tracts of country, but managed to keep its main character intact.

Expansion of this kind is governed by historical and geographical conditions and is not always on this scale. For instance, though the ancient Greeks spread to many parts of the Mediterranean and Black Seas, their poetry seems never to have taken on new leases of life in new dialects as the Germanic and Tatar poetry did. Inside its own world it spread to relatively distant countries. The poet Magnes, who lived at the court of the Lydian king, Gyges (c. 685–652), wrote a poem about a war between the Lydians and the Amazons ;[3] Stasinus of Cyprus is one of several poets credited with the composition of the *Cypria* ;[4] Eugammon of Cyrene

---

[1] Zhirmunskii-Zarifov, p. 14.   [2] *Idem*, p. 15.
[3] Nicolaus Damasc. fr. 62.   [4] Athenaeus, 334b.

wrote his *Telegony* as a sequel to the *Odyssey* in the sixth century.[1]
But since Greek did not break into different new languages and
remained restricted to a certain area, it did not encourage new
developments in the Germanic and Tatar manner. Indeed, it is
hard to see how a technique so elaborate and well adjusted as the
Homeric could have been adjusted to changes of language. On
the other hand we may surmise that the substance of Greek poetry
was taken over at least by the Etruscans, whose mirrors and vases
and paintings show a wide acquaintance with Greek heroic legend,
and it is quite possible that other " barbarians ", like the people of
Tartessus, had a similar interest in it. It may also have touched
Rome, since the story of the Dioscuri in the battle of Lake Regillus
is very similar to the Greek story of their appearance at the battle of
the Sagra at some date before 500 B.C.

These cases, where a tradition is passed by one people to
another who speak a different language and may have no ethnic
or linguistic connection with them, present a special problem.
Such is the remarkable case of *Gilgamish*. The story belongs to the
Semitic peoples, and the earliest fragments of the poem are in Old
Babylonian (Akkadian). Gilgamish himself is a Babylonian hero,
connected with the city of Erech, since an inscription earlier than
the time of Hammurabi (*c.* 2000 B.C.) tells how Anan-am " restored
the walls of Erech built of old by Gilgamish ".[2] Behind the story
in its surviving form is the much older story of the flood, which is
Sumerian and may predate the earliest fragments of the poem by
some fifteen hundred years. So even in its first Babylonian stage
the tale of Gilgamish has absorbed some Sumerian elements.
From Babylon the poem passed to other countries, notably to the
Hittites of Asia Minor, whose language is almost certainly Indo-
European and certainly not Semitic, while the Hittites themselves
were mountain-dwelling warriors very unlike the Babylonians.
Perhaps the story was taken up there because the Hittites had
adopted the cuneiform script and would thus be able to read
Babylonian documents, among which texts of *Gilgamish* in some
form may well have been included. From about 1500 B.C. come
fragments of *Gilgamish* in Hittite and another dialect from the
same part of Asia. The next appearance is in the seventh century
when the library of Assurbanipal in Nineveh provides a text in
Assyrian. Finally, there are a few fragments later than this in
New Babylonian. This is an adventurous history, and of course
Gilgamish, of which we know almost by accident, may well have

[1] Allen, v, p. 109.
[2] R. Campbell-Thompson, *C.A.H.* i, p. 562.

383

been popular elsewhere. Perhaps the reason is that it was early recorded in writing and that Babylonian texts were studied and imitated both by Hittites and Assyrians. Even so it shows how a fine story may pass far from its place of origin and be adopted by strange peoples and new civilisations.

A more mysterious case of transmission can be seen in the Uzbek poem *Kun-batyr*, which we know from a prose version made by the bard Ergash from a poem which he heard in his youth. In this King Darius of Persia sends an army under his general Kaisar against Turania, which is ruled by the queen Oi-Sulu. He falls in love with her and wishes to marry her, but his proposals are rejected. War develops and the queen's son, Kun-batyr, is taken prisoner when he is drunk, but he escapes and joins his mother, who conducts the war. They find Kaisar on the battle-field and cut off his head, and soon afterwards kill Darius.[1] Now despite many differences of detail, this is surprisingly like the story of Cyrus and Tomyris, queen of the Massagetae, as it is told by Herodotus.[2] In his story Cyrus proposes marriage to Tomyris, but is rejected; her son, Spargapises, is captured when sleeping after heavy drink, and, though liberated later, kills himself; his mother continues the war, defeats the Persians, and, finding Cyrus' body on the battlefield, casts his head into a skin filled with blood which she has brought with her, and, while blaming him for the death of her son, says that he can now glut himself with blood. The two stories have too many points of similarity for them to be accidental. Even such small divergences, as when the Uzbek poet attributes to a general of Darius what Herodotus attributes to Cyrus, only confirm the conviction of some close connection, since what matters is that the villain should be a powerful Persian. The story does not occur elsewhere and has no signs of being a folk-tale. It may even be significant that while Herodotus says that the Massagetae call the sun " lord of the Massagetae ", the name Kun-batyr means " sun-warrior " and Oi-sulu " moon-beauty ". It is of course just possible that the bard from whom Ergash got the story had somehow become acquainted, not necessarily at first hand, with Herodotus' story, but this seems unlikely in Uzbekstan in the nineteenth century. It is more likely that the story is of great antiquity and has somehow survived in central Asia. It may of course have had help from Persian poets, to whose history it belongs and whose work often passes to the Uzbeks. But in any case it presents a nice problem in the transmission of heroic stories.

In the course of a long career a tradition may vary the degree

---

[1] Zhirmunskii-Zarifov, p. 128 ff.　　　　　[2] i, 208-14.

in which it admits the creation of new subjects or keeps its main attention for what is old and familiar. On the whole this seems to be decided by the extent to which poets and their patrons believe themselves to be living in a heroic age. If they think that every-thing about themselves and their friends is wonderful, that life is so rich and grand that it must somehow be celebrated, they will demand new poems on recent subjects. This was certainly the case with the Germanic peoples in the fourth, fifth, and sixth centuries from the death of Ermanaric in about 370 to the death of Alboin, king of the Langobards, in 572. The extent of heroic material which derives from this period may be seen from various references and epitomes, from the stories touched on incidentally in *Beowulf*, the great stock of Danish legends recorded by Saxo Grammaticus, the list of kings and peoples in *Widsith*. If we add to these records the large number of songs which must have existed outside the orbit of these writers, either because they were forgotten or because they were not concerned with western Europe but with the doings of Goths or Vandals in central Europe or Spain or Italy, we can form a vague idea of the scope of this poetry. What is particularly interesting about it is that it is on the whole confined to some two hundred years, and we may surmise why. If the death of Ermanaric marked the full flood of Germanic migrations under pressure from the Huns, the death of Alboin marked their end, since after it Europe, at least in the west and south, began to settle down and to take its future shape. In this case the outburst of songs on contemporary subjects was obviously related to the sense of adventure and power which came with the conquest of new territories and the division of the imperial Roman spoils.

A similar creative liveliness may be observed elsewhere on a smaller scale in somewhat different conditions. The modern Greeks have continued to compose τραγούδια from the eleventh century to the present day; the Jugoslavs, with certain breaks in the tradition, have been almost equally lively; the Uzbeks, despite their attachment to certain ancient stories, have enjoyed composing poems on modern affairs. We may doubt if any of these cases present a richness comparable to the Germanic, but it is clear that at any rate the bards continue to compose heroic songs because they believe themselves to be living more or less in a heroic age. Nor would anyone who knows these people really dispute this. In them the rule of honour is still paramount, and a man is respected for the risks which he takes and for his skill in over-coming them. On the other hand they preserve the relics of the past in a way which the Germanic peoples seem not to have done. The fact that *Widsith* knows nothing about Arminius or the Gothic heroes mentioned by Jordanes suggests that his authorities were not interested in them but preferred more recent events. In Germany the great heroic age largely obliterated earlier memories, but among the Greeks, the Jugoslavs, and the Uzbeks the past survives as an inspiration and example to the present, and one of the excuses for modern heroic songs is that they celebrate men who have behaved in the noble manner of their great ancestors and deserve similar honours.

In contrast to these fertile traditions we may set others where at a certain point bards seem to have given up celebrating the present and confined themselves entirely to an almost canonised and certainly limited past. This is the case among the ancient Greeks, the Norsemen of Iceland, the Armenians, the Kalmucks, and the Kara-Kirghiz. The Greeks possessed a mass of heroic legends about some four generations of which the heroes of Troy belong to the third. Beyond this they hardly ever strayed. With it their epic poets were almost entirely concerned, and when epic yielded to tragedy, the tragedians observed the same limits. Nor was this because the Greeks lacked thrilling events in their own time. It was rather because they regarded this heroic age as having a special quality and distinction which had been lost. This is clear enough from Homer who regards " men as they now are " [1] as necessarily inferior to the old heroes who had divine blood in their veins and consorted freely with gods in their homes and on the battlefield. In Iceland the poems of the *Elder Edda* are all concerned with events which took place on the Germanic mainland before 500. The age of the Vikings produced no heroic poetry for its appalling and fantastic achievements. The reason for this may be that the Icelanders held the legends of their first home in a peculiar veneration and felt that they must be preserved in a class of their own without modern additions. Great as their own deeds were, they had a colonial, nostalgic feeling for the old stories of their people, even though they concerned places which they had never seen and men with whom their own connection was remote and shadowy. Perhaps something of the same kind explains the conservatism of the Kalmucks, whose chief poems deal with the prince Dzhangar and his kingdom on the borders of Tibet. The bards who sing them live on the shores of the Caspian, whither the Kalmucks moved in the great migration of the seventeenth century. They know nothing of central Asia, and the

[1] *Il.* v, 304 ; xii, 383, 449 ; xx, 287.

past of which they sing belongs to no familiar system of history. But it is none the less their past, a treasure to be guarded jealously and not degraded by competition. The Armenian case is different. Though once the Armenians seem to have covered a wide range of subjects in their poetry, it is now confined to four generations of which David of Sasoun is in the third. Here perhaps something is due to the real decay of a heroic outlook. The Armenians may still be bellicose, but they are not heroes in any real sense. They look back with pride to a time when they were, and draw comfort from it. And after all this is natural enough in a people which has for some centuries been under either Russian or Turkish dominion. Finally, the Kara-Kirghiz seem to confine themselves to a cycle of poems round Manas and his son. Unlike the Armenians and like the Uzbeks, the Kara-Kirghiz are still in many senses a heroic people, despite the efforts of the Soviets to tame them. Their poems reflect a contemporary spirit but embody it in a distant past. This art is far more elastic and expansive than the *Elder Edda* and recalls rather the scope of Greek heroic stories. Perhaps the explanation is that the Kara-Kirghiz, feeling that they are no longer the great people which they once were, need the inspiration of the past to keep up their pride and confidence.

Between these two extreme methods of dealing with legends we may put two cases where a kind of compromise has been reached, the Anglo-Saxons and the Russians. In Anglo-Saxon England the main subjects of song were the old subjects that came from the continent. These provide the matter not only for *Beowulf*, *Finnsburh*, and *Waldhere*, but for the whole catalogue in *Widsith*. Though these extant poems seem to have been composed about 700, the art was still popular in the time of Alfred, who was educated on the old songs,[1] had them taught to his children,[2] and recommended others to learn the " Saxon lays " by heart.[3] That they were still popular at the time of the Norman Conquest is clear from a chronicler who writes after it :

In those days when Valentinian ruled as emperor or prince, the kingdom of the barbarians and Germans grew up. The rising peoples and nations settled through all Europe. To this witness the doings of Rudolf and Hunlaf, Unwen and Wudga, Horsa and Hengest, Waltef and Hama, of whom some in Italy, some in Gaul, others in Britain, others in Germany, were renowned for arms and warlike matters.[4]

We can hardly doubt that in England the main subjects of heroic song were derived from the original, continental stock. There is

[1] Asser, ed. Stevenson, c. 22.   [2] *Idem*, c. 75.   [3] *Idem*, c. 76.
[4] MS. Cotton, Vesp. DIV (fol. 139b), quoted by R. W. Chambers, *Widsith*, p. 254.

no trace of an English hero in *Beowulf*, except Offa, and even he lives on the continent; and if the Hengest of *Finnsburh* is the conqueror of Kent, the poet does not say so but sets his adventures in Friesland. On the other hand this solid core of traditional material is sometimes supplemented by poems on recent events, especially by *Brunanburh* in 937 and *Maldon* in 991, to say nothing of the short poems in the Anglo-Saxon Chronicle which tell about Edmund's reconquest of the five boroughs in 973, his death in 975, the death of Alfred, son of Ethelred, in 1036, and the death of Edward the Confessor in 1065. In the case of *Brunanburh* and *Maldon* no problem arises. We can well understand that battles of this kind were felt to be equal to any battle fought in the heroic age and demanded celebration in the same kind of song. The four pieces from the Chronicle are less easily explained, but perhaps their existence is ultimately due to Alfred's patronage of the old art and a feeling that the present must be celebrated in the same way, even though the poets lacked the old impetus and the authentic heroic spirit.

To this situation Russia presents something of a parallel. The heroic age of Russia centres round Vladimir of Kiev in the twelfth century. Nor is it difficult to understand why. At this time Kiev was an energetic and expanding power, which, while it derived its art, law, religion, and writing from Byzantium, kept much of the spirit of Rurik and his Norse companions in its conflicts with invading Tatars or Lithuanians. Kiev was surrounded by formidable enemies and survived for a while by its heroic achievements. This in itself would be enough to create the conviction that a heroic age existed, and to such no doubt the companions of Vladimir actually believed themselves to belong. When Kiev fell to the Mongols in 1250, its power came to an abrupt and violent end, and nothing took its place for over a century. In these circumstances Kiev became the centre of heroic stories, from which bards have ever since derived the greater part of their repertories. How much they owe to it can be seen from Trofim Ryabinin, who deals with only some .five subjects of later provenance. But gradually this main stock of stories has been supplemented by others about recent events. In most cases these tell of men like Ivan the Terrible or Ermak or Peter the Great, who have reasonable claims to be called heroic and who certainly captured the popular imagination by their adventurous achievements. The tales of Lenin and other heroes of the revolution in modern times may be explained on the same hypothesis.

Most heroic poems have behind them a long tradition, which

provides, among other useful aids, the main elements of the vocabulary which the poets use. Since this is shaped for the most part into formulae, it enables the poets to speak about times with which they have no personal acquaintance, and preserves, as it were, fossilised relics of past ages. This is made easier by the character of the language used in most heroic poetry. In very few countries is this the common speech of men; it has nearly always an element of artificiality, of selection and adaptation for the uses of poetry. Just as the Russian *byliny* use many archaic words and prefixes which have no real function, so the Anglo-Saxon poems contain elements which come from more than one dialect, and rejoice in kennings and paraphrases just because they are useful. Even in the short space of *Hildebrand* words from more than one dialect have been found, and it is as likely that this is a " Kunstsprache " as that it has been translated from one dialect into another. The classic case of such a language is that of Homer, which can never have been spoken by any man, not even in the island of Chios,[1] where Ionic and Aeolic elements met and mixed. The different forms of the genitive singular or the infinitive, the use or not at will of the augment, the variations in the use of the definite article, the many synonyms and the survival of archaic forms all point to an elaborately constructed language which was meant for poetry and for nothing else. Such languages would take time to create, and it is significant that the language of *Roland* is simpler and closer to the vernacular than that of heroic poems composed in other countries. A language so constructed might seem to present difficulties to the simple people who hear it, but in fact it does not; it is known to them from childhood and becomes familiar with usage. If for them it has the dignity of antiquity, for modern readers it is a repository of relics from a distant past.

It is possible that this conception of a " Kunstsprache " may throw light on some poems which scholars tend to treat as if they had passed through various stages and changes from one dialect to another. Such is *Beowulf*. It seems now to be generally agreed that it is composed in a kind of literary West Saxon, and no doubt this is partly due to the fact that our manuscript dates from about 1000 and presents in its spelling the forms current in monasteries at the time. But there are forms in the text which resist such treatment and keep their archaic individuality,[2] either because of their meaning or because the metre will not allow them

---

[1] This view is held by T. W. Allen, *Origins*, pp. 98-109.
[2] C. L. Wrenn, in Clark Hall, *Beowulf* (London, 1950), p. 12.

to be transformed and brought up to date. Such are words like *regnheard*, " wondrously strong " (326), and *ealuscerwen*, " panic " (769), or forms like the instrumental *wundini*, " twisted " (1382), or uncontracted forms, demanded by the metre, although current speech would have used contracted forms. The language of *Beowulf* suggests that, though many forms have been modernised superficially, other, older ones remain because sense or metre demand them. Something of the same kind is said to occur in the Kalmuck poems.[1] At the modern end we find a few obviously recent words, including a few from Russian, like *ura*, " hurrah ", *khan-knes* (" prince-khan "), *beder*, " cask ", but there are a large number of words and phrases, especially synonyms, which indicate a composite, artificial language. Silver is expressed in seventeen different ways, silk in eleven, sandalwood in five. Since these synonyms are very helpful to the metre, which uses both parallelism and a certain amount of rhyme, it seems clear that their survival is due to this reason. If we add to this the very large number of formulaic phrases and the relics of a past enshrined in them, we may be sure that this is no spoken vernacular but a language created for poetry and skilfully adapted to its needs and uses.

Through its formulae heroic poetry may maintain for centuries memories which would otherwise be lost. They need not necessarily be of anything very important, and indeed they usually are not. When a poetical tradition is young, it incorporates much that is commonplace enough in its day simply because this gives verisimilitude and solidity to its story, but gradually this passes out of use and is preserved by convention as an antique oddity. For instance, the Ossete poems tell of certain customs which are not to be found among the Ossetes of to-day but seem to be derived from a distant past. What this past is we may surmise from some illuminating parallels between customs described in the poems and others described by Herodotus as existing among the Scyths of what is now South Russia in the fifth century B.C. Both the Narts, as the Ossetes tell of them, and the Scyths of Herodotus make cloaks of their enemies' scalps,[2] swear by the hearth,[3] practise divination by sticks,[4] sacrifice horses at funerals,[5] cut off the right arms of their enemies,[6] and take oaths in a special way, the Scyths by dipping their arms in a mixture of blood and

---

[1] S. A. Kozin in *Dzhangariada*, p. 70 ff.
[2] Hdt. iv, 64 ; Dumézil, p. 82.
[3] Hdt. iv, 68 ; Dumézil, p. 154.
[4] Hdt. iv, 67 ; Dumézil, p. 155.
[5] Hdt. iv, 72 ; Dumézil, p. 161.
[6] Hdt. iv, 62 ; Dumézil, pp. 61 and 93.

wine and the Narts by throwing silver into brandy or beer.[1] These survivals suggest that the legends of the Narts, as told to-day in the Caucasus, go back to a Scythian origin, and it is indeed possible that the Ossetes, who speak an Indo-European language, are themselves descendants of the Scyths or somehow related to them. Nor are the resemblances confined to customs. In one case at least there is something more like a traditional belief. An Ossete poem tells of a marvellous cup called Uacimonga :

> The Narts had many treasures.
> One treasure was the best of the best,
> The best of the best, the cup Uacimonga.
> That cup was no ordinary cup ;
> If any man told the truth about himself,
> Spoke about his triumphs without falsehood,
> The cup arose with its own strength,
> Of its own accord drew near to the truth-teller's lips,
> But if you tell an untruth, it will not move from its place.[2]

This remarkable cup has its parallel in Scythian lore. Herodotus records :

> Once every year each ruler in his own province mixeth a bowl of wine, whereof all the Scythians that have slain enemies drink ; but those that have not performed this deed taste not of that wine but sit apart in disgrace. And this is a very great reproach to them. But those that have slain exceeding many, have two cups at once and drink from both together.[3]

Herodotus, as we might expect, is more rationalistic than the Ossete poet, and between the two accounts many centuries have passed, but the essential theme remains the same — the hero is connected with drinking from a cup, and, if he does this, he is much honoured. This is a more special case than the others and has suffered a greater change, but we can hardly doubt that the cup " Uacimonga " is a distant descendant of the cups of the Scythian warriors.

Sometimes a custom will be remembered because of its unusual character, as indeed that of the Scythian cup has been. This is perhaps the best explanation of the careful account which the poet of *Beowulf* gives of the hero's funeral.[4] The passage is precise and factual and tells how the Geats first burn the body on a pyre, then place the remains in a barrow together with a rich treasure, and finally twelve chieftains ride round the barrow lamenting the dead king and praising him for his virtues. On this passage some-

[1] Hdt. iv, 70 ; Dumézil, p. 165.   [2] Dynnik, p. 66.
[3] Hdt. iv, 66. Trs. J. E. Powell.   [4] *Beowulf*, 3156-77.

thing needs to be said. First, the poet, despite his avowed Christianity, describes a purely heathen practice. It is true that among the continental Saxons the practice of cremation lasted into the eighth century, to the horror of the Church, but the poet of *Beowulf*, who may well have seen cremation practised among his own people, must have known that it was disapproved by the Church and inappropriate to his own views. But in this matter his respect for tradition overrode his religious beliefs and made him follow his poetical predecessors, who must often have described the burning of dead bodies, since it was the normal practice of the Germanic tribes,[1] and regarded as a fit subject for poetry in such poems as the *Short Lay of Sigurth*.[2] Secondly, the rite, as the poet describes it, is highly unusual. It seems to combine two elements, first the burning of the body with the consignment of the ashes to a barrow, and secondly the horsemen's songs of praise. The first is normal and recalls the treatment of the bodies of Hnaef and his followers;[3] the second is more peculiar. In some ways it resembles the funeral rites of Attila as Jordanes describes them.[4] The dead body was laid in a silken tent, and horsemen, chosen for their skill, galloped round it, "like circus-riders", to gladden the heart of the dead king. A song of lament was sung, of which Jordanes gives a Latin version, presumably drawn from the Greek account of Priscus, which may itself be drawn from a Hunnish original in substance if not in detail. In the meantime a barrow was erected, in which the body was laid together with gold, silver, and iron. Attila's funeral resembles Beowulf's in the use of horsemen, the song of praise, the building of the barrow, and the placing of treasure with the body. It differs in that Attila is not burned but buried, and the rite of the horsemen accompanies, instead of succeeding, the disposition of the body. It is possible that the poet of *Beowulf* had heard through poetical tradition of some burial like Attila's, but either his information had been distorted by time, or he tried to adjust it to his own idea of what a hero's funeral should be. In any case he presents an unusual state of affairs, and we can hardly doubt that he does so because tradition insists on it.

Sometimes topographical details contain frozen relics of the past which are of some interest. For instance, most Russian poems on the fight of Ilya of Murom with his son place it on the *zastava* of Kiev. This *zastava* is assumed to be a rampart or barrier outside Kiev, on which the foremost warriors are gathered

---

[1] Tacitus, *Germania*, 27.   [2] *Sigurtharkvitha en Skamma*, 64-9.
[3] *Beowulf*, 1110 ff.   [4] *Getica*, 49; cf. Thompson, p. 149 ff.

on guard-duty. A *zastava* does not appear in other places, except once or twice by mistake, when the same story is transferred elsewhere. It is associated by tradition with Kiev and with this particular story. It has indeed some point, since it gives a reason why various famous warriors should be gathered together on duty, and this is necessary to the subject, since each warrior, except at last Ilya, shrinks from fighting the unknown young man who arrives and challenges them. But the *zastava* is historical enough, though it was not at Kiev. It was a fortified frontier between western Russia and Lithuania in the thirteenth and fourteenth centuries.[1] It survives in the poetical tradition because it is connected with the story of Ilya and his son, and that is why the poets speak of it, though of course they have no historical knowledge of it. They introduce it with assurance in some such opening as

> From the famous city of Kiev,
> Three versts away by measurement
> There stood a tall rampart,[2]

but the measurements are invented. What matters is that the *zastava* belongs to the story and is expected to make an appearance.

A special case of such geographical details is to be seen in the Kalmuck poems on Dzhangar. Poets performing in the Caspian region repeat from tradition a remarkable quantity of names which come from central Asia but have been jealously preserved through long years of migration and exile. They are, so far as we can see, consistent and credible and seem to be derived from a real state of affairs in the thirteenth century.[3] The poems contain some sixty different phrases to describe Dzhangar's kingdom, and each seems to be based on fact. The Altai mountains have a prominent place, whether as " the anvil Altai ", or " the tall Altai ", or " the silken dress of Altai ". The river Irtish, which has its source in the Altai, is mentioned with its many tributaries, each of which is marked with some distinguishing phrase as providing water for Dzhangar's herds of horses and cattle. Tibet is known as " the land of the Buddha ", or " the land of the three khans ", or " the blessed land of the pipe ". The town and district of Kobdo are " the black tress of Kobdo ". These phrases preserve not only geographical details but other associations, religious and political, which reflect real conditions. The poets are proud of their tradition and preserve its gifts with care.

Another case of geographical reminiscence can be seen in the

---

[1] Trautmann, i, p. 308. [2] Speranski, i, p. 146.
[3] S. A. Kozin in *Dzhangariada*, p. 72 ff.

Norse *Battle of the Goths and the Huns*. Ordinarily the Norse poems preserve only the vaguest details about the country in which their events take place, but this poem, which must be in some sense derived from a Gothic original, not only tells of a Hunnish king, Humli, who is otherwise not famous and therefore the more likely to be historical, but sets its events with some care in a central European scene. When Hlöthr sets out his claims, he includes Myrkwood, which is the great forest of central Europe, to the east of which the Huns lived. When he proceeds to demand " the beautiful stones which stand by the Danpr ", he almost certainly refers to the Dnêpr, and it is even possible that the stones are Kiev. The battle fought on Dunheithr may be on the Danube, which is called Duna in Norse, and Harfatha Hills are surely the Carpathians.[1] Other names like Arheimar, Dylgja, and Jössurr remain without elucidation, but it is likely that they too have genuine connections with a battle about which nothing else is known but which survived in poetical tradition.

Heroic poetry sometimes preserves memories of material objects which belong to a time much earlier than the poet's, who may never have seen anything like them. So in the Yakut *Er Sogotokh* the hero sits on a seat made of mammoth-bone, which is " adorned with carved figures ".[2] In the *Elder Edda* the jewels fashioned by Völund have been connected with a period before A.D. 550.[3] Russian ships have eyes painted on them, a relic of mediaeval times. Uzbek heroes are sometimes armed with a club, sometimes with bow and arrows. They also carry shields and wear coats of mail, of which the first are " made of rhinoceros hide " or " adorned with golden plates " and the second have a layer of gold.[4] There are many cases of such survivals, but the Homeric poems, largely owing to their great scope and wide range of formulae, present them in unusual abundance and raise interesting questions about the Greek past. Because Homer likes to linger on material objects and is well provided with phrases for doing so, he is an almost unique repository of information on some things which he can hardly have seen with his own eyes.

Homer treats of armour often and fully. In the main he observes a consistent scheme and arms his warriors in bronze, makes them carry a round shield and one or two spears, and wear helmets which have knobs or horns and a horse-hair plume, bronze breast-plates, greaves and swords. This is not the historical armour of the eighth century B.C., when iron was in general use, but

[1] De Vries, i, p. 37. [2] Yastremski, p. 21.
[3] Philpotts, p. 78. [4] Zhirmunskii-Zarifov, p. 374.

it suits the thirteenth and twelfth centuries, and recalls in different degrees the equipment of the Philistine warrior, Goliath of Gath,[1] the Aegean mercenaries of Rameses II,[2] the Sea-Raiders depicted on the pylon of Medinet Habu after the victory of Rameses III in 1194 B.C.,[3] an Arimaspian on an ivory mirror from Enkomi in Cyprus,[4] the figures on the Warrior Vase [5] (c. 1250), and the Warrior Stele from Mycenae.[6] These examples are at least three hundred years older than Homer, but they are sufficiently like what he describes for us to be able to say that the armour of the Homeric warriors must be derived in the main from this period. On the other hand certain Homeric formulae go back to a more distant past and a different system of armour. In the Minoan and early Mycenean ages warriors did not wear body-armour or greaves but relied for defence on a large shield which covered their whole body. Memories of such shields survive in the shield of Ajax, which is " like a tower ",[7] in the case of the warrior ὑπασπίδια προποδίζων " edging himself forward under his shield ",[8] in the fate of Periphoetes, who comes to disaster by tripping over his shield,[9] in the shield of Hector, which reaches from neck to ankle.[10] Homer is not consistent in his treatment of such shields, and there are times when Hector and even Ajax seem to have round shields of the familiar kind. Nor is the large shield historically appropriate to body-armour such as Homer's heroes all wear. The explanation must be that he is using formulae which he does not fully understand, though he sees their immediate relevance to the narrative. These formulae come from an older age than those for his usual armour and reflect what was in fact a different kind of warfare.

A special case of arming, which is at least as old as the big shield, comes when Odysseus and Diomedes go out on an armed reconnaissance at night. While Diomedes wears a leather cap, called καταῖτυξ, Odysseus wears something more unusual, a helmet fitted with felt inside and covered outside with swine's teeth.[11] No doubt the reason for this is that a bronze helmet might shine at night and betray its wearer, but with such a helmet there is no such risk. Archaeology presents several parallels to Odysseus' unusual head-gear, notably in ivory heads from Mycenae and Spata, a silver vase from Shaft Grave IV at Mycenae, a gem from

[1] I Samuel xvii, 5-7.
[2] Lorimer, Figs. IV, 1 ; V.
[3] Bossert, pp. 248-9.
[4] Lorimer, Fig. II, 4.
[5] *Idem*, Fig. III, 1.
[6] *Idem*, Fig. II, 2.
[7] *Il.* vii, 219 ; xi, 485 ; xvii, 128.
[8] *Ibid.* xiii, 158.
[9] *Idid.* xv, 645.
[10] *Ibid.* vi, 117.
[11] *Ibid.* x, 257 ff.

Vaphio, and a sealing from Hagia Triadha in Crete.[1] Actual boars' teeth, which must have formed part of such helmets, have been found in a number of places from Boeotia to Messenia. Since this type of helmet seems to have fallen out of use before 1400 B.C., Homer's memory of it must have travelled a long road before he made use of it. Perhaps he does not understand it correctly or see that it is a helmet for common use. In fact the Mycenean cap was fitted with teeth simply for protection, since they might well break the blow of a weapon, but Homer, who has heard of such things through his formulae, uses it because it is appropriate to the special conditions of armed reconnaissance at night.

A peculiar case of Greek tradition may be seen in the great shield which Hephaestus makes for Achilles. It is made of gold, silver, tin, and some kind of blue enamel or κύανος. In general the technique of working pictorial scenes in such a mixture of metals has a parallel in the dagger-blades from Mycenae with their pictures of lion-hunts. This art existed some seven hundred years before Homer, and though specimens may have survived till his time, it is more likely that he knew of it through traditional formulae. He applies it to the shield of Achilles and in so doing probably goes beyond the limits of realism. Such a shield is not likely to have existed in Mycenean times. In the first place, it is round instead of being figure-of-eight or cylindrical; and in the second place such a shield could never have been used in battle. On the other hand, much nearer to Homer's own time, votive shields, not indeed made with this Mycenean technique but depicting various scenes of action in concentric circles, existed in Cyprus and Crete and other parts of the eastern Mediterranean. It looks as if Homer, knowing through his formulae of some ancient kind of metal-work, proceeded to describe a work of art which owed something to this in its technique but owed something else in its shape and design to a kind of art with which he himself was familiar.

Homer's handling of the shield of Achilles suggests that, though a poet may learn much about even a distant past from his formulae, he is not confined to it and may, if he wishes, stray into more recent times and derive new material from them. The result is that memories of ancient usage may be combined with other elements which are historically incompatible with them and are indeed anachronisms. Since the poet cannot be expected to be an archaeologist or a historian, he may sometimes depict the past as acquainted with things which it can in fact never have known.

[1] Lorimer, p. 212 ff.

For instance, in *Beowulf*, when the poet says that " the street was stone-paven ",[1] he must refer to a Roman road, since the Romans were the only people to pave streets in the first centuries A.D. But since the Romans were never in Jutland, such a street cannot have existed there, and what the poet has done is to transfer to Jutland the kind of street of which remains were still visible in England in his time. Again, as we all know, the telescope was invented by Galileo in the seventeenth century, but that does not prevent Russian poets from supplying it to heroes of a considerably earlier date like Nightingale Budimirovich,[2] who is connected with Prince Vladimir of Kiev in the twelfth century. The same kind of mistake is made by Jugoslav poets who make Marko Kraljević carry a rifle in the fourteenth century or even by Homer, who, despite his general picture of an age of bronze weapons, has a formula that " iron drags a man on "[3] which is certainly derived from a time when iron weapons were the rule. Such anachronisms are common enough in heroic poetry, but they are not important. What matters is that the poets use formulae which may be old or new and hardly distinguish between them. Fortunately, once a formula has come into use, it tends to continue, and this means that heroic language preserves many elements from a distant past. Nor are the poets quite unconscious of this. Just as Homer consistently clothes his warriors in bronze, so the Russian heroes of the cycle of Vladimir use weapons appropriate to the time, such as bows, swords, and helmets.

Formulae may also preserve relics of lost beliefs and outmoded theological ideas. Though the Kara-Kirghiz poems are avowedly and demonstratively Mohammedan, there are moments in them when they reflect older creeds, not merely when they deal with the gods of death, who are after all almost indispensable to such poetry, but in smaller and less essential matters. Among the enemies whom Manas, according to the prophets, is to conquer is a mysterious being called Jelmogus. Other poems, of a shaman-istic character, give information about him. Altyn Sibäldi, " the Golden Witch ", known as the " leaden-eyed and copper-nosed ", is the mother of nine sons, the Jelbagan, of which the singular is Jelmogus. They have a large number of heads, and their house is guarded by dogs who breathe flames. They seem to be connected with dragons, but Radlov was told by the Chern Tatars that Jel-mogus is a powerful demon with seven heads who has destroyed the moon but is forced by Ülgen to restore it.[4] This is a clear case

---

[1] *Beowulf*, 320.
[3] *Od.* xvi, 294 ; xix, 13.
[2] Gilferding, i, p. 517.
[4] Chadwick, *Growth*, iii, p. 84.

of a cosmological demon, and no doubt his name has survived because of his interest. But the poet of Manas seems to be ill acquainted with him, and identifies him with the Uigur people whom Manas is to conquer.[1] He has learned the relevant formulae but does not understand them and puts his own interpretation on them.

Something of the same kind may be observed in Homer. His gods and goddesses not only behave like human beings but resemble them in appearance. It is therefore the more extraordinary that he should call Hera βοῶπις and Athene γλαυκῶπις, since these words should mean " cow-faced " and " owl-faced " and indicate a theology whose figures had the heads of animals and birds. It is true that tradition explains the words as meaning " soft-eyed " and " bright-eyed ", and such was no doubt their meaning to the classical Greeks and perhaps to Homer himself. But this cannot have been their original meaning, and here we may surely see how a formula preserves an ancient belief whose meaning is lost to a later generation which still continues to use it. The ancient legends which connect Hera with cows and Athene with owls suggest that once they themselves were thought to look like cows or owls, and this belief survives in the two adjectives. So when Apollo is called λυκηγενής it is possible that, as the dictionaries say, it means " Lycian-born ", though what point this has is not clear, nor is the form quite impeccable. Its obvious meaning is " wolf-born ", but since Homer makes Apollo look like a man, he can hardly have given this sense to the word. That it is right follows not only from the form of the word but from Apollo's connection with wolves.[2] It is at least probable that Apollo was once believed to have the shape of a wolf and that was why he received the epithet of λυκηγενής, but Homer can have known nothing about this and must have used the epithet simply because it was traditional.

If formulae help to keep alive experience which has long lost its precise significance, the substance of stories is no less sturdy and capable of surviving the centuries. A story will pass not only from generation to generation in one language but from one language to another and take on many new forms. On the whole what passes round the world in this way is not a character with a name but a theme which can be adapted to many circumstances. It is true that certain heroes pass from country to country and from

[1] Radlov, v, p. 2.
[2] Schol. Soph. *El.* 6, sacrifices of wolves to Apollo ; Aristotle, *H.A.* vi, 35, his mother, Leto, is changed into a wolf at the time of his birth.

language to language. This happens not only to Gilgamish in Asia, but to other heroes no less renowned. Marko Kraljević, who began life as a Serb, has multiplied his existence in Bulgaria, Albania, and Greece. The Persian hero, Amran, has become a favourite of the Ossetes, where, with his two brothers, he is the central figure in a cycle of poems. The Tatar warrior, Kurroglou, has passed from the Turkomans to the Turks of Asia Minor and to the Greeks. Roland has found renown in most parts of western Europe. Great heroes may extend their careers in this way, and it need awake no surprise. But more interesting, because it is more complex, is the way in which a theme may travel many thousands of miles, changing its persons and its details but preserving some constant elements and a fundamental identity.

It is not always easy to say when such a theme, which has taken many forms, comes from a single source. It is often possible that a theme may have been born independently in more than one place from some fundamental element in human nature. For instance, the story of the father who fights with his son is found in many countries and takes many forms. In Greece the son, Oedipus, kills the father, and discovers later what he has done. Among the Ossetes Uryzmag kills a boy by accident and discovers later that it is his son. In Persia Sohrab has already delivered the fatal blow when he sees who his opponent, not yet dead, is. When Hildebrand fights Hadubrand, he knows the truth, but Hadubrand does not, and in some versions the fight ends with the son's death. In Ireland Cuchulainn kills his son without knowing who he is, and when he finds out, goes mad and dies fighting the waves. In Russia Ilya of Murom first fights his son in ignorance, then discovers his identity, and spares his life, only to kill him later when, at his mother's instigation, he returns to murder his father. In Armenia David fights Mher the Younger without either knowing who the other is, but the fight is stopped, and all ends happily. In these stories the constant element is that a father fights his son and that up to some point neither knows who the other is. This is a very elastic theme, which maintains its identity in a number of wide variations.

In his story of Odysseus and the Cyclops Homer has included many traditional themes, from the trick of " No Man " to the escape from the cave under the ram's belly. But once he brought these themes together into a single story, it was likely that others would take advantage of his inventiveness. This seems to have happened in a story of Uryzmag told by the Ossetes. Here the constant element is that a hero ventures into the cave of a one-eyed giant and is in danger of being eaten by him, when he blinds the giant and escapes by using his ram. The Ossete story keeps these elements, but varies the story in some minor but not unimportant respects. Whereas Odysseus puts out the Cyclops' eye with a long pole which he finds in the cave, sharpens, and heats in the fire, Uryzmag uses a different instrument:

> The giant dragged Uryzmag into the cave,
> He set him on the self-turning spit,
> The spit hung between his clothes and his skin;
> The one-eyed giant gives orders to the spit:
> " Turn now, my spit, roast the dainty morsel,
> I cannot, my eye hurts so;
> I will go and lie down and sleep till supper ".
> The spit began to turn itself, to turn Uryzmag,
> And soon his clothes smouldered in the flames;
> Uryzmag fell flat on the embers.
> Then he seized the spit, stole towards the giant,
> And thrust at his one eye with the hot iron,
> He burned it, he picked out the single eye.[1]

This is of course less rich and less dramatic than the story of Odysseus and the Cyclops. The way in which the giant goes to sleep is less ingeniously motivated than the drunken sleep into which the Cyclops falls after drinking of Odysseus' excellent wine. But this version is none the less neat and agreeable, and maintains the essential theme of blinding the giant with a new poetic justice in the use of the spit on which he is roasting the hero.

The same Ossete poem also uses the theme of the escape from the cave. In this the essential element is that the hero escapes by using the giant's ram for cover and so deceives its owner. In Homer Odysseus hangs under the ram's belly and so passes out of the cave, with an awkward moment when the Cyclops stops the ram and speaks to it. Once out of the cave, he regains his ship and defies the Cyclops from it. In the Ossete version the situation is slightly different. Uryzmag is alone and has no comrades to think about; he has only to plot his own escape. After he has blinded the giant, he is still a captive in the cave:

> Old Uryzmag lay down with his thoughts . . .
> Before the herd the giant's ram was on guard.
> The Nart carves him up at night stealthily.
> He takes off the skin, like a leather bottle, all in one piece,
> And all night till morning he eats kid's meat,
> But with morning he gets into the ram's skin,
> Puts his hands into the fore-feet,
> And with his own feet gets into the hind-feet.

[1] Dynnik, p. 16.

The giant stirs the herd to pasture,
He rises up, he places his legs by the entrance,
He lets the herd pass between his legs from the cave,
He himself feels, searches, whether Uryzmag is there.
Then on all fours — say, what a ram is this ? —
Behind all the goats Uryzmag goes to the entrance
And lightly butts the giant with his horns.
Then the giant lets the ram pass, lets him go on his way :
" My friend, my friend, look, be a good guard,
Keep my herd for me, look after all of it,
I myself cannot come, my eye is put out ! "
But with a bound Uryzmag answered him
From the ram's skin with a human voice :
" Yes, even if your eye had not been put out,
Your herd will never see you again ".[1]

The Ossete poet provides a charming variation on the static theme. Uryzmag is in his way as ingenious and as daring as Odysseus. Like Odysseus he makes use of the ram to escape, and once he is clear of the cave, boldly reveals what he has done. So far as the actual action is concerned, there is little to choose between the trick of Odysseus and the trick of Uryzmag.[2]

Another far-travelled theme which has kept its essential nature may be traced back to *Gilgamish* and is presumably of great antiquity. We have seen how Gilgamish spurns Ishtar when she offers him her love, with the consequence that he wins her hatred and pays for it with the death of Enkidu. The fundamental theme is that of a hero who rejects overtures from a goddess and suffers because of it. This theme, in a different dress, appears in fragments of the Canaanite epic on Aqhat from Ras-Shamra. The young hero, Aqhat, has acquired by accident a bow which is meant only for gods. The goddess 'Anat seeks to get it from him. First she offers him wealth, but, as a hero should, he spurns it. Then she offers him immortality, but he is sceptical of this and spurns it too, on the ground that men are bound to die, and concludes none too politely :

" A bow is a thing for warriors.
Are women then taking up hunting ? "[3]

'Anat takes this quite well, but warns Aqhat that he had better do what she asks. She then complains of Aqhat's behaviour to her father, the god El, who behaves just as Anu does when Ishtar

[1] *Idem*, p. 17.
[2] For other versions of the theme cf. L. Radermacher, *Die Erzählungen der Odyssee* (Vienna, 1915), p. 13 ff.
[3] Gaster, p. 282 ff., who shows some similarities with the story of Orion, whom Artemis kills for insulting her.

complains about Gilgamish.   After refusing to treat her seriously
at first, he gives in :

> " My daughter, I know that thou art gentle,
> And against goddesses must there be no insult.
> Now one has arisen, my daughter, of insolent heart.
> Grasp inwardly things as they are,
> Set them in thy breast ;
> He that has defrauded thee must surely be crushed." [1]

The result is that 'Anat prepares a plan to make Aqhat unconscious
and get the bow from him.   She has no wish to kill him, but the
plan goes wrong : Aqhat is killed by 'Anat's agent, and the bow
is lost in the sea.   In its details this story differs from that of
Gilgamish and Ishtar, but the fundamental theme is constant.
The mortal repels the goddess, and neither he nor she gains by
the result.

A last theme of some antiquity is that of " Potiphar's wife ".
A woman makes proposals to a man, and when he rejects them,
denounces him to her husband.   The theme seems to have arisen
in Egypt,[2] but its first appearance in poetry is in the *Iliad*, where
the wife of Proetus revenges herself on Bellerophon by telling a
false story to her husband, with the result that Bellerophon is
sent to Lycia where his exploits secure his reprieve from death.[3]
A similar story was told about Peleus, who is denounced by
Hippolyte to her husband, Cretheus, and sent by him to what looks
like death on the mountains, where he is in fact saved by the
centaur, Chiron.[4]   This theme has come to Armenia, though we
cannot say from what source, and is told both of David and of his
son, Mher the Younger.[5]   In both cases a young man is tempted
by his foster-mother, and treats her less with contempt than with
a nice sense of absurdity.   She makes him pour water over her in
her bath, but he rejects her advances and thinks no more of it.
When her husband returns, she complains to him that the young
man has assaulted her.   And at this point the story, which has
already shown a touch of comedy in making the woman old
enough to be the hero's mother, reaches a pretty climax.   When
she tells her husband that David has assaulted her, he does not at
first believe her :

> " Now, woman, that's unclean.   You are lying to me."
> She answered : " I am not lying to you.

---

[1] Gaster, p. 289.
[2] T. E. Peet, in *C.A.H.* ii, p. 223, quotes the story of Anubis and Bet in
the d'Orbiny papyrus.
[3] *Il.* vi, 156 ff.   [4] Hesiod, fr. 78 ; Pindar, *Nem.* iv, 49 ff.
[5] *David Sasunskii*, p. 195 ff. ; Macler, ii, p. 92.

He laid his hand upon me,
And I did not give myself to him."
" If that is so, we will shut the door at night."
Ovan shut the door at night,
He did not allow David into the house.
" Hey, father," said David,
" I could knock down the door with my foot,
Your door and you yourself would fall to the ground.
But how can I come to your help, father,
If you are deceived by a whore ? " [1]

The door is opened, and the episode ends without further trouble. The Armenian poet knows the theme well enough, but treats it in a light-hearted spirit. What is in Homer a serious story which involves heroic honour and gallant exertion, becomes a domestic comedy.

The passage of themes from one language or country to another illustrates in a special way the conservatism of the heroic tradition. Just as a single language is remarkably tenacious of its formulae, so a theme which breaks the bounds of a language or a linguistic group still tends to keep its essential character. This shows that, when he learns his technique, the bard learns not only formulae but stories which he must respect within certain limits. Just as he can, if he chooses, invent new formulae and adapt old ones to new uses, so he can also vary the whole character and persons of a narrative-theme, provided that he keeps the theme itself more or less intact. What matters is its structure — not its temper or its setting or its personalities. Even when such a theme comes not from the poet's own tradition but has somehow drifted in from abroad, its essential quality must still be preserved. A tradition of heroic poetry may pass through many phases and stages and places, but it somehow succeeds in keeping its main possessions intact.

[1] *David Sasunskii*, p. 196.

XI

THE BARD

ANONYMITY has been claimed as a characteristic of heroic poetry. We do not know who were the authors of the Anglo-Saxon poems or the *Elder Edda* or the *Cid*, and modern bards hardly ever mention their names in the text of a poem. So unless the recording witness makes a note of it, the poem soon becomes anonymous. It has been thought that this anonymity is a necessary element in heroic poetry and is to be explained by the theory that " however inventive he [the bard] may be, he seems to be regarded as a reciter or artist rather than as an author ".[1] In this there is some truth. Oral poets, who derive so much of their art from what others have sung before them, make no claim to copyright and are not much troubled about being thought original.[2] They are content if they can give a new variation of an old tale ; their chief task is to maintain a tradition in the correct way. If they admit the conditions of their performance, they can hardly grudge others the use of their inventions. Since a bard often claims the past or a god as the source of his information, he is not in a position to make any great claims for himself. But this does not mean that heroic poetry is necessarily anonymous, or that bards are always too modest to claim their creations for themselves. In fact they are often far from modest, but even if they were, their audiences would not allow them to remain unknown. Among simple peoples the fame of a bard spreads easily to quite distant regions, and his arrival in a place is an occasion of some importance. However anonymous their poems may be, the bards themselves are often well known, and that makes it unlikely that they disclaim any share in works of their own composition.

The anonymity of oral poems is easily explained. Each poem has one existence, when it is recited, and then the audience knows who the poet is. He has no need to mention his name in his poem since it is familiar to those who listen to him and are the only people who matter on each occasion. He does not foresee a time

---

[1] Chadwick, *Growth*, iii, p. 751.
[2] The Ainu bard, Wakarpa, who recited *Kutune Shirka*, disclaimed any responsibility for its composition ; cf. Arthur Waley, *Botteghe Oscure*, vii (1951), p. 236.

when his poem will be written down and people will wish to know the author's name, since he is unacquainted with the practice of writing poems down and may not know what reading is. Oral poets are known by name to us only when scholars have noted who recited the pieces which they record. Radlov, for instance, did not take down the names of the Tatar bards whose works he collected and may thereby have done injustice to some distinguished performers. When, however, poems are ascribed to authors, as they are in Gilferding's and Rybnikov's collections of *byliny*, we not only have some useful information but are able in some cases, as with Trofim Ryabinin, to note certain personal characteristics in their art. For though this art is traditional and conventional, it none the less allows some scope to the individual poet and enables him to indulge his own taste and judgment and inventiveness. It is easy to understand why we do not know the names of many composers of oral poems, since time has obliterated memories and even in modern times scholars have not always recorded names. But this is a different thing from saying that heroic poetry is necessarily anonymous because the poets make no claim to be responsible for what they sing.

Indeed in certain conditions the names of poets are known and remembered. Among the Achins the famous bard, Dokarim, who composed the poem *Prang Kompeuni* about his countrymen's wars with the Dutch, was known both for his work in general and for his authorship of this poem.[1] The modern Kara-Kirghiz poets, Sagymbai Orozbakov and Sayakbai Karalaev, were well known for their work even when they were in exile in China. When Karadžić made his collection of Jugoslav poems, two at least of his poets, Savo Martinović and Djuko Srdanović, were well known, if only because they also held high positions at Cetinje. Milman Parry found that a bard who had lived some forty or fifty years earlier, called Ćor Huso, was well remembered in several districts and that more than one bard paid a tribute to what he had learned from him. The Russian bards, Trofim Ryabinin and Kuzma Ivanov, whom Rybnikov interviewed in the 'seventies, both admitted a great debt to their teacher, Ilya Elustafevich. Nor are such acknowledgments confined to modern times. The author of the *Tale of Igor's Raid* speaks of the songs of Boyan and knows their characteristics, but they can have been known to him only through recitation. If a bard does his work well, there is a good chance that his name will be known even outside his own district and associated not indeed with individual poems but with subjects

[1] Hurgronje, ii, p. 100 ff.

which he has made his own or with certain ways of telling a tale.

The Greeks certainly ascribed poems, which must in the first case have been recited orally, to bards by name. It is enough to mention Eumelus of Corinth, who was credited with a *Corinthiaca*, Arctinus, Hegesias, and Stasinus, who were reputed authors of different epics in the Homeric cycle, and Cinaethon, who was said to have composed poems on Oedipus and Heracles. Such attributions may well have been wrong, and in some cases, where more than one author is claimed for a single poem, cannot all be right, but the fact remains that it was customary to ascribe poems to poets by name. So, too, certain pieces of Norse poetry are assigned by reputable tradition to such poets as Thorbjörn Hornklofi and Thjotholfr of Hvin, who were in the train of Harold Fairhaired in the ninth century.[1] Nor is there any call to dispute the tradition that Hornklofi wrote the *Hrafnsmal* about his royal patron. It is also possible that the *Hákonarmál*, which tells of a battle fought by Haakon I about 960, was composed by one Eyvindr Finnsson, who played a prominent part in his master's last fight. It is true that Finnsson was called " Skáldaspillir " or " Plagiarist ",[2] and that his poem seems to justify the name, since it is full of literary reminiscences, but none the less the poet's name was passed to posterity. The names of poets are as subject to the depredations of time as any other historical facts, but enough survive to show that for one reason or another a poet's name may sometimes be associated in popular memory with certain works after his death.

In this context the name of Homer deserves special attention. It occurs first in the seventh century when Callinus of Ephesus attributed the *Thebaid* to him.[3] Later it is used commonly, and no Greek thought of disputing the tradition that a bard called Homer composed the *Iliad* and the *Odyssey*. Attempts have indeed been made both in ancient and modern times to explain the name Ὅμηρος as a nickname or a title. While Ephorus explained it as meaning " blind "[4] and Aristotle is said to have taken it to mean " follower ",[5] and others " hostage ",[6] these efforts are as unsound as modern claims that it means " accompanist " or " putter together ". That the Greeks invented titles for poets is clear enough from such cases as Phemius, Eumolpus, and Musaeus, but Homer does not belong to this class. The word in its Ionic form, Ὅμηρος, is almost certainly a real name, and it is hard

---

[1] *Egils Saga*, 8. *Fagrskinna*, 2.   [2] *Fagrskinna*, 11.

[3] Pausanias, ix, 9, 5.   [4] Fr. 164.

[5] Fr. 76, Rose.   [6] Hesychius, *s.v.* Ὅμηρος.

to believe that it was used as a general title for any poets who wrote heroic epics and was in fact a " Sammelbegriff ". That poems which he did not compose were attributed to Homer is natural enough, but that surely implies that there were poems which he did compose and that his name was remembered because of them.

When poems are written down, the name of the author is sometimes, though not commonly, introduced into the text, no doubt because the poet or his editor desires it. A curious case of this can be seen in a Greek poem *Master John* from Crete, which tells a tale of Turkish oppression in 1770. The poem was composed in 1786 by a poet who could not write, called Patzelios, but was actually written down by Anagnostis Kordylis, who was a dealer in milk and cheese at Papura. The scribe makes his own position quite clear and claims no more than his fair share of credit :

And it was I that held the pen, 'twas I that held the paper,
But he dictated me the tale, and word by word I wrote it,
For he dictated me the tale of the schoolmaster Johannes,
And ever tears streamed from his eyes, as he the deed remembered,
Till all his speech was broken off, his narrative was ended,
And all his bitter heart was poured in black and bitter groaning.[1]

Literacy has come to the aid of the illiterate bard and preserved his name with his poem. Since the poem is of little merit, the name would not otherwise have been remembered. Of more distinction in its own land is the Achin poem *Pochut Muhamat*, which tells of warlike adventures in Sumatra in the early years of the seventeenth century. In it the poet speaks of himself, says that, though he was not present at the achievements which he celebrates, he has derived his information from eye-witnesses, and adds that his name is Teungku Lam Rukam, which title " shows him to have been a man distinguished from the general mass of the people by a certain amount of religious knowledge and devotion ".[2]

Though the earlier French *chansons de geste* tend to be anonymous, it is noteworthy that some fifteen names of poets are contained in texts as belonging to men who claim to be their authors.[3] One of these, Adenet le Roi, takes credit for three poems, *Ogier the Dane*, *Berthe aux grands pieds*, and *Bovon de Comarchis*, and there is no need to disbelieve him. These French bards sometimes make boasts about their learning, which we cannot treat very seriously, sometimes about their social position, which

[1] Entwistle, p. 10.   [2] Hurgronje, ii, p. 88.   [3] Faral, p. 177 ff.

may have some truth. No doubt most of them compose poems on subjects which have been treated before, and are not very original or creative authors, but it is worthy of notice that in the existing *remaniement* of the *Song of Antioch* the author ascribes the poem to a certain Richard the Pilgrim, known to history in connection with Arnold, who distinguished himself at Antioch.[1] The poet quotes Richard as his authority :

> He who composed the song knew well to tell the names,
> Richard the Pilgrim, he, from whom we have the tale.

In general, the French poets who give their names seem to be the authors of the texts in which they give them. It is possible that those poets who thus introduce themselves belonged to aristocratic circles where the *jongleur* was a person of importance, who could take such a risk without being thought presumptuous, while the authors of the many other poems, where no name is given, come from a humbler level of society which did not expect its poets to claim much credit for themselves.

Among French poems *Roland* presents a peculiar problem. In its last line it preserves a name which must have something to do with the poem :

> Ci falt la geste que Turoldus declinet.

Turoldus, or Thorold, is a name of Germanic origin, which occurs quite frequently in the eleventh and twelfth centuries. The beginning of the line probably means " so ends ", but everything else is obscure and disputed. It is not even clear that " la geste " is the actual poem, which now comes to an end, and not the *Gesta Francorum*, which the poet claims elsewhere to have used as his source. " Declinet " is an insoluble puzzle. It has been taken variously to mean " composes ", " sings ", " recites ", " transcribes ", and " translates ".[2] Though any of these gives sense of a sort, it is difficult to see why the present tense is used when the meaning demands a past. More ingenious is the suggestion that it means " declines " in the sense that the poet was declining in health when he finished the poem.[3] But this is not only difficult grammatically but introduces a personal, intimate note which seems very out of place. Despite all the efforts of scholars the last line of *Roland* remains obscure. None the less it looks as if Turoldus did one of two things. Either he was the

[1] Faral, p. 183.
[2] Bédier, *Commentaire*, p. 32 ff. ; Mireaux, p. 64 ff.
[3] Jenkins, p. 280.

author of a *Gesta Francorum*, which the poet turned into verse and may have translated, no doubt freely, from Latin, or he is the actual poet who calls his own poem, reasonably enough, a " geste ". Of these alternatives the second is perhaps more probable, since the aristocratic poet seems more likely to make us acquainted with his own name than with that of the author whom he uses, especially in so emphatic a place as the last line of his poem. Moreover, the poet asserts elsewhere that the book which he uses was written by St. Giles. Though we need not believe this, the poet evidently wishes us to, and in that case would not give an alternative authorship for it. So despite all the uncertainties it seems probable that Turoldus is the author of the poem as we have it. Four men of the name have been regarded as possible claimants : Thorold, abbot of Peterborough, the nephew of Odo of Bayeux, who died in 1098, with the reputation of being " an exceedingly stern man " ; Thorold, a Benedictine, abbot of Coulombs, who lived at the same time ; Thorold of Envermeu, bishop of Bayeux from 1097 to 1104, whom Pope Honorius I thought insufficiently devout ; a fourth Thorold, who has been identified as living about 1128 at Tudela in Navarre.[1] If the poem, as is possible, was written in the early years of the reign of Henry II, none of these is a likely candidate, with the possible exception of the last, about whom almost nothing is known. What is reasonably certain is that Turoldus was a Norman ; for, though the name is found in Brittany, Spain, and the Holy Land, it seems always to have been borne by Normans from Normandy or England. There are many unsolved mysteries in the authorship of our *Roland*, but it may well be ascribed to a Norman poet called Turoldus.

Once a poem was committed to writing and became well known, it might be associated with the name of a poet through some independent tradition and not through any statement in the text. Such a tradition need not necessarily be oral, as it seems to have been with Homer, but might derive support from written documents. Such a tradition existed about Hesiod. A kind of corporation owned the land at Thespiae connected with him, preserved local traditions of him, and showed to visitors like Pausanias such relics as the official copy of the *Works and Days*.[2] Hesiod is hardly a heroic poet, but he dates back to a generation or two after Homer, and this cult of his memory illustrates how a poet's name can be preserved. A more striking case is that of *Gilgamish*. The actual tablets do not contain any author's name, but a separate document from the library of Assurbanipal at

[1] Bédier, *Commentaire*, p. 33 ; Jenkins, p. xlvi ff.   [2] Paus. ix, 27.

Nineveh names as the author a priest called Sin-liqi-unninni.[1]
Since his name is said to be Assyrian, it is unlikely that he is the
old Babylonian poet and is more likely to be the Assyrian who
refashioned *Gilgamish* in his own language. It is possible that
another case shows that the Semitic peoples liked to record the
names of poets. At the end of the Canaanite *Keret* the tablet
records : " The scribe is 'Il-Mlk (Ilimilku) . . . the T‘-ite ".[2]
Of course Ilimilku may be no more than the scribe who wrote the
poem down, but it is at least possible that he is the poet who added
his name at the end of his work.

The survival of a poet's name may in some cases be due to his
superior social position, but, when we look at bards, we find that
they may come from almost any class, nor does their variety of
status conform to any sociological scheme. In some circumstances
heroic songs are sung by kings and princes. This happens when
the art is enjoyed by a whole society and patronised by rulers who
see themselves as heroes, inspired by the prowess of the past and
eager to celebrate it. Literature gives examples of this. When the
Achaeans come to Achilles in his tent, they find him with a lyre :

With this he made glad his heart and sang of men's glorious doings.[3]

Achilles, no doubt, sings of the great deeds of the past. This too is
what Hrothgar does in his great hall :

> at times a strange tale
> Read us aright   the roomy-hearted king.[4]

Nor are examples lacking from history. When Gelimer, last king
of the Vandals, was besieged at Mount Pappua in 534, he asked
his opponent, the Herulian chief, to send him a harp that he might
accompany with it a song which he had composed on his own
sufferings.[5] In the nineteenth century two Prince Bishops of
Montenegro, Peter I and Peter II, were themselves poets, and the
tradition was maintained into this century by King Nikola.[6] So
too T. E. Lawrence gives a vivid account of the Arabian chieftain,
Auda :

He saw life as a saga. All the events in it were significant ; all
personages in contact with him heroic. His mind was storied with
poems of old raids and epic tales of fights, and he overflowed with them
on the nearest listener. If he lacked listeners, he would very likely sing
them to himself in his tremendous voice, deep and resonant and loud.[7]

---

[1] Gressmann, p. 13.   [2] Gordon, p. 83.
[3] *Il.* ix, 189.   [4] *Beowulf*, 2109-10.
[5] Procopius, *Bell. Vand.* ii, 6.   [6] Chadwick, *Growth*, ii, p. 442.
[7] *Revolt in the Desert* (London, 1927), p. 94.

When princes live in a heroic age, and act by heroic standards, they may well express their interests and ideals in this kind of song.

When a prince sets an example, his companions and courtiers may follow it. The Kara-Kirghiz Manas and his forty companions accompany their drinking with songs :

> To this they join their songs,
> Make gay at the place of feasting,
> Till the noon is overpast.[1]

At Hrothgar's court, when Beowulf has routed Grendel, a thegn sings :

> A man boast-laden,   of ballads mindful
> Who almost all   of the olden sayings
> Could well remember,[2]

and his subjects are the hero's recent achievement and the tale of Sigemund. The *Nornagests Saga* relates how Gestr sings several songs on heroic subjects, including *Brynhild's Hell Ride* and the *Second Lay of Guthrun*, to King Olaf Tryggvason. It is true that the king, who is a Christian, says : " You need not tell us any more things of that kind ",[3] but it is clear that such songs were customary at courts in his time. Russian poets, who are not always very good authorities on the habits of a remote past, may be not far from the truth when they depict something similar happening at Vladimir's court. Churilo Plenkovich, in his capacity as groom of the bed-chamber, beguiles Vladimir and the princess Apraxya :

> Churilo lives as groom of the bed-chamber,
> Makes the downy feather-bed,
> Piles the high pillow,
> And sits by the high pillow,
> Plays on his gusli of maple-wood,
> Diverts Prince Vladimir
> And especially Princess Apraxya.[4]

It is true that Vladimir and Apraxya do not themselves sing songs but they expect them from their attendants as part of the ritual of court life. That the poets are not wrong about actual conditions follows not only from the esteem in which the " wise " Boyan is held in the courtly *Tale of Igor's Raid* but from the entry in the Chronicle of Hypatios under the year 1241, that there was " a famous singer Mitusa, who out of pride refused to serve the prince Daniel ".[5] If a bard could so treat a prince, he would be of some social standing.

[1] Radlov, v, p. 237.   [2] *Beowulf*, 868-70.
[3] N. Kershaw, *Ballads and Stories of the Far Past*, p. 33 ff.
[4] Rybnikov, ii, p. 462 ff.   [5] Edition of 1908, p. 794.

A court may equally use professionals. Such is he who at Hrothgar's court tells the tale of Finn.[1] Such too are the Homeric bards, Demodocus and Phemius, in the princely houses of Alcinous and Odysseus. Their social status is below that of the great people round the king, but they are not slaves. They occupy an intermediate state of δημιοεργοί[2] or craftsmen and are classed with seers, physicians, and workers of wood. They may be forced to act against their real inclinations, as Phemius is when the Suitors compel him to sing for them,[3] but they are not negligible, since Agamemnon leaves a bard to look after Clytaemestra when he goes to Troy.[4] A similar position was held by Deor at one time of his career :

> And I of myself will say this thing,
> That a while I was the Heodenings' bard ;
> To my duke was I dear ; and Deor was my name,
> I had, for many winters, a worthy office,
> A handsome lord, until Heorrenda now,
> A man skilled in lays, the land-right has taken
> Which the Guardian of Earls of old had given me.[5]

Professional bards were probably employed also at the courts of the Mongol kings and khans in the middle ages. Pian de Carpini, who visited Batu Khan during the years 1245–7, says that the Khan never drank in public except to the accompaniment of songs and the music of guitars,[6] while Ibn Batuta tells how the Kipchak Turks drank to the accompaniment of songs,[7] and Friar William of Rubruck observed a similar practice at the court of the Mongol prince, Mangu Khan, in 1254.[8] We do not know that these songs were heroic, but since heroic song was practised by these peoples, some of them probably were.

In Gaul before the Roman conquest bards held a place of special honour in the entourage of kings and princes. When in 121 B.C. Bituitus, son of the king of the Arverni, went on an embassy to Domitius Ahenobarbus, he took with him a bard, who sang praises of the prince and his royal father.[9] A stray light on the treatment of bards in Gaul comes from Posidonius' account of Bituitus' father, Luerius, king of the Arverni. Luerius, who was renowned for his display and generosity, gave a feast :

---

[1] *Beowulf*, 1063 ff.   [2] *Od.* xvii, 382 ff.   [3] *Ibid.* xxii, 351 ff.
[4] *Ibid.* iii, 267 ff.   [5] *Deor*, 35-41.
[6] W. W. Rockhill, *The Journey of Friar John of Pian de Carpini* (London, 1903), p. 11.
[7] *Idem, Journey of Friar William of Rubruck* (London, 1903), p. 62.
[8] *Ibid.* p. 138.   [9] Appian, *Gall.* iv, 12.

When he had passed the time allotted for the feast, there arrived late a poet of the barbarians, who greeted the king and began to sing a song about his pre-eminence, and bewailed himself that he had come too late. The king was pleased and called for a bag of gold and threw it to him as he was running off. The bard picked it up and again sang of the king, saying that the tracks on the earth where he drove his chariot brought gold and benefactions to men.[1]

The Gaulish bards seem to have been a privileged class, since in their songs they were allowed to distribute abuse as well as praise.[2] This may have been a tribute to their magical powers and a permission to avert the evil eye or other bad luck by anticipating it with abuse. It is not clear whether bards were closely connected with the Druids, who exerted considerable power in Gaul, as in Britain, before the Roman conquest, but were eliminated after it. Perhaps the Gaulish bards were a special case in a social system where song was still credited with magical properties and associated with peculiar privileges and liberties. They evidently made some impression upon their Roman conquerors, since in the time of Nero, when Gaul was largely Romanised, Lucan mentions bards as singers who transmit to distant ages the fame of brave spirits who have perished in war.[3]

Though bards sing for kings and princes, their songs are enjoyed by the whole company present and create a special diversion in courtly life. In the first place, they show the devotion of his followers to their ruler, and it is instructive to note how the Kalmuck poet tells of a feast at Dzhangar's court, where, after two boys have passed cups of red porcelain, filled with wine, to the assembled warriors :

> Then the ministers flowed with red sweat,
> They became drunk on the right side and the left.
> Again they ran round in five circles,
> And all the ministers on the right side
> Began to extol their leader,
> And all the ministers on the left side
> Began to glorify their Shining One.[4]

In the second place, such songs inspire a love for prowess and glory. So Vambéry describes the effect of songs of battle on the Turkomans :

The hotter the battle, the fiercer grew the ardour of the singer and the enthusiasm of his youthful listeners ; and really the scene assumed the appearance of a romance, when the young nomads, uttering deep

---

[1] Athenaeus, iv, 152.　　　　[2] Diodorus, v, 31.
[3] *Pharsalia*, i, 447 ff.　　　　[4] *Dzhangariada*, p. 181.

groans, hurled their caps to the ground, and dashed their hands in a passion through the curls of their hair, just as if they were furious to combat with themselves.[1]

This scene recalls another, when Priscus went on his embassy to Attila and heard two bards reciting, and marked the effect of their songs :

> The banqueters fixed their eyes upon them, some being charmed with the songs, while others were roused in spirit, as the recollection of their wars came back to them. Others again burst into tears, because their bodies were enfeebled by age and their martial ardour had perforce to remain unsatisfied.[2]

In courts heroic songs are more than a mere pastime ; they are an important link between the ruler and the ruled whose common interest in war they reflect and inspire.

In war itself the bard may come into his own more than in peace, since he is able to inflame his own side against the enemy by singing songs of the great past. So Raoul le Tourtier records that when a party of Burgundians went to war with the men of Châtillon, they sent a *jongleur* in front of them who sang the deeds of their ancestors.[3] In his account of the battle of Hastings in 1066 William of Malmesbury, writing before 1127, says that the " cantilena Rollandi ", the song of Roland, was begun that " the warlike example of the man might inflame those who were about to fight ",[4] and Wace reports that the song was sung by Taillefer, who demanded the favour of striking the first blow against the enemy.[5] So too the minstrel in the *Song of William*, who has a long repertory of songs about Floovant, Charlemagne, Pepin, Roland, and Oliver, is also a distinguished soldier :

> Not in all France is singer good as he,
> Nor warrior who fights more valiantly.[6]

In *Ogier the Dane* the bard speaks of himself in highly favourable terms :
> Gentle he was, most high his lineage,
> Many songs made he of great baronage.[7]

In mediaeval France the bard might also be a warrior who used his songs to inspire his companions and did not shrink from setting an

---

[1] *Travels*, p. 322 ; Chadwick, *Growth*, iii, p. 175.
[2] Müller, *F.H.G.* iv, p. 92 ; cf. Chadwick, *H.A.* p. 84.
[3] *Miracula S. Benedicti*, 37. [4] Ed. Stubbs, iii, p. 302.
[5] *Rou*, ii, 8035 ff. ; cf. Gui d'Amiens, *Carmen de Hastingae proelio*, ed. F. Michel, in *Chroniques anglo-normandes*, iii, p. 18 ; Henry of Huntingdon, *Historiae Anglorum*, vi, 30 ; Geoffroi Gaimar, *Estorie des Engleis*, 5271 ff.
[6] 1260-61. [7] L. Gautier, *Les Épopées françaises*, i, p. 351.

example himself. An Asiatic counterpart to this may be seen in the *Manas* of the Kara-Kirghiz poet, Sayakbai Karalaev. In the character of Dzhaisan-yrchi he presents a bard who is also a warrior, who rides to war on his camel and celebrates important events as they happen. The scale of his songs is shown by the statement that he takes a whole noon to praise the trappings of a tent, which surely bears some relation to his inventor's own expansive art.[1] In war the bard, whatever his origin and status, may have a special prominence if he carries out his duties properly.

Courts may also provide employment for wandering bards who make a living by passing from one prince to another. So the speaker in *Widsith* presents himself as one who has made a good thing of his profession. Some of his boasts are demonstrably false, but, while we need not believe that he received a jewel from Guthere and bracelets from Aelfwine and Ermanaric, we may still accept his words as an idealised account of what success in his calling means :

> So wandering far   by fate are driven
> Men's lay-singers   over lands many,
> Their thrifts say they,   thankful words speak they,
> Ever, south or north,   with some one meet they
> Apt in glees,   of gifts unsparing,
> Who before the fighters wishes   his fame to exalt,
> Earlship to achieve,   until all is scattered,
> Light and life together ;   laud he gaineth,
> Hath under the heavens   high fame and fast.[2]

Widsith would like us to think him the chief of bards, the welcome guest of many kings, who reward him handsomely because he tells of their great doings, but behind his exaggeration and dreams of success we can discern the genuine practice of the Germanic world. The Slavonic princes too seem to have encouraged visiting minstrels. At the court of Vladimir, at least as the poets present it, Dobrynya Nikich disguises himself as a *skomorokh* or entertainer and sings at a wedding feast, where his own wife is on the point of being married to Alyosha Popovich :

> He began to wander over the strings,
> He began to lift up his voice . . .
> And all at the feast sat still and were silent,
> They sat and watched the entertainer . . .
> And everyone listened to his playing . . .
> Such playing had never been heard in the world,
> In the white world, such playing had never been known . . .

[1] *Manas*, p. 19.   [2] *Widsith*, 135-43.

Dobrynya played mournfully,
Mournfully, softly,
So that everyone, even princes and boyars,
Even those Russian heroes,
Were all deceived :
" Ah, young entertainer,
For your glorious playing,
For your sweet delights,
Drink green wine without measure,
Accept golden treasure untold." [1]

Dobrynya of course is a noble amateur, but nobody knows it, and the treatment of him no doubt reflects a genuine custom in Russia.

If the bard's position depends largely on kings and courts, it may equally well be exercised in other surroundings. In an aristocratic society, which takes itself seriously and pursues heroic ideals without a prince to guide it, the bard may have a position very like what he has at court. For instance, Jurij Križanić, writing about 1660, records that in his youth Croat and Serb nobles used to have soldiers behind them at banquets who sang of the doings of their ancestors and of such national heroes as Marko Kraljević, Novak Debeljak, and Miloš Kobilić.[2] But later the same world seems to have given up soldiers for this purpose and to have allowed the chief men themselves to sing such songs. So in the poems on the revolt against the Turks we find that the warriors refresh themselves with songs :

Then the Serbs sat down to rest in comfort ;
On their steeds the saddle girths they slackened,
Let them wander o'er the plain in hobbles,
And the heroes pulled out other garments,
Took their waist-bands off, put on fresh footwear ;
Who was sleepy, laid him down to slumber,
Who was not, would like to dance a little,
Called for bagpipes, called for Turkish fiddles . . .
Others of them sought the maple gusle
Some old song to sing, or else to listen
To the doings of their famous forbears.[3]

This is far removed from court life, but it shows how men of independent standing sing songs for pleasure and derive inspiration from them. The Serbs recall the past in a present which is for them no less glorious. If a man wins glory, they see in him an example of what they themselves wish to be :

[1] Miller, i, p. 59 ff.   [2] Chadwick, *Growth*, ii, p. 444.
[3] Morison, p. x.

> And his name will never be forgotten
> But in years to come will be remembered
> While there still exists the Serbian spirit ;
> Never will the Serbians forget him.[1]

Like Achilles, the Serb patriots console themselves with songs about the glorious doings of men.

In a bourgeois society such songs are much rarer, no doubt because merchants and traders are not very interested in heroic doings. None the less the transition from a princely society to a mercantile may sometimes be so rapid that something survives from the old manners and tastes. This happened when Novgorod succeeded Kiev as the centre of Russian civilisation in the thirteenth century. There the art of heroic song continued to be practised, and a great prominence is given to Sadko, who is both a merchant and a minstrel, or rather begins by being a poor minstrel and ends by becoming a rich merchant. When he first comes to Novgorod, he relies on his songs to find him a living, but before long his situation is serious :

> Once Sadko had no goods ;
> He had only his gusli of maple-wood ;
> Sadko went to play at the banquets.
> One day they did not ask Sadko to the gay banquet,
> The second day they did not ask him to the gay banquet,
> The third day they did not ask him to the gay banquet.[2]

The rich men of Novgorod are even more fickle than the prince who dismissed Deor. In their society the minstrel is paid by being invited to banquets, and when he ceases to amuse and is no longer asked, he is ruined.

Nowadays most bards belong to the people and practise their art among them. With such it is not always easy to distinguish between amateurs and professionals. In some countries, notably in Russia, bards seem on the whole to have some other work and to sing songs in their spare time. Two families, which have produced a number of bards, the Ryabinins and the Kryukovs, make their ordinary living from activities connected with fishing on Lake Onega and the White Sea respectively, but on winter nights or at local festivals sing songs to please the populace. Trofim Ryabinin, indeed, thought it below his dignity to receive any pay.[3] The same seems to be true of Jugoslavia and Greece, where bards are often men of some standing who would refuse payment for what they regard as a social accomplishment. Such

---

[1] *Idem*, p. 10.   [2] Rybnikov, ii, p. 345.   [3] *Idem*, i, p. lxxix.

were, no doubt, some of the bards known to Karadžić, and the Greek, Patzelios, who composed *Master John*. But of course in any society which lives close to the level of subsistence, a man may well wish to supplement his income by singing songs, like the Russian, Kuzma Romanov, who complained to Gilferding that a man had made him chant several songs and then had given him only ten kopecs.[1]

Sometimes a bard may, even in a proletarian society, be a professional and rely on his songs for his living. Such a class seems to have been recognised in the Dark Ages by the Frisians, since the last clause of the *Lex Frisonum* fixes a compensation for injury to the hand of a harper,[2] and it would hardly do this if the harper were not a professional. Such a Frisian was Bernlef, who became a disciple of St. Leger before 785. Before that he had been blind for three years and " was greatly loved by his neighbours for his geniality and his skill in reciting to the harp stories of the deeds of the ancients and the wars of kings ".[3] Such men could be seen recently in Bosnia and Montenegro, and the impression made by a modern Greek bard on an observant foreigner can be seen from a description by G. F. Abbott at the end of the last century:

> Some time ago I was fortunate enough to come across one of these curious relics of a bygone age — probably among the last of his race. . . . Barba Sterios (this was my minstrel's name) seemed to embody in himself all the characteristics of Homer's Demodocus. Like his proto-type, he was old and blind. But neither age nor infirmity prevented him from regularly taking up his favourite station outside the Gate of Kalamaria at Thessalonica. Every afternoon he might be seen sitting cross-legged by the road-side under the shadow of the old Venetian walls, forming the centre of a ring of admiring listeners whom the shrill strains of his lyre drew from far and near. . . . Less fortunate than his predecessor of the *Odyssey*, he was not the guest of kings, his only hearers being a crowd of the lowest class, most of them as poor as the bard himself. They never failed, however, to reward his efforts with a few coppers or with a present in kind for which Barba Sterios' bag hung always open by his side.[4]

If Barba Sterios represents a common type of bard in humble societies, he is not the only type. Against him we may set the Jugoslav, Ćor Huso, who travelled from place to place on a horse, clothed in rich trappings which were said by local gossip to have been given to him at the court of the Emperor Franz Josef II.[5]

Singing is not necessarily confined to men. It is true that

---

[1] Chettéoui, p. 21.   [2] Mon. Germ. *Legg.* iii, p. 699.
[3] *Vita S. Ludgeri*, ii, 1.   [4] Abbott, p. 5 ff.
[5] Information from Mr. A. B. Lord.

there is no evidence that women sang heroic songs in the ancient Greek or Germanic worlds, or that they do so now in Greece or Jugoslavia. Their normal outlet seems to be some kind of lyrical poetry, such as they sing in the *Iliad* and still sing in Jugoslavia with their *ženske pjesme*, which differ greatly in their subjects and often in their form from the songs sung by men. On the other hand women seem to sing heroic songs in some parts of Asia. A Kalmuck poet tells how at the court of the great chief Dzhangar, one of his wives, Orchilangin-migmiyan, which is said to mean " flowering beauty ", sings at a feast :

> She sings that song and plays,
> Lifts a sandalwood pipe to her red lips.
> She sings, and that song is wafted
> To all six thousand valleys of the Altai mountains,
> As if they sang and played near by.[1]

Since her song is in praise of Dzhangar, as the peerless ruler and heroic defender of the Buddhist faith, it has presumably some qualities of heroic song, even if it is no more than panegyric. Another Asiatic case comes from the Yakuts, of whom Shklovsky says :

> To this day in the farthest north-east of Siberia, you will still hear in some dark hut, lighted only by the fire, the story of the dreadful Djennik, told in monotonous recitative by an old blind woman. . . . The old woman describes in minute detail the terrible operation of flaying, and what kinds of knives were used ; and on the seats by the wall are the listening Yakuts, with pale terrified faces, too frightened to utter a word.[2]

It is perhaps surprising that a woman should tell the tale of Djennik, who led a revolt of the Yakuts on the Yenisei in the seventeenth century, but when we remember the special position of women among these peoples as repositories of wisdom, it is perhaps only natural that they should hold among other offices that of singing about the past and its great events. Among the Yakuts a poet is still close enough to a shaman to be expected to know things which are concealed from others, and women, with their peculiar position, are well fitted to be singers.

Different causes must account for the considerable part which women have taken in Russian recitations for at least the last century. When Rybnikov began his researches into *byliny* in 1860, women were already prominent, and since then their number

[1] *Dzhangariada*, p. 154.
[2] I. V. Shklovsky, *In Far North-East Siberia* (London, 1916), p. 209 ; Chadwick, *Growth*, iii, p. 186.

has either increased or become more noticeable. The second alternative is at least possible in a country where women have been emancipated within living memory and before that were shy to appear before a stranger and sing to him. Recent enquirers have not been afraid to enter the huts of peasants and talk to the women in them, with the result that a large number of songs by women have now been recorded. In Rybnikov's collection women have 8 per cent of the names; in Gilferding's, made ten years later, 18 per cent; in that of the Sokolov brothers, made in 1926–8, 60 per cent; in Astakhova's made from the Pudozhsk region in 1941 there are six women and eight men. Not too much must be deduced from these figures, but it is clear that for nearly a hundred years women have sung *byliny* in Russia, and it is not surprising that the number of them is increasing. On the other hand women do not seem always to have done this. The *byliny* themselves say nothing about female minstrels, nor do any of the documents from the past which touch on the subject. The development looks like a purely proletarian growth, due to the equality of life which hard conditions impose on a nation of peasants and fisher-folk. Since women have to work like men, they seem also to have taken over some of men's other tasks, like that of reciting songs. Nor do they reveal any inferiority in it. If no woman is so good a performer as Ryabinin, yet in our own time Marfa Kryukova is far more original and productive than most of her male contemporaries.

In considering the social condition of bards, we have noticed incidentally that some, like Bernlef or Barba Sterios or the Yakut women, are blind, and indeed the bard's profession is often associated with blindness. The first examples come from the Greeks, who had their legends of prehistoric poets like

> Blind *Thamyris* and blind *Maeonides*,
> And *Tiresias* and *Phineus* Prophets old.

Such legends seem to have been known to Homer, who tells the story of Thamyris, how he tried to surpass the Muses in song and was in consequence punished by them, being robbed both of his gift for song and of his sight.[1] More significant is Homer's account of his own Demodocus:

> Him did the Muse love abundantly, but gave to him both good and evil;
> Him she robbed of his eyes, but gave him the gift of sweet singing.[2]

Homer knew of blind bards, and it was perhaps inevitable that he too was thought to be blind. The old etymology which explains

[1] *Il.* ii, 594 ff.   [2] *Od.* viii, 63-4.

his name, Ὅμηρος, as meaning " blind " has little to recommend it, and the Greek *Lives of Homer*, which speak of his blindness, are almost worthless as authorities since they reconstruct an imaginary Homer from incidents in his poems.[1] Nor in fact are all Homer's bards blind. Demodocus is, but Phemius is not, and it is just as possible that Homer modelled Phemius on himself as that he modelled Demodocus. On the other hand the poet of the Homeric Hymn to Apollo speaks of himself as " a blind man who lives in rocky Chios ".[2] This proves at least that some poet who recited heroic songs was blind, but it may prove more. Though it is hard to believe that a blind man composed the *Iliad* and the *Odyssey* with their many visual effects and their keen eye for the visible world, yet he may have owed much to formulae, even if it is hard to see how he used them so aptly. He may even have become blind in later life and lived on his earlier memories. And is there not in the *Odyssey* some dimming of visual impressions such as we find in the later work of Milton?

In modern times blind bards are quite common, though perhaps less common than is sometimes thought. They are sometimes found among the Turkomans and the Ainus.[3] Among the Sundanese of western Java they are said to be more usual than sighted persons.[4] Among the Jugoslavs an early example comes from 1547, when a blind soldier, conducted by his daughter, sang of Marko Kraljević in Splijt to a large crowd.[5] In the present century Murko says that they are rare, but a number of travellers have seen them. In Russia some bards of considerable renown have been blind, notably Ivan Feponov, whom Gilferding met in 1870 and who was known as " blind Ivan "; Kuzma Romanov, the rival of Trofim Ryabinin; [6] Mina Efimov, who lived in the eighteenth century, travelled a great deal and was said to have learned his *byliny* in Moscow.[7] Nor is it difficult to see why some bards are blind. If a child is born blind in a simple society, he can do nothing useful either as a worker or a soldier and is barred from helping his family and himself to live. He can, however, learn and practise the art of song, and, since blindness tends to strengthen the memory, it may even help a man to master the traditional formulae and themes. If he becomes blind in mature years, he can, if he becomes a bard, have a profession which will keep him from

---

[1] G. Wiemer, *Ilias und Odyssee als Quelle der Biographen Homers*, Marienburg, 1905/1908.
[2] *Hom. Hymn*, iii, 172; cf. *inf.* p. 432.
[3] Chadwick, *Growth*, iii, p. 176; *Botteghe Oscure*, vii (1951), p. 236.
[4] Hurgronje in a letter to Drerup, p. 57.
   Chadwick, *Growth*, ii, p. 444.   [6] *Idem*, ii, p. 252.
   Gilferding, i, p. 468.

starvation and win him respect among his people.

The social position of bards is not always secure. In some societies they have been viewed with suspicion and hostility, especially by religious authorities. In the early centuries of English Christianity the Church was fully conscious of the existence and popularity of heroic poetry and not always well disposed towards it. Perhaps that is why the early Anglo-Saxon poets go out of their way to display their devoutness. Just as *Widsith* says that God gave government to men, so *Waldhere* says that He cares for them, and *Deor* that rewards and punishments await them after death. These tributes may be no more than attempts on the part of the bard to avoid clerical anathema. With *Beowulf* it is different. The poet has tried hard to adapt his old heroic subject to a Christian point of view. His heroes are models of what princes ought to be; his monsters are of the breed of Cain. He presents what is in fact a compromise between two hostile interests. The great men of the Dark Ages were proud of their ancestors and their heroic doings, but found that the Church condemned both and disapproved of attempts to glorify them. It was quite reasonable of the Frisian king, Redbad, to withdraw from the font in 718 when he heard that his ancestors were in Hell, " in Tartarea damnatione ".[1] When the Church told him that his fathers were wicked, he decided that the Church was wrong. About the same time Bede censures monks and priests for listening to *fabulae* and *fabulationes*,[2] whose matter cannot have been far removed from traditional tales of fights and adventures. How bitter the controversy was can be seen from a letter written in 787 by Alcuin to Hygebald, bishop of Lindisfarne, denouncing the clergy for inviting harpists to entertain them at dinner and adding :

> What has Ingeld to do with Christ ? Strait is the house, it will not be able to hold them both. The king of heaven will have no part with the so-called kings who are heathen and damned ; for the one king reigns eternally in heaven, the heathen is damned and groans in hell.[3]

Ingeld, to whom *Beowulf* makes a passing reference,[4] is no doubt named because his story was one of intestine fights and a fierce revenge conducted in no Christian spirit. Alcuin was of course an extremist, and not everyone would go all the way with him. For instance, King Alfred shows his taste for the old stories when

---

[1] Cf. Plummer, *Baedae Op. Hist.* ii, p. 289.
[2] *Hist. Eccl.* iv, 25.
[3] Mon. Germ. *Epist. Carol.* ii, p. 124.
[4] *Beowulf*, 2064 ; cf. *Widsith*, 45 ff. ; Saxo, pp. 205-13.

in his translation of Boethius he replaces the Latin words " Where are the bones of Fabricius the true-hearted ? " with " Where are the bones of Weyland Smith, and who knows where they be ? " Yet the opposition of the Church to the old stories must have done much to curb the activity of the poetical tradition and may have been responsible for the decay of the old stories. Up to a point it seems to have made amends for this by encouraging a new kind of heroic poem on contemporary events like that on the death of Edward the Confessor. The Church had no objection to heroic poetry as such but did not like its heathen heroes.

The conflict with the Church did not make things easy for those bards who followed the old ways and told the old stories. Not only did King Olaf Tryggvason change the subject when Gestr recited *Brynhild's Hell Ride*,[1] which has after all been touched by Christian sentiment in its conception of a love stronger than death, but according to the *Hallfrethar Saga*,[2] he reproved the Icelandic poet Hallfrethar for introducing the old gods into his poems. The poet might well have to adapt his matter to suit his patrons, and perhaps some such situation may account for one of the less happy anomalies in *Beowulf*. Though on the whole the poet makes his characters Christians, he is uncertain about the Danes. Twice indeed they are Christians,[3] but once he goes out of his way to make them heathens and denounces them for it. After telling of Grendel's raids on Hrothgar's hall, he says :

At whiles they vowed   in the heathen-tents
Of idol-worship,   prayed with words
That the Slayer of Spirits   succour would send them
Against that plague of the people.   Such was their practice,
The hope of the heathen ;   'twas hell they remembered
In the thoughts of their minds.   Their Maker they knew not,
The Dempster of deeds,   nor wist of Divine God.[4]

When he says that the Danes prayed to idols and especially to the Devil, he contradicts much that he says elsewhere about Hrothgar and his men and denies his own high appreciation of their many virtues. It has been surmised that he did this because the Danes of his own time were not Christians, but his emphatic outburst is more probably to be attributed to his desire to show some patron how true a Christian he is. The effort spoils his presentation of Hrothgar and introduces a discordant, unheroic note. The poet of *Roland*, in his instinctive and unquestioning Christianity, would not make the mistake of calling his heroes heathen.

[1] Cf. *sup.* p. 411.   [2] Cap. 6.
[3] *Beowulf*, 90 ff., 316 ff.   [4] *Ibid.* 175-81.

Another conflict between Church and bards can be seen at a lower level of society in Russia in the sixteenth and seventeenth centuries, when the *skomorokhi* who sang *byliny* were much in demand as entertainers in Moscow and seem to have presumed on their position to cause trouble by their unbridled habits.[1] They would form themselves into large companies and rob countrymen and townsmen. This led to conflict with the ecclesiastical authorities. In 1551 the *skomorokhi* were solemnly condemned at the council of Stoglov, and there was a current proverb " *Skomorokh* and priest are no comrades ".[2] For a time their situation was saved by Ivan the Terrible, who, according to Fletcher, " recreateth himself with the empresse till supper time, with jesters and dwarfes, men and women, that tumble before him, and sing many songs after the Russe manner ".[3] In due course the civil power took action, and the Tsar Alexei Mikhailovich (1645–76) initiated persecution. This was doubtless due to ecclesiastical persuasion, and a reflection of it can be seen in a *bylina* in which St. Nicholas tells Sadko to cease playing and throw away his *gusli* since it causes destruction.[4] In Russia there seems to have been little hostility towards the old stories as such; the case was entirely against the bards. But this had a lasting effect. It meant that heroic poetry went underground and ceased to have royal or noble patrons. In due course it disappeared from cities and survived only in remote districts where it could not be controlled, and no one of importance was much interested in it.

Something of the same kind might have happened in France if special circumstances had not saved the situation. The *jongleurs* who sang heroic poems were liable to be regarded as dangerous and immoral persons. Though they had powerful patrons like Robert of Normandy[5] and Philip Augustus,[6] they were the victims of denunciations and enactments from the eleventh to the fourteenth century.[7] This was no doubt due to their low jokes and lewd songs and had probably nothing to do with their recitation of heroic poems. Indeed, when they took this up in the eleventh century, they seem to have been encouraged in it. This may partly be because in addition to *chansons de geste* they sang metrical tales of saints and were tolerated in the first because of the second. At least in the thirteenth century the English casuist Thomas Cabham, who condemns *jongleurs* in principle, makes an exception : " sunt qui dicuntur ioculatores, qui cantant gesta principum et vitas

---

[1] Chadwick, *Growth*, ii, p. 266 ff.   [2] A. Mazon, *Bylines*, p. 686.
[3] *Russia at the Close of the Sixteenth Century* (London, 1856), p. 142.
[4] Rybnikov, ii, p. 27.   [5] Ordericus Vitalis, x, 18.
[6] Rigord, *De Gestis Philippi Augusti*, p. 21.   [7] Faral, p. 18 ff.

sanctorum. Bene possunt sustineri tales." [1] A similar point of view can be seen in the same century in the treatise *De septem sacramentis*, whose author makes a distinction between those who " disfigure the image of God " by their low tricks and others who are more serious : " sed si cantant cum instrumentis et de gestis ad recreationem et forte ad informationem, vicini sunt excusationi ".[2] Indeed it is reported that at this time ministers of the Church spoke favourably of *jongleurs* and compared them to the evangelists.[3] That such distinctions were possible is clear enough from *Roland* and the *Cid*, which not only provide their own brands of historical information but display an impeccable piety in their outlooks. The bad name of the *jongleurs* goes back at least to 813 when the third council of Tours forbade the clergy to watch their profane spectacles,[4] but in the eleventh and twelfth centuries they seem to have become respectable and to have been tolerated provided that they performed heroic poems.

Christianity is not the only religion which sometimes causes inconvenience to its bards. Islam is capable of doing something of the same kind. The Uzbek bard, Fazil Yuldashev, was in the early years of this century summoned before the spiritual judge of his district, called Safar. Fazil began to sing of Rustam, but was interrupted by Safar, who asked : " Did Rustam live before the prophet Mohammed or after ? " Knowing that Rustam was a heathen, he forbade Fazil to sing this song. Later Fazil was again summoned and again began to sing of Rustam. The judge stopped him and asked if he had forgotten that he was forbidden to sing of this subject. When Fazil explained that this was another Rustam, the judge said : " But this Rustam, of whom you sing, also lived before Mohammed and was a heathen ". Fazil replied that Rustam was a Mohammedan and a great warrior, the son of a sultan, and this satisfied the judge sufficiently to let him bid Fazil proceed. Knowing the temper and convictions of his audience, Fazil gave to his hero all the qualities of a true-believing Mohammedan. His hearers were quite satisfied when they heard from him that in boyhood Rustam studied with a mullah and was a god-fearing man. They advised the poet in future to give more careful preparation to his poems, but otherwise he was allowed to go in peace.[5] This little episode shows that at times the Mohammedan bard must be as careful as his Christian predecessors of the Middle

---

[1] *Pénitentiel*, quoted by Faral, p. 44.
[2] Quoted by L. Gautier, *Épopées françaises*, ii, p. 11.
[3] Quoted from MS. Bibl. Nat. Lat. 16481 by L. de la Marche, *La Chaire française au XIIIe siècle*, p. 445.   [4] Mansi, xiv, p. 84.
[5] Zhirmunskii-Zarifov, p. 34.

Ages, and that if he wishes to keep his popularity, he must shape his stories to suit the religious views of his superiors.

Politics seem to interfere with heroic poetry less than religion does, but at times they make themselves felt. The Uzbeks again provide interesting examples. The beys, who for most purposes governed the country, were afraid of democratic tendencies and disliked poems which displayed them, and particularly any which told how a poor and humble man became a bey himself and won victories over some khan. Once the bard, Sultan-Murad, was summoned by the local beys to sing a poem from the cycle of Gorogli, but, when he told that his hero became the head of his people, one of the beys struck him on the lips with the hard heel of his slipper, crying out : " How dare you call that beggar Gorogli a sultan ! " [1] When the political situation in Uzbekstan became more critical and bards tended to take the proletarian side, they might well get into considerable trouble by their songs. The poet Nurman often voiced in his poems protests against the old social order. He had a great popular success with his poem *Namoz*, in which he celebrated the warlike exploits of that rebel-leader as worthy of the great Gorogli. Rumours of this reached the governing powers, and on their instructions Nurman was arrested and thrown without preliminary enquiry into prison, where he spent some four years in hard physical labour, was often beaten and bullied, and had his health so impaired that, when he was released, he was physically broken, though he continued to compose poems and did not die until 1940.[2] Such situations as this can themselves become subjects for poems, and it is instructive to see how in his *Mamatkarim-pavlan* Fazil Yuldashev brings his hero into conflict with the authorities against whom he has formed a conspiracy. The police receive orders to watch him as he goes to town to meet his companions. Ten soldiers " each with a rifle in one hand and a sword in the other " arrest him and lead him off to prison, while the crowd accompanies him with words of encouragement. In prison he is kept alive by fruit, bread, butter, and other gifts from outside. He remains under lock and key until the revolution comes and brings his release.[3] The story is based on what must have been a common enough experience in 1916 and 1917, when the Uzbeks anticipated what was to happen in Russia by revolting against their local khans. The bards, who had once been the favourites of these khans, seem to have lost much of their old position and to have surrendered their places to more modern

---

[1] Zhirmunskii-Zarifov, p. 33.
[2] *Idem*, p. 53. Gorogli is the same as Kurroglou.   [3] *Idem*, p. 463 ff.

artists. This may help to account for their discontent and vigorous espousal of the revolutionary cause.

We may now turn to the question of the training of bards in their craft, though it is a matter on which evidence is by no means abundant. The ancient authorities say next to nothing either in actual poems or in references to them. Indeed the only relevant case is Homer's Phemius, who says that he is self-taught and that his songs come from a god.[1] That his songs come from a god is intelligible enough, since that is Phemius' way of describing his ability to improvise. But that he was entirely self-taught is hard to believe. For this kind of poetry has so many conventions and is so traditional that the bard can hardly teach himself everything. He must at least observe how other bards work and learn their various devices and aids. Perhaps Phemius means no more than that he acknowledges no master but has picked up the art of song in many places and relies on the god to do the rest, that his actual performances are his own and not repetitions of other men's work. This is a legitimate view and recalls Radlov's Kara-Kirghiz bard who claimed that the god gave him words and that he spoke directly from his inner being.[2] Indeed though ancient poets might be so convinced of their inspiration as to feel no obligation to any teachers and believe themselves to derive everything from the Muse or a god, we can hardly admit that this is a fair statement of the facts in a society which practises traditional heroic poetry. Just because it is traditional, such a poetry is passed from one bard to another and, whether the younger bard has a single teacher or picks up his art where he can, it is clear that he must learn it from somebody. Otherwise he would lack the technique which enables him to improvise at short notice and to provide the kind of song which his audience expects. Phemius in fact seems to have been boasting and must not be taken literally as a witness to the way in which such poetry is composed.

On the other hand it cannot be disputed that at least in some primitive societies bards may believe that they have been inspired to their calling by a divine visitation or vision. Some Uzbek bards, often illiterate shepherds, claim that they have been visited in dreams by unknown figures, usually in the guise of Mohammedan holy men, who give them a *dombra* or stringed instrument and say, " You will be a bard ! " When they awake, they find that they are able to compose songs and sing them. So too the Kara-Kirghiz have tales of men in like positions who have dreams in which Manas and his forty companions command them to sing of their

[1] *Od.* xxii, 347.   [2] Cf. *sup.* p. 41.

achievements.[1] Such stories recall Caedmon, who too was a shepherd and so unable to sing that when others began to do so he left the company, until one night an angel came to him in a dream and dictated to him a hymn which he afterwards sang.[2] So too Norse legend tells that a shepherd used to visit the tomb of the poet Thorleifr in the hope of being inspired to write an elegy on him, until eventually the barrow opened and the poet came out and granted his wish.[3] There is no need to deny an element of truth in such stories. Dreams may well give a man the confidence and impulse which he needs to start poetical composition. He will regard them with great awe as coming from the gods and remember them clearly, and, what is more, he will feel that the gods have chosen him for a task, and this will give him a special sense of his own importance and ability. It is largely a psychological question of overcoming certain inhibitions and misgivings, and once a dream has done this with divine authority, the man may well take to singing songs to the best of his newly discovered ability.

Once a poet has found himself and his calling, he will still need to be trained in some way or other. Our best information on this in modern times comes from Russian bards of the last and present centuries. Trofim Ryabinin gave Rybnikov an account of his own development, which may well be typical of his kind. When he was still a boy, Trofim used to go round villages mending fishing-nets, and in this pursuit made the acquaintance of a poor old man, Ilya Elustafevich, who did the same kind of work, and, while he worked, sang. He was much renowned for his songs and died in 1830 at the age of about ninety. From him Ryabinin learned many of his songs. But he had also other masters — Fedor Trepalin of the hamlet of Migury; Ivan Kokozhin, who once kept an inn at St. Petersburg and transcribed a number of *byliny*, which he used to read aloud; and his own uncle, Ignatii Andreev, who was said to be an even better bard than Ilya Elustafevich.[4] Ryabinin clearly possessed a gift and a taste for song from the start, and probably nothing could have stopped him from learning it, but we can see how he picked it up as opportunity offered and profited from all the local masters.

In recent years evidence is more plentiful, and two accounts, coming from the bards themselves, may help to show what

---

[1] Zhirmunskii-Zarifov, p. 26.
[2] Bede, *Hist. Eccl.* iv, 24.
[3] Chadwick, *Growth*, iii, p. 902; cf. the story, ascribed by Isocrates, *Helena*, 64, to the Sons of Homer, that Helen appeared to Homer in a dream and bade him tell of the expedition to Troy.
[4] Chettéoui, p. 17 ff.

happens. Both are from the region of Pudozhзk. The first is Anna Pashkova :

" I knew *byliny* but did not sing them. Another time, after work, I made variations on them. But I was instructed by my aunt, then by Ilya Zubov. He was an old man at Yarcheva ; he was very proud. There was also a haberdasher, Danilo, who sang. Day passes, in the evening the men gather together and sing. I learned everything when I was still a girl. Afterwards Abrosim Kuplyansky sang, and I listened. They told tales in a small company : you sit and sit, and sleep over the spinning, and begin to tell stories. I did not like stories, but I liked *byliny*. Of *byliny*, that of Churilo Plenkovich pleased me most." [1]

The second is Mikhail Pavkov :

" I heard *byliny* from Yakushov. When I was eleven and thirteen I worked with him at a timber-mill. I sang ' Sukhmanty Odikhman-tevich ' and ' Dobrynya Nikitich ' (not all of it). I sang earlier than others, but when I went to the German war and became a prisoner, I began to forget. They smiled at me and said : ' What use are they to you ? ' In 1939, on March 9th, I sang to the women about Sukhman, and the women collected in our village to hear me. Yakushov was from our village. The motifs of my *byliny* come from him." [2]

While Pashkova learns her art from various people and picks it up as well as she can, Pavkov is fortunate in having lived in the same village as Yakushov, who is said by the Sokolovs to have been one of the finest singers known. In their main outlines these two careers are quite similar to Rybnikov's. The young aspirant picks up his art by listening to his elders and then tries his own hand at it.

These scanty and not very informative examples suggest one or two conclusions about the training of bards. First, it seems to begin early in life, no doubt because if a boy has a taste and a talent for this art, he will show it early, but also because the claims which it makes on the memory are in most cases too great for a man who starts in mature years. Indeed the ability to produce songs at short notice and to sustain them for several hours must require a training in its own way as difficult as any other artistic pursuit, and it is essential to start early. Secondly, the aspirant seems usually to pick up his craft for himself where he can. If the home or the village is the most natural place for this, there is no reason why he should not learn also from visiting singers or from men in other places. Local tradition may be powerful, but it need not prevent him from picking up useful material elsewhere. Thirdly, such bards must be born with a special assortment of talents. They must have good memories, be able to sing at least audibly, have a taste for words and their management, understand the kind of

---

[1] Astakhova, p. 62.   [2] *Idem*, p. 445.

subject which will appeal to their audiences. Fourthly, such an art thrives on a popular love of it. The greater the love, the more abundant the art. This at least is the case among the Kara-Kirghiz and to a lesser degree among the Russians and the Jugoslavs. Just because a people takes pride and pleasure in the use of words, the task is made much easier for those who wish to become poets.

The ways in which a bard can learn his craft illustrate the nature of a poetical tradition. Such a tradition may work through a family, as it does with the Russian Kryukovs and Ryabinins. Perhaps Homer indicates something of the same kind when he makes Phemius the son of Terpius, an imaginary name meaning " the delighter ".[1] Sometimes such a tradition may last for centuries. The Uzbek bard, Ergash Dzhumanbulbul (1870–1938), traced his descent back through five generations of bards. His father, Dzhuman (c. 1830–88), was sufficiently famous to win the addition of the word *bulbul*, " nightingale ", to his name, and his two brothers were renowned both as singers and as teachers.[2] But such family traditions are often strengthened by other traditions derived from place. Just as Trofim Ryabinin learned some of his songs from local singers not in his family, so the elder Dzhuman learned much from a bard called Buran, who lived in the district of Samarcand and died about 1860, having been the master of some ten famous Uzbek bards. Singing may prosper in certain districts, as it does in the Pudozhsk district of Russia, which has produced most of the famous recent bards and is still a lively home of them, or the Kurgan district in Uzbekstan, where in the middle of the nineteenth century there were more than twenty bards in seven large households or groups of families.[3] The different places in which poetry flourishes may develop their own tastes and characteristics and produce something which looks like a local school of bards. For instance, the Uzbeks of Kurgan are famous for poems of a religious character, but they have also their own repertory of heroic subjects, which fill about twenty-eight different poems, while the bards in the district of Khorezm are specially devoted to epic themes and use some which have parallels in poems from Azerbaijan and the Turkomans but not among other Uzbeks.[4] Indeed the strength of local taste may be seen in some words of Fazil, who belongs to Samarcand :

" Get rid of those boring stories of lovesick lamentations of a madman who weeps for love ! Better sing us a song of heroic exploits, which exalt the soul." [5]

---

[1] *Od.* xxii, 330.   [2] Zhirmunskii-Zarifov, p. 44.
[3] *Idem*, p. 45.   [4] *Idem*, 54 ff.   [5] *Idem*, p. 35.

Whatever a man's family may do for him, he will undoubtedly widen his range and strengthen his art if he is fortunate enough to live in a district where song is a popular art.

From a local school of the Uzbek kind it is but a little step to some kind of organisation like a guild. This normally implies that the bard is a professional and earns money through his performances and that he is assisted in this by other men engaged on the same work. The Russian *skomorokhi* of the sixteenth and seventeenth centuries were such professionals, organised in companies which provided instruction and worked together to produce a variety of entertainments of which heroic poetry was one. It is possible that the Gaulish bards were connected with the Druids, and in that case they would belong to a separate class and enjoy special privileges. The French and Spanish troubadours of the Middle Ages resembled the *skomorokhi* in being largely professionals, who performed at ecclesiastical festivals and on pilgrimage-routes as well as in the houses of princes and nobles. Something of the same sort but more elaborate seems to have existed in Greece, at least after Homer's time. In Chios the Sons of Homer claimed to be his true descendants, to possess private poems, to know of his life, and to have the right to bestow crowns on those who deserved well of him. They were known to Pindar in the fifth century B.C. and to Plato's Ion, and seem to have been closely connected with the rhapsodes who both recited the Homeric poems and composed poems of their own.[1] These men recited the Homeric poems but composed for them preludes, which survive as Homeric Hymns, and were themselves sometimes authors of new poems. Whether the Sons of Homer were actually descended from him cannot be proved and is of no great importance. What matters is that the bards who sang his poems and composed others of the same kind were believed to belong to his family and claimed special rights because of it. In this case the family tradition became self-conscious and organised itself in a way to which there is no close parallel elsewhere.

The results of this tradition may account for certain important elements in Homer's influence, and especially for the early spread of his renown. That his name and works were famous early in the seventh century is clear from two facts. First, other poems like the *Cypria*, *Little Iliad*, *Sack of Troy*, *Returns*, and *Telegony*, were formed round the *Iliad* and *Odyssey* to form a cycle which told a more or less continuous story from the abduction of Helen to the

---

[1] Pindar, *Nem.* ii, 1 ff. with scholia; Harpocration, *s.v.* Ὁμηρίδαι; Strabo, 645; Plato, *Rep.* 599 D; *Ion*, 530 C; cf. Allen, *Origins*, pp. 42-50.

death of Odysseus. This may have happened early in the seventh century and certainly not much later than Homer himself. This would not have happened if the *Iliad* and the *Odyssey* had not won a peculiar renown and an almost canonical place in popular regard. They must soon have been well known far outside their place of origin, and there is good evidence that they were known even in Sparta by the middle of the seventh century, when echoes of them can be heard in Tyrtaeus and Alcman. It looks as if Homer's example inspired other poets to do the same kind of thing, and, even if, as Aristotle suggests,[1] they were not very successful, it merely shows how pre-eminent he was. Secondly Homer, no doubt because of the fame of his two great poems, was credited with the authorship of others like the *Thebaid*, on the war of the *Seven against Thebes*, the *Successors* on the second war against Thebes, and the *Cypria* on the preliminaries to the Trojan War. It is unlikely that Homer composed these poems, which have in some cases names of other poets attached to them, but since they were ascribed to him, it looks as if they owed much to his example and influence, and their connection with him was a tribute to this. Though Homer himself seems to have come towards the end of a long tradition, he set an example which encouraged others to compose in his manner and kept heroic poetry alive for two or three more generations.

The peculiar fame and position of Homer may account for a remarkable passage in the Hymn to Apollo, which is a composite work but contains in its first part a complete poem composed for performance at a festival in Delos. It is almost certainly a prelude intended to be sung before the singing of the Homeric poems.[2] After telling of the birth of Apollo, the bard continues in the usual way by invoking the gods, but, more unusually, adds some words with a personal note :

> Now Apollo have mercy, and Artemis be thou kind :
> And so farewell to you all. Yet bear me in mind,
> Maidens, whenever there comes in after-days
> A son of this earth, inured to pain, and says :
> " Tell me, maidens, of poets that visit here
> Who sings you the sweetest, whom do you hold most dear ? "
> Remember me then, one answer, one only, giving :
> " A man that is blind, in scarry Chios living,
> Supreme in song both now and in times to come ".
> And I to you shall give honour, wherever I roam
> Among fine cities of men, telling ever of you ;
> And all shall believe, for the thing that I speak is true.[3]

---

[1] *Poetics*, 1459b, 2. [2] Pindar, *Nem.* ii, i.
[3] *Hom. Hymn*, iii, 165-75. Trs. T. F. Higham.

There is no certain way of fixing the date of this poem. It may possibly be as early as 700 B.C., since at that time the Ionian assembly, to which it refers, was already prominent in Greek life. Nor is there anything in the text to contradict this view. There is therefore at first sight no strong reason to reject the view of Thucydides that the poem is actually the work of Homer, who speaks of himself in the lines quoted.[1] This is an attractive view, but there are difficulties about it. First, Thucydides' authority on a matter of literary history is not final. He does no more than report current opinion, which was inclined to ascribe many poems to Homer. Secondly, though the poem has many Homeric formulae, it has others which are not Homeric, and in view of Homer's rigorous consistency in the use of formulae such a divergence is an obstacle to accepting Homer's authorship. For instance, Homer does not use ἑκάτοιο ἄνακτος (63, 90) or λιμένες τε θαλάσσης (24) or κῦμα κελαινόν (27) or ἂν νήσους τε καὶ ἀνέρας (142). The phrase μείδησε δὲ γαῖ᾽ ὑπένερθεν (118) looks like a variation on the Homeric γέλασσε δὲ πᾶσα πέρι χθών. πρυτανευσέμεν (68) is highly unusual, and other words and phrases such as χρηστήριον (81) look Hesiodic (fr. 134, 6), as does ἀγνῶς καὶ καθαρῶς (121, Theogony, 337). Small though these differences are, they suggest that the poet was not the author of the Iliad and the Odyssey, but someone else who betrays his personal touch and taste in these variations from the Homeric norm, though he is certainly well acquainted with the main elements of the Homeric style.

We might then resort to a second hypothesis that in these lines the poet, whose name we do not know, speaks about himself and claims a pre-eminence for his own songs, assuming that he is well known as " the blind man of Chios ". He may well be a Son of Homer, and his blindness is natural enough. Such a claim is not impossible, especially if the hymn was sung in competition against other poets. But there seem to be two objections to it. First, it is hard to believe that on hearing of a bard renowned for his songs and living in Chios the audience would not take him to be Homer, who was the " man of Chios " without further explanation for Semonides of Amorgos in the seventh century [2] and would presumably have the same renown at a pre-eminently Ionian festival. Secondly, if the bard is really advertising himself, it is odd that he does not give his own name but only this vague description. Of course convention may have forbidden him to say who he is,

---

[1] iii, 104.

[2] Fr. 29, 1, Diehl. The tradition of Homer's blindness may be derived from the hymn, since all other references to it are late and untrustworthy.

but none the less the account which he gives is inadequate if it is intended as a means of identification.

A third possibility is that the bard somehow identifies himself with Homer. Since the poems which he is about to recite are Homer's, he puts himself in the master's position and speaks of him in the first person. Of course the audience will know that the bard himself is not Homer, but it will recognise the songs which he recites as Homer's. No doubt too the bard, being a Son of Homer, is expected to have a closer knowledge of the master than other men. Of course this theory presents serious difficulties. First, the bard speaks of the blind singer of Chios in the first person, as if he were alive, but he was in all probability dead. Perhaps this need not be taken too literally. The songs are indubitably alive, and their creator may be assumed to live in them. Nor would such an idea seem odd to the Greeks, who regarded the immortality conferred by fame as more certain than most other forms of immortality. Secondly, the bard asks that he himself shall be remembered, and presumably by this asks for remembrance of his master. We might expect him to be more explicit and detailed on this point. Yet if he is really accepted as a representative of Homer, his claim is not absurd nor expressed in too fanciful a way. Once the audience thinks of the blind bard of Chios and his songs, the rest follows easily enough. This is all speculative and doubtful, but it is hard to see what else a Greek audience would find in the lines than a reference to the great bard of Chios whose songs were known to all men.

Something of the same kind may perhaps be seen in *Widsith*. The poem purports to be a personal record and consists largely of three lists: first, of kings and peoples to the number of thirty-seven, of whom the poet has heard; next, of fifty-eight tribes, whom he claims to have visited; finally, of thirty-nine hosts, by whom he claims to have been entertained. Between these lists he inserts some pieces of information, including accounts of gifts which he asserts to have been given him. Though not all the names can be identified with certainty, we cannot accept the list as an accurate record of personal experience, since, apart from the difficulty of extensive travel as here described, it is impossible that the poet should have met both Ermanaric, who died in 370, and Alboin, who died in 572. The poem cannot be a record of the poet's own life, but that need not mean that it is an imposture, or that the poet wishes his audience to take it literally. It seems indeed unlikely that they would, even if they were ill acquainted with the history of the times. The poem presents what is in fact a catalogue of kings and peoples of the Germanic heroic age, but this is set out in an unusual form which has been explained in more than one way.

First, it has been thought that the poem has received additions and accretions, that originally it was a work of the fourth century and that the poet speaks truly when he says :

> And I was with Eormanric   all the time,
> There the Gothic king   was good to me ;
> A bracelet he gave me,   the burgher's lord,
> Wherein were six hundred   of smelted gold
> Coins reckoned,   counted in shillings.
> This I to Eadgils'   ownership gave,
> To my lord and helper,   when to my home I came,
> To my friend as a fee   for that he furnished land to me,
> My father's heritage,   the Head of the Myrgings.[1]

From this we might argue that since Eadgils, who receives such prominence, is a comparatively unimportant figure, the poet's emphasis on his relation with him may imply something real. But even if Eadgils was the poet's patron, it cannot be true that the poet served with Ermanaric, since Eadgils belongs to the fifth century and Ermanaric to the fourth. Nor is it possible to understand why any redactor should treat an old poem in this way and turn what was reasonably accurate and possible into something quite impossible and easily recognised as such. Surely his audience would contain men sufficiently versed in heroic stories to know that the travels described are impossible for any single, real man, and no sensible bard would take the risk of trying such an imposture on them.

It looks then as if some other explanation should be found, and two are possible. The first is that the poet speaks not literally about the real world which he knows but metaphorically about the world of heroic song. He has indeed visited and known these princes and their peoples, but in the imagination through the songs which he sings of them. In that case the gifts of which he boasts are the rewards which he has received for singing about them. In favour of this view is that the name Widsith is not a real name but a *nom de plume*, which means " Far Way " or " the far traveller ". That the bard's travels are in the mind or in the world of song rather than on the map need not necessarily trouble an audience for whom the stories of the heroic world exist in a peculiar sphere of their own and who are not very critical about dates or details of geography. On the other hand it is notable that the poem does not

---

[1] *Widsith*, 88-96.

start straightway in the first person, as *Deor* does, but has an introduction, which suggests that Widsith is not a mask assumed by the actual poet but an imaginary character introduced by him :

> Widsith made utterance,   his word-hoard unlocked,
> He who most of men   among meinies on the earth
> And folks had wandered.[1]

Only after he has been so described, does Widsith begin to speak. This suggests that he is not the poet but an ideal figure, such as every bard perhaps would wish to be, far-travelled, and famous and rich.

This consideration suggests an alternative explanation. If Widsith is not the actual poet but an ideal bard, he is used by the poet to make certain claims for his art. This, it seems, is what poetry does and is. It enables the poet to be acquainted with the whole world as it is known to heroic song and gives him rich rewards. The kings and peoples enumerated are the subjects of which an ideal bard would be able to sing, and indeed suggest an enormous range of possible themes. In presenting his ideal bard in this way the poet may perhaps imply something of an old view that the bard has a special knowledge denied to other men. He may have felt, dimly and uncertainly, that the bard is a kind of shaman, who can somehow transcend the limitations of space and time and see all the kings of the earth. That traces of such a belief may have survived in Anglo-Saxon poetry is not impossible. The old Norse religion had its mantic aspects, which were associated with Othin and practised by skalds who were often singers. Be that as it may, it seems probable that *Widsith* is not intended to be taken literally but gives a picture of an ideal bard and his range of subjects. In that case it shows how many subjects were available to a bard in the heyday of Germanic heroic poetry.

Widsith's range is indeed large, and as R. W. Chambers' learned study [2] has shown, it draws on many branches of Germanic legend — on Goths, Burgundians, the sea-folk, Franks, and Langobards. Yet wide though the range of subjects is, it is limited in two ways. First, there are many places and peoples which the poet omits. He knows nothing about the Herulians or the Slavs or the Avars or the Sciri or the Turcilingi, though these peoples would have been known to any Gothic poet who lived in central Europe. The English poet draws on a different range of geography, and, though he derives it from continental sources, those sources probably belong to some region not far from the North Sea. It is the kind of world that would be known to Angles and Frisians

---

[1] *Widsith*, 1-3.   [2] *Widsith*, Cambridge, 1912.

before they crossed the water. Secondly, the poet has his own taste in stories. He does not mention any monsters, nor even Beowulf. His taste is not for the supernatural but for human relations, and especially for tales in which character and passion play a large part, like Ermanaric's vengeance on his young bride; the strife between Hagena and Heoden, between the young chief and the father of his betrothed; the mischief caused between Ingeld and Hrothgar. Especially he likes tales with contrasts of devotion and disloyalty, like the retainers of Guthhere who fall round their lord; the loyalties aroused for Hnaef and Finn; the contrast between Hrothgar and Hrothulf. The poet of *Widsith* shows how large a choice of themes may lie open to a heroic poet in a living art of song.

Though most bards learn their art by listening to others and rely entirely on the heard song, we must not rule out completely the possibility that a few may have learned from books. This must to some degree be true of the later versions of *Gilgamish*; it is also likely for mediaeval French epics. The question is whether bards derive their stories and their technique from written texts. In some modern cases we may suspect that they do. In recent years Russian bards have learned to read and write, and this has extended the range of their otherwise local and traditional repertories. Just as Ryabinin learned something from the retired inn-keeper who had copied out *byliny*, so recently Nikifor Kigachev has said of himself:

" I know thirty-six old *byliny*, and I have invented four new ones.... I know many stories, but I do not know the number. I know twelve historical poems, simple songs which are my own. A number of *byliny* I read in a book, *National Poetry*; the rest I got from old men, also stories. I liked to read, I collected books at the merchant's. My father also told stories and sang songs. I tell *byliny*, but sing few. I told a new *bylina* about Stalin at a women's holiday. I have invented only one old *bylina*. I have told a tale, and from it I have made a *bylina*. Ilya of Murom had a son, but of how he was born the *byliny* say nothing. I invented a little *bylina*, ' The Marriage of Ilya of Murom '. I worked at another also, how the Poles advanced to Moscow after the Pretender. I know songs of Grishka Rasstrig, Ermak, Stepan Razin. I learned them from a book." [1]

Kigachev is not a unique case, and it is interesting to notice that the book which he uses is a collection of *byliny*. We do not know if he alters them when he recites them or whether he has really memorised them. The first alternative seems more likely since he is proud of inventing his own pieces. What he does is no doubt

[1] Astakhova, p. 333.

done by others, and we know that, for instance, the distinguished bard, Marfa Kryukova, can read and has learned several stories from books. In her case, however, her reading is countered by her training in a family of bards and her tendency to try to tell a story as her grandfather and other relations told it.

When he begins to recite, a bard may sometimes find himself unable to get exactly the words which he needs. Among the Asiatic Tatars this is said to be regarded as a grave fault, but elsewhere it is not treated very seriously, and the bard usually recovers himself at once. While he hesitates, he may break into prose. Even so accomplished a performer as Marfa Kryukova says in the middle of her *bylina* on *Vanya Zaleshanin* that she cannot remember what happens at one point; so she goes on gaily without it.[1] The bard may begin a tale in verse and then break into prose and continue in it to the end, as Chukov did in his recitation of *Tsar Salaman* to Rybnikov.[2] Sometimes the bards interrupt their songs to make comments on the action in the way of admiration or amazement at what their heroes do, or, having come to the end, add a comment, as Nikita Remizov does in his poem on Ilya of Murom, which he finishes and then says: " Truth or falsehood, I do not know; but he went alive to heaven, be sure of it ".[3] What these Russian bards do may be paralleled in the records of Jugoslav bards made by Parry, and obviously such falterings are natural in oral performance.

There seem to be no clear rules about the rate at which a bard can recite or the quantity which he can produce without a pause for rest. It is said that a good Jugoslav minstrel does from 13 to 28 lines a minute and that a normal rate is from 16 to 20. Some Mohammedan poems take from three to five hours to recite, and the bards seem able to do this at one sitting. On the other hand, if they are performing a long poem, as Avdo Mededović did for Parry, he rations himself to four hours a day and rests for five or ten minutes every half-hour. A similar rate of progress must have been followed by the Yakut bard, Grigoi Svinoboev, in reciting the poem *Er Sogotokh*, which has about 5000 lines and took him from November 24th to 29th, 1895.[4] It seems, too, a normal practice for reciters of long poems to finish each separate performance at an appropriate place like the end of an episode. Such must have been Homer's way. The *Iliad* falls into obvious sections, which have clear beginnings and ends, and though the *Odyssey* is not so easily divisible, it can still be divided without much trouble. The

[1] Kryukova, ii, p. 45. [2] Rybnikov, i, p. 230 ff.
[3] Astakhova, p. 327. [4] Yastremski, p. 13.

present arrangement of the Homeric poems in 24 books each is due to Alexandrian editors, but it does not run counter to the structure of the poems. No doubt the editors followed actual practice to a certain extent and made the books end at appropriate points, which partly accounts for the considerable differences of length between one book and another. A similar division may be observed in *Manas*, which, as recently edited, falls into well-marked, separate sections, which may correspond with the way in which Orozbakov or Karalaev recited their versions.

Modern bards seem on the whole to have a more or less fixed repertory of songs which they are prepared to sing. Such a repertory may be quite large. In Jugoslavia some Mohammedan minstrels have a repertory of seventy or eighty poems, and one Orthodox Christian could produce a poem every evening for three months and claimed to have enough for a year.[1] The most famous Mohammedan minstrel is said to have known over three hundred poems. In Russia minstrels do not seem to have so large repertories, though Marfa Kryukova has over one hundred and thirty songs. Trofim Ryabinin is known to have had over thirty different songs; F. A. Konashkov sang nineteen; Yakushov thirty-seven. On the other hand, other bards, less distinguished, seem to be content with smaller repertories. In the Pudozhsk region, for instance, some bards seem to be limited to half a dozen. In Russia, if not in Jugoslavia, this may perhaps be a sign that the tradition of composition is not so lively as it was, or at least that it needs some stimulus from outside, such as Kryukova has had, to keep the art lively and abundant.

On the other hand when the tradition is still lively bards seem able to extend their repertory without any great effort. If the bards among the Kara-Kirghiz whom Radlov interviewed did not produce a large number of songs, it is possibly because they were not given time to do so. The fact that one could produce a poem on the birth of Manas almost without preparation, although the subject was unfamiliar to him, shows a more adaptable art than on the whole now prevails in Russia. In the same way both Orozbakov and Karalaev, in composing their long poems, show an inventive ingenuity which would produce a large number of shorter poems if called to do so. A similar vigour can be seen in the Yakuts, who compose on quite a large scale and fill their poems of 4000 to 5000 lines with a wealth of different episodes which presuppose a large range of possible topics. It was not too presumptuous of one Kara-Kirghiz minstrel to tell Radlov that

[1] Chadwick, *Growth*, ii, p. 437.

2 F

he knew all kinds of songs. He meant that, if he was provided with a theme, he could produce a poem on it through the usual devices of oral narrative. The same abundance can be seen in the Armenian poems. The number of episodes connected with Mher and David implies a lively art which deals with its heroes in many situations and under different aspects. It is a sign that a poetical tradition is still healthy and vigorous when bards are able to produce a wide range of topics and are not confined to a few which they have inherited from their predecessors.

We have seen that bards tend to limit themselves to a certain number of subjects, and this is understandable, if they wish to do their work well. If they know a subject and feel thoroughly at home with it, their performance will be more assured and more evenly sustained than if they are not quite certain what to say next. If a bard gets a name for telling some story, he will often be called upon for it, and practice will increase his confidence and his competence. No doubt this accounts for the admirable way in which Trofim Ryabinin tells some of his tales, or why some of Radlov's Kara-Kirghiz bards have so rich a style of narrative. When the poem is comparatively short, the bard may in due course reach an almost final version, though of course he is not likely to produce a complete unchangeable text as a literary poet would. But when it comes to the long epic, a special problem arises. How does a bard compose a poem on such a scale? And how does he succeed, as some undoubtedly have, in giving a polish to the smallest details? Of course it is hard for us to imagine what men can do with memory when they do not know how to read and write. There are even cases of men who can read and write but are compelled by circumstances to use their memories and do wonders with them. If we wish to understand how Homer composed, it is useful to remember that Milton composed *Paradise Lost* when he was blind and, though his daughters took it down from his dictation, the actual composition was done in his head with no aid from writing. The illiterate composers of oral epics on a large scale must do something of this kind. But they differ from Milton in one important respect. When they have composed part of a poem, they cannot have it written down and done with, and then pass on to the next section. They must carry the whole thing in their memories and work at it in their minds. They must not only plan the main shape and episodes and characters, but to a large extent the actual words. Even if they are much helped in the last respect by formulae, it is clear from some of the poets that even these have received individual thought and attention. Such a process may well take years and implies an extraordinary gift not only of memory but of concentration and judgment.

In one case something of such a process has been witnessed by a judicious observer.[1] The Achin poet, Dokarim, who was killed in 1897 for helping the Dutch against his local rajah, could neither read nor write, but he composed a famous poem, *Prang Kompeuni*, on the wars of his people against the Dutch. This poem took him, on his own statement, five years to compose. As he consulted eye-witnesses of the events described in it, he added fresh matter, and he began to recite the poem before it had reached its final form. It soon became popular, and its recitation frequent. At each recitation Dokarim would modify or omit or add as he felt suitable. He is said to have had a good memory, and this would help him in fixing the main features of the poem in his mind. But he was also a gifted poet, who was able to criticise his own work and make the right changes in it when he felt that something was amiss. This process of modification is not unlike what a literate poet does as he corrects his poem on paper, omits or alters his first ideas, and adds second and third ones. When Snouck Hurgronje knew Dokarim, he had not yet finished the poem to his own satisfaction. It is true that one Achin chief has caused parts of it to be written down, but it is not clear that this was done with the poet's permission. Hurgronje himself took down a complete version of it as it existed up to date, but even this did not satisfy the poet, and Hurgronje notes that " it may be noticed here and there, in regard to the language in which the poem is at present couched, that the ' latest hand ' has not yet left its mark upon it ". Perhaps in such a process of composition, the last and greatest difficulty is the precise words to be used at a given place. The rest — plot and characters and details — can be formed and settled, but to get the right word always must indeed be difficult with no written text to guide. Perhaps Dokarim's case may throw some light on this obscure subject and show why an oral poem can attain to a fineness of texture which we might think impossible without the aid of writing.

Of course it remains possible, at least with shorter poems, for an illiterate bard to compose them in his head and then recite them more or less by heart. Some such conditions may lie behind one or two unusual cases of recitation. When Priscus visited the court of Attila in 448, the Hunnish king had two " barbarians " who recited poems, which they had composed, on his victories.[2]

[1] Hurgronje, ii, p. 100 ff. [2] Müller, *F.H.G.* iv, p. 92.

Priscus' words, ᾄσματα πεποιημένα, suggest that the songs were ready in the men's minds before they were recited, and in that case they would probably be short. But he does not make it clear whether they recited them in unison or in turn. The first alternative is undoubtedly difficult, since a poem of action thus recited might not be easy to hear, and we can hardly imagine that Attila would like his deeds to be celebrated in a way which would prevent his guests from hearing everything about them. It is therefore tempting to accept the second alternative, and perhaps some enlightenment on the method used can be found in Finnish practice. It seems that in Finland the singer has an assistant who sits at his side and holds his hand; the singer begins a line and his assistant joins him in finishing it, then repeats the verse complete.[1] This is clearly an elaborate technique which need not be generally practised, but it shows that a singer may still keep his pre-eminence and for all practical purposes do most of the composition while his assistant helps him to emphasise what he says. Perhaps the Hunnish method was on these lines, though not necessarily resembling them closely. Something of the same kind is implied in *Widsith* when the imaginary bard describes how he and another bard, called Scilling, used to perform before Eadgils:

> When Scilling and I   with sheer voices
> Before our royal Lord   upraised the song,
> When loud to the harp   the lilt made melody,
> Then many men   whose minds were proud
> In words did say,   who well had knowledge,
> That they never a sweeter   song had heard.[2]

Here there is no question of Widsith singing one song and Scilling another; it is clear that together they sing a single song, and their method may have borne some resemblance to that of the Finns, though doubtless differing from it in detail. It has even been suggested that something of the same kind was practised in Greece, since, when Achilles sings his heroic songs, Patroclus sits opposite him in silence:

> Waiting for Aeacides, when he should cease from his singing.[3]

It has been argued that Patroclus waits for Achilles to cease, in order that he himself may take up the song.[4] If this is so, Homer has not made his point very clearly, and we may wonder if this was after all a Greek practice. This habit of singing songs with two bards is certainly not usual, but it shows that in certain circumstances improvisation may give place to more careful preparation.

---

[1] Comparetti, p. 70.   [2] *Widsith*, 103-8.
[3] *Il.* ix, 191.   [4] Drerup, p. 47.

XII

INSIDE THE TRADITION

A TRADITION of oral poetry may be maintained through a family or a place or a guild or books or other less definable means, but in each case there is a continuity which means that one generation tells the stories of another in much the same way with many of the same details. But a bard who belongs to such a tradition is free to make changes and to introduce variations. The way in which he does so and the degree of liberty which he allows himself may be illustrated from Russia. The Ryabinin family has practised the art of *byliny* for at least four generations. The first known exponent is the famous Trofim Grigorevich Ryabinin, who lived from about 1800 to 1885; the second is his son, Ivan Trofimovich Ryabinin, who was born about 1840; the third is Ivan's stepson, Ivan Gerasimovich Ryabinin, who died in 1926; and the fourth is this Ivan's son, Peter Ivanovich Ryabinin-Andreev, who was born in 1905 and is still alive. Poems by the first, second, and fourth of this succession have been recorded, and though we possess none by the third, we know something about them, including a list of titles. The first of these four bards was known to the great scholars, Rybnikov and Gilferding; the second travelled outside Russia in other Slavonic countries and gave public recitations of his work; the fourth has a considerable fame to-day. But though they have had opportunities for extending their art beyond their family tradition, they have remained remarkably faithful to it and preserved a homogeneous manner which is derived from that of the great Trofim. They thus present an illuminating case of a bardic family at work and show how it manages its own tradition.

First, we may note that the later generations tend to tell the same stories as the earlier. It is true that Trofim had a larger repertory than his successors, but, allowing for a certain shrinkage, which may after all be due to some inferiority of talent in his descendants, we see a considerable coherence in the lists of subjects treated by the four different bards. Thus of the fifteen subjects known to have been told by Ivan Trofimovich, the nine told by Ivan Gerasimovich, and the ten told by Peter Ivanovich,

all are to be found in Trofim's repertory. It is true that Peter has
added some five new subjects of his own, but these are on contemporary, revolutionary themes and lie outside the actual scope of
the tradition. The Ryabinins show how stories are passed from
one generation to another and are regarded as a family possession.
Peter says that he has learned some of his subjects from his father
and some from his step-grandfather, and as the step-grandfather
learned them from old Trofim, the tradition is unbroken. This
faithfulness to a family art helps to explain how in some places
certain stories have a great vogue, while others, which are common
elsewhere, are unknown. The tradition is a real tradition in that
it passes a repertory of stories from one generation to another.

Secondly, among these stories are some which seem to be
confined to the Ryabinins or at least not to be known elsewhere.
Thus, though the fight between Ilya of Murom and his son is a
widespread and popular tale and takes various forms in different
parts of Russia, it is important to note that the Ryabinins tell not
of this but of a fight between Ilya and his daughter. Since all four
bards do this, it is clearly a family possession. The story, it must
be admitted, is not so effective as the usual version, and it is hard
to explain why the Ryabinins have taken it up. It has been suggested that it is due to some confusion between the masculine word
polenits and its feminine form *polenitsa*, each meaning " warrior ",
and that at some stage a member of the family or his teacher heard
the tale and failed to remember it correctly. Be that as it may, the
unusual version of a popular tale shows how traditional the
Ryabinins are and how independent of other bards. For if they
had conformed to usual practice, they would surely have substituted
a son for the daughter.

Thirdly, such a tradition is conservative in quite small matters,
such as the attachment of certain formulaic passages to this or that
story. Peter Ryabinin-Andreev uses phrases which his step-
great-grandfather used nearly a hundred years earlier. For
instance, he opens the story of Ilya's quarrel with Vladimir in six
lines which are verbally almost identical with Trofim's opening.[1]
His version of Volga and Mikula repeats not only the familiar
lines about Volga's ability to change his shape into fish, bird, or
animal but the lines about Volga's effect on physical nature :

> All fish swam away into the blue sea,
> All birds flew away under the clouds,
> All wild beasts ran away to the dark woods.[2]

[1] Gilferding, ii, p. 38.
[2] Rybnikov, i, p. 10 ; Ryabinin-Andreev, p. 35.

Later, Peter uses Trofim's words to describe how Volga is asked by Mikula to get his plough from the furrow where it has stuck :

" Listen, Volga Svyatoslavich !
I have left my plough in the furrow —
Not for the wayfarer, be he on foot or on horse,
But for the labouring peasant." [1]

So too in his version of Ilya and Nightingale the Robber, Peter again uses an effective phrase of Trofim's :

Nightingale whistles like a nightingale,
He screeches, the dog, like a wild beast.[2]

Some of these phrases may be found in the works of other bards and are of course a national possession, but in the Ryabinin family they are treasured and kept intact. No doubt they are valued for their vividness and thought worthy of repetition for that reason, but they show how easily a later poet can repeat the words of his forebears.

Fourthly, the various Ryabinins keep closely to the same outline for any given story and neither add nor detract nor make any serious changes. Thus, though Ilya's quarrel with Vladimir is a common subject, it is usually no more than an episode in a longer story. With the Ryabinins it occupies a whole poem and has developed an individuality of its own in which the great hero becomes a rowdy ruffian and breaks up churches. So too the story of Staver's wife, who rescues her husband from prison by disguising herself as a man, is constant in all its main features, notably in the three tests by which Vladimir tries to find out if she is really a man or not, — first in the bath, next in a fight, and lastly in the marks which she leaves on a feather-bed. Here again the younger poet sees the advantages of the version which he has inherited and uses it with a full sense of its worth.

On the other hand this tradition allows a certain elasticity and freedom in the invention of new details. These are usually of minor importance, but add something to the variety and vividness of the story. For instance, when the wife of Staver disguises herself, Trofim gets through it quickly, but Peter has a little more to say :

She clothed herself in a man's dress,
She put on a well-worn dress,
A well-worn dress, a soldier's,
She took up a sharp sword,
Her long Tatar spear,
She took up many tempered arrows.[3]

---

[1] Ryabinin-Andreev, p. 37.   [2] *Idem*, p. 42.   [3] *Idem*, p. 85.

Here the wife disguises herself as a warrior, and that gives a slightly different character to her venture. Later, when she discloses her identity to Vladimir, she indulges in an unexpected impertinence :

> " Foolish prince Vladimir of royal Kiev,
> I am not frightened of that dog, Tsar Kalin,
> I am the young wife of Staver,
> The young woman, Vasilissa Mikulichna,
> And I have come to play at a wedding." [1]

In this there is a touch of revolutionary contempt for princes, of which old Trofim Ryabinin might not have approved. So, too, when Ilya of Murom brings Nightingale the Robber to Vladimir, in Trofim's version Vladimir behaves with dignified decorum, but in Peter's version there is a touch of comedy in Vladimir's fright when Nightingale speaks :

> Then Prince Vladimir of royal Kiev
> Ran to the courtyard, ran in circles,
> Wrapped himself in his marten-fur. [2]

Peter at times provides a touch of satire which is a little alien to his great forebear's art.

If the Ryabinins illustrate the strength and tenacity of a family tradition, another Russian family, the Kryukovs, shows that it can work rather differently. The Kryukovs have practised *byliny* for several generations, and a family-tree may help to set them out :

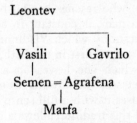

All these have been bards of some sort, and since Marfa Kryukova was born in 1876, the tradition goes back over a century or more. Marfa, whose own poems number about one hundred and thirty, admits debts to most of her relatives, but chiefly to Gavrilo and her mother. But she has supplemented her family inheritance with songs from other sources and pays acknowledgments to several men and women in her own district who are not her relatives. Moreover, since she is able to read, she may also owe something to books. In her case we can observe a tradition which is more expansive and more assimilative than that of the Ryabinins.

---

[1] Ryabinin-Andreev, p. 89.   [2] *Idem*, p. 46.

Since we are able to compare her poems with those of her mother and her great-uncle Gavrilo, we can see how the family tradition of the Kryukovs works and in what respects it differs from that of the Ryabinins.

The Kryukovs resemble the Ryabinins in their adherence to certain stories and to their manner of telling them, but they allow themselves more liberty both in detail and in scale, so that, though the traditional subjects are maintained, the presentation of them may vary considerably from poet to poet. If the main outlines are preserved, the details are varied, and the individual poets seem to enjoy giving a personal imprint to the stories. For instance, Agrafena, Gavrilo, and Marfa all tell of the death of the Empress Nastasya Romanovna, the mother of Ivan the Terrible. Their versions of it are all substantially different from versions found elsewhere and have indeed a strong family likeness, but are none the less varied to suit the singers' personal tastes. All three begin with a scene of grief which is mirrored in natural phenomena. Agrafena's version is simplest:

> The blue sea has become silent, has become sad,
> The rushing streams have become silent, become sad,
> The passing clouds have become silent, become sad;
> The Orthodox Empress makes ready to die.
> They have kindled a candle of bright wax before her.[1]

In Gavrilo's version a slightly more adventurous spirit is at work:

> Why, brothers, has every rushing stream become sad?
> Why do they not roar, the running rapids?
> Why, brothers, is the green sea silent and sad?
> Why, brothers, are they sad, why do the dark woods not whisper?
> Why, brothers, has a star under the sky fallen from the sky?
> Why, brothers, does the candle of bright wax hang its head?
> The Orthodox Empress makes ready to die.[2]

Marfa pursues the same manner and ideas with a more torrential eloquence:

> Look, the blue sea has become silent and sad,
> The black ships are weary of passing,
> There the fine white sails do not travel,
> There are no flags to be seen, no silken flags,
> The wild winds do not blow,
> The trees do not bloom in the green garden,
> The people, the good folk, have not risen to go out,
> To ride in our mother, in stone-built Moscow,
> In the clouds the red sun has not risen,
> The moon, they say, is covered with clouds,

[1] Markov, p. 182.   [2] *Idem*, p. 456.

And the wonderful image has begun to hover,
The wonderful image, even the pure Saviour Himself,
Has risen over the courtyard of the rulers,
His form comes in haste thither,
He has stopped over the bedroom of the rulers,
He has flamed in the wax of the bright candles ;
The Orthodox Empress makes ready to die.[1]

Marfa, on her own statement, learned this poem from Gavrilo, and that explains why her version is closer to his than to her mother's. But it is clear that all three bards share a common tradition, which has more elasticity than we find among the Ryabinins.

This element of freedom can also be seen in the differences of scale in the three poems. Agrafena's version of this poem has 81 lines and Gavrilo's 86, while Marfa's has 333. While there is little difference of plan or structure between Gavrilo's and Agrafena's versions, Marfa agrees with them up to a point and then follows her own devices. All three tell how the dying empress sends for her son Ivan and from her death-bed gives him advice and orders. Marfa differs partly in her characteristic elaboration of the minor details, but more substantially in the way in which she carries the story for a hundred lines beyond the point where Gavrilo and Agrafena end it. After the empress has spoken her dying speech, they close the story neatly, Agrafena without any further comment, Gavrilo by telling how nature, after her disturbances, resumes her usual course. But Marfa goes on to say that Ivan sits on his mother's grave, where the people join him in lamenting her. At his command they throw their gold, silver, and jewels on the grave. Then the poem ends with an account of how Ivan takes his mother's advice and shows kindness to everyone. Marfa evidently feels a need to round off her story more completely than her teachers have done. Her version adds something to the characterisation of Ivan and shows what liberties she feels herself entitled to take.

Though Marfa indulges her own taste for innovation, she is not shy of admitting her indebtedness to her teachers, and indeed pays some attention to the precedents which they set in telling a tale. For instance, she has twice told the tale of Kastryuk, and does it differently, because in one case she follows the example of her mother and in the other that of her great-uncle. The material of the story is derived from the marriage of Ivan the Terrible to the Circassian princess, Marya Temnyukovna. Her brother comes to

[1] Kryukova, ii, p. 459.

the wedding and sulks without eating or drinking, until Ivan asks him what is the matter, and he answers that he wishes to challenge a Muscovite to a wrestling-match. In due course the match takes place, and Kastryuk is thrown. So much is common to nearly all known versions of the story, and certainly to the two versions of Gavrilo and Agrafena.[1] But on this basis variations are possible, and Marfa is conscious that there are at least two ways of telling the story. So she tries both, and keeps the two poems quite separate.[2] In the version which she learned from Gavrilo she makes some ado about a visit paid by Ivan to the court of the princess's family to ask for her in marriage. Ivan behaves there in a way which is paralleled by the behaviour of Kastryuk when he comes to Moscow. This gives the story a special balance and makes it fall neatly into two parts. This is the scheme which Gavrilo uses and Marfa follows, although her scale is greater than his and her details, as usual, are accumulated and abundant. In Agrafena's version there is no trace of this twofold plot. Instead the actual struggle gets more attention, and much notice is given to the way in which the wrestlers appeal to the Tsar and his bride to put up prayers for their victory, with the result that Kastryuk is defeated. This theme Marfa develops in her own way but with a full fidelity to her mother's main design. Thus her two versions of the story of Kastryuk are quite different, and she is right to distinguish between the two ways of telling it. However much she may add herself, she is fully conscious that she practises an inherited art and pays acknowledgments almost of copyright to her teachers. This is in itself a tribute to tradition and shows her sense of obligation to it.

If families show this kind of loyalty to a tradition but allow a certain freedom within it, the same may be said of places. Indeed, the tradition of a place may sometimes be more powerful than that of a family like the Kryukovs in which hereditary talent sooner or later asserts itself. In a small district bards may often not be very creative or original, and in that case they keep to the traditional stories and ways of telling them, as if it were safer to do the right thing in the old way than to take unnecessary risks. When Gilferding visited the district of Kenozero near Lake Onega he took down poems from twenty-three different bards. None of these had a large repertory, and the popularity of some stories shows a homogeneity of practice akin to that in the Ryabinin family. For instance, of these bards four told of Ilya's fight with his son, six of his three journeys, four of Dobrynya and Alyosha,

[1] Markov, p. 459 ff., p. 184 ff.　　　　[2] Kryukova, ii, p. 476 ff.

four of Dyuk Stepanovich, three of Vasili Buslaev. On the other hand certain popular stories are lacking, such as those about Svyatogor, Volga and Mikula, Sadko, Staver, Nightingale Budimirovich, and most of the episodes connected with Ivan the Terrible. A local tradition resembles that of a family in being tenacious of some stories and indifferent to others. The younger generations of bards follow the older in drawing on the same stock of subjects until an almost fixed repertory is established. This is not to say that all the poets of Kenozero told Gilferding the same tales, but, if we take the common elements in their performance, we find something like a fixed corpus.

The conservatism of such a tradition may be illustrated from three versions of the death of Churilo, each told by a different bard in the Kenozero district. In all three there is a solid basis of common action. Churilo rides out and is invited into her house by Katerina. She challenges him to a game of chess for a stake of a hundred roubles. They play three games, and each time she loses and pays up. She then makes love to him, and they go upstairs to bed. Her servant-girl goes out to warn Katerina's husband, Bermyata, who is in church. He comes back with her, finds the lovers together, and kills Churilo. All three poems tell this story at very much the same length. Nor are the resemblances confined to structure and outline. They spread even to the details, as in the accounts of the games of chess. In the first, Sivtsev Pavlovich says :

> The first time he played, Churilo gave her mate,
> And took from Katerina a hundred roubles in cash.
> The second time he played, he gave her mate again,
> And took from Katerina two hundred roubles in cash.
> The third time he played, he gave her mate a third time,
> And took from Katerina three hundred roubles in cash.[1]

In the second version, Tretyakov Grigorievich says :

> He played with Katerina in the first game,
> He took a hundred roubles from her in cash.
> He played with Katerina in the second game,
> He took two hundred roubles from her in cash.
> He played with Katerina in the third game,
> He took three hundred roubles from her in cash.[2]

In the third version, Tryapitsyn Ivanovich is shorter and omits one of the games, as well as any mention of the money taken :

> They played the first game ; Churilo gave mate to Katya.
> They played a second game ; Churilo gave mate to Katya.[3]

[1] Gilferding (3rd edn.), iii, p. 170. [2] Gilferding, iii, p. 366.
[3] *Idem*, p. 273.

Here, nevertheless, there seems to be an almost standard description of the games of chess. Two poets use it faithfully, while the third seems to find it too much of a bother to repeat entire. Many such similarities can be found in poems by different bards in this district. They show that, though there is no obligation to follow a standard form, such a form exists and is in fact usually followed.

Even in points where we might expect differences we find similarities. For instance, in all three of these poems the servant-girl summons the husband from church, and there seems to be a standard way of doing it. The husband warns the girl that she will be punished if she is not telling the truth. In the first two cases he comes as soon as she tells him the news, but in the third there is a slight variation. When she speaks to him, he does not answer :

> There stands Bermyat praying to God,
> And, while he prays to God, he does not turn round.[1]

The girl has to speak to him a second time, and then all proceeds according to convention. It is evident that Tryapitsyn Ivanovich is slightly more independent than the other two poets and likes to make his own small variations, but they are of little consequence in comparison with his general fidelity to tradition. In Kenozero the story of Churilo's death has been stabilised and reduced to a certain form, from which few deviations are made. In other places the story takes other shapes, and this shows what the power of local tradition is. No doubt the poets have learned from common masters or from each other, and that is why they follow a single pattern.

Both family and local traditions tend to keep the main lines of a story and even minor details intact from generation to generation. But of course in other conditions, when the tradition is not so firmly fixed, greater liberties will be taken and greater variations introduced. When a story has travelled from district to district and even from country to country and been passed on through a long period of years, it may change its main outline and some of its characteristics. Something of the kind can be seen in two Jugoslav poems about Musić Stefan (Bušić Stjepan) at the battle of Kosovo. The first is preserved in a Franciscan manuscript at Dubrovnik and belongs to a group of poems supplied by Jodzo Betondić, who died in 1764.[2] It is thus as early as the middle of the eighteenth century and is probably of Dalmatian origin. It is written in the old long line or *bugarštica* and is composed on a not very skilful plan. The first half tells how Stefan finds that warriors are gathering for battle and decides that he must join them; he tells

---

[1] *Idem*, p. 274.   [2] Bogišić, no. 1.

his wife, but she has had an evil dream and tries to dissuade him; he remains unmoved and goes off with his squire to King Lazar's palace. There the story leaves him, while it goes on to tell of the failure of the Empress Milića to persuade the Tsar to leave one of her brothers behind with her. Lazar goes to Kosovo, gives a banquet to his captains, and accuses Miloš of intending to betray him. Miloš leaves, and the battle follows. The second poem, which is in the ordinary decasyllabic metre, is preserved in Karadžić's collection, is probably of Serbian origin, and may date from the first years of the nineteenth century.[1] In its first part it resembles the earlier poem in its outline. Stefan insists on going to Kosovo despite his wife's dream and doubts and entreaties and is supported against her by his squire. But after this it takes a new turn. On arriving at Kosovo Stefan meets a girl carrying a warrior's helmet, and hears from her that he has arrived too late, since the battle is over. He hastens to the Turkish camp, performs a great slaughter, and is himself killed with his squire. Behind these poems we can see the common structure of a single subject — the departure of a warrior with his squire for Kosovo despite his wife's entreaties. But the sequels are entirely different. In the first case the poet has incorporated themes which are used separately in other poems; in the second we may suspect that, since the finale is not found elsewhere, it is the poet's own invention. The different patterns show what can happen when a tradition is not guided by family or local discipline. Since Musić Stefan is not an important character, and indeed seems to be known only from these two cases, the poets evidently felt that they could take greater liberties with him than with more familiar heroes.

A similar example of what tradition can do may be seen in two Russian poems on Skopin, who died in 1610 and was regarded as a national hero because of his efforts to restore order in Moscow in the time of the troubles. In 1619, soon after Skopin's death, Richard James took down a short poem on him. It portrays a situation rather than tells a story. Its theme is the confusion caused by Skopin's death. The boyars, who planned it, are pleased, but the foreigners, Swedes and Germans, who have helped Skopin to restore order, feel that with their leader's death they must leave the country:

> The Germans have fled to Novgorod,
> And have shut themselves up in Novgorod.
> And many native Russians have been ruined,
> And converted in the land of Poland.[2]

---

[1] Karadžić, ii, p. 211 ff. [2] Chadwick, R.H.P. p. 237.

This must be one of the first poems on a subject which later won some popularity. A later version of it was recorded by Kirsha Danilov in the latter part of the eighteenth century from a bard in the district of Perm near the Urals.[1] Since this version is removed from that of James by a hundred and fifty years in time and a thousand miles in space, we may expect considerable divergences, and such indeed there are. The bard from the Urals takes nearly two hundred lines and provides his story with a dramatic development and crisis. He tells how Moscow is besieged, and Skopin escapes to ask the King of Sweden for help; the King gives it, and the besiegers are routed. In the hour of Skopin's triumph, when he boasts that he has delivered Russia from her enemies, he is poisoned by the boyars and dies. This differs from the Moscow version, first in providing an account of the events which lead to Skopin's death and secondly in saying nothing of the situation after it. Here we have not two versions of a single theme but two poems derived from a single event. If James' poem reflects a contemporary state of mind and dwells only on a situation, the later poem has shaped a story from a series of events. In other words we can here see the beginning of a poem's life and observe how what seems important at the start is later abandoned for other elements in the story. Such a process of selection is necessary to any tradition, and here we see it at work.

At the same time even in these two different versions there are elements of similarity which show how the story of Skopin has begun to take on its familiar features. First, there is a small verbal point which illustrates how a tradition will hold on to a phrase or two if it thinks them useful. In James' version, when Skopin dies, the boyars say:

" Our swift hawk soared,
But he has bruised himself against damp mother earth."

In Danilov's version, the same image is used for Skopin's escape from Moscow to ask for help:

He flew away as a bright falcon,
Even as a bright gerfalcon he took to his wings and flew away.

The comparison of Skopin with a bird seems to have become an integral part of his story. So, much later, Marfa Kryukova says:

Prince Skopin, came to us then,
Prince Skopin, Mikhailo Vasilevich,
And it was not a bright falcon that flew then,
It was our warrior who hastened then.[2]

---

[1] Kireevski, vii, p. 11 ff.   [2] Kryukova, ii, p. 568.

This is a small detail, but it shows a tendency to look at Skopin in a certain way and fix his character through an apt image. Secondly, the poisoning of Skopin by the boyars assumes more importance with time, but is implicit in James' version with its reference to Skopin's death at the house of Prince Vorotinksi, the leader of the boyars :

> The princes and boyars have assembled before him,
> Before Prince Mstislavski Vorotinski,
> And among themselves they have talked together,
> They have talked together and smiled.

The smile of the boyars suggests their pleasure in what they have done, and in later poems the theme is amplified and enriched, as in Danilov's version :

> The boyars straightway did a deed ;
> They uprooted a deadly poison,
> And sprinkled it in a glass of sweet mead.

In other, later versions this theme is common, but its sources can be traced back to the time of Skopin's death.

The Jugoslav poems on Musić Stefan and the Russian poems on Skopin show what freedom can be taken with a subject over a period of years. This freedom consists largely in changing or varying the main outlines of a story by starting earlier or continuing later than the original theme demands. But within this freedom there are certain limiting factors. First, the main point of the narrative remains constant, whether in Stefan's controversy with his wife or in the murder of Skopin by the boyars. Even though a story has travelled far in time and space, it keeps some of its original character. Secondly, the personality of the hero remains constant. Neither his motives nor his actions are much changed. Just as Stefan remains the Serb patriot who insists on going to battle at Kosovo, so Skopin remains the victorious general who has delivered Moscow from its enemies by getting help from the Swedes. Thirdly, though the details of the action may differ considerably from poem to poem and the crisis be developed in various ways, there is still some measure of agreement about the character of a story's contents. The emotional effect is the same, and the story keeps its essential quality.

There is, then, a considerable divergence between subjects which are controlled by a family or a local tradition and those which have a nation-wide circulation. The latter will naturally develop a greater variety of forms and assume new characteristics. Yet on the whole there is a solid degree of constancy in the tradition, and not many poems are even so elastic as those on Musić

Stefan and Skopin. A more normal example comes from Armenia. In the cycle of stories about David of Sasoun is one which tells how he fights with his son, Mher. In a version recorded in 1900 [1] Mher, who has grown up without knowing his father, rides out and meets a man carrying a girl on his horse. Mher refuses to let him pass and demands the girl from him. The result is that they fight, and Mher is thrown to the ground. He asks his victor if he intends to kill him, and if so, how will he escape from the vengeance of his father. The victor asks who the father is, hears that it is himself, and that the young man is Mher. Recognising his son, he embraces him, and all is well. A second version, published in 1936,[2] tells the story differently. It begins in exactly the same way and follows the same lines until the fight, but in this neither combatant is victorious, and the fight seems unlikely to end, when David's wife, Khandut, hears the clash of weapons and comes out. She sees her husband and her son fighting and puts an end to it. This may be less dramatic than the earlier version but has the merit of making the son as good a warrior as his father. Despite this important difference, the two poets agree on important points. This crisis of the story is the same : the father fights his son without either knowing who the other is. The personalities of the heroes are the same : David will not accept any opposition or affront, and Mher is eager to show his prowess. The main curve of the action is the same, in that what looks like becoming a tragic contest ends happily.

Though bards usually respect the main tendencies and characteristics of a tale, that does not preclude them from developing its possibilities in ways which suit their own tastes and outlooks. Indeed, as a story passes from generation to generation, it may well be accommodated to changing points of view and receive a variety of treatment from different poets. They may still observe its main elements but interpret them differently and secure new effects from them. Such conditions may partly account for the differences between the story of Finn as it is told in *Finnsburh* and in *Beowulf*. Though the two may not be very far removed from one another in date and may both come from about 700, there is a great divergence of temper between them. *Finnsburh* is a purely heroic tale in the old Germanic tradition. It has no moralising and no Christian references; it delights in a tale of bitter fighting, and of all the Anglo-Saxon poems it is closest to *Hildebrand* and

---

[1] S. Haikouni, *Eminian, azgagrakan joghovadzou*, ii, pp. 19-50 (Moscow, 1901), quoted by Macler, ii, p. 30 ff.
[2] *David Sasunskii*, p. 294 ff.

to some pieces of the *Elder Edda*. On the whole its manner is direct, certainly more direct than the circuitous and allusive manner of *Beowulf*. *Beowulf* on the other hand not only tells the tale with a sense of its ethical implications but is uncertain in its approach to its characters and episodes. If *Finnsburh* reflects the old Germanic spirit before the conquest of Britain by the Angles and Saxons, *Beowulf* is deeply touched by Christianity and feels that it must make its story accord with the new outlook.

The original story of Finn, as it was told in Jutland in the sixth century, can be deduced from the two surviving versions. Hnaef, a vassal prince of the Danes, met his death among the Frisians at the court of their king, Finn. We do not know why he was there, though it has been surmised that it was connected with some project of marriage. Nor do we know why Finn attacked him. Treachery has been suggested on the strength of the phrase " the troth of the Eotens " at *Beowulf* 1071, but this may refer simply to some quarrel among two parties of Jutes in Friesland. In any case, a fight took place in Finn's hall, where Hnaef and his company are attacked. In this fight Hnaef is killed. Then his followers, led by Hengest, hold out in the hall and inflict such losses on the Frisians that Finn comes to terms. Peace is kept through the winter, but in spring two of Hnaef's men, Oslaf and Guthlaf, go home, collect forces, and return to Friesland, where they avenge their dead master by killing Finn and his followers. It was thus originally a story of a desperate fight and a bloody revenge. Such seems to be the outline of the story, and that it was familiar to an Anglo-Saxon audience is clear from the highly allusive way in which *Beowulf* deals with it and from the references in *Widsith* to " Finn Folcwalding (who ruled) the Frisian kindred " and to " Hnaef (who ruled) the Hoccings ".[1] On this basis the two poets of *Finnsburh* and *Beowulf* built their different versions. Since the tale was familiar, there is no need to assume that either knew the work of the other.

Since *Finnsburh* is only a fragment, we do not know how much the complete poem told of the whole tale. What survives begins with the start of the fight in the hall and ends with what looks like a new move on the part of the Frisians, who see that all is not going well with them. The fight, which is told so graphically in *Finnsburh*, is only hinted at in *Beowulf*, but we can hardly doubt that it is the same fight, in which, according to *Beowulf*, Hnaef is killed :

> The hero of Half-Danes,   Hnaef of the Shieldings,
> In Frisian fight   to fall was fated.[2]

[1] *Widsith*, 27, 29.   [2] *Beowulf*, 1069-70.

A little later, the poet, with his usual circumambience, refers again to the fight, when he tells how " the daughter of Hoc " sees the carnage :

> War took off all
> Of Finn's thegns,   except a few only,
> So that he might not   in the meeting-place
> Fight one whit   in war with Hengest,
> Nor his sorry few   by fighting save
> From the Prince's thegn.[1]

Obviously the poet of *Beowulf* is not very interested in the actual fight, and his silence on its details is as tantalising as the fragmentary condition of *Finnsburh*. None the less a comparison between the two passages yields one or two results of interest.

First, there is no reason to think that there is any serious discrepancy between the two accounts. If we assume that the " battle-young king " of *Finnsburh* is Hnaef, and that he is attacked by Finn, the substance of the fragment falls into the general scheme outlined in *Beowulf*. Among Hnaef's supporters are Ordlaf and Guthlaf, who are the same as Oslaf and Guthlaf in *Beowulf*. Hengest, who is " the prince's Thegn " in *Beowulf*, is present in the fragment, evidently in a position of some importance, since, when men move to the door to defend it, the poet adds :

> And Hengest's self,   he hied in their wake.[2]

He may also be the person whom Hnaef addresses at the beginning when a light is seen which Hnaef knows to be the reflection on the armour of the attackers. This agreement between the main events is matched by a tendency common both to *Finnsburh* and to *Beowulf* to exalt the Danes at the expense of the Frisians. The story is in either case told from the Danish point of view, and the attacked are treated in a more friendly spirit than the attackers. Of course the two accounts differ greatly in their manner of narration, but that is because *Finnsburh* gives all its attention to a single episode, while *Beowulf* gives an epitome of a long tale.

On the other hand there is a remarkable difference of temper and approach between the two versions. In *Finnsburh* the poet tells a truly heroic tale of a prodigious fight and does not conceal his admiration for the defenders :

> Nor heard I ever that more worthily   in wars of men
> Sixty battle heroes   bare themselves better,
> Nor ever did swains for their sweet mead   give seemlier payment
> Than to Hnaef was paid   by his house-fellows.

---

[1] *Ibid.* 1080-85.   [2] *Finnsburh*, 17.

> They fought five days,　　yet fell there none
> Of the doughty comrades ;　　but the doors they held.[1]

Though the fragment has only fifty lines, it touches on a range of the most authentically heroic themes, like the king who calls his men to fight, the competition among them for the posts of danger, the sound and glitter of clashing arms, the birds of prey waiting for the dead bodies, the staunch defence of the doors, the confusion of the attackers when they find that all is not going according to plan. This is a heroic poem in the strictest sense and reflects the tastes and outlook of a heroic society. But the poet of *Beowulf* is hardly interested in such things. In his selection of events from the whole tale he shows what his tastes are. He passes over the actual fight rapidly with no touch of imaginative insight ; he is equally rapid in dealing with the revenge which Hengest takes on Finn :

> Then the hall was bestrewn
> With bodies of foemen ;　　Finn likewise was slain.[2]

What really interests him are the terms of the treaty between the Danes and the Frisians, to which he gives over twenty lines, and the funeral-pyre of Hnaef and a son of the queen, Hildeburh, which he describes in detail. The second might indeed be regarded as a heroic subject, but the poet treats it not from the usual heroic standpoint as the fitting culmination to a hero's life but as the occasion for a woman's tragic grief.

Indeed the poet of *Beowulf* seems to be concerned not with the heroic aspects of the tale but with some of its human and ethical aspects. He is certainly interested in Hildeburh. As the sister of Finn and the wife of Hnaef she is indeed in a poignant position. She sees her brother killed by her husband, and in the same fight she loses a son. The poet appreciates her pathos when she gives orders for the pyre for the bodies of Hnaef and her son :

> Bade she then, Hildeburh,　　that on Hnaef's pyre
> Her own self's son　　to the flames be sent,
> Their bodies for burning　　on the bier to don ;
> Her hand on his shoulder　　sorrowed that lady,
> With lays lamented.[3]

Indeed the poet's interest in Hildeburh can be seen from the way in which he begins the episode with a full reference to her position. And it is interesting to note that, though he is fully conscious of her pathos, he also feels a need to explain that she is in no wise to blame for what has happened :

---

[1] *Finnsburh*, 37-42.　　　[2] *Beowulf*, 1151-2.　　　[3] *Ibid.* 1114-18.

No wise did Hildeburh   need to honour
The troth of the Eotens ;   unsinning, she was
Lorn of her loved ones   at that linden-play,
Of her boys and her brothers ;   they bowed to their fate,
Wounded with spears ;   that was a sorrowful woman.[1]

We can hardly imagine that the early Germanic poets who sang the tale of Finn would give this prominence to a woman's feelings or trouble to explain that she was not responsible for what happened.

    The poet of *Beowulf* is also interested in the position of Hengest. We can imagine what part he played in earlier poems. He would be the victim of a fierce conflict in himself, since on the one hand he has given his word to respect the truce with Finn and on the other hand honour demands that he should revenge his master's death by killing Finn. Indeed the interest of this part of the story would depend largely on this struggle in Hengest, which would be all the sharper because his comrades, Guthlaf and Oslaf, have not acquiesced in the truce but gone home to fetch reinforcements for the task of vengeance. This is a subject in the true heroic taste, but the poet of *Beowulf* treats it very much in his own way. He seems indeed not to be quite sure of himself or to know what exactly he ought to think of Hengest. When he first mentions him, he makes a good point, which might well be followed up, that the terms of peace were offered by Hengest to Finn. We might expect this to be a prelude for a particularly sharp struggle in Hengest between his respect for his plighted word and his devotion to his dead master. But nothing is made of it, and when Hengest next appears, as staying in Friesland after the treaty through the winter, an unexpected but not very relevant point is made that he suffers from home-sickness :

                    Hengest all through
That death-stained winter   dwelt with Finn
In strength unstriving ;   his homestead he remembered,
Although he might never   over the mere drive
His ringed-stem ;   with storms the holm weltered,
Warred with the wind.[2]

Perhaps the poet wishes to suggest that Hengest would have liked to go home with Guthlaf and Oslaf but was prevented by bad weather from doing so, but he does not make this clear. Finally, he does indeed come to the theme of revenge. It seems that, being unable to go home, Hengest turns his thoughts to revenge in Friesland and is strengthened by the acquisition of a sword, called Hildeoma :

---

[1] *Ibid.* 1071-6.   [2] *Ibid.* 1127-32.

> He of grief's avenging
> Sooner thought   than of sea-faring,
> If he a bitter meeting   might bring about,
> That the men of the Eotens   therein be remembered.
> So he did not refuse   fight to the host's ruler,
> When the son of Hunlaf   set on his lap
> Hildeoma,   the best of swords.[1]

Here too we can guess what the poet means. Hengest, who has long delayed his revenge, is stirred to action by receiving the great sword. That is heroic enough, but the poet is still more interested in Hengest's motives and moral scruples than in his vengeance. The poet of *Beowulf* treats the story of Finn with a new sense of its implications, but that does not mean that he changes its episodes to suit his own purpose.

If the two versions of Finn show how differently the inner meaning of a tale may be treated, they do not necessarily come from widely separated ages or societies. Their difference may be explained by an attachment to the old tradition in *Finnsburh* and deviations from it in *Beowulf*. But similar changes of outlook and therefore to some degree of treatment may be seen if we compare poems which are almost certainly separated by a considerable lapse of years. An example of this can be seen in the Norse *Atlakvitha* and *Atlamál*, each of which tells of the destruction of the sons of Gjuki by Atli and of Guthrun's vengeance on him. The two poems are separated in space, since the first seems to have been composed in Iceland and the second in Greenland; they are also separated in time, since *Atlakvitha* is claimed on stylistic and metrical grounds as a work of the ninth century at the latest,[2] while *Atlamál* has on similar grounds been assigned to the twelfth.[3] Behind both poems lies an ancient tradition which may well go back to the fifth or sixth century. The kernel of the story lies in two historical events: first, Attila's death on his wedding night, which was soon transformed into a belief that he was killed by his wife; second, his defeat and destruction of the Burgundians and their king, Gundahari, in 437.[4] These two events were combined in heroic song and provided the germ of *Atlakvitha* and *Atlamál*. Attila's wife, Ildico, whose name suggests a Germanic origin, is turned into Guthrun, the sister of the Burgundian king, Gunnar; and what was in fact a great national struggle between Huns and Burgundians became a family battle in Atli's hall. A story so dramatic and so rich in tragic issues naturally became

---

[1] *Beowulf*, 1138-44.   [2] De Vries, i, p. 46.   [3] *Idem*, ii, p. 157 ff.
[4] *Chron. Min.* i, p. 475; ii, p. 22; Sidonius Apollinaris, *Carm.* vii, 234 ff.; Thompson, p. 65.

popular and had a long life in Iceland and Greenland. It has some four hundred years behind it in *Atlakvitha* and seven in *Atlamál*. That the two poems reproduce the main elements of the story in the same way shows how firmly fixed these were despite their age and travels, and the differences between them illustrate what can happen to a story in the lapse of years.

Though the two poems keep what is on the whole the same outline, they vary not only in details but in important matters of motive and character. The most obvious difference is in the handling of Atli's reasons for asking Gunnar and his brothers to come to his castle. In *Atlakvitha* Atli wishes to find out from Gunnar where the gold of the Niflungs is hidden and so to get hold of it. The poet does not state this at the start but introduces it gradually by insinuation until it is made fully clear at an important crisis. The first hint comes when Gunnar, after accepting Atli's invitation, calls for wine and suggests that, if he and his men are not valiant enough to make the journey, it does not matter what happens :

> " The wolves then shall rule   the wealth of the Niflungs,
> Wolves aged and grey-hued   if Gunnar is lost." [1]

Gunnar's reference to the treasure does not necessarily mean that he has seen through Atli's plot, but to the audience it gives a hint which the quick-witted will take and bear in mind when Atli delays to kill Hogni, who knows the secret of the hoard, and later keeps Gunnar alive by throwing him into the snake-pit, because the secret may still be revealed. Though the poet keeps Atli's motives in the background, a moment comes when he brings them into the open and so explains much of what has happened and looked mysterious. When Gunnar hears that Hogni is dead and so cannot reveal the secret, he bursts into a cry of triumph :

> " To no one save me   is the secret known
> Of the Niflungs' hoard,   now Hogni is dead ;
> Of old there were two,   while we twain were alive,
> Now is none but I,   for I only am living.
>
> " The swift Rhine shall hold   the strife-gold of heroes,
> That once was the gods',   the wealth of the Niflungs,
> In the depths of the waters   the death rings shall glitter,
> And not shine on the hands   of the Hunnish men." [2]

Since our poet is not given to many words, it is important to listen to him when he spends two stanzas on a single point. At this

---

[1] *Atlakvitha*, 11, 1-2.   [2] *Ibid.* 28-9.

moment the theme of Atli's desire for the gold reaches its climax, and all is made clear.

In *Atlamál* Atli's motives are less easy to unravel. The poet makes little use of the gold of the Niflungs. That he knew of it and of its part in the story is certain, since the dying Atli says to Guthrun :

> " Thou in secret didst work,   so the treasure I won not." [1]

The poet assumes that so much is due to the tradition in which the treasure plays a large part, but it is not what really interests him. It may account for something in Atli's behaviour but not for everything. He concentrates on Atli's desire for vengeance on the sons of Gjuki, and this vengeance is almost without motive, the expression of Atli's barbarous and fearful character. Atli acts like this because it is his nature. But, of course, like others who act from " motiveless malignity ", he believes that he has reasons, and he claims that he wishes to wreak vengeance on the sons of Gjuki for the death of his sister, Brynhild. So, when he chides Guthrun for taking the side of her brothers in the last fight, he reproaches her with being a bad wife and continues :

> " Now my kin all are gone,   of my gold I am robbed ;
> Nay, and worst, thou didst send   my sister to hell." [2]

This interpretation of Atli's character is well in accord with the traditional ideas of him as a ruthless and unscrupulous king, and the poet manages it with skill and persuasiveness. In one place it might have led him into trouble. The episode in which the cook's heart is cut out is well adapted to the older version of Atli's desire to know where the gold is, since it is motivated by his wish to keep Hogni alive and extract the secret from him. When Hogni has to be killed, one hope of discovery is lost with him. In *Atlamál* the poet repeats the episode of the cutting out of the hearts, but has to find new reasons for it, and is ingenious in inventing a new version. Since Atli desires to inflict pain on Guthrun, he decides to cut out Hogni's heart, but for the moment he is frustrated by his own steward, who tries to cut out the cook's heart instead. When this is delayed by the cook's howls, Hogni insists that his own heart must be cut out and submits heroically to it. The whole episode is managed adroitly, and the danger of missing a fine dramatic moment averted. The only important change in the action is that, whereas in *Atlakvitha* the action demands the cook's death, in *Atlamál* it demands that his life should be spared.

---

[1] *Atlamál*, 90, 3.   [2] *Ibid.* 52, 2-3.

But he is an unimportant character, and the change does not matter. It is necessary to the poet's conception of Atli as a man who wishes to inflict the utmost pain on Guthrun and her brothers and has no scruples how he does it.

A second comparison between the two poems can be made in the treatment of Guthrun. In *Atlakvitha* she does not make an appearance until Gunnar and his party arrive at Atli's hall, when she warns them of the doom which awaits them. When the slaughter is over, she keeps silence and restrains her tears, but is set on revenge. On this she gets to work. She makes Atli drunk, gives him the flesh of his children to eat, then tells him what she has done, kills him, sets fire to the hall, and dies in the flames. It is a story of passionate revenge, with no subtleties or complications, told with a strong sense of heroic motives and dramatic crisis. In *Atlamál* Guthrun has a greater prominence and complexity. At the start she tries to warn the sons of Gjuki of what awaits them by sending them a runic message, but it is spoiled by Vingi and fails to make any impression. She next appears when the fight has begun outside the hall. She throws off her jewels and goes outside, in the hope that peace may yet be made. When she fails, she joins the conflict and plies her sword like a man. When Atli reproaches her, she answers proudly and contemptuously. After the slaughter is finished, she begins to hold the stage. When Atli boasts of his success, she begins by warning him that evil awaits him, refuses his offer of gifts, and laments Hogni, whom she loved in childhood. Then, with an unexpected turn she pretends to accept the situation :

> " But the fierceness of men   rules the fate of women,
> The tree-top bows low   if bereft of its leaves,
> The tree bends over   if the roots are cleft under it ;
> Now mayest thou, Atli,   o'er all things here rule." [1]

Atli is deceived, with the result that Guthrun can take her vengeance on him, first by making him eat their sons' flesh and then by telling him what he has done. The poet expands this theme, showing first Guthrun's hatred even for her own children since they are also Atli's, then the quality of her hatred for him as he lies dying. The poet is fascinated by Guthrun's character and tries to give his own interpretation of it. His Guthrun differs from the Guthrun of *Atlakvitha* in being moved not by sudden passion but by a long and bitter hate for her husband. We feel that she has long waited for this chance and that the deaths of her

[1] *Ibid.* 69.

brothers are a climax to years of suffering with Atli. That is why
she enjoys her vengeance and lingers over it. Wrong-doing has
permanently embittered her. She comes from a more subtle
world than that of *Atlakvitha*, but she is still a heroic character
and moves in a heroic setting. The later poet has so mastered the
elements of the old story that he has found his own vision of their
meaning and presents it with power and insight.

On the whole the tradition of heroic poetry, in whatever ways
it operates, tends to preserve the main elements of a story and with
it certain minor details which are recognised as belonging to it.
As a tradition gets further in time or place from its origin, it may
incorporate new inventions and yield to the demands of new
outlooks, but it still feels that it must be faithful to certain fixed
elements in a story. This is one half of the work which a tradition
does, and certainly the more usual and more popular half. But
often enough it may introduce new subjects, and here the problem
is not loyalty to a fixed scheme but ability to adapt the new subjects
to an old manner and outlook. No doubt this is easy enough when
heroic song is in its heyday and every year brings new subjects to
it from the doings of a heroic age. Such must have been the
situation when the different Germanic peoples laid the foundations
of their many heroic legends; such too may have been the situation in Kiev when Russian heroic poetry came to maturity. But
the problem becomes more complex when a cycle of stories has
been more or less established and is then supplemented by new
stories drawn from recent times.

Though the poems of the *Elder Edda* all tell of the Germanic
heroic age, there are other poems, composed in Norway, which tell
of recent events. Two of these are plainly intended to be heroic
and are more or less contemporary with the earlier Eddic poems.
The Battle of Hafsfjord seems to have been composed soon after
872,[1] and the *Hákonarmál* about 960.[2] Both write in the heroic
manner about great events, the first about the battle which made
Harold Fairhaired master of all Norway, the second about another
battle in which Haakon I, the Good, defeated his enemies but died
of his wounds. The poems come from a continental tradition
which differs from the Icelandic in being rather more elaborate in
its style and maintaining throughout the use of four-lined stanzas.
It is thus close to ballad but none the less maintains the heroic
outlook. In each case the poet's concern is to tell the main events
of a battle with due attention to its high moments. If the first is
akin to panegyric, the second is akin to lament, and this indicates

---

[1] Kershaw, p. 88 ff.   [2] *Idem*, p. 101 ff.

a certain irresolution on the poet's part about the kind of poem which he wishes to compose.

Indeed, when we look at these two poems and admit that they are intended to be heroic, we can see that the poets are neither quite happy with the old form nor fully versed in its use. No doubt they wished to use heroic song that modern events might be extolled like great events of the past, but their mastery of the art is incomplete and reveals deficiencies in more than one way. In *The Battle of Hafsfjord* the story is not told with the degree of clarity and precision which heroic narrative demands. It suffers not from the allusiveness which makes *Beowulf* and even *Finnsburh* difficult reading in places and is due to the poets' and the audience's familiarity with heroic topics, but from an imperfect grasp of the means by which vigorous action is made real and vivid. We must of course make allowances for the fact that the poet's audience knows of the events which he relates and would not have any trouble in identifying such references as " the resolute monarch . . . who dwells at Utsteinn ". But the poet fails more seriously to create a real poetry of action because he does not make the most of what happens but leaves it vague and inconclusive. The crisis comes when Harold, attacked from the sea by Kjötvi, takes to his ships and forces an issue in open sea. At this point Kjötvi resorts to a manœuvre which might be interesting if we really knew what it was, but the poet fails to make it clear :

> Then the thick-necked chief   showed no wish to keep
> His land from the Shock-head.   His shield was the island.

Then the engagement follows, and it is clear that Kjötvi's men behave in a none too gallant way, hiding under the benches and covering their backs with their shields. That is intelligible and interesting, but the main feature of the encounter remains obscure. It looks as if the poet, eager to tell a modern tale in the old style, found that he was not really able to do it. The art of his own time, elliptic and allusive, gets in his way and hinders his straightforward movement.

In *Hákonarmál* Eyvindr Finnsson, who was a century later than the poet of *The Battle of Hafsfjord*, found his task even more difficult. In the first place he feels that he must introduce some divine machinery into his story and does so by making Valkyries stand round the dying Haakon and speak of his death. He hears them, and the second half of the poem is occupied with his and their words. This of course might be regarded as a reversion to a very ancient art in which gods mingled freely with men, but it seems

more likely to be a new invention in which the figures of Valhalla
are used to point a moral and provide a theological background.
In practice it means that a large part of the poem is occupied not
by heroic action but by speculations about what will happen to
Haakon after death, and this inevitably destroys much of its heroic
character. Indeed the moral purpose reveals itself clearly at the
end when the poet says that death and waste have ravaged the land
since " Haakon passed away to the heathen gods ". These gods
look as if they were not the poet's own, and his tribute to them
shows his uneasiness with his subject. Secondly, he does not
understand the kind of metre that such a poem demands. In fact
he composes it in two kinds. The first two and last twelve
quatrains are in the new *ljóthaháttr* or " chant-metre ", while the
intervening seven stanzas are in *málaháttr* or " speech-metre ".
The poet has his reasons for this curious arrangement. He uses
" speech-metre " for his account of the battle, and " chant-
metre " for his introduction and for the scene between the king
and the Valkyries. No doubt he felt that the difference of subject
demanded a difference of metre and chose to do it in this way.
But the result is not harmonious, and the whole poem has an air
of having been written by someone who was too far removed from
the old heroic manner to be able to tell a modern story effectively
in it. In these two Norwegian poems we can see how at a time
when heroic poetry was still flourishing with many years before it
in Iceland, it had already begun to decline at home and was not
easily adapted by poets to new themes.

In contrast to these two Norwegian poems, with their uncertain
touch, we may set the Anglo-Saxon *Maldon*, composed in 991, at
least two centuries after *Beowulf*. As a heroic poem *Maldon* is a
triumphant success, and in the Anglo-Saxon tradition it has a
remarkable place. Its spirit is more heroic than that of *Beowulf*,
and, if its affinities as a tale of battle are more with *Finnsburh*, it is
even more direct and straightforward in its narrative. Its subject
and its temper are purely heroic. Both the taking of the tragic
decision and the spirit in which the battle is fought leave nothing
to be desired. The poet felt the greatness of the occasion and saw
that it could fitly be celebrated in heroic song. His problem, then,
was to adapt the traditional methods of such songs to his new
occasion. He uses the old metre and much of the old formulaic
language, but with a clear insight into its usefulness and with no
undue subservience to it. He sticks much more closely to the
sequence of events than the poet of *Beowulf* ever does, and makes
his meaning more immediately clear than the poet of *Finnsburh*.

He avoids the parentheses and circular movements which create such obscurity in earlier Anglo-Saxon poems, and his sense of construction, with its series of events leading to a crisis, is firm and clear. Though he uses an old art, he records recent events carefully and correctly, and there is no call to dispute the accuracy of his main story.

In *Maldon* traditional themes are used very sparsely, but sometimes we can trace one back to an earlier age, as in the notion that eagles and ravens hover over the battlefield, waiting to feast on the bodies of the slain. This theme is at least as old as *Beowulf* and is in all probability a heritage from the original Germanic poetry. It may be illuminating to compare the use of it in four Anglo-Saxon heroic poems. First, *Beowulf*:

> The wan raven,
> Fond over the fallen,   full of news,
> To the eagle shall say   how at the eating he sped,
> When he with the wolf   harried the corpses.[1]

Next, *Finnsburh*:

> Roamed over the corpses   the raven, wandered
> Swart and sallow-brown.[2]

Then, *Brunanburh*:

> Many a carcase   they left to be carrion,
> Left for the horn-beaked,   black-backed raven,
> Left for the white-tailed,   dun-coloured eagle,
> Gave to the greedy war-hawk   to gorge it,
> And to that grey beast   gave it for garbage,
> The wolf of the weald.[3]

Finally, *Maldon*:

> Clamour arose;   ravens were circling,
> Eagles carrion-greedy;   there was crying on earth.[4]

Each poet has his own way of putting it, but each also uses the traditional and familiar idea. If the treatment in *Beowulf* is the richest and most imaginative, that in *Maldon* has its own powerful realism in its presage of a fearful slaughter ahead.

Not all the elements of heroic tradition can have been so easy to assimilate into *Maldon*, and one in particular shows the poet's understanding and mastery of his art. His subject is a general engagement in which many different men play important parts and the rank and file are hardly less important than their leaders.

[1] 3025-8.   [2] 35-6.   [3] 60-65.   [4] 106-8.

Since he sees them as an English force fighting for king and country, he cannot dismiss the minor characters, but evolves his own way of dealing with them. He takes various persons and makes them do representative actions. For instance, Dunnere is a man of no great standing and performs no conspicuous deed, but, when Byrhtnoth is killed, it is he who speaks for everyone:

> Dunnere spoke then　and shook his spear,
> A humble churl,　over all he cried:
> Bade each warrior　wreak vengeance for Byrhtnoth:
> "Whoso purposeth　to avenge the prince,
> Must not waver　nor mourn for life." [1]

Again, when the English march to the battlefield, the different tempers among them are marked by the contrast between Offa's kinsman and Eadric: the second shows no desire to shirk his duty while the first treats it a little too lightly. So the poet brings them together and shows how each behaves:

> Then first the kinsman　of Offa found
> That the earl was not minded　to endure cowardice.
> From his hands he let　the loved hawk fly
> Into the wood　and went forth to war.
> One might know thereby　that the young man would not
> Weaken in fight　when he grasped his weapons.
> Eadric also longed　to attend his leader,
> His prince, to battle.　He began to bear
> His spear to the fight.　He had a stout heart,
> While with his hands　he still could hold
> Shield and broad sword.　He achieved his boast
> To fight before　his prince began battle. [2]

Maldon is rich in such representative characters. Through them the poet shows how a whole force of men fights, and in doing this he goes beyond the narrow scope of the old technique and makes his poem national and English.

Though the original cycle of Russian heroic poetry turned round Prince Vladimir of Kiev, it has been supplemented by new stories in most centuries since, especially since the reign of Ivan the Terrible in the sixteenth century. The poets seem to have no difficulty in accommodating the new characters to the old style. Just as the early characters have their epithets and descriptions, so have the new. The process is already clear in 1619, when Richard James recorded poems in which Ivan the Terrible is "the Orthodox Tsar" or "the terrible Tsar"; the false Dmitri is "Grisha Otrepev, the unfrocked priest". From the same period must come

---

[1] *Maldon*, 255-9.　　　　　　　　　[2] 5-16.

other titles like " the wicked heretic, the godless woman " for Dmitri's wife, Marina of Poland, and " the illustrious Boris Godunov ". The process continues through the succeeding centuries, when we find such combinations as " the great boyar, the ataman of the Streltsy " and " our dog of an enemy, King Napoleon ". So in recent years, when poets have increased their repertories with poems about the Revolution and the Civil War, they have found no difficulty in finding the right phrases for their characters. Marfa Kryukova establishes the modern heroes with suitable formulae like " Lenin the leader " and " Kolchak the admiral ", and differentiates her minor personages as " Forman the commissar " and " Katharine the machine-gunner ". In telling of Otto Schmidt's expedition to the Arctic, she makes him become " Beard-to-the-knees " and his rescuing airmen " the bright hawks ". In her *Tale of Lenin* we see the heroes of the Revolution as " Klim the locksmith, the glorious Voroshilov ", " heroic Red Cossack Budenny from the quiet Don ", and Lenin's wife, Krupskaya, " his faithful helpmate, faithful and unchanging one ". Other poets do the same kind of thing, as when Nikofor Kigachev tells how Lenin plans to deliver Moscow :

> From the gory Tsarist generals,
> From the bandit officers with gold epaulettes,
> From the bands of white robbers,
> From the counter-revolutionary spies at home.[1]

In contrast to these enemies are the champions of the Revolution, who become " mighty Soviet warriors " or " brave, strong Russian soldiers ". Many of the epithets come from the past, but are brought into new combinations and produce new effects.

In these modern poems old themes and devices are used all the time and make contemporary subjects look as if they belonged to the heroic world. Sometimes the more eminent figures of recent history look a little odd in their new guise, but the poets are justified in so treating them, since they are the peers and successors of the heroes of the past. So the revolutionary Chapaev has taken on some of the gifts of Volga and even of the wise Boyan in the *Tale of Igor's Raid*, when an unknown Karelian poet and Peter Ryabinin-Andreev both say of him :

> He could dive as a pike in the blue sea,
> Race as a grey wolf over the open plain,
> Fly as a hawk under the blue clouds.[2]

[1] Astakhova, p. 377.
[2] Nechaev, p. 291; Ryabinin-Andreev, p. 118.

So, when Lenin is wounded, his wife, Krupskaya, treats his wound in the traditional way :

> She ran forth herself from the chamber,
> She ran straight to the green garden,
> She plucked grass weeds,
> Plucked green leaves of every kind,
> Gathered and brought them in,
> And laid them on the hot little wound.[1]

So, too, when Ivan Fofanov describes how Voroshilov prepares for war, he uses the traditional account of a warrior arming himself and getting out his horse :

> He clothed himself in his warrior-clothing,
> He put on his cloak of grey dog-skin,
> And his soldier's accoutrements.
> Then he went to his horse,
> To the horse-box where his charger stood,
> He took his warrior horse,
> Took too the silken bridle,
> Led out his equine horse
> From the horse-box.[2]

The whole business is conducted in the ancient manner. After all, a modern horse is very like an antique one and has to be treated in much the same way.

From this the poets advance to something more subtle. While keeping many of the traditional appearances, they insinuate little hints of modernity and achieve a charmingly ambiguous result in which past and present are neatly blended. So, for instance, in her story of Chapaev, Marfa Kryukova tells how in his youth he became a wandering singer :

> Then Chapai got himself a merry gusli,
> He went to towns and villages,
> He played on his resounding gusli,
> He sang songs of Emelka Pugachev
> And of Stenka Razin.[3]

At first sight Chapaev seems to have become a second Sadko, the minstrel of Novgorod, but the songs which Chapaev sings have a special point, since Pugachev and Razin are famous rebels of the past and therefore fit themes for the young revolutionary singer. So, too, when Kigachev tells how Stalin gets to action in the Civil War, he adopts a nice realism which rings familiar to any Russian :

[1] Kaun, p. 189.   [2] Astakhova, p. 259.   [3] Andreev, p. 508.

> Then rose on his mettlesome legs
> The strong powerful young man,
> The warrior Josef Vissarionovich,
> He began to walk up and down the chamber,
> He began to smoothe his curly hair,
> And to twist his moustaches.
> He began to smoke his pipe,
> And to speak these words.[1]

Here perhaps we may detect an echo from poems on Ivan the Terrible which tell how he walks up and down the room and combs his hair with a tooth-comb,[2] but Kigachev advances from the old theme to his own modern version of the national hero in a familiar guise.

Sometimes the modern poets use traditional themes in a more adventurous spirit, when they shape modern experience into archaic forms with which it has perhaps more in common than we might think at first sight. This enables them to make more intelligible to their audiences modern events which might otherwise seem remote and unreal. Marfa Kryukova has a nice gift for this, especially in her *Tale of Lenin*, in which the leader's career is made to appear in many respects like that of an ancient hero. When Lenin's brother, Alexander, visits the Tsar Alexander III, the Tsar is ingeniously called Idolishche or " Big Idol " — a title used in the traditional lays for half-fabulous pagan princes who are almost monsters. The young man is admitted to his presence and greeted rather as a hero might be greeted on entering the dwelling of an ogre :

> Quickly, quickly the Tsar awoke,
> Became conscious after his fat sleep,
> Then the Tsar became angry, became furious :
> " How did you dare, you worker, you enemy,
> How did you dare to approach me ? "
> Idolishche leaped from his lofty throne,
> He waved his right hand,
> With his fist he cast the good young man on the damp earth,
> Then the Tsar lifted a steel knife from his breast,
> He wished to rip open the white breast,
> Only by chance did he not kill him.[3]

Kryukova's peasant imagination has got to work on the idea of a wicked Tsar and turned him into a traditional monster. This is no doubt how she herself sees him, and of course her version will be accepted as authentic and correct. So, too, later in the poem, when she tells of the attempt which a woman makes on Lenin's life and

---

[1] Astakhova, p. 377.   [2] Cf. *sup.* p. 100.   [3] Andreev, p. 524.

the wound which she gives him, Kryukova resorts to the same technique. She identifies the assassin with a snake and leaves it open whether she is a real snake or not:

> A fierce snake glided up,
> She stung, she struck Lenin the leader,
> She barely missed his dear little heart,
> But she made a very deep wound, the evil-doer,
> A very deep and poisonous wound.[1]

Behind this lie stories like those of Dobrynya and the snake, in which the hero fights a poisonous monster and comes near to being killed by it. Kryukova finds the old theme at hand and uses it to interpret modern experience.

Not all modern events can be treated in this way, and sometimes the poets are faced with problems of some difficulty in subjects which call for heroic song but have few connections with its traditional material. Such a case arose when Russian poets felt that the stirring story of Otto Schmidt's expedition to the Arctic demanded celebration from them. So a poet from Karelia makes much of the episode in which they abandon ship for a piece of floating ice and do their best to live on it:

> When they went onto the great hill,
> The lofty hill of ice,
> Then their ship was crushed by the strong ice.[2]

The captain is not dismayed, and prepares to make the best of the situation:

> They marked it out like a camp,
> And it was fit to sleep in through the cold night,
> On that ice, that cold ice;
> But they were tired out from disembarking
> And slept the sleep of warriors.
> Then it was like ruin — the ice came asunder,
> But that crack did not cause fear,
> The company were not frightened.[3]

The unprecedented situation is dealt with in a sensible, realistic way and falls quite easily into the old manner. In Kryukova's account of the same expedition, different aspects receive attention. She knows that the aim of the explorers is scientific, but she is chiefly interested in their heroic and dramatic aspects. So when Stalin gives orders to Schmidt and his men, he sends them out rather as Vladimir might send out his knights to an unknown world:

[1] Kaun, p. 189.   [2] Nechaev, p. 288.   [3] *Idem*, p. 288.

" Fly to the land, the far-off land,
That far-off land, that cold land,
That cold land, that northern land,
Where bright hawks have never flown,
Where brave young men have never gone,
Where good people have never lived." [1]

In the Arctic the Russians come across the Italian expedition of
General Nobile, which has been stranded on the ice and been
reduced to desperate straits :

They fell into great misfortune,
Into great unhappiness far away ;
Cruel hunger fell upon them,
They began to eat, to devour each other.[2]

From this dire condition the Russians rescue them, and then proceed to their proper task of examining the North Pole. Of this
Kryukova has formed her own simple idea, with due respect for
its powers :

They looked and saw how the earth turns round,
How it turns and winds round a pillar,
So that the sun's warmth comes to all,
So that we know when the white day comes,
When the black night advances.[3]

This is not the usual stuff of *byliny*, but it is expressed in the usual
language, and the discovery of the Pole has some affinity with the
quests on which the heroes of old set out.

Like the Russians, the Uzbeks have in recent years composed
poems about the stirring events of their own time. In these, too,
there is a mixture of old and new, of traditional phrases and
modern sentiments. The poem *Mamatkarim-pavlan*, composed
by Fazil Yuldashev, tells of the class-war at the beginning of the
revolution. Though the hero comes from a well-to-do family, he
espouses the cause of the people. Attempts are made to win him
over, especially by a rich bey called Eshmamat, who says to
him :

" You are a valiant warrior,
All hold you in honour,
But you look like a man of low class,
You seek the company of dispossessed beggars.
A warrior like you should aspire to high things.
Consort with those who are above you . . .
Wear the look of a bey.
You have great authority among the people,
They call you a great soldier,

---

[1] Andreev, p. 503.   [2] *Idem*, p. 505.   [3] *Idem*, p. 506.

> If you wish, I will take you to my house,
> I will make you my son,
> I shall be of one family with you,
> I will give you wealth,
> I will give you a horse."

Mamatkarim refuses this offer in a truly up-to-date, revolutionary spirit :

> " You are bowed down with your wealth,
> With your belly you prop up your saddle-bow.
> You have come to exalt yourself and your wealth.
> Do not humble me by saying that from my friends
> I shall have little profit.
> Do not think that your wealth will always stay with you,
> It may pass to beggars.
> I have no need of your horse or your coat —
> You know only how to make yourself rich.
> A time will come when your doom will fall on you." [1]

Mamatkarim has digested his revolutionary doctrines and has his own theories of the social situation, which he expounds to someone who deplores the sad case of the poor :

> " What they say is true.
> Money and land are all in the hands of the beys.
> We never hear that they take taxes from the beys,
> We see always that the poor, who have nowhere to live,
> Have to pay for everything." [2]

The Uzbek poet is evidently much interested in the new outlook brought by revolution and presents it in his own simple way. So far his hero is a good modern revolutionary. But that is not enough. He must be related to the world of heroic poetry, and this is done by making him a *pavlan*, a great warrior. He treats his opponents as a hero treats his enemies in war, saying to one of them :

> " If you speak again,
> You will lose your authority.
> I shall throw you from your horse on to the ground.
> I shall cut you in pieces.
> Go your way, Eshmamat !
> I shall make your face turn yellow like a flower.
> If I become angry with you, I shall tear out both your eyes." [3]

Though the modern situation is presented quite faithfully and with considerable understanding of its significance, that does not prevent the hero from behaving and speaking in the best manner of ancient warriors.

[1] Zhirmunskii-Zarifov, p. 464.　　[2] *Idem*, p. 465.　　[3] *Idem*, p. 466.

It might be thought that these modern Russian and Uzbek poems are a little too conscious of contemporary events and that their adaptation of them to the traditional technique and outlook is not entirely natural but something of a *tour de force*. Because the bards are encouraged by the political authorities, we may even suspect that this is not objective art but subtle propaganda. But this is to interpret the situation too narrowly. In so telling their stories the bards act in good faith. They are stirred by present events and wish to celebrate them, and their only available technique is what they have learned from their forefathers. In their own way they do much what the poet of *Maldon* did in his. Though some modern elements may look incongruous in this traditional setting, they need not always seem so to the bard or his audience. When the Russians tell of Polar expeditions or the Uzbeks of proletarian risings, they do not take such risks as the Jugoslav poet who, in telling of the Balkan War of 1912, says :

> To the telephone the King proceeded,
> Enver Bey by telephone he summoned.[1]

This is for him an interesting novelty, worthy of a place in his story. Yet even this is really no more of an innovation than the first mention of cannon in poems of the seventeenth century. When the circumstances of war and adventure change, the poet's duty is to take notice of them, and his traditional art is usually flexible enough to allow him to do so.

[1] Kravstov, p. 96.

XIII

VARIETIES OF HEROIC OUTLOOK

The similarities which the separate branches of heroic poetry show to one another in parts of their technique do not mean that this resemblance extends to every aspect of them. The poetry of each people develops its own special qualities and presents a kind of national uniformity. It is indeed striking how in a single country a large number of poems, composed by a number of different authors, may resemble each other so closely that we might almost believe them to be the work of a single man. For instance, though the poems of the *Elder Edda* have origins in centuries from the eighth to the twelfth and in places so far apart as Iceland and Greenland, they seem to conform to a single outlook. And their case is by no means unique. The heroic poetry of the Jugoslavs, the Russians, the Kara-Kirghiz, and the Kalmucks is the work of many poets, but in each society it has a striking homogeneity of outlook. This is of course largely due to the force of tradition which compels a poet to tell stories in a familiar way, but that is not the only cause. The local tradition in each case reflects the society which produces it. Heroic poetry flourishes in societies in which life is moulded into standard forms and follows familiar ways of thought. An unlettered people will usually have a more homogeneous outlook than a people whose tastes have been diversified by books. It takes more for granted, asks fewer questions, and has a greater body of accepted beliefs. The gatherings which listen to heroic poetry have something like a common consciousness, not merely in the sense that they all enjoy the same performance together, but in the sense that they all feel much the same about it because their own lives conform to customary rules of which they are largely unconscious and therefore uncritical. Though what the German romantics called " Volksgeist " does not create poetry, which is always the work of individual poets, yet it determines its character and sets limitations on it because the poet is really the voice of the people whom he addresses and whose feelings and thoughts are his own. For this reason heroic poetry throws an intimate light on the society to which it belongs and illustrates what its outlook and tastes are.

Heroic poetry seems to fall into three main groups which are differentiated by social structure and ways of life. The first group may be called primitive. It is commonly found among pastoral or nomadic peoples who have no towns, no settled existence, and few arts or crafts. Often with no shelter more permanent than a tent and with little wealth except flocks and herds, pastoral nomads turn naturally to a poetry which can be recited in any conditions and tells of exciting actions. Among such peoples the oral heroic poem is often a living art, guided by strict rules but well equipped to express the aspirations and interests of men who pass their lives out of doors and wish to hear of great doings. Such peoples hardly possess any written literature other than their holy books, and even these may be the concern of a small and separate class. The ordinary man, even of high station, finds his recreation in the sung or recited word which he hears from bards in his hours of leisure. Such is still more or less the case among the Kara-Kirghiz, the Uzbeks, the Kalmucks, the Yakuts, the Ainus, and the Ossetes. Even though some of these peoples have passed from a purely pastoral way of life to some kind of agricultural economy and have even established permanent abodes in villages, they keep their old homogeneity and simplicity. They are primitive societies in the sense that life is organised on simple lines with a simple social structure. In them the heroic type is still a reality in that most men seek in some way or other to realise it, even though new systems of government may discourage its more violent manifestations. Though the great man may differ from the lesser in the number of cattle or horses which he owns, or in the power which he commands or the respect in which he is held, he does not really live a different kind of life. His interests, his pleasures, his manners are those of other men in the same society. His special abilities are shown by his capacity to do better what all men do to some degree and by his superior personality which enables him to exert a control over his social inferiors. The poetry produced in such conditions reflects a whole society as hardly any other poetry does, and this is possible because such societies are composed on very simple lines.

The primitive way of life may pass into other, more elaborate forms, and, when this happens, the character of heroic poetry changes. It bifurcates into two directions, which accord with the new kinds of social structure. On the one hand the imposition of a cultivated, lettered class on a large, unlettered population may mean that heroic poetry is restricted to the proletariat; on the other hand the social structure may become secure and settled but none the less keep its old homogeneity in an aristocratic frame. This means that heroic poetry follows the social movement and becomes either proletarian or aristocratic, and there is a considerable difference between the two kinds. The Russian *byliny* are now proletarian, and must have been so at least since the seventeenth century, when the Russian ruling classes lost interest in their indigenous poetry and looked to foreign models in books. Though the material of the *byliny* dates back for many centuries, their outlook, as they now exist, reflects a humble section of society which has imposed its own philosophy on these tales of kings and princes. What has happened in Russia through the development of a ruling class and its severance from the common people, has happened elsewhere through the advent of foreign conquerors. In long years of Turkish domination the Bulgars have evolved a proletarian art which reflects the outlook of simple peasants and has little contact with the seats of power and wealth. Though the Armenian hero, David of Sasoun, is a national king who defends his country against infidels, the poems about him are deeply coloured by years of Russian or Turkish rule and are ultimately the work of men who had little first-hand knowledge of heroic life. They have little heroic confidence or grandeur. The action, though full of charm and gaiety, lacks pride and style. The poets seem to be men of humble station and simple life, who have lost the old outlook and interpret their traditional material by standards which are ultimately alien to it.

Alternatively, primitive heroic poetry may develop into something aristocratic or even princely. When pastoral habits yield to agriculture and towns become seats of government and culture, poetry may still survive but develop a new character. The old social homogeneity is preserved so long as the ruling class shares the interests and the outlook of the ruled, but poetry receives a new polish and a greater fullness, as befit a more elaborate way of life. It is perhaps at this stage that heroic poetry finds its finest and most satisfactory form. The comparative stability of social conditions allows a development of heroic ideas and an enrichment of living which widens the concept of what a man ought to be. *Gilgamish*, *Beowulf*, the *Elder Edda*, *Roland*, and the *Cid* are the classical cases by which we tend to judge all other poems of a similar kind. In these the primitive stage has been left behind for something richer and more settled. The societies of which they tell are no longer nomadic. Gilgamish is king of " high-walled Erech " and superior to Enkidu, who is a child of the wilds. The first actions of *Beowulf* take place in a well-built hall; its kings are established in high positions and have relations with other kings overseas. The *Elder Edda* groups its stories round the two monarchies of the Huns and the Burgundians with their separate courts and territories. In *Roland* Charlemagne is emperor of " sweet France " and has his capital at Aix, while the Saracens have their palaces in Spain. In the *Cid*, though the action takes place in Moorish territory, the hero comes from a feudal society and owes allegiance to a king of Castile, who reigns in well-marked frontiers. In these poems the greater sense of social security is accompanied by a more elaborate code of honour and a finer elegance in material things than is possible at the primitive stage. This is the heroic world in its ripeness, when heroic worth is matched by an external dignity of circumstance and the great man shows his superiority by visible tokens of splendour. If its poetry differs from that of the primitive stage by a wider and more elaborate outlook, it differs from that of the proletarian stage by its intimate knowledge of a heroic world as it really is, not as it is seen through distant memories and distorting changes.

The richest example of this class can be seen in the Homeric poems. Though the *Iliad* tells of heroic wrath and the *Odyssey* of heroic revenge, the poems vary the central themes with many richnesses and elegances which at times seem even to pass beyond the heroic world to a humaner order. In the *Iliad* the Achaean princes live in their tents and seem almost to have no fixed abode, but Troy is a great city with its own life and established ways. In the *Odyssey* the home of Odysseus is indeed ravaged by black-guards, but it still maintains the high hospitality and easy courtesies of an ancient civilisation. The scene is filled in with many touches which reveal that life is closely connected with the soil and expresses itself in fine arts. The palaces of Menelaus and Alcinous, with their statues and colonnades and gardens, testify to a background of wealth; the furniture and fittings, vessels, brooches, clothes, and weapons show that the craftsman practises his art at a distinguished level. The range and variety of the Homeric world are nobly portrayed in the scenes which Hephaestus fashions on the shield of Achilles. There the patriarchal king rules over subjects who practise ancient ways of livelihood, who keep cattle and reap corn and get in the vintage.[1] The common life which provides a background to the Homeric poems and even breaks unexpectedly into their heroic actions is richer than in other heroic poems. None the less the essential elements in the Homeric poems are truly heroic, and their social background is not

[1] *Il.* xviii, 550 ff.

fundamentally different from that of *Beowulf* or *Roland*. They show a homogeneous society in which the great men at the top have developed a form of life which is accepted by their subjects as right and admirable.

On a rough analysis, then, there seem to be three main classes of heroic poetry, primitive, proletarian, and aristocratic. These classes are not entirely separate, and sometimes more than one kind can be found in a single country. For instance, the Jugoslav lays on Kosovo are composed in a princely spirit with an aristocratic power of selection and sense of style, while the poems on the popular hero, Marko Kraljević, have a more homely outlook, which suggests that they belong to the proletarian class. The history of Serbia may account for this conjunction of two different kinds. The poems on Kosovo reflect the old independent spirit which existed before the Turkish domination, while the poems on Marko come from the days of that domination when poetry survived in a subject population. Something similar may be seen in modern Greece, where a considerable feeling for noble endeavours and aims is combined with something less majestic and more provincial. Here too the difference may be due to the degree of subjection which the authors suffered from the Turks. Though our analysis of poems into three classes may not be final, it is useful because it stresses certain variations in heroic poetry, and shows that, although the poets deal with the same kinds of subjects, they deal with them in different ways, which seem on the whole to correspond with different social backgrounds. If all heroic poetry treats of action, and especially of violent action, the poets vary greatly in what they admit or omit and in their approach to certain familiar topics.

A signal example of this variety may be seen in the treatment of women. Heroic poetry does not confine itself to men, and women often appear in it, but they are treated in noticeably different ways. In the primitive stage they have a place which corresponds with their actual position in primitive societies. They are the centre of such domestic life as exists, the focus of family ties, and the mistresses of home and hospitality. They have a kind of rarity-value, because it is commonly the practice in such societies to expose unwanted female children at birth, and grown women are in consequence valuable. The result is that they may become powerful and influential. Their advice is sought on important matters, and their words treated with the respect due to oracular authority. Though women play very little part in the heroic poems of the Kalmucks, the poets feel it their duty to say some-

thing about Dzhangar's wife, Ragini-Lagini. She is said to be a
sorceress, whom Dzhangar made his own by subduing her when
she changed her shape many times. Her appearance suits her
special powers :

> She is bright as the red and yellow sun at its rising,
> She is radiant as the fiery, yellow sun in its ascent.
> In her light clouds disappear
> In her look you can watch over a herd of horses.
> If she looks afar, you can count the small fish in the sea.[1]

She plays little part in the recorded poems, but it is clear that
Dzhangar's winning of her was familiar to everyone and doubtless
told in other poems not published. She is the authentic type of
the sorceress-queen.

A not dissimilar role belongs to the great woman of the Narts,
Satana, who is both the sister and the wife of the hero Uryzmag.
From this position she becomes a kind of mother to the whole
people, who bring their troubles to her and ask her to deliver them
from their anxieties through her superior knowledge. Their
respect for her is indeed great :

> " Let us all go together, let us question Satana ;
> Satana will tell us what must be done.
> She is wisest of the wise, most cunning of the cunning,
> Satana knows everything in the past and the future.
> You will find nothing under the earth or in the sky
> Which is not known already to Satana." [2]

Satana has the kind of wisdom which shamans claim for themselves, and naturally her advice is sought when the Narts are in
need :

> " You have always been a sage to our people,
> The Narts have always come to you for counsel —
> Now again we have come to you for help."

This position is well deserved. Satana is usually able to solve any
problem with which she is confronted. It is she who understands
immediately Uryzmag's cryptic message when he is imprisoned
by a giant, she who brings Batradz back to earth from the sky
when the Narts need his help, she who knows that an unknown boy
killed by Uryzmag is their son.

This special importance which women have in the primitive
stage is strengthened by other less remarkable features. A woman
may be a sorceress, but that does not prevent her from carrying out
her feminine duties. She is the head of the household and respon-

---

[1] *Dzhangariada*, p. 148. [2] Dynnik, p. 27.

sible for its conduct in such matters as the entertainment of guests. So in the Kara-Kirghiz poems Kanykai, wife of Manas, is renowned as a prophetess and consulted with some pomp and circumstance by Manas and Alaman Bet before they set out on their expedition to China. But she is also a great lady, who carries out her domestic tasks in a high style. Her different duties are recognised as equally important by Alaman Bet, who says of her:

> " She is the best of fortune-tellers,
> She is the best of embroiderers,
> She is the best of spinners and weavers.
> If we first visit her,
> It will be better for us in foreign lands ! " [1]

For Alaman Bet, telling fortunes is as much a woman's business as spinning and weaving. The result is that Kanykai is persuaded to forecast the result of the expedition and does so at some length with much useful information about weather, geography, and supplies of food and water. But this is only part of her queenly equipment. Both in the latest version of *Manas* and in other poems about her, she is a true lady of the house. In the poem *Kös Kaman*, which tells of her betrothal and marriage, she is still in her father's home but already well versed in the etiquette of dignified life. When Manas and his retinue pay a visit, she summons her maidens and does the honours with lavish hospitality. With her attendants she sets out the brandy, presents the visitors with corslets, shirts, and hose, fits them with long boots, and looks after their horses.[2] Kanykai is the exemplar of womanhood as the Kara-Kirghiz poets see it, the worthy wife of the great hero who relies on her both for counsel and for the maintenance of generous hospitality in his home.

At the same time these women may also be women of action when occasion calls. Just as Satana takes part in councils of war and outwits her husband's and son's enemies, so too Kanykai uses force when it is needed. Ties of blood require that she should look after her kin, and, when her son Semätäi is murdered by two Kalmucks, it is she who avenges his death and shows the fierce heart which beats beneath her decorous appearance. When she has the enemy at her mercy she says:

> " From the blood of Khan Tschoro
> Give me a spoonful of blood,
> I will drink of his blood, child,
> And when I have drunk, I will gladly die." [3]

---

[1] *Manas*, p. 94.   [2] Radlov, v, p. 237.   [3] *Idem*, v, p. 370.

She carries out her threat, and honour is avenged. Nor is she the only Kara-Kirghiz woman capable of violent action. In *Joloi* the hero himself is a poor fellow, but his wife, Ak Kanysh, saves his life on several occasions, and when, through his own stupidity, she can at last do nothing for him, she brings up his son to avenge him and in due course deals with her own hand the fatal stroke to their enemy.[1] Nor are such achievements confined to the Kara-Kirghiz. One Yakut poem, *Uolumar and Aigyr*,[2] tells how two women shamans conduct adventures in the spirit of male heroes, defeating demons and meeting men successfully in open fight. At the primitive stage, though a woman may have magical powers, she does not necessarily use them in moments of danger but may prefer to show her equality with men by resorting to strength of hand and arm.

When the heroic poem passes into the proletarian stage, its attitude towards women is considerably altered. In Russia and Armenia, and to a large extent in Jugoslavia, the conception of womanhood conforms to the actual conditions which the poets know. Women no longer prophesy or practise magic; they are no longer consulted on points of high policy. With the decay of their prophetic powers goes the decay of their martial prowess. The Jugoslav and Armenian women do not take to arms as their Yakut and Kara-Kirghiz sisters do. With the Russians it is a little different. It is clear that the *polenitsy*, or women warriors, once played some part in Russian heroic lays. They are usually mentioned in the formulaic openings of poems about the guests at Prince Vladimir's court, and this suggests that they had an importance similar to that of the fierce women of Norse legend. But in the actual poems which we have they are, on the whole, of little importance. Indeed, we can almost see how they have fallen in prestige and interest. In one tale a *polenitsa* fulfils the requirements of a true heroine. Dobrynya Nikich meets a warrior maiden of great strength, called Nastasya, riding in the open plain. He fails to subdue her, and she seizes him by the curls, takes him off his horse, and drops him into her leather pouch. Eventually she releases him on condition that he marries her.[3] She is clearly a survival from an age when *polenitsy* were giantesses. But it is worth noticing that, when Nastasya marries Dobrynya, she changes her character and becomes a gentle domestic creature. The imagination of recent generations has been unable to imagine what Dobrynya's married life can have been if the old idea of his wife

[1] *Idem*, v, p. 390.   [2] Yastremski, p. 122 ff.
[3] Rybnikov, i, p. 147.

must persist, and so Nastasya is reduced in stature and fearfulness.

Something of an exception to this general rule may be found in Bulgaria, where women still play heroic parts as the equals of men. One poem tells how Boyana pawns her trousseau in order to become chief of a band of warriors. Her position is disputed, and various tests are arranged, such as shooting an arrow through a ring on a tree and jumping over nine swords. Boyana defeats everyone in them, and her leadership is accepted. The proof of her courage and competence comes when a rich Turkish woman, Kerima, passes by in her carriage with a large company of guards. Boyana approaches her and asks for her money. When she refuses, Boyana resorts to force, kills the guards, and threatens Kerima's life. Kerima then offers her money, but now it is too late:

> To Boyana said Kerima:
> " Sister mine, beloved Boyana,
> To you I give up my silver,
> But take not my life, I beg you;
> I'm my mother's only daughter,
> Recently was I betrothed, too,
> Promised am I, not yet married."
> But Boyana scorns Kerima,
> With her sword she cuts her head off;
> Then she calls out to her comrades:
> " Comrades, faithful and united,
> Whereso'er you be, come hither,
> Take the gold and bear it with you,
> All the gold that you can carry,
> Then go each one to his people;
> I shall travel in this carriage." [1]

In the Bulgarian resistance to the Turks women may sometimes develop the brutal capacities of men.

The qualities which the Bulgarians attribute to their own womenfolk may also be attributed to other women of higher station who are less immediately familiar. In one poem the heroine is the Empress of Muscovy, probably Catherine II. She begins by announcing that she cares nothing for the Sultan or his vizir, with the result that seventy pashas are sent with an army against her. They challenge her to war, and her response is what a simple people might expect from a great queen:

> Then the Queen of Muscovy besought them,
> To allow her time to get her hair done,
> Get her hair done and collect an army.
> No delay they grant, the seventy pashas;

[1] Dozon, p. 24.

Like the shining sun their sword-blades glisten,
Like the heavy rain their bullets whistle.
Then the Queen of Muscovy grew angry,
Mounted on her horse with hair dishevelled,
For three days and nights she gave them combat,
And she massacred the seventy pashas,
And their seventy heads she gathered from them,
Sent them to the Sultan and his vizir.
" If the Sultan and the Sultan's vizir
Still have seventy, seventy and seven,
Let him send them, that I may so treat them ! " [1]

This is the way in which Bulgarians expect a patriotic woman to behave when she is dealing with Turks, and in it there is still something of the old *polenitsa*.

In the proletarian stage of heroic poetry wives and mothers look after their menfolk and do their best to save them from the consequences of their more reckless actions. These women may be of quite high social station, but they behave like wise and cautious peasants. They have plenty of liberty and influence, but they use them not for their own glory but to help their men. Russian poems abound in admirable women who look after their men. There are the good wives, like Staver's, who disguises herself as a man and has various adventures at court in her efforts, finally successful, to get her husband out of prison.[2] There are the good mothers, like Dyuk's, who warns him against drunken boasting and saves him from its results,[3] or the mother of Nightingale Budimirovich, who goes with her son on his trading expeditions and spends much of her leisure in praying for his welfare,[4] or the mother of Vasili Buslaev, who shuts him up that he may not in the exuberance of his spirits kill too many of the neighbours.[5] These women often find themselves in unexpected situations and are forced to strange courses of conduct, but they remain true to their type and solve their problems by devotion and common sense.

Virtues no less domestic may be found among the Jugoslavs, and specially in connection with Marko Kraljević. Though he is a great hero, his mother comes from an ordinary world and gives him counsels of prudence in the hope of modifying his more out-rageous ambitions. So she exhorts him to take up some useful and peaceful pursuit instead of harrying the Turks :

" O my son, O my Kraljević Marko,
Cease, my son, from risking these adventures ;

Idem, p. 73.   [2] Rybnikov, i, p. 202 ff.   [3] *Idem*, i, p. 98 ff.
[4] Gilferding, i, p. 517 ff.   [5] Rybnikov, i, p. 368 ff.

What is evil brings no good thing with it,
And it wearies thine own agèd mother,
That she ever washes blood-stained garments.
So do thou get out the plough and oxen,
Do thou plough the hillside and the valley,
Scatter, son, the seed of the fair wheat-crop ;
Thou shalt feed thyself and me, thy mother." [1]

Marko tries to do what he is told, but succeeds only in killing some more Turks. It is evidently his mother's fate to find that her good advice somehow goes wrong. It is the same when she tells Marko that it is time for him to get married, and hears to her delight that he intends to do so. But then things again go wrong. The mother recommends Marko to invite important witnesses, like the Doge of Venice, but, when the Doge comes, he behaves outrageously and nearly ruins the marriage by his violent attentions to the bride. Marko's mother, by her practical prudence, presents both an amusing contrast to her son's doings and a modest commentary on them. She has none of the formidable fierceness which primitive mothers display in their desperate attachment to their kin.

In the Armenian poems women play a somewhat similar role. There too the standard is that of the woman of the village or the small farm, who has a limited outlook and no great ambitions but finds herself caught in great affairs conducted by men whose aims and motives are beyond her ken. The poets adapt old stories, which reflect a more violent way of life, to their new and more unadventurous outlook, and the result is often ingenious and charming. For instance, when Tsovinar, daughter of an Armenian king, marries the Caliph of Bagdad to save her country from war, she finds herself miraculously with child before she goes to him, and in due course bears twins. This produces a grave situation, since the Caliph wishes to kill her. But the proletarian poet makes it an occasion for comedy. When the executioner comes to her and tells her of his intention, Tsovinar says :

" Truly you have no laws among you !
How can these babies at my breast grow up
If my head is cut off ?
When the children have fed at the breast,
Then you can cut off my head." [2]

The executioner takes her point and lets her off. So on each subsequent occasion when the Caliph decides to kill her or her sons, she manages to defeat him by this severely rational kind of argument. She is a woman of the people, who has no respect for

[1] Karadžić, ii, p. 403.   [2] *David Sasunskii*, p. 15.

the great and will stand no nonsense where her children are concerned. The Armenian women have usually a touch of this inspired common sense. Their menfolk may behave in the wildest manner, but the women keep their heads and exert themselves to see that all goes well.

The other side to this domestic handling of women is that they forfeit the mystery and respect which encompassed them when they were prophetesses or warriors. These women work in houses and fields and are in constant contact with men. Having lost their special position, they exist chiefly to do what their men demand of them. The man is now the superior, and, if a woman offends his vanity, it is the worse for her. She is treated with particular harshness if she departs from the strict path of decorum or behaves with anything that savours of immodesty or insolence. When the Russian maiden, Zabava, tells Nightingale Budimirovich that she wishes to marry him, he answers tartly :

> " For all things, maiden, for all things I love you,
> But for one thing, maiden, I love you not at all,
> That you a maiden have done your own wooing." [1]

Fortunately, after this display of right feeling, Nightingale has the sense to make the maiden appeal to Prince Vladimir for a decision, and all ends happily. But a hero is not always so tolerant of immodesty, especially if he feels that a woman has insulted his honour. A maiden, who is betrothed to Prince Dmitri, mocks him as he goes to Matins :

> " He is a crooked hunchback,
> He has a snub nose and squinting eyes,
> He has teeth like bundles of straw,
> And he shuffles with his feet,
> And throws up all the snow in the roadway." [2]

For this insolence Prince Dmitri gives her so sound a drubbing that she dies of it, and the principle is established that women must not insult men's honour.

An even fiercer spirit may be seen in some Jugoslav poems. In *The Marriage of Dušan*, Miloš threatens to cut off girls' arms,[3] and in the tale of Strahinja Banović a faithless wife is killed by her brothers with their swords.[4] Such cases may be excused by morality or patriotism, but other cases are more striking and can be explained only by a powerful attachment to personal honour

---

[1] Gilferding, i, p. 517 ; Chadwick, *R.H.P.* p. 121.
[2] Kireevski, v, p. 63 ; Chadwick, *R.H.P.* p. 179.
[3] Karadžić, ii, p. 138.   [4] Bogišić, no. 40.

and dignity. In *Marko Kraljević and Philip the Magyar*, when Marko receives a rude answer from Philip's wife to his enquiries about her husband, he avenges himself at once:

> In the face with his flat hand he smote her,
> And upon that hand a golden ring was,
> And upon her face it made great havoc;
> Three fine teeth it knocked out from their places.
> Then he took from her three rows of ducats
> And he put them in his silken pocket.[1]

In *The Sister of Leka Capetan*, Marko's behaviour is even more violent, since his honour is more intimately attacked, when Rosanda refuses his suit:

> Marko raged and was exceeding angry,
> Took a step and made a great spring forward,
> By her hand he laid hold of the damsel,
> Drew forth the sharp dagger at his girdle,
> And with it he then cut off her right arm,
> That right arm he cut off at the shoulder,
> And he put the right arm in her left hand;
> And her eyes he put out with his dagger,
> Wrapped them up inside a silken kerchief,
> And he thrust it with them in her bosom.[2]

When poets tell of heroes acting in this way, they assume that vengeance must be exacted even from women when honour is in question.

In some Bulgarian poems an even more brutal spirit appears. Here, too, if a hero thinks that his pride or dignity or safety is compromised by a woman, he feels entitled to exact a terrible punishment. This is perhaps understandable in the case of Nencho, who is betrayed by the widow Duda to the Turks, but manages to escape from them, comes back to exact vengeance, and says to her:

> " Duda, lie down, lie down, Duda,
> In your room across the threshold,
> So that I may cut your head off,
> And then you will learn a lesson,
> Not to treat Nencho with treason." [3]

To the same class belongs the vengeance which Stoyan takes on Nedelya, who has treated him badly when he was in need. He threatens her:

> " With my sword I'll cut your head off,
> Like a lamb to St. George offered,
> Or a chicken to St. Peter." [4]

[1] Karadžić, ii, p. 323. [2] *Idem*, iii, p. 218.
[3] Dozon, p. 43. [4] *Idem*, p. 34.

He duly carries out the threat and sends the head to Nedelya's parents. The poet enjoys the situation and approves of Stoyan's action. Nor is this the limit to which Bulgarian poets are prepared to go. When personal dignity is very sensitive and exacting, it may think that mere annoyance is deadly insult, and demand hideous reprisals. When Stoyan's mother vexes him by saying that he ought to go out and get booty, he replies with deceitful irony :

> " O my mother, my dear mother,
> All the words you say enchant me !
> Put your tongue out just a little,
> Let me set a kiss upon it,
> For you speak to me so nobly,
> And you give me such good counsels."
> His fine words deceived his mother ;
> From her mouth she put her tongue out,
> From her mouth then Stoyan tore it.[1]

This kind of brutality, which exists when a people has been oppressed by a cruel dominating class, disguises itself as a respect for personal honour.

When heroic poetry passes from the primitive stage to the aristocratic, it keeps some of its original respect for women but develops it in new directions. Its women are more awe-inspiring than their proletarian counterparts, and may even keep some relics of their old prophetic grandeur. Homer's women are indeed not usually of this kind, but that he knew of the type is clear from his account of Arete, wife of Alcinous, king of Phaeacia. Phaeacia is a peculiar place, and its inhabitants are not like Homer's Achaeans. So perhaps Arete is formed on memories from some lost Aegean society, in which the queen is at least as important as the king :

Such great honour he pays her as unto none other is given
Of all women on earth, who now keep house for their husbands.
There in the years that are past she had honour and still she receives
   it
Both from her husband, the king, and from her children who love
   her,
And from all of the people, who look upon her as a goddess,
Greet her with words of respect as she walks on her way through the
   city.
For she is gifted with wits, and often wisely composes
Quarrels of men with each other, because of her excellent judgment.[2]

We can understand why Odysseus goes straight to Arete instead of to her husband. Another case of a woman held in high honour

[1] Dozon, p. 35.   [2] *Od.* vii, 67-74.

in the aristocratic stage is Nin-sun, the mother of Gilgamish. The hero, who listens to no one else, pays great respect to her. She is able to interpret dreams, and when Gilgamish has his first two dreams about Enkidu, he takes them to his mother, and the poet shows his conception of her :

> She who knows all wisdom answered her master,
> She who knows all wisdom answered her lord.[1]

A little later, when Gilgamish and Enkidu prepare for the expedition against Humbaba, they first consult Nin-sun, for as Gilgamish says :

> " Friend, let us go to the palace of splendour,
> To the presence of Nin-sun, the glorious queen,
> To Nin-sun, wisest of clever women, all-knowing ;
> She will prescribe a well-devised path for our feet." [2]

When Nin-sun hears of the project, she makes sacrifice and offers prayers to the god Shamash. She is a priestess, but she is also a repository of wisdom like Kanykai and Satana, and it is wise to consult her before setting out on an unknown quest.

Another survival from the primitive to the aristocratic stage is that of the warrior-woman. Such indeed hardly appear in Homer, but legends about the Amazons show that the Greeks knew the type, and Homer himself refers to them in passing.[3] But in other countries the aristocratic spirit enjoys the idea of women who fight like men. If we may judge by the Latin poem of *Waltharius*, in which Ekkehard of St. Gall retold in the tenth century a story which survives in the two fragments of the Anglo-Saxon *Waldhere*, Hildegund is a heroine in the grand style who shares willingly and actively in the risks and adventures of the man whom she loves. But even she pales into insignificance beside the Norse heroine Guthrun, who is indeed a mighty warrior in her own right when she takes part in the bloody struggle in Atli's hall and, flinging off her mantle, takes up a sword :

> Then the daughter of Gjuki   two warriors smote down,
> Atli's brother she slew,   and forth then they bore him ;
> So fiercely she fought   that his feet she clove off ;
> Another she smote   so that never he stood,
> To hell did she send him,   her hands trembled never.[4]

Guthrun fights for her brothers' lives, and, when her blood is up, shows that despite her royal dignity she is under her skin a primitive

---

[1] *Gilgamish*, I, v, 39-40.   [2] *Ibid*. III, i, 16-19.
[3] *Il*. iii, 189 ; vi, 186.   [4] *Atlamál*, 47.

woman like Kanykai and Ak Kanysh, who fight desperately for their kith and kin.

Another notable example of such a woman can be seen in Hervor in *The Battle of the Goths and the Huns*.[1] Since this poem may well go back to a Gothic poem of the fifth century and reflect some real historical event, Hervor's part throws an instructive light on the spirit of a heroic age. She is the sister of Angantyr and guards a fortress for him. One morning, as she stands on a tower over the gate, she looks towards the forest, and sees clouds of dust rising from a great body of horsemen. These are the Huns who are coming with their king, Humli, to claim a kingdom for Hlöthr, bastard son of the dead Gothic king, Heithrekr. She descends, calls her trumpeter, and bids him sound the assembly. She first orders her troops out to fight the Huns, then goes out herself and is killed. When news of her death is brought to Angantyr, her seneschal, Ormarr, says ·

" More ready for strife she   than for talk with a suitor,
  Or to find her seat   at the bridal feast."

When Angantyr hears, he draws back his lips, and it is some time before he speaks. Then he says :

" Not brotherly thy treatment,   my brave sister,"

and compares her courage with the unwillingness of his own men to go to battle. Hervor is not a familiar figure either in poetry or in saga, and we can hardly doubt that the poet's picture of her is based on some truth which has filtered through to him by tradition and legend.

At this stage, however, women sometimes do more than fight for their dear ones. They may even resemble men in fighting for their own honour, not indeed openly on the battlefield but by creating havoc in their own lives and homes. This is certainly what Brynhild does. She loves Sigurth, but sends him to his death by getting her husband and his brothers to kill him. And she does this because she feels that her honour has been hideously wounded by the way in which Sigurth, by taking the form of Gunnar, has won her to be Gunnar's wife. Since she loves Sigurth, the injury is all the deeper and can be wiped out only by his death. Brynhild's action is violent in the extreme, but the Norse poet understands her motives and assumes that in her circumstances she does the right thing. This is an aristocratic outlook in which honour is of first importance. No proletarian poet would allow a

[1] Kershaw, p. 148 ff.

woman to act in this way, and still approve of her. He would feel that she is after all no more than a woman and not entitled to take his life from a man, especially from a great hero like Sigurth. But at the aristocratic level there are no limits to what a woman may do when she feels herself insulted or humiliated.

In the aristocratic stage the woman is as much the mistress of the household as in the primitive stage, but the greater complexity of life imposes new duties on her. The Homeric queens are excellent hostesses. Arete sees that Odysseus is washed and fed and given gifts, though at the same time she is a good enough housewife to notice that the clothes which he wears when he appears before her come from her own store.[1] So too Penelope, hard put though she is, does her best for the visitors who come to her house and treats even the Suitors with a sense that they are after all her guests. In *Beowulf* the type is developed with a more solemn sense of its responsibilities. Hrothgar's queen, Wealhtheow, presides gracefully and graciously over her husband's court. She is a mistress of courteous speech and welcomes Beowulf by handing him a cup and thanking him for coming to give help just as later she thanks him for what he has done, and makes him rich gifts. In her own way she has considerable authority, and interprets her husband's will when she concludes a speech with an ideal picture of loyalty in the heroic world :

> " Here every earl   to the other is true,
> Mild of mood,   to the master loyal !
> Thanes are friendly,   the throng obedient,
> Liegemen are revelling,   list and obey."[2]

Wealhtheow is created by a poet much interested in moral values, but she still belongs to the company of heroic hostesses and has much in common with them.

At the aristocratic stage, however, we find another type of woman who seems to appear here and nowhere else — the young princess who has a large allowance of liberty and uses it to display royal qualities of style and charm and courage. At the primitive stage hard conditions of life do not allow such a type to emerge, but, when the aristocratic system is settled in comparative security, it encourages young women of high birth to show their gifts. The classic case of such a woman is Homer's Nausicaa. Though she is faced with no decisions of terrifying import, she has her own problems to solve, and does so with an instinctive tact and wisdom. She alone is not afraid of Odysseus when he comes out of his

---

[1] *Od.* vii, 234 ff.   [2] *Beowulf*, 1228-31.

hiding-place, sea-worn, naked, and like a hungry lion. She listens to his eloquent words and makes an appropriate and charming answer. She sees that her maidens attend to him properly, and makes admirable arrangements for him to enter her parents' palace. She is the king's daughter as she ought to be in a kingly age. In her the qualities which make a great queen are all present at an undeveloped, youthful stage. With her we may in some ways compare the heroine of *The Stealing of the Mare*, the princess Alia. Like Nausicaa, she does not know what fear is and is prompted by warm and generous feelings. She faces far greater dangers than Nausicaa and comes near to being killed at night when two enemies trick her into coming out alone. When she is saved by Abu Zeyd, she is not only devotedly grateful to him but is clever enough to see that his first account of himself is untrue, and presses him until she finds out who he is. When she discovers that he is her father's greatest enemy, she is not deterred, but helps him to steal the famous mare, suffers torture rather than betray the truth, and shows throughout a delightfully generous and gallant spirit. In her, as in Nausicaa, we see how the fundamental heroic qualities can be combined with youthful grace and charm. This is a true product of the aristocratic stage of heroic poetry and one of its chief distinctions.

A second point of variation in the three stages of heroic poetry may be seen in the ways in which they admit humour or a sense of the ludicrous. Though the heroic outlook is based on a serious view of man, that is no reason why it should not at times make concessions to humour. And in fact it does. In the primitive stage humour is certainly rare, at least by our standards. It is of course always possible that primitive peoples may find something to laugh at in matters which we take quite seriously. But, apart from this doubt, it seems on the whole clear that among the Kalmucks and the Yakuts humour plays a small part in heroic tales. Nor is this difficult to understand. In both these peoples the heroic outlook is narrow and gains its strength from its emphatic attachment to certain dominating ideas. Among the Kalmucks the heroes are so awesome and indeed so near to being super-human that they induce a mood of solemn respect in which humour might be a disturbing and destructive element. Since Dzhangar and his fellows are so grand, their opponents must be worthy of them and equally unsuited to laughter. Among the Yakuts the dominating tone is not so much of grandeur as of mystery, of men and women in remote wastes who fight against devils and conduct dangerous journeys. The sense of effort and achievement with its emphasis on courage seems to be hostile to any attempt to belittle events with laughter. In these countries humour seems to have little, if any, place, and heroic poems do without it. The poets and the audiences are content with a single, consistent view of life and do not wish it to be broken by any distracting or disturbing element.

This is, however, not true either of the Ossetes or the Kara-Kirghiz, both of whom admit humour into their heroic worlds, but limit it to a certain class of subjects. They are willing to allow laughter if it is at the expense of the heroes' enemies, and the most characteristic kind of laugh comes when the hero outwits someone by his enterprise and cunning. On such occasions the laughter may be broad, but it is natural and genuine. The Ossetes apply it when their heroes outwit the monsters who harry them, and there is an element of genuine comedy when Uryzmag defeats his captor by an ingenious message to his friends [1] or in escaping from the one-eyed giant's cave, disguised as a ram, butts the giant's legs.[2] These episodes are none the less heroic for being amusing, since they show that in resource as in courage the hero is superior to his enemies. Something of the same kind can be seen in the Kara-Kirghiz poems. The comedy may be a little more sinister, but it is still comedy, when Alaman Bet dances so beautifully that the witch Kanyshai falls in love with him and puts herself at his mercy, or Manas humiliates his rebellious khans by making them drunk. In such cases the laughter is triumphant but none the less gay for that. It may be all that heroic poetry allows in its primitive stage, but it does something to convey the high spirits of success.

In the proletarian stage the decay of heroic pride and exclusiveness is accompanied by a great exploitation of the ludicrous. This poetry exists among simple people who are not above laughing at the misfortunes of others, if they are appropriate and deserved. So we often find heroic actions diversified by humour of a knockabout kind. As in the primitive stage, this is often applied when an enemy is discomfited, but it has a somewhat different quality. While primitive laughter is usually provoked by a skilful application of wits, in the proletarian stage a mere exhibition of violence is often enough to excite it. This is common in Slavonic poetry. The humiliation of an enemy may become a subject not for a grim triumph but for an almost clowning violence. For instance, when Dobrynya comes home after a long absence to find that his wife is about to marry Alyosha Popovich, he takes his revenge on Alyosha not so much in a spirit of injured pride as crudely and comically :

[1] Dynnik, p. 23 ff.   [2] *Idem*, p. 17.

He seized Alyoshka by his yellow curls,
He dragged Alyoshka over the oaken table,
He flung Alyoshka over the brick-built floor,
He seized his riding-whip,
And set about to belabour him with the butt-end ;
You could not distinguish between the blows and the groans.[1]

A similar tone can be seen in some Jugoslav lays. For instance, when Marko Kraljević deals with Djemo the Mountaineer, he is paying off old scores and cannot be expected to be gentle. With the help of the ale-wife, Janja, Marko makes Djemo drunk, chains him up, and then kicks him into consciousness. The action has a rude, rollicking gaiety :

Then did Djemo Mountaineer look round him,
And he saw that Marko stood above him,
Round his neck he felt the chain of iron,
To his feet then Djemo leaped up lightly,
But the chain of iron dragged him downwards.
With his arms and with his legs he struggled,
And his arms were cracking in the shoulders,
And his legs were cracking in the knee-joints,
But the stubborn iron held him downwards.[2]

The humiliation of Djemo is an occasion for raucous triumph. This laughter is cruder than laughter of the primitive kind and shows a change of outlook upon deeds of violence.

Laughter of this kind can find its subject in actions more frightening than these. Indeed, in some Jugoslav poems which tell of fighting, we must suppose that the poets' insistence on scenes of horror is prompted by a sense of their grotesque character and reflects a bizarre kind of humour. The excitement of battle certainly makes some things look comic which in ordinary life are merely horrifying, and laughter provides a welcome escape from their real character. Sometimes the poet himself turns carnage to a comic purpose by an apt comparison, as

He was smitten by a well-swung sabre ;
On the left side of his head it struck him,
And it sliced a section from his noddle,
Just as you might slice a water-melon,
And the wound a palm-breadth wide was gaping. . . .[3]

or

And he smote the Moslem well and truly
In the middle of his silken waist-band :,
Sulja then was girdled with his entrails. . . .[3]

[1] Rybnikov, i, p. 171 ; Chadwick, R.H.P. p. 90.
[2] Karadžić, ii, p. 381.   [3] Morison, p. xxxiv.

Sometimes the comedy lies in the action itself, which is told with a perfect simplicity, as if it were the most natural thing in the world. Seen from a certain angle the cutting off of a man's head is undeniably grotesque, and it is not surprising if warriors almost unconsciously respond to this and feel compelled to do something appropriate to it. So, for instance, does Stano :

> Then Stanoje drew his sword and whirled it,
> Both their heads he severed from their bodies ;
> By the roadside Stano hung their noddles,
> Hung their noddles on the white-thorn branches.[1]

So too Lazar Mutap, after beheading a Turk, treats the head with a remarkable simplicity. It is after all a trophy that should be preserved :

> Mutap took the Ethiopian's noddle,
> Threw it in his bay-skinned horse's nose-bag.[2]

Such scenes are ultimately part of the appalling farce of war, which by destroying ordinary conditions of behaviour creates new conditions to which a man must adapt himself, and, if he finds laughter in horror, it is only natural.

At the same time, in the proletarian stage the comic element opens new fields by creating characters who are half heroic and half ludicrous, being neither full heroes nor yet their enemies. They deserve some respect for their love of wild enterprise, but their conduct of it and their mistakes and failures are occasions for crude mirth. The Russian lays have such figures in Vasili Buslaev and Churilo Plenkovich. Vasili is an incurable joker who causes much trouble to his neighbours by his rough treatment of them, but the poets delight in his exploits and the way in which he maltreats the old and respectable. Despite all the efforts to restrain or reprove him, he goes his own way and remains charmingly unregenerate to the end. Churilo is equally undisciplined, and even Prince Vladimir fails to bring him to order. When he is brought to court, the result is the opposite of what is intended, since Churilo's good looks cause such havoc that the Princess Apraxya is unable to attend to her task of carving swans, and when he is sent out to summon guests to the feast, he creates chaos :

> The youthful Churilo Plenkovich
> Went through the streets and alleys,
> Tossing his yellow curls :

---

[1] Morison, p. xxxiv.
[2] Karadžić, iv, p. 266. Trs. W. A. Morison.

His yellow curls flowed freely down,
Like scattered pearls rolling hither and thither.
The nuns in their cells tore off their habits ;
As they gazed on Churilo's beauty,
The young girls uncovered themselves ;
As they gazed on Churilo's beauty,
The pretty lasses tore off their head-dresses.[1]

Churilo is in fact a half-comic figure who succeeds through excess and amuses by his effrontery. If he comes to a bad end, that too is not very serious, since it is in keeping with his life and in its own way almost amusing.

In Armenian poems this sense of comedy pierces rather deeper and touches even the great hero, David of Sasoun, who is indeed a pillar of national strength but none the less a man of the people given to behaving with a delightfully bucolic innocence which is plainly half-humorous. In childhood he is so strong and clumsy that he kills the other children who play with him,[2] or, when he takes up his uncle's mace, makes such a din that everyone is frightened.[3] Later, when he is set to watch sheep, he does it so effectively that, when he brings them home in the evening, he brings with them a large number of wild beasts whom he shuts up in the fold.[4] He does not control his appetites but eats and drinks for days on end when serious duties call him : [5] when the Sultan's emissaries demand tribute, he kills six of them and knocks the teeth out of the seventh, telling him to take them back as tribute to his master ; [6] when the Caliph makes him prisoner and puts him in a hole in the ground, he escapes by whistling to his marvellous horse, who comes to his rescue.[7] David is a child of nature, and the Armenian imagination develops his character with a nice sense of its absurdity. It makes him more lovable and certainly not less admirable. He may lack dignity, but he is bursting with life.

In the aristocratic stage of heroic poetry humour of any kind is much rarer. There is none in *Gilgamish* and very little in *Beowulf*[8] and *Roland*. When the heroic type becomes sure of itself and attaches much importance to honour, it rejects anything which may undermine its dignity. So in a way the aristocratic stage resembles the primitive in restricting the play of humour to certain well-defined spheres of action. It is allowed at the expense of an inferior or an enemy. Such persons lie outside the heroic

[1] Rybnikov, ii, p. 531 ff. ; Chadwick, *R.H.P.* p. 99 ff.
[2] *David Sasunskii*, p. 144.   [3] *Ibid.* p. 156 ff.   [4] *Ibid.* p. 174 ff.
[5] *Ibid.* p. 273.   [6] *Ibid.* p. 215.   [7] *Ibid.* p. 242 ff.
[8] Possible exceptions may be found at 138 ff., 560 ff., 793 ff., 841 ff., but we cannot be sure that the author so intended them.

code and may well be made objects of mockery. This may be
good-tempered enough if the persons concerned are not objection-
able. There is genuine comedy in the *Cid*, when the hero decides
to raise money by filling chests with sand and handing them over
as surety for a loan to the Jews, Raquel and Vidas.[1] Of course the
Jews are below the heroic level and fit victims for such a trick.
But a fiercer humour informs the episode which leads to the final
action of the poem. The Cid has married his two daughters to the
Counts of Carrión, Diego and Fernán González. At Valencia,
when the Cid is asleep, a lion breaks out of its cage, and the
brothers González are so frightened that Fernán hides under a
bench and Diego behind the beam of a wine-press. The Cid wakes
up, and his appearance so awes the lion that it allows him to put it
back into the cage. Then comes the comic climax :

> The Cid asked for his sons-in-law, but them he could not find.
> Although he called aloud to them, neither of them replied.
> When at last he discovered them, they were death-pale with fright.
> You never heard such laughter as the court laughed in delight.[2]

The Cid forbids the laughter, and the brothers González are
mortally affronted by it, but the reader is of course expected to
share it.

This kind of mockery may easily become more serious and
more sinister when the subjects of it are not so much absurd as
contemptible. Then the poet may indulge himself and make them
more contemptible by putting them in an absurd light, even though
this may seem cruel to us. In the *Iliad* Thersites is a mere
nobody, and his appearance matches his character. He is the
ugliest man who has come to Troy, and, when he reviles the
Achaean chieftains, Odysseus gives him so hard a blow with his
staff that a weal comes up on his back, and at this everyone laughs.[3]
Thersites is a butt and gets what he deserves. So too in *Atlamál*
there is a similar moment when Atli's steward counsels that they
should kill not the hero, Hogni, but the cook, Hjalli, and the story
is broken by a moment of comedy in which the cook tries to avoid
death :

> Afraid was the pot-watcher,   he fled here and yon,
> And crazed with his terror   he climbed in the corners ;
> " Ill for me is this fighting,   if I pay for your fierceness,
> And sad is the day   to die leaving my swine
> And all the fair victuals   that of old did I have."

---

[1] *Cid*, 88 ff. ; cf. *sup.* p. 346.
[2] *Ibid.* 2304-7.
[3] *Il.* ii, 211 ff.

They seized Buthli's cook,   and they came with the knife,
The frightened thrall howled,   ere the edge he did feel ;
He was willing, he cried,   to dung well the court-yard,
Do the basest of work,   if spare him they would ;
Full happy was Hjalli,   if his life he might have.[1]

The cook's life is saved, but his momentary appearance in the tragic story provides a breath of comedy. This laughter is not kind or friendly, but reflects the austerity of the heroic outlook in its contempt for anything below its own standards.

This is not quite the same kind of laughter as belongs to some passages in which punishment is given or vengeance taken and becomes an occasion for boisterous guffaws. This laughter is not so rollicking as that in the Russian poems over the humiliation of Alyosha ; it has a deeper basis of disapproval and a stronger sense that such fates are deserved by those who have fallen below heroic standards. This is different from the mockery of those who are outside the heroic world and is reserved for those in it who through treachery or some other fault have shown themselves false to its demands. Such laughter is permitted even in *Roland*, when Charlemagne at last recognises the treachery of Ganelon and hands him over to the scullions :

The Guenè's beard and both his cheeks they shaved,
And four blows each with their closed fists they gave,
They trounced him well with cudgels and with staves,
And on his neck they clasped an iron chain ;
So like a bear enchained they held him safe,
On a pack mule they set him to his shame ;
Kept him till Charles should call for him again.[2]

This is rude and rollicking, but it is also cruel, the harsh laughter of revenge.

Similar to this in temper but achieved by a less direct method are the grim gibes which heroes and heroines make in moments of crisis or triumph. The poet records these without giving his express approval, but no doubt they are expected to arouse a sympathetic echo. They have a suppressed violence which makes them ironical. So, when in *Maldon* Byrhtnoth dismisses the enemy's demand for a truce, he speaks in this spirit :

" Too shameful it seems to me
That, safe with your tribute,   you should turn to your ships
Without fighting,   seeing that thus far
Ye have come hither   to our country." [3]

[1] *Atlamál*, 58-9.   [2] *Roland*, 1823-9.
[3] *Maldon*, 55-8. I am indebted to Mr. J. B. Bamborough for pointing out this and the next example to me.

The same kind of ironical under-statement can be found in Beowulf's account of the sea-monsters which he killed in his great swimming :

> " Never their fill   with joy found they,
> Evil destroyers,   to eat of me,
> Nor sate to their supper   the sea-ground near." [1]

In this spirit *Roland* also allows a little respite from its sustained grandeur, notably when Oliver has broken his spear in killing two Saracens :

> Then says Rollant : " Companion, what do you ?
> In such a fight there's little strength in wood.
> Iron and steel should here their valour prove.
> Where is your sword, that Halteclere I knew ?
> Golden its hilt, whereon a crystal grew."
> Says Oliver : " I had not, if I drew,
> Time left to strike enough good blows and true." [2]

This is a jest made in the middle of a battle and echoes the proud assumption of heroes that they are capable of anything. Nor are such jests lacking in Homer, notably when Patroclus, after striking Cebriones with a great stone on the forehead and making him fall " like a diver ", mocks him :

> " In very truth this man is nimble, so lightly he tumbles.
> Truly, if he were now in the sea, which breeds many fishes,
> To many men would he give satisfaction, seeking for oysters,
> Leaping out of a ship, even though the water was stormy,
> Even as now on the plain he tumbles down from his horses
> Easily ; truly the Trojans also have tumblers among them." [3]

It is true that in these jests humour is swallowed up in fiercer emotions of pride and triumph, but such occasions are still worth a grim laugh.

Homer, who understands the range of human emotions, does not confine laughter to these limited fields. Characteristic of him is a quiet humour which pervades the *Odyssey* and appears at times in the *Iliad*. Though his persons are great heroes, he has often an affectionate smile for their foibles, which rises from his genuine affection for most human qualities. In the *Iliad* it is applied to Nestor, who has been a great warrior in his day but in old age is inopportunely garrulous and not so agile in battle as he once was. When his son takes part in a chariot-race, Nestor gives him none too honourable advice, and when the plan fails, makes a comic fuss.[4] Even the great Ajax is sometimes the victim of this spirit.

---

[1] *Beowulf*, 562-4.   [2] *Roland*, 1360-66.
[3] *Il.* xvi, 745-50.   [4] *Ibid.* xxiii, 626 ff.

He has his splendid occasions, but there is something uncouth about his ponderous frame and slow wits, and Homer mocks him gently when he compares his retirement before the Trojans to that of an obstinate ass which has broken into a barley-crop and has to be beaten out of it by boys.[1] Even the gallant Glaucus is a target for Homer's laughter. After he has talked to his opponent, Diomedes, in battle, they exchange armour, and Homer comments :

> Then from Glaucus his wits were taken by Zeus, son of Kronos ;
> When he exchanged his armour with Tydeus' son, Diomedes,
> Bronze for gold he received, nine oxen's worth for a hundred.[2]

The same spirit appears in the *Odyssey* at the expense both of Odysseus and of Penelope. There is admiration but also humour in the delight with which Homer tells of Odysseus' ability to outwit monsters like the Cyclops and to rise to any occasion with the right style and the right words, as when, though stark naked, he addresses Nausicaa in a " cunning and sweet speech ", or to forestall risks by telling without a blush highly circumstantial false-hoods to strangers who ask who he is. Penelope also may have her pathos, but she has too a charming element of comedy when, despite her years, she shows a girlish shyness, or, true to her sex, refuses to make up her mind, or cannot believe the overwhelming evidence that the stranger is her long-lost husband. This kind of humour is hardly to be found in heroic poetry other than Homer's and is indeed characteristic of his creative spirit.

A third sphere in which the difference of social background affects heroic poetry is that of the miraculous, in the sense of events which are known to be impossible to the modern world and to most societies which may be called civilised, but are accepted as at least possible in pre-scientific ages. Their essential quality is that in them things happen against the ordinary rules of physical existence. Of course the poets have never seen such things happen, but they none the less believe in them and sing of them in the belief that in appropriate circumstances they can happen. This use of the miraculous must be distinguished from the poetical hyperbole which is a familiar feature of oriental poetry and is really no more than an instrument of rhetoric. It must also be distinguished from the exaggeration which occurs in all heroic poetry when its heroes do what is impossible for ordinary men. For what then happens is not so much against natural laws as an extension of them in special cases. Physical strength has many untried potentialities, and if a man is marvellously strong, he will

---

[1] *Ibid.* xi, 558 ff.   [2] *Ibid.* vi, 234-6.

do what looks miraculous but is still recognisably human. The essence of the miraculous is that events happen without any relation to ordinary laws.

In its primitive stage heroic poetry abounds in miraculous elements. This may be an inheritance from pre-heroic poetry in which the chief characters are magicians, but it survives because the poets and the audiences still believe that such things can happen and like to know about them. A Tatar poet sees no difficulty in making a breast-plate speak,[1] or an Ossete in making warriors live in the sky,[2] or an Ainu in making his hero travel through the air.[3] At this stage the field of the miraculous is limited only by the poet's sense of what is due to human effort. Since his main interest is in men and their capacities, he does not stray too far into the miraculous, because it detracts from the essentially human character of his persons. In the proletarian stage the sphere of the miraculous is more limited, but it is still possible for the Jugoslav poet to give wings to a hero's horse [4] and the Russian to make Mikula carry the weight of the earth in a bag.[5] The poets have inherited many such themes from folk-lore and often use them. Indeed, since at this stage the heroic ideal tends to lose some of its grandeur, the poets are perhaps less shy than their primitive predecessors of using the miraculous to enliven a hero's adventures. In the aristocratic stage the miraculous is much less common. There is none in the *Cid* or, if we make a legitimate exception of monsters, in *Beowulf* or *Gilgamish*. In *Roland* the supernatural darkness which portends Roland's death and the delay in the sun's course for Charlemagne may at least be justified by Biblical precedents. In Homer there are miraculous moments, as when Achilles' horse speaks, but they are the work of gods and confined to a special sphere. In the *Elder Edda* they are hardly less rare, and even then the poets, who have to use them because they belong to the story, do so with considerable circumspection.

The different ways of treating the supernatural may be illustrated by the transformation of men and women into other forms whether human or animal. This has its roots very deep in the past and goes back to times when magicians were believed to be able to change their own or others' shapes at will. When the hero succeeds the magician, he may keep some of these powers. In pre-heroic poetry such transformations are common. Among the Abakan Tatars, if women or children are pursued, they become

[1] Radlov, iii, p. 253. [2] Dynnik, p. 39.
[3] *Botteghe Oscure*, vii (1951), p. 223. [4] Karadžić, ii, p. 98 ff.
[5] Chadwick, *R.H.P.* p. 51.

falcons or geese; Altyn Taidshy becomes a mouse that he may
spy upon his sister's behaviour.[1] The Tibetan hero, King Kesar
of Ling, owes much of his success to a gift for changing his shape,
and becomes at various times a raven, a boy of eight years, a
goddess, a cairn, a giant, and a bee with iron wings which enters
into the belly of an enemy and kills him.[2] Similar themes survive
in poetry which is genuinely heroic in its insistence on human
prowess. In the Kara-Kirghiz *Joloi*, which is heroic in its spirit
and most of its episodes, the theme of transformation is used with
a generous abundance when Joloi's wife, Ak Saikal, pursues the
Kalmuck Karacha:

> But Karacha turned his horse
> And escaped from Saikal's hands;
> Before Saikal turned her horse,
> That war-horse with black wings
> Turned itself into a blue dove,
> Soared on high and flew away.
> But at once the brown horse
> Turned itself into a blue falcon,
> Struck it from behind,
> Swooping high from the heaven.
> Now afresh Prince Karacha
> Became a red fox,
> And hid himself in a forest,
> But the horse became a black vulture
> And swooped from on high
> And pierced through the forest,
> His feathers fluttered in the air.
> Again the other escaped
> And became a white fish,
> And plunged and swam through the water.
> The horse became a beaver,
> Dived after him to the water's bottom,
> Seized him on the water's bottom,
> And so at last Ak Saikal
> Seized the prince Karacha.[3]

These rapid transformations are indeed in the pre-heroic manner of
magicians, but they are subordinated to a heroic interest, since the
birds and animals whose forms are taken continue to fight in the
grand style, and, when the end comes, it has the appeal of a fierce
fight finished.

What distinguishes transformations at the primitive stage is
that men and women are able to work them for themselves. They
need no help from gods, and there is nothing wrong or even

---

[1] Chadwick, *Growth*, iii, p. 127.
[2] David-Neel, pp. 98, 114, 121, 132, 145, 230.   [3] Radlov, v, p. 431.

unheroic in using such means when they are useful. Indeed, it is held to the credit of Ragini-Lagini, wife of the Kalmuck hero, Dzhangar, that she is able to change her shape; [1] it is part of her knowledge of strange secrets. If a man or a woman has this gift, there is no objection to their using it as they please; it need not be reserved for emergencies. For instance, when the Yakut hero, Er Sogotokh, comes to a strange fiery sea, he has his own technique of reconnoitring it:

> Then Er Sogotokh turned himself into a hawk
> With a white streak round his neck,
> With downy circular marks on his tail, and flew.
> By the western shore of the lake flowing with fire he went;
> Thither he flew and began to look. [2]

It is all very easy and sensible, and the poet feels no call to comment on it. Yet, though such transformations are both respectable and simple, they are not very common. They are found more than once in Yakut poems, where the heroes are often shamans, rarely in Kara-Kirghiz and Kalmuck, and not at all in Ossete. They are an item in the poet's repertory which he may use if he likes, but he does not often like. Perhaps he feels that somehow they detract from the hero's dignity and prowess, since, after all, his greatness lies mainly in doing great deeds through specifically human means of which he is a master.

In the proletarian stage transformations are less common. There seems to be a tendency to limit them in certain ways. For instance, the Jugoslav poets sometimes deal with them, but we can usually detect why they do so. One is concerned with the second battle of Kosovo fought in 1448 between the Hungarian prince, John Hunyadi, and the Turks. Hunyadi was accompanied by his nephew, John Szekely, whom the poems call Sekula, and this Sekula has magical powers. Before setting out he tells his uncle that he will turn himself into a six-winged snake and bring the Turkish king in his teeth in the form of a falcon. Sekula does this, but John Hunyadi shoots the snake, and the falcon flies away. Sekula regains his human shape, but is mortally wounded, and dies after blaming his uncle for his death. [3] This episode is peculiar because it is connected with historical persons and a historical occasion. And even as an account of transformation it has unexpected features. First, Sekula, who is undeniably a hero, is regarded as abnormal in his possession of magical gifts. He says what he is going to do before he does it. It is not a sudden,

---

[1] *Dzhangariada*, p. 148. [2] Yastremski, p. 27.
[3] Karadžić, ii, p. 467 ff.

instinctive action like transformations at the primitive stage. Secondly, Sekula is able to transform not only himself but the Turkish king and is to this degree more like a pre-heroic shaman than a wonder-working hero. Heroes, no matter how gifted, do not usually have this gift. Perhaps the explanation of these oddities is that both Sekula and his uncle are not Slavs but Hungarians, who are indeed fighting a common enemy in the Turks but do not belong to the Slav world. It may be that the poet, knowing them to be foreigners, attributes to them qualities which he would be slow to attribute to his own countrymen.

The Russian poets sometimes use the theme of transformation, but make it a quality not of real heroes but of witches and sorcerers. They do not explicitly condemn it, but they imply that it is not what normally decent men and women do. Indeed they attribute such gifts to some characters who are notorious as enemies of Russia. Such is Marina, daughter of King Sigismund of Poland, who married the " False Dmitri " and reigned with him for thirty days as queen in Moscow after the death of Boris Godunov. In an eighteenth-century poem about her and her husband, the story is told with some regard to the facts. Marina, being a Roman Catholic, is called " the wicked heretic, the godless woman ", and that gives the clue to what she does. When the patriotic crowd besieges the impostors in their palace, Dmitri shuts himself up,

> But his wicked wife, Marinka the godless,
> Changed herself into a magpie,
> And away she flew out of the palace.[1]

Marina is a witch and able to change her shape. A similar political bias may account for an even more surprising attribution of witchcraft to a famous historical figure. In 1760 the Russian armies of Krasnoshchokov defeated Frederick the Great and entered Berlin. A poem which tells of this event says that Frederick's daughter, on being questioned about her father's whereabouts, answers :

> " He has perched on the window as a blue pigeon,
> The Prussian king sits under the table as a grey cat,
> He has flown from the hall as a free bird,
> He has settled on the black marsh as a black crow,
> He has dived into the blue sea as a white fish,
> He has swum to the islands as a grey duck,
> He has embarked on his ship as a bold warrior,
> He has rolled about the ship as a white pearl." [2]

---

[1] Kireevski, vii, p. 5 ; Chadwick, *R.H.P.* p. 225.
[2] Kireevski, ix, p. 154 ; Chadwick, *R.H.P.* p. 282.

Like Marina, Frederick is credited with magical powers of changing his shape, and this is regarded as suitable to his low and crafty character.

In the aristocratic stage changes of shape are rare indeed. They do not occur in *Beowulf* or *Roland* or the *Cid* or *Gilgamish*. The heroes in these poems are so powerful in themselves that they do not need such extraneous powers. But Homer uses the theme in the *Odyssey* in his own way within certain limits. There is of course nothing surprising in his Proteus who, when attacked, turns himself into a lion, a snake, a leopard, a bear, water, and a tree; [1] for Proteus is a god, who can do what he likes. Nor is it strange that Circe, on her remote island at the end of the world, can turn human beings into swine; for, though she is of divine birth, she has her sinister side and is something of a witch. More interesting are the various changes which Athene works on Odysseus, first turning him into an old beggar and then restoring him to his former shape, with a few additional graces. The changes keep Odysseus from being recognised before the right moment comes, and his change of exterior does not in any way alter his character. He continues to be his old self in all that he does or says. But it is significant that when Homer's plot needs such a change, he makes a goddess produce it. His heroes have not this power in themselves, as they have in primitive poetry. Odysseus does not even ask Athene to do it; she does it of her own initiative. This saves Odysseus' dignity and prevents the audience from thinking that the poet tells of something incredible.

No doubt such changes of shape were dictated by poetical tradition, and the poets had to make use of them as best they could. Homer surmounts the difficulty easily enough, but in the Norse tradition at one point a more serious difficulty arose. A vital occasion in the tragic story of Sigurth is when he changes shapes with Gunnar and rides on his horse Grani through the flames which surround Brynhild and subdues her. The whole series of tragic events breaks down if this starting-point is missed; for it not only shows the superiority of Sigurth to Gunnar, who fails to pierce the flames, but accounts for the whole tragic relation between Sigurth and Brynhild. The *Elder Edda* assumes this episode. In *The Prophecy of Gripir* Gripir says to Sigurth:

> " The form of Gunnar   and shape thou gettest,
> But mind and voice   thine own remain." [2]

Though there is no complete description of this change of shapes in the extant poems, it is clear from the *Völsungasaga* that it takes

---

[1] *Od.* iv, 456 ff.   [2] *Grípisspá*, 39, 1-2.

place after Gunnar has twice failed to pass the flames, first on his own horse, then on Sigurth's Grani. When Sigurth takes Gunnar's shape, he keeps his own personality and that is why he is able to pierce the flames. A fragment of a lost poem tells how this happens :

> The fire raged,   the earth was rocked,
> The flames leaped high   to heaven itself ;
> Few were the hardy   heroes would dare
> To ride or leap   the raging flames.
>
> Sigurth urged Grani   then with his sword,
> The fire slackened before the hero,
> The flames sank low   for the greedy of fame,
> The armour flashed   that Regin has fashioned.[1]

This is the only case of change of shape in the heroic poems of the *Elder Edda*, and no doubt it survives because a wonderful story needs it. The Norse poets did not anticipate the *Nibelungenlied* and explain Sigurth's conquest of Brynhild by the " Tarnkappe " or cap of darkness. They kept the old legend, but in so doing they seem to have avoided explanations of how the change of shape took place.

These variations between the different stages of heroic poetry show how it reflects the society in which it flourishes and responds to social atmosphere. Yet none of these variations is very great, and in most there is a basis of common belief and outlook which is greater than the differences. In general we may perhaps say that the aristocratic stage has more in common with the primitive than with the proletarian, and this is natural enough since in both these stages the heroic life is an actuality, while in the proletarian stage it tends to be a memory. The Kalmucks and the Kara-Kirghiz are still, or were till recently, warrior peoples who practise what they sing, but the Russians and the Jugoslavs, no matter how bellicose, have on the whole been forced to live a different kind of life. Yet despite these differences the heroic poem keeps its essential qualities in quite various societies, and the reason for this is largely that it answers a special need and has evolved methods which keep poets inside a single tradition.

[1] *Völsungasaga*, 27.

XIV

HEROIC POETRY AND HISTORY

THE audiences of heroic poetry usually assume that it is a record
of fact, and it certainly takes the place of history in societies which
have no written annals, is believed to speak with authority about
the past, and may even be used to settle disputes on such matters
as land or ancestors. The Greeks of the sixth and fifth centuries
B.C. treated the Homeric poems as an account of real events and
real people and appealed to them as an authority on matters of
past history, like the Athenian claims to Salamis [1] and Sigeum.[2]
No doubt this was made easier because at this time the poems were
written down and could be consulted without trouble, but it shows
a respect for them as repositories of information. Herodotus
believes in the reality of the Trojan War and treats it, sensibly
enough, as one of several episodes in the age-long struggle between
Europe and Asia or between Greeks and Barbarians. Though
Thucydides approaches Homer's account of the Siege of Troy in a
scientific and even critical spirit and makes illuminating comments
on it, he accepts in the main its veracity, while allowing for some
pardonable exaggerations. We can hardly doubt that some of the
early episodes in Livy's History are derived indirectly from heroic
songs, whose characteristics may be observed in the stories of
Romulus and Remus, the fight of the Horatii and the Curiatii, the
battle of Lake Regillus, and the career of Coriolanus. In the sixth
century A.D., when heroic poetry was in its heyday among the
Germanic peoples, serious historians seem to have used it without
any great doubts about its trustworthiness. Procopius' account of
the war between the Warni and the Angli has many marks of being
derived from heroic song, and perhaps even his strange description
of the northern region of Britain as a land of ghosts may come from
a similar source.[3] In the same century the Gothic historian,
Jordanes, uses heroic songs [4] as material for his narrative. In the
seventh century Bede's account of Hengest and Horsa suggests a
similar origin,[5] and in the eighth Paul the Deacon surely derives
some of his most dramatic chapters from Langobardic lays.

[1] Plut. *Vita Solonis*, 10 ; Quintilian, v, 11, 40.
[2] Hdt. vii, 161 ; Aelian, *Var. Hist.* xiii, 14 ; Dio Chrys. ii, 45.
[3] *Bell. Goth.* iv, 20.   [4] *Getica*, 5.   [5] *Hist. Eccl.* i, 14.

There can be little doubt that at most times and in most places heroic poetry is regarded as a repository of fact and treated seriously by historians.

This trust is shared by ordinary people, who accept the poets' words as true and are confirmed in their trust by the prominence which artists give to themes canonised by heroic poetry. The colossal images of Gilgamish, which once graced Sargon's palace at Khorsabad and are now in the Louvre, and the many representations of him and Enkidu on seals are a tribute to his renown and to the general belief in his reality.[1] The great popularity of Roland in the Middle Ages, when his figure was displayed in a window of the Cathedral at Chartres and in statues outside the church of San Zenone at Verona, in the market-place at Brandenburg, and in many other towns, is a tribute to his prominence in popular legend. But heroes could be remembered by means less obvious than these. A great man might leave stories behind which were passed from generation to generation or associated with some local memory. When the Serbian armies entered the field of Kosovo in 1912, they fell on their knees, said prayers, and kissed the soil, or even thought that they saw Marko Kraljević on his famous horse, Šarac, and rushed after him.[2] The place held by Digenis Akritas in mediaeval Greek tradition is attested by the existence of a tomb, which was thought to be his, though it was actually built by a petty king of Commagene, on a hillock overlooking the river Gök-su, which flows into the Euphrates near Samosata.[3] The special regard in which Ivan the Terrible has long been held by the Russian people must in part be due to his prominence in heroic poetry. Ancient tales of Völund are ultimately responsible for the existence of Weyland Smith's cave in Berkshire and for his appearance on the Franks Casket. The part which Theodoric plays in Hildebrand and the Elder Edda is matched by an inscription on a runic stone of the tenth century from Rök in Östergötland, which describes someone, who is almost certainly he, riding armed " on the shores of the Gothic sea ",[4] and this in turn may be derived from an equestrian statue once at Ravenna but removed by Charlemagne to Aachen in 809, which was thought to be of Theodoric, though in fact it was of Marcus Aurelius. Heroic poetry gives a sanction to many legends which pass into popular currency and in due course affect the visual arts. It is therefore natural to ask how

[1] G. Contenau, La Glyptique syro-hittite (Paris, 1922), p. 51 ff.
[2] J. Lavrin, in Helen Rootham, Heroic Songs of the Serbs (Oxford, 1920), pp. 19-20.
[3] Entwistle, p. 303.
[4] Stephens, Handbook of the Old Runic Monuments (London, 1884), p. 32 ff.

much historical matter it contains and whether it can be trusted on chapters of the past for which independent evidence is lacking.

At the outset it is obvious that much recorded in heroic poetry cannot be true. Even poems which seem to concern historical persons and to have an inkling of historical events tell of some things which are plainly fabulous. Gunnar of the *Elder Edda* is almost certainly based on Gundahari, king of the Burgundians, whose activities were known to Sidonius Apollinaris,[1] but he can hardly have changed shapes with Sigurth in the winning of Brynhild. If a real Charlemagne avenged the death of a real Roland at Roncesvalles, it is unlikely that the sun stopped in its course to help him. If Gilgamish was once a king in Erech, and it is possible that he was,[2] he would hardly have fought with the monster Humbaba. If Achilles fought at Troy, his horse cannot have spoken to him in human language. Much heroic poetry has an element of the fabulous in it, and though this does not necessarily discredit the other elements, it raises doubts about the reliability of poets as witnesses to a real past. There is nothing to prevent a poet inventing if he wishes to do so, and in a non-scientific age the lack of a critical spirit makes such inventions more likely than not. The poets may honestly believe that they are telling the truth, but their idea of truth may not be the same as ours, and it is possible that we may be most disposed to doubt them when they speak with the greatest assurance in the belief that they derive their information from gods or spirits. The material of heroic poetry can be accepted as historical when it is confirmed by external evidence and hardly otherwise. If we are able to apply this test, we shall form some idea of a poet's trustworthiness and regulate our confidence in him accordingly.

At the start we may note that there are a few poems which were composed either by eye-witnesses of what they relate or by men who were so close to the actual events that they present a trustworthy account of them. In this class *Maldon* has a special place. The battle of which it tells is recorded in the Anglo-Saxon Chronicle and other reputable authorities. The site may still be seen in Essex and agrees with what the poet says of it. The chief personage, Byrhtnoth, is mentioned by more than one historian, and that justifies the presumption that characters like Offa, Oswold, and Eadwold, who are not otherwise known, did in fact exist. There is nothing in the poem which is historically impossible or even improbable. Indeed the sequence of events carries

---

[1] *Carmina*, vii, 234 ff. ; cf. Thompson, p. 65.
[2] S. H. Langdon in *C.A.H.* i, p. 366 ff.

conviction because there is no obvious artistic plan in it. Of course
the speeches, as recorded, may not have been delivered in this
form, but the manufacture of speeches was part of the historian's
business until the triumph of scientific history. The whole
narrative is so factual, careful, and realistic that it is hard to believe
that the poet himself was not present at the battle. The only
objection raised to this is that at l. 117 he says :

> I have heard said that Edward   smiting strongly.
> Struck with his sword.

" I have heard " is a traditional formula and should not be
pressed too far, nor need it mean that the author was not present.
In the confusion of battle no man sees everything that happens,
and in this case the poet may record from hearsay. If anything,
this should only make us trust his word the more.

The Norse *Battle of Hafsfjord* may perhaps be regarded as
hardly less trustworthy than *Maldon*. It records a battle fought
in 872, of which other accounts survive in *Egils Saga* and the
Saga of Harold Fairhaired. The second, it is true, seems to have
taken some details from the poem, but since it contains much that
is not in the poem, it may be accounted reasonably independent.
Between the poem and the sagas there is no serious discrepancy.
The poem has no miraculous elements, but tells shortly and
decisively of a fierce fight between Harold and Kjötvi. Harold
sails into the Hafsfjord near Stavanger, and the actual struggle takes
place on an island which Kjötvi makes his defence, until he sees
that he is defeated and retreats southwards. *The Battle of
Hafsfjord* is much shorter and less factual than *Maldon*. Nor can
we be sure that the author was himself present at it. He tells what
he could easily have heard from any eye-witness. But he seems
to have lived at a date not too distant from the battle and to have
been cautious in his account of it. He was at least well acquainted
with the general politics of the time, as when he speaks of Harold as
" the resolute monarch of the men of the east, who dwells at
Utsteinn " ; for in his later years Harold was often at Utsteinn and
felt a special affection for it.

In more modern times the Greeks have shown a tendency to be
truthful and accurate in their heroic poems about contemporary
events, no doubt because their τραγούδια are often sung in camps
by men who have themselves taken part in the events of which they
sing. So far as their accounts can be tested by external evidence,
they do not stray far from historical facts. This tradition of
realism and accuracy goes back at least to the sixteenth century

when a poem celebrates Malamos who revolted in 1585 against the Turks at the instigation of the Venetians. It is maintained in the next century in poems on the execution of Bishop Serapheim of Phanari in 1612 and on the exploit of Nikolas Tsouvaras in 1672, when he attacked Louro and carried off the Turkish commander. Of course such poems may often reflect local outlooks and partisan passions, but they remain reasonably accurate in their account of events. The revolt and failure of Master John in Crete in 1770, when he hoped that Catherine II of Russia would help him, may be limited in its outlook but gives a good account of his struggle and death,[1] while the defeat of Ali Pasha by Botzaris in the defiles near Souli on July 20th, 1792, is equally historical, though it allows a certain indulgence to triumphant patriotism when the climax comes :

The Botzaris upraised his voice, his right hand shook his falchion :
" Stay, Pasha, stay ; why sneak away ? why flee among the fleetest ?
Come, turn again into our town, turn back to empty Kiapha,
And set you up your royal throne, and make yourself a sultan ! " [2]

The reliability of the Greek poems on matters on which they can be checked makes us feel some confidence in their accounts of other episodes for which external evidence is scanty or lacking. They celebrate men and women who have had their moment of glory in their own regions but whose names have left little mark on official histories. Indeed their comparative obscurity is a reason for believing that much of what is told about them is true. This is particularly relevant to the War of Independence, which was a truly national rising, when most places had their local heroes. Poems on Metsoisos, old Mpoukovalas, Demakes, Tsoulkas, Milionis, and others have a ring of authenticity and reflect the actual events in which these men took part.

Perhaps we should attach almost equal authority to the Jugoslav poems which tell of the revolt of the Serbs against the Turks in 1804–13. At least, if we do so, we have on our side the august precedent of Leopold von Ranke who used them for his classic *Serbische Revolution*, published in 1839. They certainly treat of historical characters and historical events. The taking of Belgrade and the battles of Mišar and Deligrad are as real as Kara-Djorje and the other leaders of the revolt. Moreover, the poems are almost contemporary with the events of which they tell, since Vuk Karadžić, who recorded them, began the work in 1813 on his return from Vienna and may well have met bards who took part in

---

[1] Cf. Entwistle, p. 312 ff.   [2] Politis, p. 5. Trs. Entwistle.

the actual revolt and were present at the battles of which they sang. Indeed he himself had taken service in 1804 with one of the patriot leaders and was present when this leader was killed and Tršić burned to the ground. He was prevented from taking a further part by an illness which left him lame, and his own remarks on this are instructive :

" Upheld by crutches, I could think no more of war and horses, yet had it not been for these same crutches I had surely been slain by the Turks, like so many of my contemporaries. Thanks to my crutches I had, perforce, to stay at home, and there I set down on paper what my ears had heard and what my eyes had seen." [1]

Vuk was certainly in touch with great events, and much of what he recorded rings true enough. But though to this degree the poems on the Serbian Revolt may be compared almost with *Maldon* and the Greek τραγούδια, it is dangerous to attribute quite the same authority to them. They speak of real men and real actions, but they are composed in a poetical tradition which is at once more elaborate and more conventional than the Greek or even than the Anglo-Saxon, as the poet of *Maldon* used it. This tradition insisted on the use not merely of stock phrases but of stock themes, and required of its poets that they should tell of a modern event with the apparatus canonised by time for events of the past. The result is that historical episodes are set in a frame of conventional fantasies, which we can to some extent discount, but which remain an obstacle to accepting everything said as literally true. Just as the battle-scenes are so stylised that we cannot put much trust in their details, so the literary devices are sometimes too traditional to be convincing. It is, for instance, disturbing that both *The Battle of Mišar* [2] and *The Taking of Belgrade* [3] begin with the same device by which the wife of a Turkish pasha sees ravens and foretells the coming of a Serbian army. This is part of the poet's stock-in-trade and has nothing to do either with what actually happened or with what was believed at the time to have happened. Still, within their limits these poems are reasonably historical and add something to our knowledge of the events which they relate.

The needs of art and the desire to produce a good story may lead to an even greater distortion of history than this. The Uzbek poem *Tulgan-oi* deals with events early in this century and especially with unsuccessful risings against a local khan, who becomes the villain of the piece.[4] Though the poet reflects with

[1] Quoted by Low, p. 180. [2] Karadžić, iv, p. 177.
[3] Morison, p. 104. [4] Zhirmunskii-Zarifov, p. 458 ff.

513

some truth the general conditions of the time and the kind of things which happened, he has cast his story in an imaginary form, giving to the heroine, Tulgan-oi, the role of an injured maiden who passes through a rich assortment of risks and adventures. In his pleasure at this the poet tends to forget his social and contemporary subject and to beguile his audience with ingenious imaginary scenes, as when Tulgan-oi is at last married to her betrothed because the peasants ransom her from a khan by selling a valuable horse to get the money. The poem is interesting largely because of the prominent part which these peasants play in it and because of the unsympathetic way in which the khan is depicted. It shows an immediately pre-revolutionary state of affairs and tells a story which has some basis of fact and more of fancy, but in which the fancy follows not traditional lines but the poet's political views.

Even if a poet is close in time and place to the events of which he sings, he need not necessarily be very well informed about them. When in 1619 Richard James recorded in Moscow *byliny* about recent history, he presumably got them from professional singers or *skomorokhi*, who had not yet fallen into official disfavour but still kept some of the connection with the court which they had enjoyed under Ivan the Terrible. None the less they were hardly intimates of the court, and their knowledge of political events would be derived largely from rumour and gossip. Such sources need not always be misinformed, and in the two poems on Ksenya, daughter of Boris Godunov,[1] the poet is quite close to actual facts. The contemporary writer, Sergius Kubasov, tells that, on the death of Boris, Ksenya, who had been betrothed to a brother of the king of Denmark, was imprisoned until Dmitri arrived, and when he came, he forced her to take the veil.[2] The two poems make her lament her fate and say that she does not wish to be a nun. Though her words are cast in a literary form and may have no relation to what she actually said, the main facts are correct enough. But another poem preserved by James, which tells of the failure of the Crimean khan, Devlet-Girei, to capture Moscow,[3] is less well informed. The event itself is perfectly historical and took place in 1571, but the poem, composed some fifty years later, knows little about the actual facts, and consists mainly of a dialogue between the khan and his captains about the division of the prospective spoils. At this point God calls from heaven and warns them that they will be defeated. Here there is the merest foundation of historical fact; the rest is inventive fancy. We

---

[1] Kireevski, vii, p. 58 ff. and p. 60 ff.
[2] Chadwick, *R.H.P.* p. 218 ff.   [3] Kireevski, vii, p. 56 ff.

can of course see at once where the fancy begins, since, as in the Serbian poems, it is of a traditional, formulaic character.

The poems recorded by James have a modern counterpart in the poems of Marfa Kryukova and other Russians on recent events. In addition to her *Tale of Lenin* Kryukova has composed poems on the revolutionary hero, Chapaev,[1] and the Soviet expedition under Otto Schmidt to the Arctic.[2] Nor is she alone in this. Other bards supplement their repertory of traditional tales with other tales of contemporary events. There are poems on Chapaev [3] and on Voroshilov [4] by Terentevich Fofanov, on the defeat of Denikin in the civil war [5] by Nikofor Kigachev, and on the battle of Kazan [6] by Catharine Zhuravleva. As in James' pieces, the bards of these poems were not present at the events but speak from hearsay. In some ways they are well enough informed. Kryukova, for instance, in her *Tale of Lenin* gives a more or less correct account of the events of " bloody Sunday ", January 22nd, 1905, of the treachery of the Tsar, and of the ambiguous priest, Father Gapon. On the other hand she divagates from the truth in two directions. First, legitimately enough, she introduces traditional elements and characters which do not belong strictly to history but are in fact comments on it. Thus she makes much of a Siberian peasant called Ivan, who is not historical but represents the ordinary people of Russia and behaves as they did at the time. So too when she tells that Lenin's mausoleum is built from trinkets brought by the Russian people, she is far from the actual truth but none the less adapts an old theme appropriately to her new subject. Secondly, she records what she believes to be the truth about certain events, even if it is not so in fact. Thus in the First World War she repeats the current story that, while the Tsar Nicholas II drinks and brags, his wife reveals military secrets to the Kaiser, who calls her his " blood-kindred niece ", and that the discovery by Russian soldiers of one of her treacherous letters is responsible for their decision to stop the war. Kryukova follows the Soviet myth in making Stalin a general early in his career and in ascribing a villainous part to Trotsky from the start. With the information available to her she could hardly do otherwise. The interest of her poem and of others in the same class is that they reflect the common people's version of what has happened, and this they do fairly and fully. They have a firm basis of fact, but they are not accurate reporting.

[1] Andreev, p. 508 ff.
[3] Astakhova, p. 259 ff.
[5] *Idem*, p. 377 ff.

[2] *Idem*, p. 503 ff.
[4] *Idem*, p. 261 ff.
[6] *Idem*, p. 456 ff.

There are of course a few cases where the poets may have used not hearsay but books, and if these books are reliable, the poet may preserve what they have said after the books themselves are lost. This seems to be the case with much of the *Cid*. The author must have been a cleric and may be presumed to have been able to read. His account of the Cid's departure from Castile and his conquests in Moorish territory has so factual an air that it is hard to disbelieve in it. Nor is external evidence lacking to confirm the poet's account of what happens. All the main characters, not merely King Alfonso and the Cid but Álvar Fáñez, Martín Muñoz, and Muño Gustioz, are historical. It is true that there is no independent mention of Martín Antolínez, but in such company we may presume that he too existed. The Counts of Carrión certainly did, and there is no reason to doubt that they were betrothed to the Cid's daughters. The *Cid* is a record of fact and seems to contain very little fancy. Even in its moments of comedy it may reflect actual events ; for the poet seems to be too conscientious for reckless invention. The Spanish chronicles on which he drew and such oral tradition as he may have known must have been remarkably careful and truthful, and that no doubt is why the *Cid* bears so realistic and factual an air.

The *Cid*, however, is exceptional. Most of our older heroic poems present more complicated problems. That they nearly all have some basis of fact can hardly be denied. Even *Gilgamish* bears some relation to recorded history in that Gilgamish himself appears in Babylonian records as a king of Erech after Tammuz, though his reign is said to have lasted for 126 years.[1] Though in *Hildebrand* neither the hero himself nor his son are known to history, both Odoacer and Theodoric, who are mentioned, are well known. In *Beowulf* Hygelac is said to have led a disastrous expedition against the Franks and the Frisians,[2] and this is the same as the expedition led by Chocilaicus, king of the Danes, which ended in his defeat and death through the arrival of an army under Theodberht. Since this expedition is vouchsafed independently by Gregory of Tours [3] and the *Gesta Francorum*,[4] we cannot doubt its existence or refuse to admit that on this point the author of *Beowulf* records actual facts. Hengest, who plays a part in *Finnsburh*, has been thought by good scholars to be the same as the Hengest who began the Anglo-Saxon conquest of England as recorded by Bede.[5] In the *Elder Edda* Atli, Gunnar, and Jormunrek are the historical Attila, Gundahari, and Ermanaric, who were

[1] S. H. Langdon, *C.A.H.* i, p. 367.   [2] *Beowulf*, 2914 ff.   [3] iii, 3.
[4] Cap. 19.   [5] Chadwick, *Origin of the English Nation*, pp. 49-50.

all prominent figures in their time. Roland is certainly historical, since we know of a battle fought on August 15th, 778, when Charlemagne's army, returning from Spain, was attacked in the Pyrenees, and among those killed was " Hruodlandus Britannici limitis praefectus ".[1] In these cases some figures and some events are undeniably based on historical fact.

It may well be the case that at least among the Germanic peoples a large quantity of historical or quasi-historical material has been preserved through literary tradition. The many cross-references in *Beowulf*, the long catalogue of kings and peoples in *Widsith*, some incidental references in the *Elder Edda*, present a body of material which is on the whole self-consistent and which no poet seems to have had a good reason to invent. It is at least clear that there was a mass of information known to bards and sufficiently familiar to their audiences for oblique references to it to be intelligible. It is of course possible to find inconsistencies between different references to certain characters, but that is on the whole an argument for their reality rather than against it. It suggests that the names are of real people, even though stories about them have been a bit muddled or distorted. Indeed, the general truthfulness of the account of kings and peoples in *Widsith* is surely supported by the references to them elsewhere which R. W. Chambers has collected with assiduous care. When such a body of references exist, there is a reasonable presumption that much of it is based on fact and, even though not supported by external evidence, may be treated with some respect.

When we turn from the older poems to the more modern, we find a somewhat similar situation, though with these the evidence is usually harder to find owing to the comparative paucity of written records among such peoples. None the less there are indications that historical material, no doubt preserved by oral tradition, has been used. Many Russian poems centre on Prince Vladimir of Kiev, who may be identified with Vladimir II Monomakh, Grand Prince of Kiev from 1113 to 1125. Of his alleged followers Ilya of Murom was already known in the thirteenth century to the Norse *Thithreks Saga of Bern* and the German poem *Ortnit*, and in 1594 the German traveller, Erich Lassota, saw his tomb in the Cathedral of St. Sophia at Kiev.[2] Alyosha Popovich, after being in the service of the princes of Rostov, moved to Kiev and was killed in the disastrous battle of Kalka in 1228.[3] Staver is known to the Chronicle of Novgorod as having got into trouble

---

[1] Egginhard, *Vita Caroli Magni*, 9.
[2] Chadwick, *R.H.P.* p. 58.   [3] Miller, *Ocherki*, iii, p. 74 ff.

with Prince Vladimir Monomakh and been drowned for plundering two citizens of Novgorod, while another version of the same chronicle says that he was sent into exile.[1] Dunay Ivanovich is often mentioned in records of the thirteenth century as in the service of Prince Vladimir of Volhynia,[2] while Sukhan Domantevich has been identified with Domant, prince of Pskov, who died in 1299 and was renowned for his defence of Pskov against the pagan invaders.[3] Whatever time and the poetical imagination may have done to their dates and exploits, the Russian heroes seem to have existed as real people at some date. So too the Jugoslav poems contain names which are those of historical persons. In the period before Kosovo Stjepan Dušan was king of Serbia from 1331 to 1356. The actual heroes of Kosovo are real enough, whether Prince Lazar, who was defeated and slain by the Turks in 1389, or Miloš Obilić, who seems really to have killed the Sultan Murad, as the poets tell.[4] Marko Kraljević was a real man who was killed, fighting on the Turkish side, at the battle of Rovine in 1394.[5] The Jugoslav heroes, like the Russian, have suffered many changes, but seem originally to be no less historical.

Though outside Europe external evidence is less easy to find, certain prominent heroes have historical origins. In Armenia David of Sasoun was a genuine king of the tenth century.[6] The Yakuts have poems about Djennik, who led a disastrous revolt of his people on the river Lena in the seventeenth century.[7] Kongyr Bai in the Kara-Kirghiz poems may be a descendant of Genghiz Khan and have lived in the sixteenth century,[8] while the Kalmuck Khongor, the chief companion of Dzhangar, may be the same man seen from a different angle. The Kazak Edyg lived at the end of the fourteenth and the beginning of the fifteenth centuries.[9] The Uzbek Sheibani, who fights Babur, the sultan of Samarcand, comes from about a hundred years later.[10] The Achin prince, Ethokanda, the hero of the poem *Malem Dagang*, reigned from 1607 to 1636,[11] while *Pochut Muhamat* tells of a man of high Arab descent, called Jamalulam, who reigned from 1703 to 1735, while considerable attention is paid to three brothers, the youngest being Pochut Muhamat, who disputed the claim to the throne.[12] In Dokarim's *Prang Kompeuni*, which touches on almost modern times, one character, Panglim Tibang, was still alive when the poem

---

[1] Chadwick, *Growth*, ii, p. 113 ff. [2] *Idem*, p. 116.
[3] Miller, *Ocherki*, iii, p. 167 ff. [4] Chadwick, *H.A.* p. 316.
[5] Low, p. xxii. [6] *David Sasunskii*, p. vi ff.
[7] Chadwick, *Growth*, iii, p. 122. [8] *Idem*, p. 118 ff.
[9] Orlov, p. 128 ff. [10] Zhirmunskii-Zarifov, p. 123 ff.
[11] Hurgronje, ii, p. 80 ff. [12] *Idem*, p. 88 ff.

was composed. A Hindu by birth, he had come with a troop of conjurors to Acheh, and by winning the confidence of the sultan and becoming a Moslem made himself a man of power and influence.[1] In these Asiatic poems there are, however, many characters who have not been identified with historical persons, and indeed none of the Ossete heroes are known to history, while the Narts themselves have not been traced to any identifiable past.

It is then clear that many of the characters of heroic poetry have a historical origin, and it is possible that others, on whom external information is lacking, may have a similar origin. On the other hand, when we look carefully into these historical elements, we find that the poets have taken many liberties with them and often departed from what actually happened. Indeed this is almost inevitable in an art which derives its materials from oral tradition and allows considerable freedom in the treatment of them. When a story is passed from generation to generation, it will surely change much of its character and suffer from omissions and additions. With nothing to guide him except his memory of performances by other poets the poet cannot but present his story in a new way, and the better he is at his art, the greater are his changes likely to be. Moreover, a story which reflects conditions of a past age may not be fully intelligible to a later generation and suffer just because a poet wants to make it clear and easy. But above all, the greatest enemy of historical accuracy is the creative and artistic spirit which likes to impose its own shape and pattern on given materials and to make something new out of them. Once this happens, much that the historian would think important may be lost, and the main point of a story transformed. Indeed the bards' whole view of history is not historical but dramatic. They do not see events as historians do; they are much more interested in personalities and vivid episodes than in great movements or the vagaries of politics. In reading their work we must look out for a tendency to shape material in the interest of artistic needs.

First, the poets tend to simplify. They may unite into a single episode events which actually took place at different times, and so make their story more significant. The battle of Roncesvalles is a good example of this. The actual fight in the Pyrenees was of no great importance. Charlemagne, returning from a foray into Spain, was attacked by the Basques and lost some of his commanders. The poet makes this a great battle between Christians and Infidels, in which enormous hosts are engaged and many great heroes killed. What was merely a casual engagement becomes

[1] *Idem*, p. 103 ff.

one of the great battles of the world. In fact what the poet does is to concentrate into one great battle the experience of the first crusades. To Roncesvalles he transfers some of the events and much of the spirit which two generations had known in fighting the Saracens in Palestine. His poem is important not because it tells about Charlemagne, and in fact it tells very little about him which is historically true, but because it reflects the spirit of the twelfth century and the crusades. This single battle becomes an archetype of all battles against the heathen, and what the heroes do in it shows of what Christian warriors are capable when they fight for their faith. The poet knew that there had been a battle at Roncesvalles, but he was not concerned to tell exactly of it, even if he had the means to do so, which is most unlikely. Instead he produced a great battle which would present in dramatic form some issues which he had much at heart. *Roland* is a significant document in European history not because it contains important facts but because it shows the spirit in which the crusaders of the twelfth century set about their task of war.

A similar simplification may be seen in the Kara-Kirghiz poems on Manas and especially in Orozbakov's epic on his great expedition against China. That the Kara-Kirghiz ever invaded China on such a scale is highly improbable, and Chinese history is silent on anything of the kind; it is certain that they never took Peking. On the other hand they, and other Tatar peoples, have for centuries raided Chinese outposts and colonies in Sin-Kiang and other border territories. Perhaps in imagining this invasion the poet thinks of great emperors, like Genghiz and Kublai, who really did invade and conquer China. But he has transferred their achievements to his own Manas, because Manas is the ideal type of Kara-Kirghiz, the great king whose armies are irresistible against his hereditary foes, the Chinese. What attracts and inspires the poet is largely the contempt of the Moslem Kara-Kirghiz for the " unclean " Chinese, and he tells of a glorious victory over them. In such a poem all or nearly all the episodes are invented. Some of the characters, it is true, may be historical. Just as Kongyr Bai seems to be real, so it is possible that Alaman Bet, who is by origin a Chinese, may also be real, since he is called " the tiger-like ", and this may connect him with the five sons of Khongor, who were called " the five tigers ".[1] Nor is it unlikely that Manas himself has some relation to history. It is true that no such relation has been found and no traces of his name exist in known records, but it is none the less possible that he existed.

[1] Chadwick, iii, p. 117.

But of course the poet's presentation of him is imaginary. This is what a great conqueror ought to be, and his behaviour reflects Orozbakov's conception of a Kara-Kirghiz hero. An elaborate story is fashioned in which Manas plays a leading part, and in this actual history has little share.

The same procedure may be seen in the Achin poems on the wars against the Dutch, like *Malem Dagang*, which tells of the war between Ethokanda and the owners of Malacca, or *Prang Kompeuni*, which, as its name suggests, tells of a war against the Dutch East India Company. The leading characters in both poems come from history, but not only do both contain much fabulous and fanciful matter but each telescopes a series of historical events into a single great campaign. In this the poets obey the dictates of art which insist that a poem should have a main design, and the result adds much to their success. They have indeed some acquaintance with the events which they relate, but they temper this with invention, and indeed their information on the past is sketchy and faulty. In *Malem Dagang* the ostensible enemy are the Dutch who rule at Malacca, and that is true enough to history, but their capital is placed at Goa,[1] which was never held by the Dutch but was the seat of Portuguese power before the Dutch came to the East. The poet has heard faint echoes of Goa, but does not understand its importance, or even know where it is, or that the Portuguese are different from the Dutch. What concerns him is the struggle of his countrymen against European invaders. He concentrates into a single war of a few years' duration what was in fact a series of wars fought for more than two centuries against more than one foreign power.

A similar tendency to simplify history may be seen in two poems which reflect the long wars of the Goths against the Huns, which culminated in the suicide of Ermanaric about 370. That these wars were long and varied we can hardly doubt, but the poets treat them in various ways. On the one hand is *Widsith*, which says :

> Wulfhere sought I and Wyrmhere ;   full oft there war abated not,
> When the host of the Hreths   with hard swords
> By the Wistula Wood   must watch and ward
> Their ancient seat   from Attila's people.[2]

This passage reflects history in so far as it reports long wars between Goths (Hreths) and Huns. But beyond that it presents imaginary events, since by the time of Attila the Goths were no

---

[1] Hurgronje, ii, p. 81.   [2] *Widsith*, 119-22.

longer at war with the Huns. Of Wulfhere nothing is known, but Wyrmhere may be the same as Ormarr, who was the captain of Hervor in the fight against the Huns as the Norse version tells it. Here historical events have been connected with Attila because he was the most famous of Huns, but the connection falsifies history. In contrast to this we may set the story told in *The Battle of the Goths and the Huns*. Here the poet seems to know nothing of long wars and reduces everything to an eight days' battle fought between two brothers on a disputed inheritance. This is certainly a simplification in the interests of art and is less correct than the long wars in *Widsith*. On the other hand the Norse poet is better informed about the main characters. When he makes Humli king of the Huns, he is surely reporting truth, since Humli is otherwise unknown, though Saxo records that a certain Humblus was a son of Dan, the first king of the Danes.[1] A less traditional poet might well have substituted Attila for Humli simply because Attila was the only Hunnish king of whom everyone knew. In these two cases we see how history can be perverted in different ways, and we can extract the truth only by comparing the competing versions.

The desire for simplification may be manifested by bringing heroes together at a single time in a single society, though historically they may be separated by considerable gaps of years. In *Roland*, though Roland himself and Turpin are contemporaries of Charlemagne, they are associated with others who belong to later generations. Geoffrey of Anjou can be no other than Count Geoffrey I, " Grisegonelle ", who died in 987; Richard of Normandy is the first duke of the name, who died in 996; Gerard of Roussillon is almost certainly Gerard, regent of the kingdom of Provence in the time of Charles the Bald; Thibaut of Rheims must be the first Count of Champagne who bore the name and lived in the second half of the eleventh century; the traitor Ganelon is probably Wanilo of Sens who lived in the reign of Charles the Bald. It is even possible that Roland's betrothed, Alde, is really the daughter of William the Conqueror and the wife of Stephen of Blois. The small circle of authentic Carolingian characters has been supplemented by others of a later date. The poet is not troubled by the difficulties which such a method causes in a historical narrative. What he wants is to create a circle of heroes, and to do this he brings together men known for their prowess in the past, and it does not matter that they did not all live at the same time.

[1] Saxo, p. 10.

A similar confusion of generations may be seen in the *Elder Edda*, where it is not the work of a single poet but of several working within a tradition. That it was not original or necessary can be seen from the conflict of Atli and Gunnar, which at least shadows a real rivalry between the king of the Huns and the king of the Burgundians. Equally, when in *Hildebrand* we hear of a mortal enmity between Theodoric and Odoacer, it reflects historical fact, since Odoacer was attacked and slain by Theodoric at Ravenna in 493. But as the stories were cut off from the European mainland and took new shapes in Iceland and Greenland, chronology began to be sacrificed to dramatic effect. The Gothic king, Ermanaric, who had indeed some dramatic claims on a poet, was brought into the cycle and given a prominent part in *Guthrun's Inciting* (*Guthrúnarhvöt*) and the *Lay of Hamther* (*Hamthismál*). In these poems he is the brutal husband of Guthrun's daughter, Svanhild, and comes to a hideous end at the hands of her brothers. This brings him almost into the generation of Attila, or perhaps a little later, since the events may be presumed to take place after Guthrun has killed her husband. But in fact Ermanaric died soon after 370 and Attila died in 453. The poets' chronology is impossible, but that would not trouble them. Ermanaric was a suitable figure for the harsh and cruel world of their songs, and it would be a suitable addition to Guthrun's many sorrows that her daughter should be brutally killed by him. When a poet has many stories from which to choose his subjects, it is neat and convenient to bring them together in this way.

Some such motive may account for the way in which Russian poets attach figures to Prince Vladimir. Art demands that the great prince should be surrounded and served by great men, and they are found at various times which need not be contemporary with Vladimir, who died in 1125. Among his more famous knights are Alyosha Popovich, who died in 1228; Dunay Ivanovich, who was powerful at Moscow in 1287; Sukhan Domantevich, who died in 1299; and, at the other extreme, Michael Potyk, who flourished in the second half of the ninth century. These men cannot have had anything to do with Vladimir, but have been incorporated into his age to give dignity and interest to the stories of his cycle. Indeed poetical licence has gone further than this. Ermak, who conquered Siberia and was drowned in the Irtish in 1584, belongs by rights to the cycle of Ivan the Terrible, where indeed he is often to be found, but at times he appears in the cycle of Vladimir.[1] He is an authentic hero in the old style and,

[1] Rybnikov, i, p. 39 ff., p. 266 ff.; ii, p. 108 ff.

for artistic purposes, a suitable companion for the great men of Kiev.

Though the Jugoslav poems have a clear system of cycles and a considerable respect for families and local associations, they sometimes neglect considerations of time and place in bringing heroes together. For instance, Marko Kraljević lived in the latter part of the fourteenth century; his father was killed in 1371, and he himself is believed to have been killed in 1394. But he is made the companion or the opponent of men who lived well after his death. Janko of Sibinj, that is John Hunyadi, lived in the middle of the fifteenth century, but a poem on Marko and Mina of Kostura tells how Marko is invited by Janko to christen his children.[1] In another poem Marko fights a duel with Janko and cuts off his head.[2] Similarly, the despot Djuro was a contemporary of Janko and died in 1456, but in the poem about his marriage Marko plays a large part.[3] The poets' faulty sense of period is shown by the fact that in various references to Marko and the Sultan the Sultan's name is given as Sulejman,[4] though the first of that name succeeded to the throne in 1502. In Marko's case we can perhaps discern why these mistakes are made. Though he is a great national hero, he is not attached to any great historical event or indeed to any cycle of stories except his own. He stands for Serbia during the time of Turkish domination, and since this lasted for some centuries, it is not surprising that the poets are not very precise about his dates.

A hero is known by his name and by certain marked characteristics in his behaviour. The result is that poets tend to create a single, recognisable figure and to include in it traits which come from other men. This is all the easier when the hero shares a name with other historical figures. For instance, Vladimir of Kiev, as the Russian *byliny* tell of him, seems to be based on Vladimir II, but he may well have some traits which come from Vladimir I. Since both Vladimirs fought against pagan invaders and had close relations with Byzantium, there is some excuse for confusing them. The confusion can be seen in the poets' accounts of Vladimir's formidable opponent, Tugarin, the Dragon's Son. Actually Tugarin seems to be the historical Tugor Khan, who lived in the time of Vladimir I and, after giving his granddaughter to Vladimir's son, Andrei, invaded Kievite territory and was killed in battle in 1096.[5] He was thus a suitable

---

[1] Karadžić, ii, p. 334 ff.   [2] Bogišić, no. 88.
[3] Karadžić, ii, p. 377.   [4] *Idem*, ii, p. 537 ff.
[5] Chadwick, *Growth*, ii, p. 105 ff.

epitome of the various pagan princes against whom the Russians had to fight, and it is not surprising that he is connected not only with Vladimir II but with Alyosha Popovich in the next century, when Alyosha is presented as his slayer.[1] The Jugoslav poets also tend to identify characters in this way. For instance, one poem makes both Janko of Sibinj and a king Vladislav of Hungary fall at the second battle of Kosovo, which was fought in 1448,[2] while another makes Janko live to the capture of Buda in 1526 and King Vladislav be slain in its defence.[3] Actually Janko died in 1456 and cannot have been present at the capture of Buda, nor was there any king Vladislav at this time. It looks as if the poets had combined in this mythical figure three kings who bore the name in the fifteenth century and then transferred the composite invention to a later date.

A second peculiarity in the treatment of history by heroic poets is that they naturally select themes which appeal to them, and may often give an unexpected emphasis to events of which we know mainly from historians. It is, for instance, characteristic of the Norse poets that, though they deal with great European figures of the fourth, fifth, and sixth centuries, they do not mention Alaric or Clovis or the conquests of the Vandals and the Visigoths, while what they do mention is presented in a very special way with a peculiar bias. The campaigns of the Huns might be expected to leave some trace in poetry, but the only poem which deals in any way with them is *The Battle of the Goths and the Huns*, and even in this the poet is interested not in any struggle for political power or conflict between nations but in a personal quarrel between Angantyr, king of the Goths, and his half-brother, Hlöthr, who is supported by Humli, king of the Huns. Since both Angantyr and Hlöthr are known to *Widsith*,[4] they may have been important men in their time. The quarrel is about the share of the father's inheritance, which Hlöthr, the illegitimate son, claims from the legitimate son, Angantyr. The relations between the two brothers is the chief interest of the poem, which ends when Angantyr finds Hlöthr dying on the battlefield and, after hearing his last words, says :

> " Dire is our curse, brother ; thy death-dealer am I,
> Not to be forgotten. Ill is the doom of the Norns."

When the Norse poets deal with political characters, they are less interested in their public achievements than in their personal

---

[1] Kireevski, iv, p. cxv.   [2] Bogišić, no. 21.   [3] *Idem*, no. 28.
[4] As Incgentheow and Hlithe at 116 ; cf. Saxo, pp. 154-5.

destinies. Even the great struggle between Huns and Burgundians, which led to the destruction of the Burgundian kingdom in 437, is reduced to a personal conflict between Atli and Gunnar and their respective companions.

This sense of individuality often leads poets to rearrange history in the interests of what they believe to be the hero's nature. Russian poems treat of famous historical figures like Ivan the Terrible and Peter the Great and present them as the popular mind saw them, making them act in character according to the current conceptions of them. In a fit of rage Ivan the Terrible struck his son with his notorious pointed staff and killed him. He did not mean to do this and was overcome with remorse. The Russian conception of Ivan is of a man certainly violent and passionate but also capable of generous actions, and the poets alter the story to suit this. In the poems Ivan orders his son to be killed, not because he is angry with him but because in his deeply suspicious nature he believes him to be a traitor. Another son saves the prince's life and tells the Tsar that he has done so. Ivan, with his traditional capacity for repentance, offers to make amends :

> " O illustrious prince !
> What can I bestow upon you ?
> Shall I bestow upon you a third of my land,
> Or gold treasure, or a city,
> Or peasants, or Moscow itself ? " [1]

What is interesting here is that both Ivan's suspicious character and his remorse are consonant with what is known of him. The poet, who is informed about these elements in the Tsar, shapes his story to suit them.

Peter the Great was also a popular figure, not indeed for his ruthless, far-sighted policies but for his personal eccentricities, his great size and strength, his disregard of conventions, and his ability to deal with difficult situations. With such a view of him the poets tend to transform certain episodes in his career. For instance, in 1687 Peter visited Riga in his desire to find out about western methods. He was regarded with great suspicion by the Swedish authorities, and, when he was near the fortifications, the garrison threatened to fire on him. A poem on the subject, understandably enough, transfers the scene to Stockholm. Peter goes there disguised as a merchant, but is recognised by a Swede who hurries off to tell the king's daughter. She identifies Peter from a portrait and gives orders :

[1] Kireevski, vi, p. 55 ff. ; Chadwick, *R.H.P.* p. 194 ff.

" Hearken, my Swedish generals,
Shut the gates very securely,
Seize the White Tsar with all speed ! " [1]

Peter guesses what is happening, rushes into a peasant's hut, and
bribes him to see him safely to the sea, where he boards his ship.
His men row hard, but his ship is overtaken by two Swedish ships,
which draw alongside and whose crews beg the Tsar to take them
with him, since otherwise they will all be killed when they go home.
They plunge into the sea, and the Tsar comes home. This is
certainly a way in which Peter might have behaved, and the poem
portrays him as his subjects saw him.

Other famous historical characters have been subjected to
treatment more bold and imaginative than this. Attila is presented
in Norse poetry as the powerful and fearful king of the Huns,
which in fact he was. His followers are splendidly armed and
wear red coats. He lives on a grassy plain beyond Myrkwood.
All this is real and true enough. But poetical imagination was
inflamed by his death and told how he was killed by his wife
Guthrun in revenge for his treacherous murder of her brothers in
his halls. This is not what history relates, but we can almost see
the stages by which the story was formed. Early in 453, before
his intended attack on Byzantium, Attila added another to the
large company of his wives. Ildico, as she was called, seems to
have been of Germanic origin, but, beyond that and her reputation
for great beauty, almost nothing is known of her. After the rites
Attila drank far into the night, and the next day was found dead
with his bride weeping beside his body, her face covered with a
veil. He had bled heavily through the nose and, being drunk, had
been suffocated in his sleep ; there was no trace of a wound on his
body. This is the story told by Jordanes, who got it from Priscus,[2]
who was a contemporary of Attila and well informed about him.
We cannot doubt that this is substantially what happened. But a
great king who dies on his wedding night is a fit victim for legend,
and it is not surprising that only a century later Marcellinus Comes
quotes the view that Attila had been murdered by a woman,[3]
no doubt his recently wedded bride. It remained for the poets to
make more of the woman, and they did so by identifying her with
Guthrun, the widow of Sigurth and the sister of Gunnar. Having
done this, they created the wonderful story of Guthrun's revenge
and the fate of Attila and the sons of Gjuki. In this there is a

---

[1] Kireevski, viii, p. 164 ff. ; Chadwick, *R.H.P.* p. 260 ff.
[2] Jordanes, *Getica*, 49 ff., where Priscus is expressly named as the authority ;
cf. Thompson, pp. 148-50.   [3] *Chron. Min.* ii, p. 86.

considerable element of fancy, but the combination of Attila's death with the doom of the Burgundians is not entirely without foundation, since Attila's death in 453 had been preceded in 437 by his destruction of the Burgundians. The two events were sufficiently close for poets to connect them and weave a single story from them. The dire tale told in the *Elder Edda* provides a more than fitting end for the Scourge of God.

Similar improvements have been made with Ermanaric, the Jormunrek of the *Elder Edda*. As we know from the excellent authority of Ammianus Marcellinus,[1] Ermanaric killed himself about 373 in despair at an impending invasion of the Huns. Since he was a respected and formidable figure in his time, his death made some stir, with the result that new accounts of it were invented and given currency. Jordanes, writing in the sixth century, knows of the suicide but also knows of another story that Ermanaric punished a man for his disloyalty by having his wife, Svanhild (Sunilda), tied to wild horses and torn to pieces. In trying to wreak vengeance for this her brothers attacked Ermanaric and wounded him, and this was partly the cause of his death.[2] The Annals of Quedlinburg tell a somewhat different story, that he was actually killed by three brothers for killing their father and that they cut off his hands and his feet.[3] On these conflicting versions the poets got to work and evolved a single story that Svanhild was the wife of Ermanaric, who killed her in the way mentioned by Jordanes and was in due course killed in the brutal manner described in the Annals. This is the story known to *Guthrun's Inciting* and the *Lay of Hamther*. It implies a view that Ermanaric was a bloodthirsty and cruel tyrant, and may owe its character to such a belief. We do not know if this view corresponded with the facts, though it is likely enough in view of Ermanaric's achievements in war and conquest.[4] In any case the transformation of the story about his death shows how a man's alleged character may determine what the poets tell about him.

An equally remarkable distortion of historical events may be seen in the German and Norse treatment of Theodoric (Thjothrek), the king of the Ostrogoths, who ruled Italy from 489 to 526 and was the most prominent man of his age. The poems say next to nothing about his power and tell in the main of only two episodes in his career. *Hildebrand* alone keeps reasonably close to fact when it speaks of his long enmity for Odoacer, though even then it gives a curious account of what this meant for Theodoric. Elsewhere

---

[1] xxxi, 3, 1.
[3] *Mon. Germ. Scr.* iii, p. 31.
[2] *Getica*, 24.
[4] Cf. *Deor*, 21 ff.

Theodoric is connected with Attila, and there are two features of the story. First, in the *Third Lay of Guthrun* Atli falsely accuses Guthrun of infidelity with Theodoric :

> " It troubles me, Guthrun,   Gjuki's daughter,
> What Herkja here   in the hall hath told me,
> That thou in the bed   of Thjothrek liest,
> Beneath the linen   in lovers' guise." [1]

Guthrun is submitted to an ordeal to test her innocence and proves it triumphantly ; so by implication Theodoric also is acquitted. Secondly, even in *Hildebrand* Theodoric, out of hatred for Odoacer, leaves his own country and rides away eastward to join the Huns, with whom he stays for an unspecified period, which is clearly long, since Hildebrand, who is of his company, says that he himself has been away for thirty years. This exile is mentioned as an example of suffering by the poet of *Deor* :

> Theodoric ruled for   thirty winters
> In the Maerings' burgh ;   to many 'twas known. [2]

On the runic stone from Rök he is again called " the lord of the Maeringas ", and we can hardly doubt that this period was regarded as exile passed in some sense under the Huns. So in both stories we are faced with this mysterious connection of Theodoric with the Huns, who had for all practical purposes disappeared from history before he was born. Why was Theodoric, who after all was memorable for many good reasons, remembered for a long exile which he never suffered ? The simplest explanation is that he was confused with his father Theodemir, [3] who did at least become a subject of Attila, [4] and is mentioned by name, in contexts which seem to refer to Theodoric, in the manuscripts both of the *Third Lay of Guthrun* and in the prose introduction to the *Second Lay*. It is possible that some such confusion underlies the story, and yet this would happen only if Theodoric were regarded as the kind of man who could endure a long exile with patience. Even this distortion of history reflects a view of a great man's character.

Sometimes poets falsify history by interpreting earlier events in the light of later. Wishing to explain some notable episode, they find their material in the character of some person who is actually innocent but against whom a persuasive case can be made. This seems to be what has happened to Vuk Brancović, whom the Jugoslav poets regard as the villain of Kosovo, since in the middle

---

[1] *Guthrúnarkvitha*, iii, 2.
[2] *Deor*, 18-19.
[3] Chadwick, *H.A.* p. 154 ff.
[4] Jordanes, *Getica*, 38.

of the battle he leads away his forces from the army of Tsar Lazar
and so makes defeat inevitable. When the Tsar gives a feast
before the battle, Miloš Obilić says to him :

> " At thy very knee there sits a traitor,
> Drinks the wine from his silk-covered goblet,
> He the accursèd, Brancović, the traitor ! " [1]

After the battle Vladeta reports to the Tsaritsa Milića :

> " Brancović I did not see, O mistress,
> Did not see him — may the sun not see him !
> He betrayed the prince upon Kosovo,
> He betrayed thy lord and mine, dear lady ! " [2]

In fact Vuk did nothing of the sort. He fought at the battle, and
even after it continued his opposition to the Turks. But a
disaster like Kosovo is more easily endured if it is thought to be
due to treachery, and a scapegoat was found in Vuk. He was
perhaps suitable enough, since after 1390, when the Turks
occupied the fortress of Golubac and the death of the Bosnian
king, Tvrtko, made impossible any alliance between the Serbs and
the Hungarians and Bulgars, Vuk accepted the situation and recognised the suzerainty of the Sultan Bayezid.[3] This action, combined
with an earlier quarrel with Lazar's son, Stjepan, seems to have
been enough to brand him as a traitor and by an easy move to
transfer his treachery to the classic disaster of Kosovo.

The treachery of Ganelon presents a not dissimilar case. In
Egginhard's account of the fight in the Pyrenees there is no word
either of Ganelon or of treachery. But as the fight was magnified
into a tremendous disaster in which the greatest warriors of France
were killed, treachery would both provide a dramatic motive and
help to explain the extent of the catastrophe. The poet found
his traitor in a historical character, who perhaps did not deserve
such a part but served the purpose well enough. Ganelon seems to
be based on Wanilo, once a clerk in the chapel of Charles the Bald ;
he was made bishop of Sens in 837 and crowned Charles in the
church of Sainte-Croix-d'Orléans in 843. But in 849 the king
denounced him at the council of Sanonnières as a traitor. Wanilo
refused to appear and answer the charge, and was soon afterwards
pardoned by the king.[4] The poet of *Roland* was not, it seems, the
first to treat Wanilo in this way. The poem *Saint-Léger*, which is
certainly earlier, calls by the name of " Guenle " a man whom the
Latin original calls " Waningus ", and gives him the part of a

---

[1] Karadžić, ii, p. 284. [3] *Idem*, p. 281.
[2] Subotić, p. 85. [4] Bédier, *Légendes*, iv, p. 360 ff.

traitor. No doubt the poet introduced Ganelon mainly for artistic reasons, and indeed no one can question his success. But it has been thought that he was also moved by a political motive. It has been argued that *Roland* does a subtle propaganda for the Carolingian claimants to the French throne and that earlier versions of the poem, composed about 1000, tried to win advocates for them.[1] Since the last Carolingians suffered gravely from the treachery of Adalbéron, it is possible that the treachery of Ganelon might appeal to their supporters. This is a happy hypothesis, but no more. What remains clear is that Wanilo, bishop of Sens, has been turned into the traitor Ganelon, and that the whole course of the battle of Roncesvalles has thereby been changed.

Heroic poetry does not usually hide a political purpose of this kind, but it may well be the case in *Roland*. The text contained in the Oxford manuscript seems to have been written at the beginning of the reign of Henry II Plantagenet and to reflect some ideas of his court and circle. The young king made great claims and needed support for them, and the poet seems to have taken his share in helping. By various small touches he connects Henry II with Charlemagne and in so doing creates another piece of false history.[2] For instance, the poem says that Geoffrey of Anjou was standard-bearer to Charlemagne, and it is significant that a work written for Henry's court, the treatise of Hugues de Clers, *De majoratu et senescalcia Franciae comitibus Anaegavorum collatis*, tells how Charlemagne's banner was entrusted to the Counts of Anjou.[3] This is not true to history but an invention intended to glorify Henry's ancestors. Secondly, it is remarkable that when Roland reminds his good sword, Durendal, of all the countries which they have conquered, he enumerates Anjou, Brittany, Poitou, Normandy, Maine, Provence, Aquitaine, Scotland, Ireland, Wales, and England. Here is a complete list of the countries over which Henry II ruled or claimed to rule.[4] It is true that in the middle of the list there are other less convincing countries outside the Angevin empire, but that does not affect the fact that the main list is a full and exact account of Henry's titular domains. It is certainly possible that much of the imaginative material in *Roland* is derived from contemporary history and intended to serve a political purpose.

A third source of falsification of history lies in the simple needs of narrative. Actual facts may in themselves be insufficient to provide a good story, and the poet may often be so inadequately

[1] Mireaux, p. 125 ff.   [2] *Idem*, p. 79 ff.
[3] *Roland*, 106, 3092, 3542 ; Mireaux, p. 83 ff.
[4] *Roland*, 2322 ff. ; Mireaux, p. 99 ff.

informed about them that he must resort to invention if his plot
is to have a full shape. The result is that, though many characters
are based on real people, there are others who seem to be inventions.
This is especially true of heroes' enemies, who come from foreign
peoples about whom the poet may have no information. They are
essential to the story, if only to show by contrast the true heroes'
virtues, and if tradition preserves no names for them, the poet must
invent them as best he can. This certainly seems to have happened
in *Roland*. Egginhard provides no names for the leaders of
Charlemagne's opponents in the fight in the Pyrenees, and when
the poet refashions the story, he has to create suitable characters
for the part. He does so by inventing names for imaginary
persons, not only for the many Saracens who are described before
being killed, but even for the important figures of Marsilies, emir of
Saragossa, and Baligant, admiral of Babylon. He creates twelve
leading Saracens and gives them names and short notices just
because he needs suitable adversaries for the Twelve Peers of
Charlemagne. If some of his names cannot be traced to any
identifiable origin, others show that he may have had some
difficulty in finding suitable names from the East and found them
instead elsewhere. For instance, Turgis of Tortelose bears a
well-known Germanic name, which is said to have been common
in Normandy and was borne by Turgis, bishop of Avranches
(1094–1138); [1] Margariz of Sibilie has a Byzantine name, whose
use here may reflect the Crusaders' dislike of the Eastern Empire.[2]
In the absence of real names for his Saracens the poet finds them
or invents them as best he can.

The poet of *Roland* tells an elaborate story of war, and some
of the details in it are indeed quasi-historical, not indeed in the
sense that they have anything to do with the battle of 778 but in
being drawn from more recent times and put to a new purpose to
enliven his tale. He may have derived some of these details from
an earlier poem, since they reflect conditions which prevailed
about the year 1000,[3] notably the description of France by two
diagonals from Saint Michel to Sens and from Besançon to Wis-
sant,[4] which suits the realm of the last Carolingians; the gift of
a bow by Charlemagne to Roland,[5] which is against the fighting
practice of the twelfth century; the reference to the assassination
of the Patriarch of Jerusalem,[6] which is probably based on events
of May 29th, 966, when the Basilica of Constantine and the

[1] *Roland*, 916; Jenkin, p. 77.   [2] *Roland*, 955; Jenkin, p. 79.
[3] Mireaux, p. 115 ff.   [4] *Roland*, 1428–9.
   Ibid. 766–7.   [6] *Ibid.* 1523 ff.

Church of the Holy Sepulchre were damaged and the patriarch killed. But if he draws such materials from an earlier poem, the poet also used more recent experience to give body to his tale. His account of the slaying of Baligant's standard-bearer by Ogier the Dane surely owes something to an episode of August 12th, 1099, when Robert Courthose, duke of Normandy, killed the standard-bearer of the Fatimid Caliph of Cairo, " ammiratus Babiloniae ".[1] The division of Charlemagne's forces into ten sections resembles the contingents of the crusading army as Foucher of Chartres describes them.[2] The point of the Holy Lance which Charlemagne set in the hilt of his sword recalls the story that the Lance was found at Antioch in June 1098.[3] The giant slain by Oliver resembles a giant slain at Antioch in 1098.[4] Turpin's praise of Charlemagne's men has almost verbal reminiscences of a speech made by Pope Urban II at the council of Clermont.[5] The attempt of the Saracens to defeat the Franks by throwing large numbers against a single man resembles their usual methods in the Crusades.[6] When they are defeated and curse their own gods, they follow their historical practice.[7] We can hardly doubt that, when the poet of our *Roland* set out to describe a battle with Saracens, he made them behave as recent history had taught him they might.

The invented characters of *Roland* prompt a suspicion that other poets may have done the same kind of thing elsewhere. It has, for instance, been thought that Beowulf comes not from history but from folk-tale, since his name connects him with a bear and this suits his terrible grip.[8] There are certainly other tales in which the Bear's Son behaves rather as Beowulf does, and it is noteworthy that in the complex structure of Germanic legends he stands alone, without a wife, without children, with a name that does not begin with the same letter as the names of his alleged ancestors, and that outside the Anglo-Saxon poem he hardly exists. It is at least possible that the poet brought into a heroic tale a creature of folk-lore who was in fact quite unhistorical. The same arguments may be used of Sigurth. He too is curiously independent. Annals and legends which know of Gunnar and Atli know nothing about him. Even one of the chief stories connected

---

[1] *Roland*, 3546 ff. ; *Hist. Occ.* iii, p. 162.
[2] *Roland*, 3026 ff. ; *Hist. Occ.* iii, p. 336 ff.
[3] *Roland*, 2503 ff. ; Bédier, *Commentaire*, p. 42.
[4] *Roland*, 1218 ; *Gesta Tancredi*, 57.
[5] *Roland*, 1444 ff.
[6] *Ibid.* 2121 ; Baudri de Bourgueil, *Rec.* iv, p. 98.
[7] *Roland*, 2582 ff. ; Ordericus Vitalis, iv, p. 152 ff.
[8] Carpenter, p. 138 ff.

with him, the slaying of the dragon, is in *Beowulf* attached to Sigemund, who is elsewhere Sigurth's father; and this suggests a lack of personality and definiteness in the hero. Indeed both in slaying the dragon and in riding through flames to win Brynhild Sigurth behaves more in accordance with folk-tale than with history. On the other hand we may note that a connection with monsters and wonders does not necessarily prove that a hero never existed. David of Sasoun commonly deals with devils, and both Alyosha Popovich and Ilya of Murom fight dragons, and yet all three seem to be historical enough. It is as easy to attach miraculous stories to a man who has existed as to transfer a mythical figure into a story of actual events. The question remains open. It is possible that Sigurth and Beowulf come from folk-tale, but it is equally possible that they once existed and were credited later with miraculous actions.

Similar doubts have arisen about certain Asiatic heroes, notably the Kara-Kirghiz Manas and the Kalmuck Dzhangar. It is true that external evidence is lacking for both. No chronicles seem to mention them, and their existence is certified only by heroic poems in which there are many improbable and impossible elements. It has been thought that each is in his own way a projection of a national consciousness, that Manas is the ideal Kara-Kirghiz and Dzhangar the ideal Kalmuck. So in a sense they are. If they ever existed, it would not be in the form which the poets give to them. But that does not mean that they are not based on historical characters. Indeed arguments might be advanced for their reality. First, it is possible that Alaman Bet and Khongor are real; so why not their masters? Secondly, it is easy and common to turn a historical figure into a type of what his countrymen think a man ought to be. This is certainly the case with Vladimir in Russia, with Marko Kraljević in Serbia, with Hrothgar in Jutland, and there is *a priori* no reason why the same thing should not have happened to Manas and Dzhangar. But the matter is one on which no decisive judgment is possible, and it is wiser to leave it at that.

Of minor figures, of whom many must be imaginary if only for the purposes of narrative, there may well be others who have historical origins, even if they have been made to fit into the special needs of a story. For instance, in *Beowulf* both Unferth and Wiglaf have been thought to be creations of the poet, since each fulfils a useful function, Unferth in deriding Beowulf's account of his swimming and Wiglaf in not running away from the mere when the hero is fighting the Dam. Since otherwise they have little to do, it is easy to assume that they have been invented for these occasions when they are of some importance and add something interesting to the story. Yet such a conclusion is not inevitable. Oral tradition is so elastic that it can incorporate real characters and yet limit them to quite narrow and useful functions. Though Unferth's main role in *Beowulf* is that of the mocker, the poet is oddly informative about him, saying that he is the son of Ecglaf (519) and that he has killed his brothers (587 ff.). Since the second piece of information is out of character both with Unferth's mockery and with his subsequent recantation, it looks at least like a loan from other sources, while the attribution to him of a father called Ecglaf looks like a genuine piece of tradition. So, too, though Wiglaf is important because he does not desert Beowulf, he seems to have roots in legend and even in history, since we hear something of his father, Weoxtan, as a man who served under the Swedish king, Onela, and slew Eanmund, the brother of Eadgils (2612). When Wiglaf is called " lord of Scylfings " (2603), it is presumably an implicit tribute to his father. At least it looks as if the poet of *Beowulf* did not invent either Unferth or Wiglaf, and, even if they are in some sense legendary, they may well have a historical origin.

Heroic poetry, then, seems to be on the whole a poor substitute for history. Though it contains real persons and real events, it often connects them in unreal relations, and may even add unreal persons and unreal events when the fullness of the narrative demands them. This means that, except in a few exceptional cases, we have no right to approach heroic poetry as if it were a record of fact. Its materials are largely historical, but its arrangement and adaptation of them are not. But of course it has a great relevance to history in a different way. It does not record truthfully what happened, but it shows what men believed and felt. Indeed, it is difficult to understand peoples like the Jugoslavs or the Russians or the Armenians without studying their heroic poetry. For this enshrines a mass of human experience which is excluded from polite letters and may indeed be beyond the ken of publicists and spokesmen. What is true of the present is no less true of the past. *Roland* is quite as important a document for the understanding of the twelfth century as any chronicle, since it takes us into the workings of the crusading mentality ; *Beowulf* shows what the introduction of Christianity meant to England and what difficulties it caused in adapting an old outlook to a new ; *Gilgamish* tells much about the Assyria of Assurbanipal, which we would not guess from its chronicles or even from the splendid bas-reliefs of its palaces ; the *Cid* suggests that even in the twelfth century the

Spaniards had developed those standards of style and honour which they had at the Renaissance and still have to-day ; the *Elder Edda*, which reaches back at one end to the Germanic migrations and at the other end forward to the Vikings, shows how deeply ingrained the sense of personal worth and achievement and the tragic vision of life are in the peoples of the north ; the Homeric poems present a whole living world which in its ease and its humanity is equally different from the Athens of Pericles and the Sparta of Leonidas. Heroic poetry is a well of information on what people think and feel, and even when it reports history incorrectly, it is none the less informative because it shows how facts affected living men and women and made them find their own interpretations and form their own myths.

XV

THE DECLINE OF HEROIC POETRY

THE decline of heroic poetry is no doubt to be explained by social causes which belong to some wide historical process. Foreign conquests or religious movements or cultural influences from abroad may in a short span of years undo what has endured for centuries. Anglo-Saxon heroic poetry, which existed at least until the death of Edward the Confessor, faded before the new Norman rulers who spoke an alien tongue and had their own poetic craft; the art of heroic song which flourished in Moscow in the seventeenth century was driven by ecclesiastical persecution to remote regions and humble people; the early songs of Rome perished before the culture of the Scipionic circle and its admiration for all things Greek. But commoner perhaps than any of these collapses is the imperceptible process by which a society changes its tastes and advances from the simple to the elaborate or from the communal to the personal. Whereas hitherto men have been content to enjoy a traditional and conventional art, they now feel a need for something more original and more varied. The poet who has been happy to compose in the same way as the long line of his predecessors decides that he must assert his own individuality and set his own impress on his work. The claims of literature become more conscious, and care is taken to satisfy rigorous standards of art and technique. Before long a tradition of heroic poetry may disappear, and its place be taken by some other kind of poetry which is more elaborate, more personal, and more self-conscious. This process may take more than one form, and in each we can see how the material or outlook of heroic poetry is transformed to meet new needs.

Our own age has witnessed the beginnings of such a process in more than one country where oral heroic poetry still flourishes but has been touched in recent years by a new spirit, since the poet has begun to apply to his oral art the standards of the written word. Though he himself may have been brought up in an oral tradition and listened to the performance of many heroic poems, he is influenced by the world of books with its care for the individual phrase and its revolt against the rule of convention, and tries to tell the old stories in the old form but with a new attention to small points and a new sense of literary effect. An example of this can be seen in the Kara-Kirghiz Toktogul Satylganov (1864–1933), who began his career as a bard by learning the old technique of heroic song as it is practised among his own people. Political activities brought him into trouble with the Tsarist police, and he was sent to Siberia. There he came into contact with other kinds of poetry, notably Russian, which were quite unlike his own and had a decisive influence on him. Though he still used his national form, he tempered its spirit and its contents with something more literary, introducing new themes and paying more attention to small points of style. When he composed his epic *Kedei-Khan*,[1] he took a subject which many had used before him, and used the old metre and many of the old devices and formulae. But the result is new. It is composed with greater care than other Kara-Kirghiz poems : the language has a greater softness and flexibility ; the movement of the story is easier and more straightforward ; the characterisation is more sophisticated and more intimate. More important perhaps than any of these qualities is a subtle lyrical flavour which permeates the poem and gives to it a range of sentiment alien to the proud passions and fierce excitements of Kara-Kirghiz heroic poetry. Toktogul takes advantage of speeches spoken by characters to introduce a keener psychological insight and a finer sense of emotion. It is significant that some of the best poetry in *Kedei-Khan* consists of long conversations between the hero and his foster-mother, and that in them she is neither a sorceress nor a mistress of a great household but a poor woman who has given her all to look after the stranger child entrusted to her. The new quality of *Kedei-Khan* may be seen from phrases which are indeed derived from the traditional poetry but have richer associations and a new direction. Toktogul has a happy talent for adventurous images, as when he presents a bully :

> Death stands upon his ways,
> Death is in his blood and his bones ;

or a prosperous man :

> You have made a garden beyond compare
> Not far away from your dreams ;

or the hero's melancholy :

> Night in the world, and night in his heart.

[1] *Toktogul* (Moscow, 1940), p. 115 ff.

This is a more subtle, more feminine, more lyrical art than we find in a traditional bard like Orozbakov or Karalaev, and in it heroic poetry has begun to pass into something else.

A somewhat different case of such a change can be seen in the Albanian, Gjerj Fishta (1871–1940).[1] At once a poet and a man of affairs, he received, largely from Franciscan fathers, a good education, including a knowledge of several foreign languages. His career as an advocate of Albanian independence took him on missions to western Europe, where he studied foreign literatures and made translations from them. At the same time he was grounded from childhood in the traditional poetry of his own country, especially in its heroic lays. The result was his life-work, an epic in thirty books and 16,838 lines, called *Lahuta e Malcis* — " Voice of the Highlands " — on which he worked for thirty years. In it he uses the traditional Albanian metre to tell a complex story of stirring events. He introduces many famous or familiar themes and episodes and combines them skilfully into an artistic whole. Here are all the main elements of Albanian heroic poetry — gallant fights against the Turks or Serbs, mysterious fairies who interfere with men's lives, dreams prophetic of evil, children stolen by lions, half-comic interviews with the Sultan, heroic devotions, and bloody revenges. The poem met with a great response throughout Albania, and Fishta succeeded in pleasing a populace trained in oral lays and persuaded it that his poem was of the same kind, though on a much larger scale. His skilful handling of old stories and of a familiar technique rang true to men who had strict ideas of what poetry ought to be. In some ways Fishta looks closer to traditional poetry than Toktogul. He has not got Toktogul's prevailing lyrical tone, and he keeps nearer to the old mannerisms. But in its own world *Lahuta e Malcis* is quite as far from any predecessors as *Kedei Khan*, and in Fishta we may recognise another poet who has done much to change the character of heroic poetry.

In the first place Fishta differs from authentic heroic poets in expressing his own views and judgments on the events of which he tells. His outlook is historical and patriotic, his aim to show that the Albanian past has culminated in the Albanian present. To clarify his central theme he often delivers opinions in the first person, and issues praise, warnings, and blame. His aim is to guide his people to a glorious future by inspiring them with examples from the past and correcting them by its mistakes. He has not only put into his poem all the most characteristic elements of Albanian life, such as battles and idyllic country scenes, high

[1] M. Lambertz, *Gjerj Fishta*, Leipzig, 1949.

councils and personal vendettas, religious beliefs, whether Catholic or Mohammedan or simply pagan, tragic emotions and broad humour, but he has built it on a plan by which these different elements reach their fulfilment in the deliverance of Albania from the Turks in 1913. Though his manner suggests parallels with Homer, his temper and purpose are closer to Virgil's. His characters, although interesting enough in themselves, are also examples of various tendencies in the Albanian temperament, and his scheme of narrative is not so much an ingenious pattern of stories as a complex national myth comparable in its own way to Virgil's account of the rise of Rome. Since Fishta knew Virgil's work, these characteristics are probably due to its influence and show that he has begun the journey towards " literary " epic. *Lahuta e Malcis* differs from authentic heroic poetry because it does not tell a story merely for its own sake but aims at imparting instruction as well as delight.

Fishta parts with traditional poetry in another important respect. Though his language and its formulae are derived from tradition and look traditional, they are used in a conscious, almost sophisticated spirit, which is fundamentally alien to the ordinary bard. Fishta employs them not because they are expected of him but because they have the charm of simplicity and archaism. He selects them with skill and seldom goes beyond the familiar store of them, but he stands outside them and enjoys them as a cultivated man may enjoy some primitive art. No doubt he sees in them manifestations of the Albanian national spirit, and of course he is fully entitled to exploit them for his patriotic purpose. But their appeal has changed. They strike with a certain air of strangeness, which is undeniably moving and yet a little self-conscious. For instance, Fishta often speaks of death and likes to use two traditional Albanian ways of doing so. One is to claim that death is a bride :

> Then my mother questioned me,
> Said : " Your son has made a marriage ! "
> Asked : " Whom took he for his bride ? "
> Said : " He took for bride a bullet,
> Took a bullet in his breast " ;

the other is to assume that death is the beginning of a new life :

> Since for faith and home and honour
> The Albanian maidens perish
> Gladly, not as if death took them,
> But as if now for the first time
> Life for them were just beginning.

The traditional ideas about death, which have been used again and again, are given a slightly more polished form and with it a new emphasis, as if they were a real discovery. They do not reflect the authentic experience of simple people but have the charm almost of the quaint, of a way of life which is not ours nor even the poet's, and has an almost romantic appeal because of its difference and remoteness from the present. Fishta's great poem, despite its careful use of traditional manners, is in the last analysis as far removed from its national antecedents as Toktogul's.

A third instance of such a change may be seen in the Armenian poet, Avetik Isaakyan, who was born in 1875. As a lyrical poet Isaakyan is one of the great masters of the age, a man of whom Alexander Blok wrote : " Isaakyan is a poet of the first class, perhaps of a talent more brilliant and more unusual than any poet in the whole of Europe ".[1] Isaakyan, like Toktogul and Fishta, learned much from abroad, when he was an exile in Paris, and he applied his lessons not merely to enriching his lyrical poetry but to making his own version of an Armenian heroic poem. His *Mher of Sasoun* tells of a legendary hero, son of the great David and familiarised by many generations of bards. Isaakyan, like Toktogul and Fishta, uses the traditional metre and something like a traditional style. The narrative has an easy movement and covers Mher's career from his birth to his strange end. Yet the poem is far richer and more imaginative than traditional Armenian poems about Mher. It is true that such poems have usually a certain dryness and rigid adherence to fact which makes them less stirring than the Kara-Kirghiz and Albanian poems on which Toktogul and Fishta drew for their models, and that Isaakyan, being himself a great lyrical poet, cannot but make his poem more coloured and more varied than the traditional lays. Yet even allowing for this, it is remarkable what he does with such a form and such a story. Even when he takes up a hackneyed theme like the childhood and rapid growth of his hero, he transforms the familiar subject :

> Though Mher was as yet but a young boy,
> To all in Sasoun he was a pattern of strength,
> With bearing like his father's, his eyes brightly shining,
> His face like an eagle's, his cheeks noble,
> His curls a flame,
> His stance and his arms of steel — beware, do not touch !
> The food of seven men he ate up at once !
> All grow up by years, but he grows up by hours.
> Disobedient was he, daring and ardent.
> A fiery flame lived in him.

[1] Letter of Jan. 28th, 1916, to A. A. Izmailova.

If anyone vexes him, he darkens at once,
Like the summit of Nemrut. [1]

There is much sensitive art in this. Some of the ideas and even
the images are traditional, but Isaakyan has added several small
touches which amplify and enrich the old theme. Through *Mher
of Sasoun* Isaakyan maintains this creative touch. He knows what
is expected from a poem about Mher, and gives it, but with a new
abundance and a special care.

Isaakyan differs from his traditional models in another respect.
The traditional poems agree that Mher is indeed a mighty man of
valour who is destined for a peculiar end — he does not die but
lives in a cave until the end of the world. The existing poems do
not always give a clear explanation for this. Perhaps it is a tribute
to Mher's heroic powers ; he is a kind of Barbarossa who is thought
to be too powerful for death. But whatever the reason may be, it
has been forgotten, and traditional Armenian bards usually tell of
it without explaining it. Isaakyan seizes on this point and makes
it the foundation of his poem. He makes Mher a great hero, but
shows how his deeds turn against him and win him hatred. Since
he breaks the rules of human life, he must in the end pay for it,
and the inhabitants of Sasoun put a curse on him :

" Curses upon you,
Mher, plotter of evil !
You are like Antichrist !
You are a raging devil !
You, who grew on the earth,
May you be always thirsty, and wander hungry !
May you be without children, without heirs !
May you call for death and not find it
Till the time when Christ comes
To give judgment upon you ! " [2]

To avoid this doom Mher consults his father's spirit and is told to
retire to a cave and try to repent. When he does this, the cave
closes on him and keeps him in eternal captivity. Isaakyan has
certainly made sense of the old story, and there is something noble
and even heroic in his conception of the hero who brings this
doom on himself through his excess of strength. But there is
something else which is more sophisticated and more modern.
Mher is the enemy of his kind, the accursed outcast who is unable
to deliver himself even by repentance, the peer of Lermontov's
Demon and Byron's Cain. Though heroic poets sometimes send
their heroes to terrible deaths, they do not invest them with the

[1] Isaakyan, p. 198 ff.
[2] *Idem*, p. 218 ff. For the traditional version, cf. *sup.* p. 259.

attraction which belongs to the hated and the unforgiven. Isaakyan's impressive poem, despite its stirring story, has passed beyond
the limits of a heroic outlook.

The cases of Toktogul, Fishta, and Isaakyan show how poets
who have been brought up in a tradition of heroic poetry but
touched by foreign influence change its spirit when they practise it.
Their power comes from their ability to see the old methods from
outside and to give them a new character. Their work is literary
in a way that authentic heroic poetry never is. Indeed they illustrate the point at which heroic poetry, which is communal, traditional, and impersonal, becomes individual, enterprising, and
personal. And this is the point at which literature as a conscious
art begins. In most essential respects the poems of Toktogul,
Fishta, and Isaakyan are as consciously and deliberately artistic as
Lermontov's *Song of Ivan Vasilevich*, which is written in the metre
and manner of the Russian *byliny* but with a new brilliance.
Lermontov indeed differs from these poets in not being brought up
close to a traditional art, but he came to know it early and, like
them, saw what possibilities it offered for narrative. When
cultivated poets take up the old technique and treat it in this way,
heroic poetry becomes something else because it loses what is most
essential to it — its simple, instinctive character.

A second transformation of heroic poetry comes when it passes
into what is conveniently called romance. Romance is a vague
term, but at least it suggests anything which is not real or even
believed to be real by the poets themselves, who advance it as a
charming fancy and ask it to be accepted as such. In other words,
while strictly heroic poems claim to deal with a past which once
existed, though its date may not be known, romance claims to be
nothing but delightful and is quite content to be accepted at its
own valuation. It may still use the episodes and characters of
heroic poetry, but in a different way with a new intention. We are
expected to admire not so much the human qualities of heroes as
the brilliant inventions and tender sentiments of the poets. It is a
more personal and more subjective art and rises in more sophisticated conditions. Such a change has occurred in more than one
country, but its most famous manifestation is in mediaeval France.
At some time in the twelfth century heroic poetry began to change
its character. Whereas hitherto, in such poems as *Roland*, the
emphasis had been on the feats of great warriors, it now shifted to
fancy and sentiment. This influence, which is already clear in
such epics as *Huon de Bordeaux* and *Raoul de Cambrai*, eventually
found its full expression in the works of Guillaume de Lorris and

Chrestien de Troyes. The origins of this change may be traced to the ideal of courtly love which burst so strangely on the European scene with the Provençal poetry of such men as Guillaume IX, Duke of Aquitaine, about 1100 and reached an advanced form with Arnaut Daniel and Jaufré Rudel. From Provence it spread through western Europe, caught the imagination of northern France, of Germany with the Minnesingers, of Sicily under Frederick II, of northern Italy through men like Guido Guinizelli, and of Portugal under King Diniz " the Labourer ". It gave a new meaning and a new outlook to chivalry and courtesy. The baron of the time claimed to live not for his own glory but for the service of a lady whom he worshipped with all the force and with some of the forms of religious devotion. If he did anything glorious, it was to please her and win her smiles. Though it bore little relation to the Christianity of the time, it was in its way a religious movement. Whether it owed its origins to mediaeval Platonism or to the cult of ideal love in Moslem Spain or to stranger influences, like that of the Bogomils, from the East, it was enormously powerful and dictated its character to the poetry of the age. The terms of chivalry, of fief and homage, of lord and vassal, were transferred from the temporal prince to the adored mistress, who also enjoyed some of the titles and respect hitherto reserved for Our Lady. This influence, which began with song, moved before very long to narrative poetry and transformed the heroic poem. Love, which plays no part in *Roland*, sweeps into its successors and turns them into what can only be called romance.

With this cult of sentiment goes a delight in unreal and improbable scenes which the poet knows to be unreal and improbable but presents as charming escapes from life. This is not in the least like the art of the pre-heroic or shamanistic poet who believes in wonders and magic or at least assumes that his audience will. It is a conscious exploitation of the marvellous for pleasure. An element, which is almost entirely lacking from truly heroic poems, like *Roland*, receives great prominence and affects the whole character of poetical narrative. At first, in poems like *Raoul de Cambrai* and *Huon de Bordeaux*, the heroic and the romantic elements are uneasily combined, as if the poets had been brought up in the old school but felt that they must make concessions to the new. But, soon enough, romance takes command and dominates the scene. It gives the thrill of improbable events in remote places, especially in the mythical East known from legends of Alexander and Apollonius of Tyre. Stories, which in earlier versions may well have been straightforward accounts of heroic actions, are re-written in the new spirit, until *Garin* and *The Four Sons of Aymon* are diversified with many episodes which are not only impossible but in the excitement of the miraculous lose the old attention to heroic virtues. This spirit is combined with the cult of love, and the heroic poem becomes the poem of romance. From this change the heroic poetry of western Europe never recovered. The old theme of Roland at Roncesvalles became a peg on which to hang many startling and amusing adventures, but the old outlook and standards perished, until, when the " heroic poem " was revived at the Renaissance, it was quite different from authentic heroic poetry.

Nor was this phenomenon confined to the West. In Greece and the Greek districts of Asia Minor the most characteristic and most popular poem of the Middle Ages is the epic of *Digenis Akritas*, of which the earliest extant version may date from the twelfth century when the popularity of its theme is attested by Theodore Prodromos calling the emperor Manuel Comnenus (1143–80) " the new Akritas ". The substance of the poem may well be older and have heroic affinities, but it is itself a literary work, whose author is acquainted with the *Iliad*, the Bible, and some Greek novelists, including Achilles Tatius. Though Digenis has traces of a real hero in his use of a great club and his defence of the Euphrates marches against heathen enemies, both in its episodes and its spirit *Digenis Akritas* is romance. When the hero wins the lady Eudokia or fights with a dragon or engages a maiden warrior in single combat, the interest is much less in his martial prowess than in the strangeness of his doings. Indeed, by heroic standards Digenis falls sadly short, notably when he betrays a maiden in his charge, but this hardly matters to the poet, who is interested in other matters than nobility and honour. *Digenis Akritas* indeed recalls French romance in its accounts of the beauties of May and of a garden by the Euphrates, and, though these touches are more likely to have come from the East than from France, they reveal a genuine affinity with the spirit of romance. The great popularity of the poem, which survives in six versions and a Russian adaptation, shows that it appealed to the Greeks who found little sustenance in the formal Byzantine literature of the time. Fortunately *Digenis Akritas* did not kill the short heroic lays which told of the hero in a more martial and more manly spirit. They continued to thrive and took a new lease of life when the Turkish conquest called for heroic enterprise and its celebration in song. None the less *Digenis* remains a sad example of how the taste for romance can transform and spoil popular stories about an eminent hero.

In Asia Persia played a part similar to that of France in Europe. It had enjoyed its day of heroic epic, and the vast *Shah-Nameh* of Firdausi preserves many stories which strike a truly heroic note and indicate that an authentic heroic poetry once existed, though no examples of it survive. But the Persian spirit turned away from this art to the soft allurements of love and the thrills of impossible adventures. The strength of this movement can be illustrated from one small corner of Asia. The poet Nizami Gandjevi (1141–1203) lived in what is now Azerbaijan and wrote, in Persian, four romantic epics, in which love overrides all other considerations and gives to each its plot and character. His *Leila and Medjnun* was translated into Georgian before 1200, when this mountainous country, then enjoying a remarkable revival in letters and learning, was in touch with the most advanced thought of the time. Soon afterwards Georgia found its own national poet in Shot'ha Rust'hveli who about 1200 completed his great epic, *The Knight in the Tiger's Skin*.[1] Though the introduction says that the poem is based on a Persian original, it is characteristically Georgian and emphatically itself. It tells a complex and thrilling story and deals freely in feats of arms and bodily strength, but is permeated by a powerful conception of love for which its heroes suffer dark despair and carry out prodigious labours. In it heroic courage and heroic friendship are subordinated to the service of passionate, ideal love. Rust'hveli had many gifts of a heroic poet, but he chose to write a different kind of poetry. Whatever heroic poetry the Georgians had before him, ceased with him and was replaced by a new art of romance which in most essential qualities resembles that of mediaeval France. Despite its love of action, its powerful battle-scenes and a certain rollicking humour, *The Knight in the Tiger's Skin* is not a heroic poem; for its heroic doings are related less from a direct delight in human prowess than from the tribute which they pay to the inspiring influence of love. The parallel with French romance is indeed so close that we might almost conclude that the transition from heroic poetry to romance is a natural change, which comes when feudal society has ceased to believe in its old standards and turns for inspiration to something more courtly and more complicated.

About the same time that Rust'hveli composed his great epic, an unknown German poet of the Danube region composed the famous mediaeval epic of the *Nibelungenlied*. Using materials

[1] There is a good translation into English prose by Marjory Wardrop, published at Moscow in 1938, and an excellent translation into Russian verse by Shalva Nutsubidze (Moscow, 1943).

which must ultimately go back to the sixth and fifth centuries and are related to the original sources of Norse poetry, he produced a thrilling tale of intrigue and revenge. His poem is less obviously romantic than Rust'hveli's and reveals its heroic sources more clearly, especially in the second half, where the vengeance which Kriemhild takes for the murder of her husband, Siegfried, provides many exciting and bloody episodes. But though the *Nibelungenlied* contains many heroic elements, a close inspection shows that it has been influenced by the romantic spirit which came to Germany from France in the second half of the twelfth century. The two chief heroes, Gunther and Siegfried, fall in love with women whom they have never seen, and endure the pangs of ideal devotion in the service of perfect womanhood. Kriemhild's life-long cult of Siegfried's memory and final vengeance for his death are quite different from Guthrun's devotion to her brothers in the *Elder Edda*, and imply quite a different conception of love. Moreover, the poet accepts legendary elements, in which he hardly believes, because they are charming. Though Siegfried's " Tarnkappe ", or cap of darkness, is essential to the story, it lacks the convincing realism which an earlier poet would have given it. The poet stands outside the heroic world and treats it with a certain detachment and independence, even when he deals with the dark details of Kriemhild's revenge. The *Nibelungenlied* resembles *Huon de Bordeaux* in its mixture of heroic and romantic elements, and though on the whole it begins romantically and ends heroically, as if the poet were using two quite different sources or models for a single poem, the whole work is permeated with a spirit in which heroic prowess is not of primary importance compared with the emotion of love which first brings Siegfried to marry Kriemhild and then drives her to exact a fearful vengeance for his death. The *Nibelungenlied* stands on the frontier between heroic poetry and romance, but it has enough romantic elements to show that its poet has absorbed something of the new outlook and brought some of its themes into his tale of blood.

Though the transition from heroic poetry to romance usually takes place in a cultivated, aristocratic society, it need not necessarily do so, or at least romantic themes and the romantic spirit may well pass into popular poetry. This happened with the Uzbeks.[1] Their truly heroic poetry, like the tale of Alpamys, reflects a time when they shared the adventurous outlook of the Tatar peoples with its taste for heroism and glory. But about the fifteenth century this poetry was deeply affected by romantic

---

[1] Zhirmunskii-Zarifov, pp. 132-64.

themes from Persia. At one end of the social scale this produced the work of Alisher Navoï (1441–1501) who composed epics rich in ideal love, reckless adventures, and lyrical fancy; at the other end it introduced into the repertory of oral bards many stories of a similar character, even if they were composed in a simpler, more traditional manner. Modern bards who sing to-day of fairies and devils, of adventures with monsters and heroic rescues of beautiful women, of ideal devotions and wonderful gardens and palaces, derive their art from Navoï's time, even if they have heard, directly or indirectly, of other later stories of a similar character. These poems tell of men and women not known to the heroic cycle, of the devoted brothers, Shirin and Shakhar, of the great lover, Kuntugmysh, of the gifted prince, Arzigul. If they reflect an Islamic outlook, this too is largely romantic, since it consists of the help which angels give to the heroes in their hour of need. If they lack the rich lyrical quality of Nizami, that is largely because the oral style is ill equipped for it, but they none the less enjoy descriptions of beautiful scenes and occasions of rejoicing. Their change of spirit is reflected in their change of metre. Instead of the old Tatar technique of irregular numbers of lines grouped by rhyme or assonance, they tend to use regular rhymed couplets in the Persian manner, thus displaying both their indebtedness to Persian stories and their affinity with them.

When heroic poetry passes into romance, it is touched by a lyrical spirit which dwells on tender emotions and charming scenes and softens the stark outlines of adventure with intervals of ease and pleasure. Even in the *Nibelungenlied*, which has a truly German taste for wholesale slaughter, there are moments on the Rhine or in Gunther's castle which reflect the leisure and the amenities of mediaeval court life. Just as the French poets of romance introduce scenes of dalliance and courtesy, so do *Digenis Akritas* and *The Knight in the Tiger's Skin* and the *Nibelungenlied*. Their sense of this refined life is certainly enhanced by a spirit of courtly song, and it is significant that the last two of these poems are each composed in four-lined stanzas and not in the single lines appropriate to heroic poetry. Indeed the stanza of the *Nibelungenlied* was certainly used for song by the Minnesinger Der von Kürenberg, and, though we cannot be certain that he was earlier than the epic, it remains notable that the epic has a stanza which is perfectly appropriate for lyrical song. The whole of this transformation into romance may be regarded as the intrusion into narrative of a spirit which likes to linger on the elegances of life and belongs to a society which tries to make its customs less brutal and its manners less forthright. The twelfth century had plenty of pride and violence, but it tempered them with an art which, by turning old stories to new purposes and setting them far from actual life, did much to create a new atmosphere for men and women who lived in courts and pursued, at least in theory and imagination, high standards of behaviour in personal relations.

A third change which comes upon heroic poetry is concerned less with its spirit than with its methods and manner of perform-ance. In some countries we can mark a point at which the material of the heroic lay is transferred from the poem recited in single lines to the song composed in stanzas and often sung by a group of people. In other words, the functions of heroic poetry are taken over by ballad. In ancient Greece this happened in at least one region. Boeotia had its own school of heroic poetry, which has left traces in the work of Hesiod and told of local legends, like those of Orion, which were not popular elsewhere. After 500 B.C. the poetess Corinna told these stories in verse-forms which are the nearest Greek equivalent to ballads. She uses regular, recurring stanzas, which do not have refrains, but the end of the stanza is marked by a metre different from that used in the rest of it.[1] Nor did Corinna confine herself to Boeotian tales. Her *Daughters of Asopus* is indeed based on local legend but implies a knowledge of material used by the epic poet, Eumelus of Corinth, about 700 and derived from legends connected with the early exploration of the Black Sea. This ballad-poetry was not very powerful or even very popular and suffered from having to compete with two far greater rivals, choral song and tragedy. But its existence shows that, when the Greeks had ceased to compose heroic poetry in any authentic sense, they still made use of its stories for songs which resemble ballads. We might indeed see in this change a response to the greater change which took place in Greek life when it developed the system of the city-state. This produced a communal conscious-ness, which is not very noticeable in Homer, but came to the fore in the seventh and sixth centuries B.C. and found expression in many kinds of art but especially in poems sung by a chorus at some special occasion like a festival of the gods or a local celebration of some great event. The old Greek ballad is a minor manifestation of the spirit which produced the great and different arts of Pindar and Aeschylus.

The remains of Corinna's poetry suggest that she followed a method which is common in ballads and helps to differentiate them

[1] Cf. C. M. Bowra in *New Chapters in the History of Greek Literature*, edited by J. U. Powell (Oxford, 1933), pp. 21-30.

from heroic lays. Though to some extent she uses the epic language and certainly tells heroic stories, yet she does so in a selective, rather disjointed manner. Whereas the heroic poet moves straight through his story and does not shirk its merely machining processes, the ballad-maker may choose high spots and concentrate on them. He cannot do this unless his story is so familiar to his audience that they can take its main lines for granted and confine their interest to selected dramatic or emotional moments. So in Corinna's *Daughters of Asopus* a large part of the surviving text tells of the different destinies which await the hero's daughters who have been carried off by various gods. This theme clearly meant much to Corinna, no doubt because of the local elements in it. From it she moves abruptly to tell of the succession of gods and heroes who have held the oracular shrine of Akraiphia — again a matter of patriotic interest to Boeotians. Since much of the poem is missing, it is impossible to say whether she used this selective method throughout, but the remains suggest that she did not tell a straightforward tale in all its stages. In this respect, quite as much as in its stanzaic form, ballad differs from the heroic poem. It belongs to a more advanced stage, when the poet feels free to choose for special attention only those elements in a story which seem to him of unusual interest.

Unlike Greece, where the ballad of this kind was after all a very minor affair, Scandinavia and Iceland turned to it with enthusiasm. Signs of change are already apparent in the text of the *Elder Edda* with its tendency to fall into four-lined stanzas. When the ballads emerge at the beginning of the thirteenth century, they have taken the place of the old heroic songs. With it their subjects have much in common. The lays of heroes contained in the *Elder Edda*, or at least similar poems on the same class of subjects, seem to have been known to the ballad-makers. So Sigurth and Brynhild have a lively second life as Sigurd and Gunhild. The technique of the ballads is not like that of the Edda poems. An easy eight-six stanza with simple rhymes replaces the old heroic verse, and if some traces of alliteration survive, they are no doubt a heritage from the past and hardly even conscious. But there is a more subtle difference than these between heroic poetry and ballads — a difference of tone which seems to reflect a difference of milieu in which the two kinds of poem were performed. As W. P. Ker says of the ballads, " they have lost the grand style, and the pride and solemnity of language ",[1] and this he attributes to the fact that, while the old poetry was meant for courts, the new poetry was

[1] *E.R.* p. 125.

meant for the common people. This difference of tone is not easy to analyse, but part of it is due to the ballad-makers' lack of the old sense of heroic worth and their greater interest in situations than in people. Thus, while they are very fond of violent or tragic deaths, because they are dramatic, and often give to them an effective poetry, yet the rest of their narrative is often uncertain in its tone and may fall into triviality. The flatness which does not trouble us in heroic poetry, because it is part of an objective story, becomes more marked when the ballad-maker makes a selection of situations. We feel that he ought to make the most of them, and tend to criticise him if he fails to use his chances. Of course there are some Norse ballads in which the subject is handled with great power and economy, but the result is outside the range of heroic poetry and approximates to song. This only serves to show that, when the Norse ballad brings off its best effects, they are not really akin to those of heroic narrative. They belong to a different order of imaginative experience and are closer to music than to story-telling.

The transformation of heroic poetry into ballad is most marked in Spain, where it took a peculiar course and led to remarkable results. The Spanish *romances* emerge in the middle of the four-teenth century and treat of contemporary events in the dark years of Pedro the Cruel, 1350–1369, such as the murder of Prince Fadrique in 1358 or of Queen Blanche in 1361. They do on a briefer scale what the heroic poem did up to the time of their appearance. *The Cid's Youthful Feats* is indeed an epic *remanie-ment* of an earlier poem, but its composition in the late fourteenth century shows that for a time heroic poetry and ballad competed for popularity by treating much the same kind of theme. The ballads pick up the task of heroic poetry, treat its subjects, whether traditional or contemporary, and gradually supersede it. They derive their material partly from contemporary events, partly from heroic poetry, and partly from chronicles. The first class includes the poems on Pedro the Cruel, the second those on the Cid, and the third those on the fall of the Gothic monarchy before the Moors in 711, which was developed through various chronicles in Latin, Arabic, and Spanish until it reached a final form in the *Cronica Sarracina* in 1430. In these respects the Spanish *romance* is the legitimate heir of the old heroic epic. It differs from the Scandinavian or English ballad in its comparative lack of refrains, its objective treatment of historical events, its absence of personal emotions, its patriotic sentiment, and its abundant use of speeches for dramatic purposes. Indeed its technique in this last respect resembles some Russian *byliny* or Jugoslav lays. Above all it deals not with worlds of fancy but with familiar and often painful facts. It seems to have kept its contact with the aristocracy in a way that Scandinavian and English ballads do not. In these respects it is close to heroic poetry, but none the less it differs from it in some fundamental respects.

The first and most obvious difference is in metre. The *romances* are not indeed composed in stanzas, but they are none the less composed for a tune unlike the recitative used for heroic poems. The metre is an octosyllabic line with alternate assonance. The assonance is a heritage from heroic poetry, but the regular line is new and quite different from the elastic and irregular line of the epic. The substitution of this line for the old free measure must be due to musical considerations. Something of the kind had to be done if the poems were to be sung to proper tunes. The result is that, though the matter and spirit of the *romances* is seldom lyrical, their technique is. Secondly, the manner of narrative has undergone a great change. The old heroic poetry is expansive to the point of being garrulous. It rambles on through the career of a great man without any careful attention either to its whole shape or to the comparative interest of the different episodes in it. The *romance* selects with care and discrimination and makes the most of its selection. The *romances* on the Cid are for this reason more dramatic and more concentrated than the corresponding episodes of the epic. No doubt this conciseness is due to the high standard of achievement reached by poets of the fifteenth and sixteenth centuries, but it seems necessary to the form, since the poet had a limited time for performance at his disposal and had to make the most of it. Thirdly, though the poets of the *romances* are anonymous and seldom express their personal views, they have their own mannerisms and ways of telling a story which are different from those of the old heroic poetry. They choose their words with more care, tend to avoid formulae, and, if they use devices like repetition, do so for a conscious purpose. Though they owe much to heroic poetry, they are independent of it and show how it can be transformed when it has lost its former popularity.

The transition of heroic poetry into ballads must owe something to the development of music. As music was developed, the audiences, whether popular as in Scandinavia or England, or aristocratic as in Spain, seem to have become discontented with the methods of chanting heroic poems and demanded another kind of music which could be enjoyed for its own sake. This change may well have begun in the twelfth century and seems to have been one of the determining forces in the creation of romantic epics in regular stanzas in Germany and Georgia. We can hardly doubt that it was equally important in turning heroic poetry into ballad in Scandinavia, England, and Spain. Perhaps too the same is true of ancient Greece. The great musical pioneers of the seventh century B.C., like Terpander, must have opened men's minds to the possibilities of singing words to more complex tunes than the epic enjoyed or allowed. Indeed, the great growth of Greek lyrical poetry from the seventh century onwards is convincing testimony of such a movement, which may in the special conditions of Boeotia have helped to create the art of ballad as Corinna, and no doubt many others, practised it. Once music got this hold on poetry, poetry could not but change its form and its character. It became more formal and more lyrical and forsook the easy, expansive methods of heroic song.

A fourth kind of transformation comes when heroic poetry passes into conscious, literary narrative. This happens mainly in countries where heroic song has reached the dimensions of epic, and is undoubtedly hastened by the use of writing. The new poets take advantage of writing to compose on paper, and this means that their work has a different quality from that imposed by the conditions of oral recitation. It resembles romance in its method of composition but differs from it in giving no undue emphasis to love or the impossible. Something of this kind happened in Greece in the sixth and fifth centuries B.C. The heroic epic had long passed its heyday and its place had been largely taken by lyrical verse and even tragedy, which knew the old stories but used them in a new way with a new outlook. Yet in some places poets continued to write narrative poems on what were recognised as heroic subjects since they are drawn from the cycle of stories treated by Homer and his kind. Three practitioners of this art, of whom we know something from fragments and references, are Pisander of Rhodes, who wrote a poem on Heracles; Panyassis of Halicarnassus, the uncle of Herodotus, who also wrote about Heracles; and Antimachus of Colophon, who wrote a *Thebaid*. It is perhaps relevant that all three come from the fringes of the Greek world and none comes from Athens, where the new arts of choral song and tragedy first blossomed at the end of the sixth century and the beginning of the fifth. All three practised the same kind of art. They told familiar stories in the epic hexameter and might to this extent claim to be the heirs of Homer. Nor were they without influence or reputation. Pisander promoted the familiar conception of Heracles with club and lion-skin; Panyassis added to the picture and may have been partly responsible for the role of Heracles in Euripides' *Alcestis* and *Heracles*; Antimachus did much for the later popularity in drama and epic of the story of the Seven against Thebes. In their own day these poets made names for themselves, which is perhaps more intelligible if we remember that the average Greek was brought up on Homer and had not lost the taste for heroic poetry. He might think these poets inferior to Homer, but he would not necessarily feel that their art was out of date and without significance for a modern man.

Despite their debt to Homer and the heroic tradition, these poets show their independence in more than one respect. First, they do not use the traditional language with a Homeric exactness. What appeals to them is not its usefulness for oral recitation but its archaic quality and charm. They savour its points, use its phrases if they like them, but otherwise go their own way and coin new phrases in what they think to be the old manner. Though too little survives from Pisander to show what his methods were, the remains of Panyassis and Antimachus point a clear lesson. Although they use many Homeric words, they use many others which look Homeric but in fact are not.[1] Thus Panyassis uses or invents adjectives such as ἐνεόφρων, "stupid" (fr. 12,11), ἀβλεμέως, "feebly" (fr. 13, 8), and Antimachus has nouns in -τωρ like ἀβολήτωρ, "one who meets" (fr. 76), and ἔρκτωρ, "doer" (fr. 73), and in -τυς like ἀβολητύς, "meeting" (fr. 161), and πωρητύς, "misery" (fr. 48), which look as if they came from Homer but are in all probability modelled on the analogy of Homeric forms. In the same way, though both poets occasionally use Homeric formulae, they also invent new phrases of their own for which Homer has a perfectly adequate equivalent. So Panyassis speaks of θοοῖς ποσσί, "with swift feet" (fr. 15,1), and ταλασίφρων ἄνθρωπος, "an enduring man" (fr. 12, 10). He may even take a Homeric phrase like ταλαπενθέα θυμόν, "grievous heart", or ποταμὸς ἀργυροδίνης, "silver-eddying river", and use them to form ὑσμίνας ταλαπενθέας, "grievous struggles" (fr. 12, 5), and ἀργυρέος ποταμός, "silver river" (*Pap. Ox.* ii, 221, 64). Antimachus goes further than this and shows that by his time the real use of formulae had begun to be forgotten. Whereas Homer normally describes the same kind of event in the same words, Antimachus tends to provide a new variation each time. Thus he describes six times the business of pouring out wine to guests, and does it differently

---

[1] References for Panyassis are to H. Kinkel, *Epicorum Graecorum Fragmenta*, Berlin, 1877; and for Antimachus to B. Wyss, *Antimachi Colophonii Reliquiae*, Berlin, 1936.

each time. Homer deals with it always in the same words, but Antimachus feels a need to do something new on each occasion and so anticipates Virgil, who, despite all his devotion to Homer, did not follow him in the rigidity of his formulae.[1] This emancipation from the formulaic style was no doubt due to the poet's composing his poem in a book instead of in his head and not needing the traditional aids for improvisation. Both Panyassis and Antimachus know Homer well and borrow freely from him. They seem to have felt that any epic poem must be in some respects Homeric, but they use him more as a quarry than as a model, and indeed the more closely we examine the texture of their work, the more clearly we see their desire to emancipate themselves from the traditional formulaic manner and to produce something which is emphatically their own.

A second novelty in these poets, which shows that they are outside the authentic heroic tradition, is in their treatment of old stories. Owing perhaps something to pioneers of lyrical poetry like Stesichorus, who introduced many new and picturesque touches into familiar episodes, the writers of epic sought to diversify old themes with ingenious and unexpected details. The labours of Heracles provided a rich field for such innovations, and it is not surprising that Pisander provided him with a club and lion-skin [2] or established the canon of the twelve labours [3] or gave the hydra many heads instead of one,[4] or told how he frightened the Stymphalian birds with castanets [5] or returned from the Hesperides in a marvellous cup which he took from Ocean.[6] In the same way Panyassis makes Heracles fight against the gods,[7] struggle with Death for the life of Alcestis,[8] rob the Pythian priestess of her tripod,[9] and behave generally in a more violent way than tradition recorded. At the same time he has other little novelties, in making Heracles be attacked by a crab in his fight with the hydra [10] or kill the dragon which guards the apples of the Hesperides.[11] In treating such themes these poets may not always be original, but they move outside the strict heroic orbit and introduce an element of exaggeration, whether in the picturesque or the grotesque, which is alien to the Homeric spirit. Antimachus seems to have shown his originality by the degree of horrors which he allowed, and it is interesting to note that, when Statius wrote his *Thebaid*, with its rich assortment of violent actions, he owed something to Anti-

---

[1] John Sparrow, *Half-Lines and Repetitions in Virgil* (Oxford, 1931), pp. 67-110. [2] Fr. 1. [3] Schmid-Staehlin, i, p. 291.
[4] Fr. 2. [5] Fr. 4. [6] Fr. 5. [7] Frs. 6 and 7.
[8] Fr. 19. [9] Fr. 19. [10] Fr. 3. [11] Hyginus, ii, 6.

machus.[1] In all three cases we can see the poet's desire to create an impression of novelty by ingenious variations on the ancient themes.

A process rather similar to that in Greece took place on a greater scale and with grander results in Italy, when the old lays gave place to the new poetry of the third century B.C. Naevius and Ennius wrote their epics of Rome with Greek models in mind, but they were not ignorant of the indigenous poetry, on which Naevius drew for his metre and Ennius for some of his episodes. Of the two Naevius is closer both in spirit and technique to the local tradition. His use of the Saturnian metre shows his debt to it, and his poem, to judge by the extant fragments, makes little attempt to rival the Greek manner of writing. Indeed, its factual quality suggests that it is closer to heroic lays than to literary epic. On one subject, the defeat of Regulus at Clypea in 255 B.C., Naevius seems to tell what other poets had told before him. He catches an authentically heroic note when he describes the resolution of Regulus and his men not to return home in disgrace :

> They would rather themselves perish on that very place
> Than go back with dishonour to their own people.[2]

When the situation is discussed in the Senate, a speaker pleads in the same spirit for the distressed force :

> " If they desert those men most gallant,
> A great dishonour will it be for their race through the world." [3]

This is in a truly heroic strain, and yet even here what matters is the honour not of individuals but of Rome. It is the thought of this which deters Regulus from going home and decides the orator to demand help for the soldiers. Love of country and a feeling for its honour have displaced the individual's feeling for himself, and we can hardly believe that this was common in the early lays.

Again, though Naevius writes in a native, archaic manner, he has been touched by Greek influences which were outside the local tradition and would in his time have been thought learned and cultivated and untrue to the old tradition. At the very start of his poem he displays his Hellenism, when he invokes the Nine Muses :

> Harmonious Nine, sisters of Jove's daughter.[4]

To invoke the Muses at all is Greek, since they did not exist for the Romans at this time, and indeed there is hardly any Roman

---

[1] Schol. Statius, *Theb.* v, 466.   [2] Fr. 42, Morel.
[3] *Ibid.* fr. 43.   [4] *Ibid.* fr. 1.

divinity who corresponds to them. The difficulty had already been felt by Livius Andronicus when he translated the *Odyssey* and found himself confronted with the Muse in the first line. He solved the problem, with some regard to Latin ideas, by invoking an Italian substitute:

> Sing to me, Camena, of the crafty man.[1]

Camena is a goddess more of prophecy than of song, but she will just do to take the place of the Muse in a translation. Naevius, who is more cultivated and more conscientious about doing the right epic thing, goes straight for the Greek Muses and shows his dependence on foreign models by introducing a foreign word. Again, when Naevius, well within the rights of heroic poetry, describes a work of art, whether sculpture or a cup, in which mythological scenes are depicted, he takes his subject from Greece and uses more or less Greek forms for the intractable foreign names:

> Therein were figures carved, how the Titans,
> The two-bodied Giants, and great Atlantes,
> Runcus and Purpureus, sons of earth. . . .[2]

It is true that the names have caused him some trouble and that he gets them a bit wrong — Purpureus should be Porphyrion, and Atlantes is odd by any account — but none the less he is eager to show his cultivation and his ability to equal the Greeks in their own field. The spontaneity of heroic poetry, with its lack of learned references, is lost, and something smarter has taken its place.

Ennius was more sophisticated than Naevius and shaped his *Annals* directly on Greek models, even adapting the Greek dactylic hexameter to the obstinate Latin speech. He does, it is true, show traces of the indigenous style in his partiality for alliteration, and in his use of old stories like that of Romulus. But he is careful to make his position and his aims clear. He thinks little of the old poetry and speaks of it with contempt, contrasting his own treatment of a subject with the barbarous way in which it used to be handled:

> Others wrote of the matter
> In verses which of old the Fauns and the prophets were singing;
> Nor had anyone yet climbed up the rocks of the Muses
> Or given care to the word.[3]

Ennius refers to the First Punic War and the "others", of whom he speaks, are not only Naevius but any Latin poets who told of this in the old style. The verses which he decries are the

---

[1] *Ibid.* fr. 1.   [2] *Ibid.* fr. 19.   [3] Fr. 214, Vahlen.

Saturnians, and he ascribes them to Fauns and seers. The Fauns are not the wild spirits of the countryside but the ancient oracle-mongers and wonder-workers of Italy, akin to the seers or *vates*, who delivered prophecies in uncouth verse. Ennius turns with disdain on the old poetry and even on its modernising imitators like Naevius. He himself intends to tell his tale in a more modern, more Hellenic manner, and, if he owes much to Homer, that is because he thinks Homer far superior to any Roman traditional bard. In his *Annals* Ennius may have picked up themes which the old Italian poets had used, like that of Romulus, but he treated them in a new spirit. Like Naevius, he keeps some of the old factual and even prosaic manner, which does not shrink from dull details, but his metre demands new phrases and a new use of language, and these he provides. The claim of Ennius is not that he preserves the spirit of the early Roman republic, but that he creates the right poetry for the Scipionic age. What was once the self-contained matter of a simple heroic poetry has become a chapter in the history of Rome and is treated in a new, literary, artificial style, in which the uncouth Latin tongue is made to respond to the movements of the Greek hexameter, which was surely fashioned for a lighter and more malleable language.

Neither Naevius nor Ennius builds his epic round a single person or a single event, but each seems to have found a unity by a new means. The chief character is Rome, and the story is the story of Rome, which may be episodic in a way which Aristotle would have deplored but remains single because the rise of Rome from humble beginnings to world-wide power is after all one theme, and one only. In this respect these poets must have differed greatly from their humble predecessors. The story of Romulus or of Coriolanus concerns a single man, not a metaphysical entity like a city, and the chances are that the early poems dealt with single events in their careers. So far as their subjects were concerned, Naevius and Ennius were pioneers in a new form of poetry. It is true that in Greece poems were written about cities in the seventh and sixth centuries B.C., but there is no evidence that they were more than a string of episodes or that they had any metaphysical background. When Naevius and Ennius made Rome the central figure of their epics, they reflected a point of view alien to the heroic outlook. No doubt the idea of Rome evoked heroic qualities, and in Romulus the city had an eponymous founder of heroic breed, but the centre of emphasis and interest has shifted from individual men and their doings to a city which is almost an ideal, since it lives through the centuries and is always more important than the men who make it. In reading Naevius and Ennius the average Roman would not so much feel exalted by the remarkable performances of unusual men as strengthened by the belief that the city to which he belonged was above human claims and inspired men to exert themselves prodigiously for her sake and to do things of which otherwise they would have been incapable. In passing into this kind of poetry heroic song lost much of its old outlook and embarked on a new, mysterious, and enthralling course.

In the four different ways which we have considered, and no doubt in other ways also, heroic poetry passes into other forms and ceases to be itself. Yet different though the processes of its passing seem to be, they display on the whole certain common characteristics which illustrate what happens when heroic poetry ceases to keep its grip on a people. In the first and most important place we must note that the change comes when the individual ceases to be the single, central subject of interest and is replaced by something else — by an interest in lyrical moments or in chivalrous dreams or in a national destiny or in purely literary effects of charm and humour. In other words, what happens is that what has for long held its own as a philosophy of life and made all action look simple and easy to value is abandoned for other claims which appeal to other elements in the human heart. Narrative continues to supply the body for poetry, but is no longer centred on the doings and excellence of individual men. There are many ways of assessing human action, and admiration for great achievements is only one of them. It is equally possible to enjoy their oddity or their charm or their humour or their improbability or their moral worth. Whatever the reason may be, once the attention to the individual and his prowess loses its strength, a new kind of poetry emerges. At the least he loses his old self-sufficiency by becoming more human than a hero can legitimately be ; at the most he ceases to count as a man and becomes a cipher in some ingenious romantic pattern which deals more in abstractions than in individuals. Once the poet shifts his notice from heroic man to some other point, he destroys the assumptions on which heroic poetry thrives. He may perhaps not find anything so comprehensive to replace it, and in that case his poetry loses much even as narrative ; for narrative requires a central, dominating point of view if it is to make the most of its subject. He may equally be so absorbed with some general taste or idea that his poem is no longer concerned with the characters and doings of human beings but only with parts and elements of them, and in that case his poetry may still be good but not dramatic or, in any real sense, narrative. Heroic poetry is based on assumptions which cannot be abandoned without ruining its character.

Secondly, in most of these changes there is a shift in poetical appeal. Self-conscious narrative, romance, ballads, and literary epic excite feelings unlike those excited by heroic poetry. The love of honour and glory may still be present, as may the delight in a good story, but both are supplemented and often replaced by other kinds of attraction and appeal. Even when, as in many Spanish *romances* and many English ballads, the subject is undeniably heroic, it is made attractive by various means not used by the heroic poet. What matters is not a story but a situation, not a series of events but a single event presented sometimes from different angles and in several lights. So in *Edward, my Edward* the son who kills his father is presented as he is after the murder. Of the actual event we hear next to nothing; what matters is the son's state of mind, his sense of guilt and doom, his hatred of his mother and of himself. So in the Spanish *romance* of Doña Alda the poet has chosen a single tragic and terrible moment when Alda dreams a frightening dream and discovers that it means that Roland has been killed.[1] To it he gives a noble and moving poetry, but the effect is different, for instance, from Homer's treatment of Andromache when she sees Hector's body dragged by Achilles past the walls of Troy. Homer makes the wife's agony part of a long and tragic story and relates it in its dramatic development, but the Spanish poet builds up a single situation in which a menacing dream is suddenly found to have an all too close connection with a grim reality.

Thirdly, there is a tendency in post-heroic poetry to make the story more than a story. Of course in truly heroic poetry it is impossible not to treat the great heroes to some degree as ideal types of manhood, of men who may never have existed but would be splendid if they did. But they are hardly held out as examples for imitation. The poets are interested in them for their own sake as notable human beings. Post-heroic poetry tends to make more of them than this. Siegfried in the *Nibelungenlied* is a more ideal and more abstract figure than Sigurth in the *Elder Edda*; the noble patriots of Ennius are first of all Romans, and human beings only in the second place; even Robin Hood in the English ballads has become a symbol of the courageous and generous outlaw who is impelled by chivalrous motives to fight against an iniquitous system of society. Moreover, post-heroic poetry tends to give a

[1] Santullano, p. 146 ff.

new dimension to its story by making it in some sense symbolical or allegorical, an illustration of important metaphysical issues. The heroes are not only themselves but instruments of high designs and mysterious powers. In *The Knight in the Tiger's Skin* the two women whom the heroes admire with so ideal a passion are themselves ideal types of womanhood, destined to create devotion and havoc around them. Much of the interest in Isaakyan's delineation of Mher lies in his being a symbolical figure of a man who is so powerful and so assertive that he cannot find an abiding place in human society. Heracles, as Pisander and Panyassis depict him, seems to be not merely a powerful hero who does extraordinary feats but a type of human destiny who suffers that he may work the will of the gods and is in due course rewarded by being made their equal on Olympus. In French romance the interest shifts from heroic doings to the conflict of virtues and vices, and the human agents are replaced by abstractions who masquerade in armour and live in castles but are none the less allegorical entities who are not even disguised with human names but advertised by titles derived from the elaborate rules of courtly love. In ballads the story may take other, new directions. It may tell of men, like Thomas the Rhymer, who are hardly heroes, or of events, which are domestic and homely rather than heroic. It may even, like the Spanish ballad of Conde Arnaldos, exploit a pure effect. It is true that in a version preserved among the Spanish Jews of North Africa this story has an easy, prosaic conclusion, but in the normal Spanish version it does no more than create a mystery. A count stands on the shore and sees on the sea a ship, from which a voice sings and summons him to it :

> " No man teach I what I'm singing,
> Save he sail along with me." [1]

This is wonderful indeed but quite alien to the realistic methods of heroic narrative.

Of course heroic poetry may continue to survive at the side of these new forms, as it certainly does with primitive societies like the Kara-Kirghiz, the Uzbeks, and the Armenians, and as it seems to have done for a certain period in Spain. In due course, no doubt, it becomes unable to resist the competition of the new art and loses prestige and popularity until it fades away. Even when it is not faced with serious competition and continues to hold its own, it sometimes suffers from organic complaints and loses weight and strength. Of course the emergence of a new, gifted poet may

[1] *Idem*, p. 857.

at any time revive it in his own region, and it is not always easy to distinguish between organic decay and the natural deficiencies of inferior bards. None the less we can trace some of the ways in which this deterioration takes place. It is after all to be expected. Few arts have so long a life as heroic poetry, and it is inevitable that at times it should show marks of senility, especially when it is practised in isolated regions and weakened by inbreeding. The revival of Russian *byliny* in recent years may be no more than an ephemeral or artificial phenomenon, but it undoubtedly owes much to new blood from outside. Bards, who had hitherto been restricted to themes and techniques learned in their own regions, have received a great access of both from the improvement of communications and even from newspapers and books. The same seems to be true of Jugoslavia and Albania. But before it happened, at least in Russia, there were signs that heroic poetry was ailing and had begun to suffer from a hardening of the arteries.

The first symptom of such decay is that a poet's repertory shrinks. Stories, which were once common and popular, pass out of currency, are forgotten and no longer sung. Something of this kind seems to have happened in England in the century before the Norman Conquest. If the heyday of English heroic song was the eighth and ninth centuries, when it still drew freely on the rich resources of continental, Germanic legend, it is remarkable that after this period the many stories known to the poets of *Beowulf* and *Widsith* seem to have passed, if not out of circulation, at least into a very limited popularity. Some, of course, like that of Weyland Smith, survived in popular memory and local cult; others, like that of Offa, passed into history for genealogical and dynastic reasons. It is also true that even about the year 1000 some rich man thought it worth his while to have *Beowulf* recorded in writing, which shows that the poem was known to him, and we can hardly doubt that Alfred's interest in old songs did something to keep them alive. None the less, in the tenth and eleventh centuries the old legends seem to have lost some of their charm. The historians hardly refer to them, and they are not figured in painting or sculpture. Their place was partly taken by new poems, like *Brunanburh* and *Maldon*, on contemporary events, but, whatever the reason may have been, the Anglo-Saxons seem to have grown tired of their old stories, with the result that their poetical repertory was greatly diminished and shows no similarity to the situation in Iceland, where tales which had their origin in the fifth century had a sturdy life until the twelfth.

Something of the same kind may have happened in Russia in

the last decades of the nineteenth century and the first decade of the twentieth. Until the Revolution gave a new prominence to *byliny* as a proletarian art, the bards seem to have got into an ever narrowing groove and to have ceased to tell tales which were familiar to their ancestors. How flourishing the art of the seventies of the last century was can be seen from Rybnikov's collection. He took down twenty-three pieces from Trofim Ryabinin, fifteen from Chukov, thirteen from Kuzma Romanov, and, as we know from Gilferding's visit to the same region a few years later, these were by no means all the lays recited by these bards, but only a selection from them. In modern times a conscientious effort to discover all possible *byliny* has led to less abundant harvests. Ryabinin's great-grandson has produced twelve *byliny*, which is half the number produced by his ancestor. In the Pudozhsk region, where the poems of fourteen bards have been recorded, no bard has produced more than sixteen, and six no more than one each. It is perhaps dangerous to draw too much from this evidence. It is possible that other bards exist who are more creative but have not had their work recorded, or that the bards who produced so little have other poems in reserve. There may be something in these considerations, but a general impression remains that, apart from some special cases like Marfa Kryukova, bards of this century have smaller repertories than their predecessors in the past.

Secondly, time may impoverish the language of heroic poetry because bards forget some of the old formulae without replacing them by new ones. Something of the kind may have happened in England. Great though the language of *Maldon* and at times of *Brunanburh* is, it lacks the abundant resources of *Beowulf*. This is not to say that the straightforward, less elaborated language of *Maldon* is not in many ways more powerful and more effective than that of *Beowulf*, but that is because the poet has risen nobly to a great opportunity and made full use of his resources. The fact remains that the language of Anglo-Saxon poetry seems to have lost some of its old variety and complexity. What is true of *Maldon* and *Brunanburh* is still more true of the minor poems in the Anglo-Saxon Chronicle, which have indeed a jejune and impoverished air which is not merely because they are the work of inferior poets, since even inferior poets would use whatever formulae were available to them. Just as Anglo-Saxon poetry seems to have forgotten many of its old stories, so too it seems to have lost many of its formulae. Isolated and inbred, it tended to grow weaker as it grew older.

Something of the same kind may be seen in Russia. That much was lost between the golden days of Kiev and the eighteenth and nineteenth centuries, from which most of our first *byliny* come, can hardly be doubted. The *Tale of Igor's Raid* shows how rich the poetical language of Kiev was, and contains many phrases and passages which we might expect to find in *byliny* but which are absent from them. Omens of evil are described in a way that might well have been taken up by later poets :

> Already before his misfortune birds hide in the oaks ;
> In the ravines wolves howl in the storm ;
> Eagles with their cries summon beasts to the bones ;
> Foxes bark at the scarlet shields.

Dawn is equally memorable :

> The glow of dawn has flared up,
> Mist has covered the fields.
> The nightingales' trill has gone to sleep,
> Having awoken the chatter of daws.

Yet such passages, and others like them, which seem made for composers of *byliny*, are not used by them, and their work is done by other passages which are considerably less rich and imaginative. So too even in the last hundred years the process of impoverishment can be marked when we compare the work of men like Trofim Ryabinin and that of his successors. He describes a rich garment :

> The threads of one set of stitching were of silver,
> The other threads were of red gold ;
> The buttons were shaped as brave young men,
> The loops were shaped as lovely maidens :
> When they were buttoned, they were locked in close embrace,
> When they were unbuttoned, they merely kissed.[1]

This surely cries out for general use, but does not seem to have been taken up. So too, when Ryabinin's contemporary, Chukov, who came from the same district, makes a young man complain of the sadness of his lot, he provides a passage rich in possibilities :

> " Why, when you gave me birth, dear lady mother,
> Did you not bind me to a white-hot stone
> In a little bag of fine linen
> And throw me into the blue sea ?
> I should have slept in the sea for ever." [2]

Yet this too seems to have passed out of currency. When the modern poets touch on this theme, they use duller and less

[1] Rybnikov, i, p. 106.   [2] *Idem*, i, p. 162.

imaginative words, as if they had lost touch with a past which did things on a more bounteous scale.

A third form of deterioration may be seen in the actual handling of a subject. There is a tendency for themes to be treated less and less fully, until they may become brief statements of fact without any great poetical decoration or quality. This is certainly the case with the historical poems, other than *Brunanburh*, preserved in the Anglo-Saxon Chronicle. Of these five poems the longest, *The Death of Edgar*, has thirty-seven lines and the shortest, *The Capture of the Five Boroughs*, has thirteen. Yet the first of these poems deals with a series of important events in the year 975 — the death of the king and the accession of the young Edward, the departure from Britain of Cyneweard, bishop of Wells, the anti-monastic reaction in Mercia under Aelfhere, the expulsion of Oslac, earl of Northumbria, the comet seen in the autumn, and the great famine. The second poem tells how in 942 Edmund wins back from the Danes the Five Boroughs of Danelaw — Leicester, Lincoln, Nottingham, Stamford, and Derby. Both poems tell of a series of events, each of which was of some importance in its time and might well be expected to evoke a song on some scale. Instead of that we get what is almost a synopsis — so brief are the poems and so rigidly do they adhere to mere, bare facts. The same technique is maintained in the other three poems, and we cannot help feeling that the poets have lost opportunities in dealing with subjects not without promise, like the death of Edward the Confessor. Poems of this kind lack the expansive ease which seems to have been characteristic of Anglo-Saxon heroic poetry in its prime, and, though they are for the most part earlier than *Maldon*, they indicate that even in the tenth century the scope of this art had begun to contract and, by insisting on the mere outline of facts, to lose something essential and delightful.

In a different way the same process can be seen in the Armenian poems. The modern pieces incorporated into *David of Sasoun* are not indeed jejune like the poems of the Anglo-Saxon Chronicle, but they are remarkably factual and concise. Episodes are dealt with rapidly without much attention to poetical appeal, and though the stories are always interesting or exciting or amusing because of their matter, the treatment lacks brilliance except within a very narrow range. They are the late fruits of a tradition which goes back at least to the fourth century A.D. and has lost something in the passage of years. If we compare them with the few remains of early Armenian heroic poetry, we can see how much richness has been lost. Take, for instance, the common theme of

a hero's birth. In the modern version, when David is born, no
decoration is added to the purely factual statement :

> When the tenth month was over,
> The tenth day, the tenth hour,
> A son was born to Armagan.
> They christened him. They called him David,
> And brought him home.[1]

So much the story demands, and the poet sees no need to provide
more. But this is not the ancient manner. In a fragment of
poetry contained in the *History* of Moses Khorenatsi the hero,
Vaagn, is born in a more mysterious and more impressive manner :

> Sky and earth were in the pangs of birth,
> The purple sea was in an agony of birth ;
> From the water arose a scarlet reed,
> From its neck mist arose,
> From its neck flame arose,
> From that flame a man-child arose,
> And his hair was of fire,
> He had a beard of fire,
> And his eyes were beautiful as suns.[2]

There is a vast tract of years between this and *David of Sasoun* as
we now know it, and we can see how the heroic style has grown
thinner and poorer with time.

The decay or disappearance of heroic poetry is hardly surprising. What is surprising is its remarkable hold on life. Of all
branches of literature, except the song, it seems to last the longest,
and to maintain its character with the least changes. It seems to
endure so long as men hold a certain view of life and have reached
sufficient detachment to be able to enjoy imaginary tales of great
actions, without worrying too much about their ulterior significance. It thrives on a combination of qualities which is not
common. In the first place it tells a story which is enjoyable
because it makes us witnesses of thrilling events and risks and
climaxes ; in the second place in telling its tales it is quite sure of
what their events and the men responsible for them are worth.
Because it is so certain of its values and displays them in concrete,
persuasive shapes, it has a strength denied to many more sophisticated forms of art. The poets assay their tasks with undivided
minds, with no doubts or reservations, and the result is a delightful
simplicity which misses nothing in its subject but presents everything with a steady eye and a steady mind. Within these limits
there is room for much variety not merely between one people and

[1] *David Sasunskii*, p. 131.   [2] Arutyunyan, p. 39.

another, or one poet and another, but within a single poem. The poet presents a living world, as complete and as solid as he can make it. Of course he is limited by his own experience and outlook, but within these boundaries he can use almost any element in the familiar scene to give strength and plausibility to his story. Sometimes heroic poetry may seem narrow just because the poets lack a wide vision of life, but at other times it has an almost universal strength and attains a breadth that is uncommon in any literature. If we feel that after all *Roland* and *Beowulf* come from worlds where a fixed point of view hampers the reach of imaginative sympathy, we can hardly feel the same about the tragic tales of the *Elder Edda* or the superhuman ambitions of *Gilgamish*. And if what we want is a complete vision of life, it is to be found in Homer, who stands at the fountain-head of European poetry and sets an example which no one else has yet equalled.

LIST OF ABBREVIATIONS

Author and Title of Book	*Abbreviation*

Abbott, G. F., *Songs of Modern Greece.* Cambridge, 1900. — Abbott.

Allen, T. W., *Homeri Opera*, Tom. V. Oxford, 1912. — Allen.

Homer : The Origins and the Transmission. Oxford, 1924. — Allen, *Origins.*

Amran : Osetinskii Epos. Moscow, 1932. — Amran.

Andreev, N. P., *Byliny ; Russkii Geroicheskii Epos.* Moscow, 1938. — Andreev.

Aravantinos, P., Συλλογὴ δημώδων ᾀσμάτων τῆς Ἠπείρου. Athens, 1880. — Aravantinos.

Arutyunyan, S. S., and Kirpotin, V. Y., *Antologiya Armyanskoi Poezii.* Moscow, 1940. — Arutyunyan.

Astakhova, A. M., *Byliny Pudozhskogo Kraya.* Petrozavodsk, 1941. — Astakhova.

Baggally, J. W., *The Klephtic Ballads in Relation to Greek History.* London, 1936. — Baggally.

Bassett, S. E., *The Poetry of Homer.* Berkeley, 1938. — Bassett.

Bédier, J., *La Chanson de Roland commentée*, 5th edn. Paris, 1927. — Bédier, *Commentaire.*

Les Légendes épiques, 4 vols. 3rd edn. Paris, 1927. — Bédier, *Légendes.*

Beowulf, translated by C. K. Scott-Moncrieff. London, 1921. — *Beowulf.*

Bezsonov, P. A., *Kaleki perekhozhie*, 6 parts. Moscow, 1861–64. — Bezsonov.

Blunt, W. S., *Collected Poems*, 2 vols. London, 1914. — Blunt.

Bogišić, V., *Narodne Srpske Pjesme.* Belgrade, 1878. — Bogišić.

Bossert, H. T., *Altkreta*, 2nd edn. Berlin, 1923. — Bossert.

Bowra, C. M., *Tradition and Design in the Iliad.* Oxford, 1930. — Bowra, *T.D.*

Campbell, A., *The Battle of Brunanburh.* London, 1938. — *Brunanburh.*

Cambridge Ancient History, ed. J. B. Bury and others, 12 vols. Cambridge, 1923–39. — *C.A.H.*

Carpenter, R., *Folk Tale, Fiction and Saga in the Homeric Epics.* Berkeley, 1946. — Carpenter.

Author and Title of Book	Abbreviation
Chadwick, H. M. and N. K., *The Growth of Literature*, 3 vols. Cambridge, 1932, 1936, 1940.	Chadwick, *Growth*.
Chadwick, H. M., *The Heroic Age*. Cambridge, 1912.	Chadwick, *H.A.*
Chadwick, N. K., *Russian Heroic Poetry*. Cambridge, 1932.	Chadwick, *R.H.P.*
Chettéoui, W., *Un Rapsode russe*. Paris, 1942.	Chettéoui.
Cantar de mio Cid, ed. R. Menéndez Pidal, 3 vols. Madrid, 1924.	*Cid.*
Clarke, E. D., *Travels in Various Countries*, 8th edn., 8 vols. London, 1816–18.	Clarke.
Cohn, N., *Gold Khan*. London, 1946.	Cohn.
Comparetti, D., *The Traditional Poetry of the Finns*, Eng. Trans. London, 1898.	Comparetti.
David Sasunskii : Armyanskii Narodnyi Epos. Moscow, 1938.	*David Sasunskii.*
David-Neel, A., and Yongden, *The Superhuman Life of King Gesar of Ling*. London, 1933.	David-Neel.
De Vries, J., *Altnordische Literaturgeschichte*, 2 vols. Berlin, 1941.	De Vries.
Derzhavin, N. S., *Bolgarskaya Narodnaya Poeziya*. Moscow, 1944.	Derzhavin.
Dozon, A., *B'lgarski Narodni Pesni*. Paris, 1875.	Dozon.
Drerup, E., *Das Homerproblem in der Gegenwart*. Würzburg, 1921.	Drerup.
Dumézil, G., *Légendes sur les Nartes*. Paris, 1930.	Dumézil.
Dynnik, V., *Skazanniya o Nartakh*. Moscow, 1944.	Dynnik.
Dzhangariada : Geroicheskaya Poema Kalmykov, ed. S. A. Kozin. Moscow, 1944.	*Dzhangariada.*
Entwistle, W. J., *European Balladry*. Oxford, 1930.	Entwistle.
Faral, J., *Les Jongleurs en France*. Paris, 1910.	Faral.
Garnett, L. M., and Stuart-Glennie, J. S., *Greek Folk Poesy*, vol. i. London, 1896.	Garnett.
Gaster, T. H., *Thespis*. New York, 1950.	Gaster.
Jordanes, *Getica*, ed. C. A. Closs. Stuttgart, 1861.	*Getica.*
Gilferding, A. F., *Onezhskiye Byliny*, 2nd edn., 3 vols. St. Petersburg, 1866–1904.	Gilferding.
Gordon, Cyrus H., *Ugaritic Literature*. Rome, 1949.	Gordon.
Gressmann, H., *Das Gilgamesch-Epos*. Berlin, 1881.	Gressmann.
Hurgronje, S., *The Achehnese*, Eng. Trans. London, 1906.	Hurgronje.

Author and Title of Book	Abbreviation
Isaakyan, A., *Izbrannye Stikhi*. Moscow, 1945.	Isaakyan.
Jenkins, T. A., *La Chanson de Roland*. New York, 1934.	Jenkins.
Journal of Hellenic Studies.	*J.H.S.*
Kalevala : The Land of Heroes. Trans. by W. F. Kirby, 2 vols. London, 1907.	*Kalevala.*
Karadžić, V. S., *Srpske Narodne Pjesme*, 12 vols. Belgrade, 1932–36.	Karadžić.
Kaun, A., *Soviet Poets and Poetry*. Berkeley, 1943.	Kaun.
Ker, W. P., *The Dark Ages*. London, 1804.	Ker, *D.A.*
Epic and Romance, 2nd edn. London, 1908.	Ker, *E.R.*
Kershaw, N., *Anglo-Saxon and Norse Poems*. Cambridge, 1922.	Kershaw.
Kirby, W. F., *The Hero of Esthonia*, 2 vols. London, 1895.	Kirby.
Kireevski, P., *Pesni Sobrannya*, 7 parts. Moscow, 1860.	Kireevski.
Klaeber, F., *Beowulf and the Fight at Finnsburgh*, 3rd edn. London, 1941.	Klaeber.
Kogutei : Altaiski Epos, ed. V. Zazubrin and N. Dmitrev. Moscow, 1935.	*Kogutei.*
Krauss, F. S., *Slavische Volksforschungen*. Leipzig, 1908.	Krauss.
Kravstov, N., *Serbskii Epos*. Moscow, 1933.	Kravstov.
Kryukova, M., *Byliny*, 2 vols. Moscow, 1939 and 1941.	Kryukova.
Legrand, E., *Recueil des chansons populaires grecques*. Athens-Paris, 1874.	Legrand.
Lorimer, H. E., *Homer and the Monuments*. London, 1951.	Lorimer.
Low, D. H., *The Ballads of Marko Kraljević*. Cambridge, 1922.	Low.
Macler, F., *Contes, légendes et épopées populaires d'Arménie*, 2 vols. Paris, 1933.	Macler.
Laborde, E. D., *Byrhtnoth and Maldon*. London, 1936.	*Maldon.*
Manas : Kirgizkii Epos. Moscow, 1946.	*Manas.*
Markov, A., *Belomorskiya Byliny*. Moscow, 1901.	Markov.
Miller, V., *Byliny Novoy*. Moscow, 1908.	Miller.
Ocherki Russkoy Narodnoy Slovesnosti, 3 vols. Moscow, 1897–1924.	Miller, *Ocherki.*
Mireaux, E., *La Chanson de Roland*. Paris, 1943.	Mireaux.
Morel, W., *Fragmenta Poetarum Latinorum*. Leipzig, 1927.	Morel.
Morison, W. A., *The Revolt of the Serbs against the Turks* (1804–1813). Cambridge, 1942.	Morison.

Author and Title of Book	*Abbreviation*
Müller, K., *Fragmenta Historicorum Graecorum*.	Müller, *F.H.G.*
Murko, M., *Geschichte der älteren sudslawischen Litteraturen*. Leipzig, 1908.	Murko I.
" Bericht über eine Reise " in *Sitzungsberichte der Kais. Akademie der Wissenschaften in Wien*. Bd. 173. Abh. 3, 1913.	Murko II.
Ibid. Bd. 176. Abh. 2, 1915.	Murko III.
Nechaev, A., *Izbrannye Byliny*. Petrozavodsk, 1938.	Nechaev.
Orlov, A. S., *Kazaksii Geroicheskii Epos*. Leningrad-Moscow, 1945.	Orlov.
Parry, M., *L'Épithète traditionelle dans Homère*. Paris, 1928.	Parry, *L'Épithète*.
Les Formules et la métrique d'Homére.	Parry, *Les Formules*.
" Studies in the Epic Technique of Oral Verse-Making. I. Homer and Homeric Style ", in *Harvard Studies in Classical Philology*, 1930.	Parry, *Studies* I.
Idem. " II. The Homeric Language as the Language of an Oral Poetry." *Ibid.* 1932.	Parry, *Studies* II.
" The Traditional Metaphor in Homer ", in *Classical Philology*, 1933.	Parry, *Trad. Met.*
Passow, A., *Carmina popularia Graeciae recentioris,* 3rd edn. Athens, 1932.	Passow.
Paulus Diaconus, *Historia Langobardorum*. Hannover, 1878.	Paulus Diaconus.
Pauly-Wissowa, *Real-Encyclopädie der classischen Altertumswissenschaft*. 1894–	P.-W.
Petrović, R., *Afrika*. Belgrade, 1930.	Petrović.
Philpotts, B. S., *Edda and Saga*. London, 1931.	Philpotts.
Politis, N. G., Ἐκλογαὶ ἀπὸ τὰ Τραγούδια τοῦ Ἑλληνικοῦ Λαοῦ, 3rd edn. Athens, 1932.	Politis.
Procopius, *De Bello Vandalico,* ed. J. Haury. Leipzig, 1905.	Procopius, *Bell. Van.*
De Bello Gothico, ed. J. Haury. Leipzig, 1905.	Procopius, *Bell. Got.*
Radlov, V. V., *Proben der Volkslitteratur der türkischen Stämme*, 10 vols. St. Petersburg, 1866–1904.	Radlov.
Roland, The Song of, translated by C. K. Scott-Moncrieff. London, 1920.	Roland.
Ryabinin-Andreev, P. I., *Byliny : Russkii Geroicheskii Epos*. Petrozavodsk, 1938.	Ryabinin-Andreev.
Rybnikov, P. N., *Pesni*, 2nd edn., 3 vols. Moscow, 1909–10.	Rybnikov.
Santullano, L., *Romancero español*. Madrid, 1943.	Santullano.
Saxo Grammaticus, *Gesta Danorum*, ed. A. Holder. Strasburg, 1886.	Saxo.

LIST OF ABBREVIATIONS

Author and Title of Book	*Abbreviation*
Scherrer, M., *Les Dumy ukrainiennes*. Paris, 1947.	Scherrer.
Schmid, W., and Stählin, O., *Geschichte der griechischen Literatur*, vol. i. Munich, 1929.	Schmid-Stählin.
Sokolov, B. and Y., *Byliny : Istoricheski Ocherk, Teksty i Kommentari*. Moscow, 1918.	Sokolov.
Onezhskiye byliny. Moscow, 1948.	Sokolov, *O.B.*
Speranski, M., *Byliny*, 2 vols. Moscow, 1916.	Speranski.
Subotić, D., *Yugoslav Popular Ballads*. Cambridge, 1932.	Subotić.
Thompson, E. A., *Attila and the Huns*. Oxford, 1948.	Thompson.
Trautmann, R., *Die Volksdichtung der Grossrussen*, vol. i. Heidelberg, 1935.	Trautmann.
Vahlen, J., *Ennianae Poesis Reliquiae*, 2nd edn. Leipzig, 1928.	Vahlen.
Vambéry, A., *Travels in Central Asia*. London, 1864.	Vambéry.
Widsith, ed. R. W. Chambers. Cambridge, 1912.	*Widsith*.
Woodhouse, W. J., *The Composition of Homer's Odyssey*. Oxford, 1930.	Woodhouse.
Zhirmunskii, V. M., and Zarifov, K. T., *Uzbekskii Narodnyi Geroicheskii Epos*. Moscow, 1947.	Zhirmunskii-Zarifov.

INDEX

Printed in Great Britain by
Lowe and Brydone (Printers) Limited, London, N.W.10